Lecture Notes in Computer Science

AF136517

Lecture Notes in Artificial Intelligence   **16020**

Founding Editor

Jörg Siekmann

Series Editors

Randy Goebel, *University of Alberta, Edmonton, Canada*
Wolfgang Wahlster, *DFKI, Berlin, Germany*
Zhi-Hua Zhou, *Nanjing University, Nanjing, China*

The series Lecture Notes in Artificial Intelligence (LNAI) was established in 1988 as a topical subseries of LNCS devoted to artificial intelligence.

The series publishes state-of-the-art research results at a high level. As with the LNCS mother series, the mission of the series is to serve the international R & D community by providing an invaluable service, mainly focused on the publication of conference and workshop proceedings and postproceedings.

Bernhard Pfahringer · Nathalie Japkowicz ·
Pedro Larrañaga · Rita P. Ribeiro · Inês Dutra ·
Mykola Pechenizkiy · Paulo Cortez ·
Sepideh Pashami · Alípio M. Jorge ·
Carlos Soares · Pedro H. Abreu · João Gama
Editors

Machine Learning and Knowledge Discovery in Databases

Research Track and Applied Data Science Track

European Conference, ECML PKDD 2025
Porto, Portugal, September 15–19, 2025
Proceedings, Part VIII

 Springer

Editors

Bernhard Pfahringer ⓘ
University of Waikato
Hamilton, Waikato, New Zealand

Pedro Larrañaga ⓘ
Technical University of Madrid
Boadilla del Monte, Madrid, Spain

Inês Dutra ⓘ
University of Porto
Porto, Portugal

Paulo Cortez ⓘ
University of Minho
Guimarães, Portugal

Alípio M. Jorge ⓘ
University of Porto
Porto, Portugal

Pedro H. Abreu ⓘ
University of Coimbra
Coimbra, Portugal

Nathalie Japkowicz ⓘ
American University
Washington, D.C., WA, USA

Rita P. Ribeiro ⓘ
University of Porto
Porto, Portugal

Mykola Pechenizkiy ⓘ
Eindhoven University of Technology
Eindhoven, The Netherlands

Sepideh Pashami ⓘ
Halmstad University
Halmstad, Sweden

Carlos Soares ⓘ
University of Porto
Porto, Portugal

João Gama ⓘ
University of Porto
Porto, Portugal

ISSN 0302-9743   ISSN 1611-3349 (electronic)
Lecture Notes in Artificial Intelligence
ISBN 978-3-662-72242-8   ISBN 978-3-662-72243-5 (eBook)
https://doi.org/10.1007/978-3-662-72243-5

LNCS Sublibrary: SL7 – Artificial Intelligence

Preface

The 2025 edition of the European Conference on Machine Learning and Principles and Practice of Knowledge Discovery in Databases (ECML PKDD 2025) was held in the vibrant city of Porto, Portugal on September 15–19, 2025. This marks a significant return of the conference to Porto, following successful editions in 2005 and 2015, underscoring the city's enduring appeal as a hub for scientific exchange.

The annual ECML PKDD conference stands as a premier worldwide platform dedicated to showcasing the latest advancements and fostering insightful discussions in the fields of machine learning and knowledge discovery in databases. Held jointly since 2001, ECML PKDD has firmly established its reputation as the leading European conference in these disciplines. It provides researchers and practitioners with an unparalleled opportunity to exchange knowledge, share innovative ideas, and explore the latest technical advancements. Furthermore, the conference deeply values the synergy between foundational theoretical advances and groundbreaking practical data science applications, actively encouraging contributions that demonstrate how Machine Learning and Data Mining are being effectively employed to address complex real-world challenges.

A Hub for Responsible AI and Cutting-Edge Research

As the technological landscape continues to evolve and societal needs shift, the conference remains committed to adapting to and reflecting these dynamic changes. This year's event saw a robust engagement from the global research community with a substantial increase in the number of submissions.

The three main conference days were organised into five distinct tracks:

- The Research Track received an impressive number of 924 submissions, with 226 papers ultimately accepted, reflecting a highly competitive acceptance rate of 24.5%.
- The Applied Data Science Track received a total of 299 submissions, accepting 74 papers, resulting in an acceptance rate of 24.7%.
- The Journal Track continued to bridge the gap between conference and journal publications, accepting 43 papers (27 for the Machine Learning journal and 16 for the Data Mining and Knowledge Discovery journal) out of 297 submissions.
- The Nectar Track, focusing on recent scientific advances at the frontier of machine learning and data mining, received 30 submissions.
- The Demo Track showcased practical applications and prototypes, accepting 15 papers from a total of 30 submissions.

These proceedings cover the papers accepted in the Research and Applied Data Science tracks.

The high quality and diversity of the accepted papers across all tracks underscore the continued vitality and intellectual breadth of the machine learning and data mining communities. We extend our sincere gratitude to all authors for their valuable contributions, to the program committee members and reviewers for their diligent efforts in ensuring the rigorous double-blind review process, and to the organising committee for their tireless work in making ECML PKDD 2025 a resounding success. We believe these proceedings will serve as a valuable resource, inspiring future research and innovation in these rapidly advancing fields.

This year's conference featured seven insightful keynote talks that focused on crucial and emerging areas within Responsible AI, including trustworthy AI, interpretability, and explainability. The keynotes also explored fundamental theoretical issues, covering causality, neural-symbolic systems, large language models (LLMs), and AI for science. We were honoured to host leading experts who shared their valuable perspectives:

- Cynthia Rudin (Duke University) presented on "Many Good Models Lead to …";
- Elias Bareinboim (Columbia University) discussed "Towards Causal Artificial Intelligence";
- Francisco Herrera (University of Granada) addressed "Not Just a Trend: Institutionalizing XAI for Responsible and Compliant AI Systems";
- Mirella Lapata (University of Edinburgh) explored "Compositional Intelligence: Coordinating Multiple LLMs for Complex Tasks";
- Nuria Oliver (ELLIS Alicante Foundation, Spain) spoke on "Towards a Fairer World: Uncovering and Addressing Human and Algorithmic Biases";
- Pedro Domingos (University of Washington) shared insights on "A Simple Unification of Neural and Symbolic AI"; and
- Sašo Džeroski (Jožef Stefan Institute, Slovenia) presented on "Artificial Intelligence for Science".

Fostering Diversity and Inclusion

Our Diversity and Inclusion initiative proudly awarded 10 scholarship grants of €500 to early-career researchers. These grants enabled individuals from developing countries and communities underrepresented in science and technology to attend the conference, present their work, and become integral members of the ECML PKDD community.

Acknowledging Our Contributors and Supporters

We extend our sincere gratitude to everyone who contributed to making ECML PKDD 2025 such a success. Our heartfelt thanks go to the authors, workshop and tutorial organisers, and all participants for their valuable scientific contributions.

An outstanding conference program would not be possible without the immense dedication and substantial time investment from our area chairs, program committee, and organising committee. The smooth execution of the event was also largely due to the hard work of our many volunteers and session chairs. A special acknowledgement goes to the local organisers for meticulously handling every detail, making the conference a truly memorable experience.

Finally, we are incredibly grateful for the generous financial support from our wonderful sponsors. We also appreciate Springer's ongoing support and Microsoft's provision of their CMT software for conference management, as well as their continued assistance. Our sincere thanks also go to the ECML PKDD Steering Committee for their invaluable advice and guidance over the past two years.

September 2025

João Gama
Pedro H. Abreu
Alípio M. Jorge
Carlos Soares
Rita P. Ribeiro
Pedro Larrañaga
Nathalie Japkowicz
Bernhard Pfahringer
Inês Dutra
Mykola Pechenizkiy
Sepideh Pashami
Paulo Cortez

Organization

Honorary Chair

Pavel Brazdil — University of Porto, Portugal

General Chairs

João Gama	University of Porto, Portugal
Pedro H. Abreu	University of Coimbra, Portugal
Alípio M. Jorge	University of Porto, Portugal
Carlos Soares	University of Porto, Portugal

Research Track Program Chairs

Bernhard Pfahringer	University of Waikato, New Zealand
Nathalie Japkowicz	American University, USA
Pedro Larrañaga	Technical University of Madrid, Spain
Rita P. Ribeiro	University of Porto, Portugal

Applied Data Science Track Program Chairs

Inês Dutra	University of Porto, Portugal
Mykola Pechenisky	TU Eindhoven, The Netherlands
Paulo Cortez	University of Minho, Portugal
Sepideh Pashami	Halmstad University, Sweden

Journal Track Chairs

Ana Carolina Lorena	Instituto Tecnológico de Aeronáutica, Brazil
Arlindo Oliveira	Instituto Superior Técnico, Portugal
Concha Bielza	Technical University of Madrid, Spain
Longbing Cao	Macquarie University, Australia
Tiago Almeida	Federal University of São Carlos, Brazil

Nectar Track Chairs

Ricard Gavaldà   Amalfi Analytics, Spain
Riccardo Guidotti   University of Pisa, Italy

Demo Track Chairs

Arian Pasquali   Faktion, Belgium
Nuno Moniz   University of Notre Dame, USA

Local Chairs

Bruno Veloso   University of Porto, Portugal
Rita Nogueira   INESC TEC, Portugal
Shazia Tabassum   INESC TEC, Portugal

Workshop Chairs

Irena Koprinska   University of Sydney, Australia
João Mendes Moreira   University of Porto, Portugal
Paula Branco   University of Ottawa, Canada

Tutorial Chairs

Alicia Troncoso   Universidad Pablo de Olavide, Spain
Nikolaj Tatti   University of Helsinki, Finland

PhD Forum Chairs

Raquel Sebastião   Polytechnic Institute of Viseu, Portugal
Yun Sing Koh   University of Auckland, New Zealand

Awards Committee Chairs

André Carvalho   University of São Paulo, Brazil
Amparo Alonso-Betanzos   University of A Coruña, Spain
Katharina Morik   TU Dortmund, Germany
Vítor Santos Costa   University of Porto, Portugal

Proceedings Chairs

João Vinagre   European Commission (JRC), Spain
Miriam Santos   University of Porto, Portugal
Shazia Tabassum   INESC TEC, Portugal

Diversity and Inclusion Chairs

Inês Sousa   Fraunhofer, Portugal
Zahraa Abdallah   University of Bristol, UK

Discovery Challenge Chairs

Carlos Ferreira   Polytechnic Institute of Porto, Portugal
Peter van der Putten   Leiden University, The Netherlands
Rui Camacho   University of Porto, Portugal

Panel Chairs

Pedro H. Abreu   University of Coimbra, Portugal
Paula Brito   University of Porto, Portugal

Publicity Chair

Carlos Ferreira   Polytechnic Institute of Porto, Portugal

Sponsorship Chairs

Mariam Berry   BNP Paribas, France
Nuno Moutinho   University of Porto, Portugal
Rui Teles   Accenture, Portugal

Social Media Chairs

Luis Roque   ZAAI.ai, Portugal
Ricardo Pereira   University of Coimbra, Portugal
Dalila Teixeira   Creative Matter, USA

Web Chair

Thiago Andrade   University of Porto, Portugal

Senior Program Committee – Research Track

Adam Jatowt   University of Innsbruck, Austria
Andrea Passerini   University of Trento, Italy
Anthony Bagnall   University of Southampton, UK
Arno Knobbe   Leiden University, Netherlands
Arno Siebes   Universiteit Utrecht, Netherlands
Arto Klami   University of Helsinki, Finland
Bernhard Pfahringer   University of Waikato, New Zealand
Bettina Berendt   TU Berlin, Germany
Celine Robardet   INSA Lyon, France
Celine Vens   KU Leuven, Belgium
Cesar Ferri   Universitat Politècnica Valencia, Spain
Charalampos Tsourakakis   Boston University, USA
Chedy Raissi   Inria, France
Chen Gong   Nanjing University of Science and Technology,
                            China
Danai Koutra   University of Michigan, USA
Dimitrios Gunopulos   University of Athens, Greece
Donato Malerba   Università degli Studi di Bari Aldo Moro, Italy
Dragi Kocev   Jožef Stefan Institute, Slovenia
Dunja Mladenic   Jožef Stefan Institute, Slovenia
Eirini Ntoutsi   Universität der Bundeswehr München, Germany

Emmanuel Müller	TU Dortmund, Germany
Ernestina Menasalvas	Universidad Politécnica de Madrid, Spain
Esther Galbrun	University of Eastern Finland, Finland
Evaggelia Pitoura	University of Ioannina, Greece
Evangelos Papalexakis	University of California, Riverside, USA
Fabio A. Stella	University of Milano-Bicocca, Italy
Fabrizio Costa	Exeter University, UK
Fragkiskos Malliaros	CentraleSupélec, France
Georg Krempl	Utrecht University, Netherlands
Georgiana Ifrim	University College Dublin, Ireland
Gustavo Batista	University of New South Wales, Australia
Heikki Mannila	Aalto University, Finland
Hendrik Blockeel	KU Leuven, Belgium
Henrik Bostrom	KTH Royal Institute of Technology, Sweden
Henry Gouk	University of Edinburgh, UK
Ioannis Katakis	University of Nicosia, Cyprus
Jan N. Van Rijn	LIACS, Leiden University, Netherlands
Jefrey Lijffijt	Ghent University, Belgium
Jerzy Stefanowski	Poznań University of Technology, Poland
Jesse Davis	KU Leuven, Belgium
Jesse Read	Ecole Polytechnique, France
Jessica Lin	George Mason University, USA
Jesus Cerquides	IIIA-CSIC, Spain
Jilles Vreeken	CISPA Helmholtz Center for Information Security, Germany
João Gama	INESC TEC - LIAAD, Portugal
Jörg Wicker	University of Auckland, New Zealand
José Hernández-Orallo	Universitat Politècnica de Valencia, Spain
Junming Shao	University of Electronic Science and Technology of China, China
Kai Puolamaki	University of Helsinki, Finland
Manfred Jaeger	Aalborg University, Denmark
Marius Kloft	TU Kaiserslautern, Germany
Marius Lindauer	Leibniz University Hannover, Germany
Mark Last	Ben-Gurion University of the Negev, Israel
Matthias Renz	University of Kiel, Germany
Matthias Schubert	Ludwig-Maximilians-Universität München, Germany
Michele Lombardi	University of Bologna, Italy
Michèle Sebag	LISN CNRS, France
Nathalie Japkowicz	American University, USA
Paolo Frasconi	Università degli Studi di Firenze, Italy

Parisa Kordjamshidi	Michigan State University, USA
Pasquale Minervini	University of Edinburgh, UK
Pauli Miettinen	University of Eastern Finland, Finland
Pedro Larrañaga	Technical University of Madrid, Spain
Peer Kroger	Christian-Albrechts-Universität Kiel, Germany
Peter Flach	University of Bristol, UK
Ricardo B. Prudencio	Universidade Federal de Pernambuco, Brazil
Rita P. Ribeiro	University of Porto and INESC TEC, Portugal
Salvatore Ruggieri	University of Pisa, Italy
Sebastijan Dumancic	TU Delft, Netherlands
Sibylle Hess	TU Eindhoven, Netherlands
Sicco Verwer	Delft University of Technology, Netherlands
Siegfried Nijssen	Université catholique de Louvain, Belgium
Sophie Fellenz	RPTU Kaiserslautern-Landau, Germany
Stefano Ferilli	University of Bari, Italy
Stratis Ioannidis	Northeastern University, USA
Szymon Jaroszewicz	Polish Academy of Sciences, Poland
Tijl De Bie	Ghent University, Belgium
Ulf Brefeld	Leuphana University of Lüneburg, Germany
Varvara Vetrova	University of Canterbury, New Zealand
Wannes Meert	KU Leuven, Belgium
Wei Ye	Tongji University, China
Wenbin Zhang	Florida International University, USA
Willem Waegeman	Universiteit Gent, Belgium
Wouter Duivesteijn	Technische Universiteit Eindhoven, Netherlands
Xiao Luo	University of California, Los Angeles, USA
Yun Sing Koh	University of Auckland, New Zealand
Zied Bouraoui	CRIL CNRS and Université d'Artois, France

Senior Program Committee – Applied Data Science Track

Albrecht Zimmermann	Université de Caen Normandie, France
Andreas Hotho	University of Würzburg, Germany
Anirban Dasgupta	IIT Gandhinagar, India
Anna Monreale	University of Pisa, Italy
Annalisa Appice	University of Bari Aldo Moro, Italy
Bruno Cremilleux	Université de Caen Normandie, France
Carlotta Domeniconi	George Mason University, USA
Dejing Dou	BCG, USA
Fabio Pinelli	IMT Lucca, Italy
Fuzhen Zhuang	Beihang University, China

Vincent S. Tseng	National Yang Ming Chiao Tung University, Taiwan
Vítor Santos Costa	Universidade do Porto, Portugal
Xingquan Zhu	Florida Atlantic University, USA
Yi Chang	Jilin University, China
Yinglong Xia	Meta, USA
Yongxin Tong	Beihang University, China
Yun Sing Koh	University of Auckland, New Zealand
Zhaochun Ren	Shandong University, China
Zheng Wang	Alibaba DAMO Academy, China
Zhiwei (Tony) Qin	Lyft, USA

Program Committee – Research Track

Christoph Bergmeir	Monash University, Australia
A. K. M. Mahbubur Rahman	Independent University, Bangladesh
Abdulhakim Qahtan	Utrecht University, Netherlands
Abhishek A.	Fujitsu Research, India
Acar Tamersoy	Microsoft, USA
Ad Feelders	Universiteit Utrecht, Netherlands
Adam Goodge	I2R, A*STAR, Singapore
Adele Jia	China Agricultural University, China
Adem Kikaj	KU Leuven, Belgium
Aditya Mohan	Leibniz Universität Hannover, Germany
Ajay A. Mahimkar	AT&T, USA
Akka Zemmari	Université de Bordeaux, France
Akshay Sethi	MasterCard, USA
Alborz Geramifard	Mcta, USA
Alessandro Antonucci	IDSIA, Switzerland
Alessandro Melchiorre	Johannes Kepler University Linz, Austria
Alexander Dockhorn	Leibniz University Hannover, Germany
Alexander Schiendorfer	Technische Hochschule Ingolstadt, Germany
Alexander Schulz	CITEC, Bielefeld University, Germany
Alexandre Termier	Université de Rennes 1, France
Alexandre Verine	Ecole Normale Supérieure - PSL, France
Alexandru C. Mara	Ghent University, Belgium
Ali Ayadi	University of Strasbourg, France
Ali Ismail-Fawaz	IRIMAS, Université de Haute-Alsace, France
Alicja Wieczorkowska	Polish-Japanese Academy of Information Technology, Poland
Alipio M. G. Jorge	INESC TEC/University of Porto, Portugal

Alireza Gharahighehi	KU Leuven, Belgium
Alistair Shilton	Deakin University, Australia
Alneu A. Lopes	University of São Paulo, Brazil
Alper Demir	Izmir University of Economics, Turkey
Alvaro Figueira	CRACS and Universidade do Porto, Portugal
Amal Saadallah	TU Dortmund, Germany
Aman Chadha	Stanford University and Amazon, USA
Amer Krivosija	TU Dortmund, Germany
Amir H. Payberah	KTH Royal Institute of Technology, Sweden
Ammar Shaker	NEC Laboratories Europe, Europe
Ana Rita Nogueira	INESC TEC, Portugal
Anand Paul	Louisiana State University HSC, USA
Anastasios Gounaris	Aristotle University of Thessaloniki, Greece
Andre V. Carreiro	Fraunhofer Portugal AICOS, Portugal
André C. P. L. F. de Carvalho	University of São Paulo, Brazil
Andrea Cossu	University of Pisa, Italy
Andrea Mastropietro	University of Bonn, Germany
Andrea Pugnana	University of Trento, Italy
Andrea Tagarelli	DIMES - UNICAL, Italy
Andreas Bender	LMU Munich, Germany
Andreas Nürnberger	Otto-von-Guericke-Universität Magdeburg, Germany
Andreas Schwung	Fachhochschule Südwestfalen, Germany
Andrei Paleyes	University of Cambridge, UK
Andrzej Skowron	University of Warsaw, Poland
Andy Song	RMIT University, Australia
Angelica Liguori	ICAR-CNR, Italy
Anirban Dasgupta	IIT Gandhinagar, India
Anke Meyer-Baese	Florida State University, USA
Anna Beer	University of Vienna, Austria
Anna Krause	Universität Wurzburg and Chair X Data Science, Germany
Anna Monreale	University of Pisa, Italy
Annelot W. Bosman	Universiteit Leiden, Netherlands
Antoine Caradot	Hubert Curien Laboratory, France
Antonio Bahamonde	University of Oviedo, Spain
Antonio Mastropietro	Università di Pisa, Italy
Antonio Pellicani	Università degli Studi di Bari, Aldo Moro, Italy
Antonis Matakos	Aalto University, Finland
Antti Laaksonen	University of Helsinki, Finland
Aomar Osmani	LIPN-UMR CNRS, France
Aonghus Lawlor	University College Dublin, Ireland

Aparna S. Varde	Montclair State University, USA
Apostolos N. Papadopoulos	Aristotle University of Thessaloniki, Greece
Aritra Konar	KU Leuven, Belgium
Arjun Roy	Freie Universität Berlin, Germany
Arthur Charpentier	UQAM, Canada
Arunas Lipnickas	Kaunas University of Technology, Lithuania
Atsuhiro Takasu	National Institute of Informatics, Japan
Aurora Esteban	University of Cordoba, Spain
Baosheng Zhang	Tsinghua University, China
Barbara Toniella Corradini	University of Florence and University of Siena, Italy
Bardh Prenkaj	Technical University of Munich, Germany
Barry O'Sullivan	University College Cork, Ireland
Beilun Wang	Southeast University, China
Benjamin Halstead	University of Auckland, New Zealand
Benjamin Paassen	Bielefeld University, Germany
Benjamin Quost	Université de Technologie de Compiègne, France
Benoit Frenay	University of Namur, Belgium
Bernardo Moreno Sanchez	University of Helsinki, Finland
Bernhard Pfahringer	University of Waikato, New Zealand
Bertrand Cuissart	University of Caen, France
Bin Liu	Chongqing University of Posts and Telecommunications, China
Bin Shi	Xi'an Jiaotong University, China
Bin Wu	Zhengzhou University, China
Bin Zhou	National University of Defense Technology, China
Bitao Peng	Guangdong University of Foreign Studies, China
Bo Kang	Ghent University, Belgium
Bogdan Cautis	Université Paris-Saclay, France
Bojan Evkoski	Central European University, Hungary
Boshen Shi	Institute of Computing Technology, Chinese Academy of Sciences, China
Boualem Benatallah	Dublin City University, Ireland
Brandon Gower-Winter	Utrecht University, Netherlands
Bunil K. Balabantaray	NIT Meghalaya, India
Carlos Ferreira	INESC TEC, Portugal
Carlos Monserrat-Aranda	Universitat Politècnica de Valencia, Spain
Carson K. Leung	University of Manitoba, Canada
Catarina Silva	University of Coimbra, Portugal
Cecile Capponi	Aix-Marseille University, France
Celine Rouveirol	LIPN Université de Sorbonne Paris Nord, France

Cesar H. G. Andrade	Porto University, Portugal
Chandrajit Bajaj	University of Texas, Austin, USA
Chang Rajani	University of Helsinki, Finland
Charlotte Laclau	Polytechnique Institute, Télécom Paris, France
Charlotte Pelletier	Université de Bretagne du Sud, France
Chen Wang	DATA61, CSIRO, Australia
Cheng Cheng	Carnegie Mellon University, USA
Cheng Xie	Yunnan University, China
Chenglin Wang	East China Normal University, China
Chenwang Wu	University of Science and Technology of China, China
Chiara Pugliese	IIT Institute of National Research Council, Italy
Chien-Liang Liu	National Chiao Tung University, Taiwan
Chihiro Maru	Chuo University, Japan
Chongsheng Zhang	Henan University, China
Christian Beecks	FernUniversität in Hagen, Germany
Christian M. M. Frey	University of Technology Nuremberg, Germany
Christian Hakert	TU Dortmund, Germany
Christine Largeron	LabHC Lyon University, France
Christophe Rigotti	INSA Lyon, France
Christophe Rodrigues	DVRC Pôle universitaire Léonard de Vinci, France
Christos Anagnostopoulos	University of Glasgow, UK
Christos Diou Harokopio	University of Athens, Greece
Chuan Qin	Chinese Academy of Sciences, China
Chunchun Chen	Tongji University, China
Chunyao Song	Nankai University, China
Claire Nedellec	INRAE, MaIAGE, France
Claudio Borile	CENTAI Institute, Italy
Claudio Gallicchio	University of Pisa, Italy
Claudius Zelenka	Kiel University, Germany
Colin Bellinger	NRC and Dalhousie University, Canada
Collin Leiber	Aalto University, Finland
Cong Qi	New Jersey Institute of Technology, USA
Congfeng Cao	University of Amsterdam, Netherlands
Corrado Loglisci	Università degli Studi di Bari, Aldo Moro, Italy
Cuicui Luo	University of Chinese Academy of Sciences, China
Cuneyt G. Akcora	University of Central Florida, USA
Cynthia C. S. Liem	Delft University of Technology, Netherlands
Dalius Matuzevicius	Vilnius Gediminas Technical University, Lithuania

Dan Li	Sun Yat-sen University, China
Danai Koutra	University of Michigan, USA
Dang Nguyen	Deakin University, Australia
Daniel Neider	TU Dortmund, Germany
Daniel Schlor	Universität Würzburg, Germany
Danil Provodin	TU Eindhoven, Netherlands
Danyang Xiao	Sun Yat-sen University, China
Dario Garcia-Gasulla	Barcelona Supercomputing Center (BSC), Spain
Dario Garigliotti	University of Bergen, Norway
Darius Plonis	Vilnius Gediminas Technical University, Lithuania
Dariusz Brzezinski	Poznań University of Technology, Poland
David Gomez	Universidad Politecnica de Madrid, Spain
David Holzmüller	University of Stuttgart, Germany
David Q. Sun	Apple, USA
Davide Evangelista	University of Bologna, Italy
Debo Cheng	University of South Australia, Australia
Deepayan Chakrabarti	University of Texas at Austin, USA
Deng-Bao Wang	Southeast University, China
Denilson Barbosa	University of Alberta, Canada
Denis Huseljic	University of Kassel, Germany
Denis Lukovnikov	Ruhr-Universität Bochum, Germany
Destercke Sebastien	UTC, France
Di Jin	TikTok, USA
Di Wu	Chongqing Institute of Green and Intelligent Technology, Chinese Academy of Sciences, China
Diana Benavides Prado	University of Auckland, New Zealand
Dianhui Wang	Independent Researcher, Australia
Diego Carrera	STMicroelectronics, Switzerland
Diletta Chiaro	Università degli Studi di Napoli Federico II, Italy
Dimitri Staufer	TU Berlin, Germany
Dimitrios Katsaros	University of Thessaly, Greece
Dimitrios Rafailidis	University of Thessaly, France
Dino Ienco	INRAE, France
Dmitry Kobak	University of Tübingen, Germany
Domenico Redavid	University of Bari, Italy
Dominik M. Endres	Philipps-Universität Marburg, Germany
Dominique Gay	Université de La Réunion, France
Dong Li	Baylor University, USA
Duarte Folgado	Fraunhofer Portugal AICOS, Portugal
Duo Xu	Georgia Institute of Technology, USA

Edoardo Serra	Boise State University, USA
Edouard Fouche	Karlsruhe Institute of Technology (KIT), Germany
Eduardo F. Montesuma	Université Paris-Saclay, France
Edward Apeh	Bournemouth University, UK
Edwin Simpson	University of Bristol, UK
Ehsan Aminian	INESC TEC, Portugal
Ekaterina Antonenko	Mines Paris - PSL, France
Eliana Pastor	Politecnico di Torino, Italy
Emanuela Marasco	George Mason University, USA
Emilio Dorigatti	LMU Munich, Germany
Emilio Parrado-Hernandez	Universidad Carlos III de Madrid, Spain
Emmanouil Krasanakis	CERTH, Greece
Emmanouil Panagiotou	Freie Universität Berlin, Germany
Emre Gursoy	Koc University, Turkey
Engelbert Mephu Nguifo	Université Clermont Auvergne, CNRS, LIMOS, France
Eran Treister	Ben-Gurion University of the Negev, Israel
Erasmo Purificato	Otto-von-Guericke Universität Magdeburg, Germany
Erik Novak	Jožef Stefan Institute, Slovenia
Erwan Le Merrer	Inria, France
Esra Akbas	Georgia State University, USA
Esther-Lydia Silva-Ramirez	Universidad de Cadiz, Spain
Evaldas Vaičiukynas	Kaunas University of Technology, Lithuania
Evangelos Kanoulas	University of Amsterdam, Netherlands
Evelin Amorim	INESC TEC, Portugal
Fabian C. Spaeh	Boston University, USA
Fabio Fassetti	Università della Calabria, Italy
Fabio Fumarola	Prometeia, Italy
Fabio Mercorio	University of Milan-Bicocca, Italy
Fabio Vandin	University of Padova, Italy
Fandel Lin	University of Southern California, USA
Federica Granese	Inria, Université Côte d'Azur, France
Federico Baldo	University of Bologna, Italy
Federico Sabbatini	National Institute for Nuclear Physics (INFN), Italy
Feifan Zhang	China Agricultural University, China
Felipe Kenji Nakano	KU Leuven, Belgium
Fernando Martinez-Plumed	Universitat Politècnica de Valencia, Spain
Filipe Rodrigues	Technical University of Denmark (DTU), Denmark

Flavio Giobergia	Politecnico di Torino, Italy
Florent Masseglia	Inria, France
Florian Beck	JKU Linz, Austria
Florian Lemmerich	University of Passau, Germany
Francesca Naretto	University of Pisa, Italy
Francesco Piccialli	University of Naples Federico II, Italy
Francesco Renna	Universidade do Porto, Portugal
Francisco Pereira	DTU, Denmark
Franco Raimondi	Gran Sasso Science Institute, Italy
Frederic Koriche	Université d'Artois, CRIL CNRS, France
Frederic Pennerath	CentraleSupélec - LORIA, France
Furong Peng	Shanxi University, China
Gabriel Marques Tavares	LMU Munich, Germany
Gabriele Sartor	University of Turin, Italy
Gabriele Venturato	KU Leuven, Belgium
Gaetan De Waele	Ghent University, Belgium
Gaia Saveri	University of Trieste, Italy
Gang Li	Deakin University, Australia
Gaoyuan Du	Amazon, USA
Gavin Smith	University of Nottingham, UK
Geming Xia	National University of Defense Technology, China
Geng Zhao	Heidelberg University, Germany
Gennaro Vessio	University of Bari Aldo Moro, Italy
Geoffrey I. Webb	Monash, Australia
Georgia Baltsou	Centre for Research & Technology, Greece
Geraldin Nanfack	Concordia University, Canada
Germain Forestier	University of Haute Alsace, France
Gerrit Grossmann	DFKI, Germany
Gerrit J. J. van den Burg	Alan Turing Institute, UK
Gherardo Varando	Universitat de Valencia, Spain
Giacomo Medda	University of Cagliari, Italy
Gilberto Bernardes	INESC TEC and University of Porto, Portugal
Giorgio Venturin	University of Padova, Italy
Giovanna Castellano	University of Bari Aldo Moro, Italy
Giovanni Ponti	ENEA, Italy
Giovanni Stilo	Università degli Studi dell'Aquila, Italy
Gisele Pappa	UFMG, Brazil
Giuseppe Manco	ICAR-CNR, IT, Italy
Gizem Gezici	Scuola Normale Superiore, Italy
Gjergji Kasneci	TU Munich, Germany
Goreti Marreiros	ISEP/GECAD, Portugal

Graziella De Martino   University of Bari, Aldo Moro, Italy
Grazina Korvel   Vilnius University, Lithuania
Grigorios Tsoumakas   Aristotle University of Thessaloniki, Greece
Guangyin Jin   National University of Defense Technology,
                          China
Guangzhong Sun   University of Science and Technology of China,
                          China
Guanjin Wang   Murdoch University, Australia
Guilherme Weigert   Cassales University of Waikato, New Zealand
Guillaume Derval   UC Louvain - ICTEAM, Belgium
Guorui Quan   University of Manchester, UK
Guoxi Zhang   Beijing Institute of General Artificial Intelligence,
                          China
Gustau Camps-Valls   Universitat de Valencia, Spain
Gustav Sir   Czech Technical University, Czech Republic
Gustavo Batista   University of New South Wales, Australia
Hachem Kadri   Aix-Marseille University, France
Hadi Asghari   Humboldt Institute for Internet and Society,
                          Germany
Haifeng Sun   University of Science and Technology of China,
                          China
Haihui Fan   Institute of Information Engineering, Chinese
                          Academy of Sciences, China
Haizhou Du   Shanghai University of Electric Power, China
Hajer Salem   AUDENSIEL, France
Hakim Hacid   TII, United Arab Emirates
Hamid Bouchachia   Bournemouth University, UK
Han Wang   Xidian University, China
Hang Yu   Shanghai University, China
Hanna Sumita   Institute of Science Tokyo, Japan
Hao Niu   KDDI Research, Japan
Hao Xue   University of New South Wales, Australia
Hao Yan   Carleton University, Canada
Haowen Zhang   Zhejiang Sci-Tech University, China
Harsh Borse   IIT Kharagpur, India
Heitor M. Gomes   Victoria University of Wellington, New Zealand
Helder Oliveira   FCUP and INESC TEC, Portugal
Helge Langseth   Norwegian University of Science and Technology,
                          Norway
Hendrik Blockeel   KU Leuven, Belgium
Henrique O. Marques   University of Southern Denmark, Denmark
Henryk Maciejewski   Wroclaw University of Science and Technology,
                          Poland

Jia Cai	Guangdong University of Finance and Economics, China
Jiahui Jin	Southeast University, China
Jiang Zhong	Independent Researcher, China
Jianwu Wang	University of Maryland, Baltimore County, USA
Jiawei Chen	Tianjin University, China
Jiaxin Ding	Shanghai Jiao Tong University, China
Jidong Yuan	Beijing Jiaotong University, China
Jie Song	Zhejiang University, China
Jie Wu	Fudan University, China
Jie Yang	University of Wollongong, China
Jimeng Shi	Florida International University, USA
Jin Chen	Hong Kong University of Science and Technology, China
Jin Liang	South China Normal University, China
Jing Ren	NUDT, China
Jing Wang	Amazon, USA
Jinghui Zhong	South China University of Technology, China
Jingtao Ding	Tsinghua University, China
Jinli Zhang	Beijing University of Technology, China
Jiri Sima	Czech Academy of Sciences, Czech Republic
João Gama	University of Porto, Portugal
Joao Mendes-Moreira	University of Porto, Portugal
Joao Vinagre	European Commission (JRC), Spain
Joaquim Silva	NOVA LINCS, Universidade Nova de Lisboa, Portugal
Jochen De Weerdt	KU Leuven, Belgium
Joe Mellor	University of Edinburgh, UK
Johanne Cohen	LISN-CNRS, France
Johannes Jakubik	IBM Research, USA
John W. Sheppard	Montana State University, USA
Jonata Tyska Carvalho	Federal University of Santa Catarina, Brazil
Jordi Guitart	Barcelona Supercomputing Center (BSC), Spain
Joris Mattheijssens	Ghent University, Belgium
Jose M. Costa Pereira	University of Porto, Portugal
Jose Oramas	University of Antwerp, sqIRL/IDLab, imec, Belgium
Jose Tomas Palma	University of Murcia, Spain
Joydeep Chandra	Indian Institute of Technology, Patna, India
Juan A. Botia	University of Murcia, Spain
Juan Rodriguez	Universidad de Burgos, Spain
Jukka Heikkonen	University of Turku, Finland

Li Wang	National University of Defense Technology, China
Liang Du	Shanxi University, China
Lianyong Qi	China University of Petroleum (East China), China
Lijie Hu	King Abdullah University of Science and Technology, Saudi Arabia
Lijing Zhu	Bowling Green State University, USA
Lingling Zhang	Capital Normal University, China
Lingyue Fu	Shanghai Jiao Tong University, China
Linh Le Pham Van	Deakin University, Australia
Livio Bioglio	University of Turin, Italy
Lixing Yu	Yunnan University, China
Liyan Song	Harbin Institute of Technology, China
Longlong Sun	Chang'an University, China
Luca Corbucci	University of Pisa, Italy
Luca Ferragina	University of Calabria, Italy
Luca Romeo	University of Macerata, Italy
Lucas Pereira	LARSyS, Tecnico Lisboa, Portugal
Luciano Caroprese	ICAR-CNR, Italy
Ludovico Boratto	University of Cagliari, Italy
Luis Rei	Jožef Stefan Institute, Slovenia
Mahardhika Pratama	University of South Australia, Australia
Maiju Karjalainen	University of Eastern Finland, Finland
Makoto Onizuka	Osaka University, Japan
Manali Sharma	Samsung, South Korea
Maneet Singh	MasterCard, India
Manuel M. Garcia-Piqueras	Universidad de Castilla La Mancha, Spain
Manuele Bicego	University of Verona, Italy
Mao A. Cheng	University of California, Berkeley, USA
Marc Plantevit	EPITA, France
Marc Tommasi	Lille University, France
Marcel Wever	Leibniz University Hannover, Germany
Marcilio de Souto	LIFO/Université d'Orleans, France
Marco Lippi	University of Florence, Italy
Marco Loog	Radboud University, Netherlands
Marco Mellia	Politecnico di Torino, Italy
Marco Podda	University of Pisa, Italy
Marco Polignano	Università di Bari, Italy
Marco Viviani	Università degli Studi di Milano Bicocca, Italy
Maria Vasconcelos	Fraunhofer Portugal AICOS, Portugal
Maria Sofia Bucarelli	Sapienza University of Rome, Italy

Mariana Oliveira	Universidade do Porto, Portugal
Mariana Vargas Vieyra	MostlyAI, Austria
Marielle Malfante	CEA, France
Marina Litvak	Shamoon College of Engineering, Israel
Mario Antunes	Universidade de Aveiro, Portugal
Mario Andres Munoz	University of Melbourne, Australia
Marius Koppel	Johannes Gutenberg University Mainz, Germany
Mark Junjie Li	Shenzhen University, China
Marko Robnik-Sikonja	University of Ljubljana, Slovenia
Marta Soare	Université d'Orleans, France
Martin Holena	Czech Academy of Sciences, Czech Republic
Martin Pilat	Charles University, Czech Republic
Martino Ciaperoni	Aalto University, Finland
Marwan Hassani	TU Eindhoven, Netherlands
Masahiro Suzuki	University of Tokyo, Japan
Massimo Guarascio	ICAR-CNR, Italy
Matej Mihelcic	University of Zagreb, Croatia
Mathias Verbeke	KU Leuven, Belgium
Mathieu Lefort	Université de Lyon, France
Matteo Francobaldi	University of Bologna, Italy
Matteo Riondato	Amherst College, USA
Matteo Salis	University of Turin, Italy
Matthew B. Middlehurst	University of Southampton, UK
Matthia Sabatelli	University of Groningen, Netherlands
Mattia Cerrato	JGU Mainz, Germany
Mattia Setzu	University of Pisa, Italy
Mattis Hartwig	German Research Center for Artificial Intelligence, Germany
Matyas Bohacek	Stanford University, USA
Maximilian T. Fischer	University of Konstanz, Germany
Maximilian Münch	University of Applied Sciences, Würzburg-Schweinfurt, Germany
Maximilian Stubbemann	University of Hildesheim, Germany
Maximilian Thiessen	TU Wien, Austria
Maximilian von Zastrow	Southern Denmark University, Denmark
Megha Khosla	TU Delft, Netherlands
Meiyun Zuo	Renmin University of China, China
Meng Liu	National University of Defense Technology, China
Mengying Zhu	Zhejiang University, China
Michael Granitzer	University of Passau, Germany
Michael B. Ito	University of Michigan, USA

Michael G. Madden	National University of Ireland, Galway, Ireland
Michal Wozniak	Wroclaw University of Science and Technology, Poland
Michele Fontana	Università di Pisa, Italy
Michiel Stock	Ghent University, Belgium
Miguel Rocha	University of Minho, Portugal
Miguel Silva	INESC TEC, Portugal
Mike Holenderski	Eindhoven University of Technology, Netherlands
Milos Savic	University of Novi Sad, Serbia
Mina Rezaei	LMU Munich, Germany
Minh P. Nguyen	University of Texas, Austin, USA
Minyoung Choe	Korea Advanced Institute of Science and Technology, South Korea
Minyu Chen	Shanghai Jiaotong University, China
Miquel Perello-Nieto	University of Bristol, UK
Mira Kristin Jurgens	Ghent University, Belgium
Miriam Santos	University of Porto, Portugal
Mirko Bunse	TU Dortmund, Germany
Mirko Polato	University of Turin, Italy
Mitra Baratchi	LIACS, University of Leiden, Netherlands
Mohammed Elbamby	Telefonica Scientific Research, Spain
Moises Rocha dos Santos	University of Porto, Portugal
Monowar Bhuyan	Umeå University, Sweden
Morteza Rakhshaninejad	Ghent University, Belgium
Mounim A. El Yacoubi	Télécom SudParis, France
Muhammad Rajabinasab	University of Southern Denmark, Denmark
Muhao Guo	Arizona State University, USA
Mustapha Lebbah	Paris Saclay University-Versailles, France
Nabeel Hussain Syed	Rheinland-Pfälzische Technische Universität, Kaiserslautern-Landau, Germany
Nandyala Hemachandra	Indian Institute of Technology Bombay, India
Nannan Wu	Tianjin University, China
Nanqing Dong	Shanghai Artificial Intelligence Laboratory, China
Naresh Manwani	International Institute of Information Technology, Hyderabad, India
Natan Tourne	Ghent University, Belgium
Nate Veldt	Texas A&M, USA
Nathalie Japkowicz	American University, USA
Natthawut Kertkeidkachorn	Japan Advanced Institute of Science and Technology (JAIST), Japan
Ngoc-Son Vu	ENSEA, France
Nhat-Tan Bui	University of Arkansas, USA

Nian Li	Tsinghua University, China
Nick Lim	University of Waikato, New Zealand
Nico Piatkowski	Fraunhofer IAIS, Germany
Nicolas Roque dos Santos	University of São Paulo, Brazil
Niklas A. Strauss	LMU Munich, Germany
Nikolaj Tatti	Helsinki University, Finland
Nikolaos Nikolaou	University College London, UK
Nikolaos Stylianou	Information Technologies Institute, Greece
Nikos Kanakaris	University of Southern California, USA
Ning Xu	Southeast University, China
Nripsuta Saxena	University of Southern California, USA
Nuwan Gunasekara	Halmstad University, Sweden
Olga Kurasova	Vilnius University, Lithuania
Olga Slizovskaia	AstraZeneca, UK
Olivier Teste	IRIT, University of Toulouse, France
Oswald C.	NIT Trichy, India
Oswaldo Solarte-Pabon	Universidad del Valle, Colombia
Ozge Alacam	University of Bielefeld, Germany
P. S. Sastry	Indian Institute of Science, India
Pablo Olmos	Universidad Carlos III de Madrid, Spain
Panagiotis Karras	University of Copenhagen, Denmark
Panagiotis Symeonidis	University of the Aegean, Greece
Pance Panov	Jožef Stefan Institute, Slovenia
Paolo Bonetti	Politecnico di Milano, Italy
Paolo Merialdo	Università degli Studi Roma Tre, Italy
Paolo Mignone	University of Bari Aldo Moro, Italy
Pascal Welke	TU Wien, Austria
Patrick Y. Wu	American University, USA
Paul Caillon	LAMSADE Université Paris Dauphine - PSL, France
Paul Davidsson	Malmo University, Sweden
Paul Prasse	University of Potsdam, Germany
Paulo J. Azevedo	Universidade do Minho, Portugal
Pawel Teisseyre	Warsaw University of Technology, Poland
Pawel Zyblewski	Wroclaw University of Science and Technology, Poland
Pedro G. Ferreira	University of Porto, Portugal
Pedro Larrañaga	Technical University of Madrid, Spain
Pedro Ribeiro	University of Porto, Portugal
Pedro H. Abreu	CISUC, Portugal
Peijie Sun	Tsinghua University, China
Peng Wu	Shanghai Jiao Tong University, China

Pengpeng Qiao	Institute of Science Tokyo, Japan
Peter Karsmakers	KU Leuven, Belgium
Peter Schneider-Kamp	SDU, Denmark
Peter van der Putten	Leiden University, Netherlands
Petia Georgieva	University of Aveiro, Portugal
Philipp Vaeth	Technical University of Applied Sciences Würzburg-Schweinfurt and Universität Bielefeld, Germany
Philippe Preux	Inria, France
Phung Lai	SUNY-Albany, USA
Pierre Geurts	Montefiore Institute, University of Liège, Belgium
Pierre Monnin	Université Côte d'Azur, Inria, CNRS, I3S, France
Pierre Schaus	UC Louvain, Belgium
Pierre Wolinski	Paris Dauphine University - PSL, France
Pieter Robberechts	KU Leuven, Belgium
Pietro Sabatino	ICAR-CNR, Italy
Pingchuan Ma	HKUST, China
Piotr Habas	Amazon, USA
Piotr Lipinski	University of Wroclaw, Poland
Piotr Porwik	University of Silesia, Katowice, Poland
Prithwish Chakraborty	IBM Corporation, USA
Lucie Flek	Marburg University, Germany
Przemyslaw Biecek	Warsaw University of Technology, Poland
Qiang Sheng	Institute of Computing Technology, Chinese Academy of Sciences, China
Qiang Zhou	Nanjing University of Aeronautics and Astronautics, China
Rafet Sifa	Fraunhofer IAIS, Germany
Raha Moraffah	Arizona State University, USA
Raivydas Simanas	Vilnius University, Lithuania
Rajeev Rastogi	Amazon, USA
Ranya Almohsen	Baylor College of Medicine, USA
Raphael Romero	Ghent University, Belgium
Raquel Sebastiao	ESTGV-IPV & IEETA-UA, Portugal
Ravi Kolla	Sony Research India, India
Raza Ul Mustafa	Loyola University, USA
Remy Cazabet	Université de Lyon 1, France
Renhe Jiang	University of Tokyo, Japan
Reza Akbarinia	Inria, France
Ricardo P. M. Cruz	University of Porto (FEUP), Portugal
Ricardo B. Prudencio	Universidade Federal de Pernambuco, Brazil
Ricardo Rios	Federal University of Bahia, Brazil

Ricardo Santos	Fraunhofer Portugal AICOS, Portugal
Riccardo Guidotti	University of Pisa, Italy
Robertas Damasevicius	Vytautas Magnus University, Lithuania
Roberto Corizzo	American University, USA
Roberto Interdonato	CIRAD, France
Rocio Chongtay	University of Southern Denmark, Denmark
Rohit Babbar	University of Bath, UK and Aalto University, Finland
Romain Tavenard	Université de Rennes, LETG/IRISA, France
Rosana Veroneze	LBiC, Italy
Ruggero G. Pensa	University of Turin, Italy
Rui Meng	BNU-HKBU United International College, USA
Rui Yu	University of Louisville, USA
Ruixuan Liu	Emory University, USA
Runqun Xiong	Southeast University, China
Runxue Bao	University of Pittsburgh, USA
Ruochun Jin	National University of Defense Technology, China
Ruta Juozaitiene	Vytautas Magnus University, Lithuania
Rytis Maskeliunas	Polsl, Poland
Salvatore Ruggieri	University of Pisa, Italy
Sam Verboven	Vrije Universiteit Brussel, Belgium
Sangkyun Lee	Korea University, South Korea
Sara Abdali	University of California, Riverside, USA
Sarah Masud	LCS2, IIIT-D, India
Sarwan Ali	Georgia State University, USA
Satoru Koda	Fujitsu Limited, Japan
Sebastian Buschjager	Lamarr Institute for ML and AI, Germany
Sebastian Jimenez	Ghent University, Belgium
Sebastian Meznar	Jožef Stefan Institute, Ljubljana, Slovenia
Sebastian Ventura Soto	University of Cordoba, Spain
Sebastien Razakarivony	Safran, France
Selpi Selpi	Chalmers University of Technology, Sweden
Sergio Greco	University of Calabria, Italy
Sergio Jesus	Feedzai, Portugal
Sha Lu	University of South Australia, Australia
Shalini Priya	Indian Institute of Technology Patna, India
Shanqing Guo	Shandong University, China
Shaofu Yang	Southeast University, China
Shazia Tabassum	INESCTEC, Portugal
Shengxiang Gao	Kunming University of Science and Technology, China

Shichao Pei	University of Massachusetts, Boston, USA
Shin Matsushima	University of Tokyo, Japan
Shin-ichi Maeda	Preferred Networks, Japan
Shiwen Ni	Chinese Academy of Sciences, China
Shiyou Qian	Shanghai Jiao Tong University, China
Shu Zhao	Anhui University, China
Shuai Li	University of Cambridge, UK and University of Tokyo, Japan, Tsinghua University, China
Shuang Cheng	Institute of Computing Technology, Chinese Academy of Sciences, China
Shubhranshu Shekhar	Brandeis University, USA
Shurui Cao	Carnegie Mellon University, USA
Shuteng Niu	Mayo Clinic, USA
Siamak Ghodsi	Leibniz University of Hannover, Germany
Sihai Zhang	University of Science and Technology of China, China
Silvia Chiusano	Politecnico di Torino, Italy
Silviu Maniu	Université de Grenoble Alpes, France
Simon Gottschalk	L3S Research Center, Leibniz Universität Hannover, Germany
Simona Nistico	University of Calabria, Italy
Simone Angarano	Politecnico di Torino, Italy
Sinong Zhao	Nankai University, China
Siwei Wang	Intelligent Game and Decision Lab, China
Sofoklis Kitharidis	LIACS, Netherlands
Songlin Du	University of Melbourne, Australia
Songlin Du	Southeast University, China
Soumyajit Chatterjee	Nokia Bell Labs, USA
Sourav Dutta	Huawei Research Centre, China
Stefan Duffner	University of Lyon, France
Stefan Heindorf	Paderborn University, Germany
Stefan Kesselheim	Forschungszentrum Jülich, Germany
Stefano Bortoli	Huawei Research Center, China
Stefanos Vrochidis	Information Technologies Institute, CERTH, Greece
Steffen Thoma	FZI Research Center for Information Technology, Germany
Stephan Doerfel	Kiel University of Applied Sciences, Germany
Steven D. Prestwich	University College Cork, Ireland
Suman Banerjee	IIT Jammu, India
Sunil Aryal	Deakin University, Australia
Surabhi Adhikari	Columbia University, USA

Tsunenori Mine	Kyushu University, Japan
Tuan Le	New Mexico State University, USA
Tuwe Lofstrom	Jönköping University, Sweden
Ulf Johansson	Jönköping University, Sweden
Vadim Ermolayev	Ukrainian Catholic University, Ukraine
Vahan Martirosyan	CentraleSupélec, Belgium
Vana Kalogeraki	Athens University of Economics and Business, Greece
Vanessa Gomez-Verdejo	Universidad Carlos III de Madrid, Spain
Vasileios Iosifidis	SCHUFA Holding, Germany
Vasilis Gkolemis	ATHENA RC, Greece
Victor Charpenay	Mines Saint-Etienne, France
Vincent Derkinderen	KU Leuven, Belgium
Vincent Lemaire	Orange Research, France
Vincenzo Pasquadibisceglie	University of Bari, Aldo Moro, Italy
Virginijus Marcinkevicius	Vilnius University, Lithuania
Vitor Cerqueira	University of Porto, Portugal
Vivek Kumar	Universität der Bundeswehr München, Germany
Vivek Srikumar	University of Utah, USA
Wagner Meira Jr.	UFMG, Brazil
Wei Wu	Ben Gurion University of the Negev, Israel
Weichen Li	RPTU Kaiserslautern-Landau, Germany
Weifeng Xu	Independent Researcher, China
Weike Pan	Shenzhen University, China
Weiwei Jiang	Beijing University of Posts and Telecommunications, China
Weiwei Sun	Carnegie Mellon University, USA
Weiwei Yuan	Nanjing University of Aeronautics and Astronautics, China
Weixiong Rao	Tongji University, China
Wen-Bo Xie	Southwest Petroleum University, China
Wenhao Li	Tongji University, China
Wenhao Zheng	Shopee, Singapore
Wenjie Feng	National University of Singapore, Singapore
Wenjie Xi	George Mason University, USA
Wenshui Luo	Nanjing University of Science and Technology, China
Wentao Yu	Nanjing University of Science and Technology, China
Wenzhe Yi	Wuhan University, China
Wenzhong Li	Nanjing University, China
Wojciech Rejchel	Nicolaus Copernicus University, Torun, Poland

Xi Jiang	Southern University of Science and Technology, China
Xiang Li	East China Normal University, China
Xiang Lian	Kent State University, USA
Xiao Ma	Beijing University of Posts and Telecommunications, China
Xiao Zhang	Shandong University, China
Xiaobing Zhou	Yunnan University, China
Xiaofeng Cao	University of Technology Sydney, Australia
Xiaofeng Gao	Shanghai Jiaotong University, China
Xiaojun Chen	Institute of Information Engineering, Chinese Academy of Sciences, China
Xiao-Jun Zeng	University of Manchester, UK
Xiaoming Zhang	Beihang University, China
Xiaoting Zhao	Etsy, USA
Xiaowei Mao	Beijing Jiaotong University, China
Xiaoyu Shi	Chinese Academy of Sciences, China
Xin Du	University of Edinburgh, UK
Xin Qin	California State University, Long Beach, USA
Xing Tang	Tencent, China
Xing Xing	Tongji University, China
Xinning Zhu	Beijing University of Posts and Telecommunications, China
Xinpeng Lv	National University of Defense Technology, China
Xintao Wu	University of Arkansas, USA
Xinyang Zhang	University of Illinois at Urbana-Champaign, USA
Xinyu Guan	Xi'an Jiaotong University, China
Xixun Lin	Chinese Academy of Sciences, China
Xiyue Zhang	University of Bristol, UK
Xuan-Hong Dang	IBM T.J. Watson Research Center, USA
Xue Li	University of Queensland, Australia
Xue Yan	Institute of Automation, Chinese Academy of Sciences, China
Xuefeng Chen	Chongqing University, China
Xuemin Wang	Guilin University of Electronic Technology, China
Yachuan Zhang	East China University of Science and Technology, China
Yan Zhang	Peking University, China
Yang Li	University of North Carolina at Chapel Hill, USA
Yang Shu	East China Normal University, China
Yang Wei	Nanjing University of Science and Technology, China

Yanhao Wang	East China Normal University, China
Yanmin Zhu	Shanghai Jiao Tong University, China
Yansong Y. L. Li	University of Ottawa, Canada
Yao-Xiang Ding	Nanjing University, China
Yaqi Xie	Carnegie Mellon University, USA
Yasutoshi Ida	NTT, Japan
Yaying Zhang	Tongji University, China
Ye Zhu	Deakin University, Australia
Yeon-Chang Lee	Ulsan National Institute of Science and Technology, South Korea
Yexiang Xue	Purdue University, USA
Yi Wang	Xinjiang Technical Institute of Physics and Chemistry, Chinese Academy of Sciences, China
Yifeng Gao	University of Texas, Rio Grande Valley, USA
Yilun Jin	Hong Kong University of Science and Technology, China
Yin Zhang	University of Electronic Science and Technology of China, China
Ying Chen	RMIT University, Australia
Yinsheng Li	Fudan University, China
Yong Li	Huawei European Research Center, China
Yongyu Wang	JD Logistics, China
Youhei Akimoto	University of Tsukuba/RIKEN AIP, Japan
You-Wei Luo	Sun Yat-sen University and Jiaying University, China
Yuchen Li	Baidu, China
Yuchen Yang	Harbin Institute of Technology, China
Yudi Zhang	Eindhoven University of Technology, Netherlands
Yuhao Li	University of Melbourne, Australia
Yuheng Jia	Southeast University, China
Yujia Zheng	CMU, USA
Yulong Pei	TU Eindhoven, Netherlands
Yuncheng Jiang	South China Normal University, China
Yuntao Shou	Xi'an Jiaotong University, China
Yunyun Wang	Nanjing University of Posts and Telecommunications, China
Yutong Ye	East China Normal University, China
Yuzhou Chen	University of California, Riverside, USA
Zahraa Abdallah	University of Bristol, UK
Zaineb Chelly Dagdia	UVSQ, Paris-Saclay, France
Zehua Cheng	University of Oxford, UK
Zeyu Chen	University of Auckland, New Zealand

Zhaocheng Ge	Huazhong University of Science and Technology, China
Zhe Yang	Soochow University, China
Zhen Liu	Guangdong University of Foreign Studies, China
Zheng Chen	Osaka University, Japan
Zhenghao Liu	Northeastern University, China
Zhenyu Yang	Macquarie University, Australia
Zhi Li	Tsinghua University, China
Zhichao Han	ETHZ, Switzerland
Zhihui Wang	Fudan University, China
Zhilong Shan	South China Normal University, China
Zhipeng Yin	Florida International University, USA
Zhipeng Zou	Nanjing University of Science and Technology, China
Zhiwen Xiao	Southwest Jiaotong University, China
Zhiwen Zhang	LocationMind, Japan
Zhixin Li	Guangxi Normal University, China
Zhiyong Cheng	Shandong Academy of Sciences, China
Zhong Chen	Southern Illinois University, USA
Zhong Li	Leiden University, Netherlands
Zhong Zhang	Tsinghua University, China
Zhongjing Yu	Peking University, China
Zhuang Liu	Dongbei University of Finance and Economics, China
Zhuo Cao	Forschungszentrum Jülich, Germany
Zhuoming Xie	Guangdong University of Technology, China
Zhuoqun Li	Louisiana State University, USA
Zicheng Zhao	Nanjing University of Science and Technology, China
Zichong Wang	Florida International University, USA
Zifeng Ding	University of Cambridge, UK
Ziheng Chen	Walmart, USA
Zijie J. Wang	Georgia Tech, USA
Zirui Zhuang	Beijing University of Posts and Telecommunications, China
Zixing Song	Chinese University of Hong Kong, China
Ziyu Wang	University of Tokyo, Japan
Ziyue Li	University of Cologne, Germany
Zongxia Xie	Tianjin University, China
Zongyue Li	LMU Munich, Germany
Zuojin Tang	Zhejiang University, China

List of Editors

Bernhard Pfahringer	University of Waikato, New Zealand
Nathalie Japkowicz	American University, USA
Pedro Larrañaga	Technical University of Madrid, Spain
Rita P. Ribeiro	University of Porto, Portugal
Inês Dutra	University of Porto, Portugal
Mykola Pechenisky	TU Eindhoven, The Netherlands
Paulo Cortez	University of Minho, Portugal
Sepideh Pashami	Halmstad University, Sweden
Alípio M. Jorge	University of Porto, Portugal
Carlos Soares	University of Porto, Portugal
João Gama	University of Porto, Portugal
Pedro H. Abreu	University of Coimbra, Portugal

Program Committee – Applied Data Science Track

Nasrullah Sheikh	IBM Research, USA
Aakarsh Malhotra	MasterCard, USA
Aakash Goel	Amazon, USA
Abdoulaye Sakho	Artefact, France
Abhijeet Pendyala	Ruhr-Universität Bochum, Germany
Abu Shad Ahammed	University of Siegen, Germany
Adi Lin	Didi, China
Aditya Gautam	Meta, USA
Ahmed K. Mohamed	Meta, USA
Akihiro Yoshida	Kyushu University, Japan
Akshay Sethi	MasterCard, USA
Alejandro Kuratomi	Stockholm University, Sweden
Alessandro Gambetti	Nova School of Business and Economics, Portugal
Alessandro Leite	INSA Rouen, Inria, France
Alessio Russo	Politecnico di Milano, Italy
Alex Beeson	University of Warwick, UK
Alexander Galozy	Halmstad University, Sweden
Alexander Karlsson	University of Skovde, Sweden
Alexander Kovalenko	Czech Technical University in Prague, Czech Republic
Alexey Zaytsev	Skoltech, Russia
Alina Bazarova	Forschungszentrum Jülich, Germany
Alix Lheritier	Amadeus SAS, France

Allan Tucker	Brunel University London, UK
Alvaro Figueira	CRACS and Universidade do Porto, Portugal
Aman Gulati	Amazon, USA
Amira Soliman	Halmstad University, Sweden
Ana Gjorgjevikj	Jožef Stefan Institute, Slovenia
Anders Holst	RISE SICS, Sweden
André C. P. L. F. de Carvalho	University of São Paulo, Brazil
Andrea Seveso	University of Milan-Bicocca, Italy
Andreas Bender	LMU Munich, Germany
Andreas Henelius	Independent Researcher, Finland
Andreas Holzinger	University of Natural Resources and Life Sciences, Vienna, Austria
Andrei Shelopugin	Independent Researcher, Brazil
Angelo Impedovo	Niuma, Italy
Aniket Chakrabarti	Amazon, USA
Animesh Prasad	Roku, USA
Anisio Lacerda	UFMG, Brazil
Anli Ji	Georgia State University, USA
Antoine Doucet	La Rochelle Université, France
Anton Borg	Blekinge Institute of Technology, Sweden
Antonio Bevilacqua	Meetecho, Italy
Antonis Klironomos	University of Mannheim, Germany
Aron Henriksson	Stockholm University, Sweden
Artur Chudzik	Polish-Japanese Academy of Information Technology, Poland
Arun Venkitaraman	EPFL, Switzerland
Arunabha Choudhury	ASML, Netherlands
Asem Omari	Higher Colleges of Technology, UAE
Ashman Mehra	Birla Institute of Technology and Science, India
Ashwani Rao	Amazon, USA
Asier Rodriguez	BBVA, Spain
Asma Atamna	Ruhr-Universität Bochum, Germany
Atiye Sadat Hashemi	Halmstad University, Sweden
Atul Anand Gopalakrishnan	SUNY Buffalo, USA
Avani Wildani	Emory University, USA
Aviv Rovshitz	Ben-Gurion University of the Negev, Israel
Axel Brando	Barcelona Supercomputing Center (BSC) and Universitat de Barcelona (UB), Spain
Azadeh Alavi	RMIT University, Australia
Beihong Jin	Institute of Software, China
Benoit Frenay	University of Namur, Belgium
Berkay Aydin	Georgia State University, USA

Bijaya Adhikari	University of Iowa, USA
Bin Li	Alibaba Group, China
Bo Pang	University of Auckland, New Zealand
Bogdan Ruszczak	Opole University of Technology, Poland
Bohao Qu	Agency for Science, China
Bruno Veloso	INESC TEC, FEP-UP, Portugal
Buyue Qian	Xi'an Jiaotong University, China
Camille Kurtz	Université Paris Cité, France
Cangbai Li	Guangdong University of Technology, China
Carlo Metta	ISTI CNR, Italy
Carlos N. Silla	Pontifical Catholic University of Paraná (PUCPR), Brazil
Cecile Bothorel	IMT Atlantique, France
Cesar Ferri	Universitat Politècnica Valencia, Spain
Chang Li	Apple, USA
Chang-Dong Wang	Sun Yat-sen University, China
Chaofan Li	Karlsruhe Institute of Technology, Germany
Chaoyuan Zuo	Nankai University, China
Chen Gao	Tsinghua University, China
Chen Li	Computer Network Information Center, China
Chen Zhao	Baylor University, USA
Chen-Wei Chang	Virginia Tech, USA
Chenxi Xue	Nanjing Normal University, China
Chongke Bi	Tianjin University, China
Christian M. Adriano	Hasso-Plattner Institute, Germany
Christophe Rodrigues	DVRC Pôle universitaire Léonard de Vinci, France
Chuan Li	Sorbonne University, LIPADE, France
Chunhui Zhang	Dartmouth College, USA
Cristina Soguero Ruiz	Rey Juan Carlos University, Spain
Daheng Wang	Amazon, USA
Daifeng Li	Sun Yat-sen University, China
Damien Fay	HPE Labs, Ireland
Dania Herzalla	Technology Innovation Institute, UAE
Daniel Lemire	University of Quebec (TELUQ), Canada
Daniel Trejo Banos	SDSC, USA
Daochen Zha	Rice University, USA
Dawei Cheng	Tongji University, China
Dayne Freitag	SRI International, USA
Di Yao	Institute of Computing Technology, China
Dimitris Nick Dimitriadis	Aristotle University of Thessaloniki, Greece
Diogo F. Soares	Universidade de Lisboa, Portugal

Dirk Pflueger	University of Stuttgart, Germany
Doheon Han	University of Notre Dame, USA
Dongxiang Zhang	Zhejiang University, China
Dongxiao Yu	Shandong University, China
Dugang Liu	Guangdong Laboratory of Artificial Intelligence and Digital Economy (Shenzen), China
Ece Calikus	Uppsala University, Sweden
Edwyn Brient	Thales LAS/Mines Paris PSL, France
Efstathios Stamatatos	University of the Aegean, Greece
Elaine Faria	UFU, Brazil
Elio Masciari	University of Naples, Italy
Emilie Devijver	Université Grenoble Alpes, Inria, CNRS, Grenoble INP, LIG, France
Emmanuelle Claeys	IRIT, France
Enayat Rajabi	Halmstad University, Sweden
Enda Barrett	University of Galway, Ireland
Enyan Dai	Hong Kong University of Science and Technology (Guangzhou), China
Eric Peukert	ScaDS.AI, Germany
Eric Sanjuan	Avignon University, France
Erik Frisk	Linköping University, Sweden
Eui-Hong (Sam) Han	The Washington Post, USA
Eunil Park	Sungkyunkwan University, South Korea
Fabio Carrara	CNR-ISTI, Italy
Fabiola Pereira	Federal University of Uberlandia, Brazil
Fan Yang	Rice University, USA
Fangzhao Wu	MSRA, China
Fangzhou Shi	Didi Chuxing, China
Fathima Nuzla Ismail	State University of New York, USA
Flavio Bertini	University of Parma, Italy
Francesco Dente	EURECOM, France
Francesco Guerra	University of Modena e Reggio Emilia, Italy
Francesco Scala	CNR-ICAR, Italy
Francesco Spinnato	University of Pisa, Italy
Francesco Paolo Nerini	Sapienza University of Rome, Italy
Francisco P. Romero	UCLM, Spain
Franco Maria Nardini	ISTI-CNR, Italy
Francois Schwarzentruber	ENS Lyon, France
Fudong Lin	University of Delaware, USA
Gabriel Augusto Pinheiro	UNIFESP, Brazil
Gan Sun	South China University of Technology, China

Gargi Srivastava	Rajiv Gandhi Institute of Petroleum Technology Jais, India
Giacomo Boracchi	Politecnico di Milano, Italy
Giuseppe Garofalo	DistriNet, KU Leuven, Belgium
Giuseppina Andresini	University of Bari Aldo Moro, Italy
Goran Falkman	University of Skovde, Sweden
Grzegorz Nalepa	Jagiellonian University, Poland
Guanggang Geng	Jinan University, China
Guojun Liang	Halmstad University, Sweden
Haifang Li	Baidu, China
Haina Tang	University of Chinese Academy of Sciences, China
Hancheng Ge	Amazon, USA
Hao Li	National University of Defense Technology, China
Haohui Chen	CSIRO, Australia
Haomin Yu	Aalborg University, Denmark
Haoyi Xiong	Baidu, China
Hiba Najjar	DFKI, Germany
Hillol Kargupta	Agnik, USA
Hong Zhou	Meta, USA
Hongbin Pei	Xi'an Jiao Tong University, China
Hou-Wan Long	Chinese University of Hong Kong, China
Hua Wei	Arizona State University, USA
Huaiyuan Yao	Xi'an Jiaotong University, China
Huan Song	Amazon, USA
Hubert Baniecki	University of Warsaw, Poland
Hyunsung Kim	KAIST, Fitogether, South Korea
Ibtihal El Mimouni	Inria, France
Ildar Baimuratov	L3S Research Center, Germany
Ilir Jusufi	Blekinge Institute of Technology, Sweden
Inaam Ashraf	Bielefeld University, Germany
Ines Sousa	Fraunhofer AICOS, Portugal
Iris Heerlien	Saxion, Netherlands
Isak Samsten	Stockholm University, Sweden
Ishan Verma	TCS Research, India
Ismail Hakki Toroslu	METU, Turkey
Ivan Carrera	EPN, Ecuador
Jaakko Hollmen	Stockholm University, Sweden
Jairo Cugliari	Laboratoire ERIC, France
Jakub Nalepa	Silesian University of Technology, Poland
Jelica Vasiljević	Hoffmann-La Roche, Switzerland

Jens Lundstrom	Halmstad University, Sweden
Jesse Davis	KU Leuven, Belgium
Jiahui Bai	Meta, USA
Jiajun Gu	Carnegie Mellon University, USA
Jiali Pan	Department of Information Management, USA
Jian Yu	Auckland University of Technology, New Zealand
Jiangbin Zheng	Westlake University, China
Jianhua Yin	Shandong University, China
Jingbo Zhou	Baidu, China
Jingjing Liu	MD Anderson Cancer Center, USA
Jingwen Shi	Michigan State University, USA
Jingxuan Wei	University of Chinese Academy of Sciences, China
Jinyoung Han	Sungkyunkwan University, South Korea
Jiue-An Yang	City of Hope Beckman Research Institute, USA
Joao R. Campos	University of Coimbra, Portugal
Jochen De Weerdt	KU Leuven, Belgium
Joe Tekli	Lebanese American University, Lebanon
Joel Ky	University of Lorraine, CNRS, Inria, France
John McCall	Robert Gordon University, UK
John Mitros	University College Dublin, Ireland
Jonas Fischer	Ruhr-Universität Bochum, Germany
Jonas Nordqvist	Linnaeus University, Sweden
Joydeep Chandra	Indian Institute of Technology Patna, India
Julian Martin Rodemann	LMU Munich, Germany
Jun Shen	University of Wollongong, Australia
Junichi Tatemura	Google, USA
Junxuan Li	Microsoft, USA
Jyun-Yu Jiang	Amazon Science, USA
Kai Wang	Shanghai Jiao Tong University, China
Kaiping Zheng	National University of Singapore, Singapore
Kaiwen Dong	University of Notre Dame, USA
Katarzyna Bozek	University of Cologne, Germany
Katerina Schindlerova	UniVie, Austria
Katharina Dost	Jožef Stefan Institute, Slovenia
Katsiaryna Mirylenka	Zalando SE, Germany
Keith Burghardt	ISI, Germany
Klaus Brinker	Hamm-Lippstadt University of Applied Sciences, Germany
Koki Kawabata	Osaka University, Japan
Korbinian Randl	Stockholm University, Sweden
Krzysztof Krawiec	Poznań University of Technology, Poland

Krzysztof Kutt	Jagiellonian University, Poland
Kwan Hui Lim	Singapore University of Technology and Design, Singapore
Lamija Lemes	University of Zenica, Bosnia & Herzegovina
Le Nguyen	University of Oulu, Finland
Lei Li	Hong Kong University of Science and Technology (Guangzhou), China
Lei Liu	York University, Canada
Li Liu	Chongqing University, China
Li Zhang	University College London, UK
Liang Tang	Google, USA
Liang Tong	NEC Labs America, USA
Liang Wang	Alibaba Group, China
Lina Yao	University of New South Wales, Australia
Lingxiao Li	Michigan State University, USA
Lingyang Chu	McMaster University, Canada
Lixin Zou	Wuhan University, China
Lluis Garcia-Pueyo	Meta, USA
Lou Salaun	Nokia Bell Labs, USA
Luca Corbucci	University of Pisa, Italy
Luca Pappalardo	ISTI, Italy
Luca Romeo	University of Macerata, Italy
Luis Ferreira	Olympus Medical Products Portugal, Portugal
Luis Miguel Matos	ALGORITMI Centre, Portugal
Lukas Grasmann	TU Wien, Austria
Lukas Pensel	Johannes Gutenberg University Mainz, Germany
Maciej Grzenda	Warsaw University of Technology, Poland
Maciej Piernik	Poznań University of Technology, Poland
Madiraju Srilakshmi	Dream Sports, India
Mads C. Hansen	A.P. Moller-Maersk, Denmark
Mahardhika Pratama	University of South Australia, Australia
Mahmoud Rahat	Halmstad University, Sweden
Man Tianxing	Jilin University, China
Manish Gupta	Microsoft, USA
Manos Papagelis	York University, Canada
Manuel Lopes	Instituto Tecnico Superior, Portugal
Manuel Portela	Universitat Pompeu Fabra, Spain
Marc Tommasi	Lille University, France
Marco Fisichella	Leibniz Universität, Hannover, Germany
Maria Riveiro	Jonkoping University, Sweden
Maria Ulan	RISE Research Institutes of Sweden, Sweden
Marian Scuturici	LIRIS, France

Marianne Clausel	IECL, France
Mario Doller	University of Applied Sciences, Kufstein, Austria
Marius Schwammle	DLR/BT, Germany
Markus Gotz	Karlsruhe Institute of Technology (KIT), Germany
Markus Leyser	Technische Universität Dresden, Germany
Martin Boldt	Blekinge Institute of Technology, Sweden
Martin Mladenov	Google, USA
Martin Vita	Institute of Physics, Czech Academy of Sciences, Czech Republic
Matthias Demant	Fraunhofer ISE, Germany
Matthias Galipaud	SDSC, Switzerland
Matthias Petri	Amazon, USA
Matthieu Latapy	CNRS, France
Maurice Van Keulen	University of Twente, Netherlands
Maxime Cordy	University of Luxembourg, Luxembourg
Maxwell J. Jacobson	Purdue University, USA
Md Nahid Hasan	Miami University, USA
Md Zia Ullah	Edinburgh Napier University, UK
Mehtab Alam Syed	CIRAD, France
Melanie Neubauer	University of Leoben, Austria
Meng Chen	Shandong University, China
Mengxuan Zhang	Australian National University, Australia
Miao Fan	NavInfo, China
Michael Bain	University of New South Wales, Australia
Michele Bernardini	Uni eCampus.It, Italy
Michiel Dhont	EluciDATA Lab of Sirris, Belgium
Mickael Coustaty	L3i Laboratory, France
Miguel Couceiro	LORIA, France
Mihaela Mitici	Utrecht University, Netherlands
Min Lee	Singapore Management University, Singapore
Min Hun Lee	Singapore Management University, Singapore
Mina Rezaei	LMU Munich, Germany
Ming Ma	Inner Mongolia University, China
Minghao Chen	Tencent, China
Mirco Nanni	CNR-ISTI Pisa, Italy
Mirjam Wattenhofer	Google, USA
Mirko Marras	University of Cagliari, Italy
Mitra Heidari	University of Melbourne, Australia
Modesto Castrillon-Santana	Universidad de Las Palmas de Gran Canaria, Spain

Mohammadmehdi Saberioon	German Research Centre for Geosciences, Germany
Mohammed Amer	Fujitsu Research of Europe, Germany
Mohammed Ghaith Altarabichi	Halmstad University, Sweden
Mojgan Kouhounestani	University of Melbourne, Australia
Moonki Hong	Sogang University, South Korea
Munira Syed	Procter & Gamble, USA
Nan Li	Microsoft, USA
Narendhar Gugulothu	TCS Research, India
Nedra Mellouli	LIASD, Portugal
Ngoc Son Le	University of Hildesheim, Germany
Niklas Lavesson	Blekinge Institute of Technology, Sweden
Niraj Kumar	Fujitsu, Japan
Nitish Kumar	MasterCard, USA
Nuno Cruz Garcia	FCUL, Portugal
Nuno R. P. S. Guimaraes	INESC TEC, University of Porto, Portugal
Nuwan Gunasekara	Halmstad University, Sweden
Pablo Picazo-Sanchez	Halmstad University, Sweden
Pablo Torrijos Arenas	Universidad de Castilla-La Mancha, Spain
Pablo Jose Del Moral Pastor	Ekkono.ai, Finland
Pan He	Auburn University, USA
Panagiotis Kanellopoulos	University of Essex, UK
Panagiotis Papadakos	FORTH-ICS, Greece
Pandey Shourya Prasad	International Institute of Information Technology, Bangalore, India
Panpan Xu	Amazon AWS, USA
Paola Velardi	Sapienza University of Rome, Italy
Paolo Cintia	Kode, Italy
Pascal Plettenberg	Intelligent Embedded Systems, Italy
Paul Boniol	Inria, France
Pavel Blinov	Sber AI Lab, Russia
Pawel Parczyk	Wroclaw University of Science and Technology, Poland
Pedro M. Ferreira	University of Lisbon, Portugal
Pedro Seber	MIT, USA
Peng Qiao	NUDT, China
Pengyuan Wang	University of Georgia, USA
Petr Olegovich Sokerin	Skoltech, Russia
Philipp Bach	University of Hamburg, Germany
Philipp Froehlich	TU Darmstadt, Germany
Philipp Schmidt	Amazon Research, USA
Philipp Zech	University of Innsbruck, Austria

Pinar Karagoz   Middle East Technical University (METU), Turkey

Ping Luo   Chinese Academy of Sciences, China

Po Yang   University of Sheffield, UK

Pop Petrica   Technical University of Cluj-Napoca, Romania

Prathap Manohar Joshi R   Zoho Corporation, India

Praveen Borra   Florida Atlantic University, USA

Praveen Paruchuri   IIIT Hyderabad, India

Qian Li   Curtin University, Australia

Qihang Yao   Georgia Institute of Technology, USA

Qiwei Han   Nova School of Business and Economics, Portugal

Quentin Duchemin   Université Gustave Eiffel, France

Radu Tudor Ionescu   University of Bucharest, Romania

Rafal Kucharski   Jagiellonian University, Poland

Rafet Sifa   Fraunhofer IAIS & University of Bonn, Germany

Ramasamy Savitha   I2R A*STAR, Singapore

Ran Yu   DSIS Research Group, Singapore

Ranga Raju Vatsavai   North Carolina State University, USA

Raphael Couturier   University of Bourgogne Franche-Comte (UBFC), France

Renato M. Assuncao   ESRI, USA

Renaud Lambiotte   University of Oxford, UK

Reuben Kshitiz Borrison   ABB, Switzerland

Reza Shirvany   Zalando SE, Germany

Ricardo R. Pereira   Feedzai, Portugal

Riccardo Rosati   Università Politecnica delle Marche, Ancona, Italy

Richard Allmendinger   University of Manchester, UK

Richard Nordsieck   XITASO GmbH IT and Software Solutions, Germany

Richi Nayak   Queensland University of Technology, Australia

Roberto Trasarti   CNR, Italy

Rogerio Luis de C. Costa   Polytechnic of Leiria, Portugal

Romain Ilbert   Huawei Paris Research Center, France

Roy Ka-Wei Lee   Singapore University of Technology and Design, Singapore

Ruilin Wang   University of Aberdeen, UK

Sabrina Gaito   Università degli Studi di Milano, Italy

Sai Karthikeya Vemuri   Computer Vision Group Jena, Italy

Saisubramaniam Gopalakrishnan   Quantiphi, USA

Sajjad Shumaly   Max-Planck-Institut for Polymer Research, Germany

Salvatore Rinzivillo	KDD Lab, ISTI, CNR, Italy
Samaneh Shafee	LASIGE, Portugal
Sandra Wissing	Fachhochschule Münster, Germany
Sarwan Ali	Georgia State University, USA
Sebastian Becker	Fraunhofer ISST, Germany
Sebastian Honel	Linnaeus University, Sweden
Selin Colakhasanoglu	Saxion University of Applied Sciences, Netherlands
Senzhang Wang	Central South University, China
Sepideh Nahali	York University, Canada
Shahrooz Abghari	Blekinge Institute of Technology, Sweden
Shahroz Tariq	CSIRO, Australia
Shang Yanlei	BUPT, China
Shen Liang	Paris Cité University, France
Shengheng Liu	Southeast University, China
Shereen Elsayed	University of Hildesheim, Germany
Shi-ting Wen	NingboTech University, China
Shiv Krishna Jaiswal	Walmart Global Tech, USA
Shoujin Wang	Macquarie University, Australia
Shuai Li	University of Cambridge, UK and University of Tokyo, UK
Shuchu Han	Capital One Financial Group, Japan
Simon F. Weinberger	EssilorLuxottica, France
Siyuan Chen	Guangzhou University, China
Snehanshu Saha	BITS Pilani Goa Campus, India
Souhaib Ben Taieb	University of Mons, Abu Dhabi
Sriparna Saha	IIT Patna, India
Stefan Rueping	Fraunhofer IAIS, Germany
Stephane Chretien	Université Lyon 2, France
Sunil Aryal	Deakin University, Australia
Susana Ladra	University of A Coruña, Spain
Szymon Bobek	Jagiellonian University, Poland
Szymon Jaroszewicz	Institute of Computer Science, Poland
Szymon Wilk	Poznań University of Technology, Poland
Tanel Tammet	Tallinn University of Technology, Estonia
Thanh Thi Nguyen	Monash University, Australia
Thiago Zangato	Université Sorbonne Paris Nord, France
Theodora Tsikrika	Information Technologies Institute, Greece
Thibault Girardin	Université Jean Monnet, France
Thomas Czernichow	Darwinlabs, Portugal
Thorsteinn Rognvaldsson	Halmstad University, Sweden
Tiago Mendes-Neves	FEUP/INESC TEC, Portugal

Tianshu Yu	Chinese University of Hong Kong (Shenzhen), China
Ting Su	Imperial College London, UK
Tingrui Qiao	University of Auckland, New Zealand
Tobias Glasmachers	Ruhr-Universität Bochum, Germany
Tomas Olsson	RISE SICS, Sweden
Tome Eftimov	Jožef Stefan Institute, Slovenia
Topon Paul	Toshiba Corporation, Japan
Tsuyoshi Okita	Kyushu Institute of Technology, Japan
Unmesh Padalkar	Dream Sports, India
Vahid Shahrivari Joghan	Utrecht University, Netherlands
Valerio Bonsignori	Unipisa, Italy
Vanessa Borst	University of Würzburg, Germany
Venkata Sai Prakash Mukkamala	Quantiphi Analytics, USA
Veselka Boeva	Blekinge Institute of Technology, Sweden
Viacheslav Komisarenko	University of Tartu, Estonia
Vikas Gupta	HPCL, India
Vinayak Gupta	University of Washington, Seattle, USA
Vincent Auriau	Artefact Research Center, France
Vincenzo Pasquadibisceglie	University of Bari, Aldo Moro, Italy
Vincenzo Scotti	KASTEL, Germany
Vinothkumar Kolluru	Stevens Institute of Technology, USA
Vladimir Mic	Aarhus University, Denmark
Wang-Zhou Dai	Nanjing University, China
Wee Siong Ng	Institute for Infocomm Research, Singapore
Wei Cheng	NEC Laboratories America, USA
Wei Li	Harbin Engineering University, China
Wei Wang	Tsinghua University, China
Wei-Peng Chen	Fujitsu Research of America, USA
Wentao Wang	Michigan State University, USA
Wentao Wu	Microsoft Research, USA
Wray Buntine	VinUniversity, Vietnam
Xianchao Wu	Nvidia, USA
Xiang Lian	Kent State University, USA
Xianli Zhang	Xi'an Jiaotong University, China
Xiaobo Jin	Xi'an Jiaotong-Liverpool University, China
Xiaofei Zhou	University of Chinese Academy of Sciences, China
Xiaofeng Gao	Shanghai Jiaotong University, China
Xiaolin Han	Northwestern Polytechnical University, China
Xin Huang	Hong Kong Baptist University, China
Xin Liu	East China Normal University, China

Xing Tang	Tencent, China
Xiuqiang He	Tencent, China
Xiuyuan Hu	Tsinghua University, China
Xueping Peng	University of Technology Sydney, Australia
Yanchang Zhao	CSIRO, Australia
Yang Guo	Xidian University Hangzhou Institute of Technology, China
Yang Song	Apple, USA
Yijun Zhao	Fordham University, USA
Yinghui Wu	Case Western Reserve University, USA
Yingzhen Lin	Harbin Institute of Technology (Shenzhen), China
Yintao Yu	University of Illinois at Urbana-Champaign, USA
Yixiang Fang	Chinese University of Hong Kong, China
Yixuan Cao	Institute of Computing Technology, China
Yizheng Huang	York University, Canada
Yongchao Liu	Ant Group, China
Yu Huang	Indiana University, USA
Yu Wang	University of Oregon, USA
Yuantao Fan	Halmstad University, Sweden
Yucheng Zhou	University of Macau, China
Yue Shi	Meta, USA
Yueyuan Zheng	Beihang University, China
Yunchuan Shi	University of Sydney, Australia
Yunjun Gao	Zhejiang University, China
Yuting Ding	Southeast University, China
Yuzhuo Li	University of Auckland, New Zealand
Zahra Kharazian	Stockholm University, Sweden
Zahra Taghiyarrenani	Halmstad University, Sweden
Zahraa Abdallah	University of Bristol, UK
Zeyi Wen	Hong Kong University of Science and Technology (Guangzhou), China
Zeyu Zhu	National University of Defense Technology, China
Zhanyu Liu	Shanghai Jiao Tong University, China
Zhaogeng Liu	Jilin University, China
Zhaohui Liang	National Library of Medicine, USA
Zhen Zhang	Shandong University, China
Zhendong Chu	Squirrel Ai Learning, China
Zheng Zhang	University of California, USA
Zhengze Li	University of Göttingen, Germany
Zhibin Gu	Hebei Normal University, China

Zhuang Liu   Dongbei University of Finance and Economics, China

Ziyu Guan   Xidian University, China
Zoltan Miklos   Université de Rennes, France
Zunlei Feng   Zhejiang University, China

Program Committee – Demo Track

Andrzej Wójtowicz   Adam Mickiewicz University, Poznań, Poland
Anna Sokol   University of Notre Dame, USA
Arian Pasquali   Faktion AI, Belgium
Bruno Veloso   INESC TEC - FEP-UP, Portugal
Chongsheng Zhang   Henan University, China
Christos Doulkeridis   University of Piraeus, Greece
Danqing Zhang   PathOnAI.org, USA
Fátima Rodrigues   INESC TEC, Portugal
Grigorii Khvatskii   University of Notre Dame, USA
Joe Germino   University of Notre Dame, USA
Jungwon Seo   University of Stavanger, Norway
Ke Li   University of Exeter, England
Manfred Jaeger   Aalborg University, Denmark
Marcin Luckner   Warsaw University of Technology, Poland
Mehwish Alam   Institut Polytechnique de Paris, France
Nuno Moniz   University of Notre Dame, USA
Tânia Carvalho   FCUP, Portugal
Vitor Cerqueira   FEUP, Portugal
Wei-Wei Du   National Yang Ming Chiao Tung University, Taiwan

Additional Reviewers

Andrea D'Angelo   Meng Ding
Patrick Altmeyer   Roberto Esposito
Guiseppina Adresini   Alina Fastowski
Vedangi Bengali   Roger Ferrod
Michele Bernardini   Michele Fontana
Zhi Cao   Chang Gong
Louis Carpentier   Michal Grzejdziak-Zdziarski
Alessio Cascione   Paul Hahn
Lilia Chebbah   Antonia Hain

Md Athikul Islam
Michael Ito
Philipp Jahn
Rahul Kumar
Bishal Lakha
Yuwen Liu
Jerry Lonlac
Shijie Luo
Francesca Naretto
Navid Nobani
Diego Coello de Portugal
Joana Santos
Francesco Scala

Richard Serrano
Nuno Silva
Francesco Spinnato
Pedro C. Vieira
Xiao Wang
Yunyun Wang
Qi Wen
Jianye Xie
Huaiyuan Yao
Yutong Ye
Obaidullah Zaland
Efstratios Zaradoukas
Nan Zhang

Sponsors

Diamond

Platinum

Gold

Silver

Bronze

Other Sponsors

Partners

Keynotes

Many Good Models Leads to …

Cynthia Rudin

Duke University, USA

Abstract. As it turns out, many good models leads to amazing things! The Rashomon Effect, coined by Leo Breiman, describes the phenomenon that there exist many equally good predictive models for the same dataset.

This phenomenon happens for many real datasets, and when it does it sparks both magic and consternation, but mostly magic. In light of the Rashomon Effect, my collaborators and I propose to reshape the way we think about machine learning, particularly for tabular data problems in the nondeterministic (noisy) setting. I'll address how the Rashomon Effect impacts (1) the existence of simple-yet-accurate models, (2) flexibility to address user preferences, such as fairness and monotonicity, without losing performance, (3) uncertainty in predictions, fairness, and explanations, (4) reliable variable importance, (5) algorithm choice, specifically, providing advanced knowledge of which algorithms might be suitable for a given problem, and (6) public policy. I'll also discuss a theory of when the Rashomon Effect occurs and why: interestingly, noise in data leads to a large Rashomon Effect. My goal is to illustrate how the Rashomon Effect can have a massive impact on the use of machine learning for complex problems in society.

Towards Causal Artificial Intelligence

Elias Bareinboim

Columbia University, USA

Abstract. While a significant portion of AI scientists and engineers believe we are on the verge of achieving highly general forms of AI, I offer a critical appraisal of this view through a causal lens. In particular, building on foundational developments in the field, I will present my perspective on the relationship between intelligence and causality – and the central role of the latter in building intelligent systems and advancing credible data science.

I frame this discussion in terms of five core capabilities that we should expect from an intelligent AI system: performing causal reasoning and articulating explanations; making precise, surgical, and sample-efficient decisions; generalizing across changing conditions and environments; generating and simulating in a causally consistent manner; and learning causal structures and variables.

In this talk, I will elaborate on this perspective and share current progress toward building causally intelligent AI systems. A more detailed discussion of this thesis is provided in my forthcoming textbook, a draft of which is available here: https://causalai-book.net/.

Not Just a Trend: Institutionalizing XAI for Responsible and Compliant AI Systems

Francisco Herrera

Granada University, Spain

Abstract. As artificial intelligence (AI) systems increasingly mediate decisions in high-stakes domains – from healthcare and finance to public policy – the demand for explainable AI (XAI) has grown rapidly. Yet many current XAI approaches remain disconnected from the practical needs of stakeholders and the requirements of emerging regulatory frameworks. This talk argues that XAI must not be treated as a passing trend or optional technical add-on, but as a foundational principle in the design and deployment of AI systems. We critically examine the state of the field, exposing the gap between model-centric explainability and stakeholder-centric accountability. In response, we propose a framework that aligns explainability with legal, ethical, and social responsibilities, emphasizing co-design with affected users, sensitivity to institutional contexts, and governance over opacity. Our goal is to advance XAI from superficial compliance toward deeply integrated transparency that fosters trust, accountability, and responsible innovation.

Compositional Intelligence: Coordinating Multiple LLMs for Complex Tasks

Mirella Lapata

University of Edinburgh, UK

Abstract. Recent years have witnessed the rise of increasingly larger and more sophisticated language models (LMs) capable of performing every task imaginable, sometimes at (super)human level. In this talk, I will argue that in many realistic scenarios, solely relying on a single general-purpose LLM is suboptimal. A single LLM is likely to underrepresent real-world data distributions, heterogeneous skills, and task-specific requirements. Instead, I will discuss multi-LLM collaboration as an alternative to monolithic generative modeling. By orchestrating multiple LLMs, each with distinct roles, perspectives, or competencies, we can achieve more effective problem-solving while being more inclusive and explainable. I will illustrate this approach through two case studies: narrative story generation and visual question answering, showing how a society of agents can collectively tackle complex tasks while pursuing complementary subgoals. Additionally, I will explore how these agent societies leverage reasoning to improve performance.

Towards a Fairer World: Uncovering and Addressing Human and Algorithmic Biases

Nuria Oliver

ELLIS Alicante Foundation, Spain

Abstract. In my talk, I will first briefly present ELLIS Alicante1, the only ELLIS unit that has been created from scratch as a non-profit research foundation devoted to responsible AI for Social Good. Next, I will provide an overview of AI with a focus on the ethical implications and limitations of today's AI systems, including algorithmic discrimination and bias. On this topic, I will present a few examples of our work on uncovering and mitigating both human and algorithmic biases with AI.

On the human front, I will present the body of work that we have carried out in the context of AI-based beauty filters that are so popular on social media. On the algorithmic front, I will explain the main approaches to address algorithmic discrimination and I will present three novel methods to achieve fairer decisions.

Tensor Logic: A Simple Unification of Neural and Symbolic AI

Pedro Domingos

University of Washington, USA

Abstract. Deep learning has achieved remarkable successes in language generation and other tasks, but is extremely opaque and notoriously unreliable. Both of these problems can be overcome by combining it with the sound reasoning and transparent knowledge representation capabilities of symbolic AI. Tensor logic accomplishes this by unifying tensor algebra and logic programming, the formal languages underlying respectively deep learning and symbolic AI. Tensor logic is based on the observation that predicates are compactly represented Boolean tensors, and can be straightforwardly extended to compactly represent numeric ones. The two key constructs in tensor logic are tensor join and project, numeric operations that generalize database join and project. A tensor logic program is a set of tensor equations, each expressing a tensor as a series of tensor joins, a tensor project, and a univariate nonlinearity applied elementwise. Tensor logic programs can succinctly encode most deep architectures and symbolic AI systems, and many new combinations.

In this talk I will describe the foundations and main features of tensor logic, and present efficient inference and learning algorithms for it. A system based on tensor logic achieves state-of-the-art results on a suite of language and reasoning tasks. How tensor logic will fare on trillion-token corpora and associated tasks remains an open question.

Artificial Intelligence for Science

Sašo Džeroski

Jožef Stefan Institute, Slovenia

Abstract. Artificial intelligence is already transforming science, with its future impact expected to be even greater. Realizing this potential requires addressing key scientific challenges, such as ensuring explainability (of models and their predictions), learning effectively from limited data, and integrating data with prior domain knowledge. It also requires the provision of support for open and reproducible science through formalizing and sharing scientific knowledge.

I will present an overview of my research on the development of AI methods suitable for use in science. These include methods for explainable machine learning – including multi-target prediction and relational learning – that deliver accurate yet interpretable models suitable for complex scientific domains. These methods have been applied in environmental science, life science and materials science. Learning from limited data is critical in science. I will discuss two complementary approaches: semi-supervised learning, which leverages unlabeled data directly, together with labeled data, and foundation models, which use representations learned from vast unlabeled data to support downstream tasks with minimal supervision, i.e., limited amounts of labeled data. Both paradigms expand AI's reach into data-scarce scientific problems.

I will then present our work on automated scientific modeling, where we learn interpretable models of dynamical systems – such as process-based models and differential equations – from time series data and domain knowledge. Finally, I will highlight the role of ontologies and semantic technologies in experimental computer science, including machine learning and optimization. In these areas, we have developed ontologies for the representation and annotation of both data and other artefacts produced by science, such as algorithms, models, and results of experiments.

Contents – Part VIII

Agriculture, Food and Earth Sciences

Education

Engineering and Technology

Time Series

An Empirical Evaluation of Foundation Models for Multivariate Time Series Classification

Pinar Sungu Isiacik$^{(\boxtimes)}$, Thach Le Nguyen, Timilehin Aderinola, and Georgiana Ifrim

University College Dublin, Dublin, Ireland
pinar.sunguisiacik@ucdconnect.ie,
{thach.lenguyen,timilehin.aderinola,georgiana.ifrim}@ucd.ie

Abstract. Foundation models have recently emerged as a promising approach for time series analysis, adapting transformer architectures originally designed for natural language processing to handle continuous temporal data. While these models demonstrate strong performance across various time series tasks, their handling of multivariate time series, particularly inter-channel dependencies, remains underexplored. In this paper, we present a comprehensive analysis of current foundation models for time series, including tokenization-based, patch-based, and shape-based approaches, focusing on their mechanisms and data representations for capturing relationships between channels. Our analysis shows that even though these models have advanced architectures, they mostly process channels independently, which may prevent them from fully capturing cross-channel patterns. We examine this limitation across different model families and discuss its implications for multivariate time series analysis. Our empirical evaluation shows that foundation models perform well on simpler tasks but exhibit diminished effectiveness as channel dependencies increase, with specialized time series methods consistently outperforming them on complex datasets. These findings highlight the critical need for channel-aware architectures and more effective strategies for modeling inter-channel relationships in foundation models.

Keywords: Foundation Models · Multivariate Time Series Classification · Inter-Channel Dependencies · Evaluation

1 Introduction

The success of foundation models in natural language processing has inspired their adaptation to other domains, including time series analysis. These models, pre-trained on large-scale datasets and fine-tuned for specific tasks, have

Supplementary Information The online version contains supplementary material available at https://doi.org/10.1007/978-3-662-72243-5_1.

B. Pfahringer et al. (Eds.): ECML PKDD 2025, LNAI 16020, pp. 3–21, 2026.
https://doi.org/10.1007/978-3-662-72243-5_1

shown promising results in time series forecasting, classification, and anomaly detection [20]. Recent approaches such as Chronos [1], MOMENT [17], One Fits All [29], aLLM4TS [2], Mantis [12] and VQShape [27] demonstrate various strategies for adapting transformer architectures to handle continuous temporal data [20], ranging from tokenization schemes to patch-based processing and shape-based representations. However, as these models are increasingly applied to multivariate time series (MTS) problems, a critical question emerges: how effectively do they capture dependencies between different channels or variables? This question is particularly relevant in domains such as human activity analysis and healthcare, where relationships between multiple measurements are crucial, e.g., tracking multiple body parts during an exercise, or in financial markets, where correlations between different assets drive system behavior. Traditional time series analysis methods, including both statistical approaches and neural networks, have explicitly addressed channel dependencies through various mechanisms. Some Convolutional Neural Networks (CNNs) architectures use 2D convolutions to capture cross-channel patterns, while methods like ROCKET [5] combine channel information during convolution through weighted summation across channels and further leverage these dependencies in the classification stage. In contrast, our analysis shows that current foundation models for time series predominantly process channels independently, treating them as separate sequences in their batch dimension. This design choice, while computationally efficient and effective for capturing temporal patterns within individual channels, may limit these models' ability to learn and leverage inter-channel dependencies.

This paper makes the following contributions:

– We provide a systematic analysis of how current foundation models handle multivariate time series, categorizing their approaches into tokenization-based, patch-based, and shape-based methods.
– We examine the specific mechanisms each model employs for processing multiple channels and capturing channel dependencies.
– We identify a common limitation across these models in their treatment of inter-channel relationships, suggesting an important direction for future research in time series foundation models. We showcase this limitation through extensive experiments on synthetic and real multivariate time series classification (MTSC) datasets.
– We discuss potential solutions for addressing this limitation. We make all our data and code publicly available[1].

2   Related Work

Time series classification has seen significant methodological advances, from traditional feature-based approaches to advanced architectures, including foundation models. This section reviews key methods evaluated in our study, emphasizing their architectural design and capabilities in managing channel dependencies in MTS data.

---

[1] https://github.com/mlgig/FM4MTSC

2.1 Traditional Machine Learning Methods

Traditional machine learning (ML) approaches for time series classification (TSC) can be categorized into several families. Tree-based methods include Random Forest [3] and Gradient Boosting [15], which build ensembles of decision trees to create robust classifiers. Linear classifiers, including Logistic Regression [4] and Ridge Classifier [18] separate classes using hyperplanes in the feature space. K-Nearest Neighbors (KNN) [13] makes predictions based on proximity in the feature space without constructing an explicit model. For MTSC, these methods typically treat the data as tabular by concatenating all channels into a single feature vector, flattening the temporal and channel dimensions. While this approach may not explicitly capture temporal dependencies or channel interactions, it allows these traditional methods to be directly applied to time series data, providing baseline performance for comparison with specialized temporal models [9].

2.2 Time Series Methods

ROCKET [5] is a convolution-based algorithm which transforms time series using a large number of random convolutional kernels, where each kernel has random length, weights, bias, dilation, and padding. Its implementation for MTS combines channel information during convolution through weighted summation across channels, thus capturing channel dependencies. MiniRocket [6] follows the same principle, but is more efficient, using 84 deterministic kernels.

HYDRA [7] is a hybrid method combining ideas of dictionary and convolutional approaches. Like ROCKET, it first uses convolutional kernels for feature extraction, and then implements concepts of dictionary methods by organizing kernels into groups and counting the best-matching patterns at each timepoint.

QUANT [8] is an interval-based algorithm which serves as a strong baseline in recent TSC benchmarks [23]. It computes quantiles over fixed dyadic intervals on the input time series and its transformations (first and second difference, Fourier transform). When applied to MTS, it extracts features independently from each channel and concatenates them into a single feature vector which is fed to an Extra Trees Classifier [16].

Among feature-based methods, Catch22 [21] is a popular approach that provides a compact set of 22 statistical features designed to capture diverse time series characteristics. These features are extracted independently from each channel, lacking explicit mechanisms to capture interactions between channels.

2.3 Deep Learning Approaches

CNNs have been widely utilized in time series classification due to their ability to automatically learn hierarchical features. In multivariate settings, CNNs process multiple channels using 2D convolutions [19], where early layers operate on each channel independently, extracting local features, while deeper layers combine information across channels. This architecture allows CNNs to capture some inter-channel relationships, but the initial independent processing may limit their effectiveness in scenarios with strong channel dependencies, where interactions between channels are crucial for accurate classification.

InceptionTime [31] introduces an ensemble of five inception-based classifiers that apply convolutions with different kernel sizes in parallel to capture multi-scale temporal patterns. While achieving state-of-the-art performance on many benchmarks, it processes multivariate channels through parallel pathways without explicitly modeling inter-channel dependencies during feature extraction.

LITEMVTime [30] extends lightweight ensemble approaches to MTS, balancing accuracy and computational efficiency for resource-constrained applications. It has channel-aware design elements that better utilize inter-channel relationships while maintaining lightweight computational characteristics.

Although TimesNet [28] is described as a foundation model in its original paper, we categorize it as a deep learning approach due to its architectural design and training paradigm. Unlike foundation models, which typically rely on large-scale pre-training and transformer-based architectures to learn generalizable representations across diverse tasks, TimesNet employs a CNN-based architecture that transforms 1D time series into 2D representations through Fast Fourier Transform (FFT) based periodicity analysis. Its TimesBlocks reshape the time series based on identified periodicities and process these 2D tensors with multi-scale kernels to capture complex temporal patterns. Similar to other deep learning approaches, TimesNet processes channels separately in its initial stages, which may limit its ability to fully leverage strong inter-channel dependencies present in MTS data.

2.4   Transformer-Based Methods

ConvTran [14] combines convolutional layers and transformer blocks to capture both local and global dependencies in time series data. Initially, convolutional layers extract local features, efficiently modeling short-term dependencies within each channel. Subsequently, transformer blocks leverage self-attention mechanisms to capture long-range dependencies and complex inter-channel interactions. The integration of these components allows ConvTran to overcome the limitations of using either approach alone. This can make ConvTran effective in MTS classification, particularly in datasets with strong channel dependencies. However, for datasets with weak channel dependencies, the model's complexity might not yield substantial benefits compared to simpler architectures.

TSLANet [11] introduces a novel approach to time series representation learning by integrating the Adaptive Spectral Block (ASB) and the Interactive Convolution Block (ICB). The ASB leverages the Discrete Fourier Transform to transform time series data into the frequency domain. This process involves computing the power spectrum and applying a trainable threshold to filter out noise, followed by the Inverse FFT to reconstruct time-domain features. The ICB further refines these features using a dual-layer convolutional structure with varying kernel sizes to capture both local and long-range dependencies. This block encourages interactions between features extracted at different scales, enhancing the model's ability to capture complex temporal relationships. TSLANet may be effective in scenarios with strong channel dependencies due to its ability to model complex inter-channel interactions through its spectral and convolutional components. However, in datasets with weak channel dependencies, its architecture may not provide significant advantages over simpler models.

2.5 Foundation Models

Recent advances in foundation models have introduced various approaches to time series analysis, which we categorize here by their data representation strategies.

Tokenization-based methods convert continuous time series values into discrete tokens, similar to vocabulary-based approaches in natural language processing. Chronos [1] uses this approach by transforming continuous-valued data through scaling and quantization schemes that map values to discrete tokens while preserving probabilistic characteristics, enabling language models to process time series for downstream tasks. Despite its potential versatility, Chronos was empirically validated only on univariate time series forecasting tasks, leaving its effectiveness for MTS scenarios and other applications as an open question.

Patch-based methods segment time series into fixed-length subsequences (i.e., patches) that serve as input tokens to transformer architectures, drawing inspiration from vision transformers where image patches are treated as sequence elements. OneFitsAll [29] implements a transfer learning framework that processes time series in patches while maintaining frozen pre-trained transformer blocks, while Adapting LLMs (Large Language Models) for Time Series (aLLM4TS) [2] extends this approach through its framework for handling arbitrary temporal windows. MOMENT [17] advances patch-based processing by introducing "The Time Series Pile" for large-scale pre-training, supporting multiple tasks through various deployment modes. Mantis [12] adapts the Vision Transformer [10] architecture to time series data by generating tokens from patched time series and their differentials, employing contrastive learning during pre-training and introducing channel-level adapters to handle multivariate inputs efficiently.

Shape-based methods represent time series through abstract shape features and attributes. VQShape [27] uses vector quantization to create interpretable, reusable shape-level representations through learned codebooks that generalize across domains.

A critical limitation across all these approaches is their handling of MTS: most current foundation models process channels independently, potentially missing inter-channel dependencies crucial for multivariate analysis.

3 Systematic Analysis of Foundation Models for MTSC

This section examines how current foundation models handle MTS, focusing on their data representations and mechanisms for processing multiple channels and capturing inter-channel dependencies. We denote a MTS as $X \in \mathbb{R}^{L \times C}$, where L denotes the sequence length and C represents the number of channels.

Chronos [1] approaches time series analysis by adapting language modeling techniques through a tokenization strategy. The model processes channels independently at multiple stages. First, in the scaling operation, each channel c is normalized separately using its own scale factor s_c: $\tilde{x}_c = \frac{x_c - m}{s_c}$, $s_c = \frac{1}{L} \sum_{i=1}^{L} |x_c[i]|$, where $\tilde{x}_c$ represents the scaled values for channel c, x_c is the original time series for channel c, m is the scaling factor, s_c is the channel-specific scale factor computed as the mean absolute value, L denotes the sequence length, and $x_c[i]$ is the value at time step i in channel c.

This channel-wise processing continues in the tokenization phase, where the quantization function $q(\tilde{x})$ maps the scaled values of each channel to tokens independently:

$$q(\tilde{x}) = \begin{cases} 1 & \text{if } -\infty \leq \tilde{x} < b_1 \\ 2 & \text{if } b_1 \leq \tilde{x} < b_2 \\ \vdots \\ B & \text{if } b_{B-1} \leq \tilde{x} < \infty \end{cases} \tag{1}$$

where $q(\cdot)$ is the quantization function, B is the total number of tokens in the vocabulary, and $b_1, b_2, \ldots, b_{B-1}$ are the quantization boundaries that partition the scaled value space into discrete intervals. The dequantization function $d : \{1, 2, 3, \ldots B\} \rightarrow \mathbb{R}$ is defined as $d(j) = c_j$, which maps each token back to a representative real value. While the transformer's self-attention mechanism processes these tokenized sequences:

$$\text{Attention}(Q, K, V) = \text{softmax}(\frac{QK^T}{\sqrt{d_k}})V$$

each channel must either be processed independently or flattened into a single sequence. Unlike methods such as ROCKET [5], where cross channel processing is followed by a linear classifier that can learn channel interactions through its weights, Chronos lacks an explicit mechanism for capturing inter-channel dependencies. The model processes each channel in isolation throughout its pipeline, from initial scaling through tokenization to the final prediction phase where the categorical distribution $p(z_{t+1}|z_{1:t})$ is computed separately for each channel, with $z_{1:t}$ representing the tokenized time series.

An in-depth analysis of the Chronos implementation code confirms this critical limitation. The tokenizer class processes inputs strictly as 2D tensors of shape (batch size, time length), with no provision for a channel dimension. The normalization process calculates scaling factors along the time dimension only, confirming that normalization happens independently for each channel. Moreover, the model's input validation explicitly requires inputs to be at most 2-dimensional, forcing MTS to be processed as separate univariate sequences. For MTS applications, this architecture imposes significant constraints.

In our implementation of zero-shot feature extraction for classification tasks, this limitation requires a preprocessing approach where MTS data is converted to univariate sequences by concatenating all channels before feeding it to the model.

While this enables Chronos to process the data, it fundamentally changes the time relationships between channels.

OneFitsAll. [29] adapts pre-trained language models for time series analysis through a transfer learning framework. Given a MTS $X \in \mathbb{R}^{L \times C}$, the model first applies reverse instance normalization to each channel independently: $\tilde{X}_c = \text{InstanceNorm}(X_c) + \mu_c + \sigma_c$ where $\tilde{X}_c$ is the normalized time series for channel c, X_c is the original time series for channel c, μ_c and ω_c are the channel-wise mean and standard deviation used for reverse instance normalization, and $\text{InstanceNorm}(\cdot)$ applies instance-level normalization to the input, followed by patch creation. These patches are processed through a transformer architecture where self-attention blocks and feedforward layers are frozen, while only the positional embeddings and layer normalization are fine-tuned. The reverse instance normalization is completed by adding the channel-wise mean μ_c and standard deviation σ_c to the outputs of the transformer blocks: $\hat{X}_c = \text{TransformerOutput}_c + \mu_c + \sigma_c$, rather than directly after the initial normalization step. Similar to other foundation models, OneFitsAll processes each channel independently in the batch dimension.

aLLM4TS. [2] introduces a two-stage framework for time series analysis. Given a MTS $X \in \mathbb{R}^{L \times C}$, the model first flattens it into M univariate sequences. For each channel i, the sequence is divided into patches: $p_{tp:tp+L_p-1}^{(i)} = \{p_{tp}^{(i)}, ..., p_{tp+L_p-1}^{(i)}\} \in \mathbb{R}^{L_p \times P}$, where $p_{tp:tp+L_p-1}^{(i)}$ represents the patch sequence for channel i, $t_p = \lfloor (t-P)/S \rfloor + 1$ is the starting patch index, $L_p = \lfloor (L-P)/S \rfloor + 1$ is the number of patches, P is the patch length, S is the sliding stride, and L is the total sequence length. In the causal next-patch pre-training stage, the model predicts the next patch for each channel independently: $\hat{p}_{tp+1:tp+L_p}^{(i)} = \{\hat{p}_{tp+1}^{(i)}, ..., \hat{p}_{tp+L_p}^{(i)}\} \in \mathbb{R}^{L_p \times D}$.

The loss function is computed independently for each channel and averaged:

$$\mathcal{L}_p = \mathbb{E}_p[\frac{1}{M} \sum_{i=1}^{M} \|\hat{p}_{tp+1:tp+L_p}^{(i)} - p_{tp+1:tp+L_p}^{(i)}\|_2^2] \tag{2}$$

where $\mathcal{L}_p$ is the prediction loss, M is the number of channels, $\hat{p}_{tp+1:tp+L_p}^{(i)}$ is the predicted patch sequence for channel i, $p_{tp+1:tp+L_p}^{(i)}$ is the ground truth patch sequence, and $\| \cdot \|_2^2$ denotes the squared L2 norm.

The model explicitly adopts a "channel-independence setting" where each sequence is processed independently through the causal LLM backbone. This design choice is confirmed in the implementation, where multivariate inputs undergo a series of transformations: first transposing the time and channel dimensions, then applying padding before creating patches through unfolding operations, and finally rearranging the data to concatenate channels and patch values into a single dimension. While this concatenation operation might suggest some cross-channel modeling, it actually follows the channel-independence principle. The model simply treats the concatenated patches as longer univariate sequences, without any mechanism to learn relationships between different channels.

MOMENT [17] follows a patch-based strategy that processes channels independently. For a MTS $X \in \mathbb{R}^{L \times C}$, the model first applies reversible instance normalization to each channel separately, then segments each normalized channel into non-overlapping patches: $X_c = [p_1^c, ..., p_N^c]$, $p_i^c \in \mathbb{R}^P$ where P is the patch length and N is the number of patches. Each patch is then embedded through a linear projection or replaced with a special mask token during pretraining:

$$e_i^c = \begin{cases} \text{Linear}(p_i^c) & \text{if } M_i = 1 \\ [\text{MASK}] & \text{if } M_i = 0 \end{cases} \tag{3}$$

where e_i^c is the embedding for patch i of channel c, p_i^c is the patch, M_i is a binary mask indicator (1 for non-masked, 0 for masked), $\text{Linear}(\cdot)$ is a linear projection layer, and [MASK] is a special mask token.

A key aspect of MOMENT's design is how it handles multiple variables (channels) in time series data. Although the model uses a transformer, which could potentially capture relationships between different variables, MOMENT takes a different approach. It processes each variable separately by using a simple reshaping: Input to Transformer $= \text{reshape}(E, (B \times C, N, D))$ where E is the embedding matrix, B is the batch size, C is the number of channels, N is the number of time segments (patches), and D is the embedding dimension.

This reshaping treats each variable as if it were a separate time series. As a result, the transformer processes all variables in parallel but keeps them completely separate - like processing multiple independent univariate time series rather than a single MTS.

The model applies both relative and absolute positional encodings to the patch embeddings before processing them through the transformer encoder: $Z^c = \text{Transformer}([e_1^c, e_2^c, ..., e_N^c])$ where Z is the final representation, Z^c is the representation for channel c, and $\|$ denotes concatenation. Only at the task-specific output layer does MOMENT attempt to handle cross-channel information, primarily through two reduction strategies: mean reduction, which averages representations across channels ($Z = \frac{1}{C} \sum_{c=1}^{C} Z^c$), or concatenation, which preserves channel-specific information ($Z = [Z^1 \| Z^2 \| ... \| Z^C]$) but increases parameter count in the final layer.

This architectural decision has significant implications for MTS modeling. Processing channels independently reduces the quadratic complexity of self-attention from $O((L \cdot C)^2)$ to $O(C \cdot L^2)$, enabling the model to scale to high-dimensional MTS. However, it also means the model cannot directly capture dependencies between channels during feature extraction, which may limit its ability to model complex inter-channel relationships.

Mantis. [12] is a time series classification foundation model that functions as an encoder $F : \mathbb{R}^L \to \mathbb{R}^q$, projecting any univariate time series $x \in \mathbb{R}^L$ with fixed sequence length L to a discriminative hidden space $\mathbb{R}^q$. During pre-training, an unlabeled dataset $\mathcal{D}_0$ containing multiple time series is used to learn rich embeddings that generalize across tasks. For fine-tuning, given a dataset $\mathcal{D}$ of time series $\{X_1, X_2, ..., X_n\}$ and corresponding labels Y, either F extracts embeddings $Z = \{F(X_i) \mid X_i \in \mathcal{D}\}$ for a classifier $h : \mathbb{R}^q \to \{1, \ldots, K\}$, or a classification head $h : \mathbb{R}^q \to \mathbb{R}^K$ is appended to fine-tune $h \circ F$.

For MTS $X \in \mathbb{R}^{L \times C}$, Mantis processes each channel independently with the embedding defined as $z = \text{concat}[(F(X_c))_{1 \leq c \leq C}]$, where z is the final multivariate embedding, $F(\cdot)$ is the univariate encoder function, X_c represents the c-th channel, C is the total number of channels, and concat$[\cdot]$ denotes concatenation along the feature dimension. An adapter $a : \mathbb{R}^{L \times C} \to \mathbb{R}^{L \times C_{\text{new}}}$ compresses the original channels. The model's confidence in classifying X is $\text{conf}(X) = \max[\sigma(h \circ F(X))]$, where $\text{conf}(X)$ is the classification confidence for input X, $\sigma(\cdot)$ is the softmax function, h is the classification head, $F(X)$ is the encoded representation, and $\max[\cdot]$ returns the maximum probability across all classes.

Mantis adapts the Vision Transformer (ViT) architecture for time series data. The pre-processing involves setting the input sequence length to 512 and applying instance-level standard scaling. The token generator unit performs instance-level normalization, splits the time series into 32 patches using convolution and mean pooling, generates patches for the time series differential to reduce trend influence, and preserves information about original measurements by encoding statistics of raw patches. These features are concatenated and passed through a linear projector with layer normalization to generate 32 tokens of dimension 256. The ViT unit appends a learnable class token, applies sinusoidal positional encoding, and processes the tokens through 6 transformer layers with 8-head attention. The class token's final representation serves as the output. During pre-training, a projection layer is added for similarity calculations, while during fine-tuning, a classification head maps embeddings to class logits. Mantis is pre-trained using contrastive learning with pairwise cosine similarities computed as $s_i(\phi, \psi) = [s_{\cos}(g \circ F \circ \phi(x_i), g \circ F \circ \psi(x_j))]_{j=1}^b$, where g is a projector. The model minimizes a contrastive loss defined as $\sum_{i=1}^b l_{\text{ce}}\left(\frac{s_i(\phi, \psi)}{T}, i\right)$ with temperature $T = 0.1$, using RandomCropResize as the primary augmentation method.

For MTS, Mantis employs channel-level adapters that transform the original d channels into d_{new} channels, including Principal Component Analysis (PCA), Truncated Singular Value Decomposition (SVD), Random Projection, Variance-Based Channel Selection, and a Differentiable Linear Combiner. Despite these adapters, Mantis follows the same pattern observed in other foundation models, processing each channel independently and lacking explicit mechanisms for modeling inter-channel dependencies.

VQShape. [27] introduces a shape-based representation approach for time series analysis. For a MTS $X \in \mathbb{R}^{L \times C}$, VQShape processes each channel $x_i^m \in \mathbb{R}^T$ independently through a shape-level representation framework. Each subsequence is represented by an attribute tuple: $\tau_k = (z_k, \mu_k, \sigma_k, t_k, l_k)$ where $z_k \in \mathbb{R}^{d_{code}}$ is the shape code, μ_k is the offset, σ_k is the scale, t_k is the relative starting position, and l_k is the relative length. The model processes each channel independently through its encoding pipeline: $\{h_k \in \mathbb{R}^{d_{embed}} \mid k = 1, ..., K\} = E(x^m)$ where E is the time series encoder that transforms patches into latent embeddings. The attribute decoder processes these embeddings channel-wise: $\hat{\tau}_k = (\hat{z}_k, \mu_k, \sigma_k, t_k, l_k) = A_{dec}(h_k)$.

While VQShape introduces an innovative approach to time series representation through shape abstraction, it follows the common pattern of processing each channel independently. The model architecture, from the initial encoding through shape representation to the final reconstruction, maintains separate processing streams for each channel. Despite its novel shape-based tokenization strategy, the model lacks mechanisms for capturing dependencies between channels in MTS data. Looking at the implementation code, the model flattens all channels and time steps together into a single long sequence. This removes the clear boundaries between channels. Since the channel structure is lost in this flattening, the model cannot easily identify or learn relationships between different variables in the MTS.

The model's loss function $\mathcal{L}_{\text{pretrain}} = \lambda_x \mathcal{L}_x + \lambda_s \mathcal{L}_s + \lambda_{vq} \mathcal{L}_{vq} + \lambda_{div} \mathcal{L}_{div}$ where $\mathcal{L}_x$ is the time series reconstruction loss, $\mathcal{L}_s$ is the shape reconstruction loss, $\mathcal{L}_{vq}$ is the vector quantization loss, $\mathcal{L}_{div}$ is the shape disentanglement loss, and $\rho_x, \rho_s, \rho_{vq}, \rho_{div}$ are the respective loss weights. $\mathcal{L}_{\text{pretrain}}$ optimizes for time series reconstruction, vector quantization, shape reconstruction, and shape disentanglement, but none of these components explicitly addresses cross-channel relationships. This framework yields highly interpretable representations within each channel but sacrifices the ability to model how these representations interact across the multivariate structure of the data.

Summary. Across these various types of foundation models, we observe a consistent pattern in handling MTS data: channels are processed independently regardless of the underlying representation strategy. Even approaches that introduce specialized components for multivariate data, such as Mantis with its channel-level adapters, still maintain separate processing streams for each channel. This design choice, while computationally efficient and effective for capturing temporal patterns within individual channels, means that none of these models incorporate explicit mechanisms for learning inter-channel dependencies. The computational advantage is significant, reducing self-attention complexity from $O((L \cdot C)^2)$ to $O(C \cdot L^2)$, but it comes at the cost of potentially missing critical cross-channel interactions that characterize complex MTS data. A structured comparison of these approaches is given in the Appendix (Table 9).

4   Datasets

We study four multivariate time series classification datasets with varying degrees of channel dependency. We emphasize that in this paper **channel dependency** refers to the necessity of using multiple channels (at least two) for successful classification, rather than the statistical correlation between channels. This distinction is crucial: a dataset exhibits strong channel dependency when accurate classification cannot be achieved using a single channel alone, even if the channels themselves are not correlated (e.g., this is the case for the SYNTH dataset). In contrast, we consider a dataset to have weak channel dependency when a single channel contains sufficient discriminative information for accurate classification. Detailed dataset characteristics are provided in Table 7 in the Appendix.

CounterMovementJump (CMJ) [24] contains accelerometer data from counter-movement jump exercises with 3 classes and 3 channels (x, y, z acceleration). This dataset exhibits *weak channel dependency*, as domain experts confirm that class distinctions are primarily observable on the y-channel.

Military Press (MP) [26] includes motion capture data of exercise performances in two variants: MP8 (8 key body point coordinates) and MP50 (all 50 coordinates from 25 body parts) with 4 classes. Domain experts confirm *strong channel dependency*, requiring at minimum four channels (left/right elbow and wrist coordinates) for effective classification.

Synthetic (SYNTH) [25] is specifically designed to evaluate *strong channel dependency* scenarios. It contains 8 channels where discriminative features appear in only two randomly selected channels, making classification impossible using any single channel alone, demonstrating strong channel dependency.

5   Experiments

All experiments were run on an Apple M1 Pro with 16GB RAM. Traditional ML and time series methods were run on CPU using default parameters. For deep learning approaches, transformer-based models, and foundation models requiring fine-tuning, the MPS backend was utilized. We used the original implementations provided by each method's paper. The training process used 25% of the training set as a validation set, with early stopping applied using a patience of 10 epochs and a maximum of 100 epochs to determine the optimal training duration and mitigate overfitting. Our experimental evaluation uses four distinct MTS datasets, with three exhibiting strong channel dependency characteristics. As suggested in [9], we establish baseline performance using traditional ML methods including Logistic Regression and Random Forest.

For **traditional ML** approaches, we flattened the MTS data by concatenating all channels into a single feature vector, maintaining temporal order within each channel. All traditional models were implemented using *scikit-learn* with default hyperparameters to provide a fair and reproducible baseline. As shown in Table 1, traditional methods showed strong performance on the simpler CMJ dataset but struggled with channel-dependent datasets, highlighting the limitations of flattened representations in capturing inter-channel relationships. We next compare these baselines against specialized time series approaches, deep learning architectures, transformer-based models, and foundation models.

Time series methods utilize the *aeon* library [22] implementations with default parameters for ROCKET, MiniRocket, QUANT, HYDRA, and Catch22.

Table 1. Accuracy and Runtime Results for Traditional ML Methods

Dataset	Model	Acc	TrainTime(s)	PredTime(s)
	Random Forest	0.933	0.41	0.01
	Gradient Boosting	**0.939**	30.37	0.01
	KNN	0.620	0.01	0.01
CMJ	Logistic Regression	0.687	0.16	0.01
	Ridge Classifier	0.536	0.16	0.01
	Random Forest	0.607	2.10	0.08
	Gradient Boosting	0.605	166.72	0.01
	KNN	0.548	0.01	0.01
MP8	Logistic Regression	**0.642**	2.80	0.01
	Ridge Classifier	0.607	0.33	0.01
	Random Forest	0.476	4.73	0.01
	Gradient Boosting	0.555	964.20	0.12
	KNN	0.341	0.01	0.06
MP50	Logistic Regression	**0.622**	36.83	0.02
	Ridge Classifier	0.540	0.85	0.01
	Random Forest	0.538	17.84	0.03
	Gradient Boosting	0.518	199.24	0.01
	KNN	**0.544**	0.06	0.40
SYNTH	Logistic Regression	0.537	9.28	0.02
	Ridge Classifier	0.519	0.90	0.01

As shown in Table 2, these methods consistently outperformed traditional approaches, with ROCKET achieving superior accuracy on CMJ and MP50, while HYDRA led on MP8 and QUANT excelled on the SYNTH dataset. Notably, MiniRocket maintained competitive accuracy across all datasets while offering significantly faster computation times, making it the most balanced choice for practical applications. The results demonstrate the effectiveness of these specialized approaches in handling complex time series data, particularly in capturing channel dependencies that traditional methods struggled with.

Deep learning approaches showed varying effectiveness across datasets with different channel dependency characteristics, as shown in Table 3. Inception-Time demonstrated better performance on channel dependent datasets compared to basic CNN approaches, highlighting the benefits of its multi-scale ensemble architecture. However, CNN (aeon) achieved the best results on both weak dependency and synthetic tasks, while performing poorly on real-world strong dependent datasets. LITEMVTime showed mixed results with generally lower accuracy and unexpectedly high computational overhead on these datasets. The results show that no single deep learning architecture consistently performs well across all channel dependency scenarios.

Transformer-based methods (Table 4) showed promise, particularly ConvTran's strong performance on SYNTH and MP8, but performance varied considerably depending on the data characteristics. TSLANet generally performed worse than ConvTran, especially on the datasets with strong channel depen-

Table 2. Accuracy and Runtime Results of Time Series Methods (aeon)

Dataset	Model	Acc	TrainTime(s)	PredTime(s)
CMJ	ROCKET	**0.950**	17.67	7.37
	MiniRocket	0.944	2.26	0.49
	QUANT	0.933	2.65	0.22
	HYDRA	0.944	6.01	2.59
	Catch22	0.922	19.79	8.27
MP8	ROCKET	0.743	43.67	17.65
	MiniRocket	0.741	3.58	1.09
	QUANT	0.696	26.27	0.77
	HYDRA	**0.748**	8.79	3.17
	Catch22	0.635	29.76	11.93
MP50	ROCKET	**0.793**	50.32	20.60
	MiniRocket	0.787	4.86	1.61
	QUANT	0.740	199.30	4.68
	HYDRA	0.738	9.98	3.53
	Catch22	0.672	747.74	285.73
SYNTH	ROCKET	0.861	793.20	94.78
	MiniRocket	0.882	119.53	4.88
	QUANT	**0.964**	553.77	2.92
	HYDRA	0.912	313.10	16.96
	Catch22	0.906	58.96	4.83

dence. The performance gap expands noticeably on MP50 and SYNTH, suggesting ConvTran's architecture better handles strong channel dependencies, though at the cost of longer training times on larger datasets. Channel dependency emerges as a key factor in determining when transformer-based approaches become necessary. We note that on these datasets, MiniRocket is comparable with ConvTran regarding accuracy, but much faster to train and predict.

For the **foundation models** analyzed, we evaluated both zero-shot and fine-tuning approaches, as shown in Table 5. As a sanity check, we reproduced the experiments from the original papers using their datasets and confirmed that we achieved the same performance metrics as reported by the authors, validating our implementation before applying these models to our datasets.

5.1   Impact of Classifier Selection on Zero-Shot Performance

Our evaluation demonstrates that foundation models show distinct performance patterns that are critically influenced by both dataset complexity and classifier selection. On simpler datasets with weak channel dependencies (CMJ), zero-shot methods like Chronos perform competitively (0.927 with Random Forest), while performance declines significantly on channel-dependent datasets. Notably,

Table 3. Accuracy and Runtime Results of Deep Learning Methods

Dataset	Model	Acc	Epochs	TrainTime(s)	PredTime(s)
CMJ	CNN	0.922	12	2.07	0.05
	TimesNet	0.866	24	220.66	0.95
	CNN (aeon)	**0.950**	2000	335.61	0.25
	InceptionTime (aeon)	0.905	500	578.49	1.35
	LITEMVTime (aeon)	0.899	500	2127.92	1.08
MP8	CNN	0.810	55	27.28	0.08
	TimesNet	0.351	11	186.74	1.82
	CNN (aeon)	0.659	2000	659.40	0.31
	InceptionTime (aeon)	**0.832**	500	2472.29	1.62
	LITEMVTime (aeon)	0.812	500	2618.88	1.42
MP50	CNN	0.661	56	24.37	0.10
	TimesNet	0.245	32	530.50	1.79
	CNN (aeon)	0.252	2000	1390.24	0.45
	InceptionTime (aeon)	**0.781**	500	4167.91	2.61
	LITEMVTime (aeon)	0.579	500	4924.69	2.59
SYNTH	CNN	0.732	49	92.14	0.26
	TimesNet	0.486	17	3822.72	6.56
	CNN (aeon)	**0.868**	2000	5895.06	0.48
	InceptionTime (aeon)	0.691	500	10194.65	1.68
	LITEMVTime (aeon)	0.576	500	14895.80	2.68

classifier choice becomes increasingly important as channel dependency strengthens: while Random Forest consistently performs best on simpler datasets, Ridge Classifier demonstrates notable effectiveness when paired with aLLM4TS embeddings on complex tasks, achieving better performance on MP8 (0.689) and MP50 (0.472) compared to alternative classifier combinations. This pattern indicates that different foundation models produce embeddings with distinct characteristics: Chronos generates representations that benefit from Random Forest's ensemble approach, while aLLM4TS creates more linearly separable patterns that Ridge Classifier can effectively utilize.

Beyond classifier selection, our evaluation shows significant computational trade-offs, with fine-tuning approaches like MOMENT demonstrating better adaptability to complex data but requiring exponentially higher computational cost compared to zero-shot methods. Despite these optimization strategies, foundation models consistently underperform specialized time series methods on channel-dependent tasks, with even transformer architectures specifically designed for time series (ConvTran) outperforming general foundation models on complex multivariate data. These findings emphasize that foundation model evaluation requires careful consideration of classifier selection as a critical hyperparameter, particularly for MTS with varying channel dependencies.

Table 4. Accuracy and Runtime Results of Transformer-based Methods

Dataset	Model	Acc	Epochs	TrainTime(s)	PredTime(s)
CMJ	ConvTran	0.866	48	114.39	0.65
	TSLANet	**0.894**	34	138.45	1.39
MP8	ConvTran	**0.804**	100	296.04	0.81
	TSLANet	0.727	60	387.87	2.16
MP50	ConvTran	**0.570**	48	273.15	1.58
	TSLANet	0.424	43	287.26	2.08
SYNTH	ConvTran	**0.930**	50	3821.37	6.20
	TSLANet	0.871	20	1898.66	9.74

Due to the novel proposal of adapters to address channel dependency, **Mantis model variations** (Table 8, Appendix) were evaluated in detail across extraction approaches (with/without adapters) and fine-tuning strategies. Key findings include that adapters offer significant computational efficiency, reducing transform times by 33–95% across datasets, with the most dramatic gains on complex data like MP50. However, accuracy implications vary by dataset complexity. Adapters maintain performance on weak channel dependent data (CMJ) and improve accuracy on moderately complex data (MP8), but reduce accuracy significantly on datasets with strong channel dependence (MP50, SYNTH).

Full fine-tuning significantly outperforms adapter-head fine-tuning on strongly channel dependent datasets, despite incurring a 15–20% increase in training time. The choice of classifier also plays a crucial role in performance: Random Forest excels on simpler datasets, while Logistic Regression demonstrates effectiveness with adapters on channel-dependent data, reinforcing our findings on foundation models. The most notable disparity is in computational efficiency. Mantis adapter extraction completes in seconds, whereas full fine-tuning requires hours, underscoring the critical trade-off between accuracy and efficiency.

Table 6 summarizes performance across all methods, demonstrating that foundation models struggle to consistently outperform established approaches, particularly on datasets with strong channel dependencies. While foundation models achieve top results, the performance differences are often marginal, with time series and deep learning methods remaining highly competitive across all evaluation scenarios.

Potential Solutions to Address Strong Channel Dependence. Based on these findings, we identify several promising directions for improving foundation model performance on channel-dependent MTSC data: (1) pre-training objectives that explicitly model inter-channel relationships; (2) attention mechanisms designed specifically for channel dependencies; (3) hybrid architectures combining foundation model capabilities with channel-aware components like those in ConvTran; (4) more efficient fine-tuning strategies that mitigate the

Table 5. Accuracy and Runtime Results of Foundation Models

Dataset	Model	Classifier	Fine-tune	Acc	FeatTime(s)	TrainTime(s)	PredTime(s)
CMJ	Chronos	RandomForest	–	**0.927**	10.79	5.85	0.05
	Chronos	LogisticRegr	–	0.916	10.79	9.32	0.09
	Chronos	RidgeClassif	–	**0.927**	10.79	0.66	0.03
	MOMENT	–	50	0.855	–	81.17	2.17
	One-fits-all	–	28	0.866	–	16.39	0.29
	aLLM4TS	RandomForest	–	0.832	20.29	0.37	0.01
	aLLM4TS	LogisticRegr	–	0.844	20.29	0.06	0.01
	aLLM4TS	RidgeClassif	–	0.872	20.29	0.01	0.01
	VQSHAPE	RandomForest	–	0.922	54.35	0.22	0.01
	VQSHAPE	LogisticRegr	–	0.922	54.35	0.18	0.01
	VQSHAPE	RidgeClassif	–	0.883	54.35	0.02	0.01
MP8	Chronos	RandomForest	–	0.434	32.17	38.68	0.16
	Chronos	LogisticRegr	–	0.467	32.17	30.20	0.61
	Chronos	RidgeClassif	–	0.459	32.17	4.90	0.18
	MOMENT	–	18	0.489	–	103.52	9.56
	One-fits-all	–	33	0.644	–	64.46	0.63
	aLLM4TS	RandomForest	–	0.629	31.38	2.02	0.01
	aLLM4TS	LogisticRegr	–	0.517	31.38	0.09	0.01
	aLLM4TS	RidgeClassif	–	**0.689**	31.38	0.01	0.01
	VQSHAPE	RandomForest	–	0.659	184.68	1.09	0.03
	VQSHAPE	LogisticRegr	–	0.556	184.68	0.52	0.01
	VQSHAPE	RidgeClassif	–	0.422	184.68	0.08	0.01
MP50	Chronos	RandomForest	–	0.287	34.66	39.74	0.16
	Chronos	LogisticRegr	–	0.261	34.66	32.08	0.69
	Chronos	RidgeClassif	–	0.235	34.66	4.59	0.16
	MOMENT	–	58	**0.662**	–	1791.58	119.38
	One-fits-all	–	33	0.266	–	219.96	1.61
	aLLM4TS	RandomForest	–	0.361	32.22	1.80	0.01
	aLLM4TS	LogisticRegr	–	0.390	32.22	0.09	0.01
	aLLM4TS	RidgeClassif	–	0.472	32.22	0.09	0.01
	VQSHAPE	RandomForest	–	0.368	185.38	1.02	0.03
	VQSHAPE	LogisticRegr	–	0.341	185.38	1.22	0.01
	VQSHAPE	RidgeClassif	–	0.281	185.38	0.05	0.01
SYNTH	Chronos	RandomForest	–	0.491	144.34	697.98	2.54
	Chronos	LogisticRegr	–	0.513	144.34	859.18	4.55
	Chronos	RidgeClassif	–	0.491	144.34	178.85	2.70
	MOMENT	–	60	**0.768**	–	5164.22	61.30
	One-fits-all	–	40	0.672	–	414.87	1.19
	aLLM4TS	RandomForest	–	0.497	387.88	16.59	0.02
	aLLM4TS	LogisticRegr	–	0.500	387.88	0.32	0.01
	aLLM4TS	RidgeClassif	–	0.505	387.88	0.07	0.01
	VQSHAPE	RandomForest	–	0.644	855.21	8.32	0.14
	VQSHAPE	LogisticRegr	–	0.671	855.21	0.73	0.01
	VQSHAPE	RidgeClassif	–	0.669	855.21	0.17	0.01

Table 6. Accuracy Comparison Across All Methods and Datasets

Category	Method	CMJ	MP8	MP50	SYNTH
Traditional ML	Random Forest	0.933	0.607	0.476	0.538
	Gradient Boosting	0.939	0.605	0.555	0.518
	KNN	0.620	0.548	0.341	0.544
	Logistic Regression	0.687	0.642	0.622	0.537
	Ridge Classifier	0.536	0.607	0.540	0.519
Time Series	ROCKET	0.950	0.743	**0.793**	0.861
	MiniRocket	0.944	0.741	0.787	0.882
	QUANT	0.933	0.696	0.740	**0.964**
	HYDRA	0.944	0.748	0.738	0.912
	Catch22	0.922	0.635	0.672	0.906
Deep Learning	CNN	0.922	0.810	0.661	0.732
	CNN (aeon)	0.950	0.659	0.252	0.868
	TimesNet	0.866	0.351	0.245	0.486
	InceptionTime	0.905	**0.832**	0.781	0.691
	LITEMVTime	0.899	0.812	0.579	0.576
Transformers	ConvTran	0.866	0.804	0.570	0.930
	TSLANet	0.894	0.727	0.424	0.871
Foundation Models	Chronos (best)	0.927	0.467	0.287	0.513
	MOMENT	0.855	0.489	0.662	0.768
	OneFitsAll	0.866	0.644	0.266	0.672
	aLLM4TS (best)	0.872	0.689	0.472	0.505
	VQShape (best)	0.922	0.659	0.368	0.671
	Mantis Full FT	**0.955**	0.697	0.773	0.929
Dataset Channel Dependency		**Weak**	**Strong**	**Strong**	**Strong**
BEST MODEL		**Mantis**	**InceptionTime**	**ROCKET**	**QUANT**

prohibitive computational costs observed in our experiments; (5) data representation approaches that extend Mantis' adaptive channel compression techniques to better preserve cross-channel information, e.g., by redesigning adapters to better capture dependencies between channels. Our results emphasize that model selection should be guided by both dataset characteristics and computational constraints, with specialized approaches like MiniRocket currently still providing more reliable and efficient solutions than foundation models for MTS classification.

6   Conclusion

Our analysis of foundation models for time series demonstrates a consistent pattern in their handling of multivariate data: channels are predominantly processed independently across all three categories of tokenization-based, patch-based, and shape-based approaches. While this design choice offers computational efficiency and has proven effective for many tasks, it fundamentally limits these models' ability to capture complex relationships between channels. This limitation stands in contrast to methods like ROCKET and MiniRocket, which combine channel information during convolution through weighted summation across channels and further leverage channel interactions through the classification stage. Future development of foundation models for time series may benefit from explicitly addressing channel dependencies, either through architectural modifications or novel pre-training objectives that encourage the learning of cross-channel patterns [20]. As foundation models continue to evolve in the time series domain, addressing the challenge of modeling inter-channel dependencies while maintaining the computational advantages of current approaches remains an important area for future research. This could potentially lead to more powerful models that better capture the complex interactions present in real-world multivariate time series data.

Acknowledgments. This publication has emanated from research conducted with the financial support of Taighde Éireann – Research Ireland under Grants [ML-Labs 18/CRT/6183, Insight Centre for Data Analytics 12/RC/2289_P2]. For the purpose of Open Access, the author has applied a CC BY public copyright license to any Author Accepted Manuscript version arising from this submission.

References

1. Ansari, A.F., et al.: Chronos: learning the language of time series. TMLR (2024)
2. Bian, Y., Ju, X., Li, J., Xu, Z., Cheng, D., Xu, Q.: Multi-patch prediction: adapting LLMs for time series representation learning. In: ICML (2024)
3. Breiman, L.: Random forests. Mach. Learn. **45**, 5–32 (2001)
4. Cox, D.R.: The regression analysis of binary sequences. J. Roy. Stat. Soc.: Ser. B (Methodol.) **20**(2), 215–232 (2018)
5. Dempster, A., Petitjean, F., Webb, G.I.: ROCKET: exceptionally fast and accurate time series classification using random convolutional kernels. DAMI (2019)
6. Dempster, A., Schmidt, D.F., Webb, G.I.: MiniRocket: a very fast (almost) deterministic transform for time series classification. In: SIGKDD (2021)
7. Dempster, A., Schmidt, D.F., Webb, G.I.: Hydra: competing convolutional kernels for fast and accurate time series classification. DAMI (2022)
8. Dempster, A., Schmidt, D.F., Webb, G.I.: Quant: a minimalist interval method for time series classification. In: DAMI (2023)
9. Dhariyal B., Nguyen, T.L., Ifrim, G.: Back to basics: a sanity check on modern time series classification algorithms. In: AALTD (2023)
10. Dosovitskiy, A., et al.: An image is worth 16x16 words: transformers for image recognition at scale. In: ICLR (2021)
11. Eldele, E., Ragab, M., Chen, Z., Wu, M., Li, X.: Tslanet: Rethinking transformers for time series representation learning. In: ICML (2024)
12. Feofanov, V., et al.: Mantis: lightweight calibrated foundation model for user-friendly time series classification. arXiv:2502.15637 (2025)

13. Fix, E., Hodges, J.L.: Discriminatory analysis - nonparametric discrimination: Consistency properties. Int. Stat. Rev. **57**, 238 (1989)
14. Foumani, N.M., Tan, C.W., Webb, G.I., Salehi, M.: Improving position encoding of transformers for multivariate time series classification. In: DAMI (2023)
15. Friedman, J.: Greedy function approximation: a gradient boosting machine. Ann. Stat. **29** (2000)
16. Geurts, P., Ernst, D., Wehenkel, L.: Extremely randomized trees. MACH (2006)
17. Goswami, M., Szafer, K., Choudhry, A., Cai, Y., Li, S., Dubrawski, A.: Moment: a family of open time-series foundation models. In: PMLR (2024)
18. Hoerl, A., Kennard, R.: Ridge regression: biased estimation for nonorthogonal problems. Technometrics **12**, 55–67 (2012)
19. Ismail Fawaz, H., Forestier, G., Weber, J., Idoumghar, L., Muller, P.-A.: Deep learning for time series classification: a review. Data Min. Knowl. Disc. **33**(4), 917–963 (2019). https://doi.org/10.1007/s10618-019-00619-1
20. Liang, Y., et al.: Foundation models for time series analysis: a tutorial and survey. In: SIGKDD (2024)
21. Lubba, C.H., Sethi, S.S., Knaute, P., Schultz, S.R., Fulcher, B.D., Jones, N.S.: catch22: canonical time-series characteristics. In: DAMI (2019)
22. Middlehurst, M., et al.: aeon: a python toolkit for learning from time series. JMLR (2024)
23. Middlehurst, M., Schäfer, P., Bagnall, A.: Bake off redux: a review and experimental evaluation of recent time series classification algorithms. In: DAMI (2024)
24. Nguyen, T.L., Gsponer, S., Ilie, I., O'Reilly, M., Ifrim, G.: Interpretable time series classification using linear models and multi-resolution multi-domain symbolic representations. In: DAMI (2020)
25. Serramazza, D.I., Nguyen, T.L., Ifrim, G.: Improving the evaluation and actionability of explanation methods for multivariate time series classification. In: ECMLPKDD (2024)
26. Singh, A., et al.: Fast and robust video-based exercise classification via body pose tracking and scalable multivariate time series classifiers. In: DAMI (2022)
27. Wen, Y., Ma, T., Weng, T.W., Nguyen, L.M., Julius, A.A.: Abstracted shapes as tokens – a generalizable and interpretable model for time-series classification. In: NeurIPS (2025)
28. Wu, H., Hu, T., Liu, Y., Zhou, H., Wang, J., Long, M.: Timesnet: temporal 2d-variation modeling for general time series analysis. In: TMLR (2023)
29. Zhou, T., Niu, P., Wang, X., Sun, L., Jin, R.: One fits all: power general time series analysis by pretrained LM. In: NeurIPS (2023)
30. Ismail-Fawaz, A., Devanne, M., Berretti, S., Weber, J., Forestier, G.: Look into the lite in deep learning for time series classification. Int. J. Data Sci. Anal. (2025)
31. Fawaz, H.I., et al.: InceptionTime: finding AlexNet for time series classification. In: DAMI (2020)

Hierarchical Information-Guided Spatio-Temporal Mamba for Stock Time Series Forecasting

Wenbo Yan[1,2], Shurui Wang[1,2], and Ying Tan[1,3,4(✉)]

[1] School of Intelligence Science and Technology, Peking University, Beijing, China
wenboyan@stu.pku.edu.cn, wsr@pku.edu.cn
[2] Computational Intelligence Laboratory, Beijing, China
[3] Institute for Artificial Intelligence, Beijing, China
[4] National Key Laboratory of General Artificial Intelligence, Beijing, China
ytan@pku.edu.cn

Abstract. Mamba has demonstrated excellent performance in various time series forecasting tasks due to its superior selection mechanism. Nevertheless, conventional Mamba-based models encounter significant challenges in accurately predicting stock time series, as they fail to adequately capture both the overarching market dynamics and the intricate interdependencies among individual stocks. To overcome these constraints, we introduce the Hierarchical Information-Guided Spatio-Temporal Mamba (HIGSTM) framework. HIGSTM introduces Index-Guided Frequency Filtering Decomposition to extract commonality and specificity from time series. The model architecture features a meticulously designed hierarchical framework that systematically captures both temporal dynamic patterns and global static relationships within the stock market. Furthermore, we propose an Information-Guided Mamba that integrates macro informations into the sequence selection process, thereby facilitating more market-conscious decision-making. Comprehensive experimental evaluations conducted on the CSI500, CSI800 and CSI1000 datasets demonstrate that HIGSTM achieves state-of-the-art performance.

Keywords: Stock Time Series Forecasting · Spatio-Temporal Mamba · Decomposition · Information-Guided

1 Introduction

Stock time series forecasting, a pivotal component in investment decision-making, continues to be a primary research focus. The advancement of deep neural networks has driven the development of diverse models to tackle this challenge. Early approaches included RNN-based models such as TPA-LSTM [12] and CNN-based models like TCN [5]. Later, Transformer-based models, including Crossformer [23], iTransformer [9], and PatchTST [10], demonstrated robust performance in time series forecasting. With the introduction of Mamba

© The Author(s), under exclusive license to Springer Nature Switzerland AG 2026
B. Pfahringer et al. (Eds.): ECML PKDD 2025, LNAI 16020, pp. 22–40, 2026.
https://doi.org/10.1007/978-3-662-72243-5_2

[3], Mamba-based models such as Bi-Mamba [13] and TimeMachine [1] have emerged as highly effective solutions.

Mamba-based models demonstrate exceptional capabilities in efficient long-sequence modeling. However, given the distinctive characteristics of the stock market, there exists a pronounced interdependence among stocks within the same market. Modeling each stock's time series independently fails to capture the comprehensive market dynamics. Current Mamba models encounter two primary limitations in stock forecasting: 1. They are unable to model the influence of related stocks on each individual stock during node modeling, and 2. Their selection mechanisms depend exclusively on historical time series, lacking the capacity to integrate additional information to improve selection performance.

To address this issue, we propose the Hierarchical Information-Guided Spatio-Temporal Mamba (HIGSTM). HIGSTM incorporates a hierarchical structure that models the entire stock market from three perspectives: individual, temporal, and global. On one hand, it hierarchically aggregates neighborhood information of stock nodes, capturing both dynamic and static inter-stock relationships. On the other hand, we introduce an information-guided Mamba structure, which progressively extracts time step macro information and global macro information, integrating it into the sequence selection process.

We propose an Index-Guided Frequency Filtering Decomposition that transforms stock time series and indices into the frequency domain. Using stock indices, we derive filter parameters to decompose time series into commonality and specificity components. Each node is initially modeled independently via a Mamba block. Subsequently, the Temporal Information-Guided Spatio-Temporal Mamba (TIGSTM) integrates dynamic temporal information through: (1) leveraging sequence specificity to construct a sparse time-varying relationship graph, enabling dynamic neighborhood aggregation, and (2) aggregating time step macro information from commonality to guide Mamba's sequence selection. The Global Information-Guided Spatio-Temporal Mamba (GIGSTM) incorporates static global information by: (1) aggregating specificity across all time steps to form a global static relationship graph for comprehensive neighborhood aggregation, and (2) consolidating commonality to generate global macro information for enhanced sequence selection guidance. In summary, the main contributions are as follows:

- We propose an Index-Guided Frequency Filtering Decomposition method to effectively extract commonality and specificity from time series.
- We introduce a Hierarchical Information-Guided Spatio-Temporal Mamba structure, which extracts node-related relationships and macro-level information across multiple perspectives, aggregates neighborhood information, and enhances sequence selection.
- We conduct comprehensive experiments on multiple real-world stock datasets, demonstrating the superior performance of our model.

2 Preliminary

2.1 Definition of Stock Spatio-Temporal Forecasting Problem

We formulate the **Stock Spatio-Temporal Forecasting Problem** as follows: Given historical data across T time steps for N stocks, where each stock at each time step is described by F features, the dataset is represented as $\mathbf{X} \in \mathbb{R}^{N \times T \times F}$. The index time series for market are denoted as $\mathbf{I} \in \mathbb{R}^{T \times 1}$.

Moreover, stocks demonstrate complex interconnections that collectively constitute a graph structure. In this framework, each stock represents a node, while the correlation between stocks defines the edges. These relationships are captured by the adjacency matrix $\mathcal{G} \in \mathbb{R}^{N \times N}$, where $\mathcal{G}_{ij}$ quantifies the correlation between stock i and stock j. When an edge connects stock i and stock j ($\mathcal{G}_{ij} \neq 0$), they are identified as neighboring stocks. The set of neighbors for stock i is formally defined as $\mathbf{U}_i = \{j \mid j \neq i \text{ and } \mathcal{G}_{ij} \neq 0\}$.

2.2 Definition of Broadcast

Considering the multi-scale information aggregation presented in the article, various data components may exhibit dimensional inconsistencies. Following the definition in Sect. 2.1, we normalize all variables to conform to the three-dimensional structure [N, T, F]. We introduce matrix broadcasting as the operation of replicating a matrix along absent dimensions to achieve the target [N, T, F] format. This operation is formally expressed as:

$$\mathcal{B}^{(Dims)}(*) \tag{1}$$

For example, $\mathcal{B}^{(N)}(\mathbf{Z_{t,f}})$, where $\mathbf{Z_{t,f}} \in \mathbb{R}^{T \times F}$, denotes the operation of adding a dimension to $\mathbf{Z_{t,f}}$ and repeating it N times, resulting in a shape of $\mathbb{R}^{N \times T \times F}$.

2.3 Fast Fourier Transform and Amplitude Filter

The Fast Fourier Transform (FFT) is an efficient algorithm for computing the Discrete Fourier Transform (DFT), which maps a time-domain signal to the frequency domain. For ease of reference, we denote the FFT computation process as $FFT(*)$ and its inverse as $iFFT(*)$. Any frequency-domain matrix is denoted as $\square^f$, and its corresponding amplitude is denoted as $\square^{f,amp}$.

The amplitude filter selectively enhances or suppresses signals by directly manipulating the amplitude components in the frequency domain. Its inputs are a frequency-domain matrix and filtering parameters. For clarity, we represent the amplitude filtering operation as Θ.

2.4 Discretization and State Space Model

The computation process of Mamba involves three matrices: the state transition matrix $\mathbf{A}$, the input matrix $\mathbf{B}$, and the output matrix $\mathbf{C}$. Mamba employs the

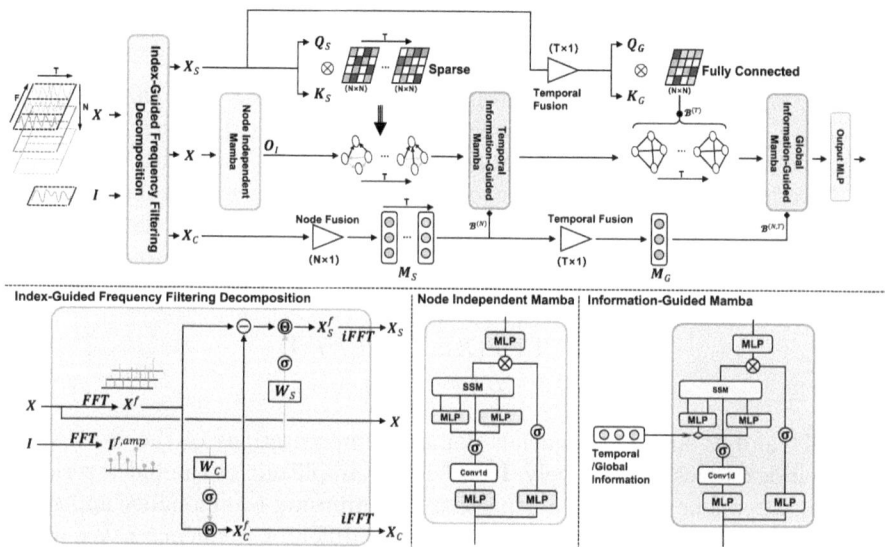

Fig. 1. The overview of the proposed Hierarchical Information-Guided Spatio-Temporal Mamba (HIGSTM)

Zero-Order Hold (ZOH) method [3] to convert the continuous parameters $\mathbf{A}$ and $\mathbf{B}$ into discrete parameters $\overline{\mathbf{A}}$ and $\overline{\mathbf{B}}$. We denote this discretization process as:

$$\overline{\mathbf{A}}, \overline{\mathbf{B}} = Discretization(\mathbf{A}, \mathbf{B}, \varDelta)$$
$$\overline{\mathbf{A}} = \exp(\varDelta\mathbf{A}), \ \overline{\mathbf{B}} = (\exp(\varDelta\mathbf{A}) - \mathbf{E})(\varDelta\mathbf{A})^{-1}(\varDelta\mathbf{B}) \tag{2}$$

where $\mathbf{E}$ is the identity matrix. Additionally, we denote the computation process of the Structured State Space Model (SSM) as $\mathbf{O} = SSM(\overline{\mathbf{A}}, \overline{\mathbf{B}}, \mathbf{C})(\mathbf{X})$, with its core computation process being (Fig. 1):

$$\mathbf{h}_t = \overline{\mathbf{A}}\mathbf{h}_{t-1} + \overline{\mathbf{B}}\mathbf{x}_t$$
$$\mathbf{o}_t = \mathbf{C}\mathbf{h}_t \tag{3}$$

3   Method

In this section, we introduce our proposed **Hierarchical Information-Guided Spatio-Temporal Mamba (HIGSTM)**.

3.1   Index-Guided Frequency Filtering Decomposition

Stocks within the same market demonstrate both commonality, reflecting shared market trends and macroeconomic information that influences all stocks' future trajectories, and specificity, capturing individual characteristics that are more effective for identifying inter-stock relationships. Eliminating commonality results in sparser stock relationships, preserving only the strongest correlations.

However, commonality and specificity are intertwined and challenging to decompose directly without a reference. Our analysis reveals that stock indices, serving as indicators of macroeconomic, can effectively guide this decomposition. Leveraging this insight, we introduce the Index-Guided Frequency Filtering Decomposition. This approach begins by transforming both the stock time series $\mathbf{X}$ and the index time series $\mathbf{I}$ into the frequency domain through the Fast Fourier Transform (FFT).

$$\mathbf{X}^f = FFT(\mathbf{X}), \ \mathbf{I}^f = FFT(\mathbf{I})$$
$$\mathbf{I}^{f,amp} = |\mathbf{I}^f| \tag{4}$$

where $\mathbf{X}^f$ and $\mathbf{I}^f$ are the frequency-domain representations of the stock series and the index series, respectively, $\mathbf{I}^{f,amp}$ is the amplitude of the index series.

From a frequency-domain perspective, decomposing commonality and specificity involves analyzing signal intensity across different frequencies. We utilize the index series' amplitude to derive the amplitude filter parameters, which are then applied to filter the stock series.

$$\mathbf{X}_c^f = \mathbf{X}^f \boldsymbol{\Theta} \sigma(\mathbf{W}_c^\top \mathbf{I}^{f,amp}) \tag{5}$$

where $\mathbf{W}_c$ is a linear transformation matrix, σ denotes the sigmoid activation function, $\boldsymbol{\Theta}$ represents the filtering operation, and $\mathbf{X}_c^f$ corresponds to the commonality. The filter parameters learned from index series' amplitude ensures that the commonality aligns more closely with macroeconomic market characteristics. Additionally, we focus on isolating the specificity from this decomposition.

$$\mathbf{X}_s^f = (\mathbf{X}^f - \mathbf{X}_c^f) \boldsymbol{\Theta} (1 - \sigma(\mathbf{W}_s^\top \mathbf{I}^{f,amp})) \tag{6}$$

where $\mathbf{W}_s$ is a linear mapping matrix and $\mathbf{X}_s^f$ denotes the specificity. Subtracting $\mathbf{X}_c^f$ from $\mathbf{X}^f$ removes the commonality, preserving each stock's specificity. Leveraging index information, we further eliminate common market trends by deriving an additional amplitude filter. Ultimately, we obtain the decomposed commonality series $\mathbf{X}_c$ and specificity series $\mathbf{X}_s$ via the inverse Fast Fourier Transform (iFFT).

$$\mathbf{X}_c = iFFT(\mathbf{X}_c^f), \ \mathbf{X}_s = iFFT(\mathbf{X}_s^f) \tag{7}$$

3.2   Node Independent Mamba

Following series decomposition, we initially model each stock's time series independently, deliberately excluding inter-stock correlations. This strategy prevents the premature introduction of neighboring node information, which could obscure intrinsic series features and compromise the stock's uniqueness. This methodology mirrors the subjective stock evaluation process: a stock's intrinsic characteristics fundamentally determine its future trajectory, and even in favorable market conditions, a fundamentally weak stock will not yield positive predictions.

We use a Mamba block [3] to independently model each time series, taking the raw stock time series $\mathbf{X}$ as input. $\mathbf{X}$ undergoes a one-dimensional convolution (Conv1d) to extract local features, followed by a Linear Projection that maps it to the input matrix $\mathbf{B}_{In}$, the output matrix $\mathbf{C}_{In}$, and the discretized time step Δ_{In}.

$$\mathbf{X}_{In} = \mu(\text{Conv1d}(\mathbf{X}))$$
$$\mathbf{B}_{In} = \mathbf{W}_{B,I}^{\mathsf{T}}\mathbf{X}_{In}, \quad \mathbf{C}_{In} = \mathbf{W}_{C,I}^{\mathsf{T}}\mathbf{X}_{In} \tag{8}$$
$$\Delta_{In} = softplus(\mathbf{W}_{\Delta,I}^{\mathsf{T}}\mathbf{X}_{In} + \mathbf{A}_{In})$$

where $\mathbf{W}_{B,I}$, $\mathbf{W}_{C,I}$, and $\mathbf{W}_{\Delta,I}$ are linear transformation matrices, $\mu(*)$ is the SiLU activation function, $softplus(*)$ denotes the Softplus activation function, and $\mathbf{A}_{In}$ is an optimizable matrix. Subsequently, the matrices $\mathbf{A}_{In}$ and $\mathbf{B}_{In}$ are discretized into $\overline{\mathbf{A}}_{In}$ and $\overline{\mathbf{B}}_{In}$.

$$\overline{\mathbf{A}}_{In}, \overline{\mathbf{B}}_{In} = Discretization(\mathbf{A}_{In}, \mathbf{B}_{In}, \Delta_{In}) \tag{9}$$

Then, $\overline{\mathbf{A}}$, $\overline{\mathbf{B}}$, $\mathbf{C}$, and $\mathbf{X}$ are fed into the State Space Model (SSM) [3].

$$\mathbf{O}_{In} = SSM(\overline{\mathbf{A}}_{In}, \overline{\mathbf{B}}_{In}, \mathbf{C}_{In})(\mathbf{X}_{In}) \tag{10}$$

where the $SSM(*)$ process is detailed in Sect. 2.4. Within the Node Independent Mamba, we utilize the Mamba block to model each stock node independently, enabling exploration of intrinsic node characteristics while preventing neighboring information from obscuring the node's unique features.

3.3   Temporal Information-Guided Spatio-Temporal Mamba

The stock market operates as an integrated system, necessitating the consideration of inter-stock interactions. We introduce the Temporal Information-Guided Spatio-temporal Mamba block (**TIGSTM**), capturing both inter-stock relationships within each time step and the influence of time step macro information on individual stocks. TIGSTM integrates two key components: Temporal Section Sparse Neighbor Aggregation and the Temporal Information-Guided Selective State Space Model.

Temporal Section Sparse Neighbor Aggregation. We utilize the decomposed specificity series $\mathbf{X}_s$ to capture inter-stock relationships. Given their dynamic evolution over time, we implement an attention mechanism to establish the correlation at each time step.

$$\mathbf{Q}_S = \mathbf{W}_{Q,S}^{\mathsf{T}}\mathbf{X}_s, \mathbf{K}_S = \mathbf{W}_{K,S}^{\mathsf{T}}\mathbf{X}_s$$
$$\mathcal{G}_S = softmax(topK(\frac{\mathbf{Q}_S^{\mathsf{T}}\mathbf{K}_S}{\sqrt{d_{kS}}}, r)) + \mathbf{E}_S \tag{11}$$

where $\mathbf{W}_{Q,S}$ and $\mathbf{W}_{K,S}$ denote linear mapping matrices, $\sqrt{d_{kS}}$ represents the dimension of the $\mathbf{K}_S$ vector, $\mathbf{E}_S$ is the identity matrix, r is a hyperparameter that controls the proportion of top neighbors, and $topK()$ ensures each node retains only the neighbors with the highest attention weights. The specificity series $\mathbf{X}_s$ eliminates commonality, resulting in sparser yet more prominent node relationships. We enforce sparsity in the graph at each time step, restricting each node to retain only r of its neighbors. We empirically set r to 30%. This enables each stock to aggregate information from its neighbors at each time step.

$$\mathbf{X}_{S,Agg} = \mathcal{G}_S \mathbf{O}_{In} \tag{12}$$

The time series after information aggregation is denoted as $\mathbf{X}_{S,Agg}$.

Temporal Information-Guided Selective State Space Model. Mamba's Selection mechanism dynamically generates the parameters of the state space model (SSM) based on the time step, with the matrices being derived from the time series, significantly enhancing SSM performance. We introduce the Temporal Information-Guided Selective State Space Model, which integrates the time step macro information into the selection mechanism to guide sequence selection. Initially, we aggregate node information from the commonality series $\mathbf{X}_c$ to form the time step macro information.

$$\mathbf{M}_S = \mathbf{W}_{F,S}^\mathsf{T}(\mathbf{W}_{(N \times 1)}^\mathsf{T} \mathbf{X}_c) + \mathbf{b}_{F,S} \tag{13}$$

where $\mathbf{W}_{(N \times 1)}$ is an $N \times 1$ mapping matrix that aggregates information from all stocks, and $\mathbf{W}_{F,S}$ is a linear mapping matrix that further blends the features to form the macro-level information $\mathbf{M}_S$ for each time step. We incorporate $\mathbf{M}_S$ into the input matrix and output matrix.

$$\mathbf{X}_S = \mu(\mathrm{Conv1d}(\mathbf{X}_{S,Agg}))$$
$$\mathbf{B}_S = <\mathbf{W}_{B,S}^\mathsf{T}\mathbf{X}_S, \mathcal{B}^{(N)}(\mathbf{M}_S)>, \ \mathbf{C}_S = <\mathbf{W}_{C,S}^\mathsf{T}\mathbf{X}_S, \mathcal{B}^{(N)}(\mathbf{M}_S)> \tag{14}$$
$$\Delta_S = softplus(\mathbf{W}_{\Delta,S}^\mathsf{T}\mathbf{X}_S + \mathbf{A}_S)$$

where $\mathbf{W}_{B,S}$ and $\mathbf{W}_{C,S}$ denote linear mapping matrices that project the input sequence $\mathbf{X}_{S,Agg}$ into the input and output matrices, $\mathbf{A}_S$ represents a learnable state transition matrix, and $< \cdots >$ indicates matrix concatenation. We broadcast and concatenate the time step macro information $\mathbf{M}_S$ into input matrix and output matrix. This ensures that the SSM process incorporates time step macro information for input and output decisions. Subsequently, we discretize the state transition matrix $\mathbf{A}_S$ and input matrix $\mathbf{B}_S$ and feed them into the SSM.

$$\overline{\mathbf{A}}_S, \overline{\mathbf{B}}_S = Discretization(\mathbf{A}_S, \mathbf{B}_S, \Delta_S)$$
$$\mathbf{O}_S = SSM(\overline{\mathbf{A}}_S, \overline{\mathbf{B}}_S, \mathbf{C}_S)(\mathbf{X}_S) \tag{15}$$

where $\mathbf{O}_S$ represents the final output of TIGSTM. The TIGSTM propagates information within localized neighborhoods, with each time step maintaining unique adjacency relationships to fully capture dynamic inter-stock correlation. Meanwhile, it extracts time step macro information to guide Mamba's sequence selection mechanism.

3.4   Global Information-Guided Spatio-Temporal Mamba

Beyond time-evolving dynamic information, static information also influences the change of the stock. To capture this, we introduce the Global Information-Guided Spatio-temporal Mamba Block **(GIGSTM)**, which extracts both global stock correlation and global macro information.

Global Neighbor Aggregation. Global Neighbor Aggregation models the global inter-stock relationships from the specificity series $\mathbf{X}_s$ and enables each stock to aggregate information from its global neighbors. Initially, we aggregate the information across all time steps in the specificity series $\mathbf{X}_s$ and construct the global stock correlations through an attention mechanism.

$$\mathbf{X}_{s,G} = \mathbf{W}_{(T \times 1)}^{\mathsf{T}} \mathbf{X}_s$$
$$\mathbf{Q}_G = \mathbf{W}_{Q,G}^{\mathsf{T}} \mathbf{X}_{s,G}, \mathbf{K}_G = \mathbf{W}_{K,G}^{\mathsf{T}} \mathbf{X}_{s,G} \tag{16}$$
$$\mathcal{G}_G = softmax(\frac{\mathbf{Q}_G^{\mathsf{T}} \mathbf{K}_G}{\sqrt{d_{kG}}}) + \mathbf{E}_G$$

where $\mathbf{W}_{(T \times 1)}$ denotes a $T \times 1$ mapping matrix that integrates information from all time steps to derive global specificity $\mathbf{X}_{s,G}$; $\mathbf{W}_{Q,G}$ and $\mathbf{W}_{K,G}$ represent linear mapping matrices; $\sqrt{d_{kG}}$ indicates the dimension of the $\mathbf{K}_G$ vector; $\mathbf{E}_G$ is the identity matrix; and $\mathcal{G}_G$ represents the adjacency matrix of the learned global correlation graph. By aggregating multiple time step information, inter-node correlation becomes more comprehensive. Consequently, we relax the sparsity constraint on $\mathcal{G}_G$, allowing a fully connected structure. Finally, we broadcast global correlation across all time steps, enabling each stock to aggregate information from all others.

$$\mathbf{X}_{G,Agg} = \mathcal{B}^{(T)}(\mathcal{G}_G)\mathbf{O}_S \tag{17}$$

The time series after information aggregation is denoted as $\mathbf{X}_{G,Agg}$.

Global Information-Guided Selective State Space Model. Global information plays a pivotal role in time step selection, as identical sequences may yield divergent decisions when incorporating versus excluding market context. We propose the Global Information-Guided Selective State Space Model, which enhances Mamba's selection mechanism through global macro information. Initially, we extract global macro information from each time step's macro data.

$$\mathbf{M}_G = \mathbf{W}_{F,G}^{\mathsf{T}}(\mathbf{W}_{(T \times 1)}^{\mathsf{T}} \mathbf{M}_S) + \mathbf{b}_{F,G} \tag{18}$$

where $\mathbf{W}_{(T \times 1)}$ denotes a $T \times 1$ mapping matrix that integrates time step macro information, and $\mathbf{W}_{F,G}$ represents a linear mapping matrix that fuses features to generate global macro information $\mathbf{M}_G$. We then incorporate $\mathbf{M}_G$ into the input and output matrix to guide the sequence selection process.

$$\mathbf{X}_G = \mu(\text{Conv1d}(\mathbf{X}_{G,Agg}))$$
$$\mathbf{B}_G = <\mathbf{W}_{B,G}^{\mathsf{T}} \mathbf{X}_G, \mathcal{B}^{(N,T)}(\mathbf{M}_G)>, \mathbf{C}_G = <\mathbf{W}_{C,G}^{\mathsf{T}} \mathbf{X}_G, \mathcal{B}^{(N,T)}(\mathbf{M}_G)> \tag{19}$$
$$\Delta_G = softplus(\mathbf{W}_{\Delta,G}^{\mathsf{T}} \mathbf{X}_G + \mathbf{A}_G)$$

where $\mathbf{W}_{B,G}$ and $\mathbf{W}_{C,G}$ represent linear mapping matrices that project the input sequence $\mathbf{X}_{G,Agg}$ into the input and output matrices, $\mathbf{A}_G$ denotes a learnable state transition matrix, and $< \cdots >$ indicates matrix concatenation. We propagate global macro information $\mathbf{M}_G$ to each stock's time step and concatenate it with both matrices. This integration ensures the SSM process incorporates global macro information for sequence selection. Finally, we discretize the state transition matrix $\mathbf{A}_G$ and input matrix $\mathbf{B}_G$ for SSM processing.

$$\overline{\mathbf{A}}_G, \overline{\mathbf{B}}_G = Discretization(\mathbf{A}_G, \mathbf{B}_G, \Delta_G)$$
$$\mathbf{O}_G = SSM(\overline{\mathbf{A}}_G, \overline{\mathbf{B}}_G, \mathbf{C}_G)(\mathbf{X}_G) \tag{20}$$

where $\mathbf{O}_G$ represents the final output of GIGSTM. The GIGSTM integrates time step macro information to learn both global macro information and static global stock correlations. Through a fully connected graph, each stock accesses information from all others, enhancing its representation. Meanwhile, global macro information guides each stock's time step selection, ensuring predictions incorporate historical patterns while aligning with market trends, thus improving stock modeling.

3.5   Prediction and Losses

Unlike conventional sequence prediction methods, we directly map all features output by GIGSTM to the prediction target through a linear layer. Considering the unique characteristics of stock prediction, we employ the mean-deviation prediction approach to achieve better forecasting performance [20].

$$mean = \mathbf{W}_{mean}^{\mathsf{T}}\mathbf{O}_G + \mathbf{b}_{mean}$$
$$dev = tanh(\mathbf{W}_{dev}^{\mathsf{T}}\mathbf{O}_G + \mathbf{b}_{dev}) \tag{21}$$
$$\hat{\mathbf{Y}} = mean + e^{dev}$$

where $\mathbf{W}_{mean}$ and $\mathbf{W}_{dev}$ are linear mapping matrices, and $\mathbf{b}_{mean}$ and $\mathbf{b}_{dev}$ are the corresponding bias matrices. The prediction target is decomposed into mean and deviation predictions. We use the Pearson correlation coefficient loss $\mathcal{L}_{pearson}$ as the loss function to learn the ranking distribution at each time step.

$$\mathcal{L}_{pearson} = -\frac{(\mathbf{Y} - \bar{\mathbf{Y}})^{\mathsf{T}}(\hat{\mathbf{Y}} - \bar{\hat{\mathbf{Y}}})}{\sqrt{(\mathbf{Y} - \bar{\mathbf{Y}})^{\mathsf{T}}(\mathbf{Y} - \bar{\mathbf{Y}})} \cdot \sqrt{(\hat{\mathbf{Y}} - \bar{\hat{\mathbf{Y}}})^{\mathsf{T}}(\hat{\mathbf{Y}} - \bar{\hat{\mathbf{Y}}})}} \tag{22}$$

4   Experiments

4.1   Experimental Setup

Datasets. We conducted experiments on three datasets: CSI500, CSI800, CSI1000. Brief statistical information is listed in Table 1. Detailed information about the datasets can be found in the appendix.

Table 1. The overall information for datasets

Dataset	Samples	Node	Partition
CSI500	3159	500	2677/239/243
CSI800	3159	800	2677/239/243
CSI1000	3159	1000	2677/239/243

Baseline. We compare our model with the following baselines: spatio-temporal models ASTGCN [4], MTGNN [18], DCRNN [7], STEMGNN [2], FC-STGNN [16] and MASTER [6], and time series models MICN [14], Filternet [21], iTransformer [9], TimeMixer [15], and TimesNet [17]. Where MASTER are specialized stock prediction models. Detailed descriptions of these models can be found in the appendix.

Metrics. We evaluate the performances of all baseline by nine metrics which are commonly used in stock prediction task including Information Coefficient (IC), Profit and Loss (PNL), Max Drawdown (MAXD), Sharpe Ratio (SHARPE), Win Rate (WINR), Profit/Loss Ratio (PL).

4.2 Main Results

We compare the proposed HIGSTM model with eight baselines across three datasets, and the experimental results are shown in Table 2. Overall, our method achieves the best performance in terms of IC, PNL, SHARPE, WINR, and PL on all datasets. For MAXD, HIGSTM just ranks second on the CSI500 dataset, slightly behind Filternet. On average, IC improves by 11%, SHARPE by 10%, and PNL and PL by over 6%. Additionally, the model's trading win rate increases by at least 2%, which represents a substantial improvement for stock trading.

More specifically, HIGSTM significantly outperforms other models in IC, with improvements of up to 18%, indicating that our method provides superior predictions. Compared to temporal models, HIGSTM incorporates cross-sectional and global information to guide sequence modeling, allowing each sequence to consider both historical patterns and overall market trends. Compared to spatio-temporal models, our proposed decomposition method extracts sequence specificity, and the hierarchical structure progressively models both dynamic and static relationships among stocks. The improvements in WINR and PL demonstrate that our model has stronger predictive capabilities for top-performing stocks, enabling more accurate identification of high-potential stocks. Regarding MAXD, HIGSTM underperforms Filternet on the CSI500 dataset, suggesting that while HIGSTM delivers higher returns, it also introduces slightly higher risk. However, this is not necessarily a drawback, as evidenced by the SHARPE metric, which measures the ratio of return to risk. HIGSTM significantly outperforms other models in SHARPE, with improvements exceeding 15%, indicating that the increase in returns far outweighs the associated risk.

Table 2. Comparison results on CSI500, CSI800 and CSI1000 datasets. ↓ indicates that the smaller the metric is better. The best result is in bold. The suboptimal results are indicated with an underline.

		CSI500					
		IC	PNL	MAXD↓	SHARPE	WINR	PL
Spatio-Temporal	ASTGCN	0.0434	0.0811	0.1387	0.4676	0.5110	1.0899
	MTGNN	0.0503	0.0797	0.1582	0.6963	0.5232	1.1866
	DCRNN	0.0521	0.1401	0.1537	0.9265	0.5162	1.1688
	STEMGNN	0.0479	0.0708	0.1308	0.7475	0.4699	1.0375
	FC-STGNN	0.0420	0.0946	0.1441	0.5858	0.5124	1.1102
	MASTER	0.0567	<u>0.1766</u>	0.1086	<u>1.2904</u>	<u>0.5579</u>	<u>1.2493</u>
Temporal	MICN	<u>0.0668</u>	0.0834	0.1390	0.6408	0.5165	1.1197
	Filternet	0.0464	0.1345	0.0688	0.8863	0.5165	1.1688
	iTransformer	0.0400	0.1214	0.1412	0.8340	0.4835	1.1574
	TimeMixer	0.0472	0.1044	0.1436	0.7657	0.5041	1.1398
	TimesNet	0.0346	0.0516	0.1250	0.3374	0.5041	1.0621
	HIGSTM	**0.0791**	**0.2619**	<u>0.1028</u>	**1.4846**	**0.5596**	**1.3207**
		CSI800					
		IC	PNL	MAXD↓	SHARPE	WINR	PL
Spatio-Temporal	ASTGCN	0.0431	0.0712	0.1380	0.5149	0.5027	1.1140
	MTGNN	0.0433	0.0939	0.1279	0.6682	0.5091	1.1409
	DCRNN	0.0373	0.0482	0.1374	0.3406	0.5098	1.0693
	STEMGNN	0.0364	0.0594	0.1289	0.3849	0.5032	1.0809
	FC-STGNN	0.0285	0.0312	0.1468	0.1803	0.5124	1.0322
	MASTER	<u>0.0628</u>	<u>0.1603</u>	<u>0.1116</u>	<u>1.2076</u>	0.4959	<u>1.2363</u>
Temporal	MICN	0.0380	0.0212	0.1493	0.1614	<u>0.5165</u>	1.0288
	Filternet	0.0302	0.0951	0.1255	0.6352	0.5083	1.1188
	iTransformer	0.0457	0.0314	0.1348	0.2192	0.4752	1.0397
	TimeMixer	0.0338	0.0487	0.1280	0.3028	0.5083	1.0548
	TimesNet	0.0253	0.0311	0.1427	0.2112	0.4793	1.0387
	HIGSTM	**0.0708**	**0.1918**	**0.1040**	**1.2602**	**0.5263**	**1.3617**
		CSI1000					
		IC	PNL	MAXD↓	SHARPE	WINR	PL
Spatio-Temporal	ASTGCN	0.0694	0.1313	0.1295	0.9434	0.4932	1.0884
	MTGNN	0.0701	0.1108	0.1406	1.1415	0.5098	1.2393
	DCRNN	0.0726	0.1426	0.1614	1.1791	0.5531	1.2593
	STEMGNN	0.0688	0.1392	0.1021	1.1334	0.4867	1.2084
	FC-STGNN	0.0733	0.1514	0.1365	0.9339	<u>0.5537</u>	1.1709
	MASTER	0.0850	0.1843	<u>0.0995</u>	<u>1.3382</u>	0.5455	<u>1.2601</u>
Temporal	MICN	<u>0.0876</u>	0.1779	0.1467	1.2339	0.5455	1.2359
	Filternet	0.0723	<u>0.1883</u>	0.1312	1.2715	0.5413	1.2392
	iTransformer	0.0747	0.1642	0.1407	1.1638	0.5289	1.2226
	TimeMixer	0.0797	0.1580	0.1178	1.0681	0.5289	1.2007
	TimesNet	0.0766	0.1512	0.1092	1.0244	0.5372	1.1922
	HIGSTM	**0.0918**	**0.2178**	**0.0759**	**1.4173**	**0.5845**	**1.3566**

4.3   Ablation Study

To validate the effectiveness of our model, we conducted ablation study on the CSI500 and CSI1000 datasets, using IC (to measure prediction accuracy) and SHARPE (to measure the return-to-risk ratio) as evaluation metrics. Specifically, we compared the following variants:

- **w/o TIGSTM:** remove Temporal Information-Guided Spatio-temporal Mamba block
- **w/o GIGSTM:** remove Global Information-Guided Spatio-temporal Mamba block
- **w/o T&GIGSTM:** remove Temporal and Global Information-Guided Spatio-temporal Mamba block
- **w/o Decomposition:** remove the Index-Guided Frequency Filtering Decomposition; both the relationships and macro-level information are extracted directly from the stock time series.
- **w/o Index:** when decomposing the stock time series, the decomposition is not guided by the stock indices.

The experimental results are shown in Table 3. It can be observed that removing either TIGSTM or GIGSTM leads to a significant decline in both IC and SHARPE, with similar magnitudes of degradation. This indicates that both temporal cross-sectional information and global information are crucial for prediction. When both TIGSTM and GIGSTM are removed, the model essentially loses its predictive capability, demonstrating the effectiveness of our proposed TIGSTM and GIGSTM. Additionally, removing the Decomposition process results in a 30% performance drop, highlighting the necessity of extracting commonality and specificity from the time series. Commonality enables better extraction of macro-level information, while specificity helps uncover more prominent relationships. Furthermore, when the Decomposition process is not guided by the Index, the model's performance also declines by over 30%, underscoring the critical role of the Index in guiding the decomposition. Using the Index to learn filter parameters is an indispensable step.

Table 3. Ablation Study

	CSI500		CSI1000	
	IC	SHARPE	IC	SHARPE
w/o TIGSTM	0.0733	0.8262	0.0745	0.9026
w/o GIGSTM	0.0604	0.6124	0.0701	1.0075
w/o T&GIGSTM	0.0409	0.0333	0.0630	0.9172
w/o Decomposition	0.0539	0.6822	0.0594	0.4605
w/o Index	0.0451	0.5711	0.0592	0.7073
HIGSTM	**0.0791**	**1.4846**	**0.0918**	**1.4173**

4.4   Hyper-parameter Study

We conducted a detailed parameter study on the model on CSI500 dataset, and the experimental results are shown in Fig. 2. We investigated the following parameters in HIGSTM: the hidden layer dimension d_{model}, the state dimension d_{state}, the convolution kernel dimension d_{conv}, the macro-level information dimension for each time step d_{te}, the global macro-level information dimension d_{ge}, and the correlation attention dimension d_{attn}.

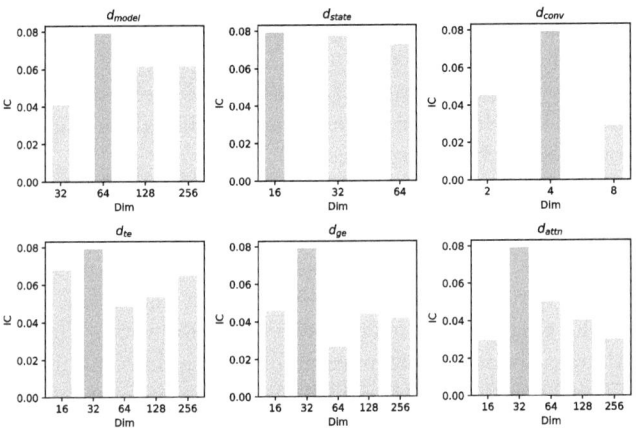

Fig. 2. Hyper-parameter Study

The results show that the optimal value for d_{model} is 64. When d_{model} is smaller than 64, the dimension is insufficient to capture all features, while when it exceeds 64, the model tends to overfit, leading to a decline in performance. For d_{state}, although the performance differences are minor, a value of 16 is recommended considering computational efficiency. The optimal value for d_{conv} is 4, as larger convolution kernels can obscure local features, degrading performance. For d_{te}, d_{ge}, and d_{attn}, the optimal dimension is 32. When these parameters are smaller than 32, the model cannot fully capture the required information, while values larger than 32 lead to overfitting, where the guiding information overshadows the unique characteristics of each node.

4.5   Analysis

Analysis of Characteristics of Temporal Section and Global Graphs.
We sampled 50 nodes and analyzed the characteristics of both the temporal section and the global graph through visualization. The visualized structure is shown in Fig. 3(a). It can be observed that the graph learned in each temporal section is sparse and prominent. Each node has only a few neighboring nodes, and most nodes exhibit 1–2 highly correlated neighbors that stand out significantly.

This aligns with the model's design intention, which is to identify a small number of truly significant neighbors at each time point, preventing the information from being overshadowed by a large number of neighbors. On the other hand, the Global Graph identifies general static relationships, measuring correlations with all nodes, and does not exhibit significantly correlated neighbors.

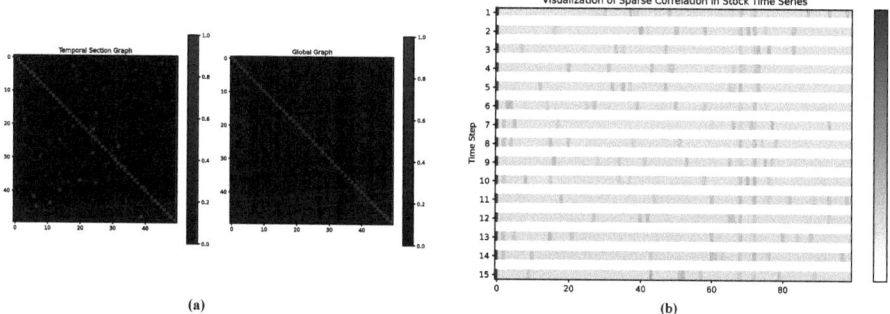

Fig. 3. (a) Visualization of Temporal Section and Global Graphs. (b) Visualization of Sparse Correlation in Stock Time Series

Analysis of Dynamic Changes in Correlations. We selected a stock (stock 0) and visualized its correlations with 100 stocks over time, as shown in Fig. 3(b). It can be observed that, on one hand, the adjacency relationships of stock 0 change significantly over time steps, indicating that the temporal section graph can capture rapidly changing relationships based on different time steps. On the other hand, stock 0 shares the same neighbors across time steps, demonstrating that the temporal graph is not only capable of capturing fast-changing relationships at the time-step level, but also relationships that persist over a period of time.

5 Related Work

5.1 Temporal Models

Research in time series forecasting has focused on improving prediction accuracy through various models. Transformer-based models include Informer [24], and FEDformer [25], which use sparse attention and decomposition techniques. CNN-based models like TimesNet [17] extract patterns via frequency and time domain segmentation. MLP-based models such as TimeMixer [15] leverage basis approximation and multi-scale decomposition. Mamba-based models like TimeMachine [1] and Bi-Mamba [13] refine content selection. Other models include PatchTST [10], which segments time series into patches, and iTransformer [9], which redefines time embeddings.

5.2 Spatio-Temporal Models

Spatio-temporal forecasting integrates temporal and spatio information for better predictions. Convolution-based models such as MTGNN [18], StemGNN [2], use gating mechanisms for feature extraction. Complex architectures like ST-GDN [22] improve performance through advanced designs. RNN+GNN models like DCRNN [7] combine temporal and spatio modeling. Transformer-based models such as ASTGCN [4] and STTN [19] integrate attention mechanisms for capturing dependencies.

5.3 Stock Price Forecasting Models

Stock price forecasting has evolved from traditional methods like ANN [26] and regularization to deep learning. Models like MTDNN [8] have shown potential. Spatio-temporal frameworks like STHAN-SR [11] and MASTER [6] capture temporal and variable dependencies.

6 Conclusion

In this paper, we propose the Hierarchical Information-Guided Spatio-Temporal Mamba (HIGSTM) to address the limitations of Mamba in stock time series forecasting. HIGSTM decomposes the series into commonality and specificity through Index-Guided Frequency Filtering Decomposition, extracting macro-level information and inter-stock relationships separately. Then, it introduces a hierarchical structure: Node Independent, Temporal Information-Guided Spatio-temporal Mamba, and Global Information-Guided Spatio-temporal Mamba, progressively modeling node features, temporal dynamic correlations, and static global relationships. Our proposed Information-Guided Mamba incorporates time step macro-level information and global information to guide the sequence selection process, ensuring decisions align with the overall market. Experimental results on real-world stock market data fully demonstrate the effectiveness of our approach.

Acknowledgments. This work is supported by the National Natural Science Foundation of China (Grant No. 62276008, 62250037, and 62076010), and partially supported by the National Key R&D of China (Grant #2022YFF0800601).

Appendix

A   Basic Informations

A.1   Datasets Feature

The stock features we utilize include: open, high, low, close, pre_close, change, pct_chg, vol, amount, turnover_rate, turnover_rate_f, and volume_ratio pe, pe_ttm, pb, ps, ps_ttm, dv_ratio dv_ttm, total_share, float_share, free_share, total_mv, and circ_mv buy_sm_vol, buy_sm_amount, sell_sm_vol, sell_sm_amount, buy_md_vol, and buy_md_amount, sell_md_vol, sell_md_amount, buy_lg_vol, buy_lg_amount, sell_lg_vol, sell_lg_amount, buy_elg_vol, buy_elg_amount, sell_elg_vol, sell_elg_amount, net_mf_vol, and net_mf_amount, up_limit, down_limit, ma5, ma10, ma15, ma20, ma25 and industry.

A.2   Experimental Setup and Parameter Settings

Our experimental environment is as follows: Ubuntu 22.04, GPU NVIDIA GeForce RTX 3090 24G, CPU AMD EPYC7282, and 256 GB of RAM. We conducted 5 repeated experiments. We set the parameters of HIGSTM as follows: the hidden layer dimension is $d_{model} = 64$, the state dimension is $d_{model} = 16$, the convolution kernel dimension is $d_{conv} = 4$, the macro-level information dimension for each time step is $d_{te} = 32$, the global macro-level information dimension is $d_{ge} = 32$, and the correlation attention dimension is $d_{attn} = 32$. The input time series length is $l_{in} = 16$.

A.3   Trading Strategies

Our simulated trading strategy involves selecting the top 10% of stocks each day, holding them for 10 days, and calculating the returns using equal-weighted simple interest for all stocks, while also taking into account transaction fees.

B   Case Study

We present the stocks most correlated with 600519.SH in the temporal section and the global graph, as shown in Fig. 4. The numerical codes in the figure correspond to individual stocks in the Chinese stock market. It can be observed that in the sparse temporal section correlation, the diversity of neighbors is low, but the correlations are prominent. The learned neighbors, such as 000596.SZ (Orange node), are stocks from the same liquor industry as 600519.SH, exhibiting significant correlations. In contrast, the Global Correlation shows higher diversity among neighbors, with no particularly dominant adjacency relationships. For instance, 000596.SZ (Orange node) has a high correlation due to belonging to the same industry as the benchmark stock, 603288.SH (Blue node) is highly correlated as it is also in the beverage sector, 601888.SH (Pink node) is correlated due to its involvement in downstream retail, and 601318.SH (Green node) is correlated as it is another industry leader.

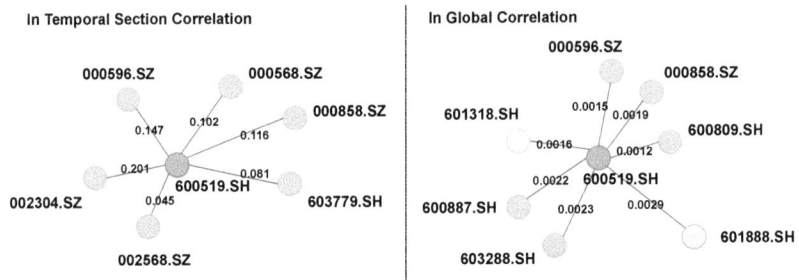

Fig. 4. Case: The neighbors of stock 600519.SH learned in the temporal section and the global graph.

C   Daily Return Rate Analysis

The box plots of daily returns (Fig. 5) show that HIGSTM achieves a significantly higher maximum return compared to other models, with its minimum return also exceeding all except MASTER. HIGSTM exhibits slightly higher return volatility, indicating greater risk, aligning with earlier findings. MASTER, in contrast, is a low-risk, low-return model, with its maximum return notably lower than HIGSTM's.

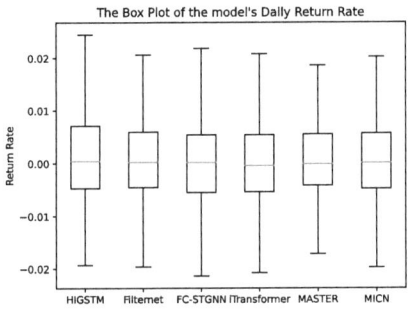

Fig. 5. The Box Plot of the model's Daily Return Rate

References

1. Ahamed, M.A., Cheng, Q.: TimeMachine: a time series is worth 4 mambas for long-term forecasting. In: ECAI 2024: 27th European Conference on Artificial Intelligence, 19-24 October 2024, Santiago de Compostela, Spain-Including 13th Conference on Prestigious Applications of Intelligent Systems. European Conference on Artificial Intelligence, vol. 392, p. 1688 (2024)
2. Cao, D., et al.: Spectral temporal graph neural network for multivariate time-series forecasting. Adv. Neural. Inf. Process. Syst. **33**, 17766–17778 (2020)

3. Gu, A., Dao, T.: Mamba: linear-time sequence modeling with selective state spaces. arXiv preprint arXiv:2312.00752 (2023)
4. Guo, S., Lin, Y., Feng, N., Song, C., Wan, H.: Attention based spatial-temporal graph convolutional networks for traffic flow forecasting. In: Proceedings of the AAAI Conference on Artificial Intelligence, vol. 33, pp. 922–929 (2019)
5. Lea, C., Vidal, R., Reiter, A., Hager, G.D.: Temporal convolutional networks: a unified approach to action segmentation. In: Hua, G., Jégou, H. (eds.) ECCV 2016, Part III. LNCS, vol. 9915, pp. 47–54. Springer, Cham (2016). https://doi.org/10.1007/978-3-319-49409-8_7
6. Li, T., Liu, Z., Shen, Y., Wang, X., Chen, H., Huang, S.: Master: market-guided stock transformer for stock price forecasting. In: Proceedings of the AAAI Conference on Artificial Intelligence, vol. 38, pp. 162–170 (2024)
7. Li, Y., Yu, R., Shahabi, C., Liu, Y.: Diffusion convolutional recurrent neural network: data-driven traffic forecasting. arXiv preprint arXiv:1707.01926 (2017)
8. Liu, G., et al.: Multi-scale two-way deep neural network for stock trend prediction. In: IJCAI, pp. 4555–4561 (2020)
9. Liu, Y., et al.: iTransformer: inverted transformers are effective for time series forecasting. arXiv preprint arXiv:2310.06625 (2023)
10. Nie, Y., Nguyen, N.H., Sinthong, P., Kalagnanam, J.: A time series is worth 64 words: long-term forecasting with transformers. arXiv preprint arXiv:2211.14730 (2022)
11. Sawhney, R., Agarwal, S., Wadhwa, A., Derr, T., Shah, R.R.: Stock selection via spatiotemporal hypergraph attention network: a learning to rank approach. In: Proceedings of the AAAI Conference on Artificial Intelligence, vol. 35, pp. 497–504 (2021)
12. Shih, S.Y., Sun, F.K., Lee, H.Y.: Temporal pattern attention for multivariate time series forecasting. Mach. Learn. 108, 1421–1441 (2019)
13. Tang, S., Ma, L., Li, H., Sun, M., Shen, Z.: Bi-mamba: towards accurate 1-bit state space models. arXiv preprint arXiv:2411.11843 (2024)
14. Wang, H., Peng, J., Huang, F., Wang, J., Chen, J., Xiao, Y.: MICN: multi-scale local and global context modeling for long-term series forecasting. In: The Eleventh International Conference on Learning Representations (2023)
15. Wang, S., et al.: TimeMixer: decomposable multiscale mixing for time series forecasting. arXiv preprint arXiv:2405.14616 (2024)
16. Wang, Y., et al.: Fully-connected spatial-temporal graph for multivariate time-series data. In: Proceedings of the AAAI Conference on Artificial Intelligence, vol. 38, pp. 15715–15724 (2024)
17. Wu, H., Hu, T., Liu, Y., Zhou, H., Wang, J., Long, M.: TimesNet: temporal 2D-variation modeling for general time series analysis. arXiv preprint arXiv:2210.02186 (2022)
18. Wu, Z., Pan, S., Long, G., Jiang, J., Chang, X., Zhang, C.: Connecting the dots: multivariate time series forecasting with graph neural networks. In: Proceedings of the 26th ACM SIGKDD International Conference on Knowledge Discovery & Data Mining, pp. 753–763 (2020)
19. Xu, K., et al.: Spatio-temporal transformer networks for traffic flow forecasting. IEEE Trans. Intell. Transp. Syst. 22(11), 7137–7147 (2021)
20. Yan, W., Tan, Y.: Double-path adaptive-correlation spatial-temporal inverted transformer for stock time series forecasting. arXiv preprint arXiv:2409.15662 (2024)
21. Yi, K., et al.: FilterNet: harnessing frequency filters for time series forecasting. arXiv preprint arXiv:2411.01623 (2024)

22. Zhang, X., et al.: Traffic flow forecasting with spatial-temporal graph diffusion network. In: Proceedings of the AAAI Conference on Artificial Intelligence, vol. 35, pp. 15008–15015 (2021)
23. Zhang, Y., Yan, J.: CrossFormer: transformer utilizing cross-dimension dependency for multivariate time series forecasting. In: The Eleventh International Conference on Learning Representations (2022)
24. Zhou, H., et al.: Informer: beyond efficient transformer for long sequence time-series forecasting. In: Proceedings of the AAAI Conference on Artificial Intelligence, vol. 35, pp. 11106–11115 (2021)
25. Zhou, T., Ma, Z., Wen, Q., Wang, X., Sun, L., Jin, R.: FedFormer: frequency enhanced decomposed transformer for long-term series forecasting. In: International Conference on Machine Learning, pp. 27268–27286. PMLR (2022)
26. Zou, J., Han, Y., So, S.S.: Overview of artificial neural networks. Artif. Neural Netw.: Methods Appl. 14–22 (2009)

G-GLformer: Transformer with GRU Embedding and Global-Local Attention for Multivariate Time Series Forecasting

Wenjun Yu[1], Jiyanglin Li[2(✉)], Wentao Gao[3], Niangxi Zhuang[4], Wen Li[1(✉)], and Shouguo Du[5]

[1] Shanghai University of International Business and Economics, Shanghai, China
liwen@suibe.edu.cn
[2] Guizhou University of Finance and Economics, Guizhou, China
jylli@mail.gufe.edu.cn
[3] University of South Australia, Adelaide, Australia
wentao.gao@mymail.unisa.edu.au
[4] Guangzhou Nanfang College, Guangzhou, China
[5] Shanghai Municipal Big Data Center, Shanghai, China

Abstract. Time series forecasting plays a vital role in various fields. Due to the special ability of its self-attention mechanism in capturing long-term dependencies, Transformer has been widely used in time series modeling. However, the majority of contemporary Transformer-based models adopt variate tokenization, where the self-attention mechanism is used to extract variable correlations, which weakens the extraction of temporal correlations. Furthermore, the self-attention mechanism extracts correlations within the look-back window. Owing to the absence of a global perspective, the correlations it captures may be influenced by local noise. To tackle these issues, we propose an advanced Transformer architecture entitled G-GLformer, which designs two novel modules, Bidirectional-Patch-GRU-Embedding (BPGE) and Global-Local-Attention (GLA), and integrates them into the Transformer to achieve more accurate forecast. Specifically, the BPGE module is mainly used to model temporal relationships and enhance local semantics. The GLA module integrates the correlation coefficients of the training set data with the data from the local look-back window. This endows the data in the look-back window with a global perspective, making it less susceptible to the influence of noise. Moreover, they can also be used as plug-ins in other models. Extensive experiments on public datasets demonstrate its superior performance over other state-of-the-art models.

Keywords: Time series forecasting · Multivariate time series · Transformer

1 Introduction

Multivariate time series forecasting holds significant importance in real-world domains such as weather [19], energy [25], transportation [1] and finance [16].

In recent years, various deep learning models have been proposed, significantly pushing the performance boundaries [4,13,14,21]. Transformers have demonstrated impressive performance in time series forecasting, primarily due to their attention mechanisms [9,11,18,26]. Traditionally, the majority of methods based on Transformer have employed temporal tokenization, which considers all variates at a specific timestamp as one single token. However, recent research findings indicate that variate tokenization, in which every variate is embedded as an individual token, surpasses temporal tokenization in terms of capturing the dependencies among variates. Due to its broad applicability to Transformers, variate tokenization has been adopted in recent advancements in multivariate time series forecasting [3,10,15]. However, these models overlook two important issues.

First, these models use the self-attention mechanism to model variable correlations instead of temporal correlations. The absence of self-attention mechanism for modeling temporal correlations undoubtedly weakens the model's ability to capture sequential relationships. Although the model adds positional encoding during embedding, this is insufficient for the model to recognize temporal relationships [23]. We contend that Recurrent Neural Networks (RNNs) may offer solutions to these issues with Transformers. This is mainly because the internal structure of RNNs is highly suitable for sequential data and hidden units can serve as an excellent representation of time series. However, when dealing with long time series, RNNs tend to encounter problems such as gradient vanishing or explosion, as well as the inability to capture long-term dependencies [12]. Therefore, we divide the time series into patches of the same size. This method can reduce the length of the sequence, mitigate the problems mentioned above, and enhance the local features of the sequence.

Secondly, these models always extract correlations within a limited look-back window. Due to the lack of a global perspective, the extraction of correlations is vulnerable to the influence of local noise. Based on the above situation, we have provided an example as shown in Fig. 1. When there is a high positive global correlation, locally, due to the presence of noise, there may be situations where the variables are uncorrelated or even negatively correlated. Therefore, we attempt to integrate global and local correlations to enhance the robustness of variable correlations extraction. Specifically, we calculate the Pearson correlation coefficients among variates in the training set. Subsequently, we take these Pearson correlation coefficients as a static graph and apply graph convolution to the query and key in the self-attention mechanism, aiming to integrate the global correlations with the local correlations.

To this end, We propose a novel Transformer architecture based on variate tokenization. The model mainly improves the performance of time series prediction through the method of GRU embedding and by integrating the global correlation with the local correlation. The main contributions are summarized as follows:

- We propose the BPGE module to enhance the temporal features of the variate-tokenized Transformer. Furthermore, the BPGE module is only used

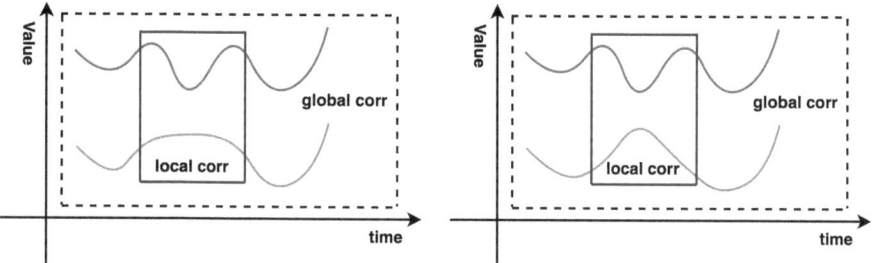

Fig. 1. The figure on the left indicates that there is no local correlation between the two time series. However, there is a high degree of positive correlation except for the locally noisy parts. The right-hand figure shows a negative correlation between the two time series locally, yet there is a high positive correlation except for the locally noisy part.

during the embedding process. Therefore, it will not significantly increase the computational burden.

- The GLA module we proposed innovatively integrates global and local correlations to improve the model's robustness to local noise. In addition, this module can also serve as a plug-in and be applied to other models that use the self-attention mechanism to extract variable correlations.
- Our model is rigorously validated on multiple standard benchmark datasets. Compared to the iTransformer (SOTA), our model achieves an average reduction in Mean Squared Error (MSE) of up to 6.12 % and Mean Absolute Error(MAE) of up to 5.08 %, demonstrating its superior ability in time series forecasting.

2   Related Work

2.1   Transformer-Based Forecasters

Inspired by the success of Transformers in natural language processing, numerous Transformers have been proposed for multivariate time series forecasting. Classic works such as Autoformer [18], Informer [25], Pyraformer [8], and FEDformer [26] represent early Transformer-based time series forecasters. These models adopt the method of temporal tokenization, encoding the values of all variates at a specific time step into an independent token. Then, the self-attention mechanism is used to extract the correlations between different tokens. However, these models fail to capture the correlations among different variates. iTransformer [9] introduces the inverted Transformer to capture multivariate dependencies and achieves accurate forecasts. Due to the good predictive performance and interpretability, an increasing number of models now adopt variate tokenization. Timer [10] combines several variates originating from diverse domains into a unified time series and regards time series as a single token. MCformer [3] performs tokenization on each individual variate and then blends these variates together, aiming to capture the correlations existing between different variates. Similarly, TimeXer [15] also makes use of variate tokenization when it comes to introducing exogenous variates.

2.2 Dependency Modeling

Time series correlations mainly includes variable correlations and temporal correlations. Some models [6,11,23] adopt a Channel Independency (CI) strategy, that is, they only consider temporal correlations. These models solely rely on the historical information of each individual sequence for prediction, overlooking the correlations among different variates. Although this method is robust, it squanders the potential information among different variates. Channel Dependency(CD) strategy [9,22,24] model the correlations among all variates, and as a result, they reduce robustness. The primary cause of the lack of robustness is the incorrect extraction of variable correlations due to local noise. Therefore, designing a robust CD method is challenging.

3   Methodology

In this section, we will describe the Bidirectional-Patch-GRU-Embedding module, the Global-Local-Attention module, and the overall architecture of the model. In multivariate time series forecasting, given historical observations $\mathbf{X} \in \mathbb{R}^{T \times N}$ with T time steps and N variates, we predict the future S time steps $\mathbf{Y} \in \mathbb{R}^{S \times N}$. The time series forecasting problem aims to learn a function $f(\cdot)$ that maps the time step T of history to the next time step S:

$$[X_{t-T+1}, X_{t-T+2}, \cdots, X_t] \xrightarrow{f(\cdot)} [\hat{X}_{t+1}, \hat{X}_{t+2}, \cdots, \hat{X}_{t+S}]. \tag{1}$$

The architecture of our proposed model, referred to as G-GLformer, is depicted in Fig. 2.

3.1   Bidirectional-Patch-GRU-Embedding

To enhance the model's ability to capture temporal relationships, we adopt the GRU model [2] with a recurrent structure. However, due to the inherent flaws of the recurrent structure, it is unable to capture long-term dependencies. Moreover, it is prone to problems such as vanishing or exploding gradients. Therefore, time series is split into non-overlapping patches, and each patch is projected to a temporal token. The patch technique can effectively reduce the sequence length, thus avoiding the above-mentioned problems. The reason for adopting bidirectional GRU is that it can extract more abundant and comprehensive features from the input sequence. During the learning process, the forward and backward GRU capture feature information from different aspects. By combining these features, a more representative feature representation can be provided for

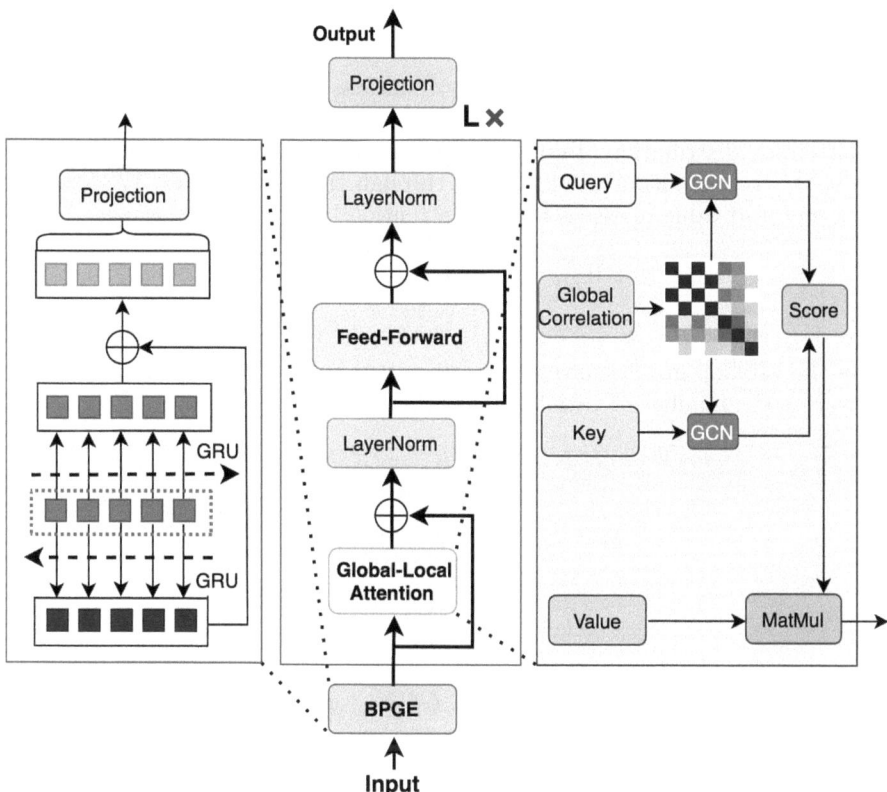

Fig. 2. G-GLformer is mainly composed of three modules: the Bidirectional-Patch-GRU-Embedding module, the Global-Local-Attention module, and the Feed-Forward module.

subsequent tasks. The overall Bidirectional-Patch-GRU-Embedding is formally stated as:

$$Patchify(\mathbf{X}) = \{P_1, P_2, \cdots, P_S\}, \tag{2}$$

$$\mathbf{P}_{forward} = GRU_{forward}(P_1, P_2, \cdots, P_S), \tag{3}$$

$$\mathbf{P}_{backward} = GRU_{backward}(P_1, P_2, \cdots, P_S), \tag{4}$$

$$\mathbf{P} = PatchEmbed(\mathbf{P}_{forward} + \mathbf{P}_{backward}). \tag{5}$$

Denote by L the length of the patch, by $S = \lfloor \frac{T}{L} \rfloor$ the number of patches split from the time series, and by P_i the i-th patch. Specifically, $Patchify(\cdot)$: $\mathbb{R}^{N \times T} \to \mathbb{R}^{N \times S \times L}$ is a process of splitting a time series into non-overlapping patches. $GRU(\cdot) : \mathbb{R}^{N \times S \times L} \to \mathbb{R}^{N \times S \times D}$ maps a patch with a length of L into a hidden state of dimension D. $PatchEmbed(\cdot) : \mathbb{R}^{N \times S \times D} \to \mathbb{R}^{N \times D}$ maps all patches into a D-dimensional vector via a trainable linear projector. Through the above operations, we complete the embedding work of the sequence.

3.2 Global-Local-Attention

To capture more reliable multivariate correlations, we introduce a new Global-Local-Attention(GLA) mechanism to calculate attention weights for more effective attention distribution. Taking the first layer of the Encoder as an example, $\mathbf{P} \in \mathbb{R}^{N \times D}$ is the output after passing through the BPGE layer. We form the query, key, and value matrices for each attention head h as:

$$Q^h = \mathbf{P}W_Q^h, \quad K^h = \mathbf{P}W_K^h, \quad V^h = \mathbf{P}W_V^h, \tag{6}$$

where $W_Q^h, W_K^h, W_V^h \in \mathbb{R}^{D \times D_H}$, D_H is the heads' hidden dimension. Then, we apply the Mixhop graph convolution [20] to $Q^h \in \mathbb{R}^{N \times D_H}$ and $K^h \in \mathbb{R}^{N \times D_H}$, where N is the number of variates. The GLA is defined as follows:

$$\tilde{Q}^h = GCN(Q^h, \tilde{A}), \tilde{K}^h = GCN(K^h, \tilde{A}), \tag{7}$$

$$S^h = Softmax(\frac{\tilde{Q}^h (\tilde{K}^h)^T}{\sqrt{D_H}})V^h, \tag{8}$$

$$GLA(\mathbf{P}) = \sum_h S^h V^h W_O^h, \tag{9}$$

where $W_O^h \in \mathbb{R}^{D_H \times D}$ is output matrix, $GCN(\cdot)$ denotes Mixhop graph convolution layer and $\tilde{A} \in \mathbb{R}^{N \times N}$ represents the adjacency matrix. The adjacency matrix learning process in our approach involves generating a learnable matrix. Then, the learnable matrix is added to the Pearson correlation coefficients of the training set. The specific process is as follows:

$$\tilde{A} = M + Pr, \tag{10}$$

where $M \in \mathbb{R}^{N \times N}$ is a learnable matrix, and $Pr \in \mathbb{R}^{N \times N}$ is the Pearson correlation coefficient matrix of the training set.

After obtaining the adjacency matrix, we use the Mixhop graph convolution layer to embed the global correlation into the local correlation. The Mixhop graph convolution layer consists of two steps: the information propagation step and the information selection step. The information propagation step is defined as follows:

$$H^{(k)} = \beta H_{in} + (1 - \beta)\tilde{A}H^{(k-1)}, \tag{11}$$

where β is a hyper parameter, which controls the ratio of retaining the root node's original states. The information selection step is defined as follows:

$$H_{out} = Linear((Concatenate(H^{(0)}, H^{(1)}, \cdots, H^{(k)}))), \tag{12}$$

where k is the depth of propagation. $H^{(0)} = H_{in}$ represents the input of the graph convolution layer, and H_{out} represents the output of the graph convolution layer. Finally, the output dimension is unified with the input dimension through a linear layer.

3.3   Feed-Forward Layer

Transformer adopts the feed-forward network (FFN) as the basic building block for encoding token representation and it is identically applied to each token. In this paper, we employ FFN to learn variable representations for time series forecasting. In order to reduce overfitting and improve the generalization ability of the model, Dropout is adopted in the FFN layer. FFN employs a Gaussian Error Linear Unit (GELU) activation function to facilitate non-linear transformations. The FFN is defined as follows:

$$X_h = Dropout(GELU(Linear(X_{in}))), \tag{13}$$

$$X_{out} = Dropout(Linear(X_h)) + X_{in}, \tag{14}$$

where X_{in} and $X_{out} \in \mathbb{R}^{N \times D}$ are the input and output of the FFN, $X_h \in \mathbb{R}^{N \times F}$, where F represents the size of the hidden layer.

3.4   Projection Prediction

A linear layer is used to obtain the final prediction $\hat{Y} = [\hat{X}_{t+1}, \hat{X}_{t+2}, \cdots, \hat{X}_{t+S}] \in \mathbb{R}^{N \times S}$. The formula is as follows:

$$\hat{Y} = Projection(X_{out}), \tag{15}$$

where $X_{out} \in \mathbb{R}^{N \times D}$ is the output of the last layer of the Encoder.

We use Mean Squared Error (MSE) to measure the difference between the predicted values $\hat{Y}$ and the ground truth Y. MSE is calculated within S time steps. The formula is as follows:

$$\mathcal{L} = \frac{1}{S} \sum_{i=1}^{S} \left\| \hat{X}_{t+i} - X_{t+i} \right\|_2^2. \tag{16}$$

4   Experiments

4.1   Datasets

We evaluate the performance of G-GLformer on 13 real-world datasets, including Weather, Exchange, ECL, Traffic, ETT (ETTh1, ETTh2, ETTm1, ETTm2) used by Autoformer [18], Solar-Energy used by LST-Net [5] and PEMS datasets (PEMS03, PEMS04, PEMS07, PEMS08) adopted by SCINet [7]. These are widely used multivariate time series datasets, and we handle the datasets the same way as iTransformer [9]. The details of datasets are as follows:

- **ETT (Electricity Transformer Temperature)** [25] includes four subsets. ETTh1 and ETTh2 collect hourly data on 7 different factors from two distinct electricity transformers from July 2016 to July 2018. ETTm1 and ETTm2 record the same factors at a higher resolution of every 15 min.

- **Traffic** [18] collects hourly data from the California Department of Transportation, describing road occupancy rates measured by 862 sensors on San Francisco Bay Area freeways.
- **ECL(Electricity)** [18] captures the hourly electricity consumption of 321 clients from 2012 to 2014.
- **Weather** [18] records 21 meteorological factors such as air temperature and humidity every 10 min throughout the year 2020.
- **Exchange** [18] records the daily exchange rates of eight different countries ranging from 1990 to 2016.
- **Solar-Energy** [5] includes data from 137 PV plants in Alabama State, with solar power production sampled every 10 min during 2006.
- **PEMS** [7] includes traffic network data from California, sampled every 5 min, focusing on four public subsets: PEMS03, PEMS04, PEMS07, and PEMS08.

The summary of the datasets is shown in Table 1.

Table 1. Detailed dataset descriptions. Dim denotes the variate number of each dataset. Dataset Size denotes the total number of time points in (Train, Validation, Test) split respectively. Prediction Length denotes the future time points to be predicted and four prediction settings are included in each dataset. Frequency denotes the sampling interval of time points.

Dataset	Dim	Prediction Length	Dataset Size	Frequency
ETTh1,ETTh2	7	$\{96, 192, 336, 720\}$	(8545, 2881, 2881)	Hourly
ETTm1,ETTm2	7	$\{96, 192, 336, 720\}$	(34465, 11521, 11521)	15 min
Exchange	8	$\{96, 192, 336, 720\}$	(5120, 665, 1422)	Daily
Weather	21	$\{96, 192, 336, 720\}$	(36792, 5271, 10540)	10 min
ECL	321	$\{96, 192, 336, 720\}$	(18317, 2633, 5261)	Hourly
Traffic	862	$\{96, 192, 336, 720\}$	(12185, 1757, 3509)	Hourly
Solar-Energy	137	$\{96, 192, 336, 720\}$	(36601, 5161, 10417)	10 min
PEMS03	358	$\{12, 24, 48, 96\}$	(15617, 5135, 5135)	5 min
PEMS04	307	$\{12, 24, 48, 96\}$	(10172, 3375, 3375)	5 min
PEMS07	883	$\{12, 24, 48, 96\}$	(16911, 5622, 5622)	5 min
PEMS08	170	$\{12, 24, 48, 96\}$	(10690, 3548, 3548)	5 min

4.2   Baselines

We compare G-GLformer with six state-of-the art models from three categories, including (1) Transformer based models: iTransformer [9], PatchTST [11], FEDformer [26], Autoformer [18] (2) CNN-based model: TimesNet [17] and (3) Linear-based models: DLinear [23].

4.3   Experimental Results

Table 2 shows the average errors for the four prediction lengths of 96, 192, 336, and 720. Due to the limitation of the length of this paper, we have not presented all the results. As can be seen from the Table 2, G-GLformer achieves a total of 13 first places and 5 s places in long-term time series prediction. However, it can also be observed that although the Mean Squared Error (MSE) of the Traffic dataset achieved the second place for G-GLformer, there is still a significant gap compared with the first-place result of iTransformer. We believe this is due to the presence of a large number of outliers in the Traffic dataset. We will discuss this issue in detail in the "Discussion" section.

Table 2. Full results for the long-term forecasting task. The input sequence length is set to 96 for all baselines. The results in the table are the averages of the prediction lengths of 96, 192, 336, and 720. The best results are in **bold** and the second best are underlined.

Models	G-GLformer (Ours)		iTransformer (2024)		PatchTST (2023)		DLinear (2023)		TimesNet (2023)		FEDformer (2022)		Autoformer (2021)	
Metric	MSE	MAE	MSE	MAE	MSE	MAE	MSE	MAE	MSE	MAE	MSE	MAE	MSE	MAE
ETTh1	**0.433**	**0.433**	0.457	0.449	0.469	0.454	0.456	0.452	0.458	0.450	0.440	0.460	0.496	0.487
ETTh2	**0.377**	**0.402**	0.384	0.407	0.387	0.407	0.559	0.515	0.414	0.427	0.437	0.449	0.450	0.459
ETTm1	0.394	0.401	0.408	0.412	**0.387**	**0.400**	0.403	0.407	0.400	0.406	0.448	0.452	0.588	0.517
ETTm2	0.283	0.328	0.293	0.336	**0.281**	**0.326**	0.350	0.401	0.291	0.333	0.305	0.349	0.327	0.371
ECL	**0.166**	**0.261**	0.176	0.267	0.205	0.290	0.212	0.300	0.192	0.295	0.214	0.327	0.227	0.338
Exchange	**0.353**	**0.400**	0.365	0.407	0.367	0.404	0.354	0.414	0.416	0.443	0.519	0.429	0.613	0.539
Traffic	0.448	**0.281**	**0.422**	0.283	0.481	0.304	0.625	0.383	0.620	0.336	0.610	0.376	0.628	0.379
Weather	**0.252**	**0.277**	0.260	0.280	0.259	0.281	0.265	0.317	0.259	0.287	0.309	0.360	0.338	0.382
Solar-Energy	**0.231**	**0.257**	0.236	0.262	0.270	0.307	0.330	0.401	0.301	0.319	0.291	0.381	0.885	0.711
1st Count	6	7	1	0	2	2	0	0	0	0	0	0	0	0

Table 3 shows the results of G-GLformer in short-term forecasting. The results show that G-GLformer achieves the best performance in all aspects of short-term prediction. Specifically, G-GLformer has an average decrease of 34.21% and 15.96% in MSE and MAE over the previous SOTA iTransformer [9] in short-term forecasting.

4.4   Ablation Study

We conducted ablation experiments to prove the effectiveness of Bidirectional-Patch-GRU-Embedding and Global-Local-Attention module. We considered 3 ablation methods and evaluated them on 4 datasets. The following will explain the variants of its implementation:

– **w/o-BPGE:** We removed the Bidirectional-Patch-GRU-Embedding module and used a linear layer as the embedding layer.

Table 3. Full results for the short-term forecasting task. The input sequence length is set to 96 for all baselines. Avg means the average results from all four prediction lengths. The best results are in **bold**.

Models		G-GLformer (Ours)		iTransformer (2024)		PatchTST (2023)		DLinear (2023)		TimesNet (2023)		FEDformer (2022)		Autoformer (2021)	
Metric		MSE	MAE	MSE	MAE	MSE	MAE	MSE	MAE	MSE	MAE	MSE	MAE	MSE	MAE
PEMS03	12	**0.065**	**0.171**	0.069	0.174	0.099	0.216	0.122	0.243	0.085	0.192	0.126	0.251	0.272	0.385
	24	**0.089**	**0.201**	0.098	0.209	0.142	0.259	0.201	0.317	0.118	0.223	0.149	0.275	0.334	0.440
	48	**0.131**	**0.244**	0.164	0.276	0.211	0.319	0.333	0.425	0.155	0.260	0.227	0.348	1.032	0.782
	96	**0.214**	**0.315**	0.240	0.338	0.269	0.370	0.457	0.515	0.228	0.317	0.348	0.434	1.031	0.796
	Avg	**0.125**	**0.233**	0.143	0.249	0.180	0.291	0.278	0.375	0.147	0.248	0.213	0.327	0.667	0.601
PEMS04	12	**0.077**	**0.184**	0.081	0.188	0.105	0.224	0.148	0.272	0.087	0.195	0.138	0.262	0.424	0.491
	24	**0.091**	**0.204**	0.100	0.212	0.153	0.275	0.224	0.340	0.103	0.215	0.177	0.293	0.459	0.509
	48	**0.111**	**0.228**	0.131	0.245	0.229	0.339	0.355	0.437	0.136	0.250	0.270	0.368	0.646	0.610
	96	**0.133**	**0.249**	0.165	0.277	0.291	0.389	0.452	0.504	0.190	0.303	0.341	0.427	0.912	0.748
	Avg	**0.103**	**0.216**	0.119	0.231	0.195	0.307	0.295	0.388	0.129	0.241	0.231	0.337	0.610	0.590
PEMS07	12	**0.066**	**0.163**	0.066	0.164	0.095	0.207	0.115	0.242	0.082	0.181	0.109	0.225	0.199	0.336
	24	**0.076**	**0.175**	0.087	0.190	0.150	0.262	0.210	0.329	0.101	0.204	0.125	0.244	0.323	0.420
	48	**0.083**	**0.181**	0.113	0.218	0.253	0.340	0.398	0.458	0.134	0.238	0.165	0.288	0.390	0.470
	96	**0.102**	**0.202**	0.140	0.246	0.346	0.404	0.594	0.553	0.181	0.279	0.262	0.376	0.554	0.578
	Avg	**0.082**	**0.180**	0.102	0.205	0.211	0.303	0.329	0.395	0.124	0.225	0.165	0.283	0.367	0.451
PEMS08	12	**0.082**	**0.185**	0.088	0.193	0.168	0.232	0.154	0.276	0.112	0.212	0.173	0.273	0.436	0.485
	24	**0.117**	**0.221**	0.138	0.243	0.224	0.281	0.248	0.353	0.141	0.238	0.140	0.236	0.467	0.502
	48	**0.183**	**0.235**	0.339	0.354	0.321	0.354	0.440	0.470	0.198	0.283	0.320	0.394	0.966	0.733
	96	**0.200**	**0.244**	0.418	0.416	0.408	0.417	0.674	0.565	0.320	0.351	0.442	0.465	1.385	0.915
	Avg	**0.146**	**0.221**	0.246	0.302	0.280	0.321	0.379	0.416	0.193	0.271	0.286	0.358	0.814	0.659
1st Count		**20**	**20**	0	0	0	0	0	0	0	0	0	0	0	0

- **w/o-GLA:** We replaced the Global-Local-Attention mechanism with the traditional self-attention mechanism.
- **w/o-BPGE&GLA:** We replaced the Bidirectional-Patch-GRU-Embedding with a linear layer and replaced the Global-Local-Attention with the traditional attention mechanism.

As can be seen from Table 4, G-GLformer achieves the best results. When the Bidirectional-Patch-GRU-Embedding module is absent, the model fails to capture the temporal relationships adequately, resulting in a decline in its performance. When the model lacks the Global-Local-Attention module, it leads to the model's lack of a global correlation perspective. As a result, the extraction of correlations is vulnerable to local noise, thus causing a decline in prediction performance. When both modules are absent, the prediction performance achieved by the model is the worst.

Table 4. Ablation analysis of ETTh2, ETTm2, Weather and Solar-Energy datasets. Results represent the average error of prediction length $\{96, 192, 336, 720\}$, with the best performance highlighted in bold black.

Datasets Metric	ETTh2 MSE	MAE	ETTm2 MSE	MAE	Weather MSE	MAE	Solar-Energy MSE	MAE
G-GLformer	**0.377**	**0.402**	**0.283**	**0.328**	**0.252**	**0.277**	**0.231**	**0.257**
w/o-BPGE	0.381	0.405	0.290	0.334	0.254	0.278	0.234	0.261
w/o-GLA	0.381	0.404	0.287	0.330	0.257	0.279	0.234	0.260
w/o-BPGE&GLA	0.383	0.407	0.291	0.335	0.260	0.281	0.238	0.263

4.5 Modules Generality

To verify the generality of the modules, we use the Bidirectional-Patch-GRU-Embedding module and the Global-Local-Attention module as plugins to enhance other models.

Global-Local-Attention. To prove the generality of the Global-Local-Attention module on other models, we applied this module to iTransformer [9] and used three different correlation coefficients. As shown in Fig. 3, we conducted tests on four datasets, namely PEMS03, PEMS04, PEMS07, and PEMS08, and then used the Pearson correlation coefficient, the Spearman correlation coefficient, and the Kendall correlation coefficient respectively. As can be found from Fig. 3, the error of iTransformer with the Global-Local-Attention module is lower than those of the original iTransformer on all the four datasets. There are no significant differences among the three correlation coefficients on PEMS03, PEMS04, and PEMS07. However, there are relatively large fluctuations on PEMS08. The reason for this situation is that the calculation methods of the three correlation coefficients are different and the situations to which they are applicable are also different. We will discuss this issue in the "Discussion" section.

Table 5. Results represent the average error of prediction length $\{96, 192, 336, 720\}$, with the best performance highlighted in bold black.

Models	iInformer		+BPGE		iReformer		+BPGE		iFlashformer		+BPGE		Impr.
Metric	MSE	MAE	MSE	MAE	MSE	MAE	MSE	MAE	MSE	MAE	MSE	MAE	
ETTh1	0.487	0.465	**0.441**	**0.435**	0.472	0.457	**0.440**	**0.436**	0.454	0.448	**0.441**	**0.438**	5.39%
ETTh2	0.390	0.410	**0.379**	**0.405**	0.384	0.409	**0.381**	**0.406**	0.389	0.410	**0.379**	**0.403**	1.75%
ETTm1	0.402	0.406	**0.389**	**0.399**	0.405	0.409	**0.394**	**0.401**	0.411	0.414	**0.406**	**0.408**	1.96%
ETTm2	0.288	0.332	**0.281**	**0.327**	0.288	0.332	**0.283**	**0.328**	0.292	0.335	**0.287**	**0.330**	1.61%
Impr.	4.02%				3.14%				1.78%				2.78%

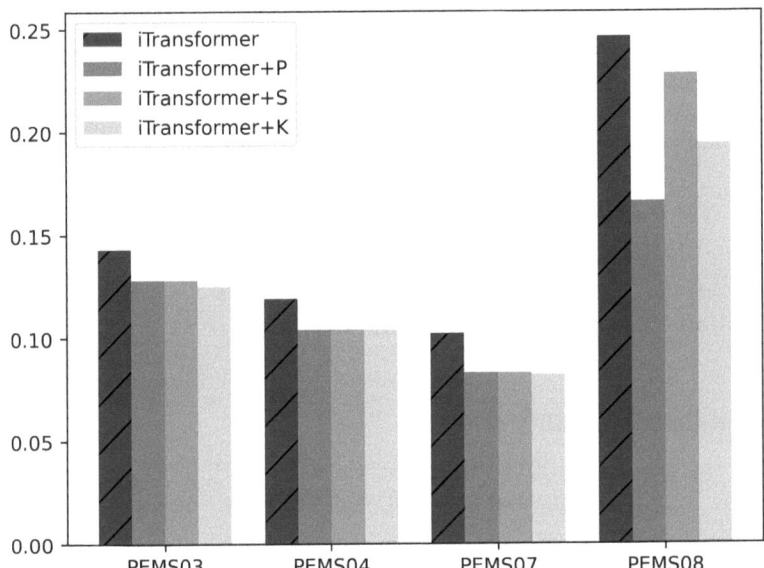

Fig. 3. The results shown in the above figure represent the average error of prediction length $\{96, 192, 336, 720\}$. P, S, and K represent the Pearson correlation coefficient, the Spearman correlation coefficient, and the Kendall correlation coefficient respectively.

Bidirectional-Patch-GRU-Embedding. To verify the generality of the BPGE module, we applied this module to iInformer [9], iReformer [9], and iFlashformer [9]. As can be found from Table 5, the BPGE module enhances the respective backbones by an average of 2.78%. Among them, the BPGE module has the most obvious effect on the ETTh1 dataset, with the error being reduced by an average of 5.39%. This fully demonstrates the effectiveness of the BPGE module.

4.6   Instance Visualization

As can be seen from Fig. 4, in the ETTh1 dataset, there is a highly positive correlation between the "MUFL" variable and the "HUFL" variable, and the Pearson correlation coefficient between them is as high as 0.99. When there are no outliers, the time-series diagrams of the "MUFL" variable and the "HUFL" variable are highly consistent.

When outliers appear in the look-back window, as shown in Fig. 5, the "HUFL" variable and the "MUFL" variable show a clear divergence in the time-series diagram. The iTransformer [9] model will be affected by local outliers when extracting correlations, because this model extracts correlations within a limited look-back window. As shown in Fig. 5, when the iTransformer model uses the self-attention mechanism to extract correlations, the presence of outliers causes it to assign lower weights to two highly correlated time series. Since G-GLformer

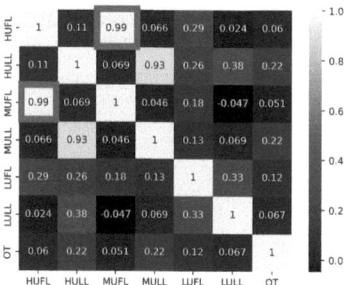
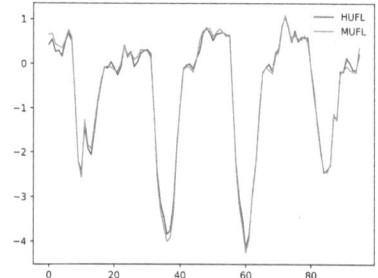

Fig. 4. The left figure shows the overall Pearson correlation coefficient on the ETTh1 training set and the right figure shows a normal look-back window without outliers.

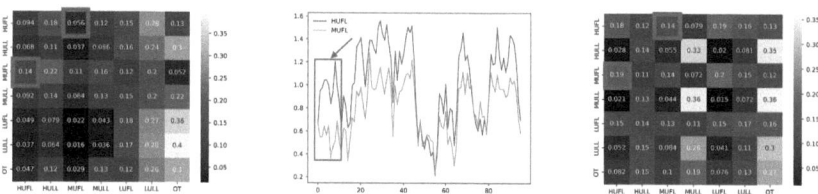

Fig. 5. The figure in the middle is a time-series diagram of a look-back window with outliers. The figure on the left is the score map of iTransformer on this look-back window, and the figure on the right is the score map of G-GLformer on this look-back window.

embeds global correlations, it is more robust to the situation of local outliers. It assigns higher weights to the two variables on the score map. This fully demonstrates that G-GLformer is more robust to local outliers.

5 Discussion

In this section, we will discuss a special case. When there are a large number of outliers in the data, the calculation of the global correlation coefficient will be affected by these outliers, which may lead to the obtained global correlation deviating from the true global correlation. We calculated the average number of outlier points for each channel in seven datasets respectively. As can be seen from Table 6, the average number of outliers per channel in the Traffic dataset is 279.29. The number of outliers in the Traffic dataset is much larger than that in other datasets. A large number of outliers in the Traffic dataset affect the calculation of global correlations, thus influencing the prediction performance of G-GLformer. This is the reason why the prediction performance of G-GLformer on the Traffic dataset in Table 2 is significantly worse than that of iTransformer [9]. Compared with the Pearson correlation coefficient, we can use the Spearman correlation coefficient, which is more robust to outliers.

As shown in Fig. 6, we replaced the Pearson correlation coefficient with the Spearman correlation coefficient on the Traffic dataset, and MSE decreased for

Table 6. Average number of extreme points per channel (Z-Score > 3).

Datasets	ECL	Solar-Energy	Traffic	PEMS03	PEMS04	PEMS07	PEMS08
Extreme Points	109.29	3.48	**279.29**	18.37	6.07	16.98	17.26

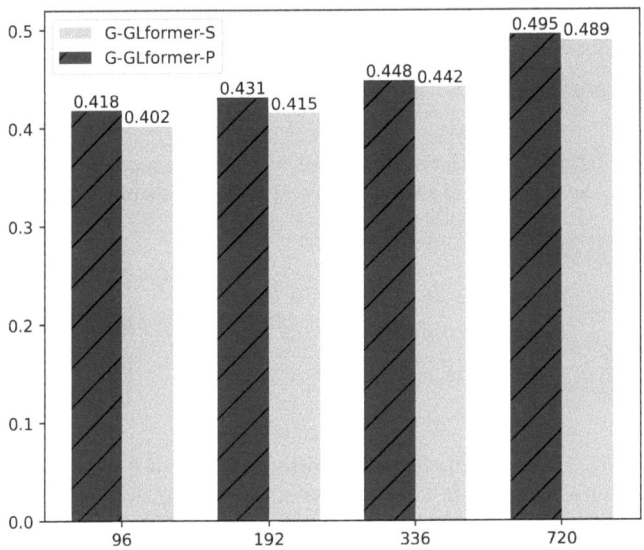

Fig. 6. The results shown in the above figure represent the Mean Squared Error of prediction length {96, 192, 336, 720} in Traffic dataset. G-GLformer-S and G-GLformer-P represent G-GLformer using the Spearman correlation coefficient and the Pearson correlation coefficient respectively.

all four prediction lengths. Therefore, in general, G-GLformer is not suitable for datasets with a large number of outliers. When there are a large number of outliers, we can use the Spearman correlation coefficient to alleviate this problem.

6   Conclusion

This paper proposes G-GLformer, a novel Transformer-based architecture that concentrates on tackling the issue of insufficient capture of time lag relationships and the impact of outliers on the extraction of local correlations. Specifically, we introduce the Bidirectional-Patch-GRU-Embedding module to enhance the ability to extract time lag relationships. Besides, we propose the Global-Local-Attention module to enhance the robustness of the model in extracting variable correlations. These innovations jointly boost the ability of G-GLformer to utilize multivariate correlations. Experiments on various datasets have demonstrated its effectiveness and accuracy. In the future, we will explore the performance of G-GLformer on large-scale real-world datasets.

Acknowledgement. This work was supported by the Degree Program Development Initiative of Shanghai University of International Business and Economics, Shanghai Action Plan for Science, Technology and Innovation (No. 24BC3200404), National Natural Science Foundation of China (12361056), and Guizhou University of Finance and Economics Introduced Talents for Scientific Research (2022YJ029).

Ethical Statement. The work of our paper focuses on more accurate time series prediction, so there are no ethical issues involved.

References

1. Chen, Y., Segovia-Dominguez, I., Coskunuzer, B., Gel, Y.: Tamp-s2gcnets: coupling time-aware multipersistence knowledge representation with spatio-supra graph convolutional networks for time-series forecasting. In: International Conference on Learning Representations (2022)
2. Chung, J., Gulcehre, C., Cho, K., Bengio, Y.: Empirical evaluation of gated recurrent neural networks on sequence modeling. arXiv preprint arXiv:1412.3555 (2014)
3. Han, W., Zhu, T., Chen, L., Ning, H., Luo, Y., Wan, Y.: Mcformer: multivariate time series forecasting with mixed-channels transformer. IEEE Internet Things J. (2024)
4. Hu, Y., et al.: Timefilter: patch-specific spatial-temporal graph filtration for time series forecasting. arXiv preprint arXiv:2501.13041 (2025)
5. Lai, G., Chang, W.C., Yang, Y., Liu, H.: Modeling long-and short-term temporal patterns with deep neural networks. In: The 41st International ACM SIGIR Conference on Research & Development in Information Retrieval, pp. 95–104 (2018)
6. Lin, S., Lin, W., Wu, W., Chen, H., Yang, J.: Sparsetsf: modeling long-term time series forecasting with 1k parameters. In: Proceedings of the 41st International Conference on Machine Learning, pp. 30211–30226 (2024)
7. Liu, M., et al.: Scinet: time series modeling and forecasting with sample convolution and interaction. Adv. Neural. Inf. Process. Syst. **35**, 5816–5828 (2022)
8. Liu, S., et al.: Pyraformer: low-complexity pyramidal attention for long-range time series modeling and forecasting. In: International Conference on Learning Representations (2022)
9. Liu, Y., et al.: itransformer: inverted transformers are effective for time series forecasting. In: The Twelfth International Conference on Learning Representations (2023)
10. Liu, Y., Zhang, H., Li, C., Huang, X., Wang, J., Long, M.: Timer: generative pre-trained transformers are large time series models. In: Proceedings of the 41st International Conference on Machine Learning, pp. 32369–32399 (2024)
11. Nie, Y., Nguyen, N.H., Sinthong, P., Kalagnanam, J.: A time series is worth 64 words: long-term forecasting with transformers. In: The Eleventh International Conference on Learning Representations (2022)
12. Pascanu, R., Mikolov, T., Bengio, Y.: On the difficulty of training recurrent neural networks. In: Proceedings of the 30th International Conference on International Conference on Machine Learning, vol. 28, pp. III–1310 (2013)
13. Qiu, X., Wu, X., Lin, Y., Guo, C., Hu, J., Yang, B.: Duet: dual clustering enhanced multivariate time series forecasting. arXiv preprint arXiv:2412.10859 (2024)
14. Wang, S., et al.: Timemixer++: a general time series pattern machine for universal predictive analysis. arXiv preprint arXiv:2410.16032 (2024)

15. Wang, Y., et al.: Timexer: empowering transformers for time series forecasting with exogenous variables. In: The Thirty-eighth Annual Conference on Neural Information Processing Systems (2024)
16. Wen, M., Li, P., Zhang, L., Chen, Y.: Stock market trend prediction using high-order information of time series. IEEE Access 7, 28299–28308 (2019)
17. Wu, H., Hu, T., Liu, Y., Zhou, H., Wang, J., Long, M.: Timesnet: temporal 2d-variation modeling for general time series analysis. In: The Eleventh International Conference on Learning Representations (2022)
18. Wu, H., Xu, J., Wang, J., Long, M.: Autoformer: decomposition transformers with auto-correlation for long-term series forecasting. Adv. Neural. Inf. Process. Syst. **34**, 22419–22430 (2021)
19. Wu, H., Zhou, H., Long, M., Wang, J.: Interpretable weather forecasting for world-wide stations with a unified deep model. Nat. Mach. Intell. **5**(6), 602–611 (2023)
20. Wu, Z., Pan, S., Long, G., Jiang, J., Chang, X., Zhang, C.: Connecting the dots: multivariate time series forecasting with graph neural networks. In: Proceedings of the 26th ACM SIGKDD International Conference on Knowledge Discovery & Data Mining, pp. 753–763 (2020)
21. Xu, Z., Zeng, A., Xu, Q.: Fits: modeling time series with $10k$ parameters. In: The Twelfth International Conference on Learning Representations (2023)
22. Yu, G., Zou, J., Hu, X., Aviles-Rivero, A.I., Qin, J., Wang, S.: Revitalizing multi-variate time series forecasting: learnable decomposition with inter-series dependencies and intra-series variations modeling. In: International Conference on Machine Learning, pp. 57818–57841. PMLR (2024)
23. Zeng, A., Chen, M., Zhang, L., Xu, Q.: Are transformers effective for time series forecasting? In: Proceedings of the AAAI Conference on Artificial Intelligence, vol. 37, pp. 11121–11128 (2023)
24. Zhang, Y., Yan, J.: Crossformer: transformer utilizing cross-dimension dependency for multivariate time series forecasting. In: The Eleventh International Conference on Learning Representations (2023)
25. Zhou, H., et al.: Informer: beyond efficient transformer for long sequence time-series forecasting. In: Proceedings of the AAAI Conference on Artificial Intelligence, vol. 35, pp. 11106–11115 (2021)
26. Zhou, T., Ma, Z., Wen, Q., Wang, X., Sun, L., Jin, R.: Fedformer: frequency enhanced decomposed transformer for long-term series forecasting. In: International Conference on Machine Learning, pp. 27268–27286. PMLR (2022)

Cross-Domain Conditional Diffusion Models for Time Series Imputation

Kexin Zhang[1], Baoyu Jing[2], K. Selçuk Candan[3], Dawei Zhou[4],
Qingsong Wen[5], Han Liu[1], and Kaize Ding[1(✉)]

[1] Northwestern University, Evanston, IL 60208, USA
{hanliu,kaize.ding}@northwestern.edu
[2] University of Illinois Urbana-Champaign, Champaign, IL 61820-5711, USA
baoyuj2@illinois.edu
[3] Arizona State University, Tempe, AZ 85281, USA
candan@asu.edu
[4] Virginia Tech, Blacksburg, VA 24061-0131, USA
zhoud@vt.edu
[5] Squirrel Ai Learning, Bellevue, WA 98004, USA

Abstract. Cross-domain time series imputation is an underexplored data-centric research task that presents significant challenges, particularly when the target domain suffers from high missing rates and domain shifts in temporal dynamics. Existing time series imputation approaches primarily focus on the single-domain setting, which cannot effectively adapt to a new domain with domain shifts.Meanwhile, conventional domain adaptation techniques struggle with data incompleteness, as they typically assume the data from both source and target domains are fully observed to enable adaptation. For the problem of cross-domain time series imputation, missing values introduce high uncertainty that hinders distribution alignment, making existing adaptation strategies ineffective. Specifically, our proposed solution tackles this problem from three perspectives: **(i) Data:** We introduce a frequency-based time series interpolation strategy that integrates shared spectral components from both domains while retaining domain-specific temporal structures, constructing informative priors for imputation. **(ii) Model:** We design a diffusion-based imputation model that effectively learns domain-shared representations and captures domain-specific temporal dependencies with dedicated denoising networks. **(iii) Algorithm:** We further propose a cross-domain consistency alignment strategy that selectively regularizes output-level domain discrepancies, enabling effective knowledge transfer while preserving domain-specific characteristics. Extensive experiments on three real-world datasets demonstrate the superiority of our proposed approach. Our code implementation is available here (https://github.com/kexin-kxzhang/CD2-TSI).

Keywords: Time Series Imputation · Domain Adaptation · Conditional Diffusion Models

K. Zhang—Research intern during the completion of this work.

© The Author(s), under exclusive license to Springer Nature Switzerland AG 2026
B. Pfahringer et al. (Eds.): ECML PKDD 2025, LNAI 16020, pp. 57–74, 2026.
https://doi.org/10.1007/978-3-662-72243-5_4

1   Introduction

Multivariate time series imputation is essential for various real-world applications, including environmental monitoring and energy management [44]. Missing values commonly arise due to sensor failures, transmission errors, or external disruptions, leading to incomplete data that could degrade the reliability of downstream tasks [18]. Effective imputation is thus critical for preserving the integrity of the data and ensuring reliable results in subsequent applications [16].

Many endeavors have been made to model the temporal patterns inherent in time series. Traditional statistical and machine learning methods for time series imputation often assume stationarity or linear relationships, which may not capture the full complexity of real-world time series data. Recurrent neural networks and attention-based models have improved the modeling of temporal dependencies by capturing nonlinear relationships [2]. More recently, deep generative models [10,38], such as variational autoencoders and generative adversarial networks, have been explored for time series imputation. Diffusion-based models [1,19,31,45] further advance imputation by learning a denoising process that iteratively refines missing values.

Despite their success, these methods struggle under high missing rates [31], as sparse observations hinder the effective modeling of the underlying temporal dependencies [7,11,45]. When observations are highly incomplete, it is natural to leverage related domains to improve imputation performance [5]. For instance, in air quality monitoring, neighboring cities' sensor networks may provide complementary temporal patterns when local sensors fail. Recent advancements in domain adaptation (DA) have shown promising results in transferring knowledge across domains in tasks such as time series forecasting and classification [14,27]. In light of this, we propose to tackle the novel cross-domain time series imputation by adapting domain discrepancies between two related domains.

However, cross-domain time series imputation remains largely underexplored and directly applying DA techniques to time series imputation may easily fail due to the following challenges: (1) *Data Challenge:* Most of the DA problems usually assume the observed data from both source and target domains are complete [41], however, in time series imputation, it is hard for existing models to well characterize the real data distributions due to the high missingness in the observed data. (2) *Model Challenge*: Existing approaches commonly rely on simply training a single shared model on mixed data, which cannot distinguish domain-shared and specific knowledge [42]. Therefore, it is necessary to develop a model that can both facilitate knowledge transfer and capture domain-specific patterns. (3) *Algorithm Challenge*: Time series data from different domains often exhibit domain-specific temporal dependencies, leading to variations in seasonality, trend shifts, or periodic patterns [40], etc. Existing domain adaptation algorithms often enforce alignment without considering such differences across domains, thus failing to capture the cross-domain knowledge required for accurate imputation in the target domain.

To address these challenges, we propose a novel **Cross-Domain Conditional Diffusion Model for Time Series Imputation (CD²-TSI)**, which improves imputation in the target domain by leveraging knowledge from a source domain while preserving domain-specific temporal patterns. Specifically, to counter the data challenge, we introduce a frequency-based time series interpolation strategy, which interpolates original missing values by integrating shared spectral components from both the source and target domains. The pre-interpolated values are used to construct the missing targets, providing more informative priors for training the imputation model. For the model challenge, we develop a diffusion-based imputation framework that learns domain-shared representations to capture common patterns across domains while maintaining dedicated denoising networks to model domain-specific temporal dependencies. To tackle the algorithm challenge, we propose a cross-domain consistency alignment algorithm that imposes alignment based on output-level discrepancy. The degree of alignment is adjusted according to the prediction difference between source and target networks for the same target samples. This approach facilitates cross-domain transfer while preserving target-specific temporal characteristics, preventing the model from overfitting to source domain patterns.

In summary, the main contributions of this work are summarized as follows: (1) We target the problem of cross-domain time series imputation, which is largely underexplored and requires research attention in the community. (2) We propose CD^2-TSI, a new diffusion model-based framework that solves the problem of cross-domain time series imputation from data, model, and algorithm perspectives. (3) We conduct extensive experiments on three real-world datasets, demonstrating that CD^2-TSI outperforms state-of-the-art models across various missing data patterns, highlighting its effectiveness in cross-domain settings.

2   Related Work

2.1   Time Series Imputation

Time series imputation (TSI) methods can be broadly categorized into predictive and generative approaches [7]: (1) Predictive methods [6,22,34] predict deterministic values but suffer from error accumulation and fail to capture the uncertainty of missing values. GRU-D [3] and BRITS [2] use deep autoregressive models with time decay, while GRIN [4] incorporates graph neural networks (GNN) for spatial relationships. (2) Generative methods, such as those based on Variational Autoencoders (VAE), Generative Adversarial Networks (GAN), and diffusion models, effectively circumvent the limitations faced by those predictive models. VAE-based methods [15,24] optimize reconstruction error and regularize the latent space. GAN-based approaches [23] use adversarial training between the generator and discriminator but can be unstable and produce unrealistic results. Diffusion models show promise due to their ability to model complex data distributions and generate varied outputs for missing values. CSDI [31] and SSD [1] use observed data as conditional information; PriSTI [19] extracts conditional information and considers spatiotemporal dependencies using geographic data; MTSCI [45] incorporates a complementary mask strategy and a mixup mechanism to realize intra-consistency and inter-consistency. However, these methods focus primarily on modeling temporal dependencies within a single domain, overlooking the complexities posed by cross-domain scenarios where domain shifts in missing patterns or temporal dynamics exist. Our CD^2-TSI framework addresses this gap by combining diffusion models with domain adaptation to enhance imputation quality across domains.

2.2   Time Series Domain Adaptation

Domain Adaptation (DA) [9] seeks to transfer knowledge to a target domain by leveraging information from source domains. These methods can be categorized into three groups: (1) Adversarial-based methods train a domain discriminator to identify domains while learning transferable features. For example, CoDATS [33] employs a gradient reversal layer for adversarial training with weak supervision on multi-source data. SLARDA [26] aligns temporal dynamics across domains via autoregressive adversarial training. (2) Discrepancy-based methods use statistical distances to align features from source and target domains. AdvSKM [20] leverages maximum mean discrepancy (MMD) with a hybrid spectral kernel for temporal domain adaptation. RAINCOAT [12] tackles feature and label shifts via temporal and frequency feature alignment. (3) Self-supervision methods incorporate auxiliary tasks. DAF [14] uses a shared attention module for domain-invariant and specific features and reconstruction. While existing DA methods have proven effective in forecasting and classification tasks, their application to imputation remains underexplored, where temporal discrepancies as well as data deficiency introduced by missing values pose additional challenges. CD^2-TSI differs from these approaches by addressing the challenges introduced by incomplete observations in cross-domain time series imputation and adaptation.

3   Problem Definition

Cross-domain time series imputation aims to reconstruct missing values in a target domain by leveraging knowledge from a related source domain. Given multivariate time series data with potential missing values, we define the time series in both domains as $\mathbf{X}_d = (\mathbf{X}_{d,1}, \ldots, \mathbf{X}_{d,K}) \in \mathbb{R}^{K \times L}$, where K is the number of features, L is the length of the time series, and $d \in \{Src, Tgt\}$ denotes the source and target domains. We assume all time series in both domains have the same length. An observation mask $\mathbf{M}_d \in \{0,1\}^{K \times L}$ indicates missing values, where $m_{k,l} = 1$ if the value is observed for the k-th feature at the l-th timestamp, and $m_{k,l} = 0$ if the value is missing. Since real-world datasets often lack ground truth for missing data, we artificially mask a subset of observed values for training and evaluation. Following previous work [31,45], the extended missing targets $\widetilde{\mathbf{X}}_d \in \mathbb{R}^{K \times L}$ include both the original missing values and artificially masked values, with a binary mask $\widetilde{\mathbf{M}}_d \in \{0,1\}^{K \times L}$.

4   Methodology

4.1   Model Overview (CD²-TSI)

As shown in Fig. 1, CD²-TSI incorporates a cross-domain diffusion-based framework, where source and target domains share representations while maintaining domain-specific denoising networks. A pre-interpolation strategy is proposed to integrate spectral components from both domains, providing priors for original missing values via cross-domain frequency mixup, while the artificial missing values are retained to construct missing targets. These targets are then corrupted by adding noise to obtain noisy inputs for training the denoising network. To ensure effective adaptation, we introduce cross-domain consistency alignment. This algorithm promotes adaptation based on output discrepancy while preventing excessive regularization that could force the target domain to overly conform to source domain patterns. Overall, CD²-TSI effectively leverages cross-domain information to improve the imputation quality in the target domain.

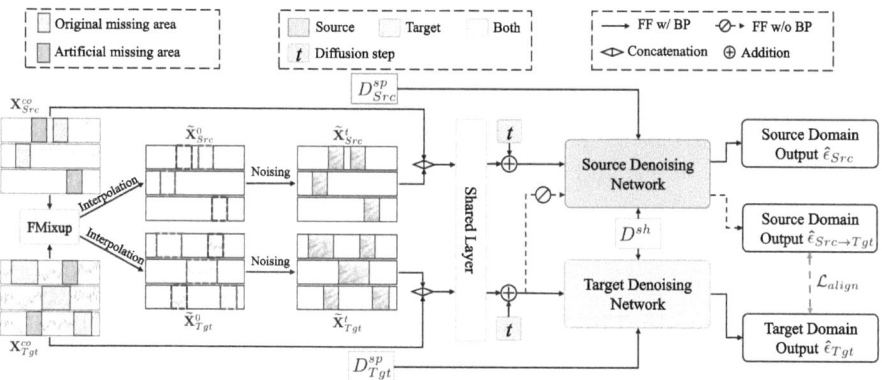

Fig. 1. Architecture of CD²-TSI. FMixup is utilized to interpolate the original missing areas (blue), while artificial missing values (red) are retained to construct the missing targets $\widetilde{\mathbf{X}}^0$. These targets are then transformed into the noisy targets $\widetilde{\mathbf{X}}^t$ to train the denoising network, with the help of conditional information $\mathbf{X}^{co}$. The framework is optimized using a combination of denoising loss and consistency alignment loss. (Color figure online)

4.2   Conditional Diffusion Model for Time Series Imputation

Imputing missing values in time series data requires capturing complex temporal dependencies while addressing challenges from data incompleteness. Our framework takes Denoising Diffusion Probabilistic Models (DDPM) [13] as the base model, where the imputation process is formulated as a conditional generative task. In the forward process, Gaussian noise is step by step added to the missing targets $\widetilde{\mathbf{X}}^0$ across T diffusion steps, gradually transforming $\widetilde{\mathbf{X}}^0$ into a noisy version $\widetilde{\mathbf{X}}^T$. This process is formalized as follows:

$$q\left(\widetilde{\mathbf{X}}^{1:T} \mid \widetilde{\mathbf{X}}^0\right) = \prod_{t=1}^{T} q\left(\widetilde{\mathbf{X}}^t \mid \widetilde{\mathbf{X}}^{t-1}\right), q\left(\widetilde{\mathbf{X}}^t \mid \widetilde{\mathbf{X}}^{t-1}\right) = \mathcal{N}\left(\widetilde{\mathbf{X}}^t; \sqrt{1-\beta_t}\widetilde{\mathbf{X}}^{t-1}, \beta_t \mathbf{I}\right) \tag{1}$$

where β_t represents the noise level, and t indicates the diffusion step. According to DDPM, $\widetilde{\mathbf{X}}^t = \sqrt{\bar{\alpha}_t}\widetilde{\mathbf{X}}^0 + \sqrt{1-\bar{\alpha}_t}\epsilon$, where $\alpha_t = 1 - \beta_t, \bar{\alpha}_t = \prod_{i=1}^t \alpha_i$, and $\epsilon \sim \mathcal{N}(\mathbf{0}, \mathbf{I})$ where $\mathcal{N}$ is Gaussian distribution. When T is large enough, $q\left(\widetilde{\mathbf{X}}^T \mid \widetilde{\mathbf{X}}^0\right)$ approximates a standard normal distribution.

The reverse process then reconstructs the missing targets by iteratively denoising imputed values, conditioned on the remaining observations $\mathbf{X}^{co}$:

$$p_\theta\left(\widetilde{\mathbf{X}}^{t-1} \mid \widetilde{\mathbf{X}}^t, \mathbf{X}^{co}\right) = \mathcal{N}\left(\mu_\theta\left(\widetilde{\mathbf{X}}^t, \mathbf{X}^{co}, t\right), \sigma_t^2 \mathbf{I}\right), \tag{2}$$

$$\mu_\theta\left(\widetilde{\mathbf{X}}^t, \mathbf{X}^{co}, t\right) = \frac{1}{\sqrt{\bar{\alpha}_t}}\left(\widetilde{\mathbf{X}}^t - \frac{\beta_t}{\sqrt{1-\bar{\alpha}_t}}\epsilon_\theta\left(\widetilde{\mathbf{X}}^t, \mathbf{X}^{co}, t\right)\right), \sigma_t^2 = \frac{1-\bar{\alpha}_{t-1}}{1-\bar{\alpha}_t}\beta_t \tag{3}$$

where $\epsilon_\theta(\cdot)$ is the denoising network with learnable parameters θ. The model is trained to estimate the added noise ϵ given $\widetilde{\mathbf{X}}^t$, conditional observations $\mathbf{X}^{co}$ and current diffusion step t, and the training objective of time series imputation is:

$$\mathcal{L}(\theta) = \mathbb{E}_{\widetilde{\mathbf{X}}^0 \sim q(\widetilde{\mathbf{X}}^0), \epsilon \sim \mathcal{N}(0,I)} \left\| \epsilon - \epsilon_\theta\left(\widetilde{\mathbf{X}}^t, \mathbf{X}^{co}, t\right) \right\|^2 \tag{4}$$

4.3   Cross-Domain Time Series Frequency Interpolation

Modeling temporal dependencies from incomplete time series is challenging, especially under high missing rates. Severe missingness disrupts the real data distribution, making it difficult for the model to capture consistent temporal dependencies. Addressing this issue is crucial, as many existing methods [1,31] simply replace original missing values with *zeros* when constructing the missing targets. However, *zeros* cannot reflect the real data distribution, and such a distribution shift makes it more challenging for the diffusion model to accurately recover missing values during the denoising process. Although linear interpolation in the time domain can partially address this issue, it often fails to capture complex non-linear temporal dynamics.

To solve this problem, our intuition is that time series data from related domains typically share low-frequency components, which represent long-term trends or periodic patterns (e.g., daily cycles in hydrology data), while high-frequency components reflect domain-specific details, such as sensor noise or transient fluctuations [35,36,43]. Formally, a signal can be decomposed into an amplitude spectrum, which captures the intensity of different frequency components, and a phase spectrum, which preserves local temporal structure. Hence, we propose a frequency-based time series interpolation strategy – FMixup. FMixup is achieved through two key steps: (1) blending *low-frequency amplitude* spectra across domains and (2) retaining each domain's *high-frequency amplitude* and *phase* spectra. The augmented data can then be used to replace original missing values and refine the missing targets.

Domain-Shared Frequency Mixup. To exchange structural information across domains, we transform the conditional observations $\mathbf{X}^{co} \in \mathbb{R}^{K \times L}$ from both domains into the frequency domain using the Fast Fourier Transform (FFT) [25]:

$$\mathcal{F}(x)(u, v) = \sum_{k=0}^{K-1} \sum_{l=0}^{L-1} x(k, l) e^{-j2\pi\left(\frac{k}{K}u + \frac{l}{L}v\right)} \tag{5}$$

where u and v are frequency indices along the two dimensions, and j is the imaginary unit. This frequency space signal $\mathcal{F}(x)$ can be further decomposed into an amplitude spectrum $\mathcal{A} \in \mathbb{R}^{K \times L}$ and a phase spectrum $\mathcal{P} \in \mathbb{R}^{K \times L}$. To integrate common patterns, we introduce a binary mask $\mathcal{M} = \mathbb{1}_{(k,l) \in [-\alpha K : \alpha K, -\alpha L : \alpha L]}$ that selects low-frequency region of the amplitude spectrum, where $\alpha \in (0, 1)$ determines the proportion of low-frequency information incorporated. The amplitude spectra of the source and target domains are then blended as follows:

$$\mathcal{A}_{Src \to Tgt} = \mathcal{A}_{Tgt} * (1 - \mathcal{M}) + (\lambda \mathcal{A}_{Tgt} + (1 - \lambda)\mathcal{A}_{Src}) * \mathcal{M} \tag{6}$$

where $\mathcal{A}_{Src}$ and $\mathcal{A}_{Tgt}$ represent the amplitude spectra of the source and target domains, respectively. $\mathcal{A}_{Src \to Tgt}$ is the newly mixed amplitude spectrum, and parameter λ adjusts the balance between the two spectra.

Domain-Specific Frequency Preserving. As mentioned above, high-frequency components often contain domain-specific fine-grained details. To preserve such information, we retain the high-frequency amplitude components of the target domain. Additionally, we do not modify the phase spectrum $\mathcal{P}_{Tgt}$, as it represents local structural information necessary for preserving the original sequence characteristics. The final augmented time series is obtained by combining the mixed amplitude spectrum $\mathcal{A}_{Src \to Tgt}$ with original phase spectrum $\mathcal{P}_{Tgt}$ of the target domain and applying the inverse Fourier transform:

$$X_{Src \to Tgt} = \mathcal{F}^{-1}(\mathcal{A}_{Src \to Tgt}, \mathcal{P}_{Tgt}) \tag{7}$$

This augmented series is used to fill in the original missing values in the target domain. Therefore, we obtain the refined missing targets $\widetilde{\mathbf{X}}^0_{Tgt}$. This frequency-based time series interpolation strategy ensures that the local temporal structure remains aligned with the target domain while benefiting from shared low-frequency trends. Similarly, we obtain the missing targets $\widetilde{\mathbf{X}}^0_{Src}$.

4.4 Cross-Domain Conditional Diffusion Model

Although cross-domain time series frequency mixup provides priors from the data perspective, it does not fully address domain shifts in temporal dynamics.

Learning a single shared model for both source and target domains often fails to capture domain-specific patterns, leading to suboptimal imputation performance in the target domain. To address this, we propose a novel cross-domain conditional diffusion model that enables domain-shared knowledge transfer while modeling domain-specific temporal dependencies.

Domain-Shared Temporal Knowledge Transfer. To facilitate knowledge transfer across domains, we try to learn domain-shared input representations using a shared convolution layer. The input representations for the source and target domains are formulated as: $H_{Src}^{in} = \text{Conv}\left(\mathbf{X}_{Src}^{co}\|\widetilde{\mathbf{X}}_{Src}^{t}\right)$ and $H_{Tgt}^{in} = \text{Conv}\left(\mathbf{X}_{Tgt}^{co}\|\widetilde{\mathbf{X}}_{Tgt}^{t}\right)$, respectively, where Conv is 1×1 convolution. To further integrate shared information and help the imputation, the model incorporates domain-shared side information D^{sh}, which includes: (1) a time embedding $s = \{s_1, \dots, s_L\} \in \mathbb{R}^{L \times 128}$ for temporal dependencies, constructed using sine-cosine temporal encoding [32]; (2) a learnable feature embedding $f = \{f_1, \dots, f_K\} \in \mathbb{R}^{K \times 16}$ to model shared feature relationships. We expand and concatenate s and f and obtain $D^{sh} \in \mathbb{R}^{K \times L \times C}$, where C is the channel size.

Domain-Specific Temporal Knowledge Modeling. After the common feature extraction, the model applies domain-specific attention mechanisms:

$$H^{tem} = \text{Attn}_{tem}\left(H^{in} + \text{Linear}(t_{emb})\right)$$
$$H^{fea} = \text{Attn}_{fea}\left(H^{tem}\right) \tag{8}$$

where $\text{Attn}_{tem}(\cdot)$ captures temporal dependencies, and $\text{Attn}_{fea}(\cdot)$ models feature interactions. These attention layers are domain-specific, enabling the model to learn unique characteristics within each domain. The diffusion step embedding t_{emb} is constructed through sine-cosine temporal encoding as well and projected through a linear layer. Additionally, domain-specific side information D^{sp} includes the conditional mask $\widetilde{\mathbf{M}}$ of each domain, which explicitly indicates missing positions. The final output of each denoising network is computed as:

$$H^{out} = H^{fea} + \text{Conv}(D^{sh}) + \text{Conv}(D^{sp}). \tag{9}$$

The domain-specific modeling stacks multiple layers, where the output H^{out} of each layer is divided into a residual connection and a skip connection after a gated activation unit. The residual connection serves as the input to the next layer, while the skip connections from each layer are summed and passed through two layers of 1×1 convolution to obtain the final output.

4.5   Cross-Domain Consistency Alignment (CDCA)

To mitigate temporal discrepancies across domains while accounting for the uncertainty caused by missing values, we further propose cross-domain consistency alignment. Unlike conventional domain adaptation methods, which enforce rigid alignment regardless of the magnitude of domain discrepancies, CDCA selectively enforces prediction consistency based on the model output discrepancy for the same target domain samples.

Let $\hat{\epsilon}_{Tgt}$ denote the target network's prediction on a given target sample, and let $\hat{\epsilon}_{Src \to Tgt}$ denote the prediction from the source network (in evaluation mode) when the same target sample is used as input. The average absolute difference between these predictions, denoted as Δ, is then computed:

$$\Delta = \frac{1}{N} \sum_{i=1}^{N} \|\hat{\epsilon}_{Tgt,i} - \hat{\epsilon}_{Src \to Tgt,i}\| \tag{10}$$

where N is the number of target domain samples.

CDCA compares Δ against two thresholds: a lower threshold τ_l and an upper threshold τ_h. If $\Delta < \tau_l$, the discrepancy is within an acceptable range, where enforcing alignment could amplify the impact of missingness-induced noise rather than improving adaptation. If $\tau_l \leq \Delta \leq \tau_h$, the discrepancy is moderate. In this case, we impose a penalty proportional to the excess difference, specifically $\Delta - \tau_l$. If $\Delta > \tau_h$, the discrepancy is large, suggesting that strict alignment could cause overfitting to source domain patterns and distort intrinsic target structures. To prevent this, the penalty is capped at $\min(\Delta - \tau_l, \tau_h)$. Thus, the alignment loss is formulated as:

$$\mathcal{L}_{align} = \begin{cases} 0, & \Delta < \tau_l, \\ \min(\Delta - \tau_l, \tau_h), & \Delta \geq \tau_l. \end{cases} \tag{11}$$

By applying regularization only when discrepancies exceed a lower threshold and capping penalties for large deviations, CDCA achieves a trade-off between imposing cross-domain alignment and preserving target-specific characteristics.

4.6 Overall Loss Function

The overall loss function for our model integrates several components: time series imputation losses (Eq. 4) for both source and target domains, and an auxiliary loss that addresses cross-domain consistency alignment (Eq. 11), re-weighted by parameters μ_{align}. The overall loss function is defined as:

$$\mathcal{L} = \mathcal{L}_{Src} + \mathcal{L}_{Tgt} + \mu_{align} \mathcal{L}_{align} \tag{12}$$

This formulation ensures that the model not only learns to impute missing values within each domain but also mitigates domain discrepancies.

5 Experiments

5.1 Experimental Setting

We evaluate our model on three real-world datasets, with details described below and the statistics of datasets are presented in Table 1.

Table 1. Dataset Characteristics

Statistics	Dataset					
	Air Quality		Hydrology		Electricity	
	Beijing	Tianjin	Discharge	Pooled	ETTh1	ETTh2
Samples	8759	8759	2726	2726	17420	17420
Length	36	36	16	16	48	48
Features	27	27	20	20	7	7
Original Missing Rate	12.36%	20.84%	0%	19.99%	0%	0%

Air Quality [37] dataset contains PM2.5 measurements from Beijing (B) and Tianjin (T). Beijing data is collected from 36 stations, while Tianjin has data from 27 stations. For cross-domain setting, 27 stations with the fewest missing values were sampled from Beijing data.

Hydrology dataset records daily river flow and sediment concentration from 20 stations in the United States, collected from United States Geological Survey [17] and Water Quality Portal [28]. It consists of two domains: Discharge (D) and Pooled (P), spanning from March 1, 2017, to September 30, 2022.

Electricity [44] dataset consists of power load and oil temperature data. It includes two years of data (from July 2016 to July 2018) from two distinct regions in China, referred to as ETTh1 and ETTh2.

We follow the dataset splitting strategy used in prior work [19,31,45]. For Air Quality dataset, we select Mar., Jun., Sep., and Dec. as the test set, the last 10% of the data in Feb., May, Aug., and Nov. as the validation set, and the remaining data as the training set. For Hydrology and Electricity, we split the training/validation/test set by 70%/10%/20%.

Evaluation Metrics. We evaluate the performance using three metrics: Mean Absolute Error (MAE), Root Mean Squared Error (RMSE), and Continuous Ranked Probability Score (CRPS). MAE and RMSE measure the error between imputed values and ground truth for deterministic methods. CRPS is used to measure how well the imputed probability distributions align with the observed values for methods that produce probability distributions.

Masking Strategy. Since original missing values within datasets lack ground truth, we consider two missing patterns to simulate the missing values for evaluation: (1) *Point missing*, where 10% of the observations is masked, and (2) *Block missing*, where we mask 5 % of the observed data and mask observations ranging from 1 to 4 data points for each feature with 0.15 % probability. For training strategies, we use two masking strategies for self-supervised learning: (1) *Point strategy* randomly selects $r(r \in [0\%, 100\%])$ of observed values; (2) *Block strategy* randomly select a sequence of length $[L/2, L]$ as missing targets with an additional 5 % of observed values randomly selected. Since Air

Quality dataset has much original missing data in the training set, we adopt point missing pattern following previous work [31]. For Hydrology and Electricity, we apply both point and block missing patterns following [19].

Baselines and Implementation Details. Baselines for DA. The chosen baselines include various state-of-the-art methods that have been widely adopted in the time series classification and forecasting tasks: CORAL [30], CDAN [21], DIRT-T [29], AdvSKM [20], CotMix [8]. **Baselines for TSI.** The baselines include RNN-based models M-RNN [39], BRITS [2], GNN-based models GRIN [4], SPIN and SPIN-H [22] and diffusion-based methods CSDI [31], SSSD [1], PriSTI [19], and MTSCI [45]. **Hyperparameters.** We set the batch size to 16 and the number of epochs to 200. The Adam optimizer is used with an initial learning rate of 1e-3, decaying to 1e-4 and 1e-5 at 75% and 90% of the total epochs, respectively. The frequency space mix ratio λ is sampled within [0.0, 1.0], and α in FMixup is empirically set as 0.003. As for the model, we use 4 residual layers, 64 residual channels (C), and 8 attention heads. For methods requiring an adjacency matrix, we use the identity matrix by default. We adopt the quadratic schedule for other noise levels following [31], with a minimum noise level $\beta_1 = 0.0001$ and a maximum noise level $\beta_T = 0.5$.

5.2   Overall Performance

The overall comparisons on three datasets are shown in Table 2. We summarize the observations as follows: (1) CD^2-TSI consistently outperforms baseline models across all datasets. Compared with existing time series imputation methods that rely solely on single-domain data, CD^2-TSI integrates cross-domain knowledge, leading to better imputation performance. Additionally, CD^2-TSI outperforms domain adaptation methods by specifically handling discrepancies in temporal dynamics and data deficiency caused by missing values, which are not adequately addressed by conventional DA approaches. (2) Incorporating domain adaptation techniques increases imputation accuracy compared to training solely on the target domain. However, the extent of this improvement varies across different missing patterns. For example, CDAN performs well on point missing but falls short on block missing scenarios due to its alignment strategy. In contrast, CD^2-TSI consistently improves upon the strongest DA baselines, with an average improvement of 1.92% (RMSE) and 1.34% (MAE), demonstrating its effectiveness in cross-domain alignment for imputation. (3) Our method achieves notable improvements over the best TSI baselines. Specifically, on the Air Quality dataset, CD^2-TSI provides a +4.41% improvement in RMSE and a +5.46% improvement in MAE. On the Hydrology dataset, it results in a +4.37% improvement in RMSE and a +4.61% improvement in MAE, while on the Electricity dataset, they are +4.13% in RMSE and +2.04% in MAE. Among TSI models, MTSCI's performance varies across datasets, with lower accuracy on Air Quality and Hydrology due to high missing rates. These results underscore CD^2-TSI's capacity to adapt effectively to different real-world datasets even under severe missing conditions.

Table 2. The overall performance comparison. Bold scores are the best performance, and underlined scores are the best time series imputation baseline performance.

Method	Air Quality	Hydrology				Electricity			
	$B \to T$	$D \to P$				$h1 \to h2$			
	Point	Point		Block		Point		Block	
	RMSE	MAE	RMSE	MAE	RMSE	MAE	RMSE	MAE	RMSE	MAE
Coral	14.814	7.374	48.353	13.579	45.484	16.370	0.645	0.381	1.230	0.548
CDAN	14.594	7.203	47.968	13.370	44.725	16.403	0.644	0.381	1.270	0.563
Dirt-T	14.945	7.429	48.506	13.659	45.394	16.227	0.672	0.396	1.194	0.559
AdvSKM	14.786	7.311	48.776	13.289	43.996	16.012	0.643	0.380	1.283	0.567
CoTMix	14.632	7.232	48.470	13.685	44.810	15.954	0.651	0.383	1.235	0.568
M-RNN	46.226	29.497	58.975	19.465	47.000	21.524	7.338	5.386	11.309	4.428
BRITS	40.067	26.355	56.749	19.249	47.207	22.251	6.988	4.428	8.109	4.893
GRIN	26.274	15.773	60.845	23.690	55.254	27.094	3.744	1.587	3.273	1.854
SPIN	27.881	16.914	59.263	22.020	53.530	25.428	6.750	2.856	7.096	3.503
SPIN-H	30.895	18.617	58.915	19.501	49.234	19.893	6.947	2.941	8.001	6.064
CSDI	<u>15.002</u>	<u>7.452</u>	<u>48.542</u>	<u>13.744</u>	<u>45.819</u>	<u>16.470</u>	<u>0.647</u>	<u>0.380</u>	1.320	0.592
SSSD	15.536	8.086	49.132	14.668	47.079	18.282	0.787	0.501	1.307	0.677
PriSTI	15.546	7.686	48.760	14.064	47.868	18.032	0.683	0.407	1.329	0.615
MTSCI	16.252	8.793	48.941	14.477	48.094	18.523	0.715	0.483	<u>1.240</u>	<u>0.562</u>
CD^2-TSI	**14.339**	**7.045**	**46.852**	**13.182**	**43.407**	**15.626**	**0.635**	**0.378**	**1.161**	**0.542**

5.3 Sensitivity and Ablation Study

Sensitivity Analysis. We investigate the sensitivity of our method to different missing rates and masking strategies. We conduct experiments on the Air Quality dataset to evaluate performance under various missing rates and on the Hydrology and Electricity datasets to assess different masking strategies.

For the Air Quality dataset, we randomly select 10/20/30/40/50% of the observed values as ground truth in the test data. Figure 2 (a) shows that our method consistently performs well across these rates. As missing data increases, imputation accuracy typically declines due to reduced availability of observed conditional information. However, our approach's use of frequency mixup interpolation and cross-domain alignment helps maintain high performance.

For the Hydrology and Electricity datasets, we use two settings: Point $\to$ Block (Point missing pattern in training set, Block missing pattern in testing set) and Block $\to$ Point (Block missing pattern in training set, Point missing pattern in testing set). Figure 2(b–c) shows that CD^2-TSI achieves relatively better performance with various missing patterns in the training and testing sets.

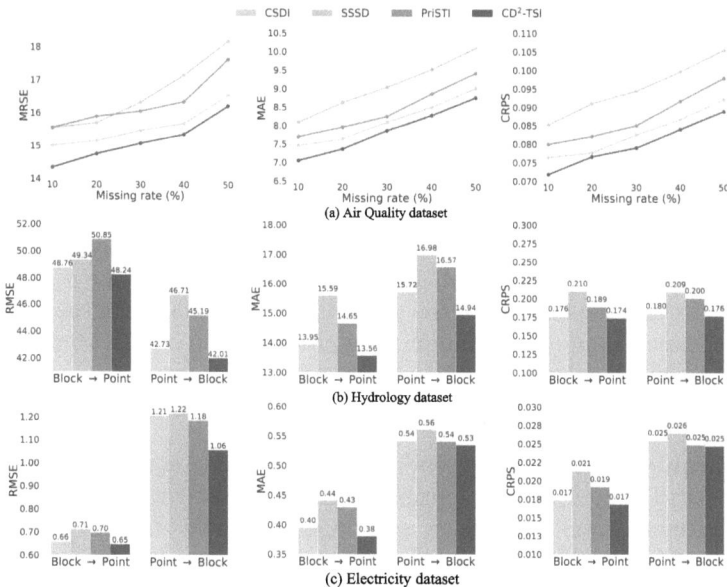

Fig. 2. Sensitivity Analysis for Air Quality, Hydrology, Electricity Datasets

Ablation Study. We evaluate the impact of key components in CD^2-TSI on imputation performance. **(1) w/o FMixup**: FMixup is excluded, and zero filling is used to construct the missing targets. **(2) w/ L.I.**: FMixup is replaced with linear interpolation to construct the missing targets. **(3) w/o CDCA**: Consistency alignment loss L_{align} is removed. Since Electricity dataset does not contain original missing values, no interpolation is required for original missing areas, and we only evaluate w/o CDCA on this dataset.

Table 3. Ablation Study of CD^2-TSI.

Method	Air Quality	Hydrology					Electricity			
	$B \to T$	$D \to P$					$h1 \to h2$			
	Point	Point		Block			Point		Block	
	RMSE	MAE	RMSE	MAE	RMSE	MAE	RMSE	MAE	RMSE	MAE
w/o FMixup	14.817	7.292	47.662	13.365	44.204	15.956	–	–	–	–
w/ L.I.	14.921	7.357	48.524	13.557	44.261	16.163	–	–	–	–
w/o CDCA	14.782	7.319	47.288	13.390	43.679	15.876	0.641	0.380	1.255	0.554
CD^2-TSI	**14.339**	**7.045**	**46.852**	**13.182**	**43.407**	**15.626**	**0.635**	**0.378**	**1.161**	**0.542**

Table 3 presents the results of our ablation study. Removing frequency mixup interpolation (w/o FMixup) significantly degrades performance across all datasets and missing patterns, confirming that frequency mixup provides informative priors that enhance imputation accuracy. When FMixup is replaced with linear interpolation (w/ L.I.), performance further declines, demonstrating that frequency-domain interpolation captures temporal dependencies more effectively than simple interpolation in the time domain. Removing the cross-domain consistency alignment loss (w/o CDCA) results in performance degradation, particularly in block missing scenarios. For instance, in the Electricity dataset, RMSE increases from 1.161 to 1.255 in block missing pattern. This confirms that cross-domain consistency alignment helps in mitigating temporal discrepancies across domains. Overall, the findings of the ablation studies underscore the importance of each proposed component in improving cross-domain imputation.

5.4 Hyperparameter and Efficiency Study

Hyperparameter Study. We conduct a hyperparameter study on key parameters in CD^2-TSI to select the optimal settings across three datasets: the frequency space mix ratio λ, the lower and upper thresholds τ_l and τ_h. The results are shown in Fig. 3. The parameter λ controls the extent of frequency mixing between the source and target domains, while the thresholds τ_l and τ_h ensure cross-domain consistency alignment while preserving domain-specific variations. Our study finds that a moderate frequency mixing ratio and properly selected alignment thresholds ensure effective cross-domain time series imputation.

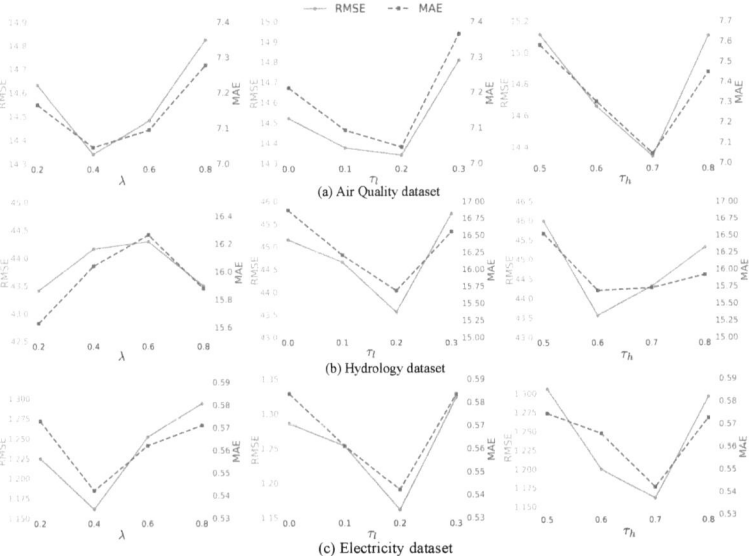

Fig. 3. Hyperparameter study on three key parameters of CD^2-TSI.

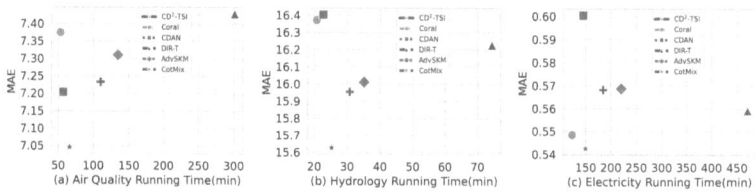

Fig. 4. Efficiency analysis on Air Quality, Hydrology and Electricity datasets.

Efficiency Study. We illustrate the total training time of DA models trained on all three datasets, and the experiments are conducted on an NVIDIA RTX 4090 GPU with 24G memory. Figure 4 shows the Time-MAE curve, indicating the relationship between time complexity and model performance. Compared with models such as Coral and CDAN, which achieve the least running time, CD^2-TSI achieves better imputation results by leveraging frequency mixup and cross-domain adaptation at the cost of marginally increased training time.

6   Conclusion

In this paper, we introduce CD^2-TSI, a novel approach for cross-domain time series imputation, addressing the limitations of existing methods in handling high missing rates and domain shifts. Our approach effectively leverages cross-domain information through a diffusion-based framework while preserving domain-specific temporal dependencies. The proposed frequency mixup interpolation and selective consistency alignment strategies contribute to improved adaptation and imputation accuracy. CD^2-TSI has demonstrated superior performance on three real-world datasets through comprehensive experiments. Future work will explore more challenging real-world conditions with extreme missing rates and complex domain shifts.

Acknowledgments. This work was supported in part by USACE under Grant No. GR40695, "Designing nature to enhance resilience of built infrastructure in western US landscapes", and by the National Science Foundation under Grant No. 2311716, "CausalBench: A Cyberinfrastructure for Causal-Learning Benchmarking for Efficacy, Reproducibility, and Scientific Collaboration".

Disclosure of Interests. The authors have no competing interests to declare that are relevant to the content of this article.

References

1. Alcaraz, J.M.L., Strodthoff, N.: Diffusion-based time series imputation and forecasting with structured state space models. arXiv preprint arXiv:2208.09399 (2022)
2. Cao, W., Wang, D., Li, J., Zhou, H., Li, L., Li, Y.: Brits: bidirectional recurrent imputation for time series. Adv. Neural Inf. Process. Syst. **31** (2018)

3. Che, Z., Purushotham, S., Cho, K., et al.: Recurrent neural networks for multivariate time series with missing values. Sci. Rep. (2018)
4. Cini, A., Marisca, I., Alippi, C.: Filling the g_ap_s: multivariate time series imputation by graph neural networks. arXiv preprint arXiv:2108.00298 (2021)
5. Ding, K., Shu, K., Shan, X., Li, J., Liu, H.: Cross-domain graph anomaly detection. IEEE Trans. Neural Netw. Learn. Syst. **33**(6) (2021)
6. Du, W., Côté, D., Liu, Y.: Saits: self-attention-based imputation for time series. Expert Syst. Appl. (2023)
7. Du, W., Wang, J., Qian, L., et al.: Tsi-bench: benchmarking time series imputation. arXiv preprint arXiv:2406.12747 (2024)
8. Eldele, E., Ragab, M., Chen, Z., Wu, M., Kwoh, C.K., Li, X.: Contrastive domain adaptation for time-series via temporal mixup. IEEE Trans. Artif. Intell. **5**(3), 1185–1194 (2023)
9. Eldele, E., Ragab, M., Chen, Z., Wu, M., Kwoh, C.K., Li, X.: Label-efficient time series representation learning: a review. IEEE Trans. Artif. Intell. (2024)
10. Fortuin, V., Baranchuk, D., Rätsch, G., Mandt, S.: Gp-vae: deep probabilistic time series imputation. In: International Conference on Artificial Intelligence and Statistics, pp. 1651–1661. PMLR (2020)
11. Gao, H., Shen, W., Qiu, X., et al.: Diffimp: efficient diffusion model for probabilistic time series imputation with bidirectional mamba backbone. arXiv preprint arXiv:2410.13338 (2024)
12. He, H., Queen, O., Koker, T., Cuevas, C., Tsiligkaridis, T., Zitnik, M.: Domain adaptation for time series under feature and label shifts. In: International Conference on Machine Learning, pp. 12746–12774. PMLR (2023)
13. Ho, J., Jain, A., Abbeel, P.: Denoising diffusion probabilistic models. Adv. Neural. Inf. Process. Syst. **33**, 6840–6851 (2020)
14. Jin, X., Park, Y., Maddix, D., Wang, H., Wang, Y.: Domain adaptation for time series forecasting via attention sharing. In: International Conference on Machine Learning, pp. 10280–10297. PMLR (2022)
15. Kim, S., Kim, H., Yun, E., Lee, H., Lee, J., Lee, J.: Probabilistic imputation for time-series classification with missing data. In: International Conference on Machine Learning, pp. 16654–16667. PMLR (2023)
16. Kong, Y., et al.: Time-MQA: time series multi-task question answering with context enhancement. arXiv preprint arXiv:2503.01875 (2025)
17. Konrad, C.P., Anderson, S.W., Restivo, D.E., et al.: Network analysis of usgs streamflow gages (2022)
18. Little, R.J., Rubin, D.B.: Statistical Analysis with Missing Data. John Wiley & Sons, Hoboken (2019)
19. Liu, M., Huang, H., Feng, H., Sun, L., Du, B., Fu, Y.: Pristi: a conditional diffusion framework for spatiotemporal imputation. In: 2023 IEEE 39th International Conference on Data Engineering (ICDE), pp. 1927–1939. IEEE (2023)
20. Liu, Q., Xue, H.: Adversarial spectral kernel matching for unsupervised time series domain adaptation. In: IJCAI (2021)
21. Long, M., Cao, Z., Wang, J., Jordan, M.I.: Conditional adversarial domain adaptation. Adv. Neural Inf. Process. Syst. **31** (2018)
22. Marisca, I., Cini, A., Alippi, C.: Learning to reconstruct missing data from spatiotemporal graphs with sparse observations. Adv. Neural. Inf. Process. Syst. **35**, 32069–32082 (2022)
23. Miao, X., Wu, Y., Wang, J., Gao, Y., Mao, X., Yin, J.: Generative semi-supervised learning for multivariate time series imputation. In: Proceedings of the AAAI Conference on Artificial Intelligence, pp. 8983–8991 (2021)

24. Miyaguchi, K., Katsuki, T., Koseki, A., Iwamori, T.: Variational inference for discriminative learning with generative modeling of feature incompletion. In: International Conference on Learning Representations (2022)
25. Nussbaumer, H.J., Nussbaumer, H.J.: The Fast Fourier Transform. Springer, Heidelberg (1982)
26. Ragab, M., Eldele, E., Chen, Z., Wu, M., Kwoh, C.K., Li, X.: Self-supervised autoregressive domain adaptation for time series data. IEEE Trans. Neural Netw. Learn. Syst. **35**(1), 1341–1351 (2022)
27. Ragab, M., et al.: Adatime: a benchmarking suite for domain adaptation on time series data. ACM Trans. Knowl. Discov. Data **17**(8), 1–18 (2023)
28. Read, E.K., Carr, L., De Cicco, L., et al.: Water quality data for national-scale aquatic research: the water quality portal. Water Resou. Res, (2017)
29. Shu, R., Bui, H.H., Narui, H., Ermon, S.: A dirt-t approach to unsupervised domain adaptation. arXiv preprint arXiv:1802.08735 (2018)
30. Sun, B., Saenko, K.: Deep CORAL: correlation alignment for deep domain adaptation. In: Hua, G., Jégou, H. (eds.) ECCV 2016. LNCS, vol. 9915, pp. 443–450. Springer, Cham (2016). https://doi.org/10.1007/978-3-319-49409-8_35
31. Tashiro, Y., Song, J., Song, Y., Ermon, S.: CSDI: conditional score-based diffusion models for probabilistic time series imputation. Adv. Neural. Inf. Process. Syst. **34**, 24804–24816 (2021)
32. Vaswani, A., et al.: Attention is all you need. Adv. Neural Inf. Process. Syst. **30** (2017)
33. Wilson, G., Doppa, J.R., Cook, D.J.: Multi-source deep domain adaptation with weak supervision for time-series sensor data. In: Proceedings of the 26th ACM SIGKDD International Conference on Knowledge Discovery & Data Mining (2020)
34. Wu, H., Hu, T., Liu, Y., et al.: Timesnet: temporal 2d-variation modeling for general time series analysis. arXiv preprint arXiv:2210.02186 (2022)
35. Xu, Q., Zhang, R., Zhang, Y., Wang, Y., Tian, Q.: A fourier-based framework for domain generalization. In: Proceedings of the IEEE/CVF Conference on Computer Vision and Pattern Recognition, pp. 14383–14392 (2021)
36. Yang, X., Sun, Y., Chen, X., et al.: Frequency-aware generative models for multivariate time series imputation. Adv. Neural. Inf. Process. Syst. **37**, 52595–52623 (2024)
37. Yi, X., Zheng, Y., Zhang, J., Li, T.: St-mvl: filling missing values in geo-sensory time series data. In: Proceedings of the 25th International Joint Conference on Artificial Intelligence (2016)
38. Yoon, J., Jordon, J., Schaar, M.: Gain: missing data imputation using generative adversarial nets. In: International Conference on Machine Learning (2018)
39. Yoon, J., Zame, W.R., Van Der Schaar, M.: Estimating missing data in temporal data streams using multi-directional recurrent neural networks. IEEE Trans. Biomed. Eng. **66**(5), 1477–1490 (2018)
40. Yue, Z., et al.: Ts2vec: towards universal representation of time series. In: Proceedings of the AAAI Conference on Artificial Intelligence, pp. 8980–8987 (2022)
41. Zhang, K., et al.: A survey of deep graph learning under distribution shifts: from graph out-of-distribution generalization to adaptation. arXiv preprint arXiv:2410.19265 (2024)
42. Zhang, K., Wang, Y., Li, X., Tang, R., Zhang, R.: Incmsr: an incremental learning approach for multi-scenario recommendation. In: Proceedings of the 17th ACM International Conference on Web Search and Data Mining, pp. 939–948 (2024)

43. Zhang, X., Zhao, Z., Tsiligkaridis, T., Zitnik, M.: Self-supervised contrastive pre-training for time series via time-frequency consistency. Adv. Neural. Inf. Process. Syst. **35**, 3988–4003 (2022)
44. Zhou, H., et al.: Informer: beyond efficient transformer for long sequence time-series forecasting. In: Proceedings of the AAAI Conference on Artificial Intelligence, pp. 11106–11115 (2021)
45. Zhou, J., Li, J., Zheng, G., Wang, X., Zhou, C.: Mtsci: a conditional diffusion model for multivariate time series consistent imputation. In: Proceedings of the 33rd ACM International Conference on Information and Knowledge Management, pp. 3474–3483 (2024)

Transfer and Multitask Learning

Task Prompt Vectors: Effective Initialization Through Multi-task Soft Prompt Transfer

Robert Belanec[1,2(✉)], Simon Ostermann[3], Ivan Srba[2], and Maria Bielikova[2]

[1] Faculty of Information Technology, Brno University of Technology, Brno, Czechia
[2] Kempelen Institute of Intelligent Technologies, Bratislava, Slovakia
{robert.belanec,ivan.srba,maria.bielikova}@kinit.sk
[3] German Research Center for Artificial Intelligence (DFKI), Saarbrücken, Germany
simon.ostermann@dfki.de

Abstract. Prompt tuning is a parameter-efficient method for adapting large language models (LLMs), where only a small continuous soft prompt is finetuned. In recent works, soft prompts have usually been trained in a task-specific way, leaving their multi-task capabilities underexplored. Our work aims to make soft prompts more *task modular* based on recent research on task vectors, where arithmetic operations are applied on full model weights to achieve the desired multi-task performance. To this end, we introduce *Task Prompt Vectors*, created by the element-wise difference between weights of tuned soft prompts and their random initialization. Experimental results on an extensive set of 19 datasets show that task prompt vectors can be used in low-resource settings to initialize prompt tuning on similar tasks effectively. In addition, we show that task prompt vectors are independent of the random initialization of prompt tuning on 3 different language model architectures. This key property of random initialization independence allows *prompt arithmetics* with the pre-trained vectors from different tasks. In this way, the arithmetic addition of task prompt vectors from multiple tasks represents a competitive and computationally more effective alternative to state-of-the-art solutions.

1 Introduction

Standard fine-tuning methods change the weights of a pre-trained language model (PLM) to increase its performance on a downstream task. There is a strong trend of improving model performance by increasing the number of parameters, which leads to a steep increase in computational resources required for training (e.g., GPT-3 [5] having 175 billion parameters). Besides this, large language models also require significant amounts of training data, which especially benefits high-resource languages [8].

To address the problem of the increasing number of parameters, *Parameter-Efficient Fine-Tuning (PEFT)* methods [17,19,24] were introduced, capable of solving multiple problems even with small amounts of labeled data while training only a fraction of the model parameters (e.g., for RoBERTa base [29], prompt tuning [24] is training only

Supplementary Information The online version contains supplementary material available at https://doi.org/10.1007/978-3-662-72243-5_5.

B. Pfahringer et al. (Eds.): ECML PKDD 2025, LNAI 16020, pp. 77–94, 2026.
https://doi.org/10.1007/978-3-662-72243-5_5

0.5% parameters, and LoRA [19] is training only 0.7% of parameters [51]). The key concept that makes many PEFT methods effective is their *task modularity* – single modules can be trained for diverse tasks and then just be swapped out inside of the same model.

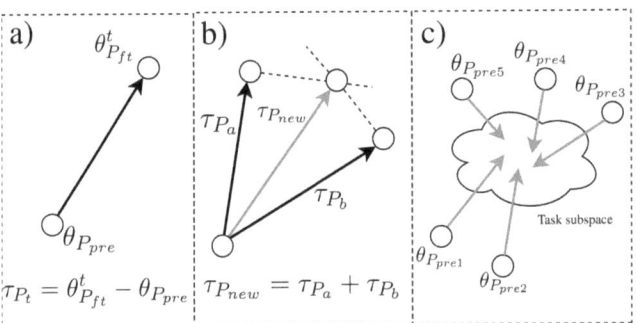

Fig. 1. An illustration of task prompt vector creation and the combination via addition that we include in our work. (a) A task prompt vector is created by subtracting the soft prompt initialization weights $\theta_{P_{pre}}$ from the soft prompt weights after prompt tuning $\theta_{P_{ft}}^t$ (Sect. 3, Eq. 2). (b) A combination via the addition of two task prompt vectors τ_{P_a} and τ_{P_b} resulting in $\tau_{P_{new}}$ (Sect. 3, Eq. 4). (c) Different task prompt vectors point into the same subspace in the embedding space of PLM (Sect. 4.2). The circles represent different random initializations.

Some of the recent PEFT methods [1,24,51] are based on fine-tuning *soft prompts*. Soft prompts are trainable (parametrized) weights that are prepended to the input embeddings while training the model. *Prompt tuning* is one of the most widely used variants of soft prompt-based tuning of large language models (LLMs).

In contrast to other PEFT methods, most soft prompt-based methods lack sufficient multi-task modularity, requiring the training process to be fully or partially repeated for each newly added task [45,47]. Other PEFT methods, while keeping their relatively high modularity, usually lack robustness, and their performance depends on the quality and the number of pre-trained soft prompts [1]. Moreover, creating a soft prompt for multiple tasks often decreases the overall multi-task performance and requires further fine-tuning.

We build on findings of research on *task vector arithmetics* [20], a suite of methods for efficiently modifying the behavior of pre-trained LLMs through **task vectors**. A task vector represents a direction in the LLM's activation space, which is obtained by subtracting the weights of a base model from its fine-tuned version. Moving along in this direction enhances performance on the corresponding task. Task vector arithmetic has mostly been applied to the full weights of computer vision models and older NLP models like T5 [37] and GPT-2 [36] trained from the same initialization, with only a limited set of machine unlearning experiments.

In our work, we fully extend this idea to the NLP domain, concretely to the efficient and modular techniques of prompt tuning [24], and propose the novel concept of **task**

prompt vectors. Task prompt vectors are created by subtracting soft prompt initializations from their fine-tuned versions, enabling *prompt arithmetics* on top of the task prompt vectors (see Fig. 1). We thoroughly investigate the properties of task prompt vectors and demonstrate their functionality in combining pairs of task prompt vectors while evaluating their in-distribution and out-of-distribution performance in full and limited data scenarios.

Our main contributions and findings are[1]:

- We introduce the novel concept of **task prompt vectors** created from fine-tuned soft prompts as a method of weight interpolation that leverages findings from task vectors. In addition, we investigate vector arithmetics on such task prompt vectors based on simple arithmetic operations as a method to reinforce PLMs to solve multi-task problems.
- We provide a comprehensive investigation of task prompt vector properties on 17 natural language understanding (NLU) and 2 natural language generation (NLG) datasets separated into 8 task types and demonstrate important properties of task prompt vectors. We show that their random initialization independence makes them robust and universally applicable, while their similarity across related problems provides a necessary base for efficient cross-task transfer.
- We show that task prompt vectors allow efficient prompt tuning initializations by leveraging multi-task combinations of the pre-trained task prompt vectors using the task prompt vector arithmetics. Experimental results show that, especially in zero- or few-shot settings, task-prompt-vector-based initializations perform better or at par with closely related techniques like SPoT (Soft Prompt Transfer learning [45]) for specific tasks while achieving high multi-task modularity.

2 Related Work

Soft Prompt-Based Fine-Tuning. After the introduction of prompt tuning [24] and prefix tuning [26] many new soft prompt-based methods [15,28,40] were introduced. Some of these methods focus on task knowledge transfer (e.g., SPoT [45] or cross-model transfer [44]) and task combinations (e.g., ATTEMPT [1], MPT [47], or BMTPT [23]). These can be classified as works on PEFT weight interpolations to increase the performance of prompt tuning in single or multi-task settings. However, they do not represent the tasks as vectors in the embedding space and require further training of the added parameters.

Model Weights Interpolation. Model weight interpolation [14,50] is a widely discussed topic in the literature since it enables combining knowledge of different fine-tuned models without or with a small amount of training. Authors of tasks vectors [20] show that it is possible to combine multiple task vectors created from fine-tuned models and still maintain the overall multi-task performance. Work [32] focuses mostly on improving task vectors by showing that training models in their tangent space contributes to the

---

[1] To support the replicability of our work, we provide a repository to store all of our implementation, results, and supplementary material: https://github.com/kinit-sk/task-prompt-vectors.

weight disentanglement and increases the performance of full model task arithmetic. Another subcategory for weight interpolation can be model merging [9,25,31,42]. In the work [39], the authors propose a strategy of merging multiple model weights from pre-trained sets of auxiliary tasks as initialization to multiple parallel fine-tunings to enhance out-of-distribution generalization. Most of these works on model weights interpolation usually focus only on the weights of the whole model or particular weights (e.g., classification heads, activation layers) of the pre-trained model.

There are also works on weight interpolation of PEFT methods [7,34,35,52], but not many of them focus on interpolation using task vectors. In the work [22], the authors present a way of combining pre-trained adapters using task vector arithmetics, but the method lacks the investigation of the dependency of their method on the random initialization of adapters. Therefore, it may require training of specific adapters from the same random initialization, which significantly limits their re-use potential.

To the best of our knowledge, there is no research on task vectors in the context of soft prompt-based fine-tuning. In this work, we address this drawback by building on the existing knowledge on prompt tuning and task vectors.

3   Task Prompt Vectors

Background. Prompt tuning, as introduced in [24], casts tasks as text generation, modeling a probability $Pr(Y|X)$, where X is a sequence of input tokens and Y is a sequence of output tokens (for classifications tasks, e.g., representing the class label). The generation $Pr_\theta(Y|X)$ is parametrized by the model weights θ. Prompting adds extra information to the generation process by prepending a series of tokens (prompt) P to the input X, such that the model maximizes the probability of getting current Y in $Pr_\theta(Y|[P; X])$, while keeping the parameters θ frozen. Prompt tuning adds another parameter θ_P to the equation, which parametrizes the prompt. During the training, only θ_P is typically updated as a negative log-likelihood loss is optimized as:

$$\mathcal{L}_{PT} = - \sum_i log Pr_{\theta,\theta_P}(Y_i|[P; X_i]) \tag{1}$$

As a method of adapting model weights without training, task vectors [20] were proposed. A task vector is defined as the element-wise difference between the pre-trained weights and the weights after fine-tuning a complete model. Task vectors can then be applied to any model weights θ of the same dimensionality (architecture) by element-wise addition. The representation of task vectors in the weight space of the model has the same properties as standard vectors. Therefore, it is possible to include them in arithmetic expressions like addition, negation, or combinations via the addition of two or more vectors. We build on findings from [20] and [24] in the following sections.

Task Prompt Vector Definition. Let $T_1, ..., T_t$ be a set of source tasks and $\theta_{P_1}, ..., \theta_{P_i}$ be a set of random soft prompt weights initializations. Intuitively, the random soft prompt weights initializations are random points in the embedding space of the PLM. During prompt tuning, we move each of these points into a task sub-space, such that the objective function in Eq. 1 is minimized. This is repeated for each task $t \in T$. These points are further denoted as *task prompts* – soft prompts fine-tuned by prompt tuning to a set of downstream tasks. We define the straight trajectory from the initial random point to the task prompt as our *task prompt vector* (see part a) of Fig. 1).

Let $\theta_{P_{pre}} \in \mathbb{R}^d$ be the weights of the soft prompt randomly initialized from the embedding vocabulary of a PLM, and $\theta^t_{P_{ft}} \in \mathbb{R}^d$ be the weights of the soft prompt P fine-tuned on a specific task t, using the standard prompt tuning formula. We formulate the task prompt vector τ_{P_t} for soft prompt P and task as an element-wise difference:

$$\tau_{P_t} = \theta^t_{P_{ft}} - \theta_{P_{pre}} \tag{2}$$

Applying a task prompt vector to the soft prompt weights of equal size would follow:

$$\theta_{P_{new}} = \theta_P + \lambda \tau_{P_t}, \tag{3}$$

where the rescaling term λ is a number from the interval $0 < \lambda \leq 1$ and when $\lambda = 1$, then $\theta_{P_{new}} = \theta_P + \tau_{P_t} = \theta^t_{P_{ft}}$

Vector Arithmetics with Task Prompt Vectors. Task prompt vectors for different tasks can be combined by simple vector addition, combining knowledge from different tasks. When we experiment with combinations, we refer to the arithmetic addition of two task prompt vectors (see part b) of Fig. 1):

$$\tau_{P_{new}} = \tau_{P_a} + \tau_{P_b} \tag{4}$$

This approach clearly results in efficient task adaptation as we perform no further training but only use vector addition. Task prompt vector combinations can also be used to initialize a new task that is sufficiently similar to an already trained task. We investigate and discuss these use cases for task prompt vectors in the upcoming sections.

4 Experiments

4.1 Experimental Setup and Implementation Details

We investigate the properties of task prompt vectors using a **T5-base** [37] model for all of our experiments since it is a widely used model in many PEFT related works, and it has a reasonable size to exdend experiments to a larger scale. To support the generalizability of our results, for origin dependency experiments in Sect. 4.2, we also include **LLaMa-3.1-8B-Instruct** [11] and **DeepSeek-LLM-7b-chat** [3] models, representing two additional LLM families. Our work covers 6 types of classification problems, as well as 2 types of generation problems covered by 19 corresponding datasets, namely **natural language inference (NLI)** – *MNLI* [49], *QNLI* [46], *SciTail* [21], *SNLI* [4], *RTE* [46]; **topic classification** – *DBPedia* [2], *TREC* [18,27], *AG News*, *Yahoo Answers* [53]; **sentiment classification** – *SST2* [41], *Yelp Polarity*, *SST5*, *IMDB* [30]; **paraphrase classification** – *QQP*[2], *MRPC* [10]; **grammatical correctness** – *CoLA* [48]; **semantic textual similarity** – *STS-B* [6]; **question answering** – *SQuADv2* [38], and **math problems solving** – *MATH* [13].

---

[2] https://quoradata.quora.com/First-Quora-Dataset-Release-Question-Pairs.

For all datasets, we report macro F1 scores, with the exception of STS-B (evaluated by Pearson Correlation) and MATH (evaluated by RougeL score). The cosine similarity between vectors (task prompts or task prompt vectors) is measured using the average pooled weights of each vector. We average all of our results across 3 different runs (i.e., different random initializations of soft prompts). To determine the statistical significance of our results, we perform a two-sample Student's t-test [43] with Bonferroni correction [12]. We denote the statistical significance by marking the corresponding result with an asterisk '*'. The subscript in our tables represents the standard deviation.

For the few-shot experiments (simulating limited labeled data scenarios), we randomly sub-sample from the data for the respective number of shots while keeping the class distribution. We consider *shot* and *sample* to be equivalent (i.e., for a 5-shot setting, we choose 5 samples overall, not 5 samples per class). When combining task prompt vectors, we evaluate their performance on the individual source tasks that formed the task combination and find the best rescaling factor λ via held-out validation sets (i.e., we randomly sample a validation subset from the evaluation dataset and select the best performing $\lambda \in \{0.1, 0.2, ..., 0.9, 1\}$).

We provide information about ethical considerations and an impact statement in Supplementary Material A. In addition, a more detailed description of our experimental setup can be found in Supplementary Material B.

4.2   Investigating Task Prompt Vectors Properties

In this section, we aim to address the following research question (RQ):

RQ1: How universally can we apply task prompt vectors to a) different prompt initializations and b) different tasks?

There are two fundamental properties that are crucial for the effectiveness of task prompt vectors: 1) If prompt vectors should be applied universally, they must be independent of random initialization (since soft prompts are usually initialized randomly, unlike PLM for task prompts in [20]). 2) The similarity of task prompt vectors between similar tasks should be high enough in order to be able to combine task prompt vectors.

To evaluate these properties, we train a set of soft prompts on specified source tasks for inference classification (*MNLI, QNLI, RTE*), topic classification (*DBPedia, TREC*), sentiment classification (*SST2, Yelp Polarity*), paraphrase classification (*QQP, MRPC*), grammatical correctness (*CoLA*), semantic textual similarity (*STS-B*), question answering (*SQuADv2*) and math problems solving (*MATH*) resulting in a set of 13 soft prompts that were trained from a single random initialization. We sample *3 random initializations* from which we create the task prompt vectors as described in Eq. 2. Since SQuADv2 and MATH are more complex tasks that T5 struggles with, we report for these tasks only results for LLaMa-3.1-8B-Instruct and DeepSeek-LLM-7B-Chat. We aggregate results by averaging across random initializations in Table 1 and Figs. 2a, 2b. At first, we evaluate task prompt vectors' independence of the random initialization and continue with experiments to confirm whether task prompt vectors trained for the same task are always pointing in a similar direction of the PLM embedding space, similar to part c) of Fig. 1.

The Performance of Task Prompt Vectors is Independent of the Random Initialization for the Majority of Observed Tasks. We conduct experiments to evaluate the performance of applying task prompt vectors to different (mixed) random initializations. For each task and each random initialization, we apply the task prompt vector (according to the Eq. 3) to all of the other random initializations and evaluate performance for each task prompt vector-initialization pair on the test set of the particular dataset. The aggregated results in the "Mixed init" rows in Table 1 differ only slightly in most tasks for all three models, compared to the results of prompt tuning in the "Original init" rows. This indicates that task prompt vectors perform well, irrespective of their initialization. The only exception is the TREC task, where the performance decreases significantly for the T5-base model. We suspect that this may be caused by the task being harder for the T5-base model to learn, which also confirms the higher standard deviation from the mean of prompt tuning performance. We can also see that for LLaMa-3.1-8B-Instruct and DeepSeek-LLM-7B-Chat, there is no statistically significant difference between using the original initialization or different task prompt vector initializations, and for SST2, CoLA, TREC, and MATH, average performance even slightly increased, but in most cases the performance remained unchanged, according to statistical significance tests. In some cases, the performance of the original initialization of the T5 model was similar or even better than for much larger instruction-fine-tuned LLaMa or DeepSeek models, which goes in line with findings of recent related work [16,33].

Table 1. Comparison of test results across 3 random soft prompt initializations for T5-base, LLaMa-3.1-8B, and DeepSeek-LLM-7B models. The first column (Original) represents the results of prompt tuning. The second column (Mixed) represents the results of moving a specific initialization in the direction of a task prompt vector created from different (mixed) initializations. N/A means that the task was too complex for the T5 model, and the results were underperforming.

	Task	T5			LLaMa			DeepSeek		
		Original	Mixed	Δ	Original	Mixed	Δ	Original	Mixed	Δ
GLUE	MNLI	$85.4_{0.1}$	$85.3_{0.2}$	-0.1	$89.7_{0.2}$	$89.7_{0.2}$	$+0.0$	$86.1_{1.9}$	$86.0_{2.0}$	-0.1
	QQP	$87.3_{0.1}$	$87.4_{0.1}$	$+0.1$	$84.6_{0.1}$	$84.6_{0.1}$	$+0.0$	$84.4_{0.1}$	$84.4_{0.1}$	$+0.0$
	QNLI	93.3_0	$93.2^*_{0.1}$	-0.1	92.0_0	$92.0_{0.1}$	$+0.0$	$90.3_{1.4}$	$90.4_{1.3}$	$+0.1$
	SST2	$93.8_{0.3}$	$93.2_{0.6}$	-0.6	$95.9_{0.4}$	$96.0_{0.5}$	$+0.1$	$95.6_{0.1}$	$95.6_{0.1}$	$+0.0$
	STS-B	$89.3_{0.2}$	$88.6^*_{0.2}$	-0.7	89.9_1	$89.8_{0.8}$	-0.1	$88.7_{0.3}$	$88.7_{0.4}$	$+0.0$
	MRPC	$90.8_{0.8}$	$83.0^*_{4.1}$	-7.8	$87.7_{0.2}$	$88.1^*_{0.1}$	$+0.4$	$87.5_{1.1}$	$87.4_{1.1}$	-0.1
	RTE	$50.3_{4.2}$	$63.4^*_{1.1}$	$+13.1$	$89.7_{0.3}$	$89.4_{0.6}$	-0.3	$84.3_{0.7}$	$84.3_{0.7}$	$+0.0$
	CoLA	$85.9_{0.2}$	$84.9^*_{0.3}$	-1.0	$87.3_{1.6}$	$87.6_{1.2}$	$+0.3$	$87.3_{0.6}$	$87.6_{0.5}$	$+0.3$
	avg	84.5_1	$84.0_{1.9}$	-0.5	$89.6_{0.7}$	$89.7_{0.6}$	$+0.1$	$88.1_{0.8}$	$88.1_{0.8}$	$+0.0$
Others	TREC	$95.5_{1.7}$	$26.5^*_{18.2}$	-69.0	$95.8_{0.3}$	$96.0_{0.3}$	$+0.2$	$95.7_{1.0}$	$95.6_{1.0}$	-0.1
	DBPedia	99.1_0	$99.0^*_{0.1}$	-0.1	99.2_0	99.2_0	$+0.0$	$99.1_{0.1}$	$99.1_{0.1}$	$+0.0$
	Yelp	97.2_0	$97.1^*_{0.1}$	-0.1	$98.6_{0.1}$	$98.6_{0.1}$	$+0.0$	$98.4_{0.1}$	$98.4_{0.1}$	$+0.0$
	SQuADv2	N/A	N/A	N/A	$66.3_{0.9}$	$66.4_{0.9}$	$+0.1$	$63.8_{0.9}$	$63.8_{0.6}$	$+0.0$
	MATH	N/A	N/A	N/A	$36.8_{0.2}$	$36.9_{0.1}$	$+0.1$	$32.1_{0.1}$	$32.2_{0.1}$	$+0.1$

Task Prompts and Task Prompt Vectors Maintain Good Performance Even If They Do Not Always Point to the Exactly Same Location in the Task Subspace. To see whether the trained task prompts end up in the same task sub-space, we evaluate cosine similarity across multiple random initializations. We train multiple task prompts for 3 different random initializations and each source task (60 task prompts in total), and compute the cosine similarity from trained task prompts for each combination of random initializations and for each combination of tasks. We then average this cosine similarity for each task combination across all random initialization combinations. If task prompts are initialized from different random initializations and point in different directions in the task sub-space, we should also witness this phenomenon with their corresponding task prompt vectors. Therefore, we repeat this process for task prompt vectors.

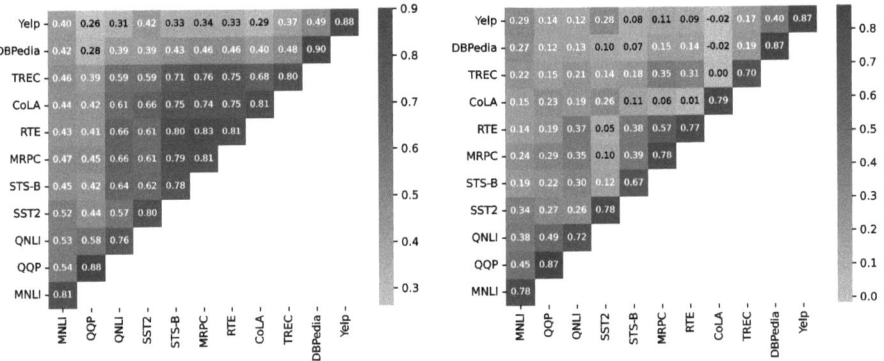

(a) Cosine similarities of *task prompts*.   (b) Cosine similarities of *task prompt vectors*.

Fig. 2. Comparison of average cosine similarities between task prompts and task prompt vectors fine-tuned on different tasks for the T5-base model. The average is calculated across all combinations of 3 random initializations (i.e., row QNLI column MNLI was calculated as the average of all cosine similarities between MNLI and QNLI for all initialization combinations, omitting the combinations of the same vectors). The diagonal represents the cosine similarities within the same task. It provides an estimate of natural in-task variation of task prompts and task prompt vectors, against which other similarities should be compared.

Results in Table 1 row 1 indicate that the downstream performance of prompt tuning on the source tasks across 3 different random initializations has a low standard deviation from the average. This shows that the task prompts end up in a subspace with sufficient task performance without necessarily residing in the same task subspace. In addition, we do not observe any difference in findings from experiments with NLI and NLG tasks.

Subsequently, Figs. 2a and 2b show the comparison of cosine similarities between task prompts and task prompt vectors from different tasks, averaged over all random initialization combinations. The cosine similarities on the diagonal serve as a baseline for comparison with the cross-task cosine similarities. We can see that cosine similarities for both task prompts as well as task prompt vectors are higher for combinations of tasks that are from similar problem domains or have similar labels and data structures. Another observation is that the cosine similarity of task prompts vectors provides a better measurement (in comparison with task prompts) of actual tasks' similarity as well as of the performance that can be achieved by a transfer between them (see also Fig. 3). For example, QNLI and TREC exhibit a relatively high similarity for their task prompts and a low similarity for task prompt vectors, which appropriately reflects their mutual diversity. In addition, we notice in Figs. 2a and 2b that task prompt vectors generally achieve lower cosine similarities than task prompts. Based on our results, we cannot determine the reason for this difference, and it can be a potential subject of future research.

More detailed and disaggregated cosine similarities of Figs. 2a and 2b can be found in Supplementary Material C, Figs. 1, and 2. We also evaluated cosine similarities of task prompts and task prompt vectors for LLaMa-3.1-8B-Instruct and DeepSeek-LLM-7B-Chat in Supplementary Material C in Figs. 3a, 3b, 4a, 4b.

Task Prompt Vectors from Similar Problems are More Similar. Additionally, we evaluate the similarity of different task prompt vectors across different tasks. Figure 2b shows that certain pairs of tasks are more similar than others, reflecting the shared properties of these tasks, such as the same number of classes, the same labels, or solving a similar problem. Problem similarity can be seen in the MNLI–QNLI task prompt vectors, and a similarity in the number of classes is observed in the MNLI task prompt vector, which tends to have higher cosine similarity with task prompt vectors for tasks with more classes (e.g., DBPedia, TREC). Increased similarity can also be seen in tasks that have common data formats (e.g., question-based QQP and QNLI). We also notice that MNLI-QQP and QNLI-QQP have even higher similarity than some tasks from common problems (e.g., MNLI–QNLI). This shows that the similarity of task prompt vectors may also appear for more dissimilar tasks. However, this phenomenon only appears in the case of the T5 model, but not necessarily in the results for LLaMa and DeepSeek models (available in Supplementary Material C).

4.3 Combination of Task Prompt Vectors via Addition for Multi-task Transfer

This section addresses the following research question: **RQ2: Can we combine multiple task prompt vectors and maintain multi-task performance on the source tasks?**

To answer this research question, we investigate the prompt arithmetics by task prompt vector addition on 55 task pair combinations from the set of NLU datasets (*MNLI, QQP, QNLI, SST2, STS-B, MRPC, RTE, CoLA, TREC Coarse, DBPedia, Yelp Polarity*). We also evaluate combinations of task prompt vectors in a simulated limited data environment by providing 0–100 training examples before evaluation on the test set.

Combinations of Task Prompt Vector Pairs Maintain Good Single-Task Performance on the Majority of Observed Task Combinations. To evaluate whether combinations of task prompt vectors maintain single-task performance, we conduct experiments where we create paired combinations from all source tasks (according to Eq. 4). We can see from the results in Fig. 3 that most binary classification tasks retain their single-task performance on both tasks, which implies that task prompt vectors can be used for

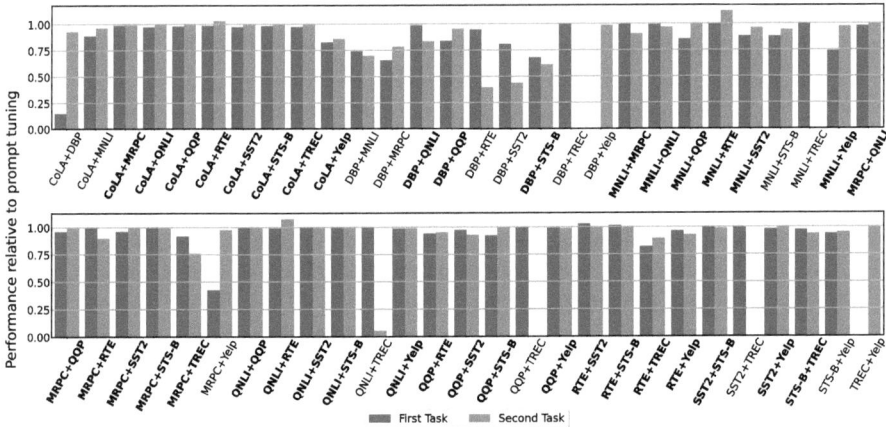

Fig. 3. Comparison of relative exact match performance of combinations of task prompt vectors across averaged across 3 different random initializations and all task combinations. The results are relative to the original single-task performance (1 is the performance of single-task prompt tuning). The task combinations in bold are the combinations that achieved over 50% of single-task performance on both of the tasks.

solving multi-task problems, and also corresponds with previous finding that state that some tasks are mutually beneficial [1, 45]. In some cases, the single-task performance was kept only for a single source task. This is, however, an expected behavior, because similar to other transfer learning approaches, a combination of task prompt vectors from too diverse tasks must inevitably end up in a negative transfer (e.g., for tasks with completely different features and meanings of labels). In some cases, the combination of two tasks even increased performance, for example, in the case of MNLI+RTE, possibly due to the shared task type (in this case, NLI/entailment). However, this increase is not clearly significant, as other NLI combinations do not show the same trend.

Task Prompt Vector Combinations are Good Initializations for Zero-Shot and Few-Shot Learning. We select two target tasks for inference classification (*SciTail, SNLI*), topic classification (*AG News, Yahoo Answers*), and sentiment classification (*SST5, IMDB*) while keeping the same set of source tasks. We compare initialization with randomly initialized soft prompts, soft prompts trained on single and multiple source tasks (equivalent to SPoT [45]), the multi-task ATTEMPT [1] method, and a combination of task prompt vectors of both of the source tasks.

The 0-shot and 100-shot results (Table 2) indicate that a combination of task prompt vectors can outperform initialization with a single-task source soft prompt on SciTail and IMDB, and the multi-task source soft prompt only for SciTail. The combination matches the SPoT baseline in cases like AG News, possibly because DBPedia and TREC together retain little TREC-specific information that could improve results. For SNLI, Yahoo Answers, and SST5 tasks, we can see that combinations of source task prompt vectors do almost match the results of the SPoT baseline.

ATTEMPT is also significantly underperforming when using a smaller set of pre-trained source soft prompts. Another observation is that ATTEMPT performs better on the AG News task. This may be caused by using the original implementation of ATTEMPT, where the authors, instead of using textual labels (i.e., "entailment", "not entailment"), used textual numbers as labels (i.e., "0", "1"), which makes the model predict numbers instead of specific words.

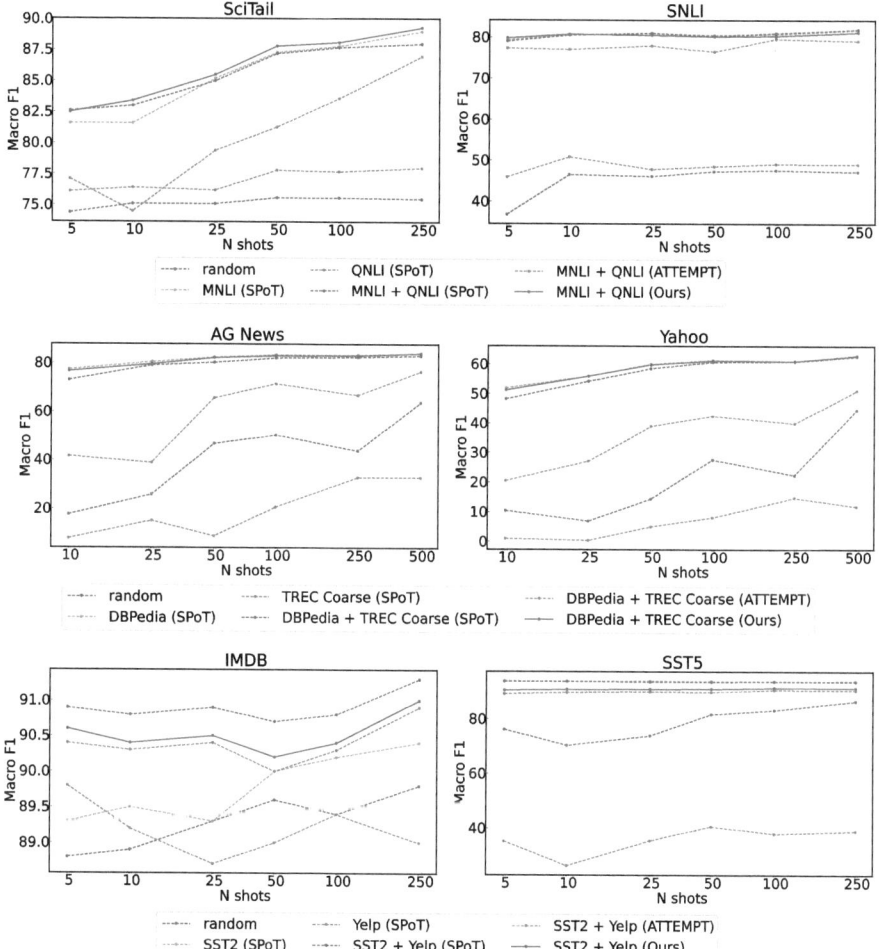

Fig. 4. Test results of training T5-base model with random, single, and multi-task soft prompt transfer (SPoT), multi-task ATTEMPT, and our task prompt vectors combination on increasing numbers of shots of data. We can see that for SciTail and IMDB tasks, a combination of task prompt vectors outperforms single task transfer.

4.4   Additional Results: Few-Shot Comparison

In this section, we study how increasing the number of demonstration data affects the performance of prompt tuning on a target task initialized by a combination of task prompt vectors of similar source tasks. We keep the same experiment setup as in the previous section and evaluate the soft prompt initialization on 5, 10, 25, 100, 250, and 500 shots.

The results in Fig. 4 indicate that the performance of the combination of task prompt vectors for SciTail and IMDB target tasks outperforms using a single-task initialization for multiple shots. We can also see that our method outperforms the multi-task initialization for the SciTail dataset across all shots of data.

Comparing the results from Fig. 3 and Fig. 4, if we choose a combination of tasks that maintains a significant amount of the source task performance (MNLI + QNLI and SST2 + Yelp), the few-shot performance of the task prompt vector combination tends to be higher than single-task transfer. In addition, we can see that in the case of the SST5 task, the SST2 initialization performs the best. We think that the reason for this may also be the similarity of SST5 and SST2, and that the combination of source tasks does not retain enough information to match the SST5 baseline.

5   Discussion and Limitations

Comparison of Task Prompt Vector Properties with Most Relevant PEFT Methods. Table 3 compares attributes beneficial for multi-task training for SPoT, ATTEMPT, and task prompt vector methods. SPoT exhibits low multi-task modularity, with a need to re-train the source soft prompt every time the set of source tasks changes. ATTEMPT, while having sufficient task modularity, depends heavily on the quality and number of source soft prompts. While task prompt vectors, in general, are able to match the results of full multi-task soft prompt transfer (SPoT), initialization of prompt tuning using task prompt vector combinations also retains high task modularity, which means that new tasks can be added without the necessity of training, ultimately decreasing computational costs considerably. **Task prompt vectors thus have both – modularity and source prompt independence – and also retain sufficient multi-task performance.**

High Reusability of the Task Prompt Vectors. In our experiments, we demonstrated multiple important properties of task prompt vectors. At first, we showed (Sect. 4.2) that task prompts and their corresponding task prompt vectors from different initializations do not necessarily point to the same space and that some vector combinations are more similar than others. Despite that, task prompt vectors created from one initialization and applied to a different initialization maintain their performance for the majority of observed tasks. The implication of this finding means that **it is possible to combine different task prompt vectors from different initializations**.

Furthermore, we showed (Sect. 4.3) that combinations of task prompt vectors for similar tasks maintain their source single-task performance (Fig. 3) and that the combinations of **task prompt vectors can be used for initialization of prompt tuning** in low resource settings (zero-/few-shot settings) on the set of target tasks (Table 2).

Table 2. Test results of training T5-base model with random, single- and multi-task soft prompt transfer (SPoT), multi-task ATTEMPT, and our task prompt vectors on 0-shot and 100-shot data for all of our observed source and target tasks. We show the initialization with different combinations for NLI classification, topic classification, and sentiment classification. The subscript represents the standard deviation from the average. The best results are bold, while the second-best results are underlined. The * in the superscript represents that the results are statistically significant from the second-best result, by two-sample Student's t-test [43].

SciTail (NLI)			SNLI (NLI)		
Source tasks	F1		Source tasks	F1	
	0 shots	100 shots		0 shots	100 shots
Random	$54.9_{6.6}$	$75.6_{0.5}$	Random	$46.5_{1.5}$	$47.6_{1.9}$
MNLI (SPoT)	$\underline{70.4_{0.4}}$	$\underline{87.8_{0.9}}$	MNLI (SPoT)	$\underline{79.5_{0.3}}$	$\underline{80.8_{0.4}}$
QNLI (SPoT)	$57.7_{13.1}$	$77.7_{1.3}$	QNLI (SPoT)	$47.1_{0.3}$	$49.1_{0.9}$
QNLI + MNLI (SPoT)	$70.4_{1.2}$	$87.7_{0.6}$	QNLI + MNLI (SPoT)	$\mathbf{79.6_{0.2}}^*$	$\mathbf{81_{0.4}}^*$
QNLI + MNLI (ATTEMPT)	$63.8_{4.2}$	83.6_3	QNLI + MNLI (ATTEMPT)	$78.5_{0.5}$	$79.6_{1.6}$
QNLI + MNLI (ours)	$\mathbf{71.5_{0.8}}^*$	$\mathbf{88.1_{0.9}}$	QNLI + MNLI (ours)	$79.2_{1.4}$	$80.3_{0.3}$

AG News (Topic)			Yahoo Answers (Topic)		
Source tasks	F1		Source tasks	F1	
	0 shots	100 shots		0 shots	100 shots
Random	0_0	$50.4_{11.2}$	Random	0_0	$27.6_{10.6}$
DBPedia (SPoT)	0_0	$\mathbf{83.4_{0.6}}^*$	DBPedia (SPoT)	0_0	$\mathbf{61.3_{1.1}}^*$
TREC (SPoT)	0_0	$65.7_{5.6}$	TREC (SPoT)	0_0	$36.5_{8.7}$
DBPedia + TREC (SPoT)	0_0	$82.1_{0.9}$	DBPedia + TREC (SPoT)	0_0	60.7_2
DBPedia + TREC (ATTEMPT)	$\mathbf{11.5_{1.7}}$	$20.7_{2.8}$	DBPedia + TREC (ATTEMPT)	$\mathbf{0.1_0}$	$8.1_{5.6}$
DBPedia + TREC (ours)	0_0	$\underline{83_{0.9}}$	DBPedia + TREC (ours)	0_0	$\underline{61.1_{0.9}}$

IMDB (Sentiment)			SST5 (Sentiment)		
Source tasks	F1		Source tasks	F1	
	0 shots	100 shots		0 shots	100 shots
Random	$77.2_{9.6}$	$89.4_{0.4}$	Random	0_0	$83.2_{5.8}$
SST2 (SPoT)	$88_{0.6}$	$90.2_{0.3}$	SST2 (SPoT)	$\mathbf{94_{0.3}}^*$	$\mathbf{93.9_{0.3}}^*$
Yelp (SPoT)	$90_{0.3}$	$90.3_{0.2}$	Yelp (SPoT)	$88.6_{0.8}$	$90.6_{0.5}$
SST2 + Yelp (SPoT)	$\mathbf{90.8_{0.2}}$	$\mathbf{90.8_{0.2}}$	SST2 + Yelp (SPoT)	$\underline{93.7_{0.5}}$	$\underline{93.8_{0.5}}$
SST2 + Yelp (ATTEMPT)	79.2_6	$89.4_{0.8}$	SST2 + Yelp (ATTEMPT)	$16.4_{4.5}$	37.8_7
SST2 + Yelp (ours)	$\underline{90.1_{0.5}}$	$\underline{90.4_{0.2}}$	SST2 + Yelp (ours)	$89.9_{0.8}$	$91.5_{0.5}$

Table 3. Task prompt vectors maintain high task modularity and multi-task performance and are independent of the number of pre-trained source soft prompts.

Method	Modularity	Multi-task performance	Source prompt independence
SPoT	✗	✓	✓
ATTEMPT	✓	✓	✗
TPV (ours)	✓	✓	✓

Based on both of these observations, we can very effectively re-use pre-trained task prompt vectors for different tasks and use them in downstream scenarios (even without a need for any further training). Since task prompt vectors are independent of their initialization, we can also **re-use pre-trained task prompt vectors shared by other researchers and practitioners** (e.g., on a designated vector hub).

Identification of Appropriate Source Task Prompt Vectors. High reusability of task prompt vectors, however, requires identifying an appropriate source task prompt vector or a combination of them. To identify such a single vector/a combination of vectors, we propose to perform an evaluation on held-out validation sets. Another possible factor that can be included in the identification of an appropriate combination is the similarity of combined tasks. This similarity can be determined by data analysis by looking at commonalities in the task domain, data structure, or labels. Additionally, similarity can be quantified using the cosine similarities of task prompt vectors, which tend to correlate better with the resulting performance when compared to task prompts.

Theoretical Implications and Analysis. It lies beyond the scope of our work to further deliver theoretical analyses for diverse properties of task prompt vectors, which we will leave for future work. However, we still want to discuss some hypotheses that arise from the empirical results achieved during the experiments with task prompt vectors.

At first, we can derive from the obtained findings that the **sub-space with optimal values in the soft prompt space has probably a convex shape**. This may be indicated by the fact that task prompts trained from different random initializations for the same task do not necessarily point in the same direction (based on Figs. 2a and 2b), but still achieve identical results.

Second, prompt arithmetics (task prompt vector addition) is possible even though the soft prompt space is non-linear. The rationale behind this could be that **task prompt vectors are linear approximations of how soft prompts change** during training. Another possibility may be that the task prompt vectors are sparse, and a combination of 2 sparse task prompt vectors creates a vector that contains more information about both tasks. These findings can be further useful for **machine unlearning tasks**, where one could also exploit task prompt vector subtraction.

Limitations. To keep our focus on the evaluation of task prompt vectors, we utilize only monolingual models in the scope of our work, as well as 12 NLU and 2 NLG datasets in the English language only. Extension to multilingual models and datasets may reveal additional interesting findings about task prompt vectors features in multilingual settings.

In this work, we employed the set of 3 common NLU problems, each covering 4 different tasks, and 2 common NLG problems, covering 2 different tasks. We consider this set as sufficient to evaluate the properties of task prompt vectors, also taking computational costs into account – adding more tasks would also result in more computational costs. Nevertheless, additional tasks may still strengthen findings presented in this paper.

Even though there are many other PLMs capable of conditional generation that beat T5 models in performance on various benchmarks, we focus our experiments on the T5-

base model as it is commonly used as a representative model in many PEFT methods. Additional experiments on a larger set of models, therefore, represent another potential extension of our work.

6   Conclusion

In our work, we introduce and investigate task prompt vectors as a method of multi-task transfer from prompt tuning. We show that the task prompt vectors are not dependent on random initialization and that the performance across different random initializations does not change significantly in the majority of observed source tasks. We show that for similar and mutually related tasks, the combination via arithmetic addition maintains the single-task performance or even improves it. Finally, we show that certain combinations of task prompt vectors can be a better option for initialization for certain tasks while maintaining higher multi-task modularity than other soft prompt-based methods like SPoT and ATTEMPT.

In the future, we would like to evaluate the cross-model performance of task prompt vectors. We think that further experiments with generation tasks may be another interesting extension. Moreover, task prompt vector arithmetic has the highest potential for improving the unlearning in PLMs by negating the task prompt vectors for the tasks we want to unlearn. Such an option is enabled by introducing task prompt vectors, which would not be possible with the existing state-of-the-art methods.

Acknowledgments. This work was partially funded by European Union under the project DisAI, GA No. 101079164, and the project CEDMO 2.0, GA No. 101158609; by the European Union NextGenerationEU through the Recovery and Resilience Plan for Slovakia under the project No. 09I01-03-V04-00006; and by the Slovak Research and Development Agency under the Contract no. APVV-22-0414.

Part of the research results was obtained using the computational resources procured in the national project funded by the Ministry of Education, Youth and Sports of the Czech Republic through the e-INFRA CZ (ID:90254); and the national project National competence centre for high performance computing (project code: 311070AKF2) funded by ERDF, EU Structural Funds Informatization of Society, Operational Program Integrated Infrastructure.

The authors also wish to acknowledge the TAILOR project funded by the European Union under the EU Horizon 2020, GA No. 952215, which supported the research mobility that started the collaboration on this paper under the TAILOR Connectivity fund.

References

1. Asai, A., Salehi, M., Peters, M., Hajishirzi, H.: ATTEMPT: parameter-efficient multi-task tuning via attentional mixtures of soft prompts. In: Goldberg, Y., Kozareva, Z., Zhang, Y. (eds.) Proceedings of the 2022 Conference on EMNLP, pp. 6655–6672. ACL, Abu Dhabi (2022). https://doi.org/10.18653/v1/2022.emnlp-main.446
2. Auer, S., Bizer, C., Kobilarov, G., Lehmann, J., Cyganiak, R., Ives, Z.: DBpedia: a nucleus for a web of open data. In: Aberer, K., et al. (eds.) ISWC ASWC 2007. LNCS, vol. 4825, pp. 722–735. Springer, Heidelberg (2007). https://doi.org/10.1007/978-3-540-76298-0_52

3. Bi, X., et al.: DeepSeek LLM: scaling open-source language models with longtermism. arXiv preprint arXiv:2401.02954 (2024)
4. Bowman, S.R., Angeli, G., Potts, C., Manning, C.D.: A large annotated corpus for learning natural language inference. In: Proceedings of the 2015 Conference on EMNLP (EMNLP). ACL (2015)
5. Brown, T., et al.: Language models are few-shot learners. Adv. Neural. Inf. Process. Syst. **33**, 1877–1901 (2020)
6. Cer, D., Diab, M., Agirre, E., Lopez-Gazpio, I., Specia, L.: SemEval-2017 task 1: semantic textual similarity multilingual and crosslingual focused evaluation. In: Bethard, S., Carpuat, M., Apidianaki, M., Mohammad, S.M., Cer, D., Jurgens, D. (eds.) Proceedings of the 11th International Workshop on Semantic Evaluation (SemEval-2017), pp. 1–14. ACL, Vancouver (2017). https://doi.org/10.18653/v1/S17-2001
7. Chronopoulou, A., Pfeiffer, J., Maynez, J., Wang, X., Ruder, S., Agrawal, P.: Language and task arithmetic with parameter-efficient layers for zero-shot summarization. arXiv preprint arXiv:2311.09344 (2023)
8. Costa-Jussà, M.R., et al.: No language left behind: scaling human-centered machine translation. arXiv preprint arXiv:2207.04672 (2022)
9. Davari, M., Belilovsky, E.: Model breadcrumbs: scaling multi-task model merging with sparse masks (2023). arXiv:2312.06795 [cs]
10. Dolan, W.B., Brockett, C.: Automatically constructing a corpus of sentential paraphrases. In: Proceedings of the International Workshop on Paraphrasing (2005)
11. Dubey, A., et al.: The LLaMA 3 herd of models. arXiv preprint arXiv:2407.21783 (2024)
12. Dunn, O.J.: Confidence intervals for the means of dependent, normally distributed variables. J. Am. Stat. Assoc. **54**(287), 613–621 (1959)
13. Fourrier, C., Habib, N., Wolf, T., Tunstall, L.: LightEval: a lightweight framework for LLM evaluation (2023). https://github.com/huggingface/lighteval
14. Frankle, J., Dziugaite, G.K., Roy, D., Carbin, M.: Linear mode connectivity and the lottery ticket hypothesis. In: ICML, pp. 3259–3269. PMLR (2020)
15. Gu, Y., Han, X., Liu, Z., Huang, M.: PPT: pre-trained prompt tuning for few-shot learning. In: Muresan, S., Nakov, P., Villavicencio, A. (eds.) Proceedings of the 60th Annual Meeting of the ACL (Volume 1: Long Papers), pp. 8410–8423. ACL, Dublin (2022). https://doi.org/10.18653/v1/2022.acl-long.576
16. Gurgurov, D., Vykopal, I., van Genabith, J., Ostermann, S.: Small models, big impact: efficient corpus and graph-based adaptation of small multilingual language models for low-resource languages. arXiv preprint arXiv:2502.10140 (2025)
17. Houlsby, N., et al.: Parameter-efficient transfer learning for NLP. In: ICML, pp. 2790–2799. PMLR (2019)
18. Hovy, E., Gerber, L., Hermjakob, U., Lin, C.Y., Ravichandran, D.: Toward semantics-based answer pinpointing. In: Proceedings of the First International Conference on Human Language Technology Research (2001)
19. Hu, E.J., et al.: LoRA: low-rank adaptation of large language models. In: ICLR (2022). https://openreview.net/forum?id=nZeVKeeFYf9
20. Ilharco, G., Ribeiro, M.T., Wortsman, M., Schmidt, L., Hajishirzi, H., Farhadi, A.: Editing models with task arithmetic. In: The Eleventh ICLR (2022)
21. Khot, T., Sabharwal, A., Clark, P.: SciTaiL: a textual entailment dataset from science question answering. In: AAAI Conference on Artificial Intelligence (2018). https://api.semanticscholar.org/CorpusID:24462950
22. Klimaszewski, M., Andruszkiewicz, P., Birch, A.: No train but gain: language arithmetic for training-free language adapters enhancement. arXiv preprint arXiv:2404.15737 (2024)

23. Lee, H., Jeong, M., Yun, S.Y., Kim, K.E.: Bayesian multi-task transfer learning for soft prompt tuning. In: Bouamor, H., Pino, J., Bali, K. (eds.) Findings of the ACL: EMNLP 2023, pp. 4942–4958. ACL, Singapore (2023). https://doi.org/10.18653/v1/2023.findings-emnlp.329

24. Lester, B., Al-Rfou, R., Constant, N.: The power of scale for parameter-efficient prompt tuning. In: Moens, M.F., Huang, X., Specia, L., Yih, S.W.T. (eds.) Proceedings of the 2021 Conference on EMNLP, pp. 3045–3059. ACL, Online and Punta Cana (2021). https://doi.org/10.18653/v1/2021.emnlp-main.243

25. Li, M., et al.: Branch-train-merge: embarrassingly parallel training of expert language models (2022). arXiv:2208.03306 [cs]

26. Li, X.L., Liang, P.: Prefix-tuning: Optimizing continuous prompts for generation. In: Zong, C., Xia, F., Li, W., Navigli, R. (eds.) Proceedings of the 59th Annual Meeting of the ACL and the 11th International Joint Conference on Natural Language Processing (Volume 1: Long Papers), pp. 4582–4597. ACL, Online (2021). https://doi.org/10.18653/v1/2021.acl-long.353

27. Li, X., Roth, D.: Learning question classifiers. In: COLING 2002: The 19th International Conference on Computational Linguistics (2002)

28. Liu, X., et al.: GPT understands, too. AI Open (2023)

29. Liu, Y., et al.: RoBERTa: a robustly optimized BERT pretraining approach. arXiv preprint arXiv:1907.11692 (2019)

30. Maas, A.L., Daly, R.E., Pham, P.T., Huang, D., Ng, A.Y., Potts, C.: Learning word vectors for sentiment analysis. In: Lin, D., Matsumoto, Y., Mihalcea, R. (eds.) Proceedings of the 49th Annual Meeting of the ACL: Human Language Technologies, pp. 142–150. ACL, Portland (2011)

31. Matena, M., Raffel, C.: Merging models with fisher-weighted averaging (2022). arXiv:2111.09832 [cs]

32. Ortiz-Jimenez, G., Favero, A., Frossard, P.: Task arithmetic in the tangent space: improved editing of pre-trained models. In: Advances in Neural Information Processing Systems, vol. 36 (2024)

33. Pecher, B., Srba, I., Bielikova, M.: Comparing specialised small and general large language models on text classification: 100 labelled samples to achieve break-even performance. arXiv preprint arXiv:2402.12819 (2024)

34. Pfeiffer, J., Kamath, A., Rücklé, A., Cho, K., Gurevych, I.: AdapterFusion: non-destructive task composition for transfer learning. In: Merlo, P., Tiedemann, J., Tsarfaty, R. (eds.) Proceedings of the 16th Conference of the European Chapter of the ACL: Main Volume, pp. 487–503. ACL, Online (2021). https://doi.org/10.18653/v1/2021.eacl-main.39

35. Qin, Y., et al.: Exploring universal intrinsic task subspace for few-shot learning via prompt tuning. IEEE/ACM Trans. Audio, Speech and Lang. Process. 32, 3631–3643 (2024). https://doi.org/10.1109/TASLP.2024.3430545

36. Radford, A., Wu, J., Child, R., Luan, D., Amodei, D., Sutskever, I., et al.: Language models are unsupervised multitask learners. OpenAI blog 1(8), 9 (2019)

37. Raffel, C., Shazeer, N., Roberts, A., Lee, K., Narang, S., Matena, M., Zhou, Y., Li, W., Liu, P.J.: Exploring the limits of transfer learning with a unified text-to-text transformer. J. Mach. Learn. Res. 21(140), 1–67 (2020)

38. Rajpurkar, P., Jia, R., Liang, P.: Know what you don't know: unanswerable questions for SQuAD. In: Gurevych, I., Miyao, Y. (eds.) Proceedings of the 56th Annual Meeting of the ACL (Volume 2: Short Papers), pp. 784–789. ACL, Melbourne (2018). https://doi.org/10.18653/v1/P18-2124

39. Ramé, A., Ahuja, K., Zhang, J., Cord, M., Bottou, L., Lopez-Paz, D.: Model ratatouille: recycling diverse models for out-of-distribution generalization. In: ICML, pp. 28656–28679. PMLR (2023)

40. Shi, Z., Lipani, A.: DePT: decomposed prompt tuning for parameter-efficient fine-tuning. In: The Twelfth ICLR (2024). https://openreview.net/forum?id=KjegfPGRde
41. Socher, R., et al.: Recursive deep models for semantic compositionality over a sentiment treebank. In: Proceedings of the 2013 Conference on EMNLP, pp. 1631–1642 (2013)
42. Stoica, G., Bolya, D., Bjorner, J., Ramesh, P., Hearn, T., Hoffman, J.: ZipIt! Merging models from different tasks without training (2024). arXiv:2305.03053 [cs]
43. Student: The probable error of a mean. Biometrika 1–25 (1908)
44. Su, Y., et al.: On transferability of prompt tuning for natural language processing. In: Carpuat, M., de Marneffe, M.C., Meza Ruiz, I.V. (eds.) Proceedings of the 2022 Conference of the North American Chapter of the ACL: Human Language Technologies, pp. 3949–3969. ACL, Seattle (2022). https://doi.org/10.18653/v1/2022.naacl-main.290
45. Vu, T., Lester, B., Constant, N., Al-Rfou', R., Cer, D.: SPoT: better frozen model adaptation through soft prompt transfer. In: Muresan, S., Nakov, P., Villavicencio, A. (eds.) Proceedings of the 60th Annual Meeting of the ACL (Volume 1: Long Papers), pp. 5039–5059. ACL, Dublin, Ireland (2022). https://doi.org/10.18653/v1/2022.acl-long.346
46. Wang, A., Singh, A., Michael, J., Hill, F., Levy, O., Bowman, S.: GLUE: a multi-task benchmark and analysis platform for natural language understanding. In: Linzen, T., Chrupała, G., Alishahi, A. (eds.) Proceedings of the 2018 EMNLP Workshop BlackboxNLP: Analyzing and Interpreting Neural Networks for NLP, pp. 353–355. ACL, Brussels (2018). https://doi.org/10.18653/v1/W18-5446
47. Wang, Z., Panda, R., Karlinsky, L., Feris, R., Sun, H., Kim, Y.: Multitask prompt tuning enables parameter-efficient transfer learning. In: The Eleventh ICLR (2023). https://openreview.net/forum?id=Nk2pDtuhTq
48. Warstadt, A., Singh, A., Bowman, S.R.: Neural network acceptability judgments. Trans. ACL 7, 625–641 (2019). https://doi.org/10.1162/tacl_a_00290
49. Williams, A., Nangia, N., Bowman, S.: A broad-coverage challenge corpus for sentence understanding through inference. In: Walker, M., Ji, H., Stent, A. (eds.) Proceedings of the 2018 Conference of the North American Chapter of the ACL: Human Language Technologies, Volume 1 (Long Papers), pp. 1112–1122. ACL, New Orleans (2018). https://doi.org/10.18653/v1/N18-1101
50. Wortsman, M., et al.: Robust fine-tuning of zero-shot models. In: Proceedings of the IEEE/CVF Conference on Computer Vision and Pattern Recognition, pp. 7959–7971 (2022)
51. Xu, L., Xie, H., Qin, S.Z.J., Tao, X., Wang, F.L.: Parameter-efficient fine-tuning methods for pretrained language models: a critical review and assessment. arXiv preprint arXiv:2312.12148 (2023)
52. Zhang, J., Liu, J., He, J., et al.: Composing parameter-efficient modules with arithmetic operation. Adv. Neural. Inf. Process. Syst. 36, 12589–12610 (2023)
53. Zhang, X., Zhao, J., LeCun, Y.: Character-level convolutional networks for text classification. Adv. Neural. Inf. Process. Syst. 28 (2015)

Gradient Similarity Surgery in Multi-task Deep Learning

Thomas Borsani[1]([✉]) [iD], Andrea Rosani[1] [iD], Giuseppe Nicosia[2] [iD], and Giuseppe Di Fatta[1] [iD]

[1] Free University of Bozen-Bolzano, Bozen-Bolzano, Italy
`{tborsani,Andrea.Rosani,Giuseppe.DiFatta}@unibz.it`
[2] University of Catania, Catania, Italy
`nicosia@dmi.unict.it`

Abstract. The multi-task learning (MTL) paradigm aims to simultaneously learn multiple tasks within a single model capturing higher-level, more general hidden patterns that are shared by the tasks. In deep learning, a significant challenge in the backpropagation training process is the design of advanced optimisers to improve the convergence speed and stability of the gradient descent learning rule. In particular, in multi-task deep learning ($MTDL$) the multitude of tasks may generate potentially *conflicting gradients* that would hinder the concurrent convergence of the diverse loss functions. This challenge arises when the gradients of the task objectives have either different magnitudes or opposite directions, causing one or a few to dominate or to interfere with each other, thus degrading the training process. Gradient surgery methods address the problem explicitly dealing with conflicting gradients by adjusting the overall gradient trajectory. This work introduces a novel gradient surgery method, the Similarity-Aware Momentum Gradient Surgery (SAM-GS), which provides an effective and scalable approach based on a gradient magnitude similarity measure to guide the optimisation process. The SAM-GS surgery adopts gradient equalisation and modulation of the first-order momentum. A series of experimental tests have shown the effectiveness of SAM-GS on synthetic problems and MTL benchmarks. Gradient magnitude similarity plays a crucial role in *regularising gradient aggregation* in $MTDL$ for the optimisation of the learning process. Code is available at https://unibzmlgroup.github.io/SAMGS/.

Keywords: Multi-Task Deep Learning · Gradient Descent Optimisation · Gradient Surgery · Gradient Aggregation · Conflicting Gradients

---

Supplementary Information The online version contains supplementary material available at https://doi.org/10.1007/978-3-662-72243-5_6.

1   Introduction

In the multi-task learning (MTL) paradigm [1] a model is trained on multiple tasks simultaneously, leveraging a shared internal representation to improve generalisation and efficiency. While training a model for a single task leverages on patterns in the data, training on multiple tasks also leverages on patterns in the tasks. MTL exploits task similarities to enhance performance, particularly when tasks share some underlying features. Utilising a shared representation for many tasks allows to improve model generalisation by capturing features that are more resilient to noise compared to a single-task approach. This concurrent learning process acts as a regularisation mechanism, reducing bias and strengthening the robustness of the model. Additionally, this approach is advantageous when data availability is particularly heterogeneous across tasks, as it enables the aggregation of data from many tasks to improve overall learning. Moreover, MTL can lead to a reduction in computational costs, training and inference time, but this depends on the specific implementation and task relationships.

The MTL paradigm has been successfully applied to many problems across various domains, including Natural Language Processing [26,34], Computer Vision [4,33], Healthcare and Medical Imaging [14,15], Fraud Detection and Finance [25]. These applications demonstrate how MTL can improve generalisation, reduce data requirements, and enhance model efficiency across diverse real-world problems. Nevertheless, there are challenges to effectively training MTL models, particularly in selecting and combining tasks, as different tasks may not always align seamlessly to produce better solutions [32].

Recent research has evidenced that one of the primary challenges for the optimisation of MTL models is the aggregation of the different gradients associated to the task-specific loss functions [37]. Typically, the task gradients are aggregated using the arithmetic mean. Indeed, it has been shown that this approach can lead to suboptimal solutions [32,37]. The underlying cause have been identified in the challenges arising from the aggregation of conflicting task gradients, i.e. gradients with opposite directions (*angle-based conflicting gradients*) and gradients dominating the aggregation (*magnitude conflicting gradients*) [37].

Current solutions to address the problem of conflicting gradients can be categorised into three sub-groups. *Task Similarity* methods focus on the selection of tasks that do not cause gradient conflicts [12,39]. *Loss Balancing* methods focus on static or dynamic weighting algorithms to weight the different loss functions [2,19], and *Gradient Surgery* methods seek to mitigate gradient conflicts by applying heuristics that modify the gradient descent learning rule to reduce their impact [20,24,37].

However, methods of *Task Similarity* tend to be computationally inefficient and limit MTL applicability, serving primarily to avoid the problem rather than addressing it to optimise the potential benefits offered by MTL models. *Loss Balancing* methods, while effective and more efficient than task similarity methods in addressing the problem [19], still ignore its underlying causes. *Gradient Surgery* methods tackle gradient conflicts directly and have been shown to be among the most effective strategies to optimise MTL models [21,24,27]. Most of these methods, however, apply the procedure indiscriminately, overlooking the proper identification of gradient conflicts, which can lead to a deterioration of the original gradient-based learning process. Additionally, some of these methodologies excessively level out the relative contributions of the tasks to the overall gradient, and inevitably miss out the inherent advantage of MTL, where tasks may provide complementary contributions in the shared representation.

To address the issue of conflicting gradients while accounting for the varying nature of task loss functions, we introduce a novel gradient surgery method, the Similarity-Aware Momentum Gradient Surgery (SAM-GS). This method dynamically adapts the gradient descent optimisation process based on the task gradient magnitude similarity. The proposed approach applies a conservative learning when gradients are dissimilar and accelerates learning when they exhibit high similarity. SAM-GS integrates gradient equalisation within conflicting scenarios and incorporates a gradient momentum, whose influence is adaptively modulated based on the task gradient similarity. Comparative experimental results demonstrate that this adaptive strategy enhances stability and efficiency in learning dynamics, yielding superior performance across diverse MTL benchmarks.

Key contributions of the proposed SAM-GS method are as follows:

- *SAM-GS Optimisation*: Introduction of a gradient similarity measure to selectively adjust gradient magnitudes, enhancing the learning process.
- *Momentum-Based Regularisation*: Integration of gradient momentum into gradient surgery, introducing a new regularisation for conflicting gradients, improving the optimisation dynamics.
- *Empirical Validation*: Analysis on synthetic problems and evaluation on four standard MTL benchmarks, achieving comparable or improving state-of-the-art (SOTA) performance over existing methods.

The remainder of the paper is organised as follows. In Sect. 2, we present the problem of conflicting gradients in $MTDL$ and the solution offered by gradient surgery methods. In Sect. 3, we discuss related work in terms of the three approaches, task similarity, load balancing and gradient surgery, to compare and contrast them. In Sect. 4, the proposed SAM-GS method is introduced and its main algorithm described. In Sect. 5, we present an experimental and comparative analysis of the proposed method with respect to other gradient surgery methods. Section 6 provides the main conclusions and indicates some areas of improvement.

2   *MTL* Optimisation

In this section, we introduce the definition of the multi-task learning paradigm, discuss the specific challenge referred to as *conflicting gradients* in deep learning models, and provide an overview of gradient surgery methods.

The MTL paradigm aims to optimise a single model $\theta \in \mathbb{R}^m$ for $K \geq 2$ numbers of tasks simultaneously. In general, the objective is to minimise the sum of the task-specific loss functions $\mathcal{L}_i(\theta) : \mathbb{R}^m \to \mathbb{R}_+$

$$\arg\min_{\theta \in \mathbb{R}^m} \left\{ \mathcal{L}_{mtl}(\theta) := \sum_{i=1}^{K} \mathcal{L}_i(\theta) \right\} \tag{1}$$

The training of a MTL model through direct optimisation of the Eq. (1) may yield to sub-optimal solutions, characterised by under-optimised tasks [37]. More specifically, MTL can be framed as a multi-objective optimisation problem [7], where optimising Eq. (1) may result in solutions that are not Pareto-efficient. In deep network models the literature has identified gradient conflicts as one of the primary causes of this sub-optimisation issue [37].

2.1   Conflicting Gradients in $MTDL$

In training deep learning models on multiple tasks simultaneously, the issue of conflicting gradients arises when different tasks produce gradients that interfere with each other, leading to inefficient or suboptimal learning. This detrimental interference hinders the performance of the model across tasks.

Two main types of conflicting gradients can be identified, respectively, caused by the relative direction of the task gradient vectors and by their different magnitudes.

Angle-Based Gradient Conflict. Let $g_i, g_j \in \mathbb{R}^d$ be the gradient vectors associated with two different tasks i and j. We define an *angle-based gradient conflict* as occurring when the angle ϕ_{ij}, in Eq. (2), between them is greater than $90°$, which corresponds to a negative cosine similarity. In this situation, the vector sum reduces the net effective learning step, slowing convergence [37].

$$\cos(\phi_{ij}) = \frac{g_i \cdot g_j}{\|g_i\|\|g_j\|} < 0. \tag{2}$$

In this scenario, the least critical case occurs when the gradients from different tasks are nearly orthogonal to each other. This still results in inefficient learning since updates get diluted rather than reinforcing progress in the common direction. The most critical case arises when the gradients from different tasks are perfectly opposite to each other, resulting in a zero vector and effectively preventing learning.

Magnitude Gradient Conflict. Let $g_i, g_j \in \mathbb{R}^d$ be the gradient vectors associated with two different tasks i and j. We quantify the *magnitude gradient conflict* by means of the magnitude similarity defined in Eq. (3):

$$\psi(g_i, g_j) = \frac{2\|g_i\|_2\|g_j\|_2}{\|g_i\|_2^2 + \|g_j\|_2^2}. \tag{3}$$

A magnitude gradient conflict occurs when the gradients associated with different tasks have significantly varying magnitudes. This imbalance can cause the model to prioritise certain tasks over others, leading to suboptimal performance.

In contrast to the *angle-based gradient conflict*, where it is clearly defined when two gradients are in conflict (i.e., negative cosine similarity), the detection of magnitude-based gradient conflicts is less straightforward. Dissimilarities in task gradient magnitudes may not be due to actual conflicts but to the lack of loss normalisation or to local topological differences in loss functions across the tasks.

2.2   Gradient Surgery Methods

Gradient surgery methods provide a heuristic aggregation function over the task gradient vectors to compute the overall gradient driving the weight update rule. The surgery function is aimed at optimising all tasks effectively by limiting the effect of gradient conflicts. We introduce a generic task gradient aggregation function, which determines how gradients from different tasks are combined according to the surgery method. The gradient of the total loss with respect to the weight matrix θ at layer is l is: $\nabla_{\theta^{(l)}}\mathcal{L} = s\left(\nabla_{\theta^{(l)}}\mathcal{L}_1, \nabla_{\theta^{(l)}}\mathcal{L}_2, \ldots, \nabla_{\theta^{(l)}}\mathcal{L}_K\right)$, where $s(\cdot)$ is a task gradient aggregation function that determines how the individual task gradients contribute to the overall optimisation.

3   Related Works

Existing solutions to deal with gradients conflicts can been categorised in three main groups, as follows.

Task Similarity. The optimisation via Task Similarity methods aims to group tasks that can be learned synergistically, thereby improving overall model performance. It is also possible that the best solution does not involve using one MTL model to solve K tasks, but rather employing K single-task models, which may lead to better outcomes [12,28,29,32,39]. In this approach, gradient conflicts are avoided by selecting a suitable combination of tasks that do not present conflicts.

Loss Balancing. Loss Balancing methods relies on weighting the different loss functions of the tasks involved in the combination. Various methodologies have been proposed to determine the optimal weights for different tasks. The method **UW** [5] leverages the homoscedastic uncertainty of each task to determine the weights , while **DWA** [22] utilises rate of change of task-specific loss functions. **GradNorm** [2] modulates weights based on the magnitude of the gradient. In contrast to these approaches, **RLW** [18] assigns random weights. Additionally, **FAMO** [19] learns the weights based on the quality of the loss updates. These methods mitigates gradient conflicts by preventing any single task from dominating the training process.

Gradient Surgery. These methods aim to enhance convergence in MTL by appropriately weighting the gradient components of different tasks. They focus on introducing heuristics to adjust the combination of gradient vectors, thereby influencing the optimisation process dynamics to resolve the conflicts and guiding the model more effectively through the loss landscape. Approaches like **Nash-MTL** [24] utilise game theory concepts, particularly the Nash Bargaining Solution, to equilibrate task gradients. Instead, **MGDA** [8,10] for MTL seeks a direction that minimises all objectives simultaneously, in line with the multi-objective Karush–Kuhn–Tucker (KKT) [17] conditions. These methods are computationally intensive but have proven to be effective.

Alternative approaches aim to mitigate gradient conflicts. **GDOD** [9] decomposes task gradients into shared and conflicting components, updating only the shared ones. **PCGrad** [37] reduces conflicts among task gradients by decorrelating them while **CAGrad** [20] seeks a conflict-averse gradient path to minimise task interference. **GradDrop** [3] ensures consistency in gradient signs across tasks. In addition, **IMTL** [21] identifies a gradient path in which cosine similarities among task gradients remain consistent, and **Aligned-MTL** [27] mitigates conflicts by aligning the principal components of the gradient matrix. These methods compete effectively with the more complex Nash-MTL [24] showing better performance maintaining low computational overhead.

4   Similarity-Aware Momentum Gradient Surgery

Similarity-Aware Momentum Gradient Surgery (SAM-GS) is a gradient surgery method that leverages a measure of the magnitude similarity of the task gradients to detect and address conflicts during the learning process.

Here, we first present the intuition behind the approach with an example with four scenarios, and then we introduce the SAM-GS algorithm.

The proposed approach focuses solely on *magnitude gradient conflicts*, which are arguably critical to effective $MTDL$ optimisation. *Angle-based gradient conflicts* are intentionally disregarded, as they only impact convergence speed.

The core difficulty of $MTDL$, compared to STL, stems from the presence of *magnitude gradient conflicts*, which are unique to $MTDL$ and the primary source of task-specific conflicts [11]. In contrast, *Angle-based gradient conflicts* are more characteristic of inter-sample variation typically address with mini-batch gradient descent.

Let us consider why *angle-based gradient conflicts* can slow the convergence of the learning process while *magnitude gradient conflicts* can significantly hinder the overall optimisation preventing the convergence of some tasks. When adding two vectors g_i and g_j of similar magnitude ($|g_i| \simeq |g_j|$) at an angle α greater than $90°$, the magnitude of the sum is reduced by a factor proportional to $cos(\alpha)$ compared to adding them when they are collinear, as shown in Fig. 1a and 1b. In the worst case, when $\alpha = 180$, the two vectors are in exactly opposite directions, and their magnitudes cancel out. However, this extreme case is rather unlikely. Although reduced in magnitude, the vector sum still contains useful information about the direction of optimisation for the gradient descent algorithm. Hence, to enhance the magnitude of the resulting sum vector by means of the momentum with no need to detect this type of conflict explicitly.

However, when one of the task gradients is overly greater than the others ($|g_i| \gg |g_j|$) the overall sum of the gradients will result in a direction dominated by that single vector. This case can be quite detrimental as only one task will benefit from the learning process, as shown in Fig. 1c. In this case, we introduce a conflict detection mechanism and a procedure to equalise the task gradients before their aggregation.

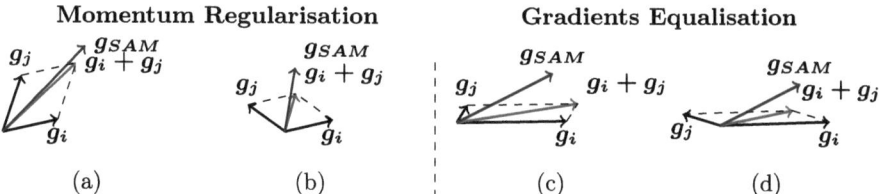

| **Momentum Regularisation** | | **Gradients Equalisation** | |
| (a) | (b) | (c) | (d) |

Fig. 1. Illustration of four scenarios for two task gradients, g_i and g_j, the standard overall gradient is denoted as $g_i + g_j$ and the overall gradient of SAM-GS is denote as g_{SAM}. (a) Ideal case: Gradients have similar magnitudes, and the angle between them is less than 90°, indicating no conflict. (b) *angle-based gradient conflict*: The angle between gradients exceeds 90°, diminishing the effectiveness of their combination. (c) *magnitude-based gradient conflict*: One gradient dominates, leading to an imbalanced gradient update. (d) Both conflicts: A combination of angle- and magnitude-based gradient conflicts, where both the directional misalignment and magnitude disparity hinder effective gradient aggregation.

As illustrated in Fig. 1, therefore, *magnitude gradient conflicts* have the potential to steer the optimisation process away from a fair convergence of all tasks, while *angle-based gradient conflicts* only influence the pace of convergence.

For this reason, SAM-GS ignores *angle-based gradient conflicts* and introduces two mechanisms: momentum regularisation and gradients equalisation. In particular, the momentum is modulated by the magnitude similarity, and the gradients equalisation is triggered by the detection of *magnitude gradient conflicts* by means of the magnitude similarity.

In cases where task gradients exhibit significantly different magnitudes, our approach equalises their magnitudes to compute a balanced direction not dominated by one task. The resulting sum vector is then scaled by the average magnitude to prevent the occurrence of near-zero gradients.

SAM-GS follows a general structure that is similar to ADABelief [40]. SAM-GS is specifically designed for multi-gradient optimisation, while ADABelief is applied to a single gradient (STL). ADABelief adopts a regularisation of the momentum that is based on the gradient, whereas SAM-GS applies a regularisation technique based on a gradient similarity measure.

Accordingly, SAM-GS is presented in Algorithm 1, where γ is a learnable hyperparameter to set the threshold on the gradient similarity to detect *magnitude gradient conflicts*. Let the model parameter vector at step t be represented by θ_t, it follows that for each of the $K \geq 2$ tasks, there exist a differentiable loss function, $\{l_i\}_{i=1}^K$. Consequently, for each task, the gradients $g_k = \nabla_\theta \mathcal{L}_k$ can be computed. The average magnitude similarity of the gradients, denoted as Ψ_t, is computed from the gradient magnitude similarities of Eq. (3). Furthermore, we indicate the momentum with $m_{k,t}$, which is the exponential moving average (EMA) of $g_{k,t}$, and with h_t the EMA of $(1 - \Psi_t)^2$ (similarity momentum coefficient) with β_1 and β_2 the smoothing parameters and $\hat{\cdot}$ represents the bias-corrected value of the respective quantity.

Algorithm 1 Similarity-Aware Momentum Gradient Surgery

Hyperparameters: $\beta_1 \leftarrow 0.9, \beta_2 \leftarrow 0.99, \gamma \leftarrow 0.1$
Initialise: $\theta_0, m_0 \leftarrow 0, h_0 \leftarrow 0, t \leftarrow 0, \epsilon \leftarrow 1e-8$
repeat
    $t \leftarrow t + 1$
    $g_k \leftarrow \nabla_{\theta_t} \mathcal{L}_k, \forall k$
    $\Psi = \frac{1}{K^2} \sum_{i,j} \psi(g_i, g_j)$
    $m_{k,t} \leftarrow \beta_1 m_{k,t-1} + (1 - \beta_1) g_k, \forall k$
    $h_t \leftarrow \beta_2 h_{t-1} + (1 - \beta_2)(1 - \Psi)^2 + \epsilon$
    $\widehat{m}_{k,t} \leftarrow \frac{m_{k,t}}{1 - \beta_1^t}, \widehat{h}_t \leftarrow \frac{h_t}{1 - \beta_2^t}$
    if $\Psi < \gamma$ **then**
        $w_k = \frac{\overline{\|g_k\|_2}}{\|g_k\|_2} g_k, \forall k$
    else
        $w_k = \frac{|\widehat{m}_{k,t}|}{\sqrt{\widehat{h}_t} + \epsilon}, \forall k$
    end if
    Update: $\theta_t = \theta_{t-1} - \alpha \sum_{k=1}^K w_k \odot g_k$
until convergence

The proposed SAM-GS approach mitigates gradient dominance by adopting cautious updates with smaller step sizes. Conversely, when gradients are well-balanced, it leverages the momentum to accelerate learning and compensate for prior conservative updates. h_t acts as a regularisation term, where, if the gradients are dissimilar, the momentum is trusted less. Conversely, when the gradients exhibit good magnitude similarity, the momentum retains its full potential. The parameter γ plays a crucial role in determining the threshold at which gradients are considered well-balanced. We provide an ablation study on this parameter in Sect. 5.2.

5   Computational Experiments and Comparisons

We conduct a series of experiments to empirically demonstrate the effectiveness of SAM-GS compared to other methods on synthetic problems and on common multi-task supervised benchmarks. Two variants of a synthetic problem based on two parameters are used to highlight the effect of gradient conflicts and how different methods fair under such conditions. The benchmarks based on real-world problems allow a comparative performance analysis of the proposed method against many state-of-the-art optimisation methods for MTL. An ablation study of SAM-GS hyperparameter γ allows to investigate its impact on the performance of the method. In the following, each experimental setup is described and the results are presented.

5.1 Synthetic Problem

To illustrate the gradient surgery problem in a simplified setting, we adopt the 2D multi-task optimisation problem proposed in Nash-MTL [24]. This problem provides a controlled environment for the study of conflicting gradient across tasks, highlighting the challenges of multi-task optimisation. In addition, we introduce a novel variant of that problem with a similar loss landscape structure, featuring two global minima, providing a different problem setting to analyse the impact of multiple optima on optimisation dynamics.

Two-Task Problem with One Global Optimum. The synthetic problem proposed in [24] provides a useful toy problem to investigate and visualise the behaviour of multi-task optimisation methods in a complex yet comprehensible loss landscape. The problem consists of two loss functions with two parameters, and the objective is to minimise both using an MTL optimisation approach; a detailed formulation is reported in [20].

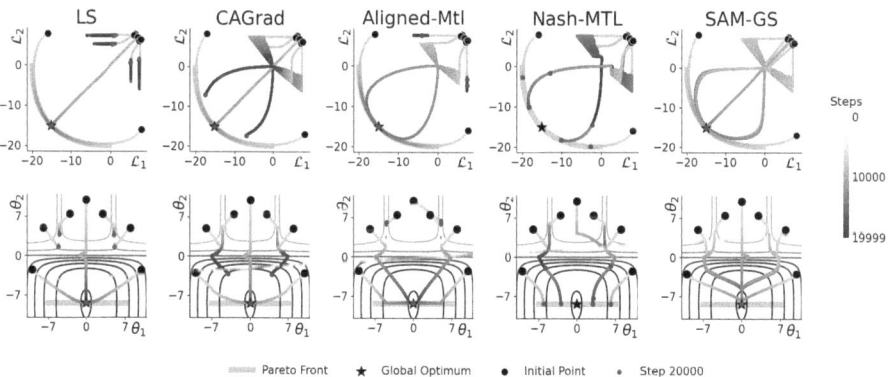

Fig. 2. Trajectories for different methods starting from 7 different initial points: Linear Sum (LS) approach using Adam [16], Nash-MTL [24], CAGrad [20], Aligned-MTL [27], and SAM-GS, from the starting points to the global optimum at the centre of the Pareto front in the loss space (top row) and parameter space (bottom row). The red dots show the end state of the trajectory after 20,000 iterations.

In the experimental results shown in Fig. 2, indicate that the proposed approach exhibits behaviour comparable to CAGrad [20]. The maximum number of

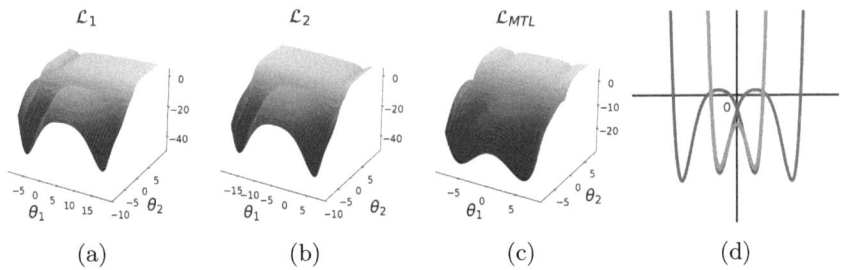

Fig. 3. Illustration of the multi-task optimisation problem ($\mathcal{L}_{MTL}$) computed as the sum of $\mathcal{L}_1$ and $\mathcal{L}_2$. In panel (d), the loss functions, $\mathcal{L}_1$ and $\mathcal{L}_2$ are displayed in red and blue, respectively, as a function of θ_1 given $\theta_2 = -5$, and $\mathcal{L}_{MTL}$ is displayed in orange.

steps is set to 20,000: SAM-GS converges within 18,000 steps, and the simulation was run for 10% more steps to ensure a good comparison. Our method is the only one that consistently reaches the global optimum from all the considered starting points. This superior performance highlights the effectiveness of SAM-GS in navigating complex loss scenarios over existing methods.

Two-Task Problem with Two Global Optima. We propose a novel inspired by Nash-MTL [24], where we introduce two distinct global optima to evaluate the MTL optimisation methods in a multi-optima scenario. In this setup, two loss functions, each dependent on two parameters, exhibit one global optimum and one local optimum. The combination of these functions forms a multi-task optimisation problem with two global optima corresponding to the two local optima of the single task problems, as illustrated in Fig. 3. This problem setup is interesting because the MTL optima correspond to the single-task local minima, thus challenging the optimisation process. Additionally, this setup presents a saddle point, which is absent in the first synthetic problem, introducing a further complexity. The complete formulation of this setup is detailed in the supplementary material.

We compare our SAM-GS with LS using Adam [16], Nash-MTL [24], CAGrad [20], and Aligned-MTL [27] across six different initialisation points, running the algorithm for a maximum of 20,000 steps.

As shown in Fig. 4, SAM-GS is the method that reaches one of the two global optima for most of the considered initial points within the maximum number of iterations. The ability of the method to consistently and efficiently identify a global optimum across different initialisations highlights its potential for solving complex multi-task optimisation problems with multiple optima, ensuring faster and more reliable convergence than existing approaches.

5.2   Performance Analysis

We tested the effectiveness of SAM-GS on three different multi-task supervised benchmarks, which have been used by various competitive optimisation methods

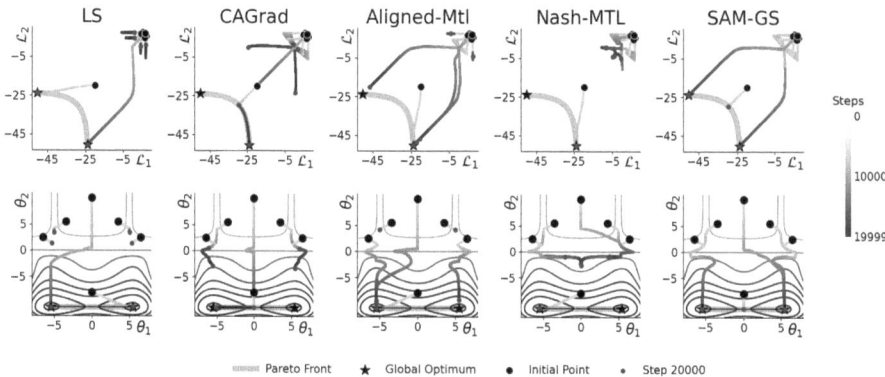

Fig. 4. Trajectories for different methods in the second synthetic problem: Linear Sum (LS) approach using Adam [16], Nash-MTL [24], CAGrad [20], Aligned-MTL [27], and SAM-GS, starting from six initial points and converging to one global optima at the extremes of the Pareto front in the loss space (top row) and parameter space (bottom row).

[19, 21, 24, 27], CelebA [23] (40 tasks), NYU-v2 [30] (3 tasks) and CityScapes [6] (2 tasks). We compare SAM-GS against 14 different optimisation methods for multi-task learning. These include loss balancing methods such as UW [5], DWA [22], GradNorm [2], and RGW [18], as well as FAMO [19]. Additionally, we evaluate gradient surgery methods, including PCGrad [37], CAGrad [20], GradDrop [3],MGDA [8], IMTL [21], Nash-MTL [24] and Aligned-MTL [27].

In the remainder of this section we present the evaluation metrics used for the comparative analysis, the results on three benchmarks and, finally, the ablation study on SAM-GS hyperparameter.

Evaluation Metrics. To evaluate the performance of the optimisation methods, we use the Mean Ranking (**MR**) and the **Δm%** metrics, similar to Nash-MTL [24]. The MR metric is the average rank of each method across tasks, where an MR of 1 indicates that the method ranks first on all tasks. The Δm% metric, defined in Eq. (4), quantifies the percentage improvement or degradation in performance of a method compared to the baseline single-task models.

$$\Delta m\% = \frac{1}{K} \sum_{k=1}^{K} (-1)^{\nu_k} \frac{m_{mtl,k} - m_{stl,k}}{m_{stl,k}} \cdot 100 \tag{4}$$

Here, $m_{mtl,k}$ and $m_{stl,k}$ represent the performance metrics for the MTL optimisation method and single-task models, respectively, for task k. The binary indicator ν_k is set to 1 when a higher value of m indicates better performance (e.g., accuracy), and 0 when a lower value is preferable (e.g., error).

CityScapes (2 Tasks). The CityScapes dataset [6] contains $5,000$ street-level RGBD images with per-pixel annotations across 19 semantic segmentation categories, grouped into 7 main categories. We adopt a similar experimental setup used in Nash-MTL [24], training a single Multi-Task Attention Network (MTAN) [22] model to simultaneously perform depth estimation and semantic segmentation. We identify that the best hyperparameter for SAM-GS are, $\beta_1 = 0.9$, $\beta_2 = 0.9$, $\gamma = 0.9$. Results in Table 1 shows that in this settings SAM-GS it is competitive with other methodology, but not superior in term of $\Delta m\%$. Some methods (e.g. UW [5]) have strictly better $\Delta m\%$ by excelling in one task; our approach has more balanced competitive performance across all tasks. The superior performance of Aligned-MTL [27], which focuses only on *angle-based gradient conflicts*, indicates that in this dataset inter-sample conflicts are more relevant, as also shown in [11]. This may explain the limitations of the proposed approach for this dataset.

Table 1. CityScapes results

	Segmentation		Depth		MR ↓	$\Delta m\%$ ↓
	mIoU ↑	PixAcc ↑	AbsErr ↓	RelErr ↓		
STL	74.01	93.16	0.0125	27.77		
LS	71.0	91.7	0.0161	33.8	11.8	14.1
SI	71.0	91.7	0.0161	33.8	11.8	14.1
RLW	74.6	93.4	0.0158	47.8	11.0	24.4
DWA	75.2	93.5	0.016	44.4	8.5	21.4
UW	72.0	92.8	0.014	**30.1**	7.75	5.89
MGDA	68.8	91.5	0.0309	33.5	12.5	44.1
PCGrad	75.1	93.5	0.0154	42.1	9.12	18.3
GradNorm	73.7	93.0	0.0124	34.1	7.75	5.63
GradDrop	75.3	93.5	0.0157	47.5	7.75	23.7
CAGrad	75.2	93.5	0.0141	37.6	7.88	11.6
IMTL-G	75.3	93.5	0.0135	38.4	6	11.1
Nash-MTL	75.4	**93.7**	**0.0129**	35.0	3.75	6.82
FAMO	74.5	93.3	0.0145	32.6	7.50	8.13
Aligned-MTL	**75.8**	93.7	0.0133	32.66	**2**	**5.27**
SAM-GS	75.2	93.5	0.0136	33.1	5.00	6.41

NYU-V2 (3 Tasks). The NYU-v2 dataset [30] comprises $1,449$ RGBD images of indoor scenes, with dense pixel-level annotations across 13 classes. We follow a similar experimental setup to Nash-MTL [24], training a single MTAN [22] model to perform depth estimation, image segmentation, and surface normal

Table 2. NYU-V2 results

	Segmentation		Depth		Surface Normal					MR ↓	$\Delta m\%$ ↓
	mIoU↑	Pix Acc ↑	Abs Err ↓	Rel Err ↓	Angle Dist ↓		Within t° ↑				
					Mean	Median	11.25	22.5	30		
STL	38.3	63.76	0.6754	0.278	25.01	19.21	30.14	57.2	69.15		
LS	39.29	65.33	0.5493	0.2263	28.15	23.96	22.09	47.5	61.08	11.4	5.59
SI	38.45	64.27	0.5354	0.2201	27.6	23.37	22.53	48.57	62.32	10.3	4.39
RLW	37.17	63.77	0.5759	0.241	28.27	24.18	22.26	47.05	60.62	13.8	7.78
DWA	39.11	65.31	0.551	0.2285	27.61	23.18	24.17	50.18	62.39	10.2	3.57
UW	36.87	63.17	0.5446	0.226	27.04	22.61	23.54	49.05	63.65	10.0	4.05
MGDA	30.47	59.9	0.607	0.2555	24.88	19.45	29.18	56.88	69.36	7.4	1.38
PCGRAD	38.06	64.64	0.555	0.2325	27.41	22.8	23.86	49.83	63.14	10.6	3.97
GradNorm	20.09	64.64	0.7200	0.2800	**24.83**	**18.86**	**30.81**	**57.94**	**69.73**	7.2	7.22
GradDrop	39.39	65.12	0.5455	0.2279	27.48	22.96	23.38	49.44	62.87	9.6	3.58
CAGrad	39.79	65.49	0.5486	0.225	26.31	21.58	25.61	52.36	65.58	7.1	0.2
IMTL-G	39.35	65.6	0.5426	0.2256	26.02	21.19	26.2	53.13	66.24	6.3	−0.76
Nash-MTL	40.13	65.93	0.5261	0.2171	25.26	20.08	28.4	55.47	68.15	4.2	−4.04
FAMO	38.88	64.9	0.5474	0.2194	25.06	19.57	29.21	56.61	68.98	4.8	−4.1
Aligned-MTL	**40.82**	66.33	0.5300	0.2200	25.19	19.71	28.88	56.23	68.54	3.6	−4.93
SAM-GS	40.79	**66.46**	**0.5251**	**0.2169**	25.03	19.65	29.26	56.35	68.78	**2.4**	**−5.3**

prediction. We identify the following hyperparameters for SAM-GS: $\beta_1 = 0.9$, $\beta_2 = 0.9$, $\gamma = 0.9$. The results in Table 2 show superior performance of SAM-GS, compared to other methods, in cases with more than two tasks.

CelebA (40 Tasks). The CelebA dataset [23] is a collection of 200,000 facial images of 10,000 distinct celebrities, with 40 binary annotations of facial attributes for each image. We use the experimental setup outlined in FAMO [19], training a CNN model to perform 40 binary classification tasks. The hyperparameter search on the validation data identifies the following as the best hyperparameters for SAM-GS: $\beta_1 = 0.9$, $\beta_2 = 0.99$, $\gamma = 0.9$. The results in Table 3 show a superior performance of SAM-GS in handling 40 different tasks concurrently.

Ablation Study on γ**.** In this section we provide a systematic study over the values of the similarity threshold γ.

Figure 5 highlights the critical role of γ in model performance. Extreme settings ($\gamma = 0$ or $\gamma = 1$), which make the algorithm to rely exclusively on either the equalisation or the momentum component of SAM-GS, yield suboptimal results. On the other hand, intermediate values of γ, with a general trend towards higher settings, yield preferable results.

5.3 MTDL Reinforcement Learning (10 Tasks)

Finally, we tested SAM-GS on a multi-task reinforcement learning (RL) problem against the most relevant MTL methods specifically designed for RL problems and a selection of the most recent gradient surgery methods. Specifically,

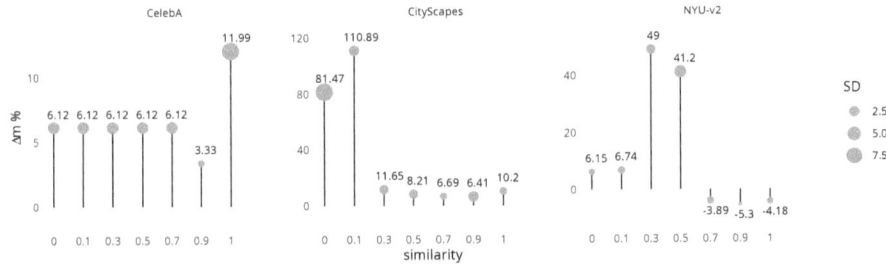

Fig. 5. Ablation study over γ. The plot shows the performance, in terms of $\Delta m\%$, of SAM-GS across three supervised learning settings with γ values of $\{0, 0.1, 0.3, 0.5, 0.7, 0.9, 1\}$, including standard deviation (SD)

Table 3. CelebA results.

Method	$\Delta m\%$ ↓
LS	6.28
SI	7.83
RLW	5.22
DWA	6.95
UW	5.78
MGDA	10.93
PCGrad	6.65
GradDrop	7.80
CAGrad	6.20
IMTL-G	4.67
Nash-MTL	4.97
FAMO	4.72
Aligned-MTL	4.58
SAM-GS	**3.33**

Table 4. Reinforcement learning (MT10).

Method	Success ($mean \pm stderr$)
STL SAC	0.90 ± 0.032
MTL SAC	0.49 ± 0.073
MTL SAC + TE	0.54 ± 0.047
MH SAC	0.61 ± 0.036
SM	0.73 ± 0.043
CARE	0.84 ± 0.051
PCGrad	0.72 ± 0.022
CAGrad	0.83 ± 0.045
Nash-MTL	0.91 ± 0.031
Aligned-MTL	$\mathbf{0.97 \pm 0.045}$
FAMO	0.83 ± 0.05
SAM-GS	0.91 ± 0.018

we applied a variation of the SAM-GS method to the MetaWorld [38] MT10 benchmark, which comprises 10 distinct robot manipulation tasks with various reward functions. The variation concerns the computation of Ψ_t; we found that using $\Psi_t = \min \psi(g_i, g_j)$ led to improved results compared to averaging in a multi-task reinforcement learning problem. The experimental setting is similar to the one used in CAGrad [20], using Soft Actor-Critic (SAC) [13] as a baseline, trained with various gradient manipulation methods [19, 20, 24, 27, 37]. We also evaluate MTL-RL [31] approaches, including MTL SAC, Multi-task SAC with task encoder (MTL SAC + TE) [35], Multi-headed SAC (MH SAC) [35], Soft Modularization (SM) [36], and CARE [31]. We identify the hyperparameters for SAM-GS: $\beta_1 = 0.9$, $\beta_2 = 0.99$, $\gamma = 0.9$. The results presented in Table 4 indicate that SAM-GS achieves performance levels on par with Nash-MTL [24], while surpassing STL baseline, FAMO [19], CAGrad [20], and the standard gradient descent baseline method.

6   Conclusions

In multi-task deep learning training a single model on many tasks can be affected by potentially conflicting task gradients that would hinder the concurrent convergence of the diverse loss functions. In this study, the importance of the gradient magnitude similarity for the effective overall optimisation of the model has been studied and highlighted. As a result, a novel gradient surgery method, the Similarity-Aware Momentum Gradient Surgery (SAM-GS), has been proposed. SAM-GS is based on a measure of the task gradient magnitude similarity and used to control and guide two mechanisms: a momentum-based regularisation and a remedy for gradient magnitude conflicts. An extensive evaluation has demonstrated that SAM-GS effectively addresses a range of challenges with respect to task gradient conflicts and outperforms previous optimisation methods in two synthetic problems, several benchmarks from real-world computer vision applications, and a benchmark for reinforcement learning tasks. Future work may include a theoretical analysis of convergence to provide optimisation guarantees. Moreover, a direction for further improvements is the analysis of the current limitations to address strict stationary states such as saddle points, where task gradients have very similar magnitude and opposite directions.

Acknowledgments. We would like to thank the anonymous reviewers for their thorough reviews and insightful comments.

References

1. Caruana, R.: Multitask learning. Mach. Learn. **28**, 41–75 (1997)
2. Chen, Z., Badrinarayanan, V., Lee, C.Y., Rabinovich, A.: GradNorm: gradient normalization for adaptive loss balancing in deep multitask networks. In: Proceedings of the 35th International Conference on Machine Learning, vol. 80, pp. 794–803 (2018)
3. Chen, Z., et al.: Just pick a sign: optimizing deep multitask models with gradient sign dropout. In: Advances in Neural Information Processing Systems, vol. 33, pp. 2039–2050 (2020)
4. Choi, W., Shin, M., Lee, H., Cho, J., Park, J., Im, S.: Multi-task learning for real-time autonomous driving leveraging task-adaptive attention generator. In: IEEE International Conference on Robotics and Automation (ICRA), pp. 14732–14739 (2024)
5. Cipolla, R., Gal, Y., Kendall, A.: Multi-task learning using uncertainty to weigh losses for scene geometry and semantics. In: Proceedings of the IEEE/CVF Conference on Computer Vision and Pattern Recognition (CVPR), pp. 7482–7491 (2018)

6. Cordts, M., et al.: The cityscapes dataset for semantic urban scene understanding. In: Proceedings of the IEEE/CVF Conference on Computer Vision and Pattern Recognition (CVPR) (2016)
7. Di Fatta, G., Nicosia, G., Ojha, V., Pardalos, P.: Multi-task deep learning as multi-objective optimization. In: Encyclopedia of Optimization (2020)
8. Dong, D., Wu, H., He, W., Yu, D., Wang, H.: Multi-task learning for multiple language translation. In: Proceedings of the 53rd Annual Meeting of the Association for Computational Linguistics and the 7th International Joint Conference on Natural Language Processing (Volume 1: Long Papers), pp. 1723–1732 (2015)
9. Dong, X., et al.: GDOD: effective gradient descent using orthogonal decomposition for multi-task learning. In: Proceedings of the 31st ACM International Conference on Information & Knowledge Management, pp. 386–395 (2022)
10. Désidéri, J.A.: Multiple-gradient descent algorithm (MGDA) for multiobjective optimization. C. R. Math. **350**(5), 313–318 (2012)
11. Elich, C., Kirchdorfer, L., Köhler, J.M., Schott, L.: Examining common paradigms in multi-task learning. In: Pattern Recognition, pp. 131–147 (2025)
12. Fifty, C., Amid, E., Zhao, Z., Yu, T., Anil, R., Finn, C.: Efficiently identifying task groupings for multi-task learning. In: Advances in Neural Information Processing Systems, vol. 34, pp. 27503–27516 (2021)
13. Guo, M., Haque, A., Huang, D.A., Yeung, S., Fei-Fei, L.: Dynamic task prioritization for multitask learning. In: Proceedings of the European Conference on Computer Vision (ECCV) (2018)
14. Hao, J., et al.: Retinal structure detection in octa image via voting-based multitask learning. IEEE Trans. Med. Imaging **41**(12), 3969–3980 (2022)
15. Kim, S., Purdie, T.G., McIntosh, C.: Cross-task attention network: improving multi-task learning for medical imaging applications. In: Celebi, M.E., et al. (eds.) MICCAI 2023. LNCS, vol. 14393, pp. 119–128. Springer, Cham (2023). https://doi.org/10.1007/978-3-031-47401-9_12
16. Kingma, D.P.: Adam: a method for stochastic optimization. The third International Conference on Learning Representations (2015)
17. Kuhn, H.W., Tucker, A.W.: Nonlinear programming. In: Proceedings of the Second Berkeley Symposium on Mathematical Statistics and Probability (1951)
18. Lin, B., Ye, F., Zhang, Y., Tsang, I.W.: Reasonable effectiveness of random weighting: a litmus test for multi-task learning. Trans. Mach. Learn. Res. 2835–8856 (2022)
19. Liu, B., Feng, Y., Stone, P., Liu, Q.: FAMO: fast adaptive multitask optimization. In: Advances in Neural Information Processing Systems, vol. 36, pp. 57226–57243 (2023)
20. Liu, B., Liu, X., Jin, X., Stone, P., Liu, Q.: Conflict-averse gradient descent for multi-task learning. In: Advances in Neural Information Processing Systems, vol. 34, pp. 18878–18890 (2021)
21. Liu, L., et al.: Towards impartial multi-task learning. In: International Conference on Learning Representations (2021)
22. Liu, S., Johns, E., Davison, A.J.: End-to-end multi-task learning with attention. In: Proceedings of the IEEE/CVF Conference on Computer Vision and Pattern Recognition (CVPR), pp. 1871–1880 (2019)
23. Liu, Z., Luo, P., Wang, X., Tang, X.: Deep learning face attributes in the wild. In: Proceedings of the 2015 IEEE International Conference on Computer Vision (ICCV), pp. 3730–3738 (2015)

24. Navon, A., et al.: Multi-task learning as a bargaining game. In: Proceedings of the 39th International Conference on Machine Learning, vol. 162, pp. 16428–16446 (2022)
25. Ong, J., Herremans, D.: Constructing time-series momentum portfolios with deep multi-task learning. Expert Syst. Appl. **230**, 120587 (2023)
26. Ruder, S.: An overview of multi-task learning in deep neural networks (2017). http://arxiv.org/abs/1706.05098
27. Senushkin, D., Patakin, N., Kuznetsov, A., Konushin, A.: Independent component alignment for multi-task learning. In: Proceedings of the IEEE/CVF Conference on Computer Vision and Pattern Recognition (CVPR), pp. 20083–20093 (2023)
28. Shen, J., Zhen, X., Worring, M., Shao, L.: Variational multi-task learning with gumbel-softmax priors. In: Advances in Neural Information Processing Systems, vol. 34, pp. 21031–21042 (2021)
29. SHI, G., Li, Q., Zhang, W., Chen, J., Wu, X.M.: Recon: reducing conflicting gradients from the root for multi-task learning. In: The Eleventh International Conference on Learning Representations (2023)
30. Silberman, N., Hoiem, D., Kohli, P., Fergus, R.: Indoor segmentation and support inference from RGBD images. In: Fitzgibbon, A., Lazebnik, S., Perona, P., Sato, Y., Schmid, C. (eds.) ECCV 2012. LNCS, vol. 7576, pp. 746–760. Springer, Heidelberg (2012). https://doi.org/10.1007/978-3-642-33715-4_54
31. Sodhani, S., Zhang, A., Pineau, J.: Multi-task reinforcement learning with context-based representations. In: Proceedings of the 38th International Conference on Machine Learning, vol. 139, pp. 9767–9779 (2021)
32. Standley, T., Zamir, A., Chen, D., Guibas, L., Malik, J., Savarese, S.: Which tasks should be learned together in multi-task learning? In: Proceedings of the 37th International Conference on Machine Learning, vol. 119, pp. 9120–9132 (2020)
33. Tian, Y., Bai, K.: End-to-end multitask learning with vision transformer. IEEE Trans. Neural Netw. Learn. Syst. **35**(7), 9579–9590 (2024)
34. Wang, A., Singh, A., Michael, J., Hill, F., Levy, O., Bowman, S.: GLUE: a multi-task benchmark and analysis platform for natural language understanding. In: Proceedings of the 2018 EMNLP Workshop BlackboxNLP: Analyzing and Interpreting Neural Networks for NLP, pp. 353–355 (2018)
35. Wulfmeier, M., et al.: Compositional transfer in hierarchical reinforcement learning. In: Proceedings of Robotics: Science and Systems (2020)
36. Yang, R., Xu, H., WU, Y., Wang, X.: Multi-task reinforcement learning with soft modularization. In: Advances in Neural Information Processing Systems, vol. 33, pp. 4767–4777 (2020)
37. Yu, T., Kumar, S., Gupta, A., Levine, S., Hausman, K., Finn, C.: Gradient surgery for multi-task learning. In: Advances in Neural Information Processing Systems, vol. 33, pp. 5824–5836 (2020)
38. Yu, T., Quillen, D., He, Z., Julian, R., Hausman, K., Finn, C., Levine, S.: Meta-world: a benchmark and evaluation for multi-task and meta reinforcement learning. In: Proceedings of the Conference on Robot Learning (2020)
39. Zamir, A.R., Sax, A., Shen, W., Guibas, L.J., Malik, J., Savarese, S.: Taskonomy: disentangling task transfer learning. In: Proceedings of the IEEE/CVF Conference on Computer Vision and Pattern Recognition (CVPR) (2018)
40. Zhuang, J., et al.: AdaBelief optimizer: adapting stepsizes by the belief in observed gradients. In: Advances in Neural Information Processing Systems, vol. 33, pp. 18795–18806 (2020)

A Unified View of Abstract Visual Reasoning Problems

Mikołaj Małkiński[1]([✉])[ID] and Jacek Mańdziuk[1,2][ID]

[1] Warsaw University of Technology, Warsaw, Poland
{mikolaj.malkinski.dokt,jacek.mandziuk}@pw.edu.pl
[2] AGH University of Krakow, Krakow, Poland

Abstract. The field of Abstract Visual Reasoning (AVR) encompasses a wide range of problems, many of which are inspired by human IQ tests. The variety of AVR tasks has resulted in state-of-the-art AVR methods being task-specific approaches. Furthermore, contemporary methods consider each AVR problem instance not as a whole, but in the form of a set of individual panels with particular locations and roles (context vs. answer panels) pre-assigned according to the task-specific arrangements. While these highly specialized approaches have recently led to significant progress in solving particular AVR tasks, considering each task in isolation hinders the development of universal learning systems in this domain. In this paper, we introduce a unified view of AVR tasks, where each problem instance is rendered as a single image, with no a priori assumptions about the number of panels, their location, or role. The main advantage of the proposed unified view is the ability to develop universal learning models applicable to various AVR tasks. What is more, the proposed approach inherently facilitates transfer learning in the AVR domain, as various types of problems share a common representation. The experiments conducted on four AVR datasets with Raven's Progressive Matrices and Visual Analogy Problems, and one real-world visual analogy dataset show that the proposed unified representation of AVR tasks poses a challenge to state-of-the-art Deep Learning (DL) AVR models and, more broadly, contemporary DL image recognition methods. In order to address this challenge, we introduce the *Unified Model for Abstract Visual Reasoning (UMAVR)* capable of dealing with various types of AVR problems in a unified manner. UMAVR outperforms existing AVR methods in selected single-task learning experiments, and demonstrates effective knowledge reuse in transfer learning and curriculum learning setups. Code is available at: https://github.com/mikomel/avr-unified-view.

Keywords: Abstract Visual Reasoning · Deep Learning · Transfer Learning · Curriculum Learning

Supplementary Information The online version contains supplementary material available at https://doi.org/10.1007/978-3-662-72243-5_7.

1   Introduction

Recent years have brought dynamic progress in the application of neural networks to computer vision (CV) problems. This increasing interest has led to the development of a broad family of effective vision models based on convolutional networks [6,11], transformers [5,10], and multi-layer perceptrons (MLPs) [8,23], that often generalize well to other vision tasks. The universality of these models should be primarily attributed to the simplicity and wide applicability of the typical problem representation in the CV domain, in the form of a single image.

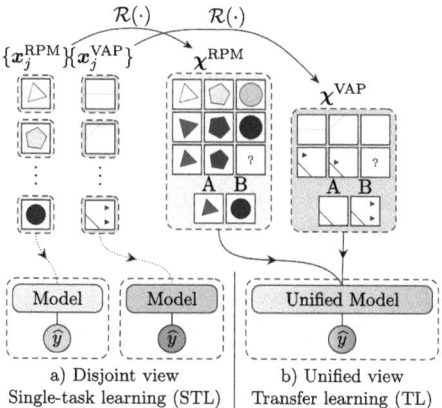

a) Disjoint view | b) Unified view
Single-task learning (STL) | Transfer learning (TL)

Fig. 1. Disjoint vs. unified perspective. Contemporary literature considers each AVR problem instance as a set of separate images (a), which leads to task-specific methods with limited applicability to other, even similar, tasks. In contrast, we propose the unified view (b), in which the problem instance is rendered as a single image (Fig. 2). This viewpoint facilitates the development of general AVR models inherently capable of incorporating advances from a broader CV field.

Abstract Visual Reasoning (AVR) is one of the CV subdomains gaining momentum in recent years. AVR encompasses problems that resemble tests used for measuring human abstract intelligence (IQ). A classical example are Raven's Progressive Matrices (RPMs) [21] that consist of simple 2D shapes (e.g., circles, hexagons, triangles) characterized by several attributes (e.g., rotation, colour, size). In most cases, an RPM problem instance is in the form of a 3 × 3 grid of panels, with the bottom-right panel missing (see Appendix D for typical examples). The test-taker has to complete the matrix by selecting one of the provided answer panels. In RPM datasets, there are usually up to 8 answer panels to choose from. In order to select the correct one, the subject has to identify various underlying abstract rules (e.g., progression, constancy, conjunction) that govern the location and attributes of RPM shapes. The selected answer has to conform to all these rules after being placed in the bottom-right corner of the matrix.

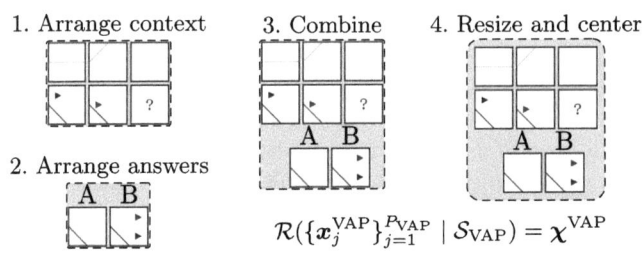

Fig. 2. Rendering algorithm. In the unified view a problem instance is rendered as a single image and without explicit division into context and answer panels.

RPMs are considered to be highly indicative for human intelligence [4], as they allow evaluating relational and abstract reasoning skills [22], and test one's ability to apply previously gained knowledge in new settings (new problem instances). Inspired by this crucial role of RPMs in designing IQ tests, recent streams of research have focused on evaluating the capacity of modern learning systems in solving RPM instances [17]. Motivated by the early successes [19], many approaches have been subsequently proposed that gradually improved the state-of-the-art (SOTA).

Despite impressive results, contemporary methods are built on a strict assumption that RPMs (or AVR tasks in general) are split beforehand into a set of individual matrix panels. In stark contrast, vision datasets typically render each problem instance as a single image. In this work, we coin these two perspectives as *disjoint* and *unified* representations, respectively (see Fig. 1). Due to inherent differences, models developed for one representation are not directly applicable to the other one. This, in turn, limits applicability of methods developed for solving AVR tasks to other vision problems and, *vice versa*, prevents evaluation of modern vision models on AVR tasks.

In addition to RPMs, other kinds of AVR benchmarks have recently been proposed [12], that specifically focus on conceptual abstraction, extrapolation, or arithmetic reasoning. This variety of AVR problems further exacerbates the issues arising from the disjoint perspective, as AVR tasks often differ w.r.t. the number and arrangement of panels the matrix is composed of. Consequently, a model constructed to handle tasks with a fixed number of panels arranged in a fixed configuration isn't directly capable of handling novel problem configurations, or problems with different numbers of panels. In effect, SOTA solutions in the AVR literature are task-specific, which limits progress towards general AVR solvers.

Contribution. In this work we pose and address the challenge of building AVR models capable of solving diverse AVR problems. To this end, we:

– Formulate a *unified view* of AVR tasks where a problem instance is represented as a single image (as opposed to a set of pre-defined panels), thus constituting a challenge for modern AVR/CV methods;

– Evaluate different CV models: convolutional networks, transformers, and MLPs on four AVR datasets with RPMs and Visual Analogy Problems (VAPs), and one real-world visual analogy dataset, represented in the unified manner, and demonstrate their limitations in this unified problem setup;
– Introduce the *Unified Model for Abstract Visual Reasoning (UMAVR)*, capable of effectively dealing with the unified problem representation, and outperforming strong baselines in this arrangement;
– Show the benefits of transfer learning (TL) and curriculum learning (CL) within the proposed unified AVR problem formulation.

On a general note, we postulate shifting the main focus of AVR research from developing dedicated task-specific models to general AVR models, capable of solving a variety of AVR problems.

2   Related Work

Tasks. Recently AVR has seen rapid expansion in terms of available benchmarks. In particular, several RPM datasets, such as PGM [1], I-RAVEN [9,33], A-I-RAVEN [15] or G-set [19,24] have been proposed. While the benchmarks differ in the number of rendered matrices, types and attributes of the objects, degree of compositional complexity, or the number of available answers, they all present matrices with the context panels arranged in the form of a 3×3 grid. VAPs [7] form a related challenge that focuses on conceptual abstraction, and are composed of a 2×3 grid of panels (see Fig. 1b and Appendix D). Other AVR problems further differ from the above two tasks in the number of context panels and their structure. For instance, the Odd One Out tests (O3) [19] present images arranged in a single row, while panels in Bongard Problems [3] are divided into left and right ones. Common to all AVR problems is their input representation in Machine Learning (ML) models, as an explicit set of distinct panels. This way of representing input data is in stark contrast to typical image recognition tasks, where each input is simply presented in the form of a single image, without further division into sub-images (though, such a division is often induced as part of a training process). In effect, existing AVR datasets cannot be easily considered when evaluating contemporary image recognition methods and are largely omitted in multi-task vision datasets. The proposed unified representation of AVR tasks enables to utilize existing AVR datasets for measuring abstract reasoning skills of current (and future) CV models.

AVR Models. Due to inherent differences in the number of panels and the task structure across AVR datasets, as well as their explicit panel-based arrangement, main AVR research lines focus on designing task-specific architectures that operate on matrices pre-segmented into individual panels. Specifically, Wild Relation Network [1] employs a convolutional encoder to generate embeddings of individual panels, which are later processed by a Relation Network. Stratified Rule-Aware Network [9] considers 3 different RPM hierarchies: single images, rows/columns, and pairs of rows/columns. For each hierarchy, a separate convolutional network is used, and a set of MLPs is employed to gradually merge the obtained embeddings. SCL [30] introduces the scattering transformation that splits panel representations, processes them in parallel with an MLP, and merges the results. Slot Transformer Scoring Network (STSN) [20] employs Slot Attention to discover objects in matrix panels and reasons about them with a transformer-based module [26]. SCAR [14] introduces the structure-aware dynamic layer that adapts its computation to the considered problem instance enabling the processing of AVR tasks with diverse structure. PoNG [16] integrates group convolution, normalization, and a parallel design.

The underlying assumption of the above approaches is that a problem instance is already pre-segmented into individual panels. Consequently, direct application of these methods to other image recognition tasks (where the input is formed by a single image), or other AVR tasks that differ in the number of panels or their structure is significantly hindered. In contrast, the proposed unified perspective facilitates and encourages the development of universal ML image recognition models that can be applied to solving diverse AVR tasks and, furthermore, other vision problems.

3   Method

We start with introducing the unified perspective that can be applied to virtually all AVR tasks, and then propose a novel image recognition model, well-suited to the proposed challenge.

3.1   Current Perspective (*Disjoint*)

In general, each AVR task $t \in \mathcal{T}$, where $\mathcal{T}$ is the family of all AVR tasks, can be defined as $t = (\{\mathcal{M}_i^t\}_{i=1}^{N_t}, \mathcal{S}_t)$, where $\{\mathcal{M}_i^t\}_{i=1}^{N_t}$ is a set of N_t different matrices (problem instances) and $\mathcal{S}_t$ is a task's structure (common for all instances). In this work, we treat each AVR dataset as a separate task. While matrices don't repeat across tasks, some tasks may have a common structure.

For each t, a single matrix (problem instance) from t can be defined as $\mathcal{M}_i^t = (X_i^t, y_i^t)$, where $X_i^t = \{x_{i,j}^t\}_{j=1}^{P_t}$ is composed of P_t panels. Each panel $x_{i,j}^t$ is a greyscale image with height h and width w, i.e. $x_{i,j}^t \in [0,1]^{h \times w}$, and y_i^t is the answer to the problem. For single-choice tasks, such as RPMs or VAPs, y_i^t is an index of the correct answer.

The above definition of a problem instance is rather general and doesn't include any information about the problem's specificity. Such problem-specific metadata is expressed by the task's structure $\mathcal{S}_t$, which defines how the images should be interpreted and arranged to form a 2D problem instance. For example, the structure of RPMs specifies that the set of images should be split into two sets: a set of 8 context panels arranged in a 3×3 grid, with a missing panel in the bottom-right corner, and a set of up to 8 answer panels also arranged in a grid.

In summary, while each AVR task t is defined as: $t = (\{(\{x_{i,j}^t\}_{j=1}^{P_t},$ $y_i^t)\}_{i=1}^{N_t}, S_t)$ its actual representation (i.e. the respective AVR dataset) is a collection of images: $t = (\{(\{x_{i,j}^t\}_{j=1}^{P_t}, y_i^t)\}_{i=1}^{N_t})$ with *implicitly* defined structure. Consequently, each AVR model $\mathcal{F}_t$ for solving matrices from t embeds the problem structure directly in its architecture. A construction of such a model using a building process $\mathcal{B}$ may be defined as a composition of functions f, given the task's structure S_t:

$$\mathcal{B}(f_* \circ f_\# \circ \ldots \circ f_\$ \mid S_t) = \mathcal{F}_t \tag{1}$$

In the AVR literature, $f_*, f_\#, \ldots, f_\$$ are most often implemented as neural network components. This leads to the following general form of a model for solving problems from t:

$$\mathcal{F}_t(\{x_{i,j}^t\}_{j=1}^{P_t}) = \widehat{y}_i^t \tag{2}$$

Due to the dependence on both S_t (implicit) and P_t (explicit), $\mathcal{F}_t$ cannot be directly applied to solving any task $t' \in T_t'$ with a different structure or number of panels: $T_t' = \{t' \in T : S_t \neq S_{t'} \vee P_t \neq P_{t'}\}$

3.2 Proposed New Perspective (*Unified*)

Instead of treating an AVR problem instance as a set of images with an associated structure, we propose to employ a rendering algorithm $\mathcal{R}$ that merges separate images, given the task's structure, into a single image $\chi \in [0,1]^{h' \times w'}$ with new height h' and width w' (see Figs. 1 and 2):

$$\mathcal{R}(\{x_{i,j}^t\}_{j=1}^{P_t} \mid S_t) = \chi_i^t \tag{3}$$

In practice, $\mathcal{R}$ defines how instances of a given task should be presented. To implement the algorithm for RPMs and VAPs considered in this work, for a given instance we first arrange the context panels, together with the missing panel (which is presented as a blank image with a centred question mark) into a grid with a small margin separating the panels. This gives a 3×3 grid accommodating 8 context panels for RPMs, and a 2×3 grid containing 5 context panels for VAPs. Next, we arrange the answer panels in another grid and position it below the context grid. Depending on the task, the number of available answers (n_a) differs, e.g. matrices from VAP, G-set, and I-RAVEN datasets, have $n_a = 4, 5, 8$, resp. To accommodate this variability, we render the answer grid with up to 4 panels in each row, resulting in up to 2 rows. A text label is placed above each answer panel. Next, we initialize a blank canvas and resize the constructed image to fit the canvas. While resizing, we keep the height to width ratio of the image in order to preserve the relative size of panel dimensions and to not distort the encompassed objects. We fix the width of the canvas to 416, and depending on the considered problem setting, set its height to 384 for VAPs, 448 for RPMs with $n_a \leq 4$, and 544 for RPMs with $4 < n_a \leq 8$, which gives enough space to clearly render the panels. All dimensions are divisible by 16 to ensure that patch-based methods (with patch size $p = 16z$, for $z \in \mathbb{N}$) can be directly applied without the need to resize the underlying image.

$\mathcal{R}$ converts a considered AVR task into a common, unified representation that (a) facilitates construction of new universal AVR models capable of solving diverse AVR tasks, and (b) enables application of TL in existing SOTA AVR models. To the best of our knowledge, neither (a) nor (b) have ever been considered in the AVR literature. Within the above unified perspective, one can view any task t as: $t = \{(\boldsymbol{\chi}_i^t, \boldsymbol{y}_i^t)\}_{i=1}^{N_t}$.

3.3   General AVR Solver

Using the proposed unified perspective, it is possible to construct a general AVR model:

$$\mathcal{B}(f_* \circ f_\# \circ \ldots \circ f_\$) = \mathcal{F} \tag{4}$$

$$\mathcal{F}(\boldsymbol{\chi}_i^t) = \widehat{\boldsymbol{y}}_i \tag{5}$$

Since $\mathcal{B}$ no longer depends on the task's structure (Eq. 1 vs Eq. 4) and the model doesn't depend on the number of panels in the matrix (Eq. 2 vs Eq. 5), the proposed unified perspective allows building a general model $\mathcal{F}$ applicable to solving diverse AVR tasks. At the same time, $\mathcal{F}$ has to support input images χ_i^t that may vary in size. Also, since $\mathcal{F}$ is no longer aware of which task it operates on, it has to provide its prediction in a common (fixed) format $\widehat{\boldsymbol{y}}$. We assume that $\widehat{y} \in \mathbb{N}$ is an index of the correct answer, which is the case of RPMs, VAPs, and many other AVR tasks [12]. This assumption may not be valid in some tasks, such as the original Bongard Problems [3], where an answer has to be provided in natural language. An extension of the unified perspective to problems with specific output formats is left for future work. Lastly, to be applicable to diverse AVR tasks, $\mathcal{F}$ has to be flexible enough to handle various structures of the tasks of interest.

3.4   Proposed Unified AVR Model

In the initial experiments, we've discovered that SOTA CV baseline models struggle to deal with the above structural diversity. Consequently, we propose UMAVR (Unified Model for Abstract Visual Reasoning) a neural architecture well-suited for the introduced unified view that takes rectangular images as input. To build *local* representations of low-level features, a convolutional backbone with depth D_L is employed. Each layer is composed of a convolution layer with kernel size 3×3, and 2×2 stride for dimensionality reduction, followed by Batch Normalization layer with ReLU activation. In the default setting, we use $D_L = 4$, and the layers have 16, 16, 32, and 128 output channels, resp. The size of the last channel determines the embedding size of a token at a given spatial location and is further referred to as d. Applying this perception backbone yields a latent representation $z_0 \in \mathbb{R}^{d \times r \times c}$, where r and c are the numbers of rows and columns in the resultant token embedding matrix, resp. For an image of size 544×416, this gives $z_0 \in \mathbb{R}^{128 \times 27 \times 25}$.

Next, we attach a component with a *global* receptive field to facilitate the discovery of patterns that span multiple panels. As a base layout, we adopt the MetaFormer architecture [31], which follows a layer-wise design, where the same layer is repeated $D_G = 4$ times, and the weights are not shared across layers. The operation performed in layer $l \in [1, D_G]$ can be formalized as:

$$z_l^* = \text{TokenMixer}\left(\text{Norm}(z_{l-1})\right) + z_{l-1} \tag{6}$$

$$z_l = \text{ChannelMixer}\left(\text{Norm}(z_l^*)\right) + z_l^* \tag{7}$$

where z_l is the output of the l'th layer, z_l^* is an intermediate representation in layer l, and Norm is the Layer Normalization. After the last layer, the token embedding matrix is passed through Layer Normalization, averaged along the width and height dimensions, and projected with a linear layer into n_a−dimensional vector. The output is passed through the softmax function, and the model is optimized end-to-end with cross-entropy. The model architecture diagram is presented in Appendix B.

TokenMixer. The input z_{l-1} is normalized and passed through a residual 2D convolution layer with a kernel of size 5×5, and 2×2 padding to enrich tokens with the context from their spatial proximity. Next, three parallel pathways are employed as introduced in the Vision Permutator (ViP) [8], which process the token matrix along the width, height, and channel dimensions, resp. In each branch, $S = 8$ segments are used. Outputs of the pathways are concatenated depthwise and a 2D convolution with 1×1 kernel and d output channels is applied to fuse information from the separate paths, in contrast to ViP which merges the branches with sum or Split Attention [34].

ChannelMixer. The above global reasoning step is followed by local processing using a two-layer non-linear feed-forward block, input normalization, and a residual connection, as popularized by the Transformer [26]: $z_l = \sigma(\text{Norm}(z_l^*)W_1)W_2 + z_l^*$, where $W_1 \in \mathbb{R}^{d \times kd}$ and $W_2 \in \mathbb{R}^{kd \times d}$ are learnable weights with an expansion factor k, and σ is a non-linearity. In the default setting, we use $k = 4$ and GELU.

4   Experiments

We conduct experiments in three learning settings: STL, TL and CL. In each case, the performance of UMAVR is compared with the baseline models belonging to distinct model families. All models are designed to return a logit vector $v \in \mathbb{R}^{n_a}$ representing a score for each answer, and the softmax function is used to compute the probability distribution $\hat{p}$ over the set of answers. The index corresponding to the highest probability is considered the predicted answer.

Table 1. Model size. The number of parameters of each model in millions (M).

MODEL	# PARAMETERS	MODEL	# PARAMETERS
RESNET-18	11.2M	MIXER S/16	20.0M
RESNET-50	23.8M	MIXER S/32	18.2M
CONVNEXT-Pico	8.7M	ViP-Nano	4.0M
CONVNEXT-NANO	15.1M	ViP-Tiny	7.9M
MAXVIT-PICO	7.3M	UMAVR	3.5M
MAXVIT-NANO	15.0M		
TINYVIT-5M	5.1M		
TINYVIT-11M	10.6M		

Baselines. The set of benchmark models includes convolutional networks, represented by ResNet [6] and ConvNext [11], Vision Transformer (ViT) [5], MaxViT [25], TinyViT [29] and Swin Transformer [10] as representatives of the Transformer family, adapted to vision tasks, and MLP-based models such as MLP-Mixer [23] and Vision Permutator (ViP) [8]. Table 1 compares the numbers of model parameters.

Table 2. Dataset details. The benchmarks differ w.r.t. their size, allocation into train/val/test splits, and the maximal number of available answers n_a^{max}.

DATASET	SIZE	TRAIN	VAL	TEST	n_a^{max}
G-SET	49K	34.4K	9.8K	4.8K	5
I-RAVEN	70K	42K	14K	14K	8
PGM	1.42M	1.2M	20K	200K	8
VAP	710K	600K	10K	100K	4
VASR	154.8K	150K	2.25K	2.55K	4

Tasks. The models are evaluated on three challenging AVR problems. Firstly, we consider the problem of solving RPMs from three datasets: G-set [19,24] with visually simple matrices following experiment 1 from [24]; I-RAVEN [9, 33] with a much richer set of available objects, attributes, and abstract rules; and the Neutral regime of PGM [1] which is of much bigger size. Secondly, we consider the VAP dataset [7] which presents a conceptual abstraction challenge with matrices that are structurally different from RPMs. Thirdly, we employ the Visual Analogies of Situation Recognition dataset (VASR) [2] that presents visual analogies comprising real-world images. We employ the dataset variant with random distractors.

Overall, the datasets vary in size, the content of the matrices (geometric shapes, real-world images), and the number of available answers (see Table 2).

This diversity allows gaining insights into models' performance in different axes. To deeper analyse the limitations of the discussed models, in some experiments we reduced the number of available answers in the matrices, expecting that this simplification would make the task more comprehensible.

Experimental Setting. The models are trained with batches of 256 matrices for PGM and VAP datasets, and of 128 matrices in all the remaining cases. Model parameters are optimized with Adam with $\beta_1 = 0.9$, $\beta_2 = 0.999$ and $\epsilon = 10^{-8}$, until the validation loss doesn't improve for 10 consecutive epochs. We tuned learning rate λ of each model separately with 3 randomly initialized runs on G-set and I-RAVEN with $n_a = 2$ and selected λ that worked best on average. We applied linear learning rate warmup starting from $\lambda = 10^{-6}$ over 500 iterations and cosine decay with $\lambda_{min} = 10^{-6}$. When learning to solve matrices from PGM, I-RAVEN and VAP, we make use of a supplementary training signal in the form of an auxiliary loss [1,33] with sparse encoding [13], where the model has to additionally predict the hidden rules that govern the matrix construction. To this end, in parallel to the answer prediction layer, a shallow rule classifier is applied. The classifier operates on the token embedding matrix z_{D_G} passed through the Layer Normalization and averaged along the width and height dimensions. The classifier is composed of a linear layer with 128 units, followed by GELU and another linear layer with $|r|$ output neurons, where $|r|$ is the size of the one-hot encoded rule vector. Depending on the dataset, this gives 50, 40 and 28 units for PGM, I-RAVEN and VAP, respectively, which corresponds to the number of unique rules in each dataset. Each training run is performed on a node with a single NVIDIA DGX A100 GPU.

In the experiments with $n_a < n_a^{max}$, in the original problem instance (with n_a^{max} answer panels) $n_a^{max} - n_a$ randomly sampled incorrect answers are deleted.

4.1   Single-Task Learning

STL experiments assess the ability of modern CV models to solve uniformly viewed AVR tasks. In preliminary experiments conducted on 4 AVR tasks (G-set, I-RAVEN, PGM, VAP) we discovered that large CV models typically struggled to perform better than chance, irrespectively of the dataset and the number of possible answers. These models included ConvNext (Tiny, Small and Base), ViT-B/16, ViT-B/32, Swin (Tiny and Small), ViP-S/7 and ViP-M/7. To overcome their limitations, in subsequent experiments we employed their smaller parameter-efficient variants including ConvNext Pico and Nano [28], MaxViT (Pico and Nano) [25] and TinyViT (5M and 11M) [29]. For ViP, variants smaller than Small weren't defined in the original paper, which lead us to construct two new variants coined Nano and Tiny. Their detailed description is provided in Appendix A.

Table 3 compares test accuracy of the models on 4 datasets with variable numbers of answers. In G-set, where the amount of available data is scarce, ConvNext and ViP models struggle to perform better than chance, while remaining models achieve high performance, typically above 90%. ResNet-50 and Mixer S/16

Table 3. Single-task learning. Test accuracy of three baseline families of models (convolutional networks, vision transformers, MLP models for vision) and UMAVR in solving matrices from five datasets with variable numbers of possible answers n_a. Results higher than a random guess by more than 0.5 p.p are highlighted with a blue background. Best results are marked in bold and the second best are underlined. P, N and T denote Pico, Nano and Tiny, resp.

MODEL	G-SET, $n_a =$			I-RAVEN, $n_a =$			PGM, $n_a =$			VAP, $n_a =$		VASR
	2	4	5	2	4	8	2	4	8	2	4	4
RESNET-18	97.0	91.5	91.1	50.0	25.0	12.5	73.8	59.0	41.2	98.3	95.4	25.0
RESNET-50	96.9	94.1	81.7	50.2	25.0	12.5	73.8	56.4	32.7	98.4	96.1	43.7
CONVNEXT-P	50.0	25.0	20.0	67.0	_29.4_	12.7	50.0	25.0	12.5	96.0	90.4	25.0
CONVNEXT-N	50.0	25.0	20.0	69.8	25.1	12.5	50.0	25.0	12.5	95.9	91.7	25.0
MAXVIT-P	97.1	_95.8_	**95.6**	50.1	25.2	12.6	85.7	**97.1**	_92.0_	**99.4**	**98.4**	**62.3**
MAXVIT-N	_97.3_	**96.1**	_95.5_	81.0	25.0	12.7	85.2	_94.6_	**97.3**	_99.3_	_98.2_	24.0
TINYVIT-5M	97.2	95.6	95.4	83.5	25.0	12.5	72.7	41.1	34.3	99.0	97.1	55.4
TINYVIT-11M	97.0	94.7	95.4	71.2	25.5	12.7	84.3	46.6	34.0	98.3	96.3	54.2
MIXER S/16	96.3	92.2	82.8	62.3	25.5	_12.9_	_88.8_	74.5	61.1	97.5	88.4	54.5
MIXER S/32	97.0	95.6	94.9	74.9	25.5	12.8	**90.1**	76.4	73.4	97.2	93.0	54.1
VIP-N	50.0	25.0	20.0	_88.3_	25.1	12.5	77.6	46.3	81.7	97.6	95.2	25.0
VIP-T	50.0	25.0	20.0	75.6	25.0	12.5	85.2	73.8	49.0	97.3	95.5	25.0
UMAVR	**97.5**	**96.1**	95.1	**95.6**	**89.4**	13.1	76.9	63.3	52.3	93.9	97.3	_59.8_

scored slightly above 80% on the most challenging dataset configuration with $n_a = 5$. In I-RAVEN, which contains visually richer matrices with a hierarchical structure, both ResNet variants and MaxViT-Pico demonstrate performance at the random guess level across all n_a, other baseline models achieve non-random results only for $n_a = 2$, while UMAVR significantly outcompetes all methods for $n_a \in \{2, 4\}$. On PGM, all models but ConvNext learned to solve some matrices, though notably the best results were achieved by MaxViT ones. On VAP, all models present satisfactory results, commonly exceeding 90%. UMAVR demonstrates consistent and strong performance across nearly all considered settings, showing its general strength in visual reasoning, rather than overfitting to a particular task. The only exception is I-RAVEN with $n_a = 8$, in which all tested models performed at the random guess level. We conclude that UMAVR is a versatile method that in spite of its simplicity outcompetes other mainstream CV models in certain settings (specifically I-RAVEN with $n_a = 4$).

Pre-trained Checkpoints. To better understand the abstract reasoning capacity of large vision models, we repeated the STL experiments for ConvNext (Tiny, Small, Base), ViT (B/16, B/32) and Swin (Tiny, Small), starting from checkpoints pre-trained on ImageNet available in the TorchVision package. However, the only setting where any of these models performed better than chance was I-RAVEN with $n_a = 2$, where ConvNext-T and ConvNext-S achieved test accuracy of 75.6% and 83.6%, resp. This shows that despite using large pre-training datasets, the contemporary large vision models are generally incapable of solving AVR tasks represented in a unified manner proposed in this paper. Since the problem of classifying real-world images formulated in ImageNet is fundamentally different from AVR tasks considered in this work, we hypothesize that pre-training of large vision models on AVR data of sufficient scale might potentially boost their performance. Until this hypothesis is validated in future work, relatively smaller, parameter-efficient supervised models remain SOTA in the domain.

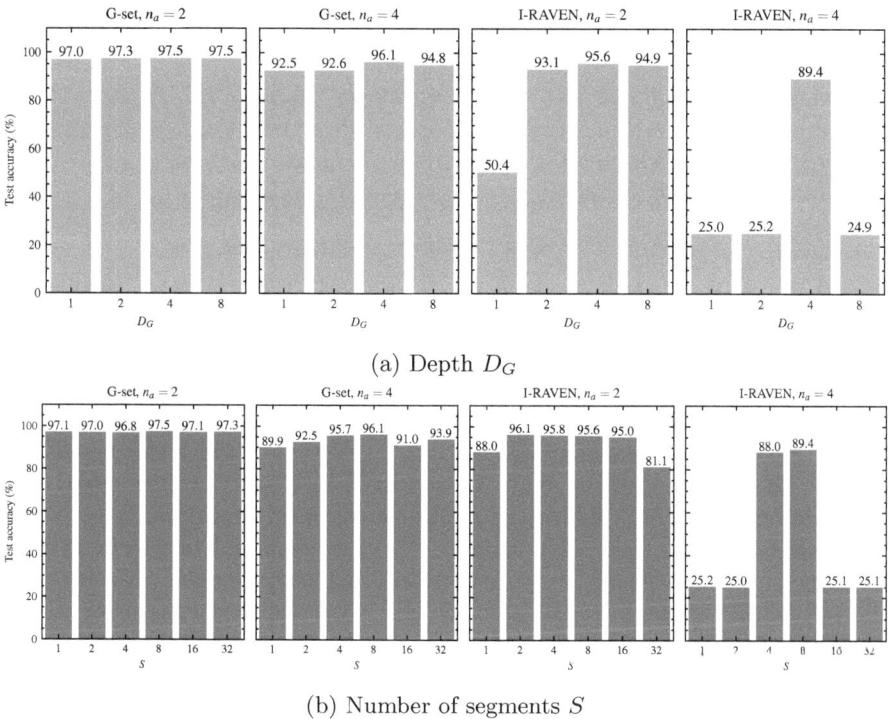

(a) Depth D_G

(b) Number of segments S

Fig. 3. Ablation study. UMAVR test accuracy with various D_G and S settings on G-set and I-RAVEN with $n_a \in \{2, 4\}$. In the default setting, we used $D_G = 4$ and $S = 8$.

Real-World Analogies. The VASR dataset [2] presents visual analogies formed from real-world images. Methods used in [2] employ pre-trained popular CV models (e.g. ViT or ConvNext) to embed each matrix image separately. The answer is predicted by applying vector arithmetics or training a shallow supervised classifier on frozen image embeddings. A limitation of these approaches is

Table 4. Transfer learning. Test accuracy of models that performed better than chance with STL on PGM (cf. Table 3). The models are first pre-trained on PGM with $n_a = 2, 4, 8$, resp., and then fine-tuned on G-set with $n_a = 2, 4, 5$ and I-RAVEN with $n_a = 2, 4, 8$, resp. TL and STL scores are shown on left/right resp.

MODEL	G-SET TEST ACCURACY (%)			I-RAVEN TEST ACCURACY (%)		
	$n_a = 2$	$n_a = 4$	$n_a = 5$	$n_a = 2$	$n_a = 4$	$n_a = 8$
RESNET-18	96.7/97.0	92.4/91.5	93.0/91.1	78.7/50.0	40.2/25.0	12.5/12.5
RESNET-50	96.7/96.9	92.9/94.1	93.8/81.7	71.2/50.2	44.6/25.0	12.5/12.5
MAXVIT-P	<u>97.5</u>/97.1	<u>96.0</u>/95.8	<u>95.6</u>/95.6	83.7/50.1	<u>67.5</u>/25.2	41.6/12.6
MAXVIT-N	97.2/97.3	**96.2**/96.1	**95.9**/95.5	<u>86.4</u>/81.0	61.3/25.0	38.5/12.7
TINYVIT-5M	95.7/97.2	92.7/95.6	92.9/95.4	56.9/83.5	29.8/25.0	26.0/12.5
TINYVIT-11M	97.4/97.0	90.6/94.7	<u>95.6</u>/95.4	82.7/71.2	46.6/25.5	27.3/12.7
MIXER S/16	96.9/96.3	93.6/92.2	91.6/82.8	78.3/62.3	46.7/25.5	20.1/12.9
MIXER S/32	96.5/97.0	93.4/95.6	94.9/94.9	79.5/74.9	45.4/25.5	36.2/12.8
VIP-N	96.3/50.0	91.8/25.0	95.0/20.0	74.0/88.3	46.4/25.1	**43.6**/12.5
VIP-T	**97.6**/50.0	95.2/25.0	94.9/20.0	81.2/75.6	60.1/25.0	28.4/12.5
UMAVR	97.3/97.5	95.9/96.1	95.4/95.1	**95.5**/95.6	**89.7**/89.4	<u>42.8</u>/13.1

the lack of ability to reason about the relations between matrix panels in early layers of the model. Instead, the reasoning is only framed as a post-processing step. Differently, we applied the proposed unified view to VASR, which enables application of CV models in an entirely different setup, in which the models reason over the whole matrix starting already from early layers of the model. The results are displayed in Table 3 (the rightmost column). Certain models, including ResNet-18, both ConvNext variants, MaxVit-Nano and both ViP variants performed indistinguishably from random guessing. Other models present performance typically exceeding 50%, with the best results achieved by MaxViT-Pico and UMAVR. We conclude that VASR matrices presented in the unified view pose a significant challenge for the contemporary vision models.

Ablation Study. We conducted additional experiments with several model variants to understand the contribution of respective components: 1) UMAVR with the convolutional backbone replaced with MetaFormer's patch emebdding layer; 2) UMAVR with TokenMixer replaced with the identity layer; 3) MetaFormer. We also considered PoolFormer-S12 [31], PoolFormerV2-S12, ConvFormer-S18, and CAFormer-S18 [32] as baselines related to UMAVR. The models were evaluated in STL on G-set and I-RAVEN with $n_a \in \{2, 4\}$. In all cases, the results were indistinguishable from random guessing, which shows the relevance of all specific UMAVR components for effective learning and reasoning. Further, we explored various model depths $D_G \in \{1, 2, 4, 8\}$ and numbers of segments $S \in \{1, 2, 4, 8, 16, 32\}$ to identify the optimal configuration. As shown in Fig. 3,

$D_G = 4$ and $S = 8$ lead to the best performance, justifying our choice of these values as the default setting for these hyperparameters.

4.2   Transfer Learning

Next, for the models that performed better than chance in at least one of the STL experiments, we explore a TL scenario, where models pre-trained on the largest dataset (PGM) are fine-tuned on the two smallest ones (G-set or I-RAVEN). For both the pre-training and fine-tuning datasets the same value of n_a is used, except for G-set with $n_a = 5$, for which pre-training on PGM is performed with $n_a = 8$. Table 4 presents the results. Application of TL leads to significant gains in multiple considered settings. Specifically, the performance of ResNet-50 and Mixer S/16 improved respectively from 81.7% and 82.8% to 93.8% and 91.6% on G-set with $n_a = 5$, while the performance of ViP Nano and Tiny improved from random guessing level to being on-par with other top performers across all n_a configurations. On I-RAVEN, significant improvement across most considered settings is observed, as after TL only ResNets struggle in the most demanding setting ($n_a = 8$).

The results signify the importance of utilizing a shared problem representation in the AVR domain, as pre-training the models on a large dataset can lead to notable performance improvements on the tasks, for which the available data is scarce. In certain cases, however, we observe the impact of the negative transfer effect, which brings attention to the need of designing robust TL techniques.

Algorithm 1. Curriculum learning. Solving matrices of gradually increasing difficulty.

Input: randomly initialized model f_θ, $n_a^{\max}$, λ_0
Output: trained model f_θ
 1: $n_a = 2$
 2: **while** $n_a \leq n_a^{max}$ **do**
 3:      $\lambda \leftarrow \lambda_0$ # reset the learning rate
 4:      $f_\theta \leftarrow \text{train}(f_\theta, n_a, \lambda)$ # until convergence with early stopping
 5:      $n_a \leftarrow n_a + 1$
 6: **end while**

4.3   Curriculum Learning

We evaluate the CL approach, in which the model is iteratively trained on gradually more demanding matrices, starting from $n_a = 2$ to $n_a = n_a^{max}$ with step 1, with the reuse of previously gathered knowledge (see Algorithm 1).

We considered all models listed in Table 3 and evaluated them with CL on G-set and I-RAVEN. On the former dataset, CL improved the performance of

ResNet-50 from 81.7% to 90.4% and Mixer S/16 from 82.8% to 95.2%. On I-RAVEN, CL improved the results of MaxViT Pico to 75.7% (+63.1 p.p.), TinyViT-5M to 28.3% (+15.8 p.p.), TinyViT-11M to 31.4% (+18.7 p.p.), Mixer S/16 to 31.7% (+18.8 p.p.), Mixer S/32 to 37.7% (+24.9 p.p.), ViP Tiny to 55.7% (+43.2 p.p.), and UMAVR to 86.9% (+73.8 p.p.). Performance in the remaining settings stayed at the STL level (±0.3 p.p.). Overall, for certain models, including the best-performing model – UMAVR, application of CL raised the STL results significantly, showing the potential of effective knowledge reuse within the unified view framework.

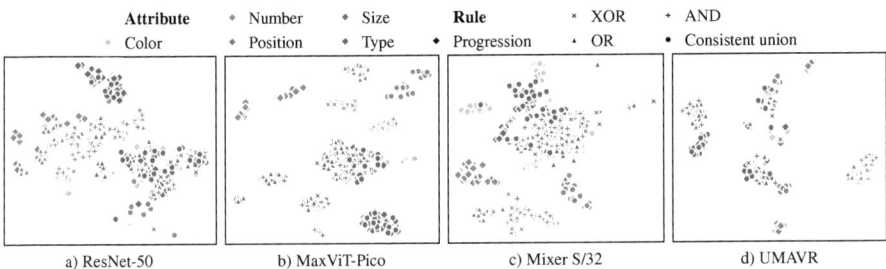

Fig. 4. PGM embeddings. The embeddings of PGM matrices ($n_a = 2$) from the test split of the Neutral regime, visualized with t-SNE. For the sake of interpretability, the figure considers matrices with a single rule applied to Shape objects.

4.4   Qualitative Analysis

Figure 4 compares UMAVR matrix embeddings ($n_a = 2$) with selected representative models on PGM. Overall, the clustering quality correlates with the model performance on the target task (cf. Table 3). Across all visualized models, the embeddings of matrices with rules applied to Number and Position attributes (green and purple, resp.) cluster into distinct groups. In addition, the embeddings of Mixer S/32 start to form distinguishable clusters for the remaining attributes as well, which aligns with the model leading performance in this setting. The visualization confirms that the models learn to identify the underlying abstract rules instead of relying on visual shortcuts or dataset biases. Appendix C extends this analysis to other relevant models and datasets.

4.5   Unified vs. Disjoint Representation

For the most demanding setting of $n_a = n_a^{\max}$, the best-performing unified approaches outperformed the state-of-the-art disjoint result on G-set (97.6% vs. 82.8% [24]), were on-par on PGM (97.3% vs. 98.2% [20]) and VAP (98.4% vs. 98.5% [20]), and were inferior on I-RAVEN (86.9% vs. 95.7% [20]) and VASR (62.3% vs. 86.0% [2]).

While the comparison shows a slight advantage of disjoint representation, it is important to note that the unified view opens several research avenues and poses challenges that extend beyond the sole performance improvement. Specifically, the use of the unified representation allows bridging the domains of broad CV and AVR by means of enabling the development of methods that could be seamlessly applied to both areas. Furthermore, the unified representation allows employing the current CV methods operating on single images to solve AVR tasks, and to use pre-trained checkpoints for their initialization. Finally, universal methods developed for solving uniformly viewed AVR tasks may accelerate progress in other domains that require relational reasoning, via knowledge reuse.

5   Conclusions and Future Work

Existing CV models that excel in solving AVR problems are generally task-specific, which prevents their application to other, even similar problems. In this work, we have formulated a unified view on AVR tasks in which an AVR instance is regarded as a single image, with no indication about the location or role of individual panels (context panels vs. answer panels). Apparently, even the SOTA CV models struggle to efficiently perform in this new setting, and in certain cases are unable to exceed a random guess level. To address this new challenge, we propose the UMAVR model, applicable to solving diverse AVR tasks within the above unified perspective. UMAVR shows its strength in the STL setup, and also demonstrates effective knowledge reuse in TL and CL setups, surpassing the performance of strong baselines.

The development of universal AVR methods has potential to foster progress in related areas via knowledge transfer. One possible target domain is document understanding that requires a high degree of relational reasoning. Large-scale datasets, with uniformly viewed AVR tasks, could be used to pre-train effective reasoning models and facilitate the development of new solutions in this area.

Moreover, AVR tasks were employed to analyze the reasoning capabilities of large language models (LLMs) using text-based task representations [27]. Recent studies extended this line of research to encompass multi-modal LLMs [18]. We believe that the proposed unified view of AVR tasks can support these advancements by providing a general problem representation, reducing the reliance on task-specific solution strategies.

Acknowledgments. This research was carried out with the support of the Laboratory of Bioinformatics and Computational Genomics and the High Performance Computing Center of the Faculty of Mathematics and Information Science Warsaw University of Technology. Mikołaj Małkiński was funded by the Warsaw University of Technology within the Excellence Initiative: Research University (IDUB) programme.

Disclosure of Interests. The authors have no competing interests to declare that are relevant to the content of this article.

References

1. Barrett, D., Hill, F., Santoro, A., Morcos, A., Lillicrap, T.: Measuring abstract reasoning in neural networks. In: International Conference on Machine Learning, pp. 511–520. PMLR (2018)
2. Bitton, Y., Yosef, R., Strugo, E., Shahaf, D., Schwartz, R., Stanovsky, G.: VASR: visual analogies of situation recognition. In: Proceedings of the AAAI Conference on Artificial Intelligence, vol. 37, pp. 241–249 (2023)
3. Bongard, M.M.: The recognition problem. Technical report, Foreign Technology Div Wright-Patterson AFB Ohio (1968)
4. Carpenter, P.A., Just, M.A., Shell, P.: What one intelligence test measures: a theoretical account of the processing in the raven progressive matrices test. Psychol. Rev. **97**(3), 404 (1990)
5. Dosovitskiy, A., et al.: An image is worth 16×16 words: transformers for image recognition at scale. In: International Conference on Learning Representations (2021)
6. He, K., Zhang, X., Ren, S., Sun, J.: Deep residual learning for image recognition. In: Proceedings of the IEEE/CVF Conference on Computer Vision and Pattern Recognition, pp. 770–778 (2016)
7. Hill, F., Santoro, A., Barrett, D., Morcos, A., Lillicrap, T.: Learning to make analogies by contrasting abstract relational structure. In: International Conference on Learning Representations (2019)
8. Hou, Q., Jiang, Z., Yuan, L., Cheng, M.M., Yan, S., Feng, J.: Vision permutator: a permutable MLP-like architecture for visual recognition. IEEE Trans. Pattern Anal. Mach. Intell. **45**(1), 1328–1334 (2023)
9. Hu, S., Ma, Y., Liu, X., Wei, Y., Bai, S.: Stratified rule-aware network for abstract visual reasoning. In: Proceedings of the AAAI Conference on Artificial Intelligence, vol. 35, pp. 1567–1574 (2021)
10. Liu, Z., et al.: Swin transformer: hierarchical vision transformer using shifted windows. In: Proceedings of the IEEE/CVF International Conference on Computer Vision, pp. 10012–10022 (2021)
11. Liu, Z., Mao, H., Wu, C.Y., Feichtenhofer, C., Darrell, T., Xie, S.: A ConvNet for the 2020s. In: Proceedings of the IEEE/CVF Conference on Computer Vision and Pattern Recognition, pp. 11976–11986 (2022)
12. Małkiński, M., Mańdziuk, J.: A review of emerging research directions in abstract visual reasoning. Inf. Fusion **91**, 713–736 (2023)
13. Małkiński, M., Mańdziuk, J.: Multi-label contrastive learning for abstract visual reasoning. IEEE Trans. Neural Netw. Learn. Syst. **35**(2), 1941–1953 (2024)
14. Małkiński, M., Mańdziuk, J.: One self-configurable model to solve many abstract visual reasoning problems. In: Proceedings of the AAAI Conference on Artificial Intelligence, vol. 38, pp. 14297–14305 (2024)
15. Małkiński, M., Mańdziuk, J.: A-I-RAVEN and I-RAVEN-Mesh: two new benchmarks for abstract visual reasoning. In: Proceedings of the Thirty-Fourth International Joint Conference on Artificial Intelligence, IJCAI-25 (2025). (Accepted)
16. Małkiński, M., Mańdziuk, J.: Advancing generalization across a variety of abstract visual reasoning tasks. In: Proceedings of the Thirty-Fourth International Joint Conference on Artificial Intelligence, IJCAI-25 (2025). (Accepted)
17. Małkiński, M., Mańdziuk, J.: Deep learning methods for abstract visual reasoning: a survey on Raven's Progressive Matrices. ACM Comput. Surv. **57**(7), 1–36 (2025)

18. Małkiński, M., Pawlonka, S., Mańdziuk, J.: Reasoning limitations of multimodal large language models. A case study of Bongard Problems. In: International Conference on Machine Learning. PMLR (2025). (Accepted)

19. Mańdziuk, J., Żychowski, A.: DeepIQ: A human-inspired AI system for solving IQ test problems. In: 2019 International Joint Conference on Neural Networks, pp. 1–8. IEEE (2019)

20. Mondal, S.S., Webb, T.W., Cohen, J.: Learning to reason over visual objects. In: International Conference on Learning Representations (2023)

21. Raven, J.C., Court, J.H.: Raven's Progressive Matrices and Vocabulary Scales. Oxford Pyschologists Press, Oxford (1998)

22. Snow, R.E., Kyllonen, P.C., Marshalek, B.: The topography of ability and learning correlations. Adv. Psychol. Hum. Intell. **2**(S 47), 103 (1984)

23. Tolstikhin, I.O., et al.: MLP-mixer: an all-MLP architecture for vision. Adv. Neural. Inf. Process. Syst. **34**, 24261–24272 (2021)

24. Tomaszewska, P., Żychowski, A., Mańdziuk, J.: Duel-based deep learning system for solving IQ tests. In: International Conference on Artificial Intelligence and Statistics, pp. 10483–10492. PMLR (2022)

25. Tu, Z., et al.: MaxViT: multi-axis vision transformer. In: Avidan, S., Brostow, G., Cissé, M., Farinella, G.M., Hassner, T. (eds.) ECCV 2022. LNCS, vol. 13684, pp. 459–479. Springer, Cham (2022). https://doi.org/10.1007/978-3-031-20053-3_27

26. Vaswani, A., et al.: Attention is all you need. Adv. Neural. Inf. Process. Syst. **30**, 5998–6008 (2017)

27. Webb, T., Holyoak, K.J., Lu, H.: Emergent analogical reasoning in large language models. Nat. Hum. Behav. **7**(9), 1526–1541 (2023)

28. Wightman, R.: PyTorch image models (2019). https://github.com/rwightman/pytorch-image-models, https://doi.org/10.5281/zenodo.4414861

29. Wu, K., et al.: TinyViT: fast pretraining distillation for small vision transformers. In: Avidan, S., Brostow, G., Cissé, M., Farinella, G.M., Hassner, T. (eds.) ECCV 2022. LNCS, vol. 13681, pp. 68–85. Springer, Cham (2022). https://doi.org/10.1007/978-3-031-19803-8_5

30. Wu, Y., Dong, H., Grosse, R., Ba, J.: The scattering compositional learner: discovering objects, attributes, relationships in analogical reasoning. arXiv:2007.04212 (2020)

31. Yu, W., et al.: MetaFormer is actually what you need for vision. In: Proceedings of the IEEE/CVF Conference on Computer Vision and Pattern Recognition, pp. 10819–10829 (2022)

32. Yu, W., et al.: MetaFormer baselines for vision. IEEE Trans. Pattern Anal. Mach. Intell. **46**(2), 896–912 (2024)

33. Zhang, C., Gao, F., Jia, B., Zhu, Y., Zhu, S.C.: RAVEN: a dataset for relational and analogical visual reasoning. In: Proceedings of the IEEE/CVF Conference on Computer Vision and Pattern Recognition, pp. 5317–5327 (2019)

34. Zhang, H., et al.: ResNeSt: split-attention networks. In: Proceedings of the IEEE/CVF Conference on Computer Vision and Pattern Recognition, pp. 2736–2746 (2022)

Multi-class and Multi-task Strategies for Neural Directed Link Prediction

Claudio Moroni[1,2](✉) , Claudio Borile[2] , Carolina Mattsson[2] ,
Michele Starnini[2,3] , and André Panisson[2]

[1] Dedagroup, Turin, Italy
claudio.moroni@dedagroup.it
[2] CENTAI Institute, Turin, Italy
{claudio.moroni,claudio.borile,carolina.mattsson,michele.starnini,
andre.panisson}@centai.eu
[3] Department of Engineering, Universitat Pompeu Fabra, 08018 Barcelona, Spain

Abstract. Link Prediction is a foundational task in Graph Representation Learning, supporting applications like link recommendation, knowledge graph completion, and graph generation. Graph Neural Networks (GNNs) have shown promising results in this domain and are widely used for learning graph representations from data. However, not all GNNs can represent edge direction and not all training strategies support the learning of directed graph representations. For this reason, Neural Directed Link Prediction (NDLP) has been divided into three sub-tasks. Models that perform well in distinguishing uncorrelated samples of positive and negative directed edges (the general DLP task) do not necessarily capture edge directionality and bidirectionality (two additional tasks). While many models can be trained to perform well on any of the sub-tasks, most fail to perform well across them all. In this work, we propose three novel training strategies that adress the three sub-tasks simultaneously and can be applied to any autoencoder-based GNN without motifying its architecture. Our first strategy, the Multi-Class Framework for Neural Directed Link Prediction (MC-NDLP) maps NDLP to a Multi-Class training objective. The second and third strategies adopt a Multi-Task perspective, either with a Multi-Objective (MO-NDLP) or a Scalarized (S-NDLP) approach. We show that these training strategies allow many models to achieve higher or more balanced performance across the three NDLP sub-tasks. The flexibility offered by our proposed training strategies provides a powerful means for improving the capabilities of NDLP models to advance the state of Neural Directed Link Prediction.

Keywords: Graph Machine Learning · Directed Link Prediction

Supplementary Information The online version contains supplementary material available at https://doi.org/10.1007/978-3-662-72243-5_8.

1 Introduction

Graphs are a natural way to represent complex systems. Examples include social networks, financial transaction networks, power grids, and neuronal connectivity [1,16]. These systems can be modeled using different types of graphs, ranging from simple networks to more sophisticated structures like Knowledge Graphs [14], Dynamic Graphs [15], or Bipartite Graphs for recommender systems [24]. Given the widespread presence of graph structures, learning representations from graph data has grown increasingly important with core applications including node classification, link prediction and graph classification.

In this work, we focus on Graph Neural Networks (GNNs) as applied to link prediction [26] on directed graphs. Recently, GNN-based models, such as Graph Autoencoders, have been devised focusing on undirected [5,7,9,20,40] and directed graphs [12,21,31,39,42,43], establishing the field of Neural Link Prediction. These models have several important applications, including completing knowledge graphs [4], serving as baseline for deep graph generation [20,33] and pre-processing transaction networks [25]. However, the recent literature primarily focuses on undirected applications [22,27,37], with few studies mentioning directed cases [3]. Direction can be core to the application itself, in some domains. With citation graphs, for instance, citing and being cited have substantively different meanings. Moreover, incorporating edge direction has been shown to improve learning for node classification across different types of graphs [30]. Even so, the nuances of link prediction on directed graphs are often overlooked and it has been argued that this limits progress in this area [31].

Neural Directed Link Prediction (NDLP) requires a model that is capable of representing edge direction and a training strategy that effectively learns directionality. Not all GNNs can represent edge direction. Graph Autoencoders, for example, often use decoder implementations where probabilities for edges (u, v) and (v, u) are the same by design [31]. We refer to these models as NDLP-incapable. But even NDLP-capable models can fail to learn edge directionality when the training strategy is adapted from link prediction on undirected graphs, where, typically, models are trained and evaluated on random subsets of positive and negative undirected edges [5,9,13,20,35,40,41]. Now, on a sparse directed graph, it is statistically unlikely that a random subset of negative directed edges would include many reverse edges of randomly sampled positive directed edges. This allows models to ignore edge direction without incurring a penalty. Indeed, using uncorrelated samples of positive and negative directed edges to train and evaluate NDLP models [12,21,39,43] can lead to NDLP-incapable models performing deceptively well.

Training and evaluation for NDLP is more complex. Three sub-tasks have been devised in the recent literature to more comprehensively evaluate performance of directed link prediction [31,41,42,44]. The "General DLP" task is the classic adaptation of the approach used in the undirected case to the directed case. This is complemented with two other binary classification sub-tasks designed to test a model's ability to distinguish edge directions. Namely, the "Directional" and "Bidirectional" sub-tasks. Prior work has shown that

NDLP-capable models can learn to perform well on each of the three sub-tasks [31,41,42,44] and that there is a trade-off among them [42]. However, prior approaches do not consider training strategies that can adress these three sub-tasks simultaneously.

Here we propose three learning strategies to improve performance across NDLP sub-tasks, simultaneously. The first strategy, *Multi-Class Directed Link Prediction (MC-NDLP)*, maps directed link prediction to a four-class classification task. This framework distinguishes between unidirectional positives, unidirectional negatives, bidirectional positives, and bidirectional negatives, ensuring balanced contributions to the training loss. The other two approaches recognize the Multi-Task nature of directed link prediction, simultaneously training on simultaneously constructed *General DLP*, *Directional* and *Bidirectional* training sets. Drawing from the literature on Multi-Objective [6] and Scalarization [17] methods, we propose *Multi-Objective Directed Link Prediction (MO-NDLP)* and *Scalarization-based Directed Link Prediction (S-NDLP)* strategies to handle these tasks more effectively. Each of our three training strategies incentivize NDLP-capable models to learn directed representations that perform well across the three sub-tasks. We find that better training strategies can be as useful as better models in advancing the state of Neural Directed Link Prediction.

The remainder of this paper is organized as follows: Sect. 2 covers the background concepts and related work, highlighting their relevance to our approach. In Sect. 3, we detail the proposed multi-class and multi-task strategies. Section 4 outlines the experimental setup, describes the datasets and presents a performance comparison of various models across all strategies and datasets. Finally, Sect. 5 provides concluding remarks.

2   Background and Related Work

In this section, we introduce the notation and review key concepts and prior research relevant to Neural Directed Link Prediction (NDLP). We briefly discuss foundational work in Graph Neural Networks and their applications in undirected link prediction, then go on to examine approaches for incorporating edge direction, in order to highlight limitations and the need for training strategies that better incentivise models to encode directed representations.

2.1   Notation

Given a directed graph $G = (V, E)$ with $N = |V|$ nodes where $E \subset V \times V$, and given $u, v \in V$ we say that:

- (u, v) is *negative bidirectional* $\iff (u, v) \notin E \wedge (v, u) \notin E$;
- (u, v) is *negative unidirectional* $\iff (u, v) \notin E \wedge (v, u) \in E$;
- (u, v) is *positive unidirectional* $\iff (u, v) \in E \wedge (v, u) \notin E$;
- (u, v) is *positive bidirectional* $\iff (u, v) \in E \wedge (v, u) \in E$;

Moreover, we denote $A \in \{0, 1\}^{N \times N}$ as G's adjacency matrix, and $X \in \mathbb{R}^{N \times F}$ as node features.

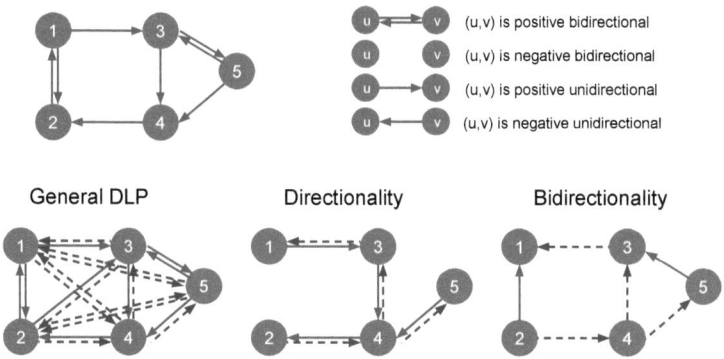

Fig. 1. From a graph G (top panel), for each task definition, green edges are the positive class and red edges are the negative class. In *General DLP*, any absent directed edge can be selected as negative. For *Directionality* prediction, unidirectional edges are positives, with their inverses as negatives. For *Bidirectionality* prediction, one direction of bidirectional edges are positives, and the reverse of unidirectional edges are negatives.

2.2   Graph Neural Networks

Graph Neural Networks (GNNs) are currently the *de facto* standard approach for learning over graph data, with applications in the pharmaceutical industry, material science [28], time series [18], and anti-money laundering [2,8,19,36].

Message Passing Neural Networks (MPNNs) [10,11,34,38] constitute the most general framework for GNNs, and elaborate successive hidden representations for each node v by aggregating messages from its neighbors. Given $z_v^{(k)}$ as the k-th layer embedding of node v (with $z_v^{(0)}$ equalling v's feature vector x_v), GNNs compute the next layer embedding $z_v^{(k+1)}$ through the following relation:

$$z_v^{(k+1)} = f^{(k)} \left(m_s^k(z_v^{(k)}), A^{(k)} \left(\left\{ m_n^{(k)}(z_u^{(k)}) | u \in N(v) \right\} \right) \right) \qquad (1)$$

where $f^{(k)}, A^{(k)}, m_s^k$ and $m_n^{(k)}$ are, respectively, the layer-specific update function, the aggregation function, the self-information and message functions. $N(v)$ indicates the neighborhood of node v.

If we consider K layers in total, the last embedding of each node $z_v \equiv z_v^{(K)}$ can be used for downstream tasks such as node classification, link prediction, and graph classification. For link prediction, a *decoder* is a function that takes as input the representation of two nodes, z_u, z_v and outputs a normalized score representing the probability of an edge (u, v) being present. For the undirected case, the decoder can be the scalar product followed by a sigmoid function, $DEC(z_u, z_v) = \sigma(z_u \cdot z_v)$, or a neural network such as a Multi-Layer Perceptron (MLP). The scalar product, being symmetric in u and v, is an example of a decoder that leaves a model unable to represent directionality in its predictions.

2.3   Neural Directed Link Prediction

This work considers three sub-tasks for NDLP, as presented in [31]. Figure 1 shows a representation of the positive and negative classes that define the *General Directed Link Prediction (General DLP)* task, the *Biased Directional Negative Samples Link Prediction (Directional)* task, and the *Bidirectionality Prediction (Bidirectional)* task. These classes are the basis for selecting the samples of (directed) edges used in the most relevant recent literature for testing and evaluation of NDLP-capable models performing directed link prediction.

We focus on NDLP-capable models that use Graph Autoencoder techniques. [21] develops an extension of the Weisfeiler-Lehman kernel [32] which is then used as a basis to define a source/target-like [31] graph autoencoder for directed graphs; however, the model is only tested on the *General DLP* sub-task. [42] defines a GCN for directed graphs where the aggregation is performed by a complex, hermitian laplacian. This model is tested across all three tasks, although for each of them, a different parameter set is inferred. To the best of our knowledge, [31] devises the earliest GNN-based autoecoders for NDLP, and is among the first to highlight the intrinsic differences between the directed and undirected cases; Their work is also responsible for one of the earliest usage of the *General DLP, Directional* and *Bidirectional* sub-tasks in a neural setting. Similarly to [42], the authors of [31] do not find one parameter set for all three tasks for each model. [41] endows cluster information in node embeddings, but, similarly to [31], trains and tests over the *Directional* and *Bidirectional* tasks using two different training graphs. [44] produces unsupervised source/target node embeddings by adversarially training a neural pair of generator and discriminator on the graph topology; the final model performs simultaneously well on the *General DLP* and *Directional* task, but it is not evaluated on the *Bidirectional* task.

Although we will experiment with different models, it is not our aim to sponsor any model in particular. Rather, we propose learning strategies that can used with *any* NDLP-capable model to encourage encoding directionality and strike a better balance among the performances on sub-tasks of NDLP. Therefore our work is much more in the spirit of [23], a representation learning framework that argues in favor of masking compared to full-graph training. Unfortunately, [23] has been developed and tested on undirected graphs only, so its extension to directed graphs could be a future research avenue.

3   Strategies for Neural Directed Link Prediction

In the previous section, we discussed that NDLP has recently been described as three distinct sub-tasks: General DLP, Directional, and Bidirectional. Simultaneously addressing these requires more than the classic approach to training for link prediction. In this section, we formalize Multi-Class and Multi-Task training strategies that are in principle applicable to every NDLP-capable encoder-based MPNN and encourage such models to learn to encode directionality.

3.1   Multi-class Strategies for Neural Directed Link Prediction

As anticipated in Sect. 1, we consider here that the reason why prior works are generally not able to infer a single model that performs well on all three sub-tasks could be related to an unaddressed imbalance between unidirectional and bidirectional edges' contributions to the training loss. We note that this imbalance should be dealt with without compromising the reweighting between positive and negative edges. Therefore we propose to simultaneously balance positives vs negatives and unidirectional vs bidirectional edges using the following Multi-Class Neural Directed Link Prediction (*MC-NDLP*) strategy.

Given a GNN model that computes d_K-dimensional embeddings z_v, $\forall v \in V$, we may compute logits for each of the four classes listed in Sect. 2.1 by applying an MLP to the concatenation of the embeddings. The MLP must take $2d_K$ input dimensions and output 4 logits, and can be arbitrarily deep:

$$[\hat{l}_{uv}^{nb}, \hat{l}_{uv}^{nu}, \hat{l}_{uv}^{pu}, \hat{l}_{uv}^{pb}] = \text{MLP}(z_u||z_v), \tag{2}$$

where $\hat{l}_{uv}^{m}, m \in \{nb, nu, pu, pb\}$ denote the model's output logits for the edge (u, v) being negative bidirectional, negative unidirectional, positive unidirectional, or positive bidirectional as defined in Sect. 2.1.

Notably, *MC-NDLP* is also compatible with any graph autoencoder that makes use of specific decoders which output only one logit $\hat{l}_{uv}$, that is, the model output for the presence of a directed edge (u, v) [21,31]. We can turn the standard binary classification task for NDLP into a 4-class classification task by transforming the output logit into a probability via e.g., a sigmoid $\hat{p}_{uv} = \sigma(\hat{l}_{uv})$ and defining:

$$\hat{p}_{uv}^{nb}, \hat{p}_{uv}^{nu}, \hat{p}_{uv}^{pu}, \hat{p}_{uv}^{pb}t= [(1 - \hat{p}_{uv})(1 - \hat{p}_{vu}), \tag{3}$$
$$(1 - \hat{p}_{uv})\hat{p}_{vu},$$
$$\hat{p}_{uv}(1 - \hat{p}_{vu}),$$
$$\hat{p}_{uv}\hat{p}_{vu}].$$

We note that Eq. 3 assumes statistical independence between $\hat{p}_{uv}$ and $\hat{p}_{vu}$, which are both conditioned on A and X. In fact, most autoencoders model $\hat{p}_{uv} = \hat{P}(e_{uv}|A, X)$ where $e_{uv} = 1 \iff (u, v) \in E$ otherwise it equals 0 [20], and Eq. 3 naturally extends these univariate autoencoders. Please refer to Appendix for details.

We can then define a weighted Multi-Class cross-entropy loss function:

$$\mathcal{L}_{MC\text{-}NDLP}(\Theta) = - \sum_{c \in C} \sum_{uv \in T} w_{y_{uv}} \mathbb{I}(y_{uv} = c) \log(\hat{p}_{uv}^{y_{uv}}), \tag{4}$$

where $C = \{nb, nu, pu, pb\}$, T is the *General DLP* training set (see Sect. 3.3), $\mathbb{I}$ is the indicator function and $y_{uv} \in C$ is the ground-truth class of the edge (u, v), and $\hat{p}_{uv}^{y_{uv}}$ is the model's output probability of edge (u, v) belonging to the ground-truth class y_{uv}. The class weight is defined as

$$w_{y_{uv}} = \frac{n_x}{n_{y_{uv}}},$$

where n_x represents the number of samples in class x, where x is the most numerous class (usually nb), and $n_{y_{uv}}$ is the number of samples in class y_{uv}. As discussed in Sect. 1, this class reweighting mitigates the statistical imbalance between all four classes defined in Sect. 2.1.

3.2 Multi-task Strategies for Neural Directed Link Prediction

Multi-Task Learning (MTL) refers to scenarios where more than one objective function must be simultaneously optimized. It is more challenging compared to single-task learning, due to the various objectives having no a priori relative importance and generally competing against each other. To simultaneously exploit the *General DLP, Directional* and *Bidirectional* training sources of information, we devise a multi-task objective over the three sub-tasks, defined by the binary cross-entropy loss functions on *General DLP* $\mathcal{L}_G$, *Directional* $\mathcal{L}_D$ and *Bidirectional* $\mathcal{L}_B$.

Multi-Task learning is usually carried out in two ways:

- *Scalarization*: it prescribes to sum and weight the losses to reduce the optimization to the single-objective case:

$$\mathcal{L} = \alpha_G \mathcal{L}_G + \alpha_D \mathcal{L}_D + \alpha_B \mathcal{L}_B$$

  The coefficients α_i, $i = G, D, B$, can be either learned or heuristically set. Despite its simplicity, heuristic implementations of Scalarization have been proven to achieve competitive performance in real use cases [17]. In this work, we set them to the validation losses (normalized between 0 and 1) of the previous epoch, to favor generalization. We name this approach *S-NDLP*;
- *Multi-Objective*: it consists in finding a parameter update rule that ensures that all losses are diminished (or left unchanged) at each optimization step. Given a model f_Θ and the objectives $\{\mathcal{L}_i(\Theta)\}_{i=1}^L$ to be simultaneously optimized, we say that Θ_1 *dominates* $\Theta_2 \iff \mathcal{L}_i(\Theta_1) \leq \mathcal{L}_i(\Theta_2) \quad \forall i \in 1, ..., L$. Therefore, a solution Θ^* is *Pareto-optimal* if it is not dominated by any other solution. The set of non-dominated solutions is called the Pareto set $\mathcal{P}$. While many Gradient-based Multi-Objective optimization algorithms with guaranteed convergence on the Pareto set have been developed, we focus for simplicity on one of the first, MGDA [6]. This algorithm is based on the observation that given the gradients associated with the individual losses, the opposite of their shortest convex linear combination points in the direction where all losses either remain constant or diminish. We name this approach *MO-NDLP*.

3.3 Simultaneous Splits

Train, validation, and test sets are constructed from the positive and negative classes associated to each of the three NDLP sub-tasks (see Fig. 1). In [31], edges are randomly sampled from the positive classes to construct the validation and test sets separately for each sub-task. Since models are separately trained on each sub-task, in that work, the training sets can be defined as what remains when the positive samples for that sub-task are reserved. In our case, the models must be trained over the graph that remains when *all* the reserved edges are removed. In order to preserve as many edges as possible for training, sampling is done together. Specifically, for each dataset, a random 10% and 5% of all unidirectional edges are reserved for testing and validation, respectively. Moreover, a random 30% and 15% of (one direction of) all bidirectional edges are reserved for testing and validation, respectively.

Validation and test sets for the three sub-tasks are constructed using the reserved edges. All the sampled edges (unidirectional and bidirectional) are used as positives for the *General DLP* task, complemented with an equal number of randomly sampled absent directed edges as negatives. The sampled unidirectional edges are used as positives for the *Directional* task, complemented with their reverses as negatives. The randomly sampled bidirectional edges are used for the *Bidirectional* task, complemented with an equal number of the reverses of unidirectional edges randomly sampled from the remaining graph as negatives. To perform well on this task, the model must distinguish between directed edges whose reverse edge exists from those whose reverse edge does not.

Multi-class learning requires a single training set. As in the *General DLP* task of [31], and in the classic formulation of directed link prediction, the training set is constructed out of all remaining directed edges and all the absent edges in the incomplete training graph. In our case, these edges are sorted into the four classes defined in Sect. 2.1 for multi-class classification as described in Sect. 3.1.

Multi-task learning requires training sets for each sub-task. Here, we take the opportunity to construct our own versions of the training sets for the *Directional* and *Bidirectional* tasks. This is done to give the training set similar edge statistics as their respective validation and test sets. In particular: for the *Directional* task, the training set is composed of all the remaining unidirectional edges (as positives) and their reverses (as negatives). This is similar to the training set for the *General DLP* task, but with the bidirectional edges removed. Finally, for the *Bidirectional* task, one direction of all the remaining bidirectional edges are used, as positives, together with an equal amount of the reverses of unidirectional edges randomly sampled from the remaining graph, as negatives.

These modifications to the sampling described in [31] make simultaneous training possible while ensuring no overlap between train and test data.

4   Experiments

In this section, we evaluate the effectiveness of our proposed strategies through comparative experiments using well-known datasets and NDLP models. We aim to demonstrate the performance improvements of our approaches across multiple tasks and models, highlighting their ability to handle the challenges of edge directionality and directionality. All code and results are publicly available at https://github.com/ClaudMor/MTMC-NDLP.

4.1 Datasets

Our experiments are conducted on three publicly available datasets, each of which is a directed graph. As in [31], we consider two small citation networks (Cora and CiteSeer) and a larger hyperlink network (Google).

Table 1. Statistics of the datasets used.

Dataset	Nodes $|V|$	Edges $|E|$	Edges (undirected)	Reciprocity	Density $|E|/|V|^2$	Clustering
Cora	2,708	5,429	5,278	0.056	0.000741	0.131
CiteSeer	3,327	4,732	4,676	0.024	0.000428	0.074
Google	15,763	171,206	149,456	0.254	0.000689	0.343

Table 1 gives the key network statistics. The Cora and CiteSeer graphs have few bidirectional edges. For the Google graph, however, a randomly sampled directed edge will be part of a bidirectional edge around 25% of the time.

Despite the difference in size, the graph density is similar across the datasets. The local density is higher for the Google dataset, as measured by the average (directed) clustering coefficient. Edge weights and/or node attributes are not considered. In all experiments, we use one-hot encoding of the node IDs as node features [31], except for the MAGNET model for which we used in- and out-degree as prescribed by the authors [42]. While employing node IDs means the models are transductive, all the strategies can be extended to inductive settings by using other node features as appropriate; an avenue for future development.

4.2 Models

We evaluate our proposed training strategies using several NDLP-capable models from the literature, all of which follow the Graph Autoencoder paradigm. These include the Gravity-Inspired Graph Autoencoder (Gr-GAE) [31], Source/Target Graph Autoencoder (ST-GAE) [31], the DiGAE Directed Graph Auto-Encoder from [21], MAGNET [42] and our custom MLP-GAE, which uses a decoder based on concatenating the encoder outputs followed by a multilayer perceptron. We also consider a recently introduced undirected model, MPLP [7], that achieves the current state-of-the-art in undirected link prediction computing approximations of graph heuristics, following the idea introduced in [40]. Altough the original implementation is not natively NDLP-capable, we introduce a modification of the decoder (dMPLP) that allows for NDLP and achieves competitive results. Each model is tested under various experimental conditions to evaluate its performance within our proposed framework. The standard graph autoencoder (GAE) [20] is included to provide a baseline NDLP-incapable model. Further details on model implementations and settings are provided in Appendix.

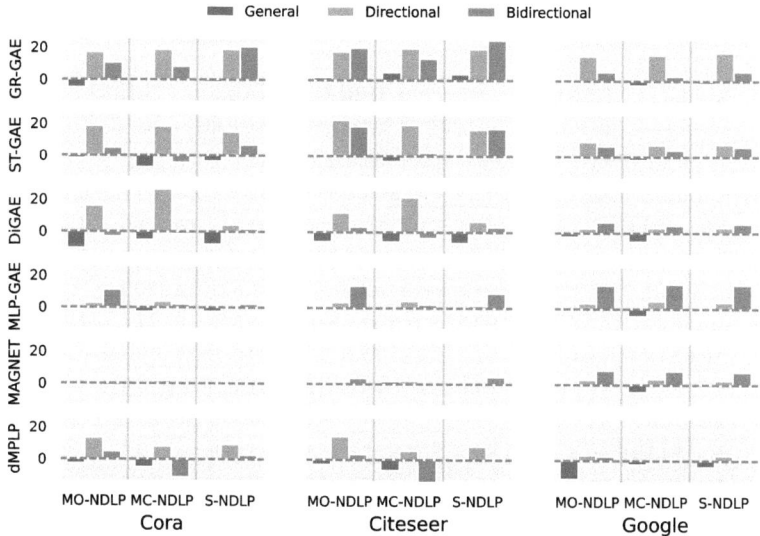

Fig. 2. Performance difference of each proposed strategy compared to the baseline strategy, measured in ROC-AUC (x100). Each bar represents the change in ROC-AUC - either an increase or decrease - when applying one of the proposed strategies to a specific sub-task, NDLP model, and dataset, relative to the same model's baseline performance. Scores are averaged over 5 runs. Error bars are omitted for visual clarity.

4.3   Experimental Settings

For the three tasks described in Fig. 1, under the sampling defined in Sect. 3.3, we measure ROC-AUC (Receiver Operating Characteristic - Area Under the Curve) to evaluate a model's ability to distinguish between classes, while AUPRC (Area Under Precision-Recall Curve) evaluates precision across different recall levels. We train the models according to the strategies defined in Sect. 3, as well as a *Baseline* strategy. Namely, the model is trained on the *General DLP* training set with rebalancing of positive and negative edges' contributions to training loss (Binary Cross Entropy). For each novel training strategy, we perform early stopping on the sum of ROC-AUC and AUPRC metrics over the *General DLP*, *Directional* and *Bidirectional* validation sets. Missing self-loops are always inserted for message passing, and they are also used as positive supervision samples in both *MO-NDLP* and *S-NDLP*, while they are treated as bidirectional negative supervision samples in *MC-NDLP*.

4.4   Results

The performance results are summarized in Table 2 (Cora dataset), Table 3 (Cite-Seer dataset), Table 4 (Google dataset) and in Fig. 2. Performances are averaged over 5 random splits, keeping the same seed for all models. All ROC-AUC and AUPRC values are scaled by 100 for compactness and clearer visualization. In

Table 2. ROC-AUC and AUPRC test scores of various models on Cora Dataset, trained with the *Baseline* strategy and our proposed strategies.

MODEL	STRATEGY	GENERAL		DIRECTIONAL		BIDIRECTIONAL	
		ROC-AUC	AUPRC	ROC-AUC	AUPRC	ROC-AUC	AUPRC
GAE	BASELINE	84.6 ± 0.4	88.6 ± 0.3	50.0 ± 0.0	50.0 ± 0.0	62.4 ± 3.0	64.0 ± 3.1
GR-GAE	BASELINE	**89.2 ± 0.4**	**92.4 ± 0.2**	63.4 ± 2.5	61.5 ± 2.7	69.1 ± 3.1	66.5 ± 3.3
	MO-NDLP	84.5 ± 1.1	86.3 ± 1.1	80.6 ± 0.7	80.2 ± 0.9	79.6 ± 4.3	84.6 ± 3.5
	MC-NDLP	88.6 ± 0.4	90.0 ± 0.4	82.1 ± 0.5	**81.8 ± 0.7**	77.3 ± 2.2	76.3 ± 1.7
	S-NDLP	87.8 ± 0.6	89.5 ± 0.5	**82.3 ± 0.5**	81.6 ± 0.4	**89.6 ± 1.6**	**92.4 ± 1.1**
ST-GAE	BASELINE	**87.8 ± 0.7**	**90.1 ± 0.5**	60.8 ± 0.5	64.5 ± 0.6	74.6 ± 1.8	74.1 ± 2.2
	MO-NDLP	86.3 ± 0.5	86.2 ± 0.4	**79.3 ± 1.0**	80.0 ± 0.9	79.3 ± 0.5	79.5 ± 1.9
	MC-NDLP	80.7 ± 2.0	80.1 ± 2.1	79.0 ± 2.3	**81.6 ± 1.9**	70.3 ± 3.0	68.1 ± 2.1
	S-NDLP	84.5 ± 0.4	84.9 ± 0.7	75.8 ± 1.0	78.4 ± 0.9	**81.1 ± 0.9**	**80.4 ± 1.6**
DiGAE	BASELINE	**80.4 ± 1.1**	**85.3 ± 0.8**	57.5 ± 1.3	63.0 ± 1.4	70.4 ± 2.2	68.6 ± 1.2
	MO-NDLP	70.2 ± 3.8	72.6 ± 3.6	73.6 ± 5.4	76.0 ± 4.2	67.3 ± 4.6	69.6 ± 4.1
	MC-NDLP	75.4 ± 0.9	77.4 ± 1.0	**84.3 ± 0.6**	**85.4 ± 0.8**	68.9 ± 1.5	69.3 ± 1.1
	S-NDLP	72.5 ± 4.0	77.4 ± 4.4	61.6 ± 1.3	69.2 ± 1.4	**72.1 ± 5.6**	**74.4 ± 5.7**
MLP-GAE	BASELINE	**77.1 ± 0.9**	**78.2 ± 0.6**	90.7 ± 0.6	90.7 ± 0.6	69.9 ± 3.2	69.7 ± 3.7
	MO-NDLP	76.0 ± 0.8	76.4 ± 0.7	93.4 ± 0.6	93.5 ± 0.6	**80.7 ± 1.6**	**79.2 ± 2.4**
	MC-NDLP	74.5 ± 0.7	75.6 ± 0.7	**94.3 ± 0.6**	**94.4 ± 0.5**	71.7 ± 2.4	65.7 ± 1.8
	S-NDLP	74.7 ± 1.0	74.9 ± 0.9	90.5 ± 0.7	90.0 ± 0.9	72.0 ± 2.6	70.5 ± 2.9
MAGNET	BASELINE	**75.2 ± 1.4**	**77.8 ± 1.0**	90.4 ± 0.9	89.8 ± 0.8	**71.9 ± 2.3**	**70.4 ± 2.8**
	MO-NDLP	74.4 ± 1.4	77.4 ± 1.1	91.3 ± 1.0	90.9 ± 1.0	70.6 ± 2.7	68.6 ± 2.7
	MC-NDLP	74.4 ± 1.0	77.4 ± 1.0	**92.1 ± 0.7**	**91.6 ± 0.7**	71.8 ± 2.6	70.0 ± 2.6
	S-NDLP	74.6 ± 1.3	77.5 ± 1.1	91.0 ± 1.0	90.4 ± 1.0	71.8 ± 2.8	70.2 ± 2.9
dMPLP	BASELINE	**86.1 ± 0.5**	**88.0 ± 0.9**	75.7 ± 2.2	76.8 ± 1.6	81.1 ± 3.6	82.2 ± 5.3
	MO-NDLP	83.5 ± 0.6	85.1 ± 0.6	**89.1 ± 1.7**	**89.0 ± 2.1**	**85.8 ± 3.3**	**89.3 ± 2.5**
	MC-NDLP	81.4 ± 1.7	82.0 ± 1.5	83.7 ± 4.2	83.7 ± 3.6	70.0 ± 4.3	71.5 ± 3.9
	S-NDLP	85.6 ± 1.0	86.9 ± 1.0	84.8 ± 2.7	86.3 ± 2.3	83.6 ± 4.7	87.0 ± 4.3

bold we highlight the best training strategy for each metric/model/task combination, while the underlined scores indicate the best training strategy across all models.

For comparison, we evaluated an NDLP-incapable graph autoencoder (GAE) model trained under the baseline strategy. While GAE performs deceptively well on the *General DLP* task, it fails to capture edge directionality, as expected. This is reflected in its random performance on the *Directional* task, with a ROC-AUC of 0.5. This limitation arises from the inner product decoder used by GAE [20], which always assigns the same probability to edges (u, v) and (v, u). Results from this experiment are reported in the first rows of Tables 2, 3 and 4.

Our proposed strategies consistently improved performance on the *Directional* and on the *Bidirectional* tasks across all datasets and models, only slightly compromising (at times even benefiting) *General DLP* performance [42], with a

Table 3. ROC-AUC and AUPRC test scores of various models on CiteSeer Dataset, trained with the *Baseline* strategy and our proposed strategies.

MODEL	STRATEGY	GENERAL		DIRECTIONAL		BIDIRECTIONAL	
		ROC-AUC	AUPRC	ROC-AUC	AUPRC	ROC-AUC	AUPRC
GAE	BASELINE	78.6 ± 0.7	84.1 ± 0.6	50.0 ± 0.0	50.0 ± 0.0	56.2 ± 3.8	59.3 ± 1.9
GR-GAE	BASELINE	77.0 ± 0.7	84.3 ± 0.6	55.7 ± 2.3	58.2 ± 3.2	72.5 ± 3.7	71.3 ± 4.4
	MO-NDLP	78.6 ± 0.8	82.6 ± 1.3	73.4 ± 1.6	76.8 ± 1.2	92.6 ± 2.1	94.6 ± 1.5
	MC-NDLP	**81.9 ± 0.8**	**85.1 ± 0.5**	**75.5 ± 0.7**	**78.9 ± 0.6**	85.9 ± 2.8	85.1 ± 3.1
	S-NDLP	80.8 ± 0.9	84.4 ± 0.7	75.2 ± 1.0	78.2 ± 0.9	**97.5 ± 1.1**	**98.0 ± 0.7**
ST-GAE	BASELINE	80.9 ± 0.8	**85.2 ± 0.7**	56.0 ± 0.3	61.1 ± 0.5	72.0 ± 4.5	73.0 ± 3.7
	MO-NDLP	**81.4 ± 1.5**	82.6 ± 2.0	**78.5 ± 2.3**	**80.1 ± 1.8**	90.5 ± 4.4	92.2 ± 4.1
	MC-NDLP	77.8 ± 1.8	79.3 ± 2.4	75.5 ± 4.0	79.5 ± 2.8	73.9 ± 5.1	75.1 ± 4.9
	S-NDLP	80.0 ± 1.3	82.0 ± 1.4	72.6 ± 1.6	77.4 ± 1.1	88.9 ± 4.3	90.3 ± 3.9
DiGAE	BASELINE	**78.5 ± 0.9**	**83.5 ± 0.8**	56.6 ± 1.0	65.2 ± 1.5	62.3 ± 3.3	65.8 ± 3.8
	MO-NDLP	72.6 ± 5.0	74.9 ± 5.2	68.7 ± 3.4	71.7 ± 4.1	**65.6 ± 4.5**	70.8 ± 5.2
	MC-NDLP	72.7 ± 1.3	74.6 ± 0.9	**78.3 ± 2.9**	**80.1 ± 1.8**	58.6 ± 3.8	61.6 ± 3.3
	S-NDLP	71.8 ± 3.9	75.4 ± 4.6	63.3 ± 1.4	69.7 ± 2.2	65.5 ± 5.1	**71.5 ± 5.8**
MLP-GAE	BASELINE	73.3 ± 0.8	**76.1 ± 0.7**	88.4 ± 0.7	89.8 ± 0.6	76.5 ± 1.1	76.5 ± 2.6
	MO-NDLP	**74.0 ± 0.9**	75.2 ± 1.0	91.8 ± 0.5	92.2 ± 0.5	**90.2 ± 0.9**	**90.0 ± 1.4**
	MC-NDLP	73.7 ± 0.8	74.3 ± 0.9	**92.6 ± 0.5**	**92.9 ± 0.4**	78.5 ± 1.1	73.6 ± 2.4
	S-NDLP	73.3 ± 0.7	74.8 ± 0.9	89.8 ± 0.3	90.1 ± 0.3	85.5 ± 2.5	85.1 ± 2.4
MAGNET	BASELINE	71.6 ± 0.7	74.9 ± 0.8	89.5 ± 0.6	89.9 ± 0.6	70.9 ± 6.1	68.9 ± 6.6
	MO-NDLP	72.3 ± 0.6	74.7 ± 0.6	91.0 ± 0.6	91.2 ± 0.5	74.6 ± 7.1	73.4 ± 7.7
	MC-NDLP	**73.2 ± 0.9**	**75.2 ± 0.9**	**91.6 ± 0.6**	**91.7 ± 0.6**	71.1 ± 7.5	69.7 ± 7.5
	S-NDLP	71.3 ± 0.8	74.6 ± 0.8	89.6 ± 0.6	90.0 ± 0.5	**75.3 ± 6.2**	**73.5 ± 7.0**
dMPLP	BASELINE	83.9 ± 0.9	86.8 ± 0.9	72.3 ± 1.5	73.8 ± 1.7	84.3 ± 7.0	86.2 ± 6.0
	MO-NDLP	81.2 ± 1.6	83.7 ± 1.7	**86.9 ± 2.1**	**87.6 ± 1.8**	87.7 ± 4.6	90.8 ± 2.9
	MC-NDLP	77.5 ± 1.9	80.8 ± 1.9	77.8 ± 3.3	77.0 ± 2.7	63.7 ± 8.6	65.5 ± 8.8
	S-NDLP	**84.9 ± 1.7**	**87.2 ± 1.8**	80.7 ± 1.4	82.9 ± 1.0	85.2 ± 7.1	88.8 ± 5.0

few exceptions. For instance, MAGNET showed similar performance on Cora and CiteSeer, regardless of the training strategy, while it achieved significant improvement in the *Bidirectional* task on the Google dataset when trained using our strategies. This highlights that even though some models, like MAGNET, show limited gains on specific datasets, the overall benefits might be more pronounced in larger datasets like Google. dMPLP shows good results with a balanced performance across all tasks for the *S-NDLP* and *MO-NDLP* strategies, while *MC-NDLP* seems less effective especially for the *Bidirectional* task. Reflecting the representational power of the original undirected model, dMPLP achieves the best performances in the *General* task both for Citeseer and Google datasets.

For other models like DiGAE, we observed a trade-off: its performance on the *Directional* task improved, but often at the expense of lower *General* task scores. Notably, on the Google dataset, especially with the *S-NDLP* strategy,

Table 4. ROC-AUC and AUPRC test scores of various models on Google Dataset, trained with the *Baseline* strategy and our proposed strategies.

MODEL	STRATEGY	GENERAL		DIRECTIONAL		BIDIRECTIONAL	
		ROC-AUC	AUPRC	ROC-AUC	AUPRC	ROC-AUC	AUPRC
GAE	BASELINE	93.5 ± 0.2	94.9 ± 0.2	50.0 ± 0.0	50.0 ± 0.0	54.8 ± 0.8	53.6 ± 1.4
GR-GAE	BASELINE	**98.3 ± 0.1**	**98.9 ± 0.0**	76.5 ± 0.8	69.1 ± 0.9	92.0 ± 0.2	91.9 ± 0.2
	MO-NDLP	97.4 ± 0.1	98.1 ± 0.1	91.9 ± 0.2	90.3 ± 0.4	97.6 ± 0.1	97.6 ± 0.1
	MC-NDLP	95.7 ± 0.1	95.7 ± 0.1	92.6 ± 0.2	92.8 ± 0.1	95.1 ± 0.1	94.2 ± 0.1
	S-NDLP	96.9 ± 0.1	97.7 ± 0.0	**94.3 ± 0.1**	**94.7 ± 0.1**	**98.0 ± 0.0**	**98.5 ± 0.0**
ST-GAE	BASELINE	**98.4 ± 0.1**	**98.7 ± 0.0**	87.2 ± 0.2	86.2 ± 0.1	92.2 ± 0.3	89.6 ± 0.4
	MO-NDLP	97.6 ± 0.2	97.4 ± 0.3	**96.6 ± 0.1**	**96.8 ± 0.1**	**98.8 ± 0.1**	**98.6 ± 0.1**
	MC-NDLP	96.6 ± 0.1	96.4 ± 0.2	94.6 ± 0.1	96.1 ± 0.1	96.4 ± 0.1	95.9 ± 0.1
	S-NDLP	97.6 ± 0.0	97.5 ± 0.1	95.0 ± 0.1	96.0 ± 0.1	98.3 ± 0.1	96.8 ± 0.1
DiGAE	BASELINE	**97.0 ± 0.1**	**97.8 ± 0.1**	92.9 ± 0.2	94.5 ± 0.2	90.9 ± 0.3	87.7 ± 0.4
	MO-NDLP	94.7 ± 0.1	95.7 ± 0.2	95.9 ± 0.1	96.9 ± 0.1	**97.7 ± 0.1**	**97.9 ± 0.1**
	MC-NDLP	91.7 ± 0.6	92.4 ± 0.5	96.3 ± 0.2	**97.2 ± 0.1**	95.7 ± 0.3	95.5 ± 0.4
	S-NDLP	96.8 ± 0.1	97.3 ± 0.1	**96.5 ± 0.1**	97.0 ± 0.1	96.7 ± 0.2	96.3 ± 0.3
MLP-GAE	BASELINE	90.8 ± 0.1	91.6 ± 0.0	93.5 ± 0.1	94.4 ± 0.1	81.2 ± 0.2	77.8 ± 0.4
	MO-NDLP	90.4 ± 0.1	91.0 ± 0.1	97.0 ± 0.0	97.3 ± 0.0	95.6 ± 0.1	95.1 ± 0.1
	MC-NDLP	86.3 ± 0.1	87.9 ± 0.1	**98.4 ± 0.1**	**98.5 ± 0.1**	96.4 ± 0.2	95.4 ± 0.1
	S-NDLP	**91.2 ± 0.1**	**91.9 ± 0.1**	97.6 ± 0.0	97.8 ± 0.0	96.0 ± 0.1	**95.5 ± 0.1**
MAGNET	BASELINE	**89.1 ± 0.1**	**90.1 ± 0.0**	93.8 ± 0.6	94.3 ± 0.4	83.9 ± 2.0	77.7 ± 2.3
	MO-NDLP	88.5 ± 0.2	89.8 ± 0.1	97.1 ± 0.1	97.2 ± 0.1	**92.9 ± 0.1**	**91.1 ± 0.3**
	MC-NDLP	84.7 ± 0.7	86.2 ± 0.4	**97.6 ± 0.0**	97.3 ± 0.1	92.5 ± 0.2	88.9 ± 0.3
	S-NDLP	87.9 ± 0.3	89.4 ± 0.2	96.7 ± 0.1	96.8 ± 0.1	91.9 ± 0.5	88.3 ± 0.9
dMPLP	BASELINE	**98.7 ± 0.1**	**98.9 ± 0.2**	93.6 ± 0.9	92.3 ± 2.2	95.6 ± 0.7	93.4 ± 0.8
	MO-NDLP	87.3 ± 2.8	85.1 ± 2.9	**97.0 ± 0.2**	**97.1 ± 0.3**	**98.1 ± 0.6**	**97.7 ± 0.8**
	MC-NDLP	96.6 ± 0.6	97.6 ± 0.4	93.6 ± 0.4	93.7 ± 0.5	96.1 ± 0.4	96.0 ± 0.5
	S-NDLP	94.9 ± 1.0	95.0 ± 1.0	96.7 ± 0.3	96.8 ± 0.2	96.3 ± 0.8	94.5 ± 1.6

DiGAE maintained its *General* task performance while delivering modest gains in *Directional* and *Bidirectional* tasks. Both MLP-GAE and MAGNET performed well on the *Directional* task but struggled on the *General* task, where their scores were systematically lower than those of the NDLP-incapable baseline GAE. DiGAE also struggled with the *General* task, surpassing GAE's baseline performance only on the Google dataset.

Selecting the right model-strategy combination depends on how much one is willing to sacrifice *General* task performance for improvements in *Directional* and *Bidirectional* tasks. Interestingly, this trade-off is not always necessary. For example, with the CiteSeer dataset, Gravity-GAE with *MC-NDLP* achieved the best *General* task performance while significantly improving *Directional* and *Bidirectional* scores. However, the optimal combination of model and strategy varies by dataset. For the Cora dataset, Gravity-AE with *S-NDLP* offers a balanced solution, delivering strong *Directional* and *Bidirectional* performance with only a slight reduction in *General* task scores. On the CiteSeer dataset, ST-GAE with *MO-NDLP* provides a good balance, offering competitive *General* task performance alongside noticeable gains in *Directional* and *Bidirectional* tasks. Similarly, for the Google dataset, ST-GAE with *MO-NDLP* proves to be an excellent choice, delivering significant improvements in *Directional* and *Bidirectional* tasks with minimal sacrifice in performance on the *General* task.

5 Conclusions

In this paper, we introduced and evaluated new training strategies to improve performance on Neural Directed Link Prediction tasks, addressing the limitations of current models in learning edge directionality. By extending existing models to handle multiple sub-tasks simultaneously, we demonstrated that the proposed strategies – Multi-Class (MC-DLP), Scalarization-based (S-DLP), and Multi-Objective (MO-DLP) Directed Link Prediction – consistently improve performance on both *Directional* and *Bidirectional* tasks, although at times with a trade-off in *General DLP* task performance.

While no single approach universally outperforms across all settings, the flexibility offered by our proposed training strategies provides a powerful means for improving NDLP model capabilities, and adopting any of the strategies is likely to yield meaningful benefits over the models trained without our optimization strategies. The proposed strategies do not require any modifications in the original models' architecture and are thus applicable to most MPNN models and versatile. The three proposed strategies affect the computational complexity of training differently. While *MC-NDLP* has a minimal impact, both *S-NDLP* and *MO-NDLP* require the computation of three losses, increasing the total memory needed. Nevertheless, also these two strategies can be effectively trained by parallizing the computation of the losses and implementing batching.

Future work can focus on refining these strategies to minimize trade-offs, particularly for applications that demand robust handling of directed graphs and directed link prediction. Our training strategies for learning edge directionality might also be usefully combined with approaches that allow GNNs to better represent edge directionality. Many alternative encodings [4, 5] and labeling tricks [1, 2, 3] have been proposed to enhance the expressiveness of GNNs, also for performing DLP, and it would be interesting to explore a wider range of augmented models. Simultaneous training across the three facets of DLP enables more concise comparative studies on the ability of models and various enhancements to provide balanced performance across these facets. Also, an interesting area for future exploration is knowledge graphs (KG), which could greatly benefit from our methods. Since KG-oriented tasks often employ specialized losses with margin terms [4] and involve complex query answering rather than basic link prediction [29], studying how enhanced directionality learning impacts KG performance would be a valuable direction.

Acknowledgements. M. S. acknowledges support from Grants No. RYC2022-037932-I and CNS2023-144156 funded by MCIN/AEI/10.13039/501100011033 and the European Union NextGenerationEU/PRTR.

References

1. Albert, R., Barabási, A.L.: Statistical mechanics of complex networks. Rev. Mod. Phys. **74**(1), 47 (2002)
2. Altman, E., Blanuša, J., Von Niederhäusern, L., Egressy, B., Anghel, A., Atasu, K.: Realistic synthetic financial transactions for anti-money laundering models. In: Advances in Neural Information Processing Systems, vol. 36 (2024)
3. Arrar, D., Kamel, N., Lakhfif, A.: A comprehensive survey of link prediction methods. J. Supercomput. (2023)
4. Bordes, A., Usunier, N., Garcia-Duran, A., Weston, J., Yakhnenko, O.: Translating embeddings for modeling multi-relational data. In: Advances in Neural Information Processing Systems, vol. 26 (2013)
5. Cai, L., Ji, S.: A multi-scale approach for graph link prediction. In: Proceedings of the AAAI Conference on Artificial Intelligence, vol. 34, no. 04, pp. 3308–3315 (2020)
6. Désidéri, J.A.: Multiple-gradient descent algorithm (MGDA) for multiobjective optimization. C. R. Math. **350**(5), 313–318 (2012)
7. Dong, K., Guo, Z., Chawla, N.: Pure message passing can estimate common neighbor for link prediction. In: Advances in Neural Information Processing Systems, vol. 37, pp. 73000–73035 (2024)
8. Egressy, B., Von Niederhäusern, L., Blanuša, J., Altman, E., Wattenhofer, R., Atasu, K.: Provably powerful graph neural networks for directed multigraphs. In: Proceedings of the AAAI Conference on Artificial Intelligence, vol. 38, pp. 11838–11846 (2024)
9. Fu, X., Zhang, J., Meng, Z., King, I.: MAGNN: metapath aggregated graph neural network for heterogeneous graph embedding. In: WWW 2020, pp. 2331–2341. Association for Computing Machinery, New York (2020)
10. Gilmer, J., Schoenholz, S.S., Riley, P.F., Vinyals, O., Dahl, G.E.: Neural message passing for quantum chemistry. In: Proceedings of the 34th International Conference on Machine Learning, ICML 2017, vol. 70, pp. 1263–1272 (2017)
11. Hamilton, W., Ying, Z., Leskovec, J.: Inductive representation learning on large graphs. In: Advances in Neural Information Processing Systems, vol. 30 (2017)
12. He, C., Zeng, J., Li, Y., Liu, S., Liu, L., Xiao, C.: Two-stream signed directed graph convolutional network for link prediction. Phys. A: Stat. Mech. Appl. **605**, 128036 (2022)
13. He, C., Cheng, J., Fei, X., Weng, Y., Zheng, Y., Tang, Y.: Community preserving adaptive graph convolutional networks for link prediction in attributed networks. Knowl.-Based Syst. **272**, 110589 (2023)
14. Hogan, A., et al.: Knowledge graphs. ACM Comput. Surv. (CSUR) **54**(4), 1–37 (2021)
15. Holme, P., Saramäki, J.: Temporal Network Theory. Springer (2019)
16. Hu, W., et al.: Open graph benchmark: datasets for machine learning on graphs. In: Advances in Neural Information Processing Systems, vol. 33, pp. 22118–22133 (2020)

17. Hu, Y., Xian, R., Wu, Q., Fan, Q., Yin, L., Zhao, H.: Revisiting scalarization in multi-task learning: a theoretical perspective. In: Advances in Neural Information Processing Systems, vol. 36 (2024)
18. Jin, M., et al.: A survey on graph neural networks for time series: forecasting, classification, imputation, and anomaly detection. IEEE Trans. Pattern Anal. Mach. Intell. (2024)
19. Johannessen, F., Jullum, M.: Finding money launderers using heterogeneous graph neural networks. arXiv preprint arXiv:2307.13499 (2023)
20. Kipf, T.N., Welling, M.: Variational graph auto-encoders. arXiv preprint arXiv:1611.07308 (2016)
21. Kollias, G., Kalantzis, V., Id'e, T., Lozano, A.C., Abe, N.: Directed graph auto-encoders. In: AAAI Conference on Artificial Intelligence (2022)
22. Kumar, A., Singh, S.S., Singh, K., Biswas, B.: Link prediction techniques, applications, and performance: a survey. Phy. A: Stat. Mech. Appl. **553**, 124289 (2020)
23. Li, J., et al.: What's behind the mask: understanding masked graph modeling for graph autoencoders. In: Proceedings of the 29th ACM SIGKDD Conference on Knowledge Discovery and Data Mining, pp. 1268–1279 (2023)
24. Li, X., Chen, H.: Recommendation as link prediction: a graph kernel-based machine learning approach. In: Proceedings of the 9th ACM/IEEE-CS Joint Conference on Digital Libraries, JCDL 2009, pp. 213–216. ACM, New York (2009)
25. Lin, D., Wu, J., Xuan, Q., Tse, C.K.: Ethereum transaction tracking: inferring evolution of transaction networks via link prediction. Phys. A: Stat. Mech. Appl. **600**, 127504 (2022)
26. Lü, L., Zhou, T.: Link prediction in complex networks: a survey. Phys. A: Stat. Mech. Appl. **390**(6), 1150–1170 (2011)
27. Qin, M., Yeung, D.Y.: Temporal link prediction: a unified framework, taxonomy, and review. ACM Comput. Surv. **56**(4) (2023)
28. Reiser, P., et al.: Graph neural networks for materials science and chemistry. Commun. Mater. **3**(1) (2022)
29. Ren, H., Hu, W., Leskovec, J.: Query2box: reasoning over knowledge graphs in vector space using box embeddings. arXiv preprint arXiv:2002.05969 (2020)
30. Rossi, E., Charpentier, B., Giovanni, F.D., Frasca, F., Günnemann, S., Bronstein, M.M.: Edge directionality improves learning on heterophilic graphs. In: Proceedings of the Second Learning on Graphs Conference, pp. 25:1–25:27. PMLR (2024). iSSN: 2640-3498
31. Salha, G., Limnios, S., Hennequin, R., Tran, V.A , Vazirgiannis, M.. Gravity-inspired graph autoencoders for directed link prediction. In: Proceedings of the 28th ACM International Conference on Information and Knowledge Management, pp. 589–598 (2019)
32. Shervashidze, N., Schweitzer, P., Leeuwen, E.J., Mehlhorn, K., Borgwardt, K.M.: Weisfeiler-Lehman graph kernels. J. Mach. Learn. Res. **12**(77), 2539–2561 (2011)
33. Simonovsky, M., Komodakis, N.: GraphVAE: towards generation of small graphs using variational autoencoders. In: Kůrková, V., Manolopoulos, Y., Hammer, B., Iliadis, L., Maglogiannis, I. (eds.) ICANN 2018. LNCS, vol. 11139, pp. 412–422. Springer, Cham (2018). https://doi.org/10.1007/978-3-030-01418-6_41
34. Veličković, P., Cucurull, G., Casanova, A., Romero, A., Liò, P., Bengio, Y.: Graph attention networks. In: International Conference on Learning Representations (2018)
35. Wang, J., Liang, J., Yao, K., Liang, J., Wang, D.: Graph convolutional autoencoders with co-learning of graph structure and node attributes. Pattern Recogn. **121**, 108215 (2022)

36. Weber, M., et al.: Anti-money laundering in bitcoin: experimenting with graph convolutional networks for financial forensics. arXiv preprint arXiv:1908.02591 (2019)
37. Wu, H., Song, C., Ge, Y., Ge, T.: Link prediction on complex networks: an experimental survey. Data Sci. Eng. **7**(3), 253–278 (2022)
38. Xu, K., Hu, W., Leskovec, J., Jegelka, S.: How powerful are graph neural networks? In: International Conference on Learning Representations (2019)
39. Yi, T., Zhang, S., Bu, Z., Du, J., Fang, C.: Link prediction based on higher-order structure extraction and autoencoder learning in directed networks. Knowl.-Based Syst. **241**, 108241 (2022)
40. Zhang, M., Chen, Y.: Link prediction based on graph neural networks. In: Advances in Neural Information Processing Systems, vol. 31 (2018)
41. Zhang, S., Zhang, W., Bu, Z., Zhang, X.: ClusterLP: a novel cluster-aware link prediction model in undirected and directed graphs. Int. J. Approximate Reasoning **172**, 109216 (2024)
42. Zhang, X., He, Y., Brugnone, N., Perlmutter, M., Hirn, M.: MagNet: a neural network for directed graphs. In: Advances in Neural Information Processing Systems (2021)
43. Zhang, Y., Tan, Y., Jian, S., Wu, Q., Li, K.: DGLP: incorporating orientation information for enhanced link prediction in directed graphs. In: ICASSP 2024-2024 IEEE International Conference on Acoustics, Speech and Signal Processing (ICASSP), pp. 6565–6569. IEEE (2024)
44. Zhu, S., Li, J., Peng, H., Wang, S., He, L.: Adversarial directed graph embedding. In: Proceedings of the AAAI Conference on Artificial Intelligence, vol. 35, no. 5, pp. 4741–4748 (2021)

ChordPrompt: Orchestrating Cross-Modal Prompt Synergy for Multi-domain Incremental Learning in CLIP

Zhiyuan Wang and Bokui Chen[✉]

Tsinghua Shenzhen International Graduate School, Tsinghua University,
Beijing, China
{wang-zy22,chenbk}@tsinghua.edu.cn

Abstract. Continual learning (CL) empowers pre-trained vision-language models to adapt effectively to novel or previously underrepresented data distributions without comprehensive retraining, enhancing their adaptability and efficiency. While vision-language models like CLIP show great promise, they struggle to maintain performance across domains in incremental learning scenarios. Existing prompt learning methods face two main limitations: 1) they primarily focus on class-incremental learning scenarios, lacking specific strategies for multi-domain task incremental learning; 2) most current approaches employ single-modal prompts, neglecting the potential benefits of cross-modal information exchange. To address these challenges, we propose the ChordPrompt framework, which facilitates a harmonious interplay between visual and textual prompts. ChordPrompt introduces cross-modal prompts to leverage interactions between visual and textual information. Our approach also employs domain-adaptive text prompts to select appropriate prompts for continual adaptation across multiple domains. Comprehensive experiments on multi-domain incremental learning benchmarks demonstrate that ChordPrompt outperforms state-of-the-art methods in zero-shot generalization and downstream task performance.

1 Introduction

Continual Learning (CL) is a crucial paradigm in machine learning that aims to develop models capable of sequentially learning from various domains without the need for complete retraining from scratch.

However, continual learning faces a critical challenge known as catastrophic forgetting [7], which severely undermines the model's ability to master distinct tasks sequentially. Catastrophic forgetting occurs when neural networks lose their ability to perform previously learned tasks after training on new ones. This leads to a significant deterioration in performance on the initial tasks. This problem becomes particularly challenging when the model must adapt to new or under-represented data distributions, a common requirement in real-world deployments.

B. Pfahringer et al. (Eds.): ECML PKDD 2025, LNAI 16020, pp. 147–164, 2026.
https://doi.org/10.1007/978-3-662-72243-5_9

Vision-language models like CLIP [22] have shown remarkable performance on various multi-modal tasks, excelling in visual and linguistic knowledge. Consequently, they exhibit impressive zero-shot generalization performance on unseen datasets [27]. Nevertheless, continually training Vision-Language (V-L) models like CLIP is critical. It helps keep the model up-to-date as new data emerges in real-world deployments. Unfortunately, during the continual fine-tuning of CLIP, its impressive zero-shot generalization performance substantially declines due to catastrophic forgetting. In addition, retraining large-scale vision-language models such as CLIP, pre-trained on 400M image-text pairs, for every new task would require computational resources often unavailable in real-world scenarios. Our approach provides a scalable solution by enabling continual learning without requiring access to the original training dataset or complete model retraining.

Continual learning for vision-language models is an emerging field presenting many open challenges and opportunities. For the CLIP model, the use of replay methods is limited, as pre-training datasets are often private and inaccessible. Therefore, recent studies focus on fine-tuning the entire model [20,36]. As shown in Fig. 1a, this method can inefficiently use both computational resources and the model's original capabilities.

To address these challenges, we introduce ChordPrompt for Continual Learning framework. Our approach is motivated by the multi-modal hypothesis in cognitive psychology. This cognitive framework suggests that perception and learning are not isolated processes confined to individual sensory channels but somewhat interactive processes where information from one modality can modulate the processing of another [25]. In traditional continual learning methods, as illustrated in Fig. 1a, the entire model typically requires fine-tuning. This process can be computationally expensive and may lead to inefficient use of the model's original capabilities. Contrastingly, as shown in Fig. 1b, single-modal prompts operate within the confines of a single modality, potentially missing valuable cross-modal insights. As shown in Fig. 1c, our proposed cross-modal approach ChordPrompt leverages the synergistic relationship between visual and textual information, overcoming these limitations and enabling the model to learn and adapt more comprehensively across different scenarios. ChordPrompt emulates the integrative nature of human cognition by fostering cross-modal interaction. This approach enables the model to develop more detailed and refined representations, significantly enhancing its performance in continual learning scenarios. Our work's main contributions are as follows:

- We introduce a cross-modal prompt strategy ChordPrompt to facilitate continual learning in vision-language models.
- We propose a domain-adaptive text prompt approach, which enables the model to adapt to specific characteristics of different domains, addressing the lack of strategies for multi-domain task incremental learning.
- We design an Aligner module and cross-modal prompts in visual and textual encoders, addressing the limitation of single-modal prompts and leveraging the benefits of cross-modal information exchange.

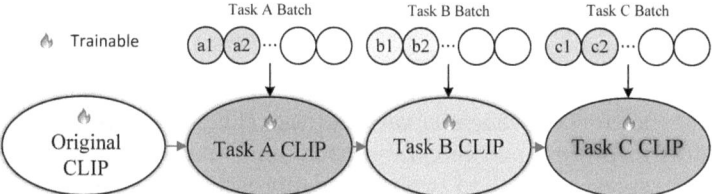

(a) Traditional continual learning strategies require fine-tuning the entire model - a process that can be computationally expensive.

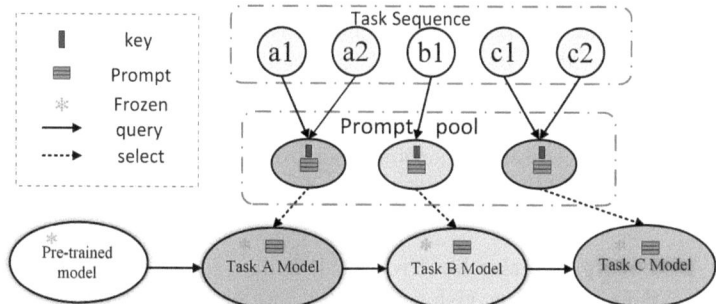

(b) The single-modal prompt restricts the model to learning within the confines of a single modality, potentially missing valuable cross-modal insights.

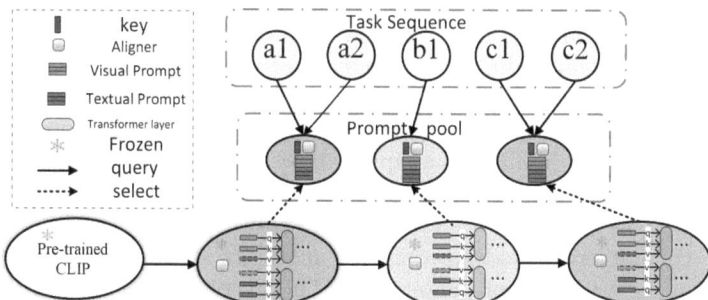

(c) ChordPrompt's cross-modal approach enables the model to benefit from the rich interplay between different modalities, leading to more robust and comprehensive learning.

Fig. 1. Comparison of traditional methods and ChordPrompt.

- We demonstrate ChordPrompt's effectiveness across various tasks and datasets, particularly highlighting its performance in multi-domain task incremental learning scenarios with vision-language models.

2   Related Work

Vision-Language Models. Beyond CLIP, other V-L models like ALIGN, ViL-BERT have shown effectiveness in various tasks. These models employ different architectures to process and integrate visual and textual information, ranging from unified representations to two-stream approaches with cross-modality layers [10,19]. The recent advancements in V-L models have played a crucial role in empowering a wide range of tasks that involve image and text processing [1,14,17]. However, these V-L models often face challenges when deployed in continual learning scenarios. Many studies have proposed continual learning methods to aid the adaptation of the model to new tasks. Our proposed framework, ChordPrompt, is tailored to continual learning (CL) setups for vision-language models, particularly those with dual-encoder architectures like CLIP. We chose CLIP as our base model due to its robust performance in aligning image and text embeddings and its widespread adoption and proven effectiveness in a variety of multimodal tasks like VQA.

Prompt Learning Methods. Prompt learning originating from NLP has become crucial in improving vision-language model performance through carefully selecting input prompts. For example, approaches like soft prompting [13] and prefix tuning [15] help streamline large language models' training by introducing learnable tokens that steer the model's outputs, making it more convenient to tailor the model to new downstream tasks. In the context of vision-language models, prompt learning has been utilized to guide the models towards better understanding and alignment of visual and language modalities. For instance, CoOp and Co-CoOp [37,38] train CLIP for few-shot transfer by prompt vectors at the language branch. However, these single modal prompts can limit the model's ability to adapt to new tasks dynamically. Recent work [12,33,39] has begun to explore the potential of cross-modal prompt learning to fully leverage the power of the cross-modal nature of vision-language models. However, current cross-modal prompting methods lack ways to select appropriate prompts for continual adaptation. They typically lack the adaptability and flexibility needed to handle the dynamic shifts in the environment during continual learning.

Continual Learning Methods. Multiple approaches are put forward to address the issue of catastrophic forgetting in continual learning. Replay-based methods [3,9,23,26] store and replay previous data to maintain knowledge. Notably, in the case of the CLIP model, replay methods to re-access original private pre-training datasets face limitations, as these datasets are often inaccessible. Regularization-based methods [2,5,16] mitigate catastrophic forgetting by aligning the current output with previous ones. Architecture-based methods [24,34] manipulate the model's architecture, such as dynamically expanding capacity or allocating model parts to each task. Prompt-based methods [6,11,29,31] have emerged to mitigate catastrophic forgetting. However, these prompt-based approaches ignore preserving the zero-shot learning capability, a crucial strength of vision-language models. Furthermore, existing approaches lack mechanisms for domain-adaptive selection, making them unsuitable for multi-domain task-incremental learning scenarios. Unlike previous methods primarily focusing on single-modal prompts or architectural modifications, our ChordPrompt framework introduces a novel cross-modal prompting strategy to facilitate continual learning.

3   Methodology

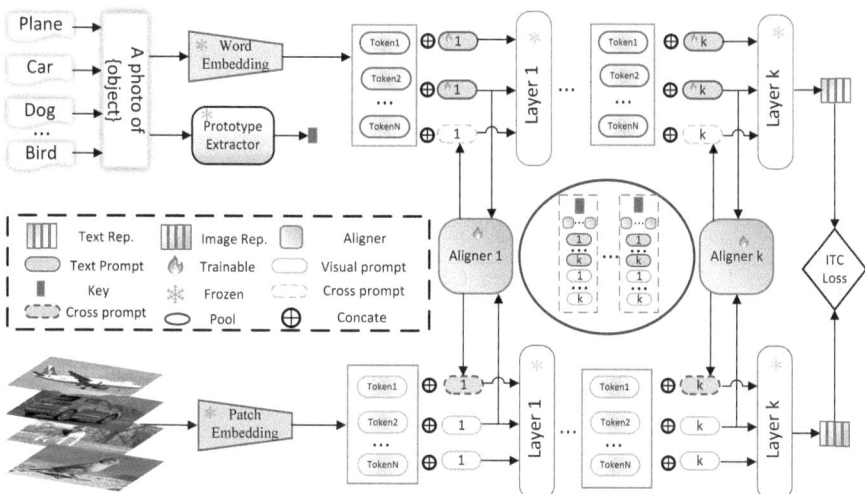

Fig. 2. Our proposed ChordPrompt approach. The detailed training process follows (a) Start by feeding all labels' text from the current dataset into the PrototypeExtractor. It transforms the text labels into one-dimensional vectors as keys. (b) Store these keys in a pool, which will later be used for querying during the inference phase. (c) Add trainable tokens as prompts at each layer of the text encoder, which are then stored in the memory pool. (d) Introduce the Aligner module, which projects text encoder prompts to the vision encoder and vision encoder prompts to the text encoder. The projected cross-modal prompts are added to each layer's value (V) component in both encoders.

In the field of continual learning (CL) for vision-language models, the goal is to develop models capable of sequentially mastering a series of distinct datasets, denoted as $\{\mathcal{D}_1, \mathcal{D}_2, \ldots, \mathcal{D}_N\}$. The $\mathcal{D}_i$ represents the dataset for the ith task, containing N_i labeled samples. For multi-domain task-incremental learning, the objective is for the model to classify images from all domains it has encountered without knowing the specific task ID during inference. The optimization problem can be formulated as (Fig. 2):

$$\min_{\theta} \mathbb{E}_{(x,y)\sim\cup_{i=1}^{N} \mathcal{D}_i} \left[- \log \frac{\exp(s_\theta(x, \hat{y})/\tau)}{\sum_{y_c \in \mathbb{C}} \exp(s_\theta(x, y_c)/\tau)} \right] \tag{1}$$

Here, $\mathcal{D}_i = (x_j^i, \hat{y}_c^i)_{j=1}^{N_i}$ represents the set of data for domain $\mathcal{D}_i$, which contains N_i input-label pairs. x_j^i is the jth input sample of domain $\mathcal{D}_i$, and $\hat{y}_c^i$ is the corresponding class label. The set of classes is denoted as $\mathbb{C} = \bigcup_{c=1}^{N_c} y_c$. N_c represents the total number of classes, and y_c denotes a specific class label within the set of classes. θ denotes the parameters of the model F_θ. The loss function $\mathcal{L}$ measures the predictive discrepancy, traditionally the negative log-likelihood of the correct class in the context of contrastive learning.

In our CL formulation, we continually fine-tune the CLIP model on a sequence of datasets $\{\mathcal{D}_1, \mathcal{D}_2, ..., \mathcal{D}_N\}$.

The similarity score $s_{j,c}^i$, between visual X_j^i and textual Y_c^i representations is defined as $s_{j,c}^i = \text{sim}(X_j^i, Y_c^i)$. The prediction probability is calculated as follows:

$$p(\hat{y}|x_j^i) = \frac{\exp(s_{j,\hat{y}}^i/\tau)}{\sum_{c=1}^{N_c} \exp(s_{j,c}^i/\tau)} \tag{2}$$

where τ represents the temperature coefficient.

Algorithm 1. Training Process for ChordPrompt

Require: Sequence of datasets $\{D_1, D_2, ..., D_N\}$; Pre-trained image encoder and text encoder; Trainable Aligner with θ_A; Prototype extractor ProtoExtrac; Text Prompt parameters θ_T; Vision Prompt parameters θ_V; Temperature coefficient τ;
Ensure: Updated CLIP parameters
1: **for** $i = 1$ to N **do**
2:     Initialize trainable prompts T_i and V_i
3:     Load dataset D_i with samples $\{(x_j, y_j)\}_{j=1}^{N_i}$
4:     $K_i \leftarrow \text{ProtoExtrac}(D_i)$
5:     Add key K_i to prompt pool $\mathcal{P}$
6:     **for** $t = 1$ to T_{iter} **do**
7:         **for** each (x_j, y_j) in D_i **do**
8:             $\hat{T}_i, \hat{V}_i \leftarrow \text{Aligenr}(V_i; T_i)$
9:             $Y_i \leftarrow \text{TextEncoder}(y_j; T_i, \hat{T}_i)$
10:            $X_{i,j} \leftarrow \text{ImageEncoder}(x_j; V_i, \hat{V}_i)$
11:            $s_{i,j} \leftarrow \text{sim}(X_{i,j}, Y_i)$
12:            Compute loss $\mathcal{L} \leftarrow \mathcal{L}_{\text{CE}}(s_{i,j}, y_j; \tau)$
13:            $\theta_A, \theta_V, \theta_T \leftarrow \text{GradientDescent}(\mathcal{L}, \eta)$
14:        **end for**
15:    **end for**
16:    Update prompt pool $\mathcal{P}$ with new prompts T_i and V_i and key K_i
17: **end for**
18: **return** $\mathcal{P}$

3.1   Domain-Adaptive Cross-Modal Text Prompt

Domain-adaptive text prompts are designed to dynamically adjust to the unique characteristics of each domain during training and inference. By associating each task with a prototype feature, these prompts ensure that the model can retrieve domain-specific knowledge, enabling task-specific adaptation and robust transfer across diverse domains.

CLIP's text encoder converts text into feature representations by tokenizing input text and projecting tokens into word embeddings $\mathbf{E}_0^i \in \mathbb{R}^{N_t \times d_t}$.

We introduce a novel Domain-Adaptive Text Prompt method to advance the conventional continual learning process. This methodology augments CLIP's text encoder with learnable tokens T_l^i in l^{th} layer of text encoder, each $T_l^i \in \mathbb{R}^{d_t}$, with lengths aligned to the visual prompts for cross-modality correspondence. Consequently, the input embeddings are a concatenation of the learnable prompts: $[\mathbf{E}_0^i, T_1^i]$, where $\mathbf{E}_0^i$ denotes the static input tokens.

Specifically, we add new learnable tokens to each transformer layer TextLayer$_l(\cdot)$ in the text encoder, up to L layers in depth. The output embeddings $\mathbf{E}_{l-1}^i$ are sequentially fed into the lth transformer layer TextLayer$_l$, for $l = 1, 2, \cdots, L$.

We introduce an Aligner module that projects visual prompts into the text space to enhance cross-modal interaction. The projected visual prompt $\hat{T}_l^i$ is computed as:

$$\hat{T}_l^i = A_{\text{V2T}} V_l^i \tag{3}$$

where $A_{\text{V2T}} \in \mathbb{R}^{d_t \times d_v}$ is a learnable matrix that aligns the visual prompt space to the text prompt space.

We incorporate the projected visual prompt into the value (V) component of the self-attention mechanism in the text encoder. This design choice is particularly effective because it does not interfere with the core attention computation. Specifically, Query (Q) and Key (K) are used to compute attention weights, so altering them could disrupt the attention alignment, whereas modifying V does not affect this crucial calculation. This approach preserves original attention patterns in Q and K while enhancing cross-modal information integration, allowing efficient information flow from the visual to the textual domain without disrupting the established attention mechanisms.

The text encoder is then modified to incorporate both the original text prompt and the projected visual prompt:

$$\mathbf{E}_l^i = \text{TextLayer}_l([\mathbf{E}_{l-1}^i, T_l^i, \hat{T}_l^i]), \quad l = 1, 2, \ldots, L. \tag{4}$$

Upon reaching the Lth layer, the final textual representation Y^i is obtained as:

$$Y^i = \text{TextProj}\left(\mathbf{E}_L^i\right). \tag{5}$$

When the learnable tokens are only introduced at the initial textual embedding, our approach is similar in structure to the CoOp method [38], which uses learnable class templates to replace manually designed templates. Our approach distinguishes itself through domain-adaptive prompts, which empower the model to flexibly adapt its responses to the unique characteristics of each domain, ultimately enabling more efficient continual learning.

Prototype Extractor. To capture the essence of each task's textual characteristics and to enable efficient retrieval of relevant prompts during inference,
we introduce the Prototype Extractor. As can be seen from Fig. 3, we utilize
the original CLIP model's text encoder TextEnc to acquire text feature representation $\hat{Y}_c^i$. Prototypes serve as compact representations of each task's textual
characteristics. They enable efficient retrieval of relevant prompts during inference, ensuring the model can quickly adapt to the current task without losing
previously acquired knowledge. The process is as follows:

$$\hat{Y}_c^i = \text{TextEnc}(y_c^i) \tag{6}$$

Herein, $\hat{Y}_c^i$ represents the feature embedding for the cth class of task i.

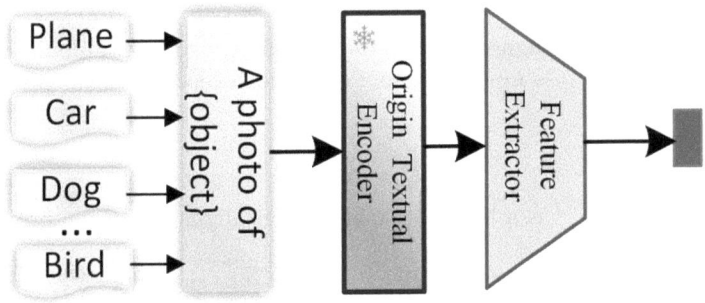

Fig. 3. The architecture of our Prototype Extractor.

The prototype feature for task i, denoted as P^i, is computed as follows:

$$P^i = \frac{\sum_{c=1}^{N_c} Y_c^i}{\left| \sum_{c=1}^{N_c} Y_c^i \right|} \tag{7}$$

In this equation, P^i is the normalized prototype feature for the ith task. This is
derived by calculating the sum of the feature representations Y_c^i for all classes
c in task i and then normalizing this sum to unit length. The normalization
ensures that the prototype feature vector norm is one. These prototype features
and their corresponding domain-specific prompts are stored in a prompt pool.
The memory pool is designed to store only compact prototype features and
corresponding prompts rather than raw data or task-specific checkpoints. This
significantly reduces storage requirements and ensures scalability, even as the
number of tasks increases. During inference, the model selects the prompt with
the most similar key based on the maximum cosine similarity between the input
and stored prototype features.

3.2   Cross-Modal Visual Prompt

Cross-modal prompts with mixed visual and textual information are essential in vision-language models. By incorporating visual and projected text prompts, ChordPrompt enables richer cross-modal interactions, leading to more robust and adaptable representations.

Image patches U_b^j of x_j^i, where N_b is the total number of patches, are initially embedded as $\mathbf{H}_{0,j}^i$:

$$\mathbf{H}_{0,j}^i = \text{Embedding}(U_1^j, ..., U_{N_b}^j) \tag{8}$$

To facilitate cross-modal learning, we introduce an Aligner module that projects text prompts into the vision space. The Aligner module, a key innovation in ChordPrompt, facilitates bidirectional information flow between visual and textual modalities, enabling more robust and comprehensive representations. The projected text prompt $\hat{V}_l^i$ is computed as:

$$\hat{V}_l^i = A_{\text{T2V}} T_l^i \tag{9}$$

where $A_{\text{T2V}} \in \mathbb{R}^{d_v \times d_t}$ is a learnable matrix that aligns the text prompt space to the visual prompt space.

The vision encoder is then modified to incorporate both the original visual prompt and the projected text prompt:

$$\mathbf{H}_{l,j}^i = \text{VisLayer}_l([\mathbf{H}_{l-1,j}^i, V_l^i, \hat{V}_l^i]), \quad l = 1, 2, \ldots, L. \tag{10}$$

Similar to the text encoder, we incorporate the projected text prompt into the value (V) component of the self-attention mechanism in the vision encoder.

Upon reaching the Lth layer, the prompts, and embeddings are combined to get the final visual representation X_j^i:

$$X_j^i = \text{VisProj}\left(\mathbf{H}_{L,j}^i\right). \tag{11}$$

where VisProj is the visual projection layer, transforms the output of the visual encoder into a visual representation that can be directly compared with text embeddings in a shared embedding space.

In the end, We store the learned prompts and their corresponding keys for each task in a memory pool. We use cosine similarity during inference to retrieve the most suitable prompt from the pool based on the current task's input.

3.3   Algorithm Architecture

The detailed training process of our algorithm is illustrated in 1. The detailed inference process is presented in Algorithm 2. Notably, our approach's image encoder of CLIP differs from that in conventional continual learning methods, as the latter do not utilize prompts in the vision branch. The more distinguishable image embeddings of ChordPrompt emphasize that adding complementary visual

---

Algorithm 2. Inference Process for ChordPrompt

Require: The dataset class categories $\mathbb{C}=\{y_1, ..., y_{N_c}\}$; Image x for inference; Prototype extractor ProtoExtrac; Discrimination threshold γ; Prompt pool $\mathcal{P}$ with keys K_i and domain-specific prompts; Original model CLIP; Aligner matrices A_{V2T}, A_{T2V};

Ensure: Predicted class label $\hat{y}$ for image x;

1: $P_x \leftarrow$ ProtoExtrac$(y_1, ..., y_{N_c})$
   # Query the prompt pool and select the prompts
2: $\mathcal{S}_{\max} \leftarrow -\infty; i_{\max} \leftarrow$ null
3: **for all** $K_i \in \mathcal{P}$ **do**
4:     $\mathcal{S} \leftarrow \frac{P_x \cdot K_i}{\|P_x\|\|K_i\|}$
5:     **if** $\mathcal{S} > \mathcal{S}_{\max}$ **then**
6:         $\mathcal{S}_{\max} \leftarrow \mathcal{S}$; $i_{\max} \leftarrow i$ # i is the index of the key
7:     **end if**
8: **end for**
   # Inference using original CLIP
9: **if** $\mathcal{S}_{\max} < \gamma$ **then**
10:     **return** $\hat{y} = $ CLIP$(x, y_1, ..., y_{N_c})$
11: **else**
12:     $V^{i_{\max}}, T^{i_{\max}}, A_{\text{V2T}}, A_{\text{T2V}} \leftarrow \mathcal{P}[i_{\max}]$ # Retrieve prompts
13:     $\hat{T}^{i_{\max}} \leftarrow A_{\text{V2T}} V^{i_{\max}}$ # Project visual prompt to text space
14:     $\hat{V}^{i_{\max}} \leftarrow A_{\text{T2V}} T^{i_{\max}}$ # Project text prompt to visual space
15: **end if**
16: $Y^{i_{\max}} \leftarrow$ TextEncoder$(\mathbb{C}, T^{i_{\max}}, \hat{T}^{i_{\max}})$ # Generate text representation
17: $X^{i_{\max}} \leftarrow$ ImageEncoder$(x, V^{i_{\max}}, \hat{V}^{i_{\max}})$ # Generate image representation
18: $\hat{y} \leftarrow \arg\max($softmax$(sim(Y^{i_{\max}}, X^{i_{\max}})/\tau))$
19: **return** $\hat{y}$

---

prompts and domain-level text prompts leads to better adaptation of CLIP in continual learning scenarios.

We can define our learning objective to optimize the parameters for independent visual prompts V, separate textual prompts T, and the parameters of the Aligner component θ_A. The learning objective can be formulated using the CE loss function. This optimization can be concisely represented as:

$$\min_{V,T,\theta_P} \mathcal{L}_{\text{CE}}\left(\mathcal{F}(x; V, T, \theta_A), y\right) \tag{12}$$

where $\mathcal{L}_{\text{CE}}$ is the CE loss [21] that measures the predictive discrepancy in a contrastive learning setup, F is the function representing the vision-language model parameterized by the prompts, and the Aligner, x is the input data, and y is the label or target data used for contrastive prediction.

By minimizing this objective, ChordPrompt optimizes the visual and textual prompts and the Aligner parameters. This approach enables the model to adapt to new tasks while preserving knowledge from previous tasks, effectively addressing catastrophic forgetting in continual learning settings. The CE loss ensures the model learns discriminative features across different modalities and tasks.

Table 1. Transfer, Average, and Last accuracy (%) of various continue learning approaches on MTIL benchmark.

Method	Param.	Aircraft	Caltech101	CIFAR100	DTD	EuroSAT	Flowers	Food	MNIST	OxfordPet	Cars	SUN397	Average
CLIP ViT-b/16													
Zero-shot	-	24.3	88.4	68.2	44.6	54.9	71.0	88.5	59.4	89.0	64.7	65.2	65.3
full fine-tuning	-	62.0	96.2	89.6	79.5	98.9	97.5	92.7	99.6	94.7	89.6	81.8	89.2
Transfer													
Continual-FT	211M	-	67.1	46.0	32.1	35.6	35.0	57.7	44.1	60.8	20.5	46.6	44.6
LwF [16]	211M	-	74.5	56.9	39.1	51.1	52.6	72.8	60.6	75.1	30.3	55.9	58.9
iCaRL [23]	211M	-	56.6	44.6	32.7	39.3	46.6	68.0	46.0	77.4	31.9	60.5	50.4
LwF-VR [3]	211M	-	77.1	61.0	40.5	45.3	54.4	74.6	47.9	76.7	36.3	58.6	57.2
WiSE-FT [32]	211M	-	73.5	55.6	35.6	41.5	47.0	68.3	53.9	69.3	26.8	51.9	52.3
Dist. only	211M	-	80.1	62.2	40.2	39.9	58.1	80.8	53.4	74.6	38.1	61.9	58.9
ZSCL [36]	211M	-	86.0	67.4	45.4	50.4	69.1	87.6	**61.8**	86.8	60.1	**66.8**	68.1
DDAS [35]	59.8M	-	87.9	68.2	44.4	49.9	70.7	**88.7**	59.7	**89.1**	64.5	65.5	68.9
ChordPrompt	9.5M	-	**88.9**	**68.6**	**45.6**	**54.0**	**71.1**	88.5	59.9	89.0	**64.8**	64.8	**69.5**
Avg.													
Continual-FT	211M	25.5	81.5	59.1	53.2	64.7	51.8	63.2	64.3	69.7	31.8	49.7	55.9
LwF [16]	211M	36.3	86.9	72.0	59.0	73.7	60.0	73.6	74.8	80.0	37.3	58.1	64.7
iCaRL [23]	211M	35.5	89.2	72.2	60.6	68.8	70.0	78.2	62.3	81.8	41.2	62.5	65.7
LwF-VR [3]	211M	29.6	87.7	74.4	59.5	72.4	63.6	77.0	66.7	81.2	43.7	60.7	65.1
WiSE-FT [32]	211M	26.7	86.5	64.3	57.1	65.7	58.7	71.1	70.5	75.8	36.9	54.6	60.7
Dist. only	211M	48.1	90.6	79.8	63.2	75.6	72.5	84.7	70.2	79.8	46.9	63.7	70.5
ZSCL [36]	211M	45.1	92.0	80.1	64.3	79.5	81.6	89.6	**75.2**	88.9	64.7	**68.0**	75.4
DDAS [35]	59.8M	50.2	91.9	**83.1**	69.4	78.9	84.0	89.1	73.7	89.3	67.7	66.9	76.7
ChordPrompt	9.5M	**54.5**	**96.9**	82.0	**70.3**	**82.1**	**84.5**	**90.1**	74.1	**90.5**	**68.1**	66.1	**78.1**
Last													
Continual-FT	211M	31.0	89.3	65.8	67.3	88.9	71.1	85.6	99.6	92.9	77.3	81.1	77.3
LwF [16]	211M	26.3	87.5	71.9	66.6	79.9	66.9	83.8	99.6	92.1	66.1	80.4	74.6
iCaRL [23]	211M	35.8	93.0	77.0	70.2	83.3	88.5	90.4	86.7	93.2	81.2	**81.9**	80.1
LwF-VR [3]	211M	20.5	89.8	72.3	67.6	85.5	73.8	85.7	99.6	93.1	73.3	80.9	76.6
WiSE-FT [32]	211M	27.2	90.8	68.0	68.9	86.9	74.0	87.6	99.6	92.6	77.8	81.3	77.7
Dist. only	211M	43.3	91.9	81.3	72.4	95.1	90.5	90.4	**99.7**	92.5	85.1	81.8	84.0
ZSCL [36]	211M	40.6	92.2	81.3	70.5	94.8	90.5	91.9	98.7	93.9	**85.3**	80.2	83.6
DDAS [35]	59.8M	49.8	92.2	**86.1**	78.1	95.7	94.3	89.5	98.1	89.9	81.6	80.0	85.0
ChordPrompt	9.5M	**54.5**	**97.1**	85.0	**79.5**	**98.2**	**95.8**	**92.0**	99.1	**94.4**	83.0	79.0	**87.0**

4   Experiments

4.1   Datasets and Models

MTIL Benchmark. Given that different classes from a single dataset usually have a common image source and a similar style [8,28], we suggest a cross-domain version of task incremental learning called Multi-domain Task Incremental Learning (MTIL). This benchmark presents a significant challenge for continual learning methods, as it requires the model to adapt to multiple domains while preserving its performance on previous tasks. In this framework, various tasks are gathered from distinct domains, each necessitating unique domain knowledge for humans to obtain high precision. Our MTIL benchmark comprises 11 tasks, including several tasks depicted in Table 1.

The MTIL benchmark presents a significant challenge, with 1,201 classes. We employ a fixed sequence for evaluation. The datasets in Order I are organized in alphabetical sequence. Conversely, the Table 3 uses a random order (Order-II): StanfordCars, Food, MNIST, OxfordPet, Flowers, SUN397, Aircraft, Caltech101, DTD, EuroSAT, CIFAR100. Experiments are done in Order I by default. Order II simulates real-world scenarios with unpredictable task arrivals, testing the robustness of domain-adaptive prompts to task order variations.

Models. We implement the CLIP model with a ViT-B/16 image encoder [4] and optimize it using the AdamW optimizer [18]. We used a learning rate of 2e-3 for each task and a batch size of 64. We allocated 2000 iterations per task for multi-domain task incremental learning and followed the evaluation framework outlined in [36].

Metrics. The measures for MTIL are displayed in Table 1, where the rows indicate training steps, and each column represents the performance for a specific dataset. For traditional continual learning, only the scores below the diagonal of the accuracy matrix carry significance since they do not allow for zero-shot predictions on unknown tasks. However, the zero-shot transfer capability of vision-language models allows them to generate predictions across all datasets. The **"Avg"** metric represents the mean accuracy across all datasets evaluated at every training step, providing an overall measure of the model's performance throughout the continual learning process. The **"Last"** metric represents the performance of every task after the continual learning process, indicating the model's flexibility in adapting to downstream tasks. The **"Transfer"** metric is computed as the average task performance in the upper-right triangle of the accuracy matrix, assessing the model's ability to maintain its zero-shot transfer capability before learning task i, disregarding tasks learned after task i. A model that excels in both the "Last" and "Transfer" metrics exemplifies the ideal continual learner, adapting to new tasks while retaining past knowledge and generalization abilities.

4.2   Ablation Study

Layer Depth. As shown in Fig. 4a, we examine the effect of different layer depths on the ChordPrompt methodology. As the model's feature space is more

Table 2. Comparison with state-of-the-art methods on few-shot MTIL benchmark in terms of "Transfer", "Average", and "Last" scores (%). Ours converges in 500 iterations on few-shot. We label the best and second methods with bold and underline styles. The top block indicates the upper-bound solutions to adapt the CLIP on each task.

Method	Param.	Aircraft	Caltech101	CIFAR100	DTD	EuroSAT	Flowers	Food	MNIST	OxfordPet	Cars	SUN397	Average
Transfer													
Continual-FT	211M	-	72.8	53.0	36.4	35.4	43.3	68.4	47.4	72.6	30.0	52.7	51.2
LwF [16]	211M	-	72.1	49.2	35.9	44.5	41.1	66.6	50.5	69.0	19.0	51.7	50.0
LwF-VR [3]	211M	-	82.2	62.5	40.1	40.1	56.3	80.0	60.9	77.6	40.5	60.8	60.1
WiSE-FT [32]	211M	-	77.6	60.0	41.3	39.4	53.0	76.6	58.1	75.5	37.3	58.2	57.7
ZSCL [36]	211M	-	84.0	68.1	44.8	46.8	63.6	84.9	61.4	81.4	55.5	62.2	65.3
DDAS [35]	59.8M	-	87.9	68.2	44.1	48.1	64.7	**88.8**	**69.0**	**89.1**	64.5	**65.1**	68.9
ChordPrompt	9.5M	-	**88.5**	**68.6**	**45.6**	**54.0**	**71.1**	88.5	59.9	89.0	**64.8**	64.9	**69.5**
Avg.													
Continual-FT	211M	28.1	86.4	59.1	52.8	55.8	62.0	70.2	64.7	75.5	35.0	54.0	58.5
LwF [16]	211M	23.5	77.4	43.5	41.7	43.5	52.2	54.6	63.4	68.0	21.3	52.6	49.2
LwF-VR [3]	211M	24.9	89.1	64.2	53.4	54.3	70.8	79.2	66.5	79.2	44.1	61.6	62.5
WiSE-FT [32]	211M	32.0	87.7	61.0	55.8	68.1	69.3	76.8	71.5	77.6	42.0	59.3	63.7
ZSCL [36]	211M	28.2	88.6	66.5	53.5	56.3	73.4	83.1	56.4	82.4	57.5	62.9	64.4
DDAS [35]	59.8M	30.0	89.6	73.9	58.7	69.3	79.3	**88.1**	**76.5**	89.1	65.3	**65.8**	71.4
ChordPrompt	9.5M	**39.3**	**93.8**	**74.5**	**59.2**	**75.0**	**83.0**	87.8	71.4	**89.8**	**66.7**	65.6	**73.3**
Last													
Continual-FT	211M	27.8	86.9	60.1	58.4	56.6	75.7	73.8	93.1	82.5	57.0	66.8	67.1
LwF [16]	211M	22.1	58.2	17.9	32.1	28.1	66.7	46.0	84.3	64.1	31.5	60.1	46.5
LwF-VR [3]	211M	22.9	89.8	59.3	57.1	57.6	79.2	78.3	77.7	83.6	60.1	69.8	66.9
WiSE-FT [32]	211M	30.8	88.9	59.6	60.3	80.9	81.7	77.1	**94.9**	83.2	62.8	70.0	71.9
ZSCL [36]	211M	26.8	88.5	63.7	55.7	60.2	82.1	82.6	58.6	85.9	66.7	70.4	67.4
DDAS [35]	59.8M	30.0	89.6	73.9	58.7	69.3	79.3	**88.1**	76.5	89.1	65.3	65.8	71.4
ChordPrompt	9.5M	**39.3**	**94.1**	**75.8**	**64.3**	**87.0**	**92.9**	87.0	91.6	**91.8**	**75.3**	72.8	**79.3**

mature and stable, inserting prompts into deeper layers of the frozen model leads to a less significant impact. Therefore, we add the prompts in a front-to-back manner. In this context, ChordPrompt generally attains optimal performance with a layer depth of 12 across most datasets. A shallower depth of 10 leads to slightly inferior accuracy compared to a depth of 12. It is observed that when increasing the layer depth from front to back, the performance improves consistently until saturation.

Prompt Length. As illustrated in Fig. 4b, we present the influence of prompt length within the ChordPrompt framework. An interesting pattern emerges where the performance on the test set relative to the original classes declines as the prompt length increases. This trend indicates that longer prompts may lead to overfitting, which harms the model's ability to generalize to unseen test samples. Therefore, we use relatively shorter prompts that may provide an ideal balance between learnability and generalizability. These findings highlight the importance of carefully tuning layer depth and length to balance model adaptability and generalization capability in continual learning scenarios.

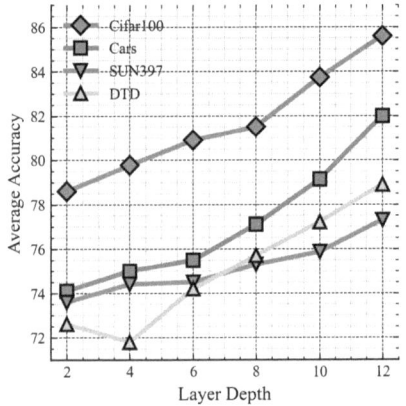 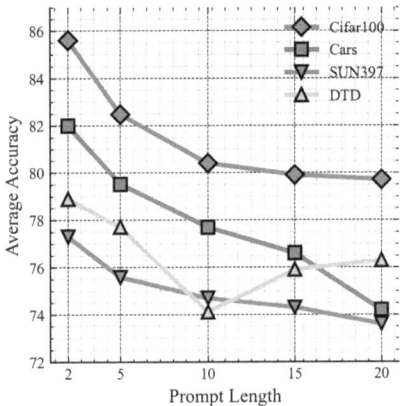

(a) The relationship between accuracy and the layer depth. (Prompt length=2. For better readability, we only display four tasks with close accuracy.)

(b) The relationship between accuracy and the prompt length. (layer depth=12. For better readability, we only display four tasks with close accuracy.)

Fig. 4. Comparisons of Performance

Effectiveness of Domain-Adaptive Text Prompt. The effectiveness of our domain-adaptive text prompt is demonstrated in Table 4, where ChordPrompt significantly outperforms other prompt-based methods such as L2P (-13.2% in Transfer accuracy), DualPrompt (-13.0%), and S-Prompts (-13.2%). These competing prompt methods lack domain-adaptive capabilities, resulting in their inability to select appropriate prompts for different domains, which explains their substantial performance degradation in multi-domain scenarios. MaPLe, despite using multi-modal prompts, still falls short in the Last accuracy metric (83.9% vs. our 86.0%) due to its unidirectional information flow and absence of domain-adaptive mechanisms for prompt selection across varied domains.

Parameter Analysis. Parameter Analysis in Table 1 showcases the computational complexity comparison among different methods. ChordPrompt introduces 9.48M trainable parameters, ChordPrompt's trainable parameter count is substantially lower than methods like iCaRL, LWF, and ZSCL, which require fine-tuning the entire CLIP model (211M parameters). ChordPrompt substantially improves in continual learning scenarios while only requiring updates to

Table 3. Compare methods on MTIL in Order II.

Method	Transfer	Δ	Avg.	Δ	Last	Δ
Zero-shot	65.4	0.0	65.3	0.0	65.3	0.0
CL.	46.6	−18.8	56.2	−9.1	67.4	2.1
LwF	53.2	−12.2	62.2	−3.1	71.9	6.6
iCaRL	50.9	−14.5	56.9	−8.4	71.6	6.3
LwF-VR	53.1	−12.3	60.6	−4.7	68.3	3.0
WiSE-FT	51.0	−14.4	61.5	−3.8	72.2	6.9
ZSCL	64.2	−1.2	74.5	9.2	83.4	18.1
ChordPrompt	**65.4**	**0.0**	**75.6**	**10.3**	**85.1**	**19.8**

a small portion of the overall model parameters, making it more efficient than full model fine-tuning approaches. This lightweight design ensures compatibility with resource-constrained environments while maintaining superior performance in continual learning scenarios.

Few-shot Multi-domain Task Incremental Learning. We further assess our method in a few-shot multi-domain task incremental learning scenario, where the CLIP model is restricted to only a handful of samples per task. Under the 5-shot setting, Table 2 presents the results based on the same evaluation metrics as Table 1. Our approach consistently achieves better performance than leading existing methods across most datasets. These findings indicate that the proposed methods are highly effective at mitigating the forgetting problem in continual learning. Moreover, the domain-adaptive prompt in our framework is able to efficiently distinguish between data distributions of different tasks, demonstrating robust distribution discrimination capabilities even with limited training examples.

Other Prompt Methods and Ablation Study. Our experimental results demonstrate that the cross-modal prompt approach consistently outperforms other continual learning methods across various tasks.

Table 4. Ablation Study on MTIL in Order I.

Method	Transfer	Δ	Avg.	Δ	Last	Δ
Zero-shot	69.5	0.0	65.3	0.0	65.3	0.0
L2P	53.2	−16.3	67.9	2.6	82.0	16.7
Dualp.	52.4	−17.1	68.0	2.7	82.3	17.0
S-Prompts	52.2	−17.3	68.3	3.0	82.4	17.1
ChordPrompt	**69.4**	**−0.1**	**77.2**	**11.9**	**86.0**	**20.7**

In Table 4, L2P [31], DualPrompt [30], and S-Prompts [29] all use single-modal prompts without domain-adaption. This neglects the benefits of cross-modal synergy and domain feature. As a result, these methods perform poorly in multi-domain task incremental learning (MTIL) scenarios, as they were primarily designed for class-incremental learning and fail to adapt effectively across different domains.

ChordPrompt's superior performance stems from its unique cross-modal information sharing mechanism. Unlike traditional methods that allow multi-modal interaction at the final stage, ChordPrompt shares prompt information across all CLIP model layers. This cross-layer sharing of prompts enables a more comprehensive exchange of information between the visual and textual modalities, allowing the model to capture fine-grained correspondences and interactions at various levels of abstraction. By facilitating this deep integration of cross-modal information, ChordPrompt can better align the visual and textual representations, leading to more robust and adaptable continual learning. The performance gain is particularly notable in complex, multi-domain tasks like the MTIL benchmark, demonstrating ChordPrompt's effectiveness in integrating diverse knowledge types. This underscores its potential for real-world applications with blurred task boundaries and crucial multi-modal processing.

5   Conclusion

ChordPrompt enhances the deployment of vision-language models by addressing continual learning challenges and eliminating the need for costly retraining. Its strong performance in zero-shot transfer and downstream tasks highlights its practicality and versatility. Our experiments validate the effectiveness of domain-adaptive text and cross-modal visual prompts in preserving task-specific and general knowledge.

While achieving significant improvements in classification tasks, future work will explore extending ChordPrompt to generative vision-language models, such as visual question answering and image captioning, to handle more open-ended and complex multi-modal interactions.

References

1. Alayrac, J.B., et al.: Flamingo: a visual language model for few-shot learning. Adv. Neural. Inf. Process. Syst. **35**, 23716–23736 (2022)
2. Dhar, P., Singh, R.V., Peng, K.C., Wu, Z., Chellappa, R.: Learning without memorizing. In: Proceedings of the IEEE/CVF Conference on Computer Vision and Pattern Recognition, pp. 5138–5146 (2019)
3. Ding, Y., Liu, L., Tian, C., Yang, J., Ding, H.: Don't stop learning: towards continual learning for the CLIP model. arXiv preprint arXiv:2207.09248 (2022)
4. Dosovitskiy, A., et al.: An image is worth 16×16 words: transformers for image recognition at scale. In: International Conference on Learning Representations (2020)

5. Douillard, A., Cord, M., Ollion, C., Robert, T., Valle, E.: PODNet: pooled outputs distillation for small-tasks incremental learning. In: Vedaldi, A., Bischof, H., Brox, T., Frahm, J.-M. (eds.) ECCV 2020. LNCS, vol. 12365, pp. 86–102. Springer, Cham (2020). https://doi.org/10.1007/978-3-030-58565-5_6

6. Douillard, A., Ramé, A., Couairon, G., Cord, M.: DyTox: transformers for continual learning with dynamic token expansion. In: Proceedings of the IEEE/CVF Conference on Computer Vision and Pattern Recognition, pp. 9285–9295 (2022)

7. French, R.M.: Catastrophic forgetting in connectionist networks. Trends Cogn. Sci. **3**(4), 128–135 (1999)

8. Hendrycks, D., et al.: The many faces of robustness: a critical analysis of out-of-distribution generalization. In: Proceedings of the IEEE/CVF International Conference on Computer Vision, pp. 8340–8349 (2021)

9. Jeeveswaran, K., Bhat, P.S., Zonooz, B., Arani, E.: BiRT: bio-inspired replay in vision transformers for continual learning. In: International Conference on Machine Learning, ICML 2023, pp. 14817–14835. PMLR (2023). https://proceedings.mlr.press/v202/jeeveswaran23a.html

10. Jia, C., et al.: Scaling up visual and vision-language representation learning with noisy text supervision. In: International Conference on Machine Learning, pp. 4904–4916. PMLR (2021)

11. Jung, D., Han, D., Bang, J., Song, H.: Generating instance-level prompts for rehearsal-free continual learning. In: Proceedings of the IEEE/CVF International Conference on Computer Vision, pp. 11847–11857 (2023)

12. Khattak, M.U., Rasheed, H., Maaz, M., Khan, S., Khan, F.S.: MaPLe: multimodal prompt learning. In: Proceedings of the IEEE/CVF Conference on Computer Vision and Pattern Recognition, pp. 19113–19122 (2023)

13. Lester, B., Al-Rfou, R., Constant, N.: The power of scale for parameter-efficient prompt tuning. In: Proceedings of the 2021 Conference on Empirical Methods in Natural Language Processing, pp. 3045–3059 (2021)

14. Li, J., Li, D., Savarese, S., Hoi, S.: BLIP-2: bootstrapping language-image pretraining with frozen image encoders and large language models. In: International Conference on Machine Learning, pp. 19730–19742. PMLR (2023)

15. Li, X.L., Liang, P.: Prefix-tuning: optimizing continuous prompts for generation. In: Proceedings of the 59th Annual Meeting of the Association for Computational Linguistics, pp. 4582–4597 (2021)

16. Li, Z., Hoiem, D.: Learning without forgetting. IEEE Trans. Pattern Anal. Mach. Intell. **40**(12), 2935–2947 (2017)

17. Liu, H., Li, C., Wu, Q., Lee, Y.J.: Visual instruction tuning. Adv. Neural Inf. Process. Syst. **36** (2024)

18. Loshchilov, I., Hutter, F.: Decoupled weight decay regularization. In: International Conference on Learning Representations (2018)

19. Lu, J., Batra, D., Parikh, D., Lee, S.: ViLBERT: pretraining task-agnostic visiolinguistic representations for vision-and-language tasks. Adv. Neural Inf. Process. Syst. **32** (2019)

20. Ni, Z., Wei, L., Tang, S., Zhuang, Y., Tian, Q.: Continual vision-language representation learning with off-diagonal information. In: International Conference on Machine Learning, ICML 2023, pp. 26129–26149. PMLR (2023). https://proceedings.mlr.press/v202/ni23c.html

21. Oord, A.V.D., Li, Y., Vinyals, O.: Representation learning with contrastive predictive coding. arXiv preprint arXiv:1807.03748 (2018)

22. Radford, A., et al.: Learning transferable visual models from natural language supervision. In: International Conference on Machine Learning, pp. 8748–8763. PMLR (2021)
23. Rebuffi, S.A., Kolesnikov, A., Sperl, G., Lampert, C.H.: iCaRL: incremental classifier and representation learning. In: Proceedings of the IEEE Conference on Computer Vision and Pattern Recognition, pp. 2001–2010 (2017)
24. Rusu, A.A., et al.: Progressive neural networks. arXiv preprint arXiv:1606.04671 (2016)
25. Shams, L., Seitz, A.R.: Benefits of multisensory learning. Trends Cogn. Sci. **12**(11), 411–417 (2008)
26. Shin, H., Lee, J.K., Kim, J., Kim, J.: Continual learning with deep generative replay. Adv. Neural Inf. Process. Syst. **30** (2017)
27. Thengane, V., Khan, S., Hayat, M., Khan, F.: CLIP model is an efficient continual learner. arXiv preprint arXiv:2210.03114 (2022)
28. Van de Ven, G.M., Tolias, A.S.: Three scenarios for continual learning. arXiv preprint arXiv:1904.07734 (2019)
29. Wang, Y., Huang, Z., Hong, X.: S-prompts learning with pre-trained transformers: an Occam's Razor for domain incremental learning. Adv. Neural. Inf. Process. Syst. **35**, 5682–5695 (2022)
30. Wang, Z., et al.: DualPrompt: complementary prompting for rehearsal-free continual learning. In: Avidan, S., Brostow, G., Cissé, M., Farinella, G.M., Hassner, T. (eds.) ECCV 2022. LNCS, vol. 13686, pp. 631–648. Springer, Cham (2022). https://doi.org/10.1007/978-3-031-19809-0_36
31. Wang, Z., et al.: Learning to prompt for continual learning. In: Proceedings of the IEEE/CVF Conference on Computer Vision and Pattern Recognition, pp. 139–149 (2022)
32. Wortsman, M., et al.: Robust fine-tuning of zero-shot models. In: Proceedings of the IEEE/CVF Conference on Computer Vision and Pattern Recognition, pp. 7959–7971 (2022)
33. Xing, Y., et al.: Dual modality prompt tuning for vision-language pre-trained model. IEEE Trans. Multimed. (2023)
34. Yoon, J., Yang, E., Lee, J., Hwang, S.J.: Lifelong learning with dynamically expandable networks. In: 6th International Conference on Learning Representations, ICLR (2018)
35. Yu, J., et al.: Boosting continual learning of vision-language models via mixture-of-experts adapters. In: Proceedings of the IEEE/CVF Conference on Computer Vision and Pattern Recognition, pp. 23219–23230 (2024)
36. Zheng, Z., Ma, M., Wang, K., Qin, Z., Yue, X., You, Y.: Preventing zero-shot transfer degradation in continual learning of vision-language models. In: Proceedings of the IEEE/CVF International Conference on Computer Vision (ICCV), pp. 19125–19136 (2023)
37. Zhou, K., Yang, J., Loy, C.C., Liu, Z.: Conditional prompt learning for vision-language models. In: Proceedings of the IEEE/CVF Conference on Computer Vision and Pattern Recognition, pp. 16816–16825 (2022)
38. Zhou, K., Yang, J., Loy, C.C., Liu, Z.: Learning to prompt for vision-language models. Int. J. Comput. Vision **130**(9), 2337–2348 (2022)
39. Zhu, J., Lai, S., Chen, X., Wang, D., Lu, H.: Visual prompt multi-modal tracking. In: Proceedings of the IEEE/CVF Conference on Computer Vision and Pattern Recognition, pp. 9516–9526 (2023)

Progressive Dual-Space Discovering of Unknowns for Source-Free Open-Set Domain Adaptation

Qianshan Zhan[1], Qian Wang[2], and Xiao-Jun Zeng[1(✉)]

[1] The Department of Computer Science, University of Manchester,
Manchester M13 9PL, UK
{qianshan.zhan,x.zeng}@manchester.ac.uk
[2] Luca Healthcare, Shanghai 200000, China

Abstract. Open-set domain adaptation (OSDA) transfers knowledge to an unlabeled target domain under both distribution shift and unknown classes absent in the source domain. Most OSDA methods require access to both source and target data and rely on either feature-space or logit-space information for known-unknown separation. However, source data is often restricted due to storage or privacy constraints, and single-space reliance can weaken separation, as unknown samples may be distinguishable in one space but not the other. To address these limitations, we propose Progressive Dual-Space Discovering (PDD), a source-free OSDA method that progressively adapts a pre-trained model for improved domain alignment and known-unknown separation. PDD iteratively builds a credible domain by selecting target samples close to the known-class distribution through dual-space selection: energy-based filtering in logit space followed by prototype-based refinement in feature space. Besides, PDD performs clustering using feature-space information from the credible domain and logit-space information from previously trained models, forming known and unknown domains. With these established domains, cross-entropy loss optimizes learning within the credible domain, while HSIC loss aligns the credible and known domains. Additionally, dual-space uncertainty losses enhance the separation between known and unknown classes. Extensive experiments on three OSDA benchmarks demonstrate the effectiveness of dual-space discovering, known-unknown separation, and progressive updates, facilitating PDD to achieve state-of-the-art performance. Code is available at https://github.com/qszhan/PDD.

Keywords: Source-free domain adaptation · Unknown classes · Known-unknown separation · Progressive dual-space discovering

Supplementary Information The online version contains supplementary material available at https://doi.org/10.1007/978-3-662-72243-5_10.

B. Pfahringer et al. (Eds.): ECML PKDD 2025, LNAI 16020, pp. 165–181, 2026.
https://doi.org/10.1007/978-3-662-72243-5_10

1 Introduction

Unsupervised domain adaptation (UDA) improves performance in an unlabeled target domain by transferring knowledge from a labeled source domain. A key challenge in UDA is handling distribution shifts, often addressed by domain-invariant features learning [20,35] or adversarial learning [5,21]. Despite their advances, these methods assume a closed-set setting [15] with identical label spaces in both domains, limiting applicability when the target domain includes unknown classes.

Open-set domain adaptation (OSDA) [13] addresses this scenario where the target domain includes unknown classes absent from source data. OSDA aims to align data from known classes across domains (domain alignment) and separate data from known and unknown classes (known-unknown separation). Existing OSDA methods employ strategies such as adversarial feature alignment [18,28], domain similarity measures [12], or learning a shared subspace [32]. Despite their advances, most methods require source data during training, raising storage and privacy concerns, especially in sensitive fields like healthcare [14]. This highlights the need for source-free OSDA [17,24], which operates without access to source data. However, source-free OSDA is still under-explored, with only a few methods like SHOT [17], AaD [34], USD [9], UPUK [30], and LEAD [24]. Without source data, source-free OSDA faces greater challenges in both domain alignment and known-unknown separation due to absent source features and known classes.

In addition to being source-dependent, current OSDA methods usually discover unknown samples using either **(1)** logit space information, such as the data similarity based on maximum class probabilities [18], prediction variances [28], entropy values [17,33], confidence scores [2,10], the Jensen-Shannon distance between logits and pseudo labels [9]; or **(2)** feature space information, including factorized representations [1], distances between source and target features from unknown data [12], a common feature space [32], or decomposed feature components [24]. Relying solely on logit-space or feature-space information is often insufficient for known-unknown separation, as unknown samples may be easier to identify in one space but harder in the other. Virtual-logit Matching (ViM) [31] first introduced the use of dual-space information for Out-of-Distribution (OOD) detection by constructing a virtual logit to represent an OOD class. However, ViM cannot be directly applied to source-free OSDA since it relies on in-distribution data, which is unavailable in source-free settings. Moreover, ViM requires a user-specified threshold for separation, limiting its practicality. Therefore, a new known-unknown separation method is needed by leveraging dual-space information without depending on source data or threshold tuning.

To overcome these limitations, we propose Progressive Dual-space Discovering (PDD), which leverages information from both logit and feature spaces to achieve domain alignment and known-unknown separation in source-free OSDA. Without source feature and known-class information, PDD progressively selects credible target samples that closely align with the known-class distribution. This selection is guided by a progressive dual-space discovering strategy, which integrates energy-based selection in logit space with prototype-based refinement in feature space, utilizing logits and features obtained from previously trained models. Through this iterative process, PDD constructs a series of credible domains with gradually shifting distributions across multiple stages (Fig. 1), progressively enhancing the domain alignment for known classes.

With the constructed credible domain, PDD performs clustering by leveraging both feature-space information from the credible domain and logit-space information from the pre-trained models. This clustering process divides the target samples into known and unknown parts, forming known and unknown domains. Given these established domains, we employ cross-entropy loss to optimize learning within the credible domain and HSIC loss to align the known domain with the credible domain, reinforcing the learning of known classes. Furthermore, dual-space uncertainty losses facilitate effective separation between known and unknown classes. Extensive experiments on three benchmarks demonstrate that our PDD method achieves new state-of-the-art performance. Contributions are summarized below:

(1) We propose Progressive Dual-space Discovering (PDD) for source-free OSDA, leveraging feature and logit space information to enhance domain alignment and known-unknown separation. The framework of PDD is provided in Fig. 2.

(2) To address the absence of source data and the resulting lack of source feature and known-class information, PDD constructs credible domains that are close to the known-class distribution using the previously trained models, progressively enhancing the domain alignment for known classes over multiple stages.

(3) To facilitate known-unknown separation, PDD performs clustering by leveraging both feature-space information from the credible domain and logit-space information from previously trained models.

(4) Extensive experiments on three OSDA benchmarks confirm that PDD achieves state-of-the-art performance, validating the effectiveness of dual-space discovering, known-unknown separation, and progressive updates.

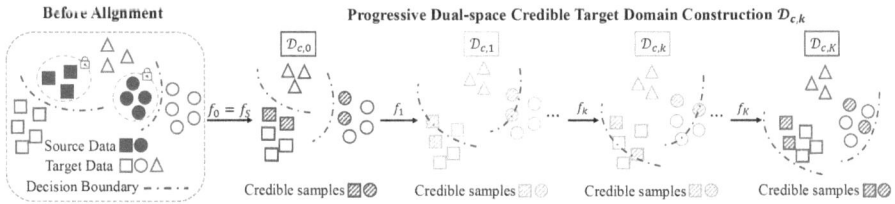

Fig. 1. Progressive dual-space credible target domain construction.

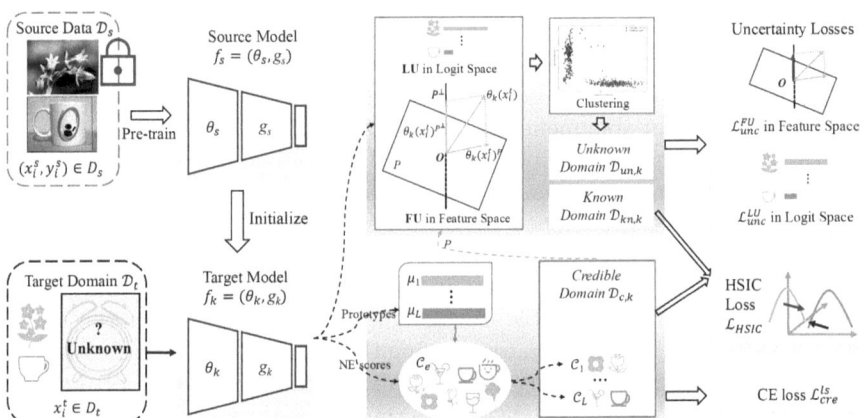

Fig. 2. PDD framework for constructing target model f_k. Before constructing f_k, a credible domain $\mathcal{D}_{c,k} \subset \mathcal{D}_t$ is constructed by selecting samples close to known-class distribution. Unknown classes are identified by discovering in both feature and logit spaces, resulting in unknown domain $\mathcal{D}_{un,k}$ and known domain $\mathcal{D}_{kn,k}$ with $\mathcal{D}_{un,k} \cup \mathcal{D}_{kn,k} = \mathcal{D}_t$ and $\mathcal{D}_{un,k} \cap \mathcal{D}_{kn,k} = \varnothing$. For the discovered unknowns in feature space (**FU**), each representation $\theta_k(\mathbf{x}_i^t)$ in $\mathcal{D}_t$ decomposes into $\theta_k(\mathbf{x}_i^t)^P$ (principal space component) and $\theta_k(\mathbf{x}_i^t)^{P^\perp}$ (deviation component). In logit space, the discovered unknowns **LU** are obtained from negative energy scores. Cross-entropy loss $\mathcal{L}_{cre}^{ls}$ trains on credible samples in $\mathcal{D}_{c,k}$. HSIC loss $\mathcal{L}_{HSIC}$ aligns $\mathcal{D}_{kn,k}$ with $\mathcal{D}_{c,k}$ to improve the learning of known classes. Dual-space uncertainty losses $\mathcal{L}_{unc}^{FU}$ and $\mathcal{L}_{unc}^{LU}$ facilitate known-unknown separation.

2   Method

2.1   Problem Formulation

Domains, Datasets, and Source Model. Suppose that there is a source domain $\mathcal{D}_s$ and a target domain $\mathcal{D}_t$. For $\mathcal{D}_s$, the input space and discrete label space are respectively denoted by $\mathcal{X}_s$ and $\mathcal{Y}_s \in \{1, 2, \cdots, L\}$. For $\mathcal{D}_t$, the input space and discrete label space are respectively denoted by $\mathcal{X}_t$ and $\mathcal{Y}_t \in \{1, 2, \cdots, L'\}$. The target dataset for $\mathcal{D}_t$ is denoted by $D_t = \{(\mathbf{x}_i^t, y_i^t)\}_{i=1}^{n_t}$. The source dataset for $\mathcal{D}_s$ is given by $D_s = \{(\mathbf{x}_i^s, y_i^s)\}_{i=1}^{n_s}$. With the source dataset D_s, a source model $f_s : (\theta_s, g_s)$ is pre-trained with two canonical stages: representation followed by classification. The feature extractor, denoted as $\theta_s : \mathcal{X}_s \rightarrow \mathbb{R}^d$, maps the input data to a d-dimensional representation in the feature space $\mathcal{Z}$. This representation is then passed through the classifier $g_s : \mathbb{R}^d \rightarrow \mathbb{R}^L$, which transforms the representation into a logit vector $\delta \in \mathbb{R}^L$. The transformation is achieved through a fully connected layer with weight matrix $\mathbf{W} \in \mathbb{R}^{d \times L}$ and bias vector $\mathbf{b} \in \mathbb{R}^L$, formally expressed as $\delta_i = \mathbf{W}^T \mathbf{x}_i^s + \mathbf{b}$. The final soft predictions, yielding the probability distributions $\mathcal{P} = \{\mathbf{p}_i\}_{i=1}^{n_s} = \{[p_{i,1}, p_{i,2}, \ldots, p_{i,L}]\}_{i=1}^{n_s}$, are obtained by applying the softmax function to the logits.

Source-Free Open-Set Unsupervised Domain Adaptation. Due to the source-free and unsupervised constraints, source data D_s and true target labels $\{y_i^t\}_{i=1}^{n_t}$ are unavailable during adaptation. Besides, the source label set $C_s \subset \mathcal{Y}_s$ and target label set $C_t \subset \mathcal{Y}_t$ satisfy $C_s \subset C_t$, with the target-private label set $\overline{C}_t = C_t \backslash C_s$. Our goal is to adapt the source pre-trained model to obtain a target model f_t that can classify target samples into L known classes in C_s and identify them as "unknown" if they belong to $\overline{C}_t$.

Adaptative Training Process. To obtain the target model $f_t : (\theta_t, g_t)$, we freeze the classifier ($g_t = g_s$) and train only a target-specific feature extractor θ_t to ensure that target features from known classes align with the source features through same decision boundaries [17]. The adaptation process is divided into K successive stages, initializing θ_0 as the source feature extractor θ_s and performing a training step to obtain f_1. This process continues iteratively, updating model from f_{k-1} at stage $k-1$ to f_k at stage k.

2.2   Progressive Credible Domain Construction

This section progressively constructs a credible domain, $\mathcal{D}_{c,k}$, at each stage k to select target samples that are more likely to belong to, or close to, the distribution captured by the previous model, f_{k-1}, initialized from a source model pre-trained on known-class data. Consequently, the selected credible samples inherently reflect the characteristics of known-class distribution. Through this iterative process, PDD constructs a series of credible domains with gradually shifting distributions across multiple stages (Fig. 1), enhancing domain alignment for known classes. This selection is performed in dual-space: energy-based selection in the logit space, followed by prototype-based refinement in the feature space, which together enhance the reliability of the credible domain.

Energy-Based Selection in Logit Space. We begin by operating in logit space, selecting samples with high negative energy (NE) scores to form a group $\mathcal{C}_e$. This method leverages the established correlation between NE scores and sample likelihood within the distribution learned by the previous model f_{k-1} [19]. A higher NE score $NE(\mathbf{x}_i^t)$ indicates that the sample $\mathbf{x}_i^t$ is more likely to belong to or closely match the distribution captured by f_{k-1}. Since f_{k-1} was initialized from a source model pre-trained on known-class data, a high NE score $NE(\mathbf{x}_i^t)$ suggests that $\mathbf{x}_i^t$ is more likely to be within the known-class distribution. Therefore, we use NE scores, $NE(\mathbf{x}_i^t)$, to identify credible samples.

For a target sample $\mathbf{x}_i^t$, the negative energy score, based on the logits δ_i from the model f_k, is computed as $NE(\mathbf{x}_i^t) = \log \sum_l^L e^{\delta_{i,l}}$, where $\delta_{i,l}$ denotes the logit of $\mathbf{x}_i^t$ for class l. A higher $NE(\mathbf{x}_i^t)$ indicates that $\mathbf{x}_i^t$ is more likely to belong to, or closely match known-class distribution and is thus a credible known-class sample, while lower values suggest reduced credibility. Accordingly, the group $\mathcal{C}_e$ is defined by selecting target samples whose negative energy values rank within the top $\sigma_e n_t$ values: $\mathcal{C}_e = \{\mathbf{x}_i^t \mid \mathbf{x}_i^t \in \mathcal{X}_t, i \in \mathrm{top}_{\sigma_e n_t}(\{NE(\mathbf{x}_i^t)\}_{i=1}^{n_t})\}$, where $\{NE(\mathbf{x}_i^t)\}_{i=1}^{n_t}$ denotes the set of negative energy scores for all target samples, and σ_e is a scaling parameter.

Prototype-Based Refinement in Feature Space. To enhance the credibility of $\mathcal{C}_e$, we further refine $\mathcal{C}_e$ by leveraging geometric prototypes for L classes in feature space. Specifically, the prototype μ_l for class l is computed as $\mu_l = \frac{\sum_{i=1}^{n_t} p_{i,l}\, \theta_k(\mathbf{x}_i^t)}{\sum_{i=1}^{n_t} p_{i,l}}$, $1 \le l \le L$, where $p_{i,l}$ represents the probability of sample $\mathbf{x}_i^t$ belonging to class l, and $\theta_k(\mathbf{x}_i^t)$ denotes its representation.

For each class l, the distance between the representation $\theta_k(\mathbf{x}_i^t)$ and the prototype μ_l is given by $d(\theta_k(\mathbf{x}_i^t), \mu_l)$, where $d(\cdot, \cdot)$ denotes the cosine distance. Using μ_l, the credible group for class l, i.e., $\mathcal{C}_l$, is defined by selecting samples from $\mathcal{C}_e$ that have the small distances to μ_l:

$$\mathcal{C}_l = \left\{ (\mathbf{x}_i^t, l) \mid \mathbf{x}_i^t \in \mathcal{X}_t, d(\theta_k(\mathbf{x}_i^t), \mu_l) \in \operatorname{top}_m \left(\{ d(\theta_k(\mathbf{x}_j^t), \mu_l) \mid \mathbf{x}_j^t \in \mathcal{C}_e \}_{i=1}^{n_t} \right) \right\},$$

where l represents the pseudo-label for $\mathbf{x}_i^t$, and top_m denotes the selection of the m samples from $\mathcal{C}_e$ with the smallest distances to μ_l. This iterative selection continues until $\mathcal{C}_l$ reaches m samples. The number of selected target samples m per class l is defined as $m = \lfloor m_0 + (k\eta) \cdot m_0 \rfloor$, where m_0 is the initial number of selected samples, k is the current epoch, and η is an enlarging factor that progressively increases credible domain size.

The final credible domain $\mathcal{D}_{c,k}$ for stage k is obtained by combining the credible groups across all classes: $\mathcal{D}_{c,k} = \bigcup_{l=1}^{L} \mathcal{C}_l = \bigcup_{l=1}^{L} \{ (\mathbf{x}_i^t, l) \mid \mathbf{x}_i^t \in \mathcal{C}_l \}$. For analysis, we denote the credible domain at stage k as $\mathcal{D}_{c,k} = \{ (\mathbf{x}_i^{t,c}, \tilde{y}_i^t) \}_{i=1}^{mL}$.

2.3   Progressive Construction of Known and Unknown Domains

Discovered Unknowns in Feature Space. To achieve known-unknown separation, we leverage the principal subspace P, obtained from the eigen-decomposition of representations in credible domain $\mathcal{D}_{c,k}$. Since the credible domain closely reflects the characteristics of known-class data as analyzed in Sect. 2.2, the principal subspace P captures the core structure of known samples. Consequently, target samples lie within or near P are likely from known classes, while those deviating significantly suggest an unknown distribution. By measuring the distance of sample representations from P, we can distinguish between samples from known and unknown classes.

Inspired by the principal subspace definition in residual score [31], we define the principal subspace P by first offsetting the feature space with the vector $\mathbf{o} = -(\mathbf{W}^T)^+\mathbf{b}$, removing the influence the bias term $\mathbf{b}$ on sample positioning. Here $\mathbf{W}$ and $\mathbf{b}$ represent the weight matrix and bias vector from the fully connected layer. The subspace P is then constructed using the adjusted representations $\tilde{\mathbf{Z}}$ from the credible domain $\mathcal{D}_{c,k}$, where each element $\tilde{\mathbf{z}}_i = \theta_k(\mathbf{x}_i^{t,c}) - \mathbf{o}$ denotes the representation of credible sample $\mathbf{x}_i^{t,c}$ in the new coordinate system with origin $\mathbf{o}$. Performing eigen-decomposition on the matrix $\tilde{\mathbf{Z}}^T\tilde{\mathbf{Z}}$ yields $\tilde{\mathbf{Z}}^T\tilde{\mathbf{Z}} = \mathbf{Q}\mathbf{\Lambda}\mathbf{Q}^{-1}$, where the eigenvalues in $\mathbf{\Lambda}$ are sorted decreasingly. The span of the first d' columns of $\mathbf{Q}$ forms the d'-dimensional principal subspace P. In this study, d' set to $d' = \lfloor \frac{d}{2} \rfloor$, capturing the main structures of the credible domain. Let $\mathbf{R} \in \mathbb{R}^{d \times (d-d')}$ be the matrix formed by the $(d'+1)$-th column to the last column of $\mathbf{Q}$.

For any target sample $\mathbf{x}_i^t$ with representation $\theta_k(\mathbf{x}_i^t)$, the orthogonal projection of $\theta_k(\mathbf{x}_i^t)$ outside the principal subspace P is given by $\mathbf{RR}^T\theta_k(\mathbf{x}_i^t)$. The unknowns discovered in feature space is defined as the norm of the component of $\theta_k(\mathbf{x}_i^t)$ that lies outside P, i.e., $fu_i = \sqrt{\theta_k(\mathbf{x}_i^t)\mathbf{RR}^T\theta_k(\mathbf{x}_i^t)}$. A larger fu_i indicates that $\mathbf{x}_i^t$ is farther away from P, suggesting it may belong to the unknown distribution. For all target samples, the discovered unknowns in feature space are denoted by $\mathbf{FU} = [fu_i, ..., fu_{n_t}]^T \in \mathbb{R}^{n_t}$.

Discovered Unknowns in Logit Space. Given the logit δ from model f_k, the negative energy scores for target domain are represented as $\mathbf{LU} = \left[NE(\mathbf{x}_1^t), NE(\mathbf{x}_2^t), \ldots, NE(\mathbf{x}_{n_t}^t)\right]^T \in \mathbb{R}^{n_t}$, where $NE(\mathbf{x}_i^t) = \log \sum_l^L e^{\delta_{i,l}}$. As discussed on Sect. 2.2, the negative energy scores is linearly correlated with the likelihood of samples being known. Higher values of $NE(\mathbf{x}_i^t)$ indicate a higher likelihood, making these samples credible for the previous target model f_{k-1} on the previous stage, thus more likely being the data from known classes. Conversely, samples with low negative energy values are less credible for model f_{k-1}, thus more likely being the data from unknown classes.

Discovery of Unknowns. The obtained $\mathbf{FU}$ and $\mathbf{LU}$ are combined into a clustering feature matrix $\mathbf{U} = [\mathbf{FU}, \mathbf{LU}] \in \mathbb{R}^{n_t \times 2}$. Using $\mathbf{U}$, a clustering algorithm, such as K-means [6] or Gaussian Mixture Model [25], is applied to divide samples into two clusters C_a and C_b, which are assigned as either the known cluster C_{kn} or unknown cluster C_{un}. The unknown cluster C_{un} is identified as the one with the lower mean negative energy score, i.e., $C_{un} = \arg\min_{C \in \{C_a, C_b\}} \left\{\frac{1}{|C|}\sum_{\mathbf{x}_i^t \in C} NE(\mathbf{x}_i^t)\right\}$, while the known cluster C_{kn} has higher mean negative energy, i.e., $C_{kn} = \arg\max_{C \in \{C_a, C_b\}} \left\{\frac{1}{|C|}\sum_{\mathbf{x}_i^t \in C} NE(\mathbf{x}_i^t)\right\}$.

The pseudo labels for samples from unknown classes can be assigned with $\tilde{y}_i^t = L + 1$ as they are considered belonging to the class $L + 1$. For identified samples from known classes, it can be further specified using the distance of each known sample to the class prototypes μ_l, which are

$$
\tilde{y}_i^t = \begin{cases} L + 1, & \text{if } \mathbf{x}_i^t \in C_{un} \text{ (unknown)}, \\ \arg\min_l d(\theta_k(\mathbf{x}_i^t), \mu_l), & \text{if } \mathbf{x}_i^t \in C_{kn} \text{ (known)}. \end{cases}
$$

This results in the unknown domain $\mathcal{D}_{un,k}$ for stage k defined as $\mathcal{D}_{un,k} = \{(\mathbf{x}_i^t, L + 1) \mid \mathbf{x}_i^t \in C_{un}\}$, and the known domain $\mathcal{D}_{kn,k}$ as $\mathcal{D}_{kn,k} = \{(\mathbf{x}_i^t, \arg\min_l d(\theta_k(\mathbf{x}_i^t), \mu_l)) \mid \mathbf{x}_i^t \in C_{kn}\}$. The designed clustering for known-unknown separation improves reliability by combining feature and logit space insights. When a sample is identified as unknown in both spaces, it strengthens our confidence in classifying it as unknown. If it aligns in only one space, the dual-space method captures this inconsistency, reducing errors. Further analysis of the separation mechanism is in Sect. 3.3. For analysis, we denote the known domain $\mathcal{D}_{kn,k}$ at stage k as $\mathcal{D}_{kn,k} = \{(\mathbf{x}_i^t, \tilde{y}_i^t)\}_{i=1}^{m_{kn}} = \{(\mathbf{x}_i^t, \arg\min_l d(\theta_k(\mathbf{x}_i^t), \mu_l))\}_{i=1}^{m_{kn}}$, unknown domain $\mathcal{D}_{un,k}$ at stage k as $\mathcal{D}_{un,k} = \{(\mathbf{x}_i^t, \tilde{y}_i^t)\}_{i=1}^{n_t - m_{kn}} = \{(\mathbf{x}_i^t, L + 1)\}_{i=1}^{n_t - m_{kn}}$, where m_{kn} is the number of known class samples selected from clustering.

2.4   Target Domain Adaptation

This section introduce the designed loss function to progressively update the model f_k for target domain adaptation.

Credible Domain Learning. To ensure effective learning on the credible domain $\mathcal{D}_{c,k}$, a cross-entropy loss with label smoothing is employed [22]: $\mathcal{L}_{cre}^{ls}(f_k) = -\mathbb{E}_{(\mathbf{x}_i^t, \tilde{y}_i^t) \in \mathcal{D}_{c,k}} \sum_{l=1}^{L} \delta_l^t \log f_k(\mathbf{x}_t)$, where $\delta_l^t = (1 - \alpha)q_l^t + \alpha/L$, with q^t as the one-hot encoding of the pseudo label $\tilde{y}_i^t$ and $\alpha = 0.1$ as the smoothing parameter. Here, $f_k(\mathbf{x}_i^t)$ is the softmax logit of model f_k.

Dual-Space Learning of Unknowns. With the defined known domain $\mathcal{D}_{kn,k}$ and unknown domain $\mathcal{D}_{un,k}$ at stage k, we define an dual-space uncertainty losses in both feature and logit spaces to enhance the differentiation of the model between the samples from known and unknown classes. Specifically, the uncertainty loss in feature space is defined as

$$\mathcal{L}_{unc}^{FU}(f_k) = \exp\left[\mathbb{E}_{(\mathbf{x}_i^t, \tilde{y}_i^t) \in \mathcal{D}_{kn,k}} fu_i\right] - \exp\left[\mathbb{E}_{(\mathbf{x}_i^t, \tilde{y}_i^t) \in \mathcal{D}_{un,k}} fu_i\right], \quad (1)$$

where fu_i, calculated using Sect. (2.3), represents the discovered unknowns in feature space of each target sample $\mathbf{x}_i^t$. This loss encourages smaller values of fu_i for samples from known classes and larger values for samples from unknown classes, thereby reinforcing separation in the feature space. Similarly, the uncertainty loss in logit space is defined as

$$\mathcal{L}_{unc}^{LU}(f_k) = \exp\left[\mathbb{E}_{(\mathbf{x}_i^t, \tilde{y}_i^t) \in \mathcal{D}_{kn,k}} \frac{-\sum_{i=1}^{L} p_{i,l} \log p_{i,l}}{\log L}\right]$$
$$- \exp\left[\mathbb{E}_{(\mathbf{x}_i^t, \tilde{y}_i^t) \in \mathcal{D}_{un,k}} \frac{-\beta \sum_{i=1}^{L} p_{i,l} \log p_{i,l}}{\log L}\right], \quad (2)$$

where $p_{i,l}$ represents the softmax probability of class l for sample $\mathbf{x}_i^t$. The scaling parameter β adjusts the emphasis on minimizing uncertainty for unknown samples. A larger β encourages faster learning for classifying uncertain samples. This loss facilitates lower entropy for samples from known classes and higher entropy for those from unknown classes, reinforcing separation in the logit space.

Domain Alignment for Knowns. As analyzed in Sect. 2.2, the distribution within credible domain $\mathcal{D}_{c,k}$ is close to the known-class distribution. Therefore, aligning $\mathcal{D}_{c,k}$ with the known domain $\mathcal{D}_{kn,k}$ facilitates the adaptation of samples from known classes. To achieve this alignment, we use the Hilbert-Schmidt Independence Criterion (HSIC), a kernel-based method that measures statistical dependence between distributions without requiring density estimation [4]. By capturing dependencies between credible and known domains, HSIC supports effective domain adaptation for samples from known classes.

To calculate the HSIC value, each class prototype $\tilde{\mu}_l$ within the credible domain $\mathcal{D}_{c,k}$ is refined as $\tilde{\mu}_l = \frac{\sum_{i=1}^{mL} p_{i,l} \theta_k(\mathbf{x}_i^t)}{\sum_{i=1}^{mL} p_{i,l}}$, $1 \leq l \leq L, \mathbf{x}_i^t \in \mathcal{D}_{c,k}$, where

$p_{i,l}$ represents the probability for sample $\mathbf{x}_i^t$ belonging to class l. Using these refined class prototypes, each target sample $\mathbf{x}_i^t$ in the known domain is assigned a prototype $\tilde{\mu}_{l_i}$ based on the nearest distance: $l_i = \arg\min_l d(\theta_k(\mathbf{x}_i^t), \tilde{\mu}_l)$. Let $\mathbf{N} = \{\theta_k(\mathbf{x}_i^t)\}_{i=1}^{m_{kn}}$ represent the target representations in the known domain, and $\mathbf{M} = \{\tilde{\mu}_{l_i}\}_{i=1}^{m_{kn}}$ represent the corresponding prototypes from the credible domain. Using $\mathbf{N}$ and $\mathbf{M}$, we compute the HSIC value to measure dependence between the two distributions and define the HSIC loss for domain alignment as: $\mathcal{L}_{HSIC} = \mathrm{HSIC}(\mathbf{N}, \mathbf{M})$. Due to space constraints, the detailed calculation of $\mathrm{HSIC}(\mathbf{N}, \mathbf{M})$ is provided in the Supplementary Material.

2.5 Overall Objective

Combining the designed losses, the overall objective function is formulated as

$$\mathcal{L}_{obj} = \mathcal{L}_{cre}^{ls} + \mathcal{L}_{HSIC} + \lambda_1 \mathcal{L}_{unc}^{FU} + \lambda_2 \mathcal{L}_{unc}^{LU}, \tag{3}$$

where λ_1 and λ_2 are regularization parameters. The pseudo code of PDD is presented in the Supplementary Material.

3 Experiments

3.1 Setup

Datasets. PDD is evaluated on three image classification benchmarks: Office-31, Office-Home, and Digits. (1) *Office-31* [26] includes three object domains: AMAZON (A), DSLR (D), and WEBCAM (W), each with 31 classes. The first 10 classes (alphabetically) are used as known classes, and the others as unknown, forming 6 OSDA tasks: A → D, $\cdots$, W→D. (2) *Office-Home* [29] includes four domains: Artistic (Ar), Clipart (Cl), Product (Pr), and Real-World (R), each with 65 classes. Classes 1–25 are labeled as known and 26–65 as unknown, creating 12 OSDA tasks: Ar→Cl, $\cdots$, R→Pr. (3) *Digits* [8] include three datasets: MNIST (M), SVHN (S), and USPS (U). Classes 0–4 are labeled as known, and classes 5–9 as unknown, forming 3 OSDA tasks: S→M, $\cdots$, U→M.

Baseline. This study compares the performance of our PDD with the standard OSDA methods such as OSBP [28], STA [18], ROS [2], OSLPP [32], DANN [5], ANNA [15], BCL [7], and source-free OSDA methods such as SHOT [17], AaD [34], USD [9], UPUK [30], and LEAD [24].

Evaluation Metrics. Three widely-used metrics are adopted for evaluation [18,28]: (1) **OS***: normalized accuracy for the known classes only; (2) **UNK**: accuracy of the unknown class; and (3) **HOS**: harmonic mean accuracy of OS* and UNK. Detailed calculations of these metrics and implementation details are provided in the Supplementary Material.

3.2 Main Results

Tables 1, 2, and 3 present HOS score comparisons on Office-31, Office-Home, and Digits datasets. ✓ denotes source-free OSDA methods, while ✗ denotes standard OSDA methods. The best performance among source-free methods is in bold blue. While standard OSDA methods often outperform source-free methods due to direct access to source data, PDD achieves HOS scores competitive with top-performing standard OSDA methods on tasks such as A → D in Office-31, Ar → Pr in Office-Home, and U → M in Digits. Among source-free OSDA methods, PDD consistently outperforms all other methods across every task in Office-Home and most tasks in Office-31 and Digits. Notably, on tasks like A → D in Office-31 and R → Ar in Office-Home, PDD shows marked improvements, validating the effectiveness of PDD in source-free OSDA.

Table 1. HOS (%) on 6 tasks from Office-31. Additional results for OS* and UNK metrics are available in Supplementary Material.

Method	SF?	A-D	A-W	D-A	D-W	W-A	W-D	AVG
OSBP [28]	✗	82.4	82.7	75.1	97.2	73.7	91.1	83.7
STA [18]	✗	75	75.9	73.2	69.8	66.1	75.2	72.6
ROS [2]	✗	82.4	82.1	77.9	96	77.2	**99.7**	85.9
DANCE [27]	✗	66.9	70.7	80	84.8	65.8	70.2	73.1
cUADAL [11]	✗	90.1	87.9	**98.2**	99.4	80.5	75.1	88.5
OSLPP [32]	✗	91.5	**89**	79.3	92.3	78.7	93.6	87.4
ANNA [15]	✗	83.8	85.5	82.5	**99.5**	81.6	98.4	88.6
BCL [7]	✗	**92.4**	88.3	84.8	**99.5**	**86.9**	**99.7**	**92.1**
SHOT [17]	✓	62	58.7	53.3	86.1	59.6	82.1	67
AaD [34]	✓	78.3	74.3	74.2	87	73	95.7	80.4
USD [9]	✓	81.2	77.9	73.9	<u>97.3</u>	74	95.2	83.3
UPUK [30]	✓	76.7	80.0	75.5	83.2	78.2	84.3	79.7
LEAD [24]	✓	<u>84.9</u>	<u>85.1</u>	**90.2**	94.8	**90.3**	<u>96.5</u>	<u>90.3</u>
PDD	✓	**93.4**	**86.5**	84	97.8	<u>81.5</u>	**99.6**	**90.5**

3.3 Further Analyses

(1) Mechanism of PDD for Known-Unknown Separation. PDD clusters known and unknown samples by discovering unknowns in both feature (FU) space and logit (LU) space, as illustrated in Fig. 3 for the W → D task on Office-31. Initially (Fig. 3a), there is obvious overlap between known and unknown samples, hindering separation accuracy. As training progresses, PDD increases

Table 2. HOS (%) on 12 tasks from Office-Home. Additional results for OS* and UNK metrics are available in Supplementary Material.

Method	SF?	Ar-Cl	Ar-Pr	Ar-R	Cl-Ar	Cl-Pr	Cl-R	Pr-Ar	Pr-Cl	Pr-R	R-Ar	R-Cl	R-Pr	AVG
OSBP[28]	✗	55.1	65.2	72.9	64.3	64.7	70.6	63.2	53.2	73.9	66.7	54.5	72.3	64.7
STA[18]	✗	56.3	63.7	62.1	57.9	62.5	66.3	61.9	53.2	69.5	67.1	54.5	64.5	61.1
DAOD[3]	✗	60.5	56.6	69.5	60.4	60.4	65.8	59.1	49.4	62.5	52.5	45.5	49.1	57.6
DANCE[27]	✗	53.1	49.8	39.4	40.9	45.9	30.2	54.2	55.7	41.2	27.5	48.3	44	44.2
ROS[2]	✗	60.1	69.3	76.5	58.9	65.2	68.6	60.6	56.3	74.4	68.8	60.4	75.7	66.2
cUADAL[11]	✗	63.6	71.6	77.5	**65**	68.3	72.6	62.9	54.6	76.8	**72.6**	59.9	76.7	68.5
OSLPP[32]	✗	61	72.8	74.3	60.9	66.9	70.4	63.6	59.3	74	67.2	59	74.4	67
ANNA[15]	✗	**69**	73.7	76.8	64.7	68.6	73	**66.5**	**63.1**	76.6	71.3	**65.7**	78.7	70.7
BCL[7]	✗	64.3	**75.4**	**79.0**	63.1	**70.0**	**73.4**	66.2	62.5	**77.3**	69.7	64.7	**82.1**	**70.8**
SHOT[17]	✓	39.5	39.8	47	54.6	40.2	39.1	57.7	40.8	46.2	59.9	40.1	42.3	45.6
AaD[34]	✓	57.6	66.9	69.9	60.5	61.4	67.8	60.1	55.9	70.6	64.6	57.5	70.1	63.6
USD[9]	✓	_61.1_	70	76.3	60.1	65.2	68.9	62.6	56.3	72.2	_67.8_	59.1	71.1	65.9
UPUK[30]	✓	55.8	_76.7_	_78.4_	_66.4_	_73.1_	_77.6_	_67.6_	55.1	_78.6_	_67.8_	_59.4_	74.4	_69.2_
LEAD[24]	✓	60.7	70.8	76.5	61.0	68.6	70.8	65.5	_59.8_	74.2	64.8	57.7	_75.8_	67.2
PDD	✓	**67.3**	**79.5**	**82.1**	**67.3**	**76.5**	**77.8**	**71.5**	**59.9**	**81.0**	**75.6**	**64.2**	**80.4**	**73.6**

Table 3. HOS (%) on tasks from Digits. Additional results for OS* and UNK metrics are available in Supplementary Material.

SF?	OSVM	DANN	ATI-λ	OSBP	STA	KASE	BADA	PDD
	[10] ✗	[5] ✗	[23] ✗	[28] ✗	[18] ✗	[16] ✗	[36] ✗	✓
S-M	18	65.5	_69.6_	58.4	63.7	65.3	**83.5**	64.9
U-M	48.5	89.8	84	**95.8**	95.1	93.9	86.3	**95.8**
M-U	83	86.8	80.4	_91.7_	91.6	_91.7_	90.8	**92.8**
AVG	61.4	80.8	78.4	82	83.6	83.7	_86.9_	**94.3**

LU and reduces FU for known samples while doing the opposite for unknowns. By Epoch 6 (Fig. 3b), this strategy reduces overlap, clustering known samples (high LU, low FU) and unknown samples (low LU, high FU) more effectively. By Epoch 15 (Fig. 3c), clusters for known and unknown samples are well-established, achieving clear separation in both spaces. This progressive dual-space adaptation enables reliable identification of known and unknown samples.

(2) Ablation on Dual-Space Discovering and Progressive Updates. We evaluate PDD against three variants on HOS scores in the Office-31 dataset, as shown in Fig. 4. (1) **PDD w/o P**. This variant skips progressive construction of credible domain $\mathcal{D}_{c,k}$, known domain $\mathcal{D}_{kn,k}$, and unknown domain $\mathcal{D}_{un,k}$ at each epoch. PDD significantly outperforms PDD w/o P, indicating the importance of updating these domains progressively for domain alignment and

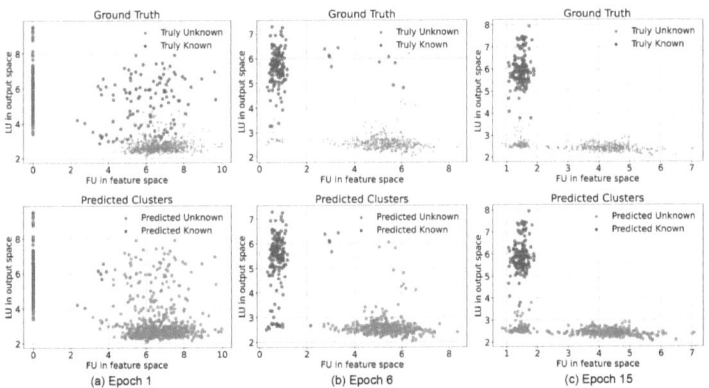

Fig. 3. Progressive clustering of known and unknown samples in dual spaces (feature and logit) across training epochs.

known/unknown separation. (2) **PDD w/o OSD** and **PDD w/o FSD**: PDD w/o OSD excludes logit space discovering when constructing known/unknown domains and the logit space uncertainty loss $\mathcal{L}_{unc}^{LU}$, while PDD w/o FSD removes feature space discovering and feature space uncertainty loss $\mathcal{L}_{unc}^{FU}$. PDD demonstrates superior performance over both variants, confirming the effectiveness of dual-space discovering and adaptation for accurately identifying unknowns.

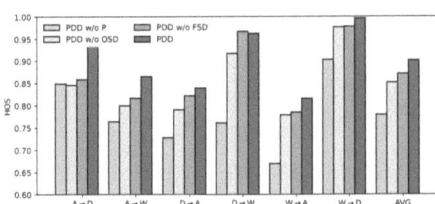

Fig. 4. HOS comparison of PDD and its three variants on Office-31.

(3) Ablation Analysis on Loss Component Contributions. We evaluate PDD with different combinations of loss components. Table 4 presents the HOS scores on the Office-31 dataset for various configurations. The results in the last row show that PDD incorporating all four loss components yields the highest overall HOS scores across most tasks. This highlights the complementary roles of each component: $\mathcal{L}_{cre}^{ls}$ improves credible data learning, $\mathcal{L}_{HSIC}$ enhances domain alignment, and $\mathcal{L}_{unc}^{LU}$ and $\mathcal{L}_{unc}^{FU}$ facilitate effective known-unknown separation.

(4) HOS During Training. As shown in Fig. 5, we present HOS curves of AaD, SHOT, and PDD on Office-31 tasks D → A, D → W, as well as Office-Home tasks Ar → Cl and Ar → Pr. HOS scores for AaD and SHOT either remain

Table 4. HOS (%) from ablation analysis of individual loss components on various tasks in the Office-31 dataset.

	A→D	A→W	D→A	D→W	W→A	W→D
PDD w/o $\mathcal{L}_{cre}^{ls}$	89.9	84.8	**84.3**	95.7	80.9	95.2
PDD w/o $\mathcal{L}_{HSIC}$	92.6	84.8	<u>84.1</u>	96.1	80.6	96.6
PDD w/o $\mathcal{L}_{unc}^{FU}$	91	85.6	83.5	93.7	81.4	95
PDD w/o $\mathcal{L}_{unc}^{LU}$	91.6	74.5	74.5	72.4	74.2	95.6
PDD	**93.4**	**86.5**	84	**97.8**	**81.5**	**99.6**

stable or decline during training. This is because SHOT, designed for closed-set settings, lacks mechanisms to explicitly separate unknown samples from known ones in OSDA. In contrast, our method consistently achieves the highest HOS scores and steadily improves over epochs, validating its training stability.

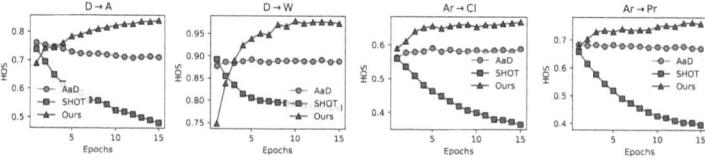

Fig. 5. HOS variation curve for methods AaD, SHOT, and PDD during training on Office-31 and Office-Home tasks.

(5) Impact of Parameters σ_e, m_0, and η. Figure 6 analyzes the impact of σ_e, m_0, and η on HOS scores, which control the sample numbers in credible domain. For m_0 (first subplot), a lower value like 5 results in fewer samples selected, restricting learning due to limited data. Conversely, a higher m_0 (e.g., 20) allows more samples but introduces noise from non-credible data, reducing HOS stability. Moderate values like 10 or 15 achieve a balance, selecting enough samples and yielding high, stable HOS scores. This trade-off also applies to η and σ_e: larger values enhance learning by increasing sample count but reduce credibility, while smaller values improve credibility but limit learning data. Therefore, optimal and stable performance is achieved with moderate parameter settings: m_0 between 10 and 15, σ_e between 0.4 and 0.8, and η between 0.1 and 0.5. These ranges provide a balanced trade-off, maximizing learning potential while preserving sample credibility.

(6) Sensitivity to Loss Coefficients β, λ_1, and λ_2. We evaluate the sensitivity of PDD to variations in loss coefficients β, λ_1, and λ_2, which influence uncertainty losses across feature and logit spaces. Figure 7 shows that HOS remains stable across varying λ_1 and λ_2 values (first and second plot), indicating robustness to these parameters. Although minor variations may occur on specific tasks,

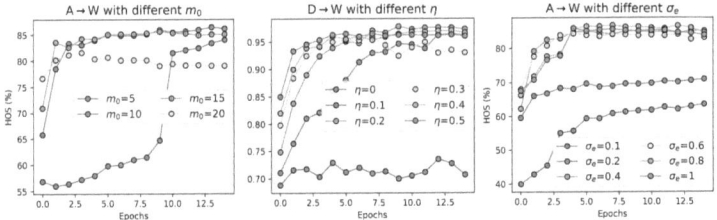

Fig. 6. Effect of σ_e, m_0, and η on HOS in Office-31 dataset.

the overall impact across multiple tasks remains minimal. For β (third plot), a higher value (e.g., 3) overemphasizes uncertainty, reducing HOS and affecting performance, while $\beta = 0$ neglects logit space uncertainty, leading to suboptimal performance. Moderate values (1 or 2) provide better balance, effectively managing uncertainty without overfitting.

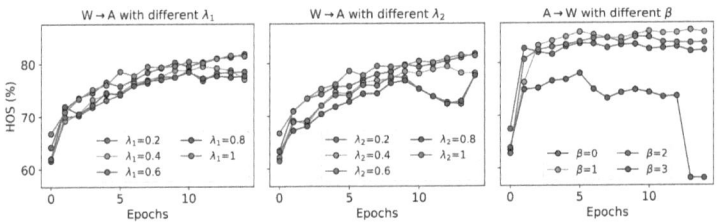

Fig. 7. HOS variation on Tasks W $\rightarrow$ A and A $\rightarrow$ W in the Office-31 dataset as the λ_1, λ_2 and β varying.

(7) Impact of Openness. To verify the robustness of PDD across varying openness levels, we conducted experiments on Office-31 dataset with openness O set to $\{0.25, 0.5, 0.75, 0.93\}$, where $O = 1 - \frac{|C_s|}{|C_t|}$, following [18]. Higher O values indicate greater challenges due to more unknown classes in target domain. Figure 8 presents HOS performance for PDD, AaD, and SHOT on tasks A→W and W→D. While AaD and SHOT degrade as openness increases, likely due to reliance on source-like samples, PDD remains stable or improves, consistently outperforming both methods across all openness levels. This stability is due to its dual-space discovering of unknowns, improving known-unknown separation. Besides, as openness increases and known classes decrease, the classification of known data is simplified, further supports the domain alignment. All these highlights its effectiveness across varying openness levels in OSDA.

(8) Feature Visualization. We visualize the last-layer features of ResNet-50, AaD, SHOT, and PDD on W → D task using t-SNE embeddings, as shown in Fig. 9. For ResNet-50, AaD, and SHOT methods, we observe overlapping features between known and unknown classes, along with the misalignment between

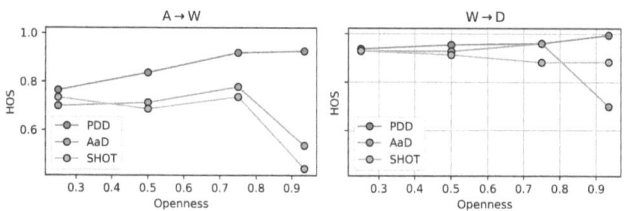

Fig. 8. HOS performance comparison of PDD, AaD, and SHOT on Office-31 dataset across different openness levels.

source and target features within the same known classes. In contrast, PDD achieves an obvious separation between known and unknown classes. Besides, within each known class, PDD closely aligns source and target samples, demonstrating effective domain alignment. These results indicate that PDD successfully identifies unknown samples and achieves consistent alignment of source and target features for known classes, validating its effectiveness.

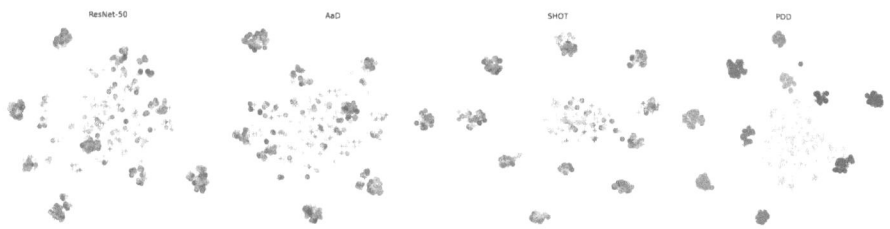

Fig. 9. Visualization of the features extracted by ResNet-50, AaD, SHOT, and PDD on Office-31 task W → D using t-SNE embeddings, respectively. ○ and + represent the source and target data. Different classes are distinguished by unique colors, with unknown samples marked in light blue. (Color figure online)

4   Conclusion

This study introduces PDD, a source-free OSDA method that leverages dual-space, i.e., both feature and logit spaces information to improve alignment and known-unknown separation. By progressively constructing a credible domain through dual-space selection and establishing known and unknown domains via dual-space discovering, PDD achieves effective alignment for known classes across domains and known-unknown separation. Extensive experiments validate the effectiveness of our dual-space consideration and progressive updates, with PDD achieving state-of-the-art performance across three OSDA benchmarks.

Disclosure of Interests. The authors have no competing interests to declare that are relevant to the content of this article.

References

1. Baktashmotlagh, M., Faraki, M., Drummond, T., Salzmann, M.: Learning factorized representations for open-set domain adaptation. In: ICLR (2019)
2. Bucci, S., Loghmani, M.R., Tommasi, T.: On the effectiveness of image rotation for open set domain adaptation. In: ECCV, pp. 422–438. Springer, Cham (2020)
3. Fang, Z., Lu, J., Liu, F., Xuan, J., Zhang, G.: Open set domain adaptation: theoretical bound and algorithm. IEEE TNNLS 32(10), 4309–4322 (2020)
4. Fukumizu, K., Gretton, A., Sun, X., Schölkopf, B.: Kernel measures of conditional dependence. In: NIPS, vol. 20 (2007)
5. Ganin, Y., Lempitsky, V.: Unsupervised domain adaptation by backpropagation. In: International Conference on Machine Learning, pp. 1180–1189. PMLR (2015)
6. Hartigan, J.A., Wong, M.A.: Algorithm as 136: a k-means clustering algorithm. J. R. Stat. Soc. Ser. C 28(1), 100–108 (1979)
7. Huang, Z.X., Ren, C.X.: Rethinking correlation learning via label prior for open set domain adaptation. In: IJCAI (2024)
8. Hull, J.J.: A database for handwritten text recognition research. IEEE TPAMI 16(5), 550–554 (1994)
9. Jahan, C.S., Savakis, A.: Unknown sample discovery for source free open set domain adaptation. In: CVPR, pp. 1067–1076 (2024)
10. Jain, L.P., Scheirer, W.J., Boult, T.E.: Multi-class open set recognition using probability of inclusion. In: ECCV, pp. 393–409. Springer, Cham (2014)
11. Jang, J., Na, B., Shin, D.H., Ji, M., Song, K., Moon, I.C.: Unknown-aware domain adversarial learning for open-set domain adaptation. In: NIPS, vol. 35, pp. 16755–16767 (2022)
12. Jing, M., Li, J., Zhu, L., Ding, Z., Lu, K., Yang, Y.: Balanced open set domain adaptation via centroid alignment. In: AAAI, vol. 35, pp. 8013–8020 (2021)
13. Jing, T., Liu, H., Ding, Z.: Towards novel target discovery through open-set domain adaptation. In: ICCV, pp. 9322–9331 (2021)
14. Kim, Y., Cho, D., Han, K., Panda, P., Hong, S.: Domain adaptation without source data. IEEE TAI 2(6), 508–518 (2021)
15. Li, W., Liu, J., Han, B., Yuan, Y.: Adjustment and alignment for unbiased open set domain adaptation. In: CVPR, pp. 24110–24119 (2023)
16. Lian, Q., Li, W., Chen, L., Duan, L.: Known-class aware self-ensemble for open set domain adaptation. arXiv preprint arXiv:1905.01068 (2019)
17. Liang, J., Hu, D., Feng, J.: Do we really need to access the source data? Source hypothesis transfer for unsupervised domain adaptation. In: ICML, pp. 6028–6039. PMLR (2020)
18. Liu, H., Cao, Z., Long, M., Wang, J., Yang, Q.: Separate to adapt: open set domain adaptation via progressive separation. In: CVPR, pp. 2927–2936 (2019)
19. Liu, W., Wang, X., Owens, J., Li, Y.: Energy-based out-of-distribution detection. In: NIPS, vol. 33, pp. 21464–21475 (2020)
20. Long, M., Cao, Y., Wang, J., Jordan, M.: Learning transferable features with deep adaptation networks. In: ICML, pp. 97–105. PMLR (2015)
21. Mei, Z., Ye, P., Ye, H., Li, B., Guo, J., Chen, T., Ouyang, W.: Automatic loss function search for adversarial unsupervised domain adaptation. IEEE TCSVT 33(10), 5868–5881 (2023)
22. Müller, R., Kornblith, S., Hinton, G.E.: When does label smoothing help? In: NIPS, vol. 32 (2019)

23. Panareda Busto, P., Gall, J.: Open set domain adaptation. In: ICCV, pp. 754–763 (2017)
24. Qu, S., et al.: Lead: learning decomposition for source-free universal domain adaptation. In: CVPR, pp. 23334–23343 (2024)
25. Reynolds, D.A.: Gaussian mixture models. In: Encyclopedia of Biometrics, pp. 741–745. Springer, Boston (2009)
26. Saenko, K., Kulis, B., Fritz, M., Darrell, T.: Adapting visual category models to new domains. In: ECCV, pp. 213–226 (2010)
27. Saito, K., Kim, D., Sclaroff, S., Saenko, K.: Universal domain adaptation through self supervision. In: NIPS, vol. 33, pp. 16282–16292 (2020)
28. Saito, K., Yamamoto, S., Ushiku, Y., Harada, T.: Open set domain adaptation by backpropagation. In: ECCV, pp. 153–168 (2018)
29. Venkateswara, H., Eusebio, J., Chakraborty, S., Panchanathan, S.: Deep hashing network for unsupervised domain adaptation. In: CVPR, pp. 5018–5027 (2017)
30. Wan, F., Zhao, H., Yang, X., Deng, C.: Unveiling the unknown: unleashing the power of unknown to known in open-set source-free domain adaptation. In: CVP, pp. 24015–24024 (2024)
31. Wang, H., Li, Z., Feng, L., Zhang, W.: Vim: Out-of-distribution with virtual-logit matching. In: CVPR (2022)
32. Wang, Q., Meng, F., Breckon, T.P.: Progressively select and reject pseudo-labelled samples for open-set domain adaptation. IEEE TAI (2024)
33. Wang, Y., Zhu, R., Ji, P., Li, S.: Open-set graph domain adaptation via separate domain alignment. In: AAAI, vol. 38, pp. 9142–9150 (2024)
34. Yang, S., Jui, S., van de Weijer, J., et al.: Attracting and dispersing: a simple approach for source-free domain adaptation. In: NIPS, vol. 35, pp. 5802–5815 (2022)
35. Zhan, Q., Zeng, X.J., Wang, Q.: Reducing bias in source-free unsupervised domain adaptation for regression. Neural Netw. 107161 (2025)
36. Zhong, L., Fang, Z., Liu, F., Yuan, B., Zhang, G., Lu, J.: Bridging the theoretical bound and deep algorithms for open set domain adaptation. IEEE TNNLS **34**(8), 3859–3873 (2021)

Target-Adaptive Structure-Semantic Consistency for Unsupervised Graph Domain Adaptation

Yan Zou[1], Yongzheng Lu[1], Na Li[1], Xiatian Zhu[2], Lan Du[3], Ming Yan[4], and Ying Ma[1(✉)]

[1] Harbin Institute of Technology, Harbin, China
{23b903066,24b903068,24s003043}@stu.hit.edu.cn, y.ma@hit.edu.cn
[2] University of Surrey, Guildford, UK
xiatian.zhu@surrey.ac.uk
[3] Monash University, Melbourne, VIC, Australia
lan.du@monash.edu
[4] Centre for Frontier AI Research (CFAR), A*STAR, Singapore, Singapore

Abstract. Unsupervised Graph Domain Adaptation (UGDA) aims to mitigate distribution shifts between domains by transferring knowledge from labeled source graphs to unlabeled target graphs. Current work indicates that enhancing target embeddings is helpful for domain generalization. However, these methods primarily focus on structure-guided enhancement but often overlook the intrinsic coupling between structural topology and node semantics in graph data, resulting in suboptimal target representations during complex structure adaptation. To address this problem, we propose a novel approach called Target-adaptive Structure-Semantic Consistency (TASSC). First, we establish bidirectional optimization, ensuring consistency between structural proximity and semantic similarity on the target graph. Specifically, we propose a hybrid contrastive learning strategy, which unifies topological neighbors and cosine-similarity features (semantic neighbors) as positive samples. Additionally, we employ entropy minimization to suppress target semantic ambiguity caused by source domain biases, creating a closed-loop optimization where 'structure guides semantics, semantics feedback structure.' Furthermore, we develop a scale-aware adaptive module to access scale disparities between domains, dynamically transferring source knowledge to mitigate target semantic insufficiency. Extensive experiments on three real-world benchmark datasets demonstrate that our method achieves state-of-the-art results.

Keywords: Graph Neural Networks · Transfer Learning · Unsupervised Graph Domain Adaptation

1 Introduction

Graph Neural Networks (GNNs) [7,16] have demonstrated remarkable effectiveness in modeling relational data, driving advances in social network analysis [25],

B. Pfahringer et al. (Eds.): ECML PKDD 2025, LNAI 16020, pp. 182–198, 2026.
https://doi.org/10.1007/978-3-662-72243-5_11

protein interaction prediction [37], and recommendation systems [24]. However, their performance heavily relies on labeled data, with cross-domain generalization hindered by label scarcity and distribution shifts. To mitigate such issues, Unsupervised Graph Domain Adaptation (UGDA) [8,13,23,31] addresses this by transferring structural knowledge from labeled source graphs to unlabeled target graphs via domain-invariant representation learning.

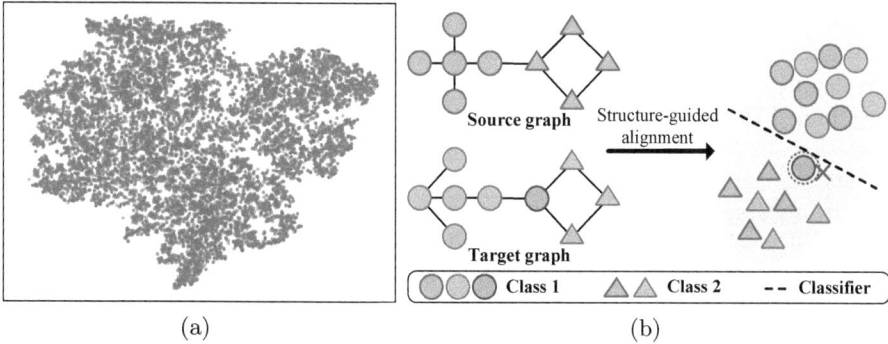

(a)   (b)

Fig. 1. Illustration of motivation. (a) The t-SNE [17] feature visualization for the task A → C on the ArnetMiner [27] dataset, where orange and blue colors represent the target and source data, respectively. (b) The performance of structure-guided alignment is limited without the semantic consistency constraint.

In real-world scenarios, such as citation networks across different publishers and time periods, variations in node attributes and graph structural properties are evident. The source graph may contain dense clusters of highly intercon-nected papers, whereas the target graph may have a more sparse, distributed structure, or vice versa. This drives recent efforts to leverage target information for better domain generalization (DG). A2GNN [11] implicitly enhances topology representation by stacking multiple message-passing layers on the target graph, while TDSS [3] further employs structural smoothing to mitigate distribution shifts. Moreover, some studies [14,15] adjust edge weights to better align target topology, mitigating conditional shifts caused by neighborhood structures.

However, these methods primarily adopt target structure-guided alignment to refine target embeddings while overlooking the importance of target-specific semantic information. As illustrated in Fig. 1(a), in the embedding space, tar-get node representations become diffusely distributed due to insufficient seman-tic constraints. This results in a situation where the source domain, benefiting from labeled supervision, could partially ignore the semantic constraint to some extent and still achieve good classification performance, as shown in the upper part of Fig. 1(b). In contrast, the target domain lacks such guidance, causing the node (marked by a green circle in Fig. 1(b)) within the same class to experi-ence shifts due to structural perturbations, which may lead to misclassification. Therefore, it is essential to not only align features based on target topology but also ensure consistency between structure and semantics. Specifically, nodes with strong structural connections should remain close in feature space, reflecting the graph topology, while semantically similar nodes should form compact clusters, preserving consistency for accurate classification.

Motivated by this analysis, we propose Target-adaptive Structure-Semantic Consistency (TASSC) for cross-domain node classification. First, we design a structure-semantic constraint module to break through the limitations of single-perspective optimization. Specifically, we introduce a hybrid contrastive learning strategy, constructing positive and negative sample pairs at both the node and embedding levels to enforce dual consistency. At the node level, positives are defined by topological neighbors, while at the embedding level, they are determined through cosine similarity. Additionally, we incorporate entropy minimization on the target graph to reduce noise from source structural priors, enhancing semantic consistency. Second, we develop an adaptive adjustment module to assess the target domain's information scale relative to the source domain. By selectively transferring high-quality source knowledge, this module adaptively enhances target semantics. These two modules are designed to preserve structure-semantic consistency during adaptation, refining target node representations through topological properties and semantic similarity, ultimately improving generalization on the target graph.

Our contributions can be summarized as follows:

1. We propose TASSC, a novel framework for UGDA, which establishes a bidirectional adaptation process, integrating structural topology and semantic representations on the target graph to enhance representation consistency and improve cross-domain generalization.
2. We design an adaptive mechanism that assesses domain complexity and refines target representations by dynamically leveraging source domain information, facilitating more effective knowledge transfer.
3. We conduct extensive experiments on three benchmark datasets. The results demonstrate that TASSC achieves state-of-the-art performance, significantly outperforming the best baseline with notable relative improvements.

2   Related Work

Unsupervised Domain Adaptation (UDA) [5,6] is a widely adopted transfer learning paradigm aimed at minimizing domain divergence. In the context of graph-structured data, UGDA [4,23] has emerged as an effective approach for addressing distribution shifts within relational networks. Existing UGDA methods can be categorized into three main groups.

Methods in the first group primarily focus on reducing source prediction risks through enhanced node embeddings [4,33]. For example, UDAGCN [31] introduces a dual-GNN that employs adversarial training to align feature distributions across domains. ACDNE [21] utilizes the k-hop PPMI matrix to capture high-order proximity, ensuring global consistency during adaptation. The

second group of methods mitigate graph domain shifts by constructing intermediate representations to bridge domain gaps effectively [30,34]. Several strategies have been proposed to achieve this. ASN [36] separates domain-private
and shared features, leveraging adversarial domain adaptation to extract the
domain-invariant shared features across networks. GGDA [10] introduces a compact domain sequence with FGW-based intermediate graphs and vertex-based
progression to minimize information loss and improve adaptation. KBL [1] adds
data augmentation with adversarial learning to align node embeddings across
domains. The last group of methods enhances target embeddings by leveraging target domain information [12,14,28]. PairAlign [15] mitigates structure and
label shifts by adjusting node influences with edge and label weights, improving
cross-domain alignment in graph adaptation. DMGNN [22] refines predictions
through a label propagation mechanism, utilizing a node classifier that improves
label consistency by aggregating the predictions of a node and its neighbors.
A2GNN [11] enhances adaptation by replacing a shared encoder with a shared
transformation layer and deeper propagation on the target graph. TDSS [3] mitigates structural shifts and improves node representation by performing structural smoothing on the target graph.

　　While these methods above have shown remarkable effectiveness in enhancing target node representations, the structure-semantic collaborative mapping
mechanism has not received sufficient attention and exploitation.

3　Preliminaries

In this section, we begin with the notation and problem definition, then present
the graph neural networks employed in this work.

3.1　Notation and Problem Definition

Consider an attributed graph $\mathcal{G} = (\mathcal{V}, \mathcal{E})$, where $\mathcal{V} = \{v_i\}_{i=1}^{|\mathcal{V}|}$ is the set of $|\mathcal{V}|$
nodes and $\mathcal{E}$ is the set of edges. Let $\mathbf{X} = \{\mathbf{x}_v | v \in \mathcal{V}\} \in \mathbb{R}^{|\mathcal{V}| \times D}$ be the node
adjacency matrix of $\mathcal{G}$, where $\mathbf{x}_i$ is the D-dimensional feature vector of node
v_i. We denote the graph structure as an adjacency matrix $\mathbf{A} \in \mathbb{R}^{|\mathcal{V}| \times |\mathcal{V}|}$, where
$\mathbf{A}_{i,j} = 1$ means there exits an edge connecting v_i and v_j, otherwise $\mathrm{A}_{i,j} = 0$.

　　Given two different but related source domain $\mathcal{S}$ and target domain $\mathcal{T}$, both
domains share the same C categories. The source graph with m labeled nodes
is denoted as $\mathcal{G}_S = (\mathcal{V}_S, \mathcal{E}_S, \mathcal{Y}_S)$ and target graph with n unlabeled nodes is
denoted as $\mathcal{G}_T = (\mathcal{V}_T, \mathcal{E}_T)$. In practice, $\mathbb{P}(\mathcal{G}_S) \neq \mathbb{P}(\mathcal{G}_t)$ but $\mathbb{P}(\mathcal{Y}_S | (\mathcal{V}_S, \mathcal{E}_S)) = \mathbb{P}(\mathcal{Y}_T | (\mathcal{V}_T, \mathcal{E}_T))$, where $\mathbb{P}$ denotes the probability distributions. Our goal is to
build a function $\mathcal{F} : (\mathcal{G}_S, \mathcal{G}_T) \rightarrow \mathcal{Y}$ for the node classification task, using the
labeled source graph $\mathcal{G}_s$ and unlabeled target graph $\mathcal{G}_T$ during adaptation.

3.2　Graph Neural Networks

Inspired by the previous work [11], we construct our model $\mathcal{F}$, which adopts
an asymmetric strategy that increases the number of message passing layers

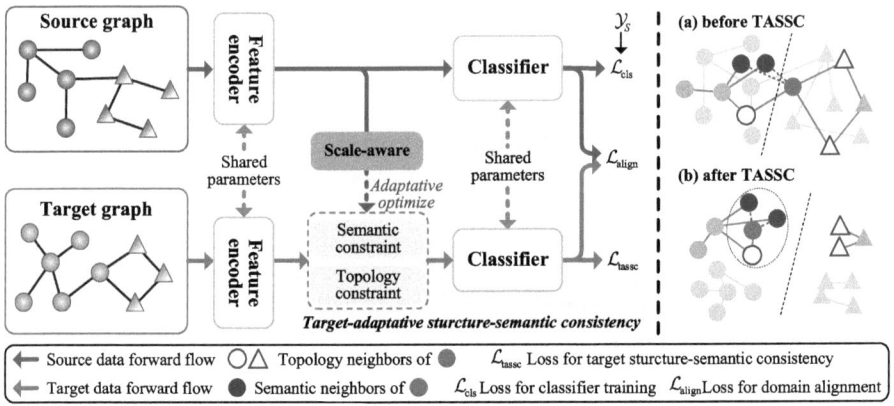

Fig. 2. The framework of the proposed method to learn $\mathcal{F}$.

on the target graph while reducing those on the source graph. Specifically, the feed-forward neural network $\mathcal{F}$ with parameter Θ consists of two modules: a feature encoder $g(\cdot;\theta) : \mathbf{X} \rightarrow \mathbb{R}^d$ and a node classifier $h(\cdot;\xi) : \mathbb{R}^d \rightarrow \mathbb{R}^C$, i.e. $\mathcal{F} = h \circ g\,(\cdot;\Theta)$ where $\Theta = \{\theta,\xi\}$ represents the shared parameters across both the source and target graphs, and d denotes the dimension of the input features.

Without loss of generality, we update the representation of node v at l-th hidden layer in the network $\mathcal{F}$, which can be formulated as:

$$\mathbf{h}_v^l = \mathcal{C}^l\left(\mathbf{h}_v^{l-1}, \mathcal{A}^{(k)}\left(\{h_u^{l-1}|u \in \mathcal{N}\,(v)\}\right)\right), \tag{1}$$

where $\mathbf{h}_v^l = \mathcal{F}^l\,(v;\Theta)$, $\mathcal{N}\,(v)$ represents the neighbors of node v and $\mathcal{C}^l$ serves as the combination function at layer l. The aggregation function $\mathcal{A}^{(k)}$ comprehensively processes the features of the k-hop neighbors of v. Notably, the value of node k in the source graph branch is significantly smaller than in the target graph branch, i.e., $k_S \ll k_T$.

4   Methodology

In this section, we introduce our method, Target-adaptive Structure-Semantic Consistency (TASSC). The overall framework of TASSC is shown in Fig. 2. In the following sections, we provide a detailed explanation of its components.

4.1   Target Structure-Semantic Consistency Learning

The core contribution of this paper is to efficiently preserve the consistency between target structural proximity and semantic similarity, to achieve better generalization. Notably, we observe that graph contrastive learning [24,32] provides distinct theoretical advantages. By explicitly defining structure-guided similarity relationships, this approach inherently incorporates local topological constraints into the representation learning process. For instance, by forming positive pairs within local neighborhoods, the contrastive loss encourages the latent space distance between adjacent nodes to be proportional to their structural similarity, thereby reinforcing the alignment between the learned representations and the underlying graph structure.

However, relying solely on topological neighbors as positive samples may propagate structural noise, especially under cross-domain distribution shifts. As shown on the right side of Fig. 2, the green-circled node is connected to three other nodes, but only one of them shares the same class. This could lead to misclassification due to source-biased structural alignment, affected by the hollow red-triangled nodes. In contrast, the solid red-circled nodes, though not directly connected to the green-circled node (as shown by the red dashed line in Fig. 2), are semantically similar to it, as indicated by their proximity in the feature space. Therefore, the solid red-circled nodes can provide meaningful semantic information to the green-circled node, effectively acting as its semantic neighbors.

Motivated by this observation, we propose a hybrid positive sampling strategy for target-oriented contrastive learning. In this approach, positive pairs are constructed by combining both topological neighbors and feature-similar nodes. For any input target node v_t, we calculate its cosine similarity with all other nodes in the target graph $\mathcal{G}_t$, excluding v_t itself. Let $\hat{\mathcal{V}}_t \subset \mathcal{V}_t$ denote the set of nodes used for comparison, where $v_t \notin \hat{\mathcal{V}}_t$. Thus, we select semantic neighbors based on similarity ranking, which can be formulated as:

$$\mathcal{N}_{\text{sem}}(v_t) = \left\{ v_{t,i}^{\text{sem}} \mid v_{t,i}^{\text{sem}} \in \hat{\mathcal{V}}_t, i \in \text{topk}\left(\text{sim}\left(\mathbf{v}_t, \hat{\mathbf{V}}_t \right), k_{\text{sem}} \right) \right\}, \qquad (2)$$

where $\mathbf{v}_t = g(v_t; \theta)$ presents the target feature of v_t, $\hat{\mathbf{V}}_t = [\hat{\mathbf{v}}_{t,j}]_{j=1}^{|\mathcal{V}_t|-1}$ is the matrix containing the node feature $\hat{\mathbf{v}}_t = g(\hat{v}_t; \theta)$ for each node $\hat{v}_t \in \hat{\mathcal{V}}_t$. Additionally, $\text{sim}(\cdot, \cdot)$ is the function to evaluate cosine-similarity of the input two vectors, and $\text{topk}(\mathcal{Z}, k)$ represent an operation which selects the k elements with the highest values from set $\mathcal{Z}$ and returns the corresponding indices of these elements.

For the one-hop local neighbor set $\mathcal{N}(v_t)$, we uniformly select k_{topo} elements as the topological neighbors of v_t, forming the set $\mathcal{N}_{\text{topo}}(v_t)$ [32]. We then dynamically select positive samples for v_t as follows:

$$\mathcal{N}_+(v_t) = \mathcal{N}_{\text{topo}}(v_t) \cup \mathcal{N}_{\text{sem}}(v_t), \qquad (3)$$

where $\mathcal{N}_+(v_t)$ denotes the set of selected target neighbors for v_t.

For any input target node v_t, the regularization can be expressed as:

$$\mathcal{L}_{\text{ssc}}^{\mathcal{T}}(\mathcal{G}_T; \Theta) = -\mathbb{E}_{v_t \in \mathcal{V}_T} \mathbb{E}_{v_{t+} \in \mathcal{N}_+(v_t)} \log \frac{e^{\mathbf{v}_t^\top \mathbf{v}_{t+}/\tau}}{e^{\mathbf{v}_t^\top \mathbf{v}_{t+}/\tau} + \sum_{v_{t-} \in \mathcal{N}_-(v_t)} e^{\mathbf{v}_t^\top \mathbf{v}_{t-}/\tau}}. \qquad (4)$$

Here $\mathbf{v}_{t+}$ and $\mathbf{v}_{t-}$ are the node representations generated by $g(\cdot; \theta)$ for nodes v_{t+} and v_{t-}, respectively. τ is the temperature hyper-parameter. Typically, $\mathcal{N}_-(v_t)$

denotes the negative sample set, which is randomly selected from the target node space $\mathcal{V}_T$ [26], with the constraint that the number of negative samples, $|\mathcal{N}_-(v_t)|$, is equal to the number of positive samples, $|\mathcal{N}_+(v_t)|$, ensuring equal sample sizes for effective contrastive learning.

4.2 Target-Oriented Semantic Regularization

While the target structure-semantic consistency learning method proposed in Sect. 4.1 effectively enforces localized constraints between topological neighborhoods and semantic neighborhoods, it lacks explicit regularization of the global semantic distribution in the embedding space. Specifically, under the shared feature encoder framework, domain structural biases may cause target node representations to deviate from their true semantic distribution, resulting in blurred class boundaries.

To address this limitation, incorporating global semantic constraints or regularization mechanisms into the learning objective is essential. Such enhancements would ensure that target representations not only preserve local consistency but also maintain global discriminability, thereby mitigating the adverse effects of noise introduced by source structural priors.

Thus, we employ entropy minimization to preserve critical distinctions in the target graph's feature space, formulating this regularization as shown in Eq. (5).

$$\mathcal{L}_{\text{ent}}^{\mathcal{T}}(\mathcal{G}_T;\Theta) = -\mathbb{E}_{v_t \in \mathcal{V}_T} \sum_{c=1}^{C} \delta_c\left(\mathcal{F}(v_t;\Theta)\right) \log \delta_c\left(\mathcal{F}(v_t;\Theta)\right), \tag{5}$$

where $\delta_c(\boldsymbol{\mu}) = \exp(\mu_c)/\sum_i \exp(\mu_i)$ denotes the c-th element in the *softmax* output for a C-dimensional vector $\boldsymbol{\mu}$, and $\mathcal{F}(v_t;\Theta) = h \circ g(v_t;\{\theta,\phi\})$ denotes the C-dimensional output of target node v_t.

Due to the absence of target labels, the model may overfit to dominant classes under the optimization of Eq. (5), causing minority classes to collapse into ambiguous clusters. To tackle this issue, we integrate a diversity maximization regularization term to counteract degenerate distributions [9], which can be formulated as:

$$\mathcal{L}_{\text{bal}}^{\mathcal{T}}(\mathcal{G}_T;\Theta) = \text{KL}\left(\boldsymbol{p}, \frac{1}{C}\mathbb{I}_C\right), \tag{6}$$

where $\boldsymbol{p} = \mathbb{E}_{v_t \in \mathcal{V}_T}[\delta(\mathcal{F}(v_t;\Theta))]$ represents the mean output embedding of the whole target domain, $\mathbb{I}_C$ is a C-dimensional vector with all elements set to one. $\text{KL}(\cdot,\cdot)$ is a function outputting Kullback–Leibler(KL) divergence of the two inputted probability vectors.

Combining Eq. (5) and Eq. (6), we concisely express the target-oriented semantic regularization by Eq. (7).

$$\mathcal{L}_{\text{tos}}^{\mathcal{T}}(\mathcal{G}_T;\Theta) = \mathcal{L}_{\text{ent}}^{\mathcal{T}}(\mathcal{G}_T;\Theta) + \mathcal{L}_{\text{bal}}^{\mathcal{T}}(\mathcal{G}_T;\Theta). \tag{7}$$

By maximizing mutual information between target representations and latent labels, $\mathcal{L}_{\text{tos}}^{\mathcal{T}}$ drives the model to learn more distinct and discriminative target node representations in the latent space.

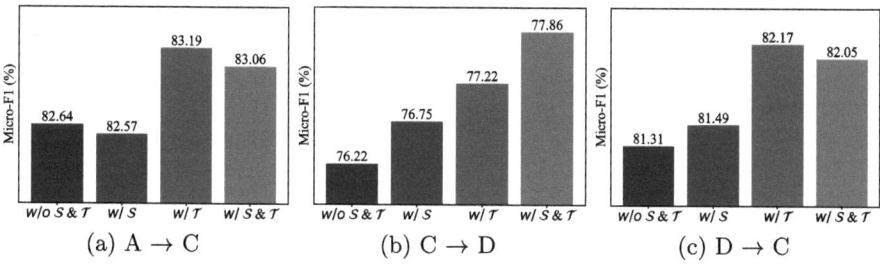

Fig. 3. The Micro-F1 scores (%) of different strategies for achieving structural and semantic consistency on the ArnetMiner dataset.

4.3 Scale-Aware Adaptive Structure-Semantic Consistency Learning

Similar to previous works [11], our method mitigates distribution shifts under the assumption of implicit homogeneity between source and target domain scales. However, we observe that this assumption overlooks the dynamic impact of scale discrepancies on semantic optimization, potentially resulting in suboptimal class separability and ambiguous node representations in the target graph.

To validate our hypothesis, we conduct experiments on the widely used ArnetMiner [27] dataset in UGDA for further investigation. Figure 3 shows the results under different strategies. Specifically, we design four distinct experiments on three tasks, where $w//w/o$ $\mathcal{S}$ or $\mathcal{T}$ indicates whether employ structure-semantic consistency learning as Eq. (4), is applied to the source or target domain data. As shown in Table 1 for the detailed dataset, domains A and C exhibit similar numbers of nodes and edges, whereas domain D is relatively smaller in scale. When we transfer knowledge from one domain to another which containing similar or larger scale information (e.g. A → C, D → C), as shown in Fig. 3(a) and Fig. 3(c), the source semantics have little impact on overall generalization. Moreover, integrating source semantics with target information may even lead to performance degradation. In contrast, enforcing both structural and semantic constraints solely on the target data significantly improves generalization. The results are explainable that when the target graph carries information on par with or exceeding that of the source graph, further enhancing the source representation introduces additional structural noise, thereby compromising target semantics. Nonetheless, as illustrated in Fig. 3(b), transferring knowledge to a smaller-scale domain in the C → D task results in insufficient informational support, leading to suboptimal performance. However, incorporating semantic optimization from the source domain can enhance cross-domain semantic commonality, thereby improving target representation.

The scale of a graph is determined by both the number of nodes and edges. Nodes serve as the main carriers of semantic information in graph-structured data, while edges serve as concrete representations of structural relationships. Guided by the aforementioned analysis, we design the weighted joint scale disparity measurement method, which is formulated as follows:

$$\lambda = \begin{cases} 1, & if \quad \omega \frac{|\mathcal{V}_S|}{|\mathcal{V}_T|} + (1-\omega)\frac{|\mathcal{E}_S|}{|\mathcal{E}_T|} \geq \epsilon \ \wedge \ \frac{|\mathcal{E}_T|}{|\mathcal{V}_T|} \leq \Upsilon \\ 0, & otherwise \end{cases} , \qquad (8)$$

where the weight coefficient $\omega = 0.7$ is used to balance the impact of nodes and edges on domain-scale measurement. ϵ is the value that represents the relative information scale of the source domain compared to the target domain and is set to 1.5. Additionally, we impose a constraint ensuring that the target degree, defined as $\frac{|\mathcal{E}_T|}{|\mathcal{V}_T|}$, remains below the threshold Υ, thereby preventing the model from neglecting extreme structural variations.

Similar to Eq. (4), we build the structure-semantic consistency learning on the source domain, which is regularized as follows, where $\mathbf{v}_s = g(v_s; \theta)$:

$$\mathcal{L}_{\text{ssc}}^{\mathcal{S}}(\mathcal{G}_S; \Theta) = -\mathbb{E}_{v_s \in \mathcal{V}_S} \mathbb{E}_{v_{s+} \in \mathcal{N}_+(v_s)} \log \frac{e^{\mathbf{v}_s^\top \mathbf{v}_{s+}/\tau}}{e^{\mathbf{v}_s^\top \mathbf{v}_{s+}/\tau} + \sum_{v_{s-} \in \mathcal{N}_-(v_s)} e^{\mathbf{v}_s^\top \mathbf{v}_{s-}/\tau}}. \qquad (9)$$

By incorporating the scale-adaptive adjustment parameter λ derived from Eq. (8), we implement Eq. 10, where α and β are trade-off parameters.

$$\mathcal{L}_{\text{tassc}}(\mathcal{G}_S, \mathcal{G}_T; \Theta) = \alpha \left(\mathcal{L}_{\text{ssc}}^{\mathcal{T}}(\mathcal{G}_T; \Theta) + \lambda \mathcal{L}_{\text{ssc}}^{\mathcal{S}}(\mathcal{G}_S; \Theta) \right) + \beta \mathcal{L}_{\text{tos}}^{\mathcal{T}}(\mathcal{G}_T; \Theta). \qquad (10)$$

4.4 Model Optimization

As aforementioned, we achieve the target-adaptive structure-semantic consistency learning by minimizing the objective $\mathcal{L}_{\text{tassc}}$. To facilitate effective knowledge transfer from the source domain to the target domain, we combine the standard cross-entropy loss and entropy minimization loss on the source domain. The resulting regularization is formulated as shown in Eq. (11).

$$\mathcal{L}_{\text{cls}}(\mathcal{G}_S; \Theta) = -\mathbb{E}_{(v_s, y_s) \in \mathcal{V}_S \times \mathcal{Y}_S} \sum_{c=1}^{C} q_c \log \delta_c \left(\mathcal{F}(v_s; \Theta) \right)$$
$$- \gamma_1 \mathbb{E}_{v_s \in \mathcal{V}_S} \sum_{c=1}^{C} \delta_c \left(\mathcal{F}(v_s; \Theta) \right) \log \delta_c \left(\mathcal{F}(v_s; \Theta) \right), \qquad (11)$$

where $\gamma_1 = 0.5$, and q denotes the one-hot encoding of $y_s \in \mathcal{Y}_S$, with q_c being '1' for the correct class and '0' for all other classes.

To summarize, the overall loss function can be expressed as:

$$\mathcal{L}(\mathcal{G}_S, \mathcal{G}_T; \Theta) = \mathcal{L}_{\text{tassc}}(\mathcal{G}_S, \mathcal{G}_T; \Theta) + \mathcal{L}_{\text{cls}}(\mathcal{G}_S; \Theta) + \gamma_2 \mathcal{L}_{\text{align}}(\mathcal{G}_S, \mathcal{G}_T; \Theta), \qquad (12)$$

where $\mathcal{L}_{\text{align}}$ is the domain alignment regularization, γ_2 functions as a weighting factor. In this paper, we follow the recent work [3] which utilizes the Maximum Mean Discrepancy (MMD) to align the source and target domains.

Table 1. Statistics of datasets, # means 'number of', 'Attr.' refers to attributes.

Datasets	Graph	#Node	#Edge	#Attr.	#Label
ArnetMiner	ACMv9(A)	9,360	15,556	6,775	5
	Citationv1(C)	8,935	15,098		
	DBLPv7(D)	5,484	8,117		
Airport	EUROPE(E)	399	11,990	241	4
	USA(U)	1,190	27,198		
Twitch	Germany(DE)	9,498	153,138	3,170	2
	England(EN)	7,126	35,324		

5   Experiments

This section briefly introduces the evaluation datasets and experimental setting, followed by a presentation of experimental results of our method. Subsequently, supporting experiments, such as analysis and ablation study, are conducted.

5.1   Experimental Setup

Datasets. This paper uses the following three datasets that are widely used for UGDA. **ArnetMiner** [27] is a middle-scale dataset, which includes papers from different sources and time periods of 5 categories shared by three domains: ACMv9(A), Citationv1(C), and DSLR(D). Our method is evaluated by performing domain adaptation on all 6 tasks. **Airport** [19] is a small-scale dataset consisting of 4 node categories in total, where each node indicates an airport and each edge represents the routes between two airports. We evaluate our method on two graphs in this dataset: EUROPE(E) and USA(U). **Twitch** [20] is a social network dataset collected from different regions, where each node represents a user and the edges indicate friendships between users. We evaluate our method on the following two graphs: Germany(DE) and England(EN). The statistics of these datasets are presented in Table 1.

Implementation Details. In practice, we adopt the same experimental settings as in previous work [3,11], with slight difference. We design the feature encoder and classifier, respectively, of 128 (except 64 for Twitch) and C units, in which C differs from one dataset to another. Υ is set to 20. The number of topology and semantic neighbors $|\mathcal{N}_+(v_t)| = 5$, where $k_{sem} = 1$. β in Eq. (10) is initialized at 0.3 starting from the middle stage of training, with the remaining periods set to 0. α and τ are searched within the sets $\{0.5, 1.0\}$ and $\{0.25, 0.5, 1.0\}$, respectively. γ_2 in Eq. (12) is set to 10. We set the message propagation layers $k \in \{1, 10\}$ in the target graph branch while $k = 0$ in the source graph branch. All experiments are implemented using PyTorch and run on a single NVIDIA RTX 3090 with 24GB. The whole network is trained by Adam with weight decay $\in \{1e-3, 5e-3\}$ and the learning rate is set to 0.01. Under random seed 200,

Table 2. Classification accuracy (%) on ArnetMiner dataset, the bold and the underline mean the best and the second-best result, respectively.

Methods	A → C		A → D		C → A		C → D		D → A		D → C		Avg.	
	Mi-F1	Ma-F1	Mi-F1	Ma-F1	Mi-F1	Ma-F1	Mi-F1	Ma-F1	Mi-F1	Ma-F1	Mi-F1	Ma-F1	Mi-F1	Ma-F1
UDAGCN [31]	72.15	60.33	66.95	64.83	66.80	67.22	71.77	69.46	58.16	55.89	73.28	61.12	68.19	63.14
SAGDA [18]	77.50	74.09	70.46	66.28	69.90	68.89	73.80	68.10	61.74	53.62	73.92	70.38	71.22	66.89
AdaGCN [4]	79.32	76.51	75.04	71.39	71.67	70.77	75.59	72.34	69.67	69.47	78.20	74.22	74.92	72.45
CWGCN [29]	80.21	78.34	74.11	71.84	71.68	71.80	76.40	73.76	68.35	68.39	76.82	73.73	74.60	72.98
ACDNE [21]	81.75	80.09	76.24	73.59	73.59	74.79	77.21	75.74	71.29	72.64	80.14	78.83	76.70	75.95
GRADE [30]	76.04	72.52	68.22	63.03	69.55	69.34	73.95	70.02	63.72	59.35	74.32	69.32	70.97	67.26
KBL [1]	77.66	75.24	69.60	65.80	70.59	69.87	74.48	70.95	63.23	57.51	74.93	70.28	71.75	68.28
ASN [36]	80.64	77.81	73.80	71.40	72.74	73.17	76.36	73.98	70.15	71.49	78.23	75.17	75.32	73.84
DMGNN [22]	81.58	80.08	76.81	74.76	72.70	73.82	76.57	74.08	70.50	71.44	80.26	78.16	76.40	75.39
GGDA [10]	81.90	80.40	77.20	74.90	**77.10**	76.60	77.40	75.90	**75.80**	**75.80**	81.50	80.30	78.48	77.32
StruRW [14]	77.35	72.07	69.10	62.51	67.81	59.77	73.81	66.89	63.27	53.82	72.41	62.94	70.63	63.00
PairAlign [15]	70.88	67.88	65.91	62.35	65.85	65.09	71.04	67.56	59.34	58.77	67.07	64.61	66.68	64.38
SpecReg [34]	80.55	78.83	75.93	73.98	72.04	73.15	75.74	73.64	71.01	72.34	79.04	77.78	75.72	74.95
A2GNN [11]	82.39	81.06	77.14	75.01	74.30	75.74	77.30	74.97	71.79	72.84	80.63	78.11	77.26	76.29
SEPA [12]	82.46	81.11	76.05	74.78	73.88	75.29	78.08	76.97	73.83	74.85	82.82	81.74	77.79	77.39
TDSS [3]	82.51	80.93	**78.14**	74.94	74.63	76.04	78.21	74.78	73.93	75.39	81.12	78.87	78.09	76.83
TASSC (*ours*)	**83.95**	**82.94**	77.91	**76.11**	75.41	**77.11**	**78.40**	**77.23**	74.16	75.68	**83.19**	**82.11**	**78.84**	**78.53**

we run the codes repeatedly for 5 rounds and report the average results using both Micro-F1 and Macro-F1 scores. Our code is available on https://github.com/YeewZ/TASSC.

Baseline Methods. To evaluate our method, we select 16 baseline methods divided into the following three groups. The first group includes 5 deep node embedding methods: ACDNE [21], UDAGCN [31], AdaGCN [4], SAGDA [18], and CWGCN [29]. The second group contains 5 methods using GNNs to aggregate topology and node attributes across source and target graphs to address distribution shifts: ASN [36], KBL [1], GRADE [30], DMGNN [22], and GGDA [10]. The third group includes 6 methods that leverage target information to enhance generalization: SpecReg [34], StruRW [14], PairAlign [15], A2GNN [11], SEPA [12], and TDSS [3].

5.2 Experimental Results

The node classification accuracies of TASSC and these comparison methods on the three benchmarks are presented from Table 2, 3 and Table 4. For the dataset ArnetMiner (Table 2), TASSC achieves competitive results. In all comparison tasks, TASSC obtains the best result on A → C, C → D, and D → C. Although GGDA performs best on C → A and D → A, its performance exhibits significant fluctuations on the others. Compared to other UGDA methods, our method achieves the best result in average accuracy and surpasses the second-best method GGDA by 0.36% in Micro-F1 and almost 1.21% in Macro-F1 on average. As shown in Table 3, TASSC further defeats other methods on Airport.

Table 3. Classification accuracy (%) on Airport dataset, the bold and the underline mean the best and the second-best result, respectively.

Methods	E → U		U → E		Avg.	
	Mi-F1	Ma-F1	Mi-F1	Ma-F1	Mi-F1	Ma-F1
CWGCN [29]	44.96	39.68	40.60	34.17	42.78	36.93
SAGDA [18]	36.30	28.18	37.09	36.10	36.70	32.14
ACDNE [21]	50.50	48.15	47.37	44.94	48.94	46.55
AdaGCN [4]	46.89	43.56	49.87	47.67	48.38	45.62
ASN [36]	46.64	43.29	42.11	38.31	44.38	40.80
KBL [1]	45.46	35.61	31.83	23.45	38.65	29.53
GRADE [30]	49.83	47.36	48.37	47.21	49.10	47.29
DGDA [2]	42.27	35.59	43.11	36.47	42.69	36.03
StruRW [14]	43.70	41.27	41.10	37.39	42.40	39.33
PairAlign [15]	39.08	36.55	38.60	35.31	38.84	35.93
A2GNN [11]	47.78	45.32	55.39	52.70	51.59	49.01
TDSS [3]	40.08	30.30	53.13	47.93	46.61	39.12
TASSC (*ours*)	**53.51**	**51.17**	**57.04**	**56.27**	**55.28**	**53.72**

Specially, our method reaches the best accuracy of 55.28% and 53.72% in Micro-F1 and Macro-F1 on average, and also obtains the best on both two tasks. Upon closer inspection of the results on Twitch (Table 4), TASSC demonstrates either the best or second-best performance. Specifically, our method achieves the highest performance on the EN → DE task and surpasses the KBL by 8.35% in the Macro-F1 score. Although KBL performs outstandingly on the DE → EN task in Twitch, it exhibits mediocre performance on the other tasks. In contrast, TASSC demonstrates the best or second-best performance among the three datasets.

5.3 Analysis

In this section, we further analyze TASSC from the following three aspects.

Feature Visualization. According to the 5-way node classification results for the A → C task, we provide the visualization of the node feature representations learned in the target domain by using t-SNE [17], comparing our method against three baselines. As shown in Fig. 4(d), TASSC effectively captures the intrinsic semantic structure of the target graph, yielding a well-clustered distribution. To quantitatively evaluate the clustering quality, we employ Normalized Mutual Information (NMI) [35], and our method achieves the highest score of 0.6249, indicating well-separated clusters and tighter intra-class groupings. In contrast, PairAlign, A2GNN, and TDSS exhibit more dispersion and overlap, with NMIs of 0.3588, 0.5880, and 0.5973, respectively, as shown in Fig. 4(a)–(c).

Parameters Sensitivity. In the objective of TASSC, two key parameters, α and β, are introduced, as defined in Eq. (10). Parameter α reflects the adjust-

Table 4. Classification accuracy (%) on Twitch dataset, the bold and the underline mean the best and the second-best result, respectively.

Methods	DE → EN		EN → DE		Avg.	
	Mi-F1	Ma-F1	Mi-F1	Ma-F1	Mi-F1	Ma-F1
ACDNE [21]	56.13	55.85	57.30	55.47	56.72	55.66
AdaGCN [4]	57.20	57.20	61.46	58.27	59.33	57.74
CWGCN [29]	57.03	55.00	62.16	55.73	59.60	55.37
UDAGCN [31]	58.32	52.81	62.68	54.04	60.50	53.43
ASN [36]	55.82	55.47	60.45	57.19	58.14	56.33
KBL [1]	**59.32**	**59.11**	<u>64.07</u>	53.90	**61.70**	56.51
GRADE [30]	58.03	57.37	58.71	56.23	58.37	56.80
DMGNN [22]	57.79	53.71	60.24	59.57	59.02	56.64
PairAlign [15]	56.33	55.77	58.28	55.16	57.31	55.47
A2GNN [11]	57.26	56.57	62.44	<u>60.32</u>	59.85	<u>58.45</u>
SEPA [12]	57.90	<u>57.44</u>	63.58	58.34	60.74	57.89
TDSS [3]	56.03	54.88	61.14	55.55	58.59	55.22
TASSC (*ours*)	<u>58.74</u>	57.08	**64.38**	**62.25**	<u>61.56</u>	**59.67**

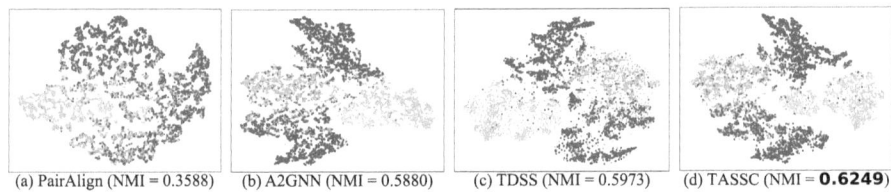

(a) PairAlign (NMI = 0.3588)   (b) A2GNN (NMI = 0.5880)   (c) TDSS (NMI = 0.5973)   (d) TASSC (NMI = **0.6249**)

Fig. 4. Visualization of the learned node embeddings for the A → C task on the ArnetMiner dataset across different models.

ment from the contrastive learning based on topology and semantic neighbors. Parameter β regulates the strength of the target semantic regularization. To evaluate their sensitivity, we carry out 60 experiments on the A → C task in the ArnetMiner dataset, varying α within $[0.1, 1.0]$ and β within $[0.05, 0.5]$. As illustrated in Fig. 5, the high-accuracy region (marked in blue) is not isolated, indicating that TASSC is not overly sensitive to specific choices of α and β.

Qualitative Study. When selecting semantic neighbors, we fix $k_{\text{sem}} = 1$ without further adjustment. In this analysis, due to space limitations, we design two sets of experiments, one for A, D → C and another for the symmetric A → D and D → A task, to examine the impact of the number of selected semantic neighbors, as illustrated in Fig. 6(a) and Fig. 6(b). We vary k_{sem} within set $\{0, 1, 2, 3, 4, 5\}$. By analyzing Fig. 6, we conclude that incorporating a moderate number of semantic neighbors effectively enhances the model's generalization

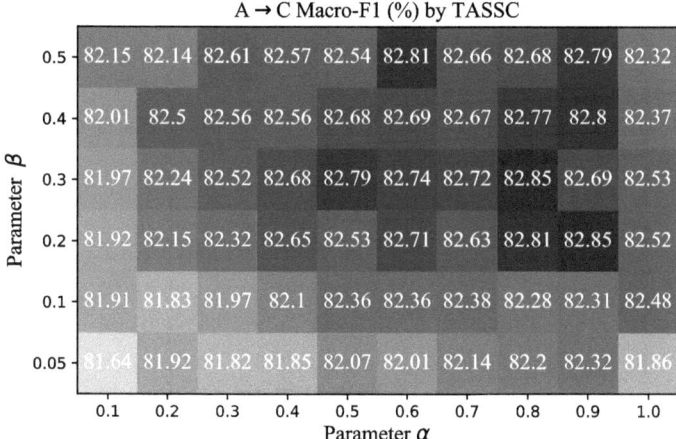

Fig. 5. The influence of parameters α and β on A $\rightarrow$ C task.

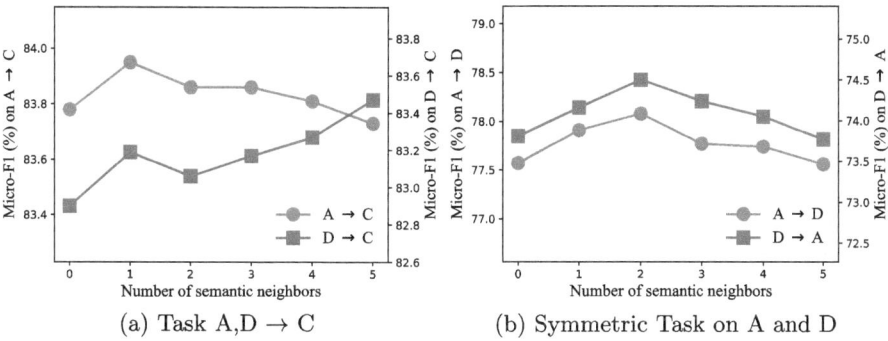

(a) Task A,D $\rightarrow$ C   (b) Symmetric Task on A and D

Fig. 6. Micro-f1 performances (%) across different transfer tasks with varying numbers of semantic neighbors.

ability in optimizing structure-semantic consistency, while excessive additions hinder it.

5.4   Ablation Study

We design an ablation experiment to isolate the effectiveness of key components in TASSC. Specifically, we decouple the combination in Eq. (3) to shield the influence of both topological and semantic neighbors. Correspondingly, we reconstruct the regularization in Eq. (10) as $\mathcal{L}_{\text{tassc}}^{\text{no-sem}}$ and $\mathcal{L}_{\text{tassc}}^{\text{no-topo}}$, respectively. $\mathcal{L}_{\text{tassc}}^{\text{no-sem}}$ indicates that the positive samples constructed for v_t only utilize the target's local neighbors $\mathcal{N}_{\text{topo}}(v_t)$, excluding semantic neighbors. In contrast, $\mathcal{L}_{\text{tassc}}^{\text{no-topo}}$ is constructed by using semantic neighbors while excluding the topological neighbors. Here we use the classification loss $\mathcal{L}_{\text{cls}}$ and domain alignment loss $\mathcal{L}_{\text{align}}$ to regulate the training of TASSC and take it as the baseline. Then we use $\mathcal{L}_{\text{tassc}}^{\text{no}-\text{sem}}$, $\mathcal{L}_{\text{tassc}}^{\text{no}-\text{topo}}$ and $\mathcal{L}_{\text{tassc}}$ to form three variation methods.

Table 5. Ablation results (Avg. %) of TASSC on the three datasets. the bold means the best result and ✓marks the available regularization term.

$\mathcal{L}_{\text{cls}} + \mathcal{L}_{\text{align}}$	$\mathcal{L}_{\text{tassc}}^{\text{no}-\text{sem}}$	$\mathcal{L}_{\text{tassc}}^{\text{no}-\text{topo}}$	$\mathcal{L}_{\text{tassc}}$	ArnetMiner		Airport		Twitch	
				Mi-F1	Ma-F1	Mi-F1	Ma-F1	Mi-F1	Ma-F1
✓				77.47	76.30	50.90	49.16	60.95	57.09
✓	✓			78.54	78.18	53.65	51.97	61.15	58.80
✓		✓		78.22	77.84	53.79	51.58	60.90	58.68
✓			✓	**78.84**	**78.53**	**55.28**	**53.72**	**61.56**	**59.67**

As shown in Table 5, we observe that the variant methods incorporating target topology preservation or semantic constraint outperform the baseline. Furthermore, enforcing both target structure and semantic consistency, represented by $\mathcal{L}_{\text{tassc}}$, significantly improves performance. This phenomenon indicates that the designed losses have a positive impact on the final results.

6   Conclusion

In this paper, we investigate the problem of UGDA by addressing the limitations of existing methods in exploiting the intrinsic interplay between structural proximity and semantic similarity within the target graph. To this end, we propose TASSC, a novel method that enforces consistency learning between structure and semantics in the feature space for enhancing domain generalization. Specifically, TASSC integrates topological and semantic neighborhood information to improve representation alignment and incorporate two self-supervised regularizations to enforce both global and local consistency. Furthermore, we introduce a scale-aware adaptive module that dynamically adjusts knowledge transfer based on domain scale discrepancies, enhancing target node representations for more effective consistency learning. Extensive experiments on three widely used datasets validate the effectiveness of TASSC, demonstrating significant performance compared to state-of-the-art baselines.

References

1. Bi, W., Cheng, X., Xu, B., Sun, X., Xu, L., Shen, H.: Bridged-GNN: knowledge bridge learning for effective knowledge transfer. In: Proceedings of the 32nd ACM International Conference on Information and Knowledge Management, pp. 99–109 (2023)
2. Cai, R., Wu, F., Li, Z., Wei, P., Yi, L., Zhang, K.: Graph domain adaptation: a generative view. ACM Trans. Knowl. Discov. Data **18**(3), 1–24 (2024)

3. Chen, W., et al.: Smoothness really matters: a simple yet effective approach for unsupervised graph domain adaptation. arXiv preprint arXiv:2412.11654 (2024)
4. Dai, Q., Wu, X.M., Xiao, J., Shen, X., Wang, D.: Graph transfer learning via adversarial domain adaptation with graph convolution. IEEE Trans. Knowl. Data Eng. **35**(5), 4908–4922 (2022)
5. Dantas, C.F., Gaetano, R., Ienco, D.: Semi-supervised heterogeneous domain adaptation via disentanglement and pseudo-labelling. In: Joint European Conference on Machine Learning and Knowledge Discovery in Databases, pp. 440–456. Springer, Cham (2024)
6. Englert, B.B., Piva, F.J., Kerssies, T., De Geus, D., Dubbelman, G.: Exploring the benefits of vision foundation models for unsupervised domain adaptation. In: Proceedings of the IEEE/CVF Conference on Computer Vision and Pattern Recognition, pp. 1172–1180 (2024)
7. Gong, C., Li, X., Yu, J., Cheng, Y., Tan, J., Yu, C.: Self-pro: a self-prompt and tuning framework for graph neural networks. In: Joint European Conference on Machine Learning and Knowledge Discovery in Databases, pp. 197–215. Springer, Cham (2024)
8. Hamilton, W., Ying, Z., Leskovec, J.: Inductive representation learning on large graphs. In: Advances in Neural Information Processing Systems, vol. 30 (2017)
9. Krause, A., Perona, P., Gomes, R.: Discriminative clustering by regularized information maximization. In: Advances in Neural Information Processing Systems, vol. 23 (2010)
10. Lei, P.I., Chen, X., Sheng, Y., Liu, Y., Guo, J., Gong, Z.: Gradual domain adaptation for graph learning. arXiv preprint arXiv:2501.17443 (2025)
11. Liu, M., et al.: Rethinking propagation for unsupervised graph domain adaptation. In: Proceedings of the AAAI Conference on Artificial Intelligence, vol. 38, pp. 13963–13971 (2024)
12. Liu, M., et al.: Structure enhanced prototypical alignment for unsupervised cross-domain node classification. Neural Netw. **177**, 106396 (2024)
13. Liu, M., Zhang, Z., Tang, J., Bu, J., He, B., Zhou, S.: Revisiting, benchmarking and understanding unsupervised graph domain adaptation. In: Advances in Neural Information Processing Systems, vol. 37, pp. 89408–89436 (2025)
14. Liu, S., et al.: Structural re-weighting improves graph domain adaptation. In: International Conference on Machine Learning, pp. 21778–21793. PMLR (2023)
15. Liu, S., Zou, D., Zhao, H., Li, P.: Pairwise alignment improves graph domain adaptation. In: Proceedings of the 41st International Conference on Machine Learning, pp. 32552–32575 (2024)
16. Longa, A., et al.: Explaining the explainers in graph neural networks: a comparative study. ACM Comput. Surv. **57**(5), 1–37 (2025)
17. Van der Maaten, L., Hinton, G.: Visualizing data using t-SNE. J. Mach. Learn. Res. **9**(11) (2008)
18. Pang, J., Wang, Z., Tang, J., Xiao, M., Yin, N.: SA-GDA: spectral augmentation for graph domain adaptation. In: Proceedings of the 31st ACM International Conference on Multimedia, pp. 309–318 (2023)
19. Ribeiro, L.F., Saverese, P.H., Figueiredo, D.R.: struc2vec: learning node representations from structural identity. In: Proceedings of the 23rd ACM SIGKDD International Conference on Knowledge Discovery and Data Mining, pp. 385–394 (2017)
20. Rozemberczki, B., Allen, C., Sarkar, R.: Multi-scale attributed node embedding. J. Complex Netw. **9**(2), cnab014 (2021)

21. Shen, X., Dai, Q., Chung, F., Lu, W., Choi, K.S.: Adversarial deep network embedding for cross-network node classification. In: Proceedings of the AAAI Conference on Artificial Intelligence, vol. 34, pp. 2991–2999 (2020)
22. Shen, X., Pan, S., Choi, K.S., Zhou, X.: Domain-adaptive message passing graph neural network. Neural Netw. **164**, 439–454 (2023)
23. Shi, B., Wang, Y., Guo, F., Xu, B., Shen, H., Cheng, X.: Graph domain adaptation: challenges, progress and prospects. arXiv preprint arXiv:2402.00904 (2024)
24. Shui, C., Li, X., Qi, J., Jiang, G., Yu, Y.: Hierarchical graph contrastive learning for review-enhanced recommendation. In: Joint European Conference on Machine Learning and Knowledge Discovery in Databases, pp. 423–440. Springer, Cham (2024)
25. Stubbemann, M., Stumme, G.: The mont blanc of twitter: identifying hierarchies of outstanding peaks in social networks. In: Joint European Conference on Machine Learning and Knowledge Discovery in Databases, pp. 177–192. Springer, Cham (2023)
26. Tang, J., Qu, M., Wang, M., Zhang, M., Yan, J., Mei, Q.: Line: large-scale information network embedding. In: Proceedings of the 24th International Conference on World Wide Web, pp. 1067–1077 (2015)
27. Tang, J., Zhang, J., Yao, L., Li, J., Zhang, L., Su, Z.: Arnetminer: extraction and mining of academic social networks. In: Proceedings of the 14th ACM SIGKDD International Conference on Knowledge Discovery and Data Mining, pp. 990–998 (2008)
28. Wang, H., Liu, G., Hu, P.: TDAN: transferable domain adversarial network for link prediction in heterogeneous social networks. ACM Trans. Knowl. Discov. Data **18**(1), 1–22 (2023)
29. Wang, W., Zhang, G., Han, H., Zhang, C.: Correntropy-induced Wasserstein GCN: learning graph embedding via domain adaptation. IEEE Trans. Image Process. **32**, 3980–3993 (2023)
30. Wu, J., He, J., Ainsworth, E.: Non-IID transfer learning on graphs. In: Proceedings of the AAAI Conference on Artificial Intelligence, vol. 37, pp. 10342–10350 (2023)
31. Wu, M., Pan, S., Zhou, C., Chang, X., Zhu, X.: Unsupervised domain adaptive graph convolutional networks. In: Proceedings of the Web Conference 2020, pp. 1457–1467 (2020)
32. Xiao, T., Zhu, H., Chen, Z., Wang, S.: Simple and asymmetric graph contrastive learning without augmentations. In: Advances in Neural Information Processing Systems, vol. 36, pp. 16129–16152 (2023)
33. Yin, N., et al.: Coco: a coupled contrastive framework for unsupervised domain adaptive graph classification. In: International Conference on Machine Learning, pp. 40040–40053. PMLR (2023)
34. You, Y., Chen, T., Wang, Z., Shen, Y.: Graph domain adaptation via theory-grounded spectral regularization. In: The Eleventh International Conference on Learning Representations (2023)
35. Zhang, P.: Evaluating accuracy of community detection using the relative normalized mutual information. J. Stat. Mech: Theory Exp. **2015**(11), P11006 (2015)
36. Zhang, X., Du, Y., Xie, R., Wang, C.: Adversarial separation network for cross-network node classification. In: Proceedings of the 30th ACM International Conference on Information & Knowledge Management, pp. 2618–2626 (2021)
37. Zhong, Z., Mottin, D.: Efficiently predicting mutational effect on homologous proteins by evolution encoding. In: Joint European Conference on Machine Learning and Knowledge Discovery in Databases, pp. 399–415. Springer, Cham (2024)

Agriculture, Food and Earth Sciences

Forecasting Irregularly Sampled Time Series with Transformer Encoders

Riccardo Benassi[✉], Francesco Del Buono, Giacomo Guiduzzi,
and Francesco Guerra

Università di Modena e Reggio Emilia, Modena, Italy
{riccardo.benassi,francesco.delbuono,giacomo.guiduzzi,
francesco.guerra}@unimore.it

Abstract. Time series forecasting is a fundamental task in various domains, including environmental monitoring, finance, and healthcare. State-of-the-art forecasting models typically assume that time series are uniformly sampled. However, in real-world scenarios, data is often collected at irregular intervals and with missing values, due to sensor failures or network issues. This makes traditional forecasting approaches unsuitable. In this paper, we introduce ISTF (Irregular Sequence Transformer Forecasting), a novel transformer-based architecture designed for forecasting irregularly sampled multivariate time series (MTS). ISTF leverages exogenous variables as contextual information to enhance the prediction of a single target variable. The architecture first regularizes the MTS on a fixed temporal scale, keeping track of missing values. Then, a dedicated embedding strategy, based on a local and global attention mechanism, aims at capturing dependencies between timestamps, sources and missing values. We evaluate ISTF on two real-world datasets, French-Piezo and USHCN. The experimental results demonstrate that ISTF outperforms competing approaches in forecasting accuracy while remaining computationally efficient.

1 Introduction

A wide range of real-world phenomena across various domains, such as environmental monitoring, finance, and healthcare, can be naturally represented as time series. Advances in sensor technology, big data collection, data cleaning, and the Internet of Things have made it increasingly accessible for practitioners to acquire and manage such data. In particular, multivariate time series (MTS) are commonly used to consolidate temporal data from multiple sources, capturing different aspects of the same phenomenon (e.g., measurements from diverse sensors or the inclusion of exogenous variables).

The availability of many reliable datasets describing such real-world scenarios has also been the driver of technological innovations in the field of time-series analytics. Many approaches have been proposed as recently published surveys demonstrate [9,18]. In particular, forecasting has been the recent focus of many innovations (e.g., see [7,9,15]) thanks to the application of the results achieved

B. Pfahringer et al. (Eds.): ECML PKDD 2025, LNAI 16020, pp. 201–217, 2026.
https://doi.org/10.1007/978-3-662-72243-5_12

in the field of Machine Learning and Deep Learning. The resulting state-of-the-art approaches can accurately describe temporal information and incorporate exogenous data to improve the forecast. However, they generally share the same requirement: time series should represent their observations with regular and uniform timestamps. Most of the approaches therefore assume that the data is collected on uniform intervals and that all the time series describing the phenomenon have the same pace. This can definitely be considered as an unrealistic condition in real-world scenarios, where sensors collect data with different intervals, paces and values may be missing in some timestamps due to failures of the network or the devices.

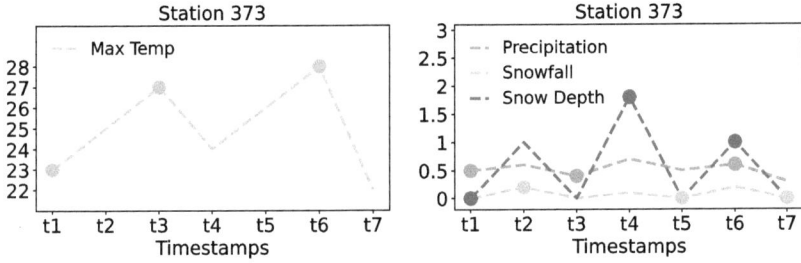

(a) Max temperature at Station 373.   (b) Exogeneous data at Station 373.

Fig. 1. Motivating scenario: time series generated by sensors at Station 373. Notice how stations collect data at a different frequency and at different timestamps.

Motivating Scenario. Let us suppose that we need to forecast the maximum temperature recorded at monitoring station 373. The station has sensors that record both the time series of the maximum temperature (Fig. 1a) and other exogenous data (Fig. 1b). The goal is to forecast the maximum temperature of the next timestamps. We observe that the stations collect data with different frequencies and in different intervals, making it impossible to directly apply traditional forecasting techniques to this scenario.

Forecasting techniques for irregular time series broadly fall into two categories. The first relies on data imputation during preprocessing, to regularize the series before applying standard models. The second includes models natively designed for irregular data, which recognize irregularities and missing values and treat them as additional information [2,5,12,17].

In this paper, we propose ISTF (Irregular Sequence Transformer Forecasting), an innovative architecture for the forecasting of irregularly sampled MTS that relies on contextual knowledge, provided by (1) other time stamps in the MTS; and (2) exogenous data sources. The architecture, described in Sect. 3, is built upon four main components: the Input Generator, responsible for extracting the relevant time series from the dataset; the Embedder and the Encoder, which generate embeddings for both the target and exogenous series; and the Forecaster, which produces the final predictions.

The approach has been experimentally evaluated against the real scenarios offered by the FrenchPiezo and USHCN datasets, regarding the water piezometric levels in France and climate data in the USA respectively. The results demonstrate that ISTF outperforms competing approaches in effectiveness while remaining computationally feasible. In particular, training time is higher than the baselines, reaching up to an order of magnitude more, but remains manageable, with a maximum of six hours in the slowest configuration. Serving time, however, is in line with the baselines. The main contributions of the approach are: 1) the design of a transformer-based encoder architecture for forecasting that can manage forms of contributions in the prediction from exogeneity neighboring; 2) the experimentation of an technique that masks irregularly sampled MTS; 3) a deep experimentation on two large datasets. The code of ISTF and the experiments presented in the paper are available in the project GitHub[1].

2   Background

2.1   Related Work

Forecasting in time series is a long-standing research problem [6]. Traditional approaches are based on probability and statistics. More recently, approaches based on machine learning and deep learning have demonstrated to achieve great accuracy levels [9]. In particular, several works have successfully applied and extended transformers-based architecture to deal with time series analytic. [18] reviews the proposed variants of transformers for modeling time series data. The main modifications include enhancement in the positional encoding, in the attention module and in the architecture.

The majority of existing forecasting techniques cannot deal with irregular time series. Typically, data preprocessing is required before of their application [9]. The field of irregular time series forecasting has experienced significant advancements in recent years, with researchers exploring a variety of methodologies to handle missing values and irregular sampling intervals.

Usually, missing values in time series are addressed through heuristic or unsupervised imputation methods. Common practices [16] include omitting missing data, smoothing, interpolation, and spline methods. However, these techniques often fail to capture variable correlations and complex patterns, leading to suboptimal performance, especially in cases with high rates of missing data [4].

A paradigm shift occurred with [8], where absence is treated as a feature rather than an artifact to be corrected. The paper demonstrates that this kind of strategy significantly enhances predictive performance, particularly in classifying diagnoses with clinical time series data. Several approaches proposing a similar idea have been proposed. Among them, we selected GRU-D [2], mTAN [14], InterpNet [13], and PrimeNet [3] as representative approaches to be used as baselines in the evaluation of our proposal. GRU-D is a deep learning approach that effectively utilizes missing patterns in time series data. By incorporating

---

[1] https://github.com/softlab-unimore/ISTF.

masking and time intervals into a Gated Recurrent Unit (GRU) framework, GRU-D is able to capture long-term temporal dependencies and utilize informative absence patterns for improving prediction accuracy. ISTF relies on masking and positional encoding to deal with irregularity, too. The main difference is the model architecture, a variant of a transformer-based model for ISTF. mTAN is based on a transformer architecture [14]. The key innovation here is using time embedding as both queries and keys in the attention mechanism, allowing the model to attend to observations at different time points. ISTF differs from mTAN at the architecture level. They are both based on a transformer, but ISTF relies on three modules to manage the contribution of exogenous data.

Other interesting DL-based approaches are InterpNet [13] and PrimeNet [3]. InterpNet is a deep learning architecture that combines a semi-parametric interpolation network with a prediction network, allowing information sharing across multiple dimensions during the interpolation stage. PrimeNet is a self-supervised learning framework that utilizes time-sensitive contrastive learning and data reconstruction task.

In summary, irregular time series forecasting has evolved from simple imputation methods to sophisticated deep learning models that effectively leverage the information in absence patterns and irregular sampling intervals.

2.2 Problem Definition

Let us start from the formalization in [17], where $\mathcal{D} = \{m_1, m_2, \ldots, m_N\}$ is a dataset of N MTS. Each MTS is defined as a sequence of observations collected over time, called features or variables, in the form of irregularly sampled univariate time series $\mathbf{m_i} = \{m_{i,1}, m_{i,2}, \ldots, m_{i,F_i}\}$, with F_i the dimension of the MTS m_i. We denote with N_{ij} as the number of data of the j-th univariate time series of m_i. The univariate time series can be represented as $m_{i,j} = [(t_{i,j,1}, x_{i,j,1}), (t_{i,j,2}, x_{i,j,2}), \ldots, (t_{i,j,N_{i,j}}, x_{i,j,N_{i,j}})]$, where $x_{i,j,k}$ is the value observed at time step k (i.e., at time $t_{i,j,k}$) of the j-th univariate time series of m_i. Since we are dealing with irregularly sampled MTS, different univariate time series may include a different number of observations collected in different times. This means that $N_{i,j} \neq N_{i,z}$ for $j \neq z$ and $t_{i,j,a} \neq t_{i,z,a} \, \forall a, j \neq z$. We define as the **target series** the time series $m_{i,j}$, which represents the variable the user aims to forecast.

Finding Exogenous time series. We assume the existence of a function $findEx$ for the target series $m_{i,j}$ that selects from the MTS in the dataset $\mathcal{D}$ the exogeneous time series $E = \{e_1, \ldots, e_e\}$, where each e_k is a univariate time series:

$$E = findEx(m_{i,j}, \mathcal{D})$$

Forecasting. ISTF predicts the values of a given time series at time step $t + n$ using its past data and the exogenous time series.

$$\hat{y}_{t+n} = f(m_{i,j,1}, m_{i,j,2}, \ldots, m_{i,j,t}, e_{1,1}, \ldots, e_{1,t'}, e_{e,1}, \ldots, e_{e,t'}) \tag{1}$$

where the $m_{i,j,t}$, and $e_{u,t'}$ points are the historical data points for the target and the exogeneous series. We recall that time step t corresponds to the actual timestamp $t_{i,j,t}$ of the univariate time series $m_{i,j}$. Since the timestamps of the series can correspond to different steps, we denote by t' all time steps associated with timestamps preceding t in the target series. To simplify the notation, we assume that all MTS have the same number of features ($F_i = F, \forall i$), and that the time steps are "normalized" for the MTS in the collection $\mathcal{D}$. This means that, the features of a MTS can assume the null value for the time steps that correspond to timestamps which are not sampled in the non-normalized series. Given a MTS m_i, we indicate with $M_i(t)$ the sequences of values for all the features composing m_i for the time steps $1, 2, \ldots, t$. The same notation is applied to exogenous ($E(t)$) series. With this simplification, Eq. 1 can be reformulated in:

$$\hat{y}_{t+n} = f(m_{i,j}(t), e_1(t), \ldots, e_e(t))$$

2.3 Overview

The architecture of ISTF is designed around two key considerations: (1) real-world time series data is often irregular, with missing values and various sampling rates; and (2) real-world phenomena are typically described by multiple interdependent variables, such as temperature, humidity, and precipitation. As highlighted in Fig. 2, ISTF expects two inputs: the target time series, which represents the phenomenon under investigation and whose future values need to be predicted, and a set of MTS exogenous series, which provide contextual environmental data.

The role of the *Embedder* component is to construct vector representations of the input time series. These embeddings provide a uniform representation of each timestamp of each variable as a fixed-size array, combining its value with information about its position in the series and its sampling date. ISTF implementation of the ISTF *Encoder* component enriches the representation provided by the embedder by incorporating knowledge of the interdependencies between the input time series. The ISTF *Encoder* extends the transformer encoder architecture with a local and global attention mechanism. In particular, local attention is the self-attention applied to each series separately, whereas global attention considers all points across all series. This way, the forecasting model (ISTF relies on a GRU model followed by a linear layer) can capture both series-specific patterns and inter-series relationships, which are crucial for accurate forecasting.

3   The ISTF Model

ISTF is conceived as a transformer model based architecture composed of 4 main components as represented in Fig. 2: the Input Generator (in Sect. 3.1), the Embedder (in Sect. 3.2), the Encoder (in Sect. 3.3) and the Forecaster (in Sect. 3.4).

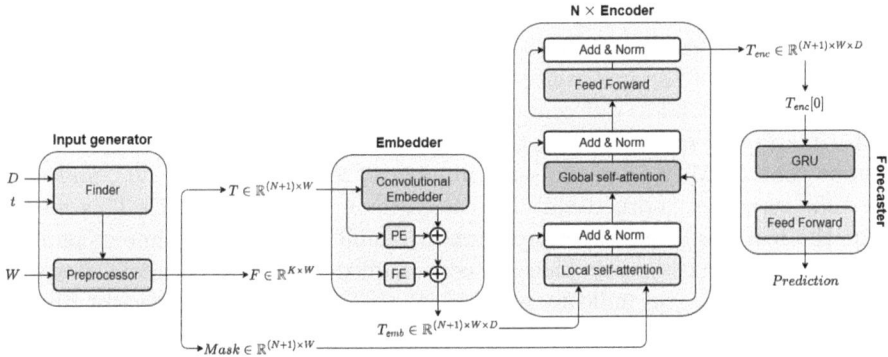

Fig. 2. ISTF Architecture

3.1 The Input Generator

The goal of the Input Generator component is to construct the input elements for ISTF from a target univariate time series and a multivariate dataset. The component consists of two modules: Finder implements the function $findEx$, which returns the n univariate time series in $\mathcal{D}$ that influence the forecasting of the target series t. Providing an implementation for $findEx$ is beyond the scope of this paper. A straightforward implementation is to select as exogenous series all signals in the MTS except for the target series. Moreover, domain knowledge can be used to identify which of these signals are actually relevant for the problem at hand. The preprocessor handles the irregular sampling of both the target and exogenous time series of interest. In particular, it addresses irregularities by aligning all series to the timestamps of the series with the highest granularity. One possible strategy to impute the missing values, which arise when aligning coarser time series to the finest resolution, is to use the last observed value prior to the missing timestamp. However, the approach is agnostic to the specific imputation method adopted. The component keeps track of the steps containing imputed values through a dedicated $Mask$ matrix and also maps the temporal features used by the original selected series into the ones with the highest granularity through the F matrix.

Finally, the *Input Generator* component computes three output matrices, considering the time window of interest W specified by the user. In particular:

- $T \in \mathbb{R}^{(N+1) \times W}$ represents the values of the target series (indexed by $T[0]$) and the exogenous series (indexed by $T[1:N]$) within the given time window.
- $F \in \mathbb{R}^{K \times W}$ contains the K temporal features extracted from the original $N+1$ univariate series.
- Mask $\in \mathbb{R}^{(N+1) \times W}$ is a boolean matrix indicating the imputed values (set to 1) during the "regularization" process of the series.

3.2 The Embedder

The goal of the ISTF Embedder is to standardize the heterogeneity of irregularly sampled input time series by generating a uniform embedding for each of them $t_{emb} \in T_{emb}$, with $T_{emb} \in \mathbb{R}^{(N+1) \times W \times D}$, where, according to the previous formalization, $N + 1$ is the set of time series, W is the time window, and D is the dimension of the embedding, hyper-parameter of the approach.

The ISTF Embedder performs two main operations. Firstly, a Convolutional Neural Network (CNN) is applied to each series $i \in I$ to create an embedding vector $i_{emb} \in \mathbb{R}^{w \times d}$. Then, two kinds of positional encodings are added to the embeddings. The first, $PE(\mathcal{P})$, with $\mathcal{P}$ the relative position associated to the time steps of i, is the positional encodings usually adopted in Transformer-based approaches. It assumes the form of Eq. 2:

$$PE_{(pos, 2i)} = \sin\left(\frac{pos}{10000^{2i/D}}\right), \quad PE_{(pos, 2i+1)} = \cos\left(\frac{pos}{10000^{2i/D}}\right), \quad (2)$$

where pos is the relative position in the time series and D the dimension of the embedding. The second positional encoding is the variation introduced in [18,19,21] to incorporate the timestamp features (such as day, month, week, year, etc.), thus acknowledging the sequential and possible cyclical nature of the series. We call this $PE(\mathcal{F})$, where $\mathcal{F}$ represents the timestamps (day, week, year,...) associated to the time steps of i through the matrix F.

The final results is the multi-faceted embedding $T_{emb} \in \mathbb{R}^{(N+1) \times W \times D}$ that encapsulates both the values of the time series and the temporal dynamics dictated by irregular sampling and missing values.

3.3 The Encoder

As in [5], the ISTF Encoder extends a vanilla transformer encoder with local attention, which captures intra-series relationships, and global attention, which models dependencies between target and exogenous series. The encoder is composed of a stack of identical layers, of which we describe a single one.

Local Attention. The intra-temporal dynamics of time series data are often complex, requiring advanced models to effectively capture the underlying patterns. The local attention mechanism is designed to learn these dynamics by generating embeddings for each time series independently, focusing exclusively on non-null values. This is achieved through the Mask matrix, which identifies missing values in the series, ensuring they are skipped during the self-attention computation. Lines 1–4 in Algorithm 1 describe the behavior of the local attention module, which applies a multi-head attention layer to the embeddings of each time series, properly masked.

Global Attention. ISTF computes new embeddings that represent interrelations between the series, starting from the embeddings generated by the Local Attention component. Lines 5–9 in Algorithm 1 describe the procedure. First, the mask and the embeddings are reshaped to represent a bidimensional

Algorithm 1. The Encoder

Input: $T_{emb} \in \mathbb{R}^{(N+1) \times W \times D}$
Output: $T_{enc} \in \mathbb{R}^{(N+1) \times W \times D}$
    // Local attention
1: **for** $i \in [0, ..., n]$ **do**
2:    $I[i, :] = \text{MultiHeadAttention}(Q = T_{emb}[i], K = T_{emb}[i], V = T_{emb}[i], \text{Mask} = Mask[i])$
3: **end for**
4: $T_{local} = \text{norm}(T_{local} + T_{emb})$
    // Global attention
5: $Mask\_global = \text{reshape}(Mask, (N+1, W) \rightarrow (N+1 \times W))$
6: $T_{local} = \text{reshape}(T_{local}, (N+1, W, D) \rightarrow (N+1 \times W, D))$
7: $T_{local} = \text{MultiHeadAttention}(Q = T_{local}, K = T_{local}, V = T_{local}, \text{mask} = Mask\_global)$
8: $T_{global} = \text{norm}(T_{global} + T_{local})$
9: $T_{global} = \text{reshape}(T_{global}, (V \times W, D) \rightarrow (V, W, D))$
    // Feedforward
10: **for** $i \in [0, ..., n]$ **do**
11:    $T_{enc}[i, :] = \text{FF}(T_{global}[i])$
12: **end for**
13: $T_{enc} = \text{norm}(T_{enc} + T_{global})$

matrix, with time steps for each series in the rows and the embeddings in the columns. Then, a Multi-Head Attention layer is applied to this data structure to generate the global attention embeddings.

Finally, the output embedding is obtained by applying a Feed-Forward layer to each embedding generated by the global attention module (lines 10–12), followed by a normalization layer that sums the global attention embeddings as residual components (line 13).

3.4 The Forecaster

The Encoder from the previous step generates an embedding for each timestamp of both the target series and the exogenous series, where each embedding has been related to the others. We preserve only the embeddings of the target series, which are then passed to a unidirectional GRU to obtain an aggregated representation of the embeddings:

$$f_E = GRU(T_{enc}[0, :]) \tag{3}$$

This is followed by a FeedForward Layer that computes the prediction

$$Prediction = FF(f_E) \tag{4}$$

4 Experimental Evaluation

The goal of the experimental evaluation is to answer the following research questions:

Table 1. Statistics about the Datasets used in the experiments.

Dataset	MTS	Points	Signals	Avg lenght	NaN percentage	Target NaN percentage
USHCN	1201	1744720	6	1453	3.97%	4.94%
FrenchPiezo	2664	6385608	4	2397	5.25%	12.1%

RQ1. **Effectiveness.** How accurate is ISTF architecture in making forecasts in scenarios with irregularly sampled time series data? (Sect. 4.2)

RQ2. **Ablation.** Are all components of ISTF architecture necessary, or can its complexity be reduced without sacrificing forecasting accuracy? (Sect. 4.3)

RQ3. **Robustness.** How sensitive is ISTF architecture to hyperparameter choices? (Sect. 4.4)

RQ4. **Efficiency.** How efficient is the ISTF architecture in terms of time performance? (Sect. 4.5)

4.1   Experimental Settings

Settings. The experiments have been performed on a Workstation with an NVIDIA L40S GPU with 48 GB of VRAM, 256 GB of RAM, and a dual AMD EPYC 9254 24-Core Processor. According to the literature in the field, the predictions are computed via single point regression [3]. Moreover, we used the hyperparameters defined for each baseline model as indicated in the original papers. For ISTF, we conducted experiments with the following configuration selected via a search on the validation set: a maximum of 100 training epochs combined with an early stopping patience of 20 epochs, a learning rate of $3 * 10^{-4}$, L2 regularization set to 10^{-2}, an embedding dimension of 32, 2 encoder layers and 4 attention heads. In all experiments, we employed the straightforward implementation of $FindEx$, which selects all signals in the MTS except for the target series as exogenous series. Each experiment was run three times with different random seeds, and the results were aggregated.

Datasets. We conducted experiments on two real MTS datasets, FrenchPiezo [10] and USHCN [11], which consist of irregularly sampled time series. Table 1 provides key statistics, including the number of MTS in each dataset, the total number of timestamps across all series, the number of signals in the MTS, the average series length, and the percentage of missing values in the dataset and in the target time series.

FrenchPiezo. is a multivariate time series dataset from mainland France that monitors groundwater levels, also known as piezometric levels. It comprises 1,026 multivariate time series, each consisting of three dimensions: piezometric level (p), precipitation (tp), and evapotranspiration (e). Each series is associated with a unique identifier (bss) corresponding to the piezometer that measures the piezometric level. The data, sampled daily from January 2015 to January 2021, span 2,221 days. The training period covers data from January 1, 2015, to January 1,

2020, and testing is conducted on data from January 1, 2020, to December 31, 2021. The objective is to forecast the piezometric levels.

The United States Historical Climatology Network (*USHCN*) dataset includes daily records from 1,218 weather stations across the US, capturing six variables: precipitation, snowfall, snow depth, minimum temperature, maximum temperature, and average temperature. Each time series (TS) features irregular time intervals ranging from one to seven days, with varying sampling rates among them. The specific goal is to accurately forecast the average temperature for New York in the following days. Utilizing the cleaning procedure described in [1], we selected a subset of 1,168 meteorological stations, focusing on data spanning four years (1990 - 1993). The training dataset encompasses the years 1990 to 1992, and testing is performed on the year 1993 [12].

Baselines. We selected four approaches for irregular time series forecasting. GRU-D [2] is the common reference baseline, one of the earliest deep-learning approaches that handles missing data patterns. We also compare against more recent approaches: InterpNet [13], mTAN [14], and PrimeNet [3], which have achieved the highest results with irregular time series. Moreover, we include DLinear [20] as a representative of traditional forecasting approaches, which has also shown strong performance in regular time series tasks.

4.2   Forecasting Accuracy

To evaluate the accuracy of ISTF, we performed multiple experiments using both the original datasets and modified versions where we artificially introduced missing values at rates of 20%, 50%, and 70% of the total data points. We then assessed its performance across different forecast horizons of 7, 30, and 60 days, using a fixed lookback window of 48 time steps. Figure 3 shows the results of the experiments: darker colors in the heatmap are associated to lower mean absolute error (MAE). Note that the Figure includes an experiment with 0% of missing value inserted. In this case the datasets still contain missing values as reported in Table 1. Table 2 reports the standard deviation only for the MAE due to space constraints, but similar trends are observed for the MSE.

Discussion. The analysis of the results highlights two main aspects: (1) ISTF typically exhibits a lower error than other approaches. Figure 3 shows that our approach is the most effective for the majority of the dataset configurations in terms of both MAE and MSE. ISTF also tends to show a lower standard deviation compared to the other methods. (2) The error typically increases as the percentage of missing values and the forecasting horizon grow. While this trend holds for all approaches, the increase is less marked for ISTF, in particular in the USHCN dataset. (3) The standard deviation of ISTF is generally lower than that of the baselines, as reported in Table 2.

Lesson learned. ISTF consistently outperforms other baselines across all experiments, demonstrating both superior forecasting accuracy and greater robustness to increasing missing values and longer forecasting horizons.

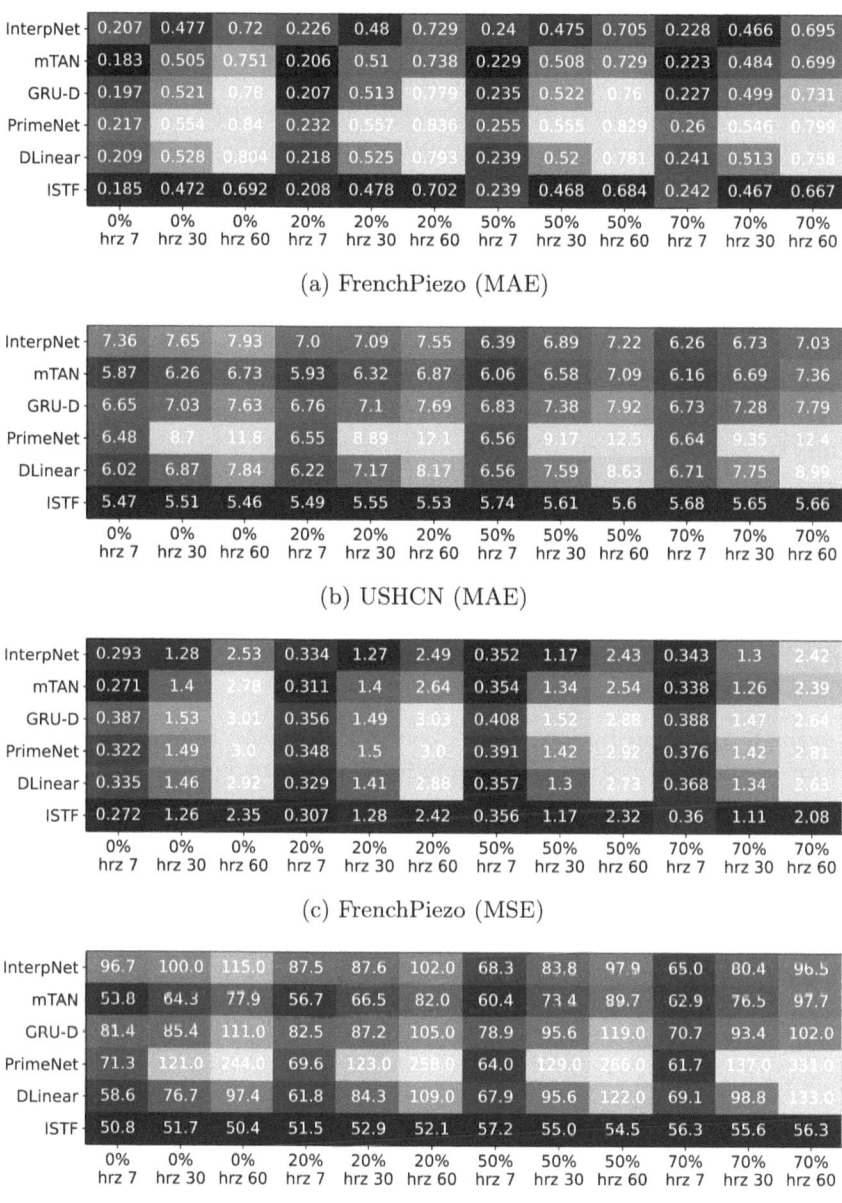

Fig. 3. Forecasting error measured using MAE and MSE. Darker colors in the heatmap indicate lower error. In the x-axis, the percentage represents the amount of inserted missing values and and *hrz* the forecast horizon.

Table 2. Standard deviation of MAE (similar for MSE).

	0% hrz 7	0% hrz 30	0% hrz 60	20% hrz 7	20% hrz 30	20% hrz 60	50% hrz 7	50% hrz 30	50% hrz 60	70% hrz 7	70% hrz 30	70% hrz 60
InterpNet	0.018	0.008	0.018	0.014	0.010	0.037	0.018	0.014	0.025	0.012	0.012	0.009
mTAN	0.006	0.010	0.005	0.018	0.010	0.019	0.014	0.033	0.035	0.006	0.013	0.014
GRU-D	0.012	0.020	0.024	0.005	0.010	0.015	0.004	0.007	0.022	0.004	0.007	0.016
PrimeNet	0.005	0.006	0.013	0.002	0.005	0.009	0.006	0.019	0.027	0.010	0.011	0.010
DLinear	0.006	0.007	0.011	0.003	0.007	0.006	0.007	0.013	0.021	0.002	0.010	0.008
ISTF	0.004	0.004	0.006	0.006	0.005	0.018	0.014	0.016	0.017	0.013	0.013	0.008

(a) FrenchPiezo (MAE)

	0% hrz 7	0% hrz 30	0% hrz 60	20% hrz 7	20% hrz 30	20% hrz 60	50% hrz 7	50% hrz 30	50% hrz 60	70% hrz 7	70% hrz 30	70% hrz 60
InterpNet	0.332	0.562	0.441	0.165	0.228	0.268	0.164	0.111	0.063	0.241	0.173	0.129
mTAN	0.330	0.386	0.430	0.166	0.181	0.272	0.068	0.118	0.041	0.236	0.216	0.115
GRU-D	0.368	0.415	0.487	0.210	0.242	0.321	0.031	0.126	0.085	0.206	0.170	0.095
PrimeNet	0.303	0.433	0.646	0.145	0.288	0.482	0.098	0.054	0.371	0.256	0.128	0.042
DLinear	0.293	0.346	0.437	0.137	0.221	0.285	0.093	0.029	0.040	0.259	0.204	0.104
ISTF	0.353	0.417	0.390	0.149	0.239	0.265	0.040	0.069	0.009	0.233	0.205	0.140

(b) USHCN (MAE)

4.3 Ablation Study

To evaluate the contribution of each component in the ISTF architecture, we performed an ablation study by systematically removing individual modules and analyzing their impact on forecasting accuracy. The complete model, without any modifications, serves as a baseline to assess the necessity of each component. The following ablation settings were considered:

1. **w/o Embedder**: The Embedder and positional encoder are removed, and the irregular time series are fed directly into the Encoder.
2. **w/o Local & Global Attention**: The attention mechanisms are replaced with a standard Transformer Encoder.
3. **w/o GRU**: The Encoder output is directly used for forecasting, bypassing the GRU component.

Figure 4 presents the MAE and MSE errors for both datasets, considering missing value rates of 0%, 20%, 50% and 70%, and future horizon of 30 days. Table 3 shows the percentage error increase due to ablations.

Discussion. The experimental results clearly indicate that the primary contributor to error reduction is the Embedder. In particular, its removal leads to a 16% increase in MAE, averaged across missing value configurations for the French-Piezo dataset (8% for USHCN), whereas the removal of other components results in a more modest error increase of 3% (7% for USHCN). Similar considerations hold when evaluating the error using MSE.

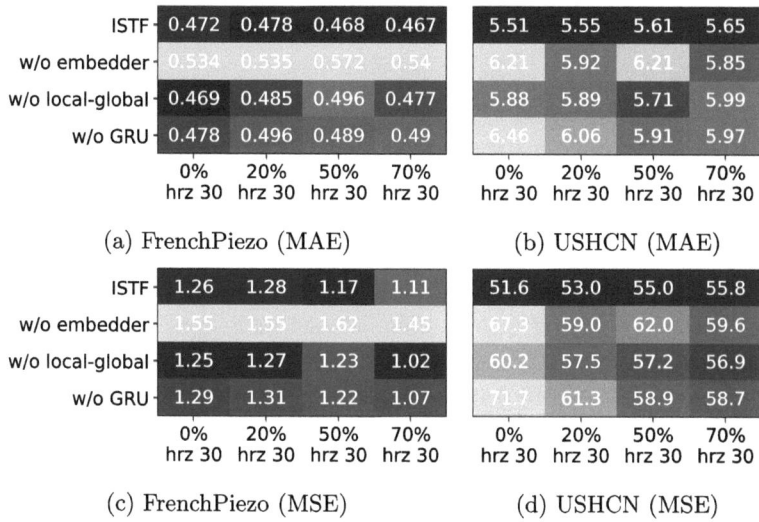

(a) FrenchPiezo (MAE)   (b) USHCN (MAE)

(c) FrenchPiezo (MSE)   (d) USHCN (MSE)

Fig. 4. Ablation study results. The rows represent the full model and its ablated versions; the columns correspond to different percentages of missing values for the FrenchPiezo and USHCN datasets. The cells report the error in terms of MAE and MSE.

Lesson learned. The results show that all components contribute to the model performance, but the Embedder is crucial for error reduction.

4.4   Robustness

To evaluate the sensitivity of ISTF to key hyperparameter changes and to identify the optimal configuration, we conducted four types of experiments on both the USHCN and FrenchPiezo datasets, as shown in Fig. 5. We experimented with a missing value percentage of 0%, 20%, 50% and 50%, a prediction horizon of 30 days, and a look-back window of 48 time steps, varying the following parameters:

1. **Attention Heads:** we tested configurations with 2, 4 (default), and 8 heads to analyze the impact of the attention mechanisms.
2. **Embedding Dimension:** we examined embedding sizes of 16, 32 (default), and 64 dimensions to assess their effect on representation capacity. The GRU hidden size was set to match the embedding dimension in each respective configuration.
3. **Encoder Layers:** we explored architectures with 1, 2 (default), and 3 transformer encoder layers to measure the effect of depth on performance.
4. **Feed-Forward internal dimension**: we varied the internal dimension of the feed-forward network within each encoder layer, exploring values of 32, 64 (default), and 128.

Table 3. Error increase due to ablations.

Model	FrenchPiezo					USHCN				
	0%	20%	50%	70%	Mean	0%	20%	50%	70%	Mean
w/o embedder	13.31%	11.91%	22.07%	15.66%	15.74%	12.62%	6.54%	10.79%	3.54%	8.37%
w/o local-global	-0.47%	1.47%	5.90%	2.23%	2.28%	6.68%	6.02%	1.78%	5.99%	5.11%
w/o GRU	1.38%	3.67%	4.49%	4.99%	3.63%	17.22%	9.07%	5.29%	5.75%	9.33%

(a) MAE

Model	FrenchPiezo					USHCN				
	0%	20%	50%	70%	Mean	0%	20%	50%	70%	Mean
w/o embedder	23.13%	21.07%	38.60%	29.97%	28.10%	30.45%	11.34%	12.88%	6.69%	15.34%
w/o local-global	-0.35%	-0.44%	5.40%	-7.97%	-0.84%	16.59%	8.36%	4.12%	1.89%	7.74%
w/o GRU	2.26%	2.91%	5.01%	-3.93%	1.56%	38.93%	15.55%	7.19%	5.12%	16.70%

(b) MSE

Discussion. All experiments confirm that the selected hyperparameters minimize the error in both datasets. Moreover, the Figure shows that variations around the chosen values do not produce significant changes in forecasting accuracy, highlighting the robustness of the model to parameter tuning.

Lesson learned. ISTF shows robustness to hyperparameter variations, with minimal impact on performance.

4.5   Time Performance

We assessed the evaluation by measuring the time needed to train the datasets with 50% missing values. Table 4 shows the time required for training the datasets, reporting the total time, the time required to complete an epoch and a batch of 64 records.

Discussion. The experimental results show that ISTF is generally less efficient than the fastest baselines. However, its efficiency is comparable to GRU-D, and overall training times remain manageable, not hindering ISTF applicability in real-world scenarios. The longest training time is observed for the FrenchPiezo dataset, reaching two hours, close to the time recorded by InterpNet and slightly less than GRU-D, the slowest baseline overall. For the USHCN dataset, training takes slightly less than an hour, which is marginally slower than GRU-D, the least efficient baseline on this dataset. It is also worth noting that the time required to process a batch, which is relevant to assessing the serving time of ISTF, is limited and in line with the average of the other baselines.

Lesson learned. ISTF trades efficiency in training for improved accuracy, but training times remain feasible for real-world applications.

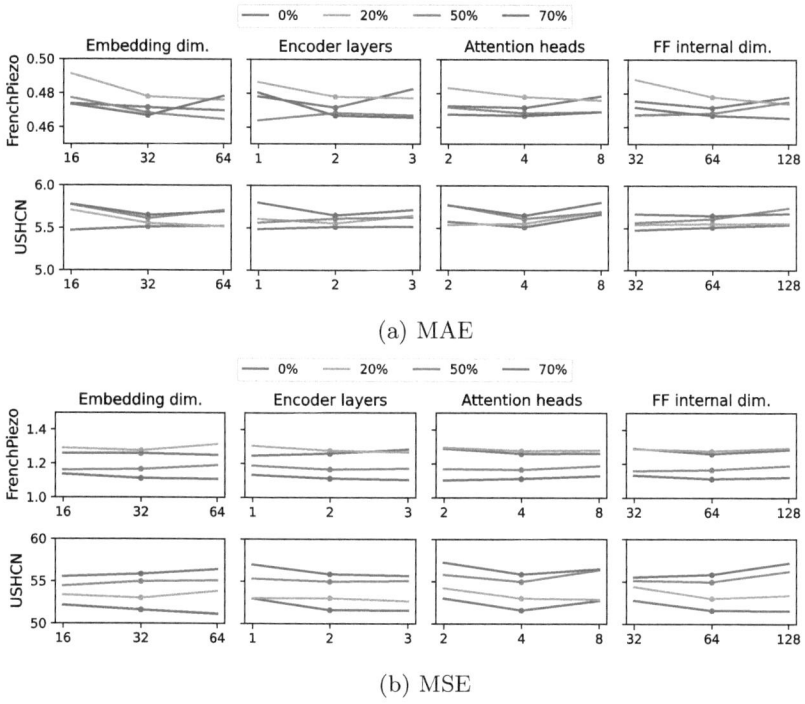

(a) MAE

(b) MSE

Fig. 5. Robustness to variations in hyperparameters. The x-axis represents the hyperparameter configurations; the y-axis the forecasting error (MAE and MSE).

Table 4. Training time (seconds): total, per epoch, per batch.

Model	FrenchPiezo			USHCN		
	total	epoch	batch	total	epoch	batch
InterpNet	5304.155	160.732	0.022	1412.895	64.223	0.023
mTAN	4585.016	127.362	0.017	1505.682	48.57	0.018
GRU-D	8202.501	356.63	0.048	3166.397	143.927	0.052
PrimeNet	3963.591	74.785	0.010	869.753	28.992	0.010
DLinear	1037.824	24.710	0.003	464.587	9.481	0.003
ISTF	7461.781	226.115	0.030	3489.839	94.32	0.034

5 Conclusions

We proposed ISTF, a transformer-based model designed to handle irregularly sampled multivariate time series by integrating local and global attention mechanisms. Experimental results on two real-world datasets show that ISTF achieves superior forecasting accuracy compared to existing approaches. This improvement comes with higher computational time, but the overall cost remains manageable for real-world applications. The ablation study highlights the importance of every architecture component, confirming its role in reducing prediction errors. Future work will focus on optimizing efficiency and extending the model to broader forecasting scenarios.

Acknowledgments. This work was partially supported by the project AnomalyFeats - FARD2023 (Department of Engineering "Enzo Ferrari", UNIMORE, IT).

References

1. Brouwer, E.D., Simm, J., Arany, A., Moreau, Y.: Gru-ode-bayes: continuous modeling of sporadically-observed time series. In: NeurIPS, pp. 7377–7388 (2019)
2. Che, Z., Purushotham, S., Cho, K., Sontag, D.A., Liu, Y.: Recurrent neural networks for multivariate time series with missing values. CoRR **abs/1606.01865** (2016)
3. Chowdhury, R.R., Li, J., Zhang, X., Hong, D., Gupta, R.K., Shang, J.: Primenet: pre-training for irregular multivariate time series. In: AAAI, pp. 7184–7192. AAAI Press (2023)
4. Du, W., et al.: Tsi-bench: benchmarking time series imputation. CoRR **abs/2406.12747** (2024)
5. Grigsby, J., Wang, Z., Qi, Y.: Long-range transformers for dynamic spatiotemporal forecasting. CoRR **abs/2109.12218** (2021)
6. Hyndman, R., Athanasopoulos, G.: Forecasting: Principles and Practice, 3rd edn. OTexts, Australia (2021)
7. Lim, B., Zohren, S.: Time series forecasting with deep learning: a survey. CoRR **abs/2004.13408** (2020)
8. Lipton, Z.C., Kale, D.C., Wetzel, R.C.: Directly modeling missing data in sequences with RNNs: improved classification of clinical time series. In: MLHC. JMLR Workshop and Conference Proceedings, vol. 56, pp. 253–270. JMLR.org (2016)
9. Liu, Z., Zhu, Z., Gao, J., Xu, C.: Forecast methods for time series data: a survey. IEEE Access **9**, 91896–91912 (2021)
10. Mbouopda, M.F., Guyet, T., Labroche, N., Henriot, A.: Experimental study of time series forecasting methods for groundwater level prediction. In: AALTD@ECML/PKDD. Lecture Notes in Computer Science, vol. 13812, pp. 34–49. Springer (2022)
11. Menne, M., Williams, Jr., C., Vose, R.: Long-term daily and monthly climate records from stations across the contiguous united states (U.S. historical climatology network) (2016). https://doi.org/10.3334/CDIAC/CLI.NDP019
12. Schirmer, M., Eltayeb, M., Lessmann, S., Rudolph, M.: Modeling irregular time series with continuous recurrent units. In: ICML. Proceedings of Machine Learning Research, vol. 162, pp. 19388–19405. PMLR (2022)
13. Shukla, S.N., Marlin, B.M.: Interpolation-prediction networks for irregularly sampled time series. In: ICLR (Poster). OpenReview.net (2019)
14. Shukla, S.N., Marlin, B.M.: Multi-time attention networks for irregularly sampled time series. In: ICLR. OpenReview.net (2021)
15. Torres, J.F., Hadjout, D., Sebaa, A., Martínez-Álvarez, F., Troncoso, A.: Deep learning for time series forecasting: a survey. Big Data **9**(1), 3–21 (2021)

16. Wang, J., et al.: Deep learning for multivariate time series imputation: a survey. CoRR **abs/2402.04059** (2024)
17. Wang, Z., et al.: Improving irregularly sampled time series learning with time-aware dual-attention memory-augmented networks. In: CIKM, pp. 3523–3527. ACM (2021)
18. Wen, Q., et al.: Transformers in time series: a survey. In: IJCAI, pp. 6778–6786. ijcai.org (2023)
19. Wu, H., Xu, J., Wang, J., Long, M.: Autoformer: decomposition transformers with auto-correlation for long-term series forecasting. In: NeurIPS, pp. 22419–22430 (2021)
20. Zeng, A., Chen, M., Zhang, L., Xu, Q.: Are transformers effective for time series forecasting? In: AAAI, pp. 11121–11128. AAAI Press (2023)
21. Zhou, H., et al.: Informer: Beyond efficient transformer for long sequence time-series forecasting. In: AAAI, pp. 11106–11115. AAAI Press (2021)

Automating Geospatial Vision Tasks with a Large Language Model Agent

Yuxing Chen[1], Weijie Wang[2], Camille Kurtz[1], and Sylvain Lobry[1(✉)]

[1] Université Paris Cité, Paris 75006, France
{yuxing.chen,camille.kurtz,sylvain.lobry}@u-paris.fr
[2] Università degli Studi di Trento, Trento 38122, Italy
weijie.wang@unitn.it

Abstract. Large Language Models (LLMs) have shown promise in automating code generation for data science tasks, yet they struggle with complex task sequences, especially in geospatial vision tasks. These difficulties stem from challenges in managing stepwise dependencies, aligning diverse data sources with spatial constraints, and accurately applying various geospatial libraries—often resulting in logical errors or hallucinations. To address these limitations, we introduce GeoAgent, an interactive framework designed to enable LLMs to automate geospatial vision tasks effectively. GeoAgent integrates a code interpreter, static analysis, and retrieval generation within a Monte Carlo Tree Search framework, creating a robust solution tailored to the geospatial data processing workflow. We introduce a new benchmark to evaluate GeoAgent's performances on single- and multi-turn tasks, including geospatial data acquisition, analysis, and visualization across multiple Python libraries. Our experiments reveal that GeoAgent significantly outperforms baseline LLMs in function call accuracy, task pass rate and task completion, marking a substantial advancement in automating geospatial vision tasks and setting a new standard for LLM-driven geospatial data analysis.

Keywords: Large Language Model · Agent · Geospatial · Data Analysis

1 Introduction

Large language models (LLMs) have demonstrated their potential to solve complex tasks in the geospatial domain [3, 13, 28]. Current approaches mainly rely on pre-defined, template-based prompts and third-party application programming interfaces (APIs), enabling LLMs to utilize external tools as foundational components for task completion. For instance, Remote Sensing ChatGPT [7] and ChangeAgent [17] leverage independent remote sensing (RS) vision model APIs while GEOGPT [31] uses geographic information system (GIS) API calls. These APIs provide single-line calls for a specific task without an understanding of the dependencies of their functionalities. Although GeoLLM-Engine [22] advances

_____

Supplementary Information The online version contains supplementary material available at https://doi.org/10.1007/978-3-662-72243-5_13.

by integrating multiple APIs into a sequential task within a real user interface, it remains constrained by fixed task-level APIs. Recent efforts in NLP, such as QwenAgent [2] and BigCodeBench [32], demonstrate LLMs' potential to handle open-domain data analysis utilizing any available Python libraries in code generation. These advancements suggest the potential for using LLM-based coding to address open-domain geospatial vision tasks in code execution environments.

Geospatial vision tasks pose significant challenges for LLMs, requiring them to understand complex instructions, manage interdependent inputs and outputs, and apply specialized libraries and models accurately [25]. These tasks often demand expert intervention for decomposing tasks and selecting appropriate libraries, as LLMs typically struggle with multi-library function calls, especially when under-trained with these libraries. Expert intervention is occasionally necessary for task decomposition and dynamic adjustments, which may involve fixing unsuccessful steps. General data analysis benchmarks [30, 32] rely heavily on popular Python libraries, but these are often limited to single-turn tasks and saturated by the recently released LLMs. These studies have a limited scope in geospatial vision tasks, which often require using less common geospatial Python libraries in sequential tasks. For less common geospatial Python libraries, LLMs frequently exhibit "API hallucinations" [11]. Retrieval-augmented generation (RAG) [8] has emerged as a method to supplement LLM's coding capability by incorporating domain-specific knowledge. However, effectively tackling specialized geospatial vision tasks still requires sequential reasoning and iterative refinement guided by execution feedback. Advanced techniques like Monte Carlo Tree Search (MCTS) further enhance LLMs' sequential reasoning, enabling feedback-driven, multi-step processing—a crucial aspect for handling complex geospatial tasks [10].

In addition to standalone API calls, most existing works on geospatial vision tasks leverage Vision-Language Models (VLMs) to process input data and task descriptions in a single step [14,15,28]. While this approach simplifies execution, it restricts detailed analysis of individual outputs and hinders integration of results across models and data sources. Key challenges arise with VLMs in geospatial applications: First, geospatial data's diverse modalities require extensive model parameters for effective initialization. Second, interdisciplinary topics often depend on domain knowledge—particularly physical models—that current VLMs cannot access. Third, geospatial tasks often require compositional reasoning, involving multiple steps like image preprocessing and analysis that are challenging to handle in a single prompt. Finally, many remote sensing data are cloud-based and accessible only via APIs, limiting VLMs' ability to query data dynamically. Unlike VLMs, LLM-based code generation offers greater flexibility, supporting multi-model integration and stepwise processing for more comprehensive geospatial data analysis.

To address these challenges, we introduce GeoAgent, an LLM-based agent that combines a code interpreter, static analysis, and RAG within an MCTS framework. We also propose a benchmark for evaluating diverse geospatial vision and vision-support tasks. GeoAgent fulfills human requirements by translating given tasks into executable Python code, utilizing dynamic task adjustment and refinement through the MCTS. This iterative refinement enables GeoAgent to manage dependencies among subtasks and dynamically refine them using execution feedback within an MCTS framework, ensuring that each code segment is logically consistent and well-developed with prior steps. The following outlines our key contributions:

- We introduce a novel LLM agent that integrates an external knowledge retriever, a code interpreter, and static analysis within an MCTS framework tailored for geospatial vision tasks. This integration enhances problem-solving, and logical capabilities in sequential task programming. Operating within Jupyter Notebook, GeoAgent enables iterative user interaction, optimizing code execution while ensuring compliance with Python libraries and best practices;
- We present GeoCode, an execution-based benchmark comprising over 18,000 single-turn and 1,356 multi-turn geospatial data analysis tasks, involving 2,313 function calls from 28 widely-used libraries across 8 task categories. GeoCode provides two evaluation models: single-turn task evaluation, which measures function call accuracy and task pass rate, and multi-turn task evaluation, which assesses task completion rates through either automatic iterative refinement or human intervention;
- We evaluate multiple LLMs on the GeoCode benchmark, showing that general-purpose LLM coders often produce incomplete workflows, while GeoAgent achieves higher task pass and completion rates. This success is attributed to its effective handling of specialized Python libraries within an MCTS framework, guided by execution feedback. The study provides a more accurate assessment of LLM coders in geospatial data processing and points to a promising future for automating geospatial vision tasks.

2 Related Work

2.1 LLM-Based Code Generation

LLMs exhibit strong abilities to generate standalone function codes while struggling with multi-step and interrelated task programming. Recent works [24,27,30] have emphasized integrating tools like code interpreters and static analysis to enhance code-based reasoning capabilities. For example, RepairAgent [4] uses static analysis for code repair, and $STALL^+$ [20] enhances generated code fixes. Execution feedback approaches like CodeAct [24] iteratively improve code through interpreter feedback, supporting symbolic computations and logical consistency. RAG has also advanced code generation by connecting LLMs to external databases, improving precision with evolving libraries [11]. However, there is no geospatial RAG database for geospatial task programming. Tools like ToolFormer [21] and CodeAgent [29] have enabled the invocation of standalone APIs within code generation, though challenges remain for open-domain tasks. Additionally, API hallucinations are prevalent, especially with less common APIs, with rates reaching up to 15% in recent studies [18].

2.2   Geospatial Vision Tasks with LLMs

Researchers have explored integrating LLMs into geospatial vision tasks [3,15, 31]. The preliminary attempt at bridging the gap between visual features and the semantic reasoning capabilities of LLMs is large VLMs [3,15], which incorporate LLMs into RS image captioning, Visual Question Answering (VQA), and visual grounding tasks. Pioneering work RS-CLIP [15] created a human-annotated RS image captioning dataset, advancing VLMs in the RS domain. To leverage LLM capabilities, RS-LLaVA [3] developed the RS-instructions dataset, a benchmark integrating captioning and VQA tasks in a LLaVA [19] framework. However, the textual outputs of LLMs often fall short of meeting users' expectations. Recent advancements in GeoChat [13] have expanded VLM tasks to referring expression, region captioning, image description, and VQA. While significant progress has been made in geospatial vision tasks, challenges persist in applying these models to open-domain scenarios, especially in using multiple professional tools, procedures, and multimodal data. Recent works [16,31] shift LLMs from operational roles to decision-makers, enabling them to select appropriate tools. For example, Change-Agent [17] directs LLMs to use segmentation and captioning tools, while GeoLLM-Engine [22] calls geospatial APIs and external knowledge bases to handle sequential tasks. However, these tools require pre-determined task-level APIs, limiting their use in open-domain tasks, especially in sequential tasks where tool calling integration becomes challenging.

3   Methodology

3.1   Framework

GeoAgent is an LLM agent designed to process geospatial vision tasks. Its architecture, shown in Fig. 1, consists of two main components: 1) Task programming (Fig. 1 a): GeoAgent starts by leveraging the parameterized knowledge of LLMs to generate code based on task instructions. External knowledge, such as specific Python libraries, can be integrated with retrieved items through RAG and execution feedback to enhance code generation. 2) Task refinement with MCTS (Fig. 1 b, c, d): GeoAgent executes code and collects feedback within the MCTS framework. MCTS explores and evaluates multiple code candidates, while LLMs serve as the reasoner, diagnosing errors, refining prompts, and correcting failed code. This integration allows dynamic adjustments during task programming.

3.2   Dynamic Refinement on MCTS

The GeoAgent employs an MCTS framework [12] to iteratively refine subtasks within the task sequence. MCTS utilizes a tree structure where nodes represent states s and edges denote actions a. The algorithm explores the state space starting from the root s^0 to identify the terminal state s^n with the highest reward $r(s^n)$. Each node contains: the visited times count v, probability p from LLMs, and state-action value $Q(s, a)$ (i.e., the maximum reward obtained by taking

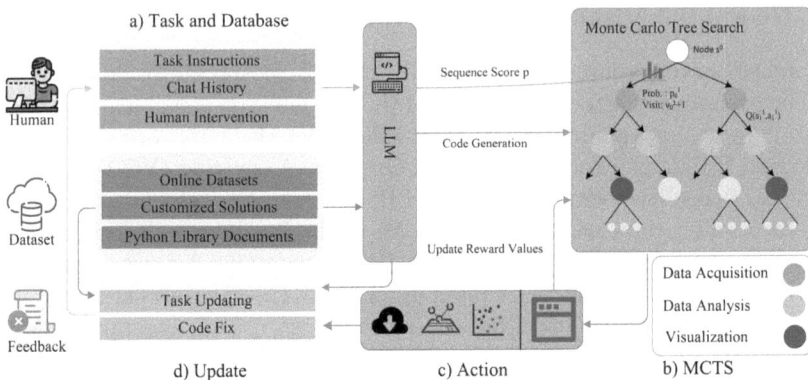

Fig. 1. GeoAgent: A geospatial vision task programming agent. This agent comprises four integral components: **a) Task and Database**, which provide LLM the task instruction and task-relevant items including Python library documents, online datasets, and solutions; **b) MCTS**, explores and evaluates multiple possible code candidates to optimize the selection of the most promising solution at each step through iterative adjustment and refinement; **c) Action**, which is an execution environment integrated with a code interpreter and static analysis and provides feedback on generated code; and **d) Update**, which suggests potential error fixes on generated code and adjustments on given tasks. In addition, the **LLM** functions as the code generator and the intelligent reasoner to propose code solutions and iteratively diagnose detected errors.

action a from state s). The reward r of state s is updated by the backpropagation of its children node's reward. Nodes with higher rewards are prioritized indicating high-quality generation. GeoAgent first transforms natural language instructions into executable codes and then dynamically refines each subtask during the MCTS selection, expansion, evaluation, and backpropagation. The full MCTS process is illustrated in Fig. 2.

First, in the selection phase, GeoAgent uses the probabilistic Upper Confidence Bound (P) algorithm to select branches starting from root node s^0, which is defined as:

$$P = \arg\max_{i \in I} \left[Q\left(s^0, a_i^0\right) + \beta\left(s^0\right) \cdot \frac{p_i^0 \sqrt{\log\left(v^0\right)}}{1 + v_i^0} \right], \tag{1}$$

$Q\left(s^0, a_i^0\right)$ denotes the maximum reward obtained at action a_i^0 and is defined as:

$$Q\left(s^0, a_i^0\right) = \frac{S_{pass} - S_{node}}{S_{all} - S_{node}}, \tag{2}$$

where S_{all} represents the total number of code steps generated during the lookahead phase, S_{pass} is the number of code steps that passed the evaluation test, and S_{node} is the number of code steps in node s^0. In addition, $\beta(s^0)$ is the weight for exploration:

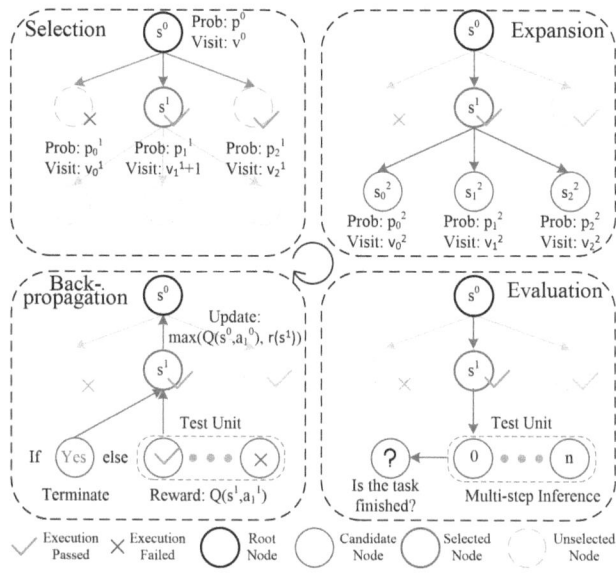

Fig. 2. Illustration of using the Monte Carlo Tree Search algorithm in geospatial vision task programming.

$$\beta(s^0) = \log\left(\frac{v^0 + c_{base} + 1}{c_{base}}\right) + c. \tag{3}$$

It depends on the visited number (v^0) and constants c_{base} and c, where a higher c encourages more exploration. In Equation (1), $\beta(s^0)$ is weighted by the probability p that is the LLM-determined sequence score. In the selection phase, GeoAgent begins at the root node s^0, recursively selecting subtrees until it reaches an unexplored node. This process uses P to balance exploration between known and less-visited states. Then, in the expansion phase, after selecting the initial node, potential codes for subsequent steps are generated and added to the child node list until the next subtask is reached. We sample n code snippets generated from the prompt and return the top $k = 3$ of them. These three code snippets (s_0^2, s_1^2, s_2^2) are added to the current node's (s^1) children list. For each child node, the reward Q is set to 0 for executable ones and -1 for non-executable ones. And then, in the evaluation phase, the selected node s^1 must be assessed, despite the node potentially representing only a partial program. Since the quality of partial programs is uncertain, the LLM performs a look-ahead search, generating a longer code snippet ("Test Unit"). This "Test Unit" is concatenated with the code of the current node for execution test. Finally, the reward of the current node is calculated based on the "Test Unit" and measured using Equation (2). The node terminates and receives a reward of 1 if the test code unit fully overlaps with its code. At last, in the backpropagation phase, this reward $r(s^1)$ is then backpropagated through the tree, updating the values of its ancestor nodes accordingly.

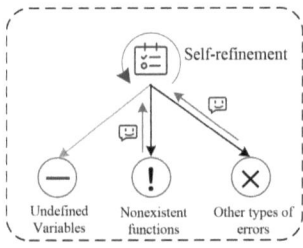

Fig. 3. The self-refinement algorithm in MCTS.

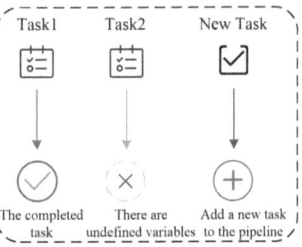

Fig. 4. Addition of new tasks to the task pool in MCTS.

The proposed MCTS framework incorporates an error traceback and analysis mechanism to refine subtasks. As shown in Fig. 3 and Fig. 4, it assesses the initial code using a code interpreter and static analysis tools. When undefined variables arise, the framework removes the affected subtree, adds a new subtask to define the variable at the top of task stacks (see Fig. 4), and retries. If non-existent functions are called, tools such as Python Jedi [9] retrieve alternative functions, which are added to the prompt to guide the LLM in correcting the function call. For other errors, the interpreter provides traceback details, allowing the LLM to diagnose and suggest fixes, such as syntactic errors, logical errors, or issues with Python libraries. The failed code snippet, with suggested corrections and original instructions, is reintroduced into the task stack. This process continues until the generated code is successfully executed or the maximum number of attempts is reached.

However, even with the integration of static analysis and execution feedback, ensuring the success of task programming remains challenging due to the non-deterministic nature of LLM inference. GeoAgent addresses this by setting a maximum attempt limit. Meanwhile, manual editing is also introduced to enhance task completeness. If the problem remains unsolved, GeoAgent generates a report detailing the task, code, and encountered errors for human intervention; these modifications are then integrated as contextual inputs in subsequent runs.

4   Benchmark Setup

4.1   Benchmark Construction

We outline the process of constructing the benchmark, which involves three primary steps: code collection, code refactoring, and instruction generation. Creating a high-quality, execution-based benchmark for geospatial vision tasks is challenging, as finding naturally self-contained geospatial tasks with detailed instructions is rare. GeoAgent gathers code snippets that utilize geospatial Python libraries and creates corresponding task descriptions for each code segment. Given the limited resources for geospatial vision tasks using Python libraries,

Table 1. Illustration of Python libraries in GeoCode. This table categorizes Python libraries used in GeoCode according to their respective domains. Each domain is associated with specific tasks.

Domain	Library
Data Acquisition,and Data Preparation	earthengine-api, cubo, pystac, GOES-2-Go, meteostat, pystac_client, pytesmo, planetary_computer
Raster Processing	earthengine-api, eemont, geetools, GeoUtils, wxee, xarray-spatial
Vector Processing	GemGIS, GeoPandas, GeoUtils
3D analysis	Gempy
Machine Learning	scikit-eo, Verde
Deep Learning	segment-geospatial, srai
Specific Alogorithm	geeet, gstools, sen2nbar, pylandtemp, eradiate, spectramap
Visualization	geemap, leafmap, Lonboard

we employ tutorials from various Python libraries and leverage LLMs to construct code-instruction pairs. In addition, we also constructed the RAG library to assess the function call performance under RAG assistance. Notably, we split GeoCode into two subsets: Google Earth Engine library-based tasks (GeoCode-GEE) and the other library-based tasks (GeoCode-Other).[1]

4.2 Benchmark Statistics

The proposed GeoCode benchmark, summarized in Table 1, encompasses 28 widely-used Python libraries across 8 key domains. These libraries extensively facilitate or support geospatial vision tasks, with code snippets often combining multiple library functions, thereby requiring considerable compositional reasoning ability. Table 2 compares GeoCode with existing executable Python programming benchmarks, highlighting the libraries and function calls referenced in these benchmarks. Notably, GeoCode includes 18,148 single-turn tasks and 1,356 multi-turn tasks as well as 2,313 function calls from 28 external libraries, reflecting a broader diversity compared to other benchmarks. This indicates that GeoCode offers diverse task prompts, which involve complex instructions and demand intricate implementation logic.[2]

We provide a simple taxonomy of GeoCode-GEE single-turn tasks without context: Data Acquisition (4.4%), Data Analysis (73.6%), and Visualization (22%). Unlike common data science programming tasks where users give clean and simple data (e.g., tables or images), GeoCode works with thousands of online geospatial datasets in many different formats. These tasks often require

---

[1] See Supplement 8 for additional details and 9.1 for used prompts.
[2] See Supplement 8.1 for the library version and 9.2 for task examples.

Table 2. Python programming benchmark statistics: analysis by external library usage, function call frequency, task count, and task type.

Benchmark	ExternalLibrary	FunctionCall	Single-turnTasks	Multi-turnTasks
DS-1000	14	540	1000	0
ODEX	13	190	439	0
BigCodeBench	62	877	1140	0
CIBench	11	171	469	73
GeoCode	28	2313	18148	1356

combining multiple datasets, and the model—not the user—must decide which data to use. This means the model must not only understand the task well, but also know what data is available and how to use it. This makes GeoCode more complex than standard data science benchmarks.

4.3   Experimental Settings

In this work, we select Llama 3.1 (8B) [5] as the LLM to support geospatial vision task programming. Additionally, we consider CodeGemma 2 (7B) [23] and Phi3.5-mini (3.8B) [1], Qwen2 (7B) [26] in our analysis of the impact of different model sizes and specialized LLMs. Inference is performed using a single NVIDIA GeForce RTX 4090 GPU, encompassing both the initial stage of instruction generation and the subsequent stage of code generation. The parameters configuration includes setting the top-p value to 0.9, the temperature parameter to 0.6, and a maximum token limit of 2048. The window size is set to at least 32k tokens, thereby supporting the retrieval of extensive contexts. For the Retriever modules, we employ the embedding model (BBAI-embedding-001) to generate high-quality embeddings for both texts and codes, enabling efficient similarity computations and retrieval processes. The constants c_{base} and c in MCTS are set as 10 and 4, the maximum attempt of each subtask is set as 3.

4.4   Metrics

This section presents the evaluation metrics for assessing function calls and task completion. To evaluate function calls in generated code, we apply multilabel classification metrics: Precision, Accuracy, Recall, F1 score, and Hamming distance[3]. Functions referenced in the generated code are extracted as predicted labels, aligning the evaluation with example-based multilabel classification [6], where partial correctness is taken into consideration. The label differences are averaged across all tasks in the test set. For a function call dataset T with n tasks (X_i, Y_i) and k classes, let h denote LLM, and $Z_i = h(X_i) = \{0, 1\}^k$ represent the set of label memberships predicted by the LLM for the task X_i. The

---

[3] See Supplement 8.7 for other metric definitions.

Table 3. Comparison of function call performance of Llama3.1 with zero (@0) and three (@3) retrieval items across all benchmarks.

	Accuracy		F1		Hamming Loss	
	@0	@3	@0	@3	@0	@3
DS-1000	0.38	0.40	0.45	0.47	0.15	0.15
ODEX	0.49	0.53	0.50	0.55	0.28	0.26
BigCodeBench	0.37	0.61	0.45	0.72	0.11	0.10
CIBench	0.54	0.57	0.62	0.66	0.14	0.14
GeoCode-GEE	0.60	0.54	0.65	0.57	0.20	0.22
GeoCode-Others	0.61	0.67	0.66	0.72	0.19	0.17

F1 score is the harmonic mean of precision and recall, is defined as:

$$F_1 = \frac{1}{n} \sum_{i=1}^{n} \frac{2 |Y_i \cap Z_i|}{|Y_i| + |Z_i|}. \tag{4}$$

For code completion, we consider task pass rate (pass@1) and task completion rate, where the task pass rate is mainly for single-turn task evaluation and the task completion rate is the primary measure of multi-turn tasks. For instance, in a 10-step task, the model is prompted step-by-step to generate 10 code blocks sequentially. The completion rate is calculated based on consecutive successful executions; if the first five steps succeed, the rate is 50%. Furthermore, the pass@1 metric, a standard for evaluating single-turn task execution correctness, where sequential tasks were converted into single-turn tasks to facilitate this evaluation.

5   Evaluation

This section presents the evaluation results for all benchmarks along with the proposed GeoCode-GEE and GeoCode-Others. GeoCode-GEE focuses exclusively on tasks within the GEE environment, while GeoCode-Others involves multiple Python libraries. Additionally, we include benchmarks relevant to general data science tasks, such as DS-1000, ODEX, BigCodeBench, and CIBench. We first assess the function call performance with RAG using Accuracy, F1 score, and Hamming loss metrics. To assess GeoAgent's performance on task-level tasks, we evaluate the pass rate (pass@1) on single-turn tasks and the qualitative function call (F1 score) while assessing the task completion rate on multi-turn tasks. Notably, RAG is not included in task-level evaluation avoiding introducing additional uncertainty.

5.1   Function Call Performance

We first evaluate the function call performances using Llama3.1 and RAG-powered Llama3.1, with metrics reported under settings involving zero (@0) and three (@3) retrieval items. As shown in Table 3, most benchmarks benefit from including retrieved function documentation, leading to improved performance across all metrics. The most significant improvement is observed on BigCodeBench, where the @3 setting achieves a 0.275 increase in F1 score and a 0.007 reduction in Hamming loss. Conversely, the improvement in F1 score for other benchmarks is minimal: GeoCode-Others shows a gain of about 0.06, CIBench and ODEX about 0.04, while DS1000 exhibits almost no increase. Notably, performance on GeoCode-GEE declines with RAG, likely because the GEE Python library is heavily represented in Llama3.1's training data. Adding RAG in this context introduces noise, which detracts from generation quality. This suggests that LLMs may not yet be robust in handling extensive context, which can lead to undesired outcomes when processing varied inputs. Most geospatial Python libraries are unlikely to reach saturation in future LLM releases due to limited online documentation, making it crucial to include library documentation in the LLM's context for accurate function calls.

5.2   Single-Turn Task Evaluation

To assess GeoAgent's performance in single-turn tasks, we conducted experiments on 100 randomly chosen single-turn tasks of each benchmark, given our limited computational resources. We first evaluated the pass rate (pass@1) of single-turn tasks using four different LLMs (Llama3.1, CodeGemma, Phi3.5-mini, and Qwen2) both with and without GeoAgent. As shown in Table 4, most benchmarks demonstrate a higher pass rate when using GeoAgent across all four LLMs. This improvement is because LLMs sometimes fail by calling incorrect or non-existent functions[4]. GeoAgent addresses this issue by allowing multiple attempts when the initial attempt fails. The most significant improvements are observed on the GeoCode and ODEX benchmarks. For GeoCode-GEE, GeoAgent achieves a 13% improvement with Llama3.1, a 6% improvement with CodeGemma, a 16% improvement with Phi3.5-mini, and a 20% improvement with Qwen2. For GeoCode-Others, GeoAgent shows an 18% improvement with CodeGemma, a 5% improvement with Phi3.5-mini, and a 21% improvement with Qwen2. Similarly, on ODEX, GeoAgent achieves a 17% improvement with Llama3.1, a 9% improvement with CodeGemma, a 7% improvement with Phi3.5-mini, and a 10% improvement with Qwen2.

Among the different LLMs, Phi3.5-mini achieves the best performance on general data science benchmarks while CodeGemma demonstrates the highest performance on the GeoCode benchmark, achieving a pass@1 rate of 86% on GeoCode-GEE and 59% on GeoCode-Others. This suggests that code instruction-tuned LLMs may perform better on geospatial task code generation. Across all benchmarks, DS-1000 exhibits a notably lower pass rate with both standalone LLMs and GeoAgent, highlighting the challenge of generating executable solutions for this benchmark. Nonetheless, GeoAgent still manages to improve performance on DS-1000.

---

[4] See Supplement 9.3 for error examples.

Table 4. Code generation pass rate (Pass@1) of the Llama3.1, CodeGemma, Phi3.5 mini, and Qwen 2 on all benchmarks.

	Llama3.1		CodeGemma		Phi3.5 mini		Qwen 2	
	LLM	Agent	LLM	Agent	LLM	Agent	LLM	Agent
DS-1000	0.05	0.34	0.10	0.19	0.03	0.06	0.15	0.18
ODEX	0.74	0.91	0.78	0.87	0.84	0.91	0.84	0.94
BigCodeBench	0.67	0.61	0.82	0.82	0.94	0.91	0.87	0.84
CIBench	0.93	0.92	0.93	0.96	0.94	0.99	0.96	0.93
GeoCode-GEE	0.76	0.89	0.86	0.92	0.66	0.82	0.61	0.81
GeoCode-Others	0.45	0.40	0.58	0.76	0.50	0.55	0.39	0.61

Table 5. Function call performance (F1 score) of the Llama3.1, CodeGemma, Phi3.5 mini, and Qwen 2 on all benchmarks.

	LLama3.1		CodeGemma		Phi3.5 mini		Qwen 2	
	LLM	Agent	LLM	Agent	LLM	Agent	LLM	Agent
DS-1000	0.83	0.86	0.75	0.75	0.80	0.80	0.79	0.79
ODEX	0.53	0.66	0.54	0.56	0.55	0.58	0.55	0.56
BigCodeBench	0.77	0.80	0.72	0.74	0.79	0.80	0.69	0.68
CIBench	0.80	0.82	0.76	0.76	0.83	0.83	0.78	0.79
GeoCode-GEE	0.78	0.86	0.75	0.71	0.70	0.77	0.76	0.74
GeoCode-Others	0.66	0.69	0.69	0.70	0.66	0.72	0.63	0.64

While the pass rate alone does not fully capture task-level performance, we also evaluate function call performance using the F1 metric. As shown in Table 5, most benchmarks benefit from GeoAgent, leading to improved function call performance. The most significant improvements are observed on GeoCode-GEE and ODEX with Llama3.1, where GeoAgent achieves a 0.08 increase on GeoCode-GEE and a 0.13 increase on ODEX. Among the different LLMs, Llama3.1 and CodeGemma demonstrated the highest function call performance on the GeoCode benchmark. Overall, considering both pass rate and function call performance, GeoAgent with Llama3.1 performs best on single-turn tasks in GeoCode-GEE, while GeoAgent with CodeGemma is the top performer across the entire GeoCode benchmark for single-turn tasks. Additionally, GeoCode-GEE consistently outperforms GeoCode-Others across all standalone LLMs and GeoAgent configurations, suggesting that tasks involving multiple libraries are more challenging than single-library tasks.

5.3 Multi-turn Task Evaluation

To assess GeoAgent's performance on multi-turn tasks[5], we use 30 randomly chosen sequential tasks from three multi-turn benchmarks. Specifically, we evaluate the completion rates of these tasks under both self-debugging and human intervention modes (see Fig. 5). When a problem remains unresolved, human intervention is introduced to move the task to the next step. Consistent with the single-turn task evaluations, GeoAgent achieves a higher completion rate on all benchmarks under both the automatic and human intervention modes.

GeoAgent with Llama3.1 improves the completion rate by 20% and 6% on CIBench, 9% and 10% on GeoCode-GEE, and 48% and 22% on GeoCode-Others, under self-debugging and human intervention modes, respectively. The improvement arises because code generated solely by Llama3.1 frequently includes undefined variables, causing execution failures. In such cases, GeoAgent dynamically adjusts by refactoring the undefined variables into new subtasks and updating failed attempts within the current task loop. Compared to the automatic mode, human intervention improves the completion rate by 20% and 7% on CIBench, 46% and 47% on GeoCode-GEE, and 40% and 14% on GeoCode-Others, under LLMs alone and GeoAgent, respectively. Nearly all cases perform better with human assistance across both vanilla LLMs and GeoAgents. These observations suggest that LLMs perform better with human interaction, highlighting a promising direction for integrating LLMs to assist humans in geospatial data analysis tasks. Although GeoCode-Others is the most challenging one among the three benchmarks, with a zero completion rate for 7 out of 10 tasks using Llama3.1 alone in automatic mode, GeoAgent significantly improves the pass rate for these tasks. In contrast, CIBench is the easiest benchmark, achieving a 100% completion rate for 6 out of 10 tasks.

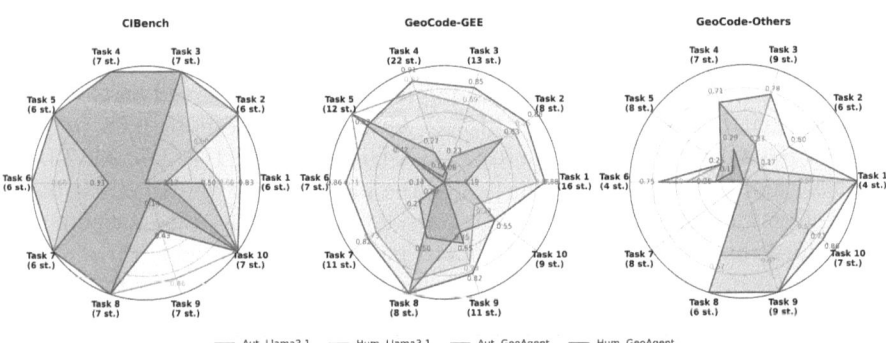

Fig. 5. Code generation complete rate (Complete@1) of the Llama3.1, GeoAgent under modes of self-debugging (Aut.) and Human Intervention (Hum.) across all benchmarks from Task 1 to Task 10 where *st.* denotes task steps.

---

[5] See Supplement 9.4 for a multi-turn task case.

We compare the computational performance of Llama3.1 and GeoAgent on the GeoCode-GEE benchmark, focusing on runtime and running steps per task (Table 6). On average, Llama3.1 completes each task in approximately 6 min, whereas GeoAgent requires about 14 min. GeoAgent also tends to require more steps: across the 10 evaluated tasks, it uses an average of 14.3 steps, compared to 11.7 steps for Llama3.1—an increase of 2.6 steps per task. This additional computational burden limited our evaluation to 10 tasks per dataset. Furthermore, GeoAgent's performance is affected by latency from remote data access on the Google Earth Engine (GEE) server.

Table 6. Runtime and step counts for multi-turn tasks using Llama3.1 and GeoAgent with self-debugging on the GeoCode-GEE benchmark.

Task No.	1	2	3	4	5	6	7	8	9	10
Aut. Llama3.1 (Steps)	16	8	13	22	12	7	11	8	11	9
Aut. GeoAgent (Steps)	16	10	15	27	16	7	15	9	11	17
Aut. Llama3.1 (Minutes)	9.0	5.5	5.2	15.0	4.4	2.6	6.5	2.9	5.8	2.7
Aut. GeoAgent (Minutes)	18.6	9.6	16.7	35.6	12.9	4.7	15.1	4.8	8.1	13.7

5.4 Discusssion

Generating code with LLMs alone is challenging, as they lag behind evolving Python libraries and datasets. Our RAG implementation, simply using vector matching with metadata filters and a pre-trained embedder, limits the retrieval performance. As shown in Table 3, function call performance shows minimal improvement in DS1000 and declines in GeoCode-GEE, likely due to the saturation of relevant libraries in recent LLMs and the noise introduced by RAG. This suggests a need for selective RAG application only when LLMs cannot find suitable functions. The proposed GeoAgent integrates RAG into a structured decision-making framework that combines a code interpreter, static analysis, and MCTS. As shown in Sect. 5.1, RAG improves function selection, while Sect. 5.2 demonstrates that the code interpreter, static analysis, and MCTS still contribute significantly to task-level performance even in the absence of RAG. However, the independent effectiveness of MCTS remains unverified, as its reward computation relies on feedback from the code interpreter.[6]

For task-level evaluation, this study focuses on process-oriented assessment. Although the generated code is executable, evaluating its performance based on output is challenging due to the variability and complexity of results. Both the quality of task instructions and the complexity of tasks can influence their results. In single-turn task evaluations, benchmarks like ODEX and GeoCode-Others exhibit the lowest function call performance, but ODEX achieves the

---

[6] See Supplement 8.2 for further discussions.

second-highest pass rate and GeoCode-Others has the lowest pass rate, apart from DS1000 (Table 4). This suggests that ODEX contains more open-ended problems that can be solved with certain Python libraries, whereas LLMs may lack sufficient knowledge of the libraries used in GeoCode-Others. For DS1000, despite having the lowest pass rate, it achieves the second-highest function call performance (Table 5). This indicates that DS1000's low pass rate stems primarily from task instructions that are not well-suited to generating executable solutions. The reasoning capabilities of LLMs further affect outcomes, as noise may be introduced during multi-step inference. As shown in Table 4, GeoAgent with Llama3.1 appears to struggle with inference noise on ODEX and GeoCode-Others. Similar issues are observed with GeoAgent using Phi3.5-mini on Big-CodeBench and with Qwen2 on CIBench. Multi-turn task evaluations, such as Task 1 in CIBench and Task 4 in GeoCode-GEE, show similar patterns. Additionally, even human intervention does not guarantee task success if tasks are too complex, as seen in Task 7 of GeoCode-Others.

To better understand failure modes, we categorize common errors into four types: (1) Instruction-following errors, where the LLM misinterprets or oversimplifies the prompt due to insufficient domain knowledge; (2) Hallucination errors, involving invalid function calls or undefined variables—often stemming from reliance on less common geospatial libraries; (3) Lack of information errors, where the prompt lacks critical input details or context; and (4) General code errors, which reflect broader limitations in LLM reasoning or syntax handling within the geospatial programming domain.

6   Conclusion

We introduce GeoAgent, an innovative approach designed to enhance access to extensive geospatial datasets and facilitate automated geospatial vision task workflows. By leveraging the capabilities of LLMs and a diverse set of evolving Python libraries, GeoAgent transforms tasks into executable units and refines the corresponding library usage through the MCTS framework. To assess the efficacy of GeoAgent, we developed a benchmark, GeoCode, focused on geospatial vision tasks using popular geospatial Python libraries. Our experimental results on GeoCode, along with existing benchmarks, demonstrate that GeoAgent outperforms LLM baselines in both data science and geospatial vision tasks. The findings highlight that GeoAgent significantly improves the pass rate and task completion for geospatial tasks. Future work will proceed along two main directions. First, we will scale GeoAgent by fine-tuning LLMs using reinforcement learning with task completion rewards, aiming to enhance planning and long-horizon decision-making. Second, we will extend the integration of geospatial libraries and improve the LLM's ability to dynamically generate new tools based on available Python packages, thereby increasing the system's adaptability to more diverse and complex geospatial workflows. With GeoAgent, we envision a future for advanced assistance tools that can seamlessly access relevant Python libraries and extensive online data for various geospatial tasks, thereby generating tailored code for researchers. We hope this work contributes to advancing the use of geospatial data in research aimed at societal benefits and environmental conservation.

Acknowledgments. This work is supported by *Agence Nationale de la Recherche* (ANR) under the ANR-21-CE23-0011 project. The GitHub repository for this work will be made available at: https://github.com/Yusin2Chen/GeoAgent.

Disclosure of Interests. The authors have no competing interests to declare that are relevant to the content of this article.

References

1. Abdin, M., et al.: Phi-3 Technical Report: a highly capable language model locally on your phone. CoRR **abs/2404.14219** (2024). https://doi.org/10.48550/ARXIV. 2404.14219
2. Bai, J., et al.: Qwen2.5 Technical Report. CoRR **abs/2412.15115** (2024). https:// doi.org/10.48550/ARXIV.2412.15115
3. Bazi, Y., Bashmal, L., Al Rahhal, M.M., Ricci, R., Melgani, F.: Rs-llava: a large vision-language model for joint captioning and question answering in remote sensing imagery. Remote Sens. **16**(9), 1477 (2024). https://doi.org/10.3390/rs16091477
4. Bouzenia, I., Devanbu, P., Pradel, M.: Repairagent: an autonomous, LLM-based agent for program repair. In: 2025 IEEE/ACM 47th International Conference on Software Engineering (ICSE), pp. 694–694. IEEE Computer Society, Los Alamitos, CA, USA (2025). https://doi.org/10.1109/ICSE55347.2025.00157
5. Dubey, A., et al.: The Llama 3 herd of models. CoRR **abs/2407.21783** (2024). https://doi.org/10.48550/ARXIV.2407.21783
6. Giraldo-Forero, A.F., Jaramillo-Garzón, J.A., Castellanos-Domínguez, C.G.: Evaluation of example-based measures for multi-label classification performance. In: Ortuño, F., Rojas, I. (eds.) IWBBIO 2015. LNCS, vol. 9043, pp. 557–564. Springer, Cham (2015). https://doi.org/10.1007/978-3-319-16483-0_54
7. Guo, H., Su, X., Wu, C., Du, B., Zhang, L., Li, D.: Remote sensing ChatGPT: solving remote sensing tasks with ChatGPT and visual models. In: IGARSS 2024 - 2024 IEEE International Geoscience and Remote Sensing Symposium, pp. 11474–11478. IEEE (2024). https://doi.org/10.1109/IGARSS53475.2024.10640736
8. Guu, K., Lee, K., Tung, Z., Pasupat, P., Chang, M.: Retrieval augmented language model pre-training. In: Proceedings of the 37th International Conference on Machine Learning, ICML 2020, 13–18 July 2020, Virtual Event. Proceedings of Machine Learning Research, vol. 119, pp. 3929–3938. PMLR (2020)
9. Halter, D.: Jedi: an awesome autocompletion tool for Python (2024). https:// github.com/davidhalter/jedi. Accessed: 2024-10-18
10. He, G., Singh, Z., Yoneki, E.: MCTS-GEB: Monte Carlo tree search is a good e-graph builder. In: Proceedings of the 3rd Workshop on Machine Learning and Systems, EuroMLSys 2023, Rome, Italy, 8 May 2023, pp. 26–33. ACM (2023). https://doi.org/10.1145/3578356.3592577
11. Jain, N., Kwiatkowski, R., Ray, B., Ramanathan, M.K., Kumar, V.: On mitigating code LLM hallucinations with API documentation. In: Proceedings of the 47th International Conference on Software Engineering: Software Engineering in Practice (ICSE-SEIP). To appear. IEEE/ACM (2025)

12. Jiang, X., et al.: Self-planning code generation with large language models. ACM Trans. Softw. Eng. Methodol. **33**(7) (2024). https://doi.org/10.1145/3672456

13. Kuckreja, K., Danish, M.S., Naseer, M., Das, A., Khan, S., Khan, F.S.: GeoChat: grounded large vision-language model for remote sensing. In: Proceedings of the IEEE/CVF Conference on Computer Vision and Pattern Recognition, pp. 27831–27840. IEEE Computer Society, Los Alamitos, CA, USA (2024). https://doi.org/10.1109/CVPR52733.2024.02629

14. Li, X., Wen, C., Hu, Y., Yuan, Z., Zhu, X.X.: Vision-language models in remote sensing: current progress and future trends. IEEE Geosci. Remote Sens. Mag. **12**(2), 32–66 (2024). https://doi.org/10.1109/MGRS.2024.3383473

15. Li, X., Wen, C., Hu, Y., Zhou, N.: Rs-clip: zero shot remote sensing scene classification via contrastive vision-language supervision. Int. J. Appl. Earth Obs. Geoinf. **124**, 103497 (2023). https://doi.org/10.1016/j.jag.2023.103497

16. Li, Z., Ning, H.: Autonomous GIS: the next-generation AI-powered GIS. Int. J. Digit. Earth **16**(2), 4668–4686 (2023). https://doi.org/10.1080/17538947.2023.2278895

17. Liu, C., Chen, K., Zhang, H., Qi, Z., Zou, Z., Shi, Z.: Change-agent: toward interactive comprehensive remote sensing change interpretation and analysis. IEEE Trans. Geosci. Remote Sens. **62**, 1–16 (2024). https://doi.org/10.1109/TGRS.2024.3425815

18. Liu, F., et al.: Exploring and evaluating hallucinations in LLM-powered code generation. CoRR **abs/2404.00971** (2024). https://doi.org/10.48550/ARXIV.2404.00971

19. Liu, H., Li, C., Li, Y., Lee, Y.J.: Improved baselines with visual instruction tuning. In: Proceedings of the IEEE/CVF Conference on Computer Vision and Pattern Recognition, pp. 26286–26296 (2024). https://doi.org/10.1109/CVPR52733.2024.02484

20. Liu, J., Chen, Y., Liu, M., Peng, X., Lou, Y.: STALL+: Boosting LLM-based repository-level code completion with static analysis. CoRR **abs/2406.10018** (2024). https://doi.org/10.48550/ARXIV.2406.10018

21. Schick, T., et al.: Toolformer: Language models can teach themselves to use tools. In: Proceedings of the 37th International Conference on Neural Information Processing Systems (NeurIPS). Curran Associates Inc., Red Hook, NY, USA (2023). https://doi.org/10.5555/3666122.3669119

22. Singh, S., Fore, M., Stamoulis, D.: GeoLLM-Engine: a realistic environment for building geospatial copilots. In: Proceedings of the IEEE/CVF Conference on Computer Vision and Pattern Recognition (CVPR) Workshops, pp. 585–594 (2024). https://doi.org/10.1109/CVPRW63382.2024.00063

23. Team, C.: CodeGemma: Open code models based on Gemma. CoRR **abs/2406.11409** (2024). https://doi.org/10.48550/ARXIV.2406.11409

24. Wang, X., et al.: Executable code actions elicit better LLM agents. In: Salakhutdinov, R., et al., (eds.) Proceedings of the 41st International Conference on Machine Learning (ICML 2024), Proceedings of Machine Learning Research, vol. 235, pp. 50208–50232. PMLR (2024). https://doi.org/10.5555/3692070.3694124

25. Wu, J., Gan, W., Chao, H.C., Philip, S.Y.: Geospatial big data: survey and challenges. IEEE J.Sel. Top. Appl. Earth Obser. Remote Sens. **17**, 17007–17020 (2024). https://doi.org/10.1109/JSTARS.2024.3438376

26. Yang, A., et al.: Qwen2 Technical Report. CoRR **abs/2407.10671** (2024). https://doi.org/10.48550/ARXIV.2407.10671

27. Yao, S., et al.: ReAct: synergizing reasoning and acting in language models. In: International Conference on Learning Representations (ICLR 2023). OpenReview.net, Kigali, Rwanda (2023)

28. Zhan, Y., Xiong, Z., Yuan, Y.: SkyEyeGPT: unifying remote sensing vision-language tasks via instruction tuning with large language model. CoRR **abs/2401.09712** (2024). https://doi.org/10.48550/ARXIV.2401.09712

29. Zhang, K., Li, J., Li, G., Shi, X., Jin, Z.: CodeAgent: enhancing code generation with tool-integrated agent systems for real-world repo-level coding challenges. In: Ku, L.W., Martins, A., Srikumar, V. (eds.) Proceedings of the 62nd Annual Meeting of the Association for Computational Linguistics (Volume 1: Long Papers), pp. 13643–13658. Association for Computational Linguistics, Bangkok (2024). https://doi.org/10.18653/v1/2024.acl-long.737

30. Zhang, S., et al.: CIBench: evaluating your LLMs with a code interpreter plugin. CoRR **abs/2407.10499** (2024). https://doi.org/10.48550/ARXIV.2407.10499

31. Zhang, Y., Wei, C., He, Z., Yu, W.: Geogpt: an assistant for understanding and processing geospatial tasks. Int. J. Appl. Earth Obs. Geoinf. **131**, 103976 (2024). https://doi.org/10.1016/j.jag.2024.103976

32. Zhuo, T.Y., et al.: BigCodeBench: benchmarking code generation with diverse function calls and complex instructions. (2025)

Fourier-Enhanced Adaptive Manifold Latent Feature Analysis for Spatiotemporal Signal Recovery

Yuting Ding[1], Jianyong Zheng[2(✉)], Fei Mei[3], and Ang Gao[2]

[1] School of Cyber Science and Engineering, Southeast University, Nanjing, China
[2] School of Electrical Engineering, Southeast University, Nanjing, China
jyzheng209@163.com, 220202894@seu.edu.cn
[3] College of Electrical and Power Engineering, Hohai University, Nanjing, China
meifei@hhu.edu.cn

Abstract. Wireless Sensor Networks (WSNs) face critical data incompleteness challenges driven by hardware failures and energy constraints, which severely undermine environmental monitoring reliability. Although are frequently employed, Low-Rank Matrix Approximation (LRMA) methods often overlook nonlinear temporal dynamics and fail to discriminate structured noise from actual anomalies. This paper introduces the Adaptive Latent Feature Analysis with Fourier Embedding (ALFA-FE) framework, featuring two principal contributions: (1) dynamic Fourier embeddings that incorporate manifold-based frequency-domain regularization to flexibly capture multi-scale temporal patterns, and (2) a robust optimization scheme unifying Huber-norm loss with anomaly-sensitive constraints. Comprehensive evaluations across four real-world datasets reveal that ALFA-FE significantly outperforms seven state-of-the-art models in both reconstruction accuracy and robustness. By effectively balancing precise signal recovery with anomaly retention, ALFA-FE demonstrates strong potential for advancing environmental sensing reliability in resource-limited IoT deployments.

Keywords: Wireless sensor networks(WSNs) · Low-rank matrix approximation(LRMA) · Manifold Regularization · Spatio-temporal correlation

1 Introduction

WSNs consist of a deluge of distributed sensor nodes that communicate wirelessly to monitor and collect environmental data [28]. Each sensor node is capable of performing preliminary data processing, such as filtering, aggregation, and fusion, to reduce redundant data and enhance data transmission efficiency [5].

Supplementary Information The online version contains supplementary material available at https://doi.org/10.1007/978-3-662-72243-5_14.

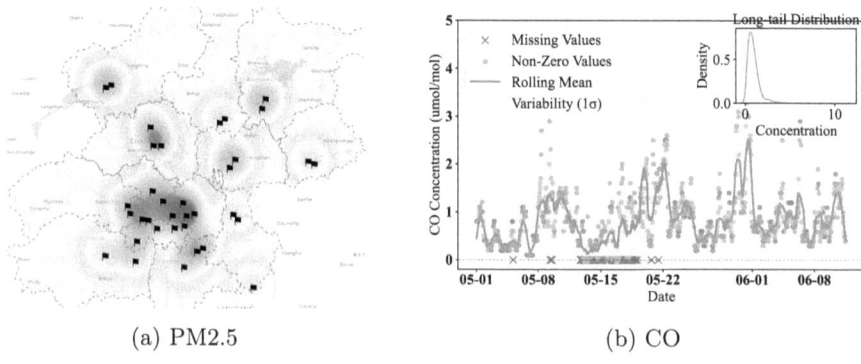

(a) PM2.5   (b) CO

Fig. 1. The data distribution of real Beijing air quality.

With the continuous evolution of WSNs, adoption has expanded across diverse domains, including environmental monitoring, smart cities [4,6,30], healthcare management [9,34], and industrial automation [19,32]. WSNs enable real-time, high-resolution data acquisition, playing a crucial role in enhancing decision-making and optimizing resource utilization across various fields. The significant advantages of WSNs have established it as a key driver of efficiency and innovation in multiple domains.

WSNs often suffer from data loss due to sensor failures, communication disruptions, and changes in network topology [10]. Ensuring reliable data collection becomes particularly challenging when monitoring dynamic environments, where measurements must be continuously captured and transmitted [29,33]. Moreover, the data collected by WSNs often exhibit complex spatiotemporal dependencies, influenced by environmental cycles or periodic industrial operations, further complicating the recovery process [18]. To tackle this issue effectively, missing data appears as an incomplete matrix, with rows corresponding to sensor nodes and columns representing time slots. Given the inherent correlations within WSN data, including nonlinear dependencies across both spatial and temporal dimensions, the resulting matrix often exhibits low-rank structure. Consequently, recovering missing values can be formulated as LRMA problem, where the missing entries are inferred based on the relationships embedded in the observed data.

LMRA establishes a mathematical framework for matrix decomposition, employing rank constraints to construct low-dimensional manifold approximations of high-dimensional data [37]. Derived from this theory, low-rank constrained optimization models enable effective missing data recovery in wireless sensor networks by leveraging subspace structures of partial observations [21,26,37]. However, current implementations ignore the intrinsic heterogeneity of anomalies across multisource sensors [12], characterized by divergent spatiotemporal signatures across sensor clusters. To be more intuitive, Fig. 1 shows a real example to demonstrate this issue.

Example 1: Air quality monitoring data from Beijing WSNs (5.1–6.8, 2014) demonstrate sensor challenges. Figure 1a reveals intensified urban gradients that indicate persistent high-concentration variability, while the suburban site remains comparatively stable. Figure 1b indicates a multimodal CO distribution ($\mu = 1.8$, $\sigma = 0.5\,\mathrm{mg/m^3}$) with 9.4% of samples above $2.7\,\mathrm{mg/m^3}$. Three transient spikes exceeding $3.5\,\mathrm{mg/m^3}$ appear around May 25–28, peaking at $3.8\,\mathrm{mg/m^3}$, contrasting the typical diurnal cycle of 1.1–$2.3\,\mathrm{mg/m^3}$. Spatial-temporal coupling between PM2.5 volatility and CO anomalies suggests distinct noise-outlier interactions.

Example 1 substantiates the challenges of strongly coupled outliers and pervasive multimodal noise within data gathered by WSNs. While conventional approaches predominantly resort to static regularization schemes, such methods prove inadequate as predetermined weighting parameters and rigid processing frameworks fail to accommodate the intricate, nonlinear dynamics intrinsic to noise–outlier coupling phenomena. A case in point is PM2.5, which exhibit a rapid increase and inconsistency with nearby sensor readings. Needless to say, such an outlier cannot uniformly treated as random noise. Alternatively, can we build adaptive LRMA architectures that improve recovery accuracy by achieving noise suppression and anomaly retention?

In response, this paper proposes an adaptive latent feature analysis (ALFA) framework with Fourier embedding (FE) for spatiotemporal signal recovery in WSN data, termed ALFA-FE, balancing noise resistance and anomaly retention. Its main idea is twofold: 1) temporal-focused Fourier integration enables the latent space to dynamically adapt to non-stationary patterns through manifold-basedfrequency-domain regularization. 2) Aggregating the huber-norm with gradient descent empowers the model to discern legitimate anomalies from coupled noise-artifacts. With such a design, it possesses the merits of both robustly capturing temporal dynamics and effectively distinguishing noise from genuine anomalies.

The primary contributions of this work are summarized as follows:

– An ALFA-FE model is constructed by integrating Fourier feature embedding with the Huber norm, facilitating dynamic frequency regulation and robust anomaly handling in spatiotemporal WSN data.
– Theoretical guarantees, including convergence analysis and generalization bounds, are provided for the ALFA-FE model.
– An efficient optimization algorithm is designed by synergizing gradient-based updates with adaptive noise suppression, ensuring scalability and real-time adaptability for large-scale WSN deployments.

The computational complexity analysis of ALFA-FE and some experimental detail are submiteed as supplemental material. ALFA-FE code and supplemental material have been published on https://github.com/adingyuting/signal-recovery.

2   Related Work

The LRMA model formulates WSN data recovery as a low-rank matrix completion problem, leveraging its intrinsic low-rank structure to represent data with a limited set of latent factors. By harnessing spatial and temporal dependencies from observed data points, LRMA optimizes an objective function to infer missing values, ensuring a globally coherent reconstruction. In recent years, LRMA has made significant strides in WSN data recovery, integrating various regularization techniques to enhance reconstruction accuracy, including graph regularization, nuclear norm minimization, sparsity constraints, weighted L1-L2 regularization, temporal smoothness enforcement, total variation regularization, and Bayesian prior modeling.

The exploitation of spatiotemporal features constitutes the cornerstone of LRMA-based data recovery in WSNs. Prevailing methods predominantly resort to graph-based regularization to encode such dependencies—ranging from graph Laplacian matrices for topology-aware smoothing [20,27] to hybrid graph constraints capturing global-local signal structures [8]. Despite their merits, these approaches intrinsically presume linear or quasi-linear temporal dependencies, often failing to accommodate the nonlinear dynamics pervasive in real-world WSN signals [7,20,25].

Regarding robustness enhancement, the community has witnessed a dichotomy between L2-norm-oriented accuracy optimization [14,44] and L1-norm-driven outlier resistance [13,36]. While L2-based models achieve superior performance under Gaussian noise, their susceptibility to anomalies has been widely documented [38,41]. Conversely, L1-regularized variants, though more robust, tend to undermine recovery fidelity due to over-conservative noise suppression [2,15,39,43]. Recent attempts to reconcile this dilemma through static L1/L2 hybrid regularization [16,45] merely mitigate rather than resolve the bias-variance tradeoff, as their fixed weighting parameters cannot adapt to skewed noise distributions. This paper introduces two innovations: Nonlinear Temporal Regularization and Adaptive Robustness via Huber Regularization. The first embeds coupled Fourier features to capture nonlinear spatiotemporal dependencies, overcoming graph-based methods' linearity assumption. The second replaces rigid L1/L2 composites with Huber loss for dynamic outlier response, synergizing with nonlinear representation learning to form a theoretically grounded framework that achieves an optimal equilibrium unattainable by prior arts.

3   The Proposed ALFA-FE Model

The proposed ALFA-FE framework advances LFA models through dual-criteria optimization. It exploits spatiotemporal manifold regularization term that captures nonlinear time-dependent patterns and employs Huber-norm for noise suppression and anomaly preservation, offering adaptive responses via self-adjusted thresholds. The next is to introduce the proposed ALFA-FE model.

3.1   Exploiting Spatiotemporal Feature

The spatiotemporal features in WSNs are characterized by spatial proximity and temporal dynamics. Spatially, sensor measurements attenuate with increasing node distance. Temporally, sensor signals show stable frequency and diverse dynamics across different time scales.

Spatial Proximity. To capture spatial proximity, we construct undirected weighted sensor graph $G = (\mathcal{V}, \mathcal{E}, A)$, where $\mathcal{V}$ represents the set of N sensor nodes, $\mathcal{E}$ denotes the set of edges representing pairwise sensor connections, and $A \in \mathbb{R}^{N \times N}$ is the weighted adjacency matrix. Each entry a_{ij} in A quantifies the relationship between sensor node i and node j. Given the sensor locations, the pairwise distance matrix $D \in \mathbb{R}^{N \times N}$ is computed based on Euclidean distances:

$$d_{ij} = \|\mathbf{x}_i - \mathbf{x}_j\|_2, \tag{1}$$

where $\mathbf{x}_i$ and $\mathbf{x}_j$ represent the coordinate vectors of the respective sensors.

Using the distance matrix D, the adjacency matrix A is constructed by selecting k nearest neighbors for each node. The edge weights are determined by a Gaussian kernel function:

$$a_{ij} = \begin{cases} \exp\left(-\frac{d_{ij}^2}{\sigma^2}\right), & \text{if } j \in \mathcal{N}_k(i) \text{ or } i \in \mathcal{N}_k(j) \\ 0, & \text{otherwise} \end{cases} \tag{2}$$

where σ is a scaling parameter controlling the decay of similarity with distance.

The spatial smoothness is characterized by the graph Laplacian matrix L, defined as:

$$L = D - A, \tag{3}$$

where D is the degree matrix, a diagonal matrix whose elements are given by:

$$D_{ii} = \sum_j a_{ij}. \tag{4}$$

Thus, L is expressed as:

$$L = \begin{bmatrix} \sum a_{1j} & -a_{12} & \cdots & -a_{1N} \\ -a_{21} & \sum a_{2j} & \cdots & -a_{2N} \\ \vdots & \vdots & \ddots & \vdots \\ -a_{N1} & -a_{N2} & \cdots & \sum a_{Nj} \end{bmatrix}_{N \times N}, \tag{5}$$

where $\sum a_{ij}$ denotes the sum of weights in the i-th row of A. The Laplacian matrix encodes the structural properties of the sensor network and enables spatial proximity modeling.

To normalize the influence of varying node degrees, we further define the normalized graph Laplacian as:

$$L_{\text{sym}} = I - D^{-1/2} A D^{-1/2}, \tag{6}$$

and the random walk Laplacian as:

$$L_{rw} = I - D^{-1} A. \tag{7}$$

Normalized Laplacians ensure scale-invariance and enhance spectral analysis of the sensor network. By constructing the graph Laplacian, ALFA-FE effectively captures spatial dependencies among sensor nodes, enabling robust graph-based signal processing techniques for spatiotemporal modeling in wireless sensor networks.

Temporal Dynamic. WSNs measurements, represented as rows in $\mathbf{W} \in \mathbb{R}^{N \times T}$, exhibit structured temporal dynamics, often containing both long-term trends and high-frequency variations. Fixed-scale representations may fail to capture this variability, leading to either the loss of fine details or excessive sensitivity to noise. To fix this issue, this paper employs Concatenated Fourier Features (CFF), which embeds time into a multi-scale sinusoidal basis, ensuring a robust representation of diverse temporal patterns.

Given a sequence of time indices $\boldsymbol{\tau} = [\tau_1, \tau_2, \ldots, \tau_T]^T \in \mathbb{R}^T$, we define the Fourier feature expansions:

$$\gamma(\boldsymbol{\tau}) = \Big[\sin(2\pi\mathbf{B}_1\boldsymbol{\tau}),\, \cos(2\pi\mathbf{B}_1\boldsymbol{\tau}),\, \ldots,\, \sin(2\pi\mathbf{B}_S\boldsymbol{\tau}),\, \cos(2\pi\mathbf{B}_S\boldsymbol{\tau})\Big]^T \quad (8)$$

where $\mathbf{B}_s \in \mathbb{R}^{d/2 \times 1}$ frequency scaling matrices are sampled from a Gaussian distribution, i.e.,

$$\mathbf{B}_s \sim \mathcal{N}(\mathbf{0}, \sigma_s^2\mathbf{I}), \quad (9)$$

ensuring multi-scale feature extraction across different frequency bands.

Using this transformation, the **temporal encoding matrix** $\mathbf{T} \in \mathbb{R}^{T \times Sd}$ is constructed as follows:

$$\mathbf{T} = \begin{bmatrix} \gamma(\tau_1) \\ \gamma(\tau_2) \\ \vdots \\ \gamma(\tau_T) \end{bmatrix} = \begin{bmatrix} \sin(2\pi B_1\tau_1) & \cos(2\pi B_1\tau_1) & \ldots & \sin(2\pi B_S\tau_1) & \cos(2\pi B_S\tau_1) \\ \sin(2\pi B_1\tau_2) & \cos(2\pi B_1\tau_2) & \ldots & \sin(2\pi B_S\tau_2) & \cos(2\pi B_S\tau_2) \\ \vdots & \vdots & \ddots & \vdots & \vdots \\ \sin(2\pi B_1\tau_T) & \cos(2\pi B_1\tau_T) & \ldots & \sin(2\pi B_S\tau_T) & \cos(2\pi B_S\tau_T) \end{bmatrix}.$$
$$(10)$$

Using the temporal encoding matrix $\mathbf{T}$, the temporal dynamic matrix C_{temp} is shown as:

$$C_{temp} = \mathbf{T}\mathbf{T}^T \in \mathbb{R}^{T \times T}. \quad (11)$$

This formulation encodes dependencies across all time steps, naturally capturing periodicity and multi-scale temporal variations.

Regularization Constraint of Spatiotemporal Feature. After obtaining the graph Laplacian matrix L_{rw} and the temporal dynamic matrix C_{temp}, they are incorporated into the Huber norm as the regularization constraints,

$$\varepsilon(P, E) = \underbrace{\beta\|J \circ (W - PE)\|_{\text{Huber}}}_{\text{Data fitting term}} + \underbrace{\lambda_{reg}\left(\|P\|_F^2 + \|E\|_F^2\right)}_{\text{Tikhonov regularization}}$$
$$(12)$$
$$+ \underbrace{\lambda_1 \operatorname{trace}\left(P^T L_{rw} P\right)}_{\text{Spatial proximity constraint}} + \underbrace{\lambda_2 \operatorname{trace}\left(E^T C_{temp} E\right)}_{\text{Temporal dynamic constraint}}$$

where λ_1 and λ_2 are two hyperparameters controlling the effects of spatial and temporal features, respectively. β is hyperparameter controlling the effects of the Huber norm.

3.2 Model Optimization

It is noteworthy that since the Huber-norm-based loss function in (12) exhibits gradient discontinuity at specific points, (12) can be reformulated into an element-wise representation, as shown in [11, 27, 41].

$$
\varepsilon(P,E) = \beta \sum_{i=1}^{N} \sum_{j=1}^{T} \left(\begin{cases} \frac{1}{2}(w_{i,j} - p_{i,.}e_{.,j})^2, & \text{if } |w_{i,j} - p_{i,.}e_{.,j}| \leq \delta \\ \delta(|w_{i,j} - p_{i,.}e_{.,j}| - \frac{1}{2}\delta), & \text{otherwise} \end{cases} \right)
$$

$$
+ \lambda_{\text{reg}} \sum_{i=1}^{N} \sum_{j=1}^{T} (\|p_{i,.}\|_F^2 + \|e_{.,j}\|_F^2) + \lambda_1 \sum_{i=1}^{N} \sum_{j=1}^{T} ((P^T L_{rw} P)_{i,i}) \quad (13)
$$

$$
+ \lambda_2 \sum_{i=1}^{N} \sum_{j=1}^{T} ((E^T C_{temp} E)_{j,j})
$$

where $p_{i,.}$ and $e_{.,j}$ denote the ith row vector of P and the jth column vector of E, respectively. Then, considering the instant loss $\varepsilon_{i,j}$ of $\varepsilon(P,E)$ on a single entry $w_{i,j}$, we define

$$
\varepsilon(i,j) = \beta \left(\begin{cases} \frac{1}{2}(w_{i,j} - p_{i,.}e_{.,j})^2, & \text{if } |w_{i,j} - p_{i,.}e_{.,j}| \leq \delta \\ \delta(|w_{i,j} - p_{i,.}e_{.,j}| - \frac{1}{2}\delta), & \text{otherwise} \end{cases} \right)
$$

$$
+ \lambda_{\text{reg}} ((p_{i,.})^2 + (e_{.,j})^2) + \lambda_1 \sum_m (L_{rw})_{im} (p_{i,.} - p_{m,.})^2 \quad (14)
$$

$$
+ \lambda_2 \sum_n (C_{temp})_{jn} (e_{.,j} - e_{.,n})^2
$$

The optimization with respect to top $p_{i,.}$ and $e_{.,j}$ can achieve it by the stochastic gradient descent (SGD) algorithm. Then, at the tth iteration, employ SGD to minimize (14) as follows:

$$
\begin{cases} p_{i,.}^t = p_{i,.}^{t-1} - \eta \dfrac{\partial \varepsilon_{i,j}^{t-1}}{\partial p_{i,.}^{t-1}} \\ e_{.,j}^t = e_{.,j}^{t-1} - \eta \dfrac{\partial \varepsilon_{i,j}^{t-1}}{\partial e_{.,j}^{t-1}} \end{cases} \quad (15)
$$

where $p_{i,.}^{t-1}$, $e_{.,j}^{t-1}$, and $\varepsilon_{i,j}^{t-1}$ denote the states of $p_{i,.}$, $e_{.,j}$, and $\varepsilon_{i,j}$ at the $(t-1)$th iteration, and η denotes the learning rate of SGD. Let $\Delta_{i,j}^{t-1} = w_{i,j} - p_{i,.}^{t-1} e_{.,j}^{t-1}$ be the estimation error on a single entry $w_{i,j}$ at the $(t-1)$th iteration. By combining (14) into (15), the updating rules of $p_{i,.}^t$ and $e_{.,j}^t$ on a single entry $w_{i,j}$ at the tth iteration are obtained as follows:

$$|\Delta_{i,j}^{t-1}| \le \delta \begin{cases} p'_{ik} = p'^{-1}_{ik} + \eta\beta\Delta_{i,j}^{t-1}e_{jk}^{t-1} - 2\eta\lambda_{\text{reg}}p_{ik}^{t-1} \\ -2\eta\lambda_1\sum_m(L_{\text{rw}})_{im}(p_{ik}^{t-1} - p_{mk}^{t-1}) \\ e'_{jk} = e_{jk}^{t-1} + \eta\beta\Delta_{i,j}^{t-1}p_{ik}^{t-1} - 2\lambda_{\text{reg}}e_{jk}^{t-1} \\ -2\lambda_2\sum_n(C_{\text{temp}})_{jn}(e_{jk}^{t-1} - e_{nk}^{t-1}) \end{cases} \qquad (16)$$

$$|\Delta_{i,j}^{t-1}| > \delta \begin{cases} p'_{ik} = p'^{-1}_{ik} + \eta\beta\delta \cdot \text{sgn}(\Delta_{i,j}^{t-1})e_{jk}^{t-1} \\ -2\lambda_{\text{reg}}p_{ik}^{t-1} - 2\lambda_1\sum_m(L_{\text{rw}})_{im}(p_{ik}^{t-1} - p_{mk}^{t-1}) \\ e'_{jk} = e_{jk}^{t-1} + \eta\beta\delta \cdot \text{sgn}(\Delta_{i,j}^{t-1})p_{ik}^{t-1} \\ -2\lambda_{\text{reg}}e_{jk}^{t-1} - 2\lambda_2\sum_n(C_{\text{temp}})_{jn}(e_{jk}^{t-1} - e_{nk}^{t-1}) \end{cases} \qquad (17)$$

where $\text{sgn}(\cdot)$ is the sign function, defined as:

$$\text{sgn}(x) = \begin{cases} 1, & x > 0 \\ -1, & x < 0 \end{cases} \qquad (18)$$

3.3   Theoretical Analysis

Error Bound Analysis with Huber-Spatiotemporal Regularization

Proposition 1. *The composite loss at iteration t combines Huber loss and spatiotemporal regularization:*

$$O_t^{H,ST} = \beta_t^H \mathcal{H}(J \circ (W - P_t E_t)) + \beta_t^{ST}\left(\lambda_1 tr(P^T L_{rw} P) + \lambda_2 tr(E^T C_{temp} E)\right) \qquad (19)$$

where $\mathcal{H}(\cdot)$ denotes Huber norm. The cumulative error $B_t^{H,ST} := \sum_{\omega=1}^t O_\omega^{H,ST}$ satisfies

$$B_T^{H,ST} \le \min B_T^H, B_T^{ST} + \ln 2\sqrt{\ln T} + \frac{T}{8\sqrt{\ln T}} \qquad (20)$$

Proof. Define potential function $F_t = e^{-\sigma B_t^H} + e^{-\sigma B_t^{ST}}$ with $\sigma = (1/\ln T)^{1/2}$. Through Hoeffding's inequality;

$$\ln\frac{F_T}{F_0} \le -\sigma B_T^{H,ST} + \frac{\sigma^2 T}{8} \qquad \le -\sigma \min B_T^H, B_T^{ST} - \ln 2 \qquad (21)$$

Rearranging terms yields the bound with $\sigma = \sqrt{1/\ln T}$.

Recovery Error Guarantee

Proposition 2. *For any corrupted matrix $H \in \mathbb{R}^{M \times N}$ satisfying $|H - \mathcal{P}(H)|_F \le \alpha|H|F$ $\alpha \in [0,1)$, the reconstruction error satisfies:*

$$|X - W|F \le \frac{\lambda\sqrt{2\,rank(W)} + z_1|LrwW|F + z_2|WCtemp|F}{1 - \alpha} \qquad (22)$$

where $\mathcal{P}(H) := \beta_1 J \circ sign(H) + \beta_2 J \circ H + z_1 LrwH + z_2 HCtemp$.

Proof. Apply KKT conditions to derive the reconstruction formula:

$$X = \text{SVT}_\lambda(W - \mathcal{P}(W)) \tag{23}$$

Use triangle inequality with SVT properties:

$$|X - W|_F \le \lambda\sqrt{2\text{rank}(W)} + |\mathcal{P}(W)|_F \tag{24}$$

Combine with spectral bounds for $\mathcal{P}(W)$.

Summary: The integration of Huber loss and spatiotemporal regularization ensures controlled cumulative errors ($\le \min B_T^H, B_T^{ST} + \mathcal{O}(\sqrt{\ln T})$) and bounded reconstruction error proportional to noise level and graph/temporal smoothness.

Table 1. Properties of Experimental Datasets.

No.	Name	$|\mathcal{M}|$	$|\mathcal{N}|$	Time	Minimum/Maximum
D1	Beijing PM2.5 concentration [1]	35	8647	2014-05–2015-04	3.0/773.7
D2	Beijing CO Concentration [42]	35	8647	2014-05–2015-04	0.1/20.0
D3	Sea surface Temperature [24]	70	1733	1976-01–2014-12	0.01/30.31
D4	Daily mean CO concentration [35]	74	365	2010-01–2010-12	0.1/2.9

4   Experiments

The experiments are designed to address the following research questions (RQs):

RQ.1. Does the proposed ALFA-FE model outperform state-of-the-art models in recovering missing data in WSNs?

RQ.2. How do noise data affect the performance of ALFA-FE and other recovery models?

RQ.3. How do different hyperparameter settings influence the performance of the proposed ALFA-FE model?

4.1   Experimental Setup

Datasets. To evaluate the performance of the proposed model, we select four benchmark datasets collected from real-world WSNs, including PM2.5, CO, and sea surface temperature. The key properties of these datasets are summarized in Table 1.

Evaluation Metrics. Mean absolute error (MAE) and root mean square error (RMSE) are widely used to assess predictive accuracy [17,23,31]. RMSE penalizes larger errors due to the squared term, making it suitable for scenarios where extreme deviations matter, while MAE treats all errors uniformly, providing a balanced evaluation [20,22,25,27,41]. In WSN missing data recovery, where outliers are common, the metric play a crucial role. The mathematical formulations are as follows:

$$
\mathrm{MAE} = \frac{\sum\limits_{w_{i,j} \in \Gamma} |w_{i,j} - \hat{w}_{i,j}|}{|\Gamma|}
$$

$$
\mathrm{RMSE} = \sqrt{\frac{\sum\limits_{w_{i,j} \in \Gamma} (w_{i,j} - \hat{w}_{i,j})^2}{|\Gamma|}}
$$

(25)

where $\hat{w}_{i,j}$ denotes the estimation of $w_{i,j}$ and Γ denotes the testing set, a lower value of RMSE/MAE indicates better accuracy.

Table 2. The comparison results of recovery accuracy on D1-D4.

Data	Metric	ST-LRMA	BR-TVGS	LRDS	RRImpu	L3F	TRSS	LFA-STSR	ALFA-FE
D1	MAE	12.3630±0.94	9.82±0.67	9.56±0.70	23.2691±1.09	13.8012±1.15	8.1215±1.50	8.2616±1.53	**7.9241±1.54**
	RMSE	22.7555±1.97	18.7477±1.01	18.0317±1.06	38.8918±1.50	25.35±1.04	16.2920±1.64	16.0696±1.64	**15.4539±1.62**
D2	MAE	0.1946±0.02	0.1658±0.02	0.1651±0.01	0.3027±0.02	0.2491±0.02	**0.1322±0.02♦**	0.1445±0.02	0.1393±0.01
	RMSE	0.4366±0.02	0.3777±0.01	0.3731±0.01	0.5507±0.02	0.5180±0.02	**0.3126±0.02♦**	0.3390±0.02	0.3220±0.02
D3	MAE	0.1268±0.02	0.1734±0.02	0.1260±0.01	0.4064±0.02	0.1255±0.02	0.1737±0.02	0.1207±0.0150	**0.1162±0.02**
	RMSE	0.1753±0.02	0.2438±0.01	0.1740±0.02	0.5449±0.01	0.1709±0.013	0.2444±0.03	0.1654±0.02	**0.16±0.02**
D4	MAE	0.1145±0.01	0.0981±0.01	0.0922±0.01	0.1064±0.01	0.0984±0.01	0.0919±0.01	0.0969±0.01	**0.0780±0.01**
	RMSE	0.1916±0.01	0.1585±0.01	0.1488±0.01	0.1667±0.01	0.1488±0.01	0.1478±0.01	0.1471±0.01	**0.1124±0.01**
Statistical	win/loss♦	8/0	8/0	8/0	8/0	8/0	6/2	8/0	âĂŤ
	p-value*	0.002	0.002	0.002	0.002	0.002	0.002	0.002	âĂŤ
Analysis	F-rank*	5.78	5.11	4.11	8.00	7.00	2.33	2.67	**1.00**

Baselines. The proposed ALFA-FE model is evaluated against seven state-of-the-art models, including ST-LRMA [25], BR-TVGS [27], RRImpu [22], L^3F [41], TRSS [7], and LFA-STSR [40]. A brief description of the competing models is provided in supplement document.

Experimental Details. To simulate missing data scenarios in WSNs, partial observations are randomly selected from the complete dataset to construct the training set, while the remaining observations are designated as the testing set. Within the training set, half of the data is utilized for model training, and the other half is reserved for performance validation and hyperparameter tuning. After determining the optimal hyperparameters, model retraining is performed using the entire training set. The maximum number of iterations is fixed at 1500, and early termination is triggered if the error difference between two consecutive iterations falls below 10^{-6}. Each experiment is conducted five times, and the average results are reported. All experiments are executed on a computing system equipped with a 3.4-GHz Intel i7 processor and 64 GB of RAM.

4.2   Performance Comparison (RQ.1)

The Recovery Accuracy of ALFA-FE. Comprehensive evaluations at a 0.8 sampling rate demonstrate superior reconstruction capability of ALFA-FE across four datasets, as shown in Table 2. Statistically significant improvements in both accuracy and stability are achieved, with MAE = 7.92 $\pm$ 1.54 and RMSE = 15.45 $\pm$ 1.62 on D1, surpassing LFA-STSR by 4.3% and 3.9%, respectively. On D4, MAE is reduced to 0.078 $\pm$ 0.006, marking a 15.1% improvement over TRSS (0.0919 $\pm$ 0.007). In D2, variance remains 50% lower than TRSS (0.139 $\pm$ 0.01 vs. 0.132 $\pm$ 0.02) while maintaining comparable accuracy. For temporal reconstruction in D3, RMSE reaches 0.1569 $\pm$ 0.0154, with 11.2% error reduction compared to LRDS (0.174 $\pm$ 0.0149). Dominance in pairwise comparisons is evident with 8/0 win-loss ratio, significant differentiation confirmed by Wilcoxon tests (p<0.002), and optimal Friedman ranking (F-rank=1.00 vs. TRSS=2.33). Despite slightly better D2 metrics (MAE=0.132 vs. 0.139), TRSS exhibits compromised robustness, reflected in 100% higher variance and inferior ranking. This systematic validation highlights the effectiveness of ALFA-FE in balancing precision-stability trade-offs through adaptive spatiotemporal regularization. Compared to TRSS, ALFA-FE yields the largest relative gain on D1 and D4, where sharp pollutant spikes are prevalent, indicating the benefit of Huber-based anomaly preservation. On smoother datasets like D3, the improvements are moderate, demonstrating Fourier embeddings' capacity to align with continuous temporal structures.

Comparison of Computational Efficiency. To evaluate the computational efficiency of all test models, we measured their CPU runtime across all datasets, as illustrated in Fig. 2. Besides, Analysis of computational complexity can be found in the supplementary document. In Our model generally achieves a lower CPU runtime compared to the baseline models, except in certain cases where L3F performs better. This is primarily due to the fact that our approach incorporates spatio-temporal smoothness characteristics, which are not considered in the L3F model.

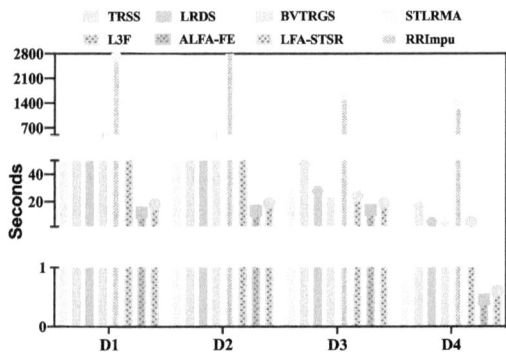

Fig. 2. The comparison CPU running time of involved models on D1–D4.

4.3   Robustness Analysis Under Noisy Conditions (RQ.2)

To rigorously evaluate the capability of ALFA-FE in handling heterogeneous anomalies and coupled noise-outlier interactions inherent in real-world WSN deployments, we design a structured noise injection protocol that emulates the spatiotemporal characteristics of sensor data corruption. The contamination process adheres to four principles: (a) Spatially randomized selection of observed entries to simulate uneven anomaly distribution across different district sensor arrays; (b) Value corruption via extremal substitution based on localized training subsets, replicating multimodal WSNs data distributions observed in Fig. 1b; (c) Controlled escalation of noise intensity from 10% to 50% contamination ratios to mimic progressive sensor degradation scenarios; (d) Strict isolation of noise injection to training data, preserving test set integrity for unbiased generalization assessment. As visualized in Fig. 4, our simulation framework preserves the baseline distribution (pink) while introducing context-aware outliers (orange) bounded by localized extremal thresholds (green). Quantitative analysis in Fig. 3 reveals that conventional low-rank models exhibit accelerated performance decay under rising contamination levels due to undifferentiated noise-anomaly processing. In contrast, our ALFA-FE framework demonstrates moderated accuracy degradation, maintaining 22% lower MAE than the best baseline at 50% noise ratio. The results confirm the dual capacity of ALFA-FE that is simultaneously recovering stable low-rank structures through Fourier-embedded manifolds

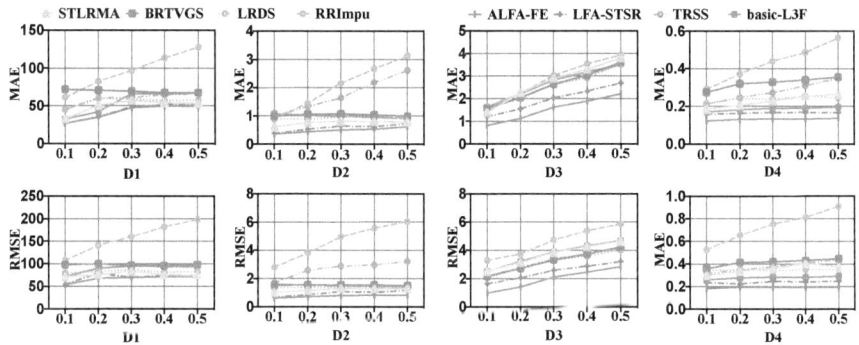

Fig. 3. Outlier data sensitivity tests on all the datasets.

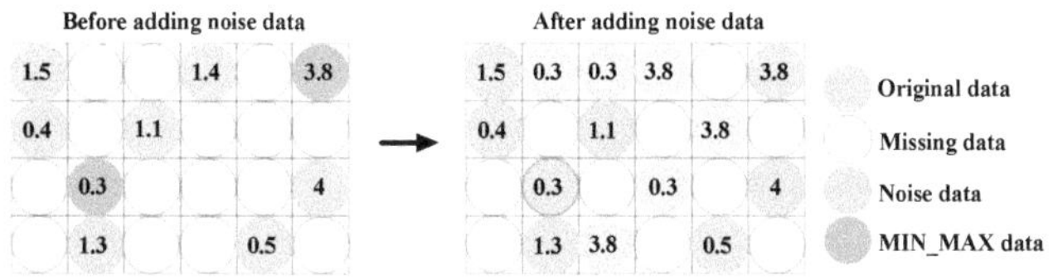

Fig. 4. An example of adding noise data. (Color figure online)

and protecting sensor-specific anomaly signatures via noise-outlier discriminative learning.

4.4 Effects by the Hyperparameters (RQ.3)

This section investigates the influence of *spatio-temporal regularization parameters* (λ_1 and λ_2) and the *latent factor dimension* (k) on model effectiveness. We systematically analyze their effects on reconstruction accuracy, stability, and adaptability to varying data patterns.

Trade-Off Analysis of Feature Dimensions. Increasing the feature dimension generally improves model recovery accuracy at the expense of increased computational time. At sampling rate of 0.9, we experimented with feature dimensions ranging from 5 to 80, and the results are presented in Fig. 5. The data indicate that both MAE and RMSE decrease as the feature dimension increases, until reaching a point beyond which further improvements become marginal. Furthermore, as analysised in Sect. 3.3 and corroborated by the violin plots in the accompanying figures, increasing the parameter k leads to a notable rise in time complexity. Therefore, a value of $k = 50$ is recommended to strike a balance between recovery accuracy and computational efficiency.

Impact of Spatiotemporal Regularization on Reconstruction Performance. Figure 6 illustrates the impact of spatiotemporal regularization on reconstruction performance under sampling rate of 0.1. A systematic parameter analysis reveals non-linear error responses to parameter variations: Incremental increases in λ_1 and λ_2 (ranging from 0.2 to 1.0) initially lead to a 14.5% reduction in MAE on dataset D3. However, beyond a critical threshold, further parameter augmentation results in performance deterioration. Dataset D4 achieves optimal performance at $\lambda_1 = 0.02$ and $\lambda_2 = 0.005$, yielding a minimum MAE of 0.1173. This result underscores the importance of balancing spatial and temporal regularization constraints to achieve optimal reconstruction accuracy. The interplay between spatial λ_1 and temporal λ_2 regularization parameters exhibits a complementary effect, where appropriately tuned values mitigate reconstruction errors

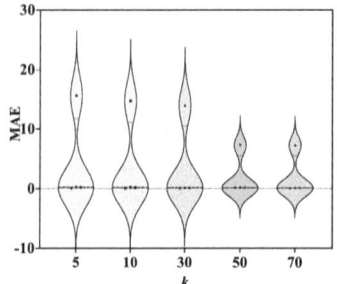 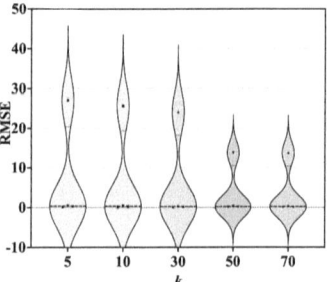

Fig. 5. The MAE/RMSE of ALFA-FE as k increases from 5 to 70 on all the datasets.

while preserving structural integrity. Overall, harmonized spatiotemporal regularization plays a pivotal role under conditions of limited sampling.

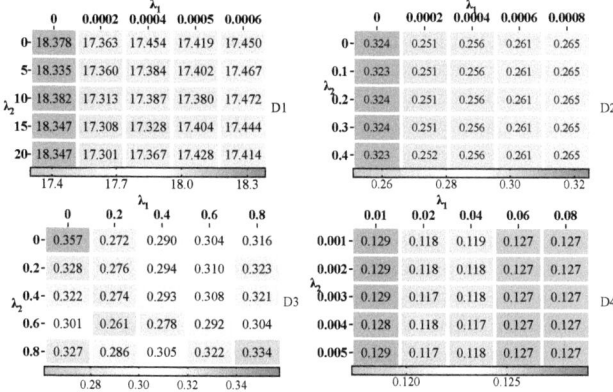

Fig. 6. The MAE of ALFA-FE with different λ_1 and λ_2 on all the datasets.

5 Conclusion

This article proposes ALFA-FE for robust spatiotemporal signal recovery in wireless sensor networks. Its main idea is twofold: 1) embedding Concatenated Fourier Features into temporal dynamics to improve the adaptability to non-stationary data patterns; 2) integrating the Huber norm with gradient descent optimization to enhance robustness against coupled noise and anomalies. By harmonizing frequency-domain regularization and adaptive robustness constraints, ALFA-FE possesses the merits of both dynamic representation learning and effective anomaly handling. In the experiments, ALFA-FE is evaluated on four benchmark datasets of varying scales from real-world WSNs. The results demonstrate that ALFA-FE significantly outperforms state-of-the-art methods in reconstruction accuracy and robustness under noisy conditions. Although ALFA-FE performs well, its deployment can be streamlined. Replacing fixed-rate SGD and grid search with adaptive optimizers (e.g., Adam) and automated tuning (e.g., Bayesian optimization) will cut training cost, while extending the framework to edge-friendly, decentralized updates and dynamic graphs will let it handle mobile or wireless WSNs and meet real-time, resource-limited constraints in large-scale IoT deployments.

References

1. Beijing Municipal Ecological and Environmental Monitoring Center: Beijing pm$_{2.5}$ data (2016). https://quotsoft.net/air/
2. Che, H., Pu, X., Ouyang, D., Li, B.: Enhanced tensorial self-representation subspace learning for incomplete multi-view clustering. In: Proceedings of the 32nd ACM International Conference on Multimedia, pp. 719–728 (2024)
3. Chen, Y., Chi, Y., Goldsmith, A.J.: Exact and stable covariance estimation from quadratic sampling via convex programming. IEEE Trans. Inf. Theory **61**(7), 4034–4059 (2015)
4. Dowlatshahi, M.B., Rafsanjani, M.K., Gupta, B.B.: An energy aware grouping memetic algorithm to schedule the sensing activity in WSNS-based IoT for smart cities. Appl. Soft Comput. **108**, 107473 (2021)
5. Fadhel, M.A., et al.: Comprehensive systematic review of information fusion methods in smart cities and urban environments. Inf. Fusion 102317 (2024)
6. Ghazal, T.M., Hasan, M.K., Alzoubi, H.M., Alshurideh, M., Ahmad, M., Akbar, S.S.: Internet of things connected wireless sensor networks for smart cities. In: The Effect of Information Technology on Business and Marketing Intelligence Systems, pp. 1953–1968. Springer, Cham (2023)
7. Giraldo, J.H., Mahmood, A., Garcia-Garcia, B., Thanou, D., Bouwmans, T.: Reconstruction of time-varying graph signalsvia sobolev smoothness. IEEE Trans. Signal Inf. Process. Netw. **8**, 201–214 (2022)
8. Gong, X., Yu, L., Wang, J., Zhang, K., Bai, X., Pal, N.R.: Unsupervised feature selection via adaptive autoencoder with redundancy control. Neural Netw. **150**, 87–101 (2022)
9. Goswami, P., Mukherjee, A., Sarkar, B., Yang, L.: Multi-agent-based smart power management for remote health monitoring. Neural Comput. Appl. **35**(31), 22771–22780 (2023)
10. Grover, A., Lall, B.: A recursive method for estimating missing data in spatio-temporal applications. IEEE Trans. Industr. Inf. **18**(4), 2714–2723 (2021)
11. He, X., Tang, J., Du, X., Hong, R., Ren, T., Chua, T.S.: Fast matrix factorization with nonuniform weights on missing data. IEEE Trans. Neural Netw. Learn. Syst. **31**(8), 2791–2804 (2019)
12. Kong, X., Wang, J., Hu, Z., He, Y., Zhao, X., Shen, G.: Mobile trajectory anomaly detection: taxonomy, methodology, challenges, and directions. IEEE Internet Things J. (2024)
13. Li, R., Zhou, G., Li, X., Jia, L., Shang, Z.: Semi-supervised multi-label dimensionality reduction learning based on minimizing redundant correlation of specific and common features. Knowl.-Based Syst. **294**, 111789 (2024)
14. Liu, F., Zhang, A., Du, R., Sun, G.: Structural sparse tensor robust PCA method based on cross-entropy for vehicular network data recovery. IEEE Trans. Veh. Technol. (2024)
15. Liu, H., Wang, P., Huang, L., Qu, Q., Balzano, L.: Symmetric matrix completion with relu sampling. In: Proceedings of the 41st International Conference on Machine Learning, ICML 2024. JMLR.org (2024)
16. Long, J., Wu, H.: Latent factor analysis enhanced graph contrastive learning for recommendation. In: 2024 IEEE International Conference on Systems, Man, and Cybernetics (SMC), pp. 547–552. IEEE (2024)
17. Luo, X., Wu, H., Wang, Z., Wang, J., Meng, D.: A novel approach to large-scale dynamically weighted directed network representation. IEEE Trans. Pattern Anal. Mach. Intell. **44**(12), 9756–9773 (2021)

18. Luo, X., Yuan, Y., Chen, S., Zeng, N., Wang, Z.: Position-transitional particle swarm optimization-incorporated latent factor analysis. IEEE Trans. Knowl. Data Eng. **34**(8), 3958–3970 (2020)

19. Majid, M., et al.: Applications of wireless sensor networks and internet of things frameworks in the industry revolution 4.0: a systematic literature review. Sensors **22**(6), 2087 (2022)

20. Mao, X., Qiu, K., Li, T., Gu, Y.: Spatio-temporal signal recovery based on low rank and differential smoothness. IEEE Trans. Signal Process. **66**(23), 6281–6296 (2018)

21. Miao, J., Kou, K.I.: Color image recovery using low-rank quaternion matrix completion algorithm. IEEE Trans. Image Process. **31**, 190–201 (2021)

22. Muzellec, B., Josse, J., Boyer, C., Cuturi, M.: Missing data imputation using optimal transport. In: International Conference on Machine Learning, pp. 7130–7140. PMLR (2020)

23. Pan, J., Gillis, N.: Generalized separable nonnegative matrix factorization. IEEE Trans. Pattern Anal. Mach. Intell. **43**(5), 1546–1561 (2019)

24. Physical Sciences Division, Earth System Research Laboratory, National Oceanic and Atmospheric Administration: Sea surface temperature (SST) v2 (2015). http://www.esrl.noaa.gov/psd/data/gridded/data.noaa.oisst.v2.html. Accessed 18 Dec 2015. [Online]

25. Piao, X., Hu, Y., Sun, Y., Yin, B., Gao, J.: Correlated spatio-temporal data collection in wireless sensor networks based on low rank matrix approximation and optimized node sampling. Sensors **14**(12), 23137–23158 (2014)

26. Qin, W., Luo, X., Li, S., Zhou, M.: Parallel adaptive stochastic gradient descent algorithms for latent factor analysis of high-dimensional and incomplete industrial data. IEEE Trans. Autom. Sci. Eng. (2023)

27. Qiu, K., Mao, X., Shen, X., Wang, X., Li, T., Gu, Y.: Time-varying graph signal reconstruction. IEEE J. Sel. Top. Signal Process. **11**(6), 870–883 (2017)

28. Rashid, B., Rehmani, M.H.: Applications of wireless sensor networks for urban areas: a survey. J. Netw. Comput. Appl. **60**, 192–219 (2016)

29. Sarkar, S., Sahay, R.R.: A non-local superpatch-based algorithm exploiting low rank prior for restoration of hyperspectral images. IEEE Trans. Image Process. **30**, 6335–6348 (2021)

30. Sharma, H., Haque, A., Blaabjerg, F.: Machine learning in wireless sensor networks for smart cities: a survey. Electronics **10**(9), 1012 (2021)

31. Shi, W., et al.: Effective prediction of missing data on apache spark over multivariable time series. IEEE Trans. Big Data **4**(4), 473–486 (2017)

32. Soares, C.A.R., de Souza Couto, R., Sztajnberg, A., do Amaral, J.L.M.: Posimnet-R: an immunologic resilient approach to position routers in industrial wireless sensor networks. Expert Syst. Appl. **188**, 116045 (2022)

33. Song, J., Xia, S., Wang, J., Patel, M., Chen, D.: Uncertainty quantification of hyperspectral image denoising frameworks based on sliding-window low-rank matrix approximation. IEEE Trans. Geosci. Remote Sens. **60**, 1–12 (2021)

34. Swami Durai, S.K., Duraisamy, B., Thirukrishna, J.: Certain investigation on healthcare monitoring for enhancing data transmission in WSN. Int. J. Wirel. Inf. Netw. **30**(1), 103–110 (2023)

35. United States Environmental Protection Agency: Air quality data (2016). https://www.epa.gov/outdoor-air-quality-data, [Online]

36. Wang, F., Xu, Z., Chen, J., Hu, R.: Semisupervised action recognition with adaptive correlation learning. Int. J. Mach. Learn. Cybern. 1–14 (2024)

37. Wang, J., Han, H., Li, H., He, S., Sharma, P.K., Chen, L.: Multiple strategies differential privacy on sparse tensor factorization for network traffic analysis in 5G. IEEE Trans. Industr. Inf. **18**(3), 1939–1948 (2021)
38. Wang, J., Ma, Z., Nie, F., Li, X.: Top-k discriminative feature selection with uncorrelated and ℓ2,0-norm equation constraints. Neurocomputing **598**, 128069 (2024)
39. Wang, Z.Y., So, H.C., Zoubir, A.M.: Robust low-rank matrix completion via sparsity-inducing regularizer. Signal Process. **226**, 109666 (2025)
40. Wu, D., Li, Z., Yu, Z., He, Y., Luo, X.: Robust low-rank latent feature analysis for spatiotemporal signal recovery. IEEE Trans. Neural Netw. Learn. Syst. (2023)
41. Wu, D., Shang, M., Luo, X., Wang, Z.: An l 1-and-l 2-norm-oriented latent factor model for recommender systems. IEEE Trans. Neural Netw. Learn. Syst. **33**(10), 5775–5788 (2021)
42. Xu, P., Ruan, W., Sheng, Q.Z., Gu, T., Yao, L.: Interpolating the missing values for multi-dimensional spatial-temporal sensor data: a tensor SVD approach. In: Proceedings of the 14th EAI International Conference on Mobile and Ubiquitous Systems: Computing, Networking and Services, MobiQuitous 2017, pp. 442–451. Association for Computing Machinery, New York (2017). https://doi.org/10.1145/3144457.3144474
43. Xu, Z., et al.: Lere: learning-based low-rank matrix recovery with rank estimation. In: Proceedings of the AAAI Conference on Artificial Intelligence, vol. 38, pp. 16228–16236 (2024)
44. Zhang, H., et al.: Learnable transform-assisted tensor decomposition for spatio-irregular multidimensional data recovery. ACM Trans. Knowl. Discov. Data **19**(1), 1–23 (2024)
45. Zhang, H., Wu, M., Feng, Q., Li, H.: Aerqp: adaptive embedding representation-based QoS prediction for web service recommendation. J. Supercomput. **80**(3), 3042–3065 (2024)
46. Zhang, R., et al.: Privacy-aware web APIS recommendation for consumer mashup creation based on iterative quantification. IEEE Trans. Consum. Electron. (2024)

Understanding Rumen Methanogen Interactions in Sheep Using Machine Learning

Katharina Dost[1,2(✉)], Steffen Albrecht[2], Paul Maclean[3], Jörg Wicker[2], and Sandeep K. Gupta[3]

[1] Jožef Stefan Institute, Ljubljana, Slovenia
`katharina.dost@ijs.si`
[2] University of Auckland, Auckland, New Zealand
`{steffen.albrecht,j.wicker}@auckland.ac.nz`
[3] Bioeconomy Science Institute, AgResearch, Grasslands, New Zealand
`{paul.maclean,sandeep.gupta}@agresearch.co.nz`

Abstract. Methane emissions from livestock pose a significant challenge globally, particularly in countries with a strong farming industry dominated by sheep farming, such as Aotearoa, New Zealand (NZ). Chemical inhibitors such as feed additives or vaccines help to decrease methane emissions. However, their successful development has been hindered by a limited understanding of the complex interactions among the microorganisms in the rumen (forestomach). This study serves as a proof-of-concept to explore the potential of using metatranscriptome data to understand the genetic basis of microbial interactions in the rumen and identify potential inhibitor targets. We analyzed a small but carefully curated dataset of 10 sheep emitting different levels of methane. We employed various statistical and machine learning techniques to uncover new contigs (continuous sequences of DNA) linked to high levels of methane output. Despite the limited sample size, our findings revealed new insights into microbial mechanisms, validated by domain experts. These preliminary results suggest that expanding the dataset and integrating machine learning can enhance our understanding of the complex microbial interactions in the rumen, ultimately contributing to the development of effective strategies to reduce methane emissions in livestock.

Keywords: Livestock Methane Emission · Chemical Inhibitors · Microbial Interactions · Applied Machine Learning

1 Introduction

Methane emissions from farmed animals pose a significant environmental challenge, contributing to global warming [23]. In Aotearoa New Zealand (NZ), these emissions are particularly pronounced, with livestock methane accounting for $\sim 35\%$ of the country's greenhouse gas output [13].

© The Author(s), under exclusive license to Springer Nature Switzerland AG 2026
B. Pfahringer et al. (Eds.): ECML PKDD 2025, LNAI 16020, pp. 253–269, 2026.
https://doi.org/10.1007/978-3-662-72243-5_15

To reduce the methane output in livestock, researchers have tested targeted breeding, leading to successfully lowered emissions; however, the genetic long-term impacts are uncertain [13]. An alternative is the administration of chemical inhibitors – substances that slow down or completely stop chemical reactions or biological processes – via feed additives [21] or vaccines [1] that specifically target the growth of methanogens. Methanogens are the main organisms responsible for producing methane in ruminants, but they rely on other microorganisms in the rumen for their survival. Therefore, understanding their interactions with other microorganisms in the rumen will help develop new ways to target them.

Developing an effective vaccine or feed additive is now a key goal for scientists, industry, and the government in NZ, but it has proven challenging due to limited knowledge of the complex interactions of the methanogens with the other microbial population in the rumen. Machine learning could help in dissecting these complex interactions and identify the specific genes of methanogens responsible for their interactions with other microbes in the rumen. The understanding of these complex genetic interactions can lead to the development of novel avenues to target methane production in ruminants.

As a proof-of-concept, we use a sheep rumen metatranscriptome dataset [26] gathered in NZ (10 sheep x 2 sampling days, yielding a total of 20 samples) to enhance our understanding of rumen microbial interactions and to identify promising contigs, continuous sequences of DNA, for further investigation. Although small for machine learning tasks, the sample size is considered large in the field, and it is sufficient as the involved sheep have been hand-selected for this task – the dataset contains sheep with low, intermediate and high methane output, which enables us to investigate the differences in interactions between contigs. This is the first study using metatranscriptome data in a sheep rumen context, but it has shown great potential for the human microbiome [28]. To the best of our knowledge, it is also the first study to apply advanced machine learning approaches to analyze metatranscriptome data from the rumen of low/intermediate/high methane-yielding sheep in general. Particularly, this is also the first study to analyze our dataset. Upon success, this study may lead to a substantially larger sample collection, yielding the foundation for inhibitor development.

Particularly, we seek to answer the following questions:

1. Hypothesis and data validation: Is there a connection between contig counts and methane output in sheep? Is it manifested in our sample?
2. Narrowing down the search: Which contigs play a role in methane production beyond methanogens?
3. Understanding patterns: Are there groups of contigs that act together?
4. Identifying causal relationships in the rumen: Are some of the identified relationships causal?

To address these questions, we employ various statistical and machine learning techniques to uncover potential drivers responsible for low or high methane production in the same breed of sheep. Despite challenges due to the small sample size, our analysis managed to provide interesting and promising insights.

Due to intellectual property (IP) restrictions, only anonymized contigs without annotations can be made publicly available alongside the paper. However, we acknowledge the need for additional data and research to validate these findings and to obtain more robust results.

Section 3 describes our dataset, Sect. 2 reviews related approaches in the literature, and Sect. 4 uses both to answer the above questions. Section 5 concludes the paper.

2   Related Research

A large body of research has been dedicated to understanding genetic interactions and revealing genetic functions in different organisms in complex communities. We provide a brief, non-exhaustive overview of approaches related to this project.

Analyzing Metatranscriptome Data: Metatranscriptome data is obtained via RNA sequencing and captures gene expression profiles of organisms within a complex microbial community. It is typically analyzed by mapping to reference genomes [20, 24] or assembly [12], which provide, among other benefits, a natural grouping, an on-gene distance metric, or insights into some specific functionalities [25, 28]. However, we are only provided with contig counts but no contig meta-information, such as genetic annotations, making such a mapping infeasible for our dataset.

Finding Genetic Interactions: To investigate contig-contig interactions, we use concepts from gene interaction or co-expression networks in which nodes are typically defined as genes, and edges are the interaction strength between adjacent nodes. This interaction strength can be defined via correlation [22], assembly graph similarities [16], or structural similarities [7]. Given our dataset, correlation is the only option as it does not require auxiliary contig information, and we include it in our analysis. Cui *et al.* [6] detect genetic interactions by capturing them in a neural network using Shapley Taylor interaction indices. We include an adapted version in our analysis.

Investigating the Rumen Microbiome in Livestock: Söllinger *et al.* [27] used quantitative metatranscriptomics with gas and volatile fatty acid profiling to investigate methanogen interactions and effects within the rumen of Holstein cows. Rather than observing natural differences between animals, the authors designed a targeted experiment allowing them to observe abundance fluctuations over time that can be linked to a specific feeding pattern. Their work follows a different path to identifying active methanogens and is not applicable to our dataset. Li *et al.* [18] investigate the breed effect on the rumen microbiome in beef cattle using metagenomics and metatranscriptomics. The authors compare observed abundancies with statistical analysis using t-tests and link these differences to feed efficiency. Our analysis extends beyond this approach using a machine learning perspective.

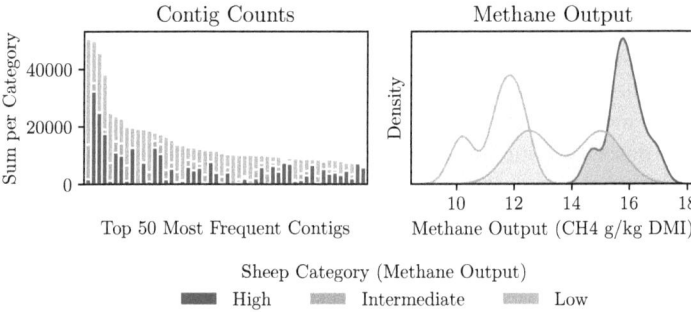

Fig. 1. Basic dataset statistics: contig counts per 1M contigs per sample, summed up per methane output category (left) and methane output distribution per sample (right)

3 Dataset Description

The dataset used in this study consists of metatranscriptome data, which represents the collection of RNA sequences from the microbial community in the sheep rumen. This data helps us understand which genes are active and what functions the microbes are performing in relation to methane production.

To obtain this data, 10 sheep with varying methane outputs were sampled on two distinct days. Specifically, RNA was extracted from the rumen of low (4), high (4), and intermediate (2) methane-yielding sheep, sampled on two dates with a 14-day gap in New Zealand. This RNA is then sequenced, producing "reads," short fragments of RNA sequences that serve as snapshots of the gene expression activity within the microbial community at the time of sampling.

The raw sequencing reads often contain errors or low-quality segments, which are first trimmed[1]. After cleaning, the reads are assembled into longer, contiguous sequences ("contigs")[2]. Contigs provide a clearer picture of which genes are being expressed and can then be used to explore how microbial activity in the rumen contributes to methane production, offering insights that could inform predictive models or strategies to reduce methane emissions in livestock. As Fig. 1 (left) highlights, some contigs are found in the samples with high frequency, while others are rarely found. Overall, there are differences in the abundance of specific contigs for sheep with different methane output levels.

To assign equal weight to all samples in subsequent tasks, we normalize the raw contig counts per sample and express them as "counts per million". Contigs with counts per million less than one for all samples were subsequently removed, leaving $686,456$ contigs.

---

[1] Reads are trimmed with Trimmomatic version 0.39.

[2] Trimmed reads are assembled into contigs using MEGAHIT version 1.2.9 with default parameters. The alignment of trimmed reads from each metatranscriptome sample to the MEGAHIT assembly was performed using the bwa aligner version 0.7.17-r1188. Aligned reads with a mapping quality of 30, indicating a 1 in 1000 chance of misalignment, were extracted using Samtools version 1.17.

Table 1. Overview of datasets used in this project after preprocessing

Table "Methane Output" Columns (20×5-dimensional)	
SampleID	Unique identifier per sample that matches the SampleID in other tables
Sheep#	Unique identifier per sheep used for training/test splits
CH_4	Average daily methane emission (in g)
CH_4 / DMI	Average daily methane emission (in g) per Dry Matter Intake (in kg)
	(feed consumed per day on a moisture-free basis)
Methane Class	Categorization based on methane output (low/intermediate/high)
Table "Contigs" Columns ($686,456 \times 21$-dimensional)	
ContigID	Unique identifier per contig
Counts $SampleID_1$	Contig counts for sample with ID_1
Counts ...	...
Counts $SampleID_{20}$	Contig counts for sample with ID_{20}

The contigs could further be annotated with corresponding genes, biological roles and functions, or (groups of) organisms from which the contig originated by comparing the sequences to known databases. However, due to IP restrictions, we cannot disclose the annotated contigs but use unique identifiers instead. Using these ContigIDs, we are able to make this dataset, as well as the code for our analysis, publicly available alongside the paper in our repository[3].

In addition to the RNA samples, we measure the sheep's methane output, CH_4, by placing them in separate sealed chambers (respiration chambers) where their breath is monitored over a day. Multiple measurements (two to three days) per sheep were taken to mitigate measurement errors, and we averaged these results. Standard deviations were found to be very low, justifying the choice of averaging. Since the methane output is highly correlated with the sheep's food intake, we also monitor the Dry Matter Intake (DMI) of the sheep during their stay in the respiration chambers. Subsequently, we use the raw methane output in grams per kilogram DMI for our analysis, i.e., CH_4 g/kg DMI, and refer to it as methane output. This entire sampling procedure was repeated for the same sheep two weeks later to rule out anomalies, leading to a total of 20 samples (10 sheep $\times$ 2 measurement rounds). Figure 1 (right) illustrates the distribution of methane output per sample.

The two measurement rounds per sheep are generally considered separate training instances in this analysis due to the small dataset size. When splitting the data into training and test sets for evaluation, however, we make sure to randomly select sheep, not the individual measurements. After filtering the rel-

---

[3] Our repository: https://github.com/KatDost/Sheep_Methane_Paper.

evant columns, we obtain the datasets described in Table 1 that can be joined on a shared ID.

The number of contigs counted per sample varies, reflecting differences in the sizes of the rumen samples. This variation may introduce bias when analyzing the data. To address this issue, we employ counts per million (CPM) normalization, which normalizes the counts per sample, mitigating the imbalance between samples. Furthermore, as is common in the field, the counts are then rounded to the nearest integer, suppressing measurement noise. This normalization technique ensures that each sample's contribution to the overall analysis is proportional to the contigs' share, not their absolute count, facilitating fair comparisons across samples.

4   Methods and Results

After preprocessing our dataset, we address the questions listed in the introduction, drawing inspiration and incorporating approaches from the related research projects discussed above.

4.1   Hypothesis and Data Validation

As a first step, we validate the existence of a connection between contig counts and methane output and the presence of meaningful signals within our dataset. We use various regression models to predict the methane output from the contig counts and evaluate their performance.

To identify suitable hyperparameters for each model while guarding against overfitting, we employ a rough hyperparameter grid search methodology using HalvingGridSearchCV [14,19]. Based on the grid search results, we decided to include the following regressors in the test: Linear Regression, Lasso Regression with $\alpha = 9339.46$, *Support Vector Regression (SVR)* with the nonlinear RBF kernel, $\gamma = 0.01$ and $C = 1000$, *Decision Tree (DT)* with different maximum depths (3 and 4), *Random Forest (RF)* with varying maximum depths (3 and 4) and 20 trees, and XGBoost [4] with 20 trees and learning rate $= 0.1$.

Employing 5-fold cross-validation, we assess the predictive capability of these models on our dataset based on *Mean Absolute Error (MAE)* for the sake of its interpretability. Mean Absolute Percentage Error (MAPE) showed similar patterns and is hence excluded. These metrics were computed for both training and test sets to gauge model performance and are presented in Fig. 2 (left).

We observe that despite our efforts in hyperparameter tuning, all models overfit the training data. This overfitting can be attributed to the stark disparity between the small sample size and the vast number of features. The limited number of samples relative to the high dimensionality of the feature space poses a significant challenge for the models to generalize effectively.

The machine learning models generally demonstrate MAE values below the baseline model, always predicting the average methane output, with the exception of SVR. However, it is worth noting that there is a significant standard

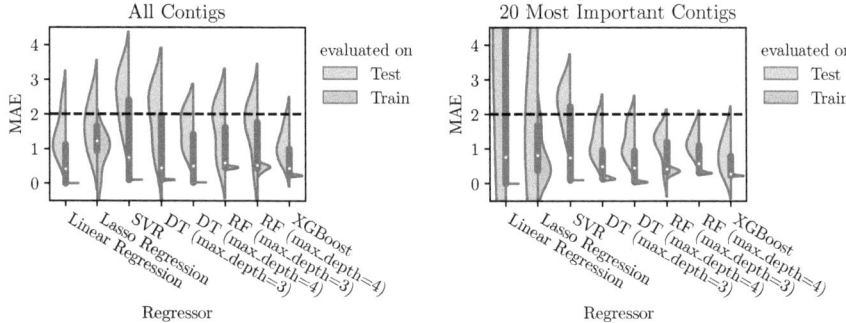

Fig. 2. MAE for multiple regressors predicting methane output trained on all features/contigs (left) and a selection of the 20 most important features based on a pretrained RF (right) for training and test set individually. The dashed black line serves as a baseline (always predict the average methane output).

deviation among folds, indicating variability in model performance that can be traced back to the small test set sizes in each fold. Linear regression performs better than the tree-based methods, leading us to suspect an adverse effect due to many highly correlated features (see our repository for Pearson correlations).

To disentangle the high correlation among contigs, we train a RF on each fold's training set and use its feature importance to select the most important features. This approach chooses a set of features (in our case, contigs) that is highly informative for the model, which mitigates high correlations by design as they would carry duplicate information. We observe a natural drop in feature importance after the 20 most important features for each fold and drop the rest before repeating the above experiment. Figure 2 (right) shows the results. While the feature selection harms the regression methods, the tree-based ones benefit largely, which may be attributed to the tree-based feature importance. We further observe that the feature selection decreases the test error substantially more than the training error, which confirms that the size of the input space is significantly contributing to the overfitting, in addition to the small dataset size. Although the models still overfit, they demonstrate a performance well below baseline, indicating that there is indeed a relationship between contig counts and methane output, validating our hypothesis.

In conclusion, while our analysis suggests the presence of a signal in the data, the small sample size, in contrast to the large number of contigs, imposes limitations on our machine learning approach to analyzing the dataset.

4.2   Identifying Essential Contigs

We can expect our dataset to contain a large number of contigs with auxiliary functions that do not play a role in methane production and are, therefore, irrelevant to this study. However, there may be non-methanogen contigs that do

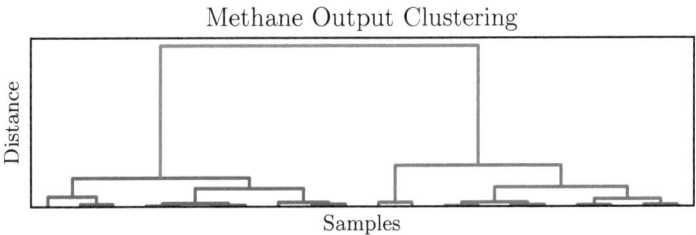

Fig. 3. Hierarchical clustering (Ward linkage) of samples based on their methane output

contribute to methane production by interacting with the methanogens in the rumen. These are the contigs we aim to identify as they provide new insights.

As evident from the previous section, predicting the raw methane output as a regression task is challenging. This can be attributed to the small sample size: Variations in methane output can either be due to (i) measurement noise (sheep are not particularly compliant with our scientific endeavors) and the sample size is insufficient to obtain a fair estimate of the underlying distribution, or (ii) the variations are true signals, and the sample size is too small to capture these signals accurately. We choose to simplify the prediction task by converting it to a binary problem to alleviate the impact of the above issues.

To obtain binary labels, we cluster the samples hierarchically based on their methane output and observe two clearly defined groups as illustrated in Fig. 3: high and low methane output samples. Note that these groups do not match the "Methane Class" categorization the dataset was originally annotated with (see Table 1 – "Methane Output"). Our hierarchical clustering reveals that there is no natural third group with "medium" methane output.

Upon training an initial decision tree classifier, we uncover decision stumps that can perfectly distinguish between low and high methane output. One example is shown in Fig. 4 (left), where a single contig suffices to discern between the two output categories, a surprising discovery. We adopt an iterative approach to tally the number of contigs with this distinguishing property, sequentially removing the contig used for the stump and retraining a new stump. This method identifies 348 contigs capable of perfectly differentiating between low and high methane output.

Motivated by these findings, we scrutinize whether these contigs represent statistically significant discoveries or mere chance occurrences. To this end, we conduct pairwise t-tests for each contig, comparing the corresponding contig counts between samples with high and low methane output. Figure 4 (right) showcases the number of contigs exhibiting significantly different values for low and high methane output samples under specified p-values. We denote these contigs as *"supercontigs"* for brevity. Subsequently, we typically limit our analysis to supercontigs.

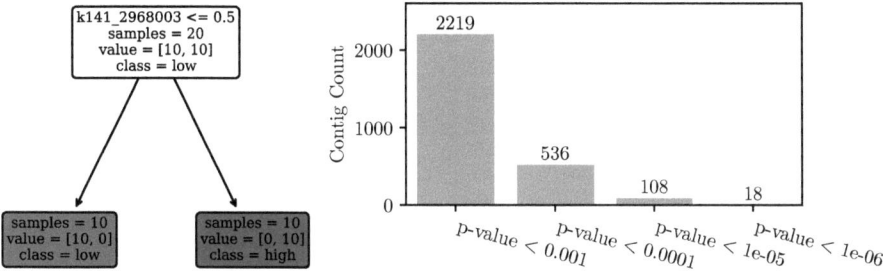

Fig. 4. Left: Decision Tree to predict high (10) and low (10) methane output using all contigs. There are 348 contigs, such as k141_2968003, that can distinguish **perfectly** between both classes. **Right:** Zoom-in on p-values for pairwise t-tests on contig counts for the cohorts high/low methane output: Displayed is the number of contigs for which the p-value lies below a specific threshold.

In conclusion, we have identified a set of contigs that play a substantial role in the sheeps' methane production. These findings are statistically significant under specified significance levels. Interestingly, our set of supercontigs contains methanogens as well as non-methanogens.

4.3 Understanding Patterns

In the previous sections, we narrowed down the set of contigs that are involved in the methanogen cycle in sheep, but we have also observed high correlations among contigs. Naturally, we seek to investigate which of the relevant contigs act together, and which ones drive different mechanisms. We explore three different approaches to find groups of contig interactions, i.e., community search in a correlation network, non-negative matrix factorization, and neural networks with Shapley Taylor interaction index [6,9] values. These approaches are not to be seen as competing but as different perspectives on the same question. The groups identified by different approaches will likely be different but can all be of interest to a domain expert and collectively help the understanding of rumen methanogen mechanisms.

Community Search in a Contig Network. We construct a contig-contig interaction network as follows: Each contig is a node. Each pair of contigs is connected by an edge indicating the p-value of a pairwise t-test between the counts of the contigs represented by the adjacent nodes. Using the Louvain method [2], we detect communities of highly interacting contigs within the network. Figure 5 shows an example. Although the displayed interactions are statistically significant, we observe an unwelcome chain effect: If $C_1 \leftrightarrow C_2$ and $C_2 \leftrightarrow C_3$ are significant interactions, we frequently observe a community containing C_1, C_2, C_3, although $C_1 \nleftrightarrow C_3$ is *not* necessarily a significant interaction.

p-Value-Based Interaction Communities (p-value > 0.9)

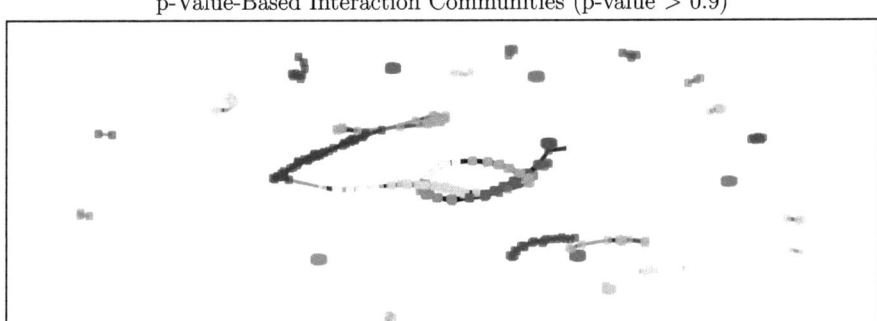

Fig. 5. Louvain-communities (colors) in a pairwise t-test-based contig interaction network. Edges with p-values < 0.9 as well as isolated nodes have been removed. Annotations are omitted to enhance readability.

Matrix Factorization. We employ *non-negative matrix factorization (NMF)* [17] to uncover latent structures and patterns within high-dimensional data, facilitating the identification of groups of similarly acting contigs and aiding in the interpretation of complex relationships between contig counts and methane output levels.

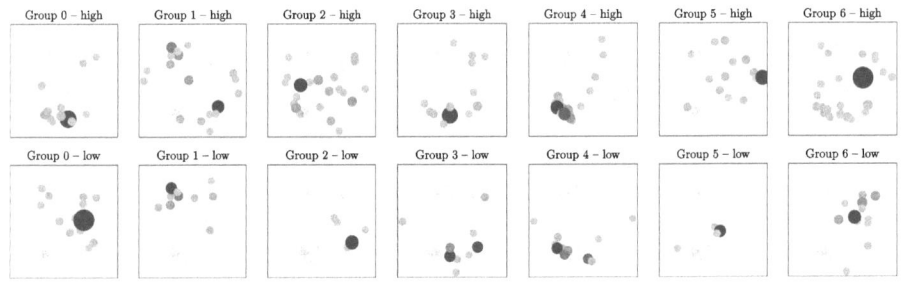

Fig. 6. NMF has been applied separately for samples with high and low methane output. Each point corresponds to a contig in MDS space. We included only supercontigs with $p < 10^{-4}$. Group members are colored; darker colors correspond to stronger group membership.

Given a matrix X, matrix factorization aims to find two matrices of lower dimensionality whose product approximates X as closely as possible. We use NMF to find mechanisms of contig behavior, i.e., groups of contigs that operate together and exhibit similar patterns by factorizing the Sample x Contig Count matrix into A (of dimension #samples$\times l$) and B (of dimension $l\times$ #contigs). The number of groups, l, is often referred to as the latent dimension and is a parameter that needs to be tuned.

Since both factors typically have a smaller dimension, the input matrix usually cannot be reconstructed perfectly, and the factors necessarily have to focus on the most important information and neglect minor variations, suppressing noise. Following the definition of matrix multiplication, the factors group rows with similar patterns since they trigger the same columns in the corresponding factor and vice versa. These groups can overlap (which distinguishes matrix factorization from standard clustering and our network community search). NMF offers nonnegative numbers expressing the strength of group memberships.

We restrict our analysis to contigs that exhibit significant differences for high and low methane outputs at a significance level of 1e-05, acknowledging the adjustability of this parameter for future experiments. Each sample is rescaled independently such that its L2 norm equals one. This normalization step is crucial to ensure each sample is considered equally.

Next, we tune the latent dimension l by maximizing the cophenetic correlation coefficient – a measure of how faithfully a dendrogram preserves pairwise distances in the original data—and select $l = 7$. We construct separate sample×contig count matrices for high and low-methane-outputting sheep and perform matrix factorization on both.

To visually represent the identified contig groups, we train a 2-dimensional embedding space using *multi-dimensional scaling (MDS)* [3,8]. An embedding space is a low-dimensional representation of high-dimensional data that preserves its inherent structure and relationships. We use MDS to position the contigs in a plot using their pairwise correlation as a similarity measure ($1 - |\text{correlation}|$ as a distance). That means close contigs are highly correlated (positively or negatively), whereas distant contigs have a low correlation.

The identified contig groups are illustrated in Fig. 6, where distinct interactions are observed for low and high methane-outputting sheep. We can observe changes in group memberships in high and low methane producing sheep and that these identified groups often stretch beyond clusters of highly correlated contigs, which has the potential to reveal interesting insights. Domain experts investigated annotated versions of these plots (that we have to omit due to IP restrictions) and confirmed this.

Neural Networks with Shapley Taylor Interaction Index. To find different contig groups and uncover interactions between these groups, we adapt the methodology proposed by Cui *et al.* [6]. The authors proposed a framework for detecting genetic interactions by considering all single nucleotide polymorphisms (SNPs) within selected genes and their complex relationships. They developed a deep learning architecture that captures these interactions using Shapley scores between hidden nodes representing genes. Their approach successfully identified significant interactions in real-world datasets and hence offers a promising avenue for us. However, since the authors use an existing mapping from SNPs to genes, the approach cannot directly be transferred to this study.

Instead, we allow the model to learn the contig grouping instead of initializing it with prior knowledge, as we lack predefined mappings. Our model architecture

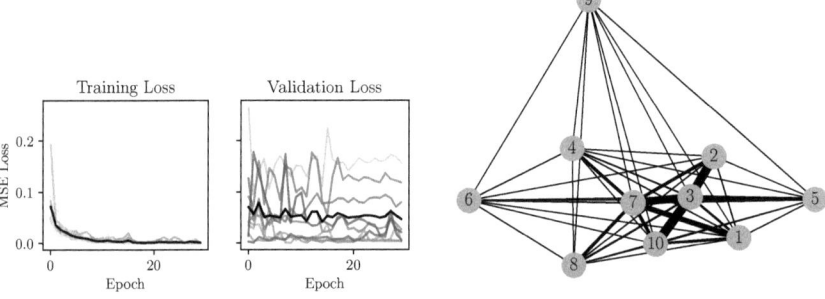

Fig. 7. Neural Network using contig groups. **Left:** Training and validation loss show poor learning performance – **the results of this neural network cannot be trusted! Right:** Nodes are groups of contigs. Edges indicate interactions between connected groups. Edge thickness displays the strength of the interaction.

consists of a sparse layer, a linear layer with softplus activation, and a linear output layer. The sparse layer creates a bottleneck to group contigs, akin to mapping single nucleotide polymorphisms (SNPs) to genes in the original framework.

We present the training and validation loss per epoch in Fig. 7 (left). We observe that the network does not train properly, as can be seen from the validation loss. We attribute this to the small sample size but include the results regardless since the approach is promising and can be reused in larger datasets.

We emphasize that results derived from this trained model cannot be considered reliable! However, for the sake of demonstration, we search for interactions between contig groups post-training using the *Shapley Taylor Interaction Index* [9]. Attribution or feature importance for neural networks generally measures the contribution of individual features to a prediction. The Shapley value measures the change in model prediction when a specific feature is included or omitted. The Shapley Taylor index identifies to what extent a set of features exert influence in conjunction as opposed to independently. Thereby, we obtain strong interactions between pairs (or higher-order groups) of features. Figure 7 (right) shows the identified interactions between groups. We have to omit the annotated version of the plot due to IP limitations.

We conclude that this network is too complex given our small sample size, and decide to drop the sparse layer. This way, we will find contig-contig interactions instead of group interactions. Although not a grouping per se, these interactions also provide us with information on contigs acting together. This network is training well – Training and validation loss are converging conjointly on all leave-one-sheep-out runs (see our repository for details). We can, therefore, expect more reliable results than previously.

As before, we carry out a post-training interaction search using the Shapley Taylor interaction index. The identified interaction network is presented in Fig. 8. We suggest filtering interactions involving specific contigs of interest when

Shapley Taylor Interactions

Zoom-In

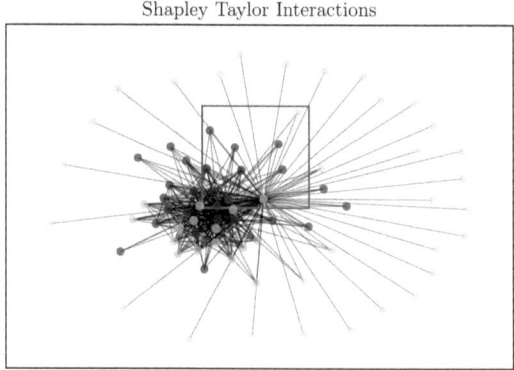
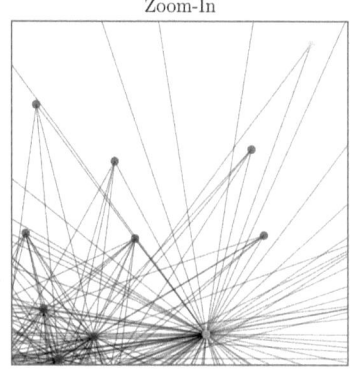

Fig. 8. Interactions between contigs identified using the Shapley Taylor interaction index with interaction strength > 0.5. The right image shows a zoom-in on a part of the left figure to reveal more detailed interactions. We included only supercontigs with $p < 10^{-4}$.

analyzing this result. We observe a densely interacting group of contigs. The surrounding ones, however, interact with only a few contigs.

4.4   Identifying Causal Relationships in the Rumen

Lastly, we seek to find stronger relationships than interactions – we are searching for causal relationships between contigs as well as between contigs and the methane output. Contigs causing an increase or decrease in methane production can be the key to designing injections that mitigate methane production in ruminants.

Initially, we normalize the data such that each sample's contig counts add up to 1. We then establish a graph skeleton using the *Graphical LASSO (GLASSO)* [10] technique. This skeleton serves as a scaffold for subsequent causal inference and reduces the computational burden.

To find causal relationships within the constructed skeleton, we employ a number of algorithms from the Causal Discovery Toolbox [15] (see the package documentation for details on the methods and the original references): Greedy Equivalence Search, *Peter-Clark (PC) Algorithm* [5], Greedy Interventional Equivalence Search, Linear Non-Gaussian Acyclic model, and Structural Agnostic Model. None of these methods identified any causal relationships within our dataset, except for the PC algorithm. PC is a score-based approach for causal discovery based on conditional tests on variables and sets of variables that is quite popular [11] and allows us to set the significance level α for the individual conditional independence tests and make up for the small sample size.

As depicted in Fig. 9, PC identified a number of causal relationships between contigs (left), but also between contigs and the methane output (right), revealing potential drivers of methane production in the rumen microbiome.

Causality Graph: PC Algorithm ($\alpha = 0.1$)   Causality Graph: PC Algorithm ($\alpha = 0.4$)

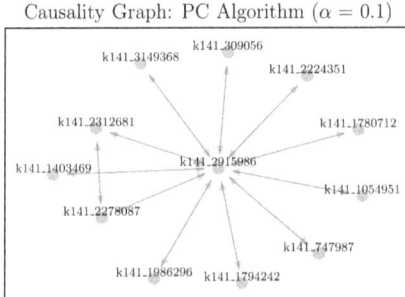 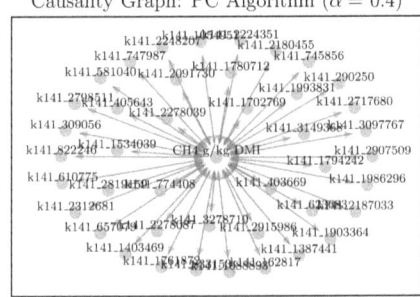

Fig. 9. Causal relationships between contigs (left) as well as between contigs and the methane output (right) using the Peter-Clark Algorithm. We included only supercontigs with $p < 10^{-4}$.

4.5 Validation

Our project is of exploratory nature, aiming to provide new insights to domain experts. Many of our results are backed up by what is already common knowledge in the fields. In addition, we revealed a number of previously unknown mechanisms that will be subject to further experimental and theoretical investigation by domain experts on the path to developing new chemical inhibitors.

5 Conclusion

As a proof-of-concept on the way to developing new chemical inhibitors for livestock to reduce their methane emissions, in this project, we aimed to explore and understand the genetic basis of the complex interplay between rumen microbes and methane production in livestock using machine learning.

Our findings are based on a small rumen metatranscriptome dataset gathered in-house from 10 sheep on two sampling days by domain experts, yielding 20 samples. Although small, the sample size is sufficient to indicate whether there is a signal in the data or not. We approached this project with a number of different statistical and machine learning techniques, identifying potential molecular drivers of methane production, with several contigs emerging as strong candidates for further investigation. Our domain experts confirmed that our results are reasonable and reveal new and interesting mechanisms.

Looking ahead, to augment our understanding of rumen microbial interactions and methane production, a larger-scale subsequent experiment could benefit from additional samples (particularly from a larger number of individual animals, but also from other ruminant species such as cattle and deer). Increasing the dataset size will enhance the reliability of machine learning models and support the training process, making it possible to train more complex models than were used in this study.

Integrating metadata on the contigs, such as their molecular structure or existing relationships, could help define a graph and open the field for graph neural networks, even on relatively small datasets.

In conclusion, this project is a step towards utilizing machine learning approaches to understand the complex interactions affecting methane production in ruminant livestock.

Acknowledgments. This study was funded by the Ministry of Business, Innovation & Employment, New Zealand (MBIE number C10X2201 awarded to SKG). KD and JW have received research funding from AgResearch, New Zealand. Although their identities are unknown to us, we would like to thank the reviewers of this paper. We found great value in the provided comments.

Disclosure of Interests. The authors have no competing interests to declare that are relevant to the content of this article.

Data and Software Availability. Data, software, and experimental scripts able to reproduce all results presented in this article are available in our repository at https://github.com/KatDost/Sheep_Methane_Paper.

References

1. Baca-González, V., Asensio-Calavia, P., González-Acosta, S., Pérez de la Lastra, J.M., Morales de la Nuez, A.: Are vaccines the solution for methane emissions from ruminants? A systematic review. Vaccines **8**(3) (2020). https://doi.org/10.3390/vaccines8030460
2. Blondel, V.D., Guillaume, J.L., Lambiotte, R., Lefebvre, E.: Fast unfolding of communities in large networks. J. Stat. Mech. Theory Exp. **2008**(10), P10008 (2008). https://doi.org/10.1088/1742-5468/2008/10/P10008
3. Cannistraci, C.V., Alanis-Lobato, G., Ravasi, T.: Minimum curvilinearity to enhance topological prediction of protein interactions by network embedding. Bioinformatics **29**(13), i199–i209 (2013). https://doi.org/10.1093/bioinformatics/btt208
4. Chen, T., Guestrin, C.: Xgboost: a scalable tree boosting system. In: Proccedings of the 22nd ACM SIGKDD International Conference on Knowledge Discovery and Data Mining, KDD '16, pp. 785–794. Association for Computing Machinery, New York (2016). https://doi.org/10.1145/2939672.2939785
5. Colombo, D., Maathuis, M.H.: Order-independent constraint-based causal structure learning. J. Mach. Learn. Res. **15**(116), 3921 3962 (2014)
6. Cui, T., Mekkaoui, K., Reinvall, J., Havulinna, A.S., Marttinen, P., Kaski, S.: Gene-gene interaction detection with deep learning. Commun. Biol. **5**(1), 1238 (2022)
7. Dai, Y., Guo, C., Guo, W., Eickhoff, C.: Drug–drug interaction prediction with Wasserstein Adversarial Autoencoder-based knowledge graph embeddings. Brief. Bioinf. **22**(4), bbaa256 (2020). https://doi.org/10.1093/bib/bbaa256
8. Davison, M.L., Sireci, S.G.: 12 - multidimensional scaling. In: Handbook of Applied Multivariate Statistics and Mathematical Modeling, pp. 323–352. Academic Press, San Diego (2000). https://doi.org/10.1016/B978-012691360-6/50013-6

9. Dhamdhere, K., Agarwal, A., Sundararajan, M.: The shapley taylor interaction index. In: Proceedings of the 37th International Conference on Machine Learning. ICML'20, JMLR (2020)

10. Friedman, J., Hastie, T., Tibshirani, R.: Sparse inverse covariance estimation with the graphical lasso. Biostatistics **9**(3), 432–441 (2007). https://doi.org/10.1093/biostatistics/kxm045

11. Glymour, C., Zhang, K., Spirtes, P.: Review of causal discovery methods based on graphical models. Front. Genet. **10** (2019). https://doi.org/10.3389/fgene.2019.00524

12. Grabherr, M.G., et al.: Full-length transcriptome assembly from rna-seq data without a reference genome. Nat. Biotechnol. **29**(7), 644–652 (2011)

13. Hickey, S.M., et al.: Impact of breeding for reduced methane emissions in new zealand sheep on maternal and health traits. Front. Genet. **13** (2022). https://doi.org/10.3389/fgene.2022.910413

14. Jamieson, K., Talwalkar, A.: Non-stochastic best arm identification and hyperparameter optimization. In: Proceedings of the 19th International Conference on Artificial Intelligence and Statistics. Proceedings of Machine Learning Research, vol. 51, pp. 240–248. PMLR, Cadiz (2016)

15. Kalainathan, D., Goudet, O., Dutta, R.: Causal discovery toolbox: uncovering causal relationships in python. J. Mach. Learn. Res. **21**(37), 1–5 (2020)

16. Lamurias, A., Sereika, M., Albertsen, M., Hose, K., Nielsen, T.D.: Metagenomic binning with assembly graph embeddings. Bioinformatics **38**(19), 4481–4487 (2022). https://doi.org/10.1093/bioinformatics/btac557

17. Lee, D.D., Seung, H.S.: Learning the parts of objects by non-negative matrix factorization. Nature **401**(6755), 788–791 (1999)

18. Li, F., Hitch, T.C.A., Chen, Y., Creevey, C.J., Guan, L.L.: Comparative metagenomic and metatranscriptomic analyses reveal the breed effect on the rumen microbiome and its associations with feed efficiency in beef cattle. Microbiome **7**(6) (2019). https://doi.org/10.1186/s40168-019-0618-5

19. Li, L., Jamieson, K., DeSalvo, G., Rostamizadeh, A., Talwalkar, A.: Hyperband: a novel bandit-based approach to hyperparameter optimization. J. Mach. Learn. Res. **18**(185), 1–52 (2018)

20. Mann, E., Wetzels, S.U., Wagner, M., Zebeli, Q., Schmitz-Esser, S.: Metatranscriptome sequencing reveals insights into the gene expression and functional potential of rumen wall bacteria. Front. Microbiol. **9** (2018). https://doi.org/10.3389/fmicb.2018.00043

21. Palangi, V., Lackner, M.: Management of enteric methane emissions in ruminants using feed additives: a review. Animals **12**(24) (2022). https://doi.org/10.3390/ani12243452

22. Park, C., Kim, J., Kim, J., Park, S.: Machine learning-based identification of genetic interactions from heterogeneous gene expression profiles. PLOS ONE **13**(7), 1–15 (2018). https://doi.org/10.1371/journal.pone.0201056

23. Reisinger, A., Clark, H.: How much do direct livestock emissions actually contribute to global warming? Glob. Change Biol. **24**(4), 1749–1761 (2018). https://doi.org/10.1111/gcb.13975

24. Salazar, G., et al.: Gene expression changes and community turnover differentially shape the global ocean metatranscriptome. Cell **179**(5), 1068–1083 (2019)

25. Shakya, M., Lo, C.C., Chain, P.S.G.: Advances and challenges in metatranscriptomic analysis. Front. Genet. **10** (2019). https://doi.org/10.3389/fgene.2019.00904

26. Shi, W., et al.: Methane yield phenotypes linked to differential gene expression in the sheep rumen microbiome. Genome Res. **24** (2014). https://doi.org/10.1101/gr.168245.113
27. Söllinger, A., et al.: Holistic assessment of rumen microbiome dynamics through quantitative metatranscriptomics reveals multifunctional redundancy during key steps of anaerobic feed degradation. mSystems **3**(4) (2018). https://doi.org/10.1128/msystems.00038-18
28. Zhang, Y., et al.: Metatranscriptomics for the human microbiome and microbial community functional profiling. Ann. Rev. Biomed. Data Sci. **4**, 279–311 (2021). https://doi.org/10.1146/annurev-biodatasci-031121-103035

Education

Text Mining from Migration Narratives

David Ing[1]([✉]), Fabien Delorme[1], Said Jabbour[1], Nelly Robin[2],
and Lakhdar Sais[1]

[1] CRIL, CNRS - Université d'Artois, Lens, France
{ing,delorme,jabbour,sais}@cril.fr
[2] Géographe, CEPED - IRD/Université Paris Cité, Paris, France
nelly.robin@ird.fr

Abstract. The pervasive proliferation of textual information, combined with the swift advancement in data acquisition methods, has resulted in an overwhelming volume of data, making it challenging to uncover relevant patterns. Text mining is a crucial process for extracting noteworthy and non-trivial patterns, as well as valuable knowledge from extensive collections of textual data. In this paper, we present a step towards a text mining approach designed to harness migration narrative texts, those collected from interviews with migrants during their journeys in English and French. Our contributions can be summarized as follows: (1) We first collaborate with experts in Humanities and Social Sciences (HSS) to annotate the essential domain concepts, their related terms, and the locations mentioned in those narratives. (2) To automatically extract such related terms embedded in the narratives, we propose adapting a set expansion algorithm in a weakly supervised manner using a tiny set of annotated terms. We then evaluate the proposed algorithm by comparing its output terms to those annotated by experts. (3) We utilize some existing frameworks to automatically identify locations crossed by migrants, followed by a disambiguation model to precisely pinpoint them on a map. To evaluate the proposed systems, we conduct the experiments by comparing their recognized locations and disambiguated locations to those annotated by experts. (4) We design a tool to visualize the itineraries of those locations on a map, enabling the observation of migration routes. Our discussions with HSS experts reveal that our proposed approach assists their analyses by automatically retrieving pertinent terms and drawing itineraries of migrants on a map, enabling a comprehensive understanding of their construction.

Keywords: Text Mining · Humanities and Social Sciences · Migration Narratives · Migration Routes

1 Introduction

More than 80 percent of the data generated and collected by organizations is in the form of unstructured data [10]. This type of data manifests in var-

Supplementary Information The online version contains supplementary material available at https://doi.org/10.1007/978-3-662-72243-5_16.

ious forms across different fields, including email bodies, press releases, contracts, medical records, speech-to-text snippets, and more. Given its ubiquitous nature, unstructured data provides a rich source of information. For example, the migration narrative texts in our study are collected from interviews with migrants during their journeys. This type of data offers valuable insights that enable experts in Humanities and Social Sciences (HSS) to analyze migration routes and gain a profound understanding of migration phenomena. However, extracting, acquiring, and formalizing knowledge from unstructured text data effectively and promptly presents several challenges. Firstly, the sheer volume of unstructured text makes manually extracting critical concepts or terms arduous. Secondly, a deep understanding of the specific domain is crucial for extracting the desired information. Lastly, unstructured text often contains noise, such as misspellings, run-on words, additional whitespace characters, and abbreviations. This paper is part of an innovative ANR HYCI (Hyper-lieux, Crises, Migrations et Inégalités) Project (ANR-22-CE55-0010) that aims to extract complex knowledge (migration routes formulated as attributed graphs) from migrants' narrative texts, focusing on their journeys towards Western Europe. The complexity of these graphs relates to the attributes that label both the *nodes* and *arcs*. More specifically, *nodes* provide information about the resources associated with migration, such as financial support (e.g. aid from family, work experiences, etc.), accommodation (e.g. legal or illegal housing, etc.) and environments (e.g. sea, forest, desert, etc.), whereas *arcs* are annotated with various types of information, including means of transport, cost, and duration. A migrant's journey transcends mere spatial and temporal dimensions; it is characterized by various events, resources, constraints, and opportunities. The unique nature of each journey, along with the richness and diversity of migratory experiences, poses significant challenges in terms of modeling and representing the concepts within this domain and the relationships that connect them.

To address the aforementioned challenges, this paper presents a step towards a text mining technique designed to harness the wealth of migration narrative texts articulated by migrants in two languages: English and French. This approach represents an initial step in unraveling the intricate structure of the migratory experiences highlighted above. Our contributions can be summarized as shown in Fig. 1 and presented as follows:

1. In Fig. 1(a), we first collaborate with experts in HSS to annotate domain concepts and their related terms based on a narrative corpus and a list of extracted terms. In Fig. 1(b), all the locations mentioned in such narratives are annotated and then disambiguated using Wikidata [31] by experts to generate the corpus of annotated and disambiguated locations.
2. In Fig. 1(c), we propose adapting a set expansion algorithm to extract the related terms embedded within the narratives in a weakly supervised manner using only a tiny set of annotated terms. We evaluate the proposed algorithm by comparing its output terms to the annotated terms.
3. In Fig. 1(d), we employ some existing models to identify those locations, and disambiguate them using a pretrained model as shown in Fig. 1(e). We

conduct the evaluations by comparing the recognized locations and disambiguated locations of the proposed systems to those annotated by experts.

4. In Fig. 1(f), we design a tool to visualize the itineraries of those locations.

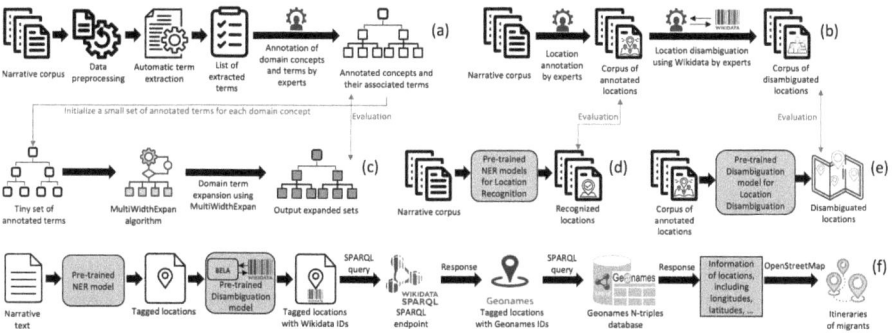

Fig. 1. The overall proposed framework for text mining from migration narratives.

The rest of this paper is organized as follows. Section 2 discusses related works on text mining in HSS. Section 3 presents the description of migration narratives. Section 4 describes our contributions for mining those narratives. Section 5 reports the evaluations of the proposed methods. Section 6 delineates the process of visualizing the itineraries of migrants on a map and discuss it with experts. Finally, Sect. 7 concludes the paper and addresses future works.

2   Related Work

This section briefly outlines the main approaches related to our works, focusing mainly on text mining in HSS and its use for migration narrative texts analysis.

In [17], the author discusses the state and the future of computational text analysis in sociology for social science by summarizing how different text mining tools have been used by sociologists in various analytical tasks across research questions and methodological traditions. The author describes five families of computational methods used in recent research: dictionary methods, semantic and network analysis tools, language models, unsupervised, and supervised machine learning. Among them, we tried the unsupervised clustering to identify the interesting concepts in our small migrant's narrative corpus. Unfortunately, the clusters that are supposed to delineate groups of terms enabling the emergence of concepts contain many noisy terms, making their identification challenging. Thus, we propose an alternative solution which we will describe in the sequel.

In [35], using a text mining approach/sentiment analysis on Twitter data, the authors investigate the public opinions and sentiments towards the Syrian refugee crisis. In [15], the authors analyze blogs to study shift in narratives within the blogosphere towards refugees or migrants during the migrant crisis in Europe. They use named-entity extraction to identify different topics and themes, followed by the use of targeted sentiment analysis to study the shift in narratives toward migrants in the blogosphere. In the two previously mentioned studies focusing on Twitter and blogosphere texts, the authors examined public sentiment regarding Europe's major refugee crises. However, our study breaks new ground by analyzing narratives directly from migrants (in their own words during the interviews) to uncover the key concepts and their associated terms. Moreover, we extract and visualize the routes taken by the migrants on a map.

3   Migration Narratives Acquisition and Description

Studies on minor migrants often use narratives to convey representations of the migratory experience; narrative texts are collected from interviews conducted during their migratory journeys. These interviews do not occur in the familiar surroundings of the minors' villages or in their country of origin, nor in the host country where they may have found security, but rather in the transit points along the migration route. The minors are in a situation of waiting and in great uncertainty. This difficult and sometimes hostile environment requires a relationship of trust, which has been established through a period of time, the use of the language spoken by the minors, and the guarantee of anonymity for their testimonies. This raises the question of tensions between the researchers' goals in their field, professional ethics and moral responsibilities. The interviewers ensured that each life story is collected in accordance with social science ethical rules. The life stories are anonymized without causing any privacy concerns. Researchers from transit countries (Algeria, Mali, Morocco, Niger, Senegal) and local associations, trained in scientific data collection, are involved in the process. More specifically, life stories are collected from sub-Saharan minors in Niger (Agadez and Arlit), Algeria (Adrar, Tamanrasset and Maghnia), Senegal (Dakar, Mbour and Ziguinchor), and Morocco (Oujda and Rabat). They focus on three corridors along the *Trans-Saharan* routes [23]: (1) *Algerian-Malian corridor*: minors arrive from West African countries (Ivory Coast, Guinea-Bissau, Guinea, Mali, Nigeria and Senegal), and from Central Africa (the Democratic Republic of Congo (DRC)). (2) *Algerian-Nigerian corridor*: minors come from Nigeria and the DRC. (3) *Morocco-Senegal corridor*: the countries of origin of the migrants are from West Africa, including Senegal. In their narratives, minors tell their stories using a selection of places, means of transports, accommodations, words that designate objects and represent subjective experience.

Using similar methodology, other migrants' narratives are collected through the *Balkan* route [2]: one of the main migratory pathways into Europe. Transit corridors from Bulgaria, North Macedonia and Serbia, as well as through Albania and Montenegro, via Bosnia and Herzegovina, became one of the most travelled mixed migration routes in the Western Balkans. The migrants present along this route generally come from Syria, Pakistan, Afghanistan, Irak, Iran and Turkey.

4   Text Mining from Migration Narratives

This section presents our framework for mining migration narrative texts in three steps: (1) Narratives preprocessing, term extraction, and annotation, (2) Automatic domain term expansion, and (3) Location recognition and disambiguation.

4.1   Narratives Processing, Term Extraction and Concept Annotation

Narratives preprocessing is an initial step before extracting high-quality terms. It consists of basic natural language processing (NLP) tasks. For our narratives, we replace multiple consecutive punctuations with a single punctuation and multiple consecutive whitespace characters with a single whitespace character. We also remove all non-ASCII characters except accent characters, and some specific characters like š, đ, č, ć, ž for both lowercase and uppercase because those characters can be the name of certain places or locations (e.g. Šid, Krnjača, etc.).

To automatically extract terms, we first discussed with HSS experts and reached a consensus that single-word and two-word terms containing part-of-speech as nouns are relevant. Therefore, we use an approach that combines linguistic and statistical information to extract terms from both types of narratives.

Linguistic Part. Inspired by [9], this approach consists of three core elements: (1) *Part-of-Speech (PoS)*: involves tagging the entire corpus with grammatical categories (e.g. noun, verb, adjective, etc.). (2) *Linguistic Filter*: filters desired terms from the resulting PoS tags, permitting only specific grammatical string for extraction. In our case, candidate terms are retained if they respect syntactic patterns such as: *Noun* and *Noun Noun*. *Noun* can be *"NN"*, *"NPS"*, *"NNP"*, etc. (3) *stop-list*: a list of words excluded as terms in a domain.

Statistical Part. We use Term Frequency-Inverse Document Frequency (TF-IDF) [25], a numerical statistic that scores terms in a text to indicate how important a term is to a document in a corpus. TF-IDF is calculated as follows:

$$TF\text{-}IDF(e, d, \mathcal{D}) = tf(e, d) * idf(e, \mathcal{D}),$$

$$tf(e, d) = \frac{f(e, d)}{\max\{f(w, d) : w \in d\}}, \quad idf(e, \mathcal{D}) = \log\left(\frac{|\mathcal{D}|}{|\{d \subset \mathcal{D} : e \in d\}|}\right),$$

where e is a term or entity (note that throughout the paper, we will use the words "term" and "entity" interchangeably), d is a document, $\mathcal{D}$ is a set of documents (i.e. a corpus), $f(e, d)$: number of occurrences of e in d, $tf(e, d)$: term frequency of e in d, and $idf(e, \mathcal{D})$: inverse document frequency of e in $\mathcal{D}$.

Following discussions with HSS migration experts on the previously extracted terms and narrative texts, we identified four essential and less sensitive domain concepts, along with a general concept, for both types of narratives as follows:

Table 1. Statistics of migration narrative texts.

Narrative type : |D|	avg-tok-len	|V|	#LOC	Domain concept : #Entities
English: 29	4148	1407	3039	Accommodation: 16, **Family or Friends:** 31, Means of transport: 28, **Environment:** 18
French: 108	1309	1719	2553	Accommodation: 20, **Family or Friends:** 35, Means of transport: 30, **Environment:** 14

- **Family or Friends**: Family members or friends who financially support migrants in starting and continuing their journeys. They can also be companions during the journey (e.g. parents, siblings, friends, etc.).
- **Accommodation**: Locations or items where migrants can stay during a stopover (e.g. house, room, bed, etc.).
- **Means of transport**: Modes of transport or infrastructure utilized by migrants during their journeys (e.g. foot, plane, bus, road, etc.).
- **Environment**: Identifies the spatial and natural environments traversed by migrants during their journey (e.g. sea, forest, jungle, desert, etc.). These indicators highlight the difficulties, dangers, and risks of the migration routes.
- **Location**: A general concept denoted as a geographical location where migrants make a stopover, or a final destination city or country where they arrive (e.g. Greece, Istanbul, Gao, etc.). Extracting such locations is essential for HSS experts to clearly analyze the migration routes.

Table 1 shows the statistics of the narrative texts considered in this paper, including the total number of narratives ($|\mathcal{D}|$) in English and French, the average number of words (*avg-tok-len*), the total number of extracted terms ($|V|$), where V is a list of extracted terms, the total number of annotated and disambiguated locations (#*LOC*), and the total number of associated terms for each domain concept (#*Entities*). Note that #*LOC* and #*Entities* are annotated by experts.

4.2   Automatic Domain Term Expansion

In this section, we aim to automatically identify all the associated terms for each domain concept. Explicitly, our goal is to initialize a small set of annotated terms for each concept, and then find a complete set of terms belonging to the same concept. To achieve this, we use an algorithm called "set expansion". It refers to a technique of expanding a given partial set of seed entities into a more complete set of entities that belong to the same semantic class [33]. Previous works for solving this task include *Google Set* [30], *SEAL* [33], and *Lyretail* [6]. Other studies [13,26,28,32] and Width Expansion in HiExpan [27] are proposed in a *corpus-based* setting where sets are expanded through an offline process.

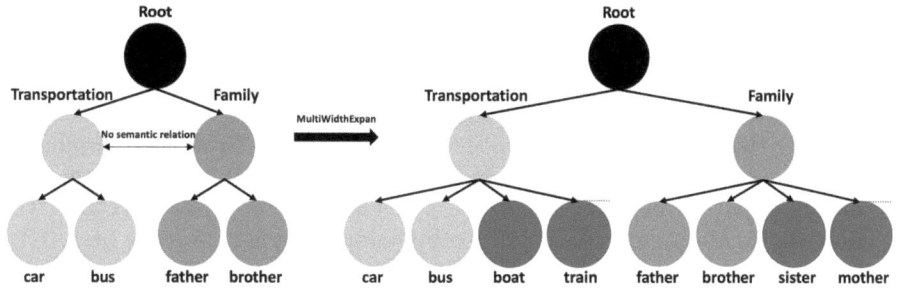

Fig. 2. Example of MultiWidthExpan with two different concepts.

Since our work does not exploit external resources and relies solely on small corpora of migration narratives (see Table 1) articulated naturally by migrants, plus a tiny set of annotated terms (seed set), we propose adapting the Width Expansion in HiExpan [27]. It is a new and modified version of SetExpan [26], which additionally incorporates the term embedding feature and enhances the entity type features. The input for WidthExpan includes three parts: (1) a list of extracted terms V, (2) a set of documents $\mathcal{D}$, each document d contains tagged entities $e \in V$, and (3) a tiny set of annotated entities S. Given V and $\mathcal{D}$, we aim to expand S into a more complete set. For example (see Fig. 2), if a given seed set S of *Transportation* is {*car, bus*}, WidthExpan should return other related entities such as *boat*, *train*, etc. Note that we made some necessary changes to the original Width Expansion algorithm to handle both types of narratives, since the original one only allows to expand terms using English texts. Precisely, we execute the WidthExpan consecutively in each iteration, denoted as *Multi-WidthExpan*. As shown in Fig. 2, each direct node from the root node does not belong to the same semantic class; they are simply the labeled concepts defined by experts to categorize related terms. Therefore, *MultiWidthExpan* executes the Width Expansion under each labeled concept successively (e.g. starting first with *Transportation*, then *Family*, and so on). We do not execute the Width Expansion separately for each concept, because at the end of each iteration, we globally optimize our *MultiWidthExpan* in case of conflict (the same term appears in multiple concepts), which we will describe in the sequel.

We now discuss the components of WidthExpan in detail, including the types of features, similarity measures, and the whole process of the Width Expansion. **Features.** We use three types of features as follows:

1. ***skip-pattern***: Given a target term e_i in a sentence, one of its skip-pattern features is "w_{-1} ___ w_1" where w_{-1} and w_1 are two context words and e_i is replaced with a placeholder. For example, one skip-pattern of term "bus" in sentence "we went by bus to the border." is "by ___ to". We extract six skip-patterns of various lengths for one target term e_i in each sentence.
2. ***term embedding***: This feature captures the semantic similarity for each term. We have conducted preliminary experiments with various word embeddings and observed that the skip-gram [3] and continuous bag-of-words

(CBOW) [12] models obtained the highest similarity scores for our English and French narratives, respectively. Thus, we utilize the pretrained skip-gram and CBOW models for the English and French corpora, respectively. Note that two-word terms (e.g. bus station) are concatenated using "_" before learning their embeddings. Since these models exploit subword information, they can handle out-of-vocabulary words, which is suitable for our case.

3. *entity type*: Given {*car*, *bus*}, one of their common types is *vehicle*. For English, we obtain each entity's type by linking it to a knowledge base (KB) called Probase [34]. To our knowledge, no probabilistic taxonomy is available for French. Inspired by [20], we propose to query a French Masked Language Model (MLM) called CamemBERT[1] [18] with cloze-style prompts [29] to obtain the types of entities for creating a KB for French. Precisely, we design a specific prompt that combines an entity and a short sentence as follows:

"[ENTITY] est le type de [MASK].",

where [ENTITY] represents an entity $e \in V$, and [MASK] represents a hidden word to be predicted as the type of e by the MLM. For example, to find types of the term "camion" in French, we submit a specific prompt: "camion est le type de [MASK]". CamemBERT will return the following results:

```
[(vehicule, 0.34907031059265137),
(camion,   0.1406002938747406),
(voiture,  0.11208264529705048),
...]
```

Similarity Measures. We want to compute the sibling similarity between two entities e_1 and e_2 denoted as $sim_{sib}(e_1, e_2)$. First, the TF-IDF weight [24] between an entity e and a skip-pattern sk is calculated as follows:

$$f_{e,sk} = \log(1 + X_{e,sk}) \left[\log|V_{sk}| - \log\left(\sum_{\substack{e' \in V_{sk} \\ e' \neq e}} X_{e',sk} \right) \right], \tag{1}$$

Similarly, the association weight between an entity e and a type tp is calculated as follows:

$$f_{e,tp} = \log(1 + C_{e,tp}) \left[\log|V_{tp}| - \log\left(\sum_{\substack{e' \in V_{tp} \\ e' \neq e}} C_{e',tp} \right) \right], \tag{2}$$

Then, we can calculate the weighted Jaccard similarity [16] of two sibling entities using *skip-pattern* features as follows:

$$sim_{sib}^{sk}(e_1, e_2 | SK) = \frac{\sum_{sk \in SK} min(f_{e_1,sk}, f_{e_2,sk})}{\sum_{sk \in SK} max(f_{e_1,sk}, f_{e_2,sk})}, \tag{3}$$

---

[1] https://huggingface.co/almanach/camembert-base.

Similarly, the weighted similarity of two sibling entities using *type* features is calculated as follows:

$$sim_{sib}^{tp}(e_1, e_2|TP) = \frac{\sum_{tp \in TP} min(f_{e_1,tp}, f_{e_2,tp})}{\sum_{tp \in TP} max(f_{e_1,tp}, f_{e_2,tp})}, \tag{4}$$

where $X_{e,sk}$ is the raw co-occurrence count between entity e and skip-pattern sk. $V_{sk} \subseteq V$ is a list of entities contained in noun phrases (NPs), and $|V_{sk}|$ denotes its size. $C_{e,tp}$ is the confidence score of entity e having type tp. $V_{tp} \subseteq V$ is a list of entities that have types in the KB, and $|V_{tp}|$ denotes its size. SK and TP are selected sets of skip-pattern and type features associated with entities in V_{sk} and V_{tp}, respectively. Note that $V_{sk} \neq V_{tp}$, since some entities are not contained in NPs but have types, and vice versa. For example, a term "refugee" has no types in Probase. Therefore, it is not included in V_{tp}.

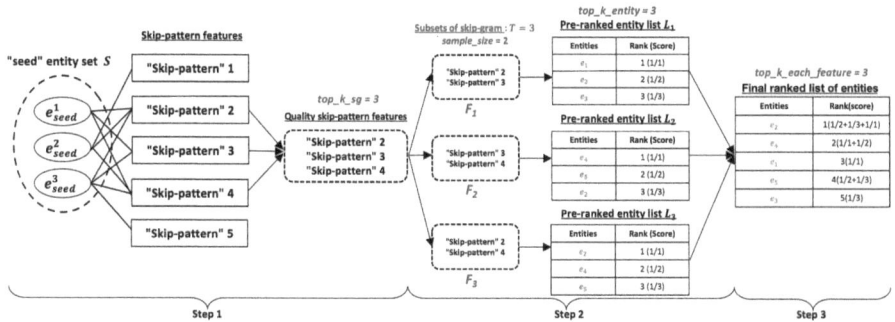

Fig. 3. Example of WidthExpan process using *skip-pattern* features.

Finally, the similarity between two entities based on their *embedding* features via cosine similarity is calculated as follows:

$$sim_{sib}^{emb}(e_1, e_2) = \frac{e_1.e_2}{\|e_1\|_2 * \|e_2\|_2}, \tag{5}$$

where $\| \|_2$ is the 2-norm, $e_1.e_2$ is a dot product of entity e_1 and entity e_2.

We combine the three similarities mentioned above by concluding that a good pair of sibling entities can appear in similar contexts, share similar embedding, and have similar types. Thus, the sibling similarity is calculated as follows:

$$sim_{sib}(e_1, e_2) = \sqrt{\left(1 + sim_{sib}^{sk}(e_1, e_2|SK)\right)\left(1 + sim_{sib}^{tp}(e_1, e_2|TP)\right)} \, sim_{sib}^{emb}(e_1, e_2) \tag{6}$$

The confidence score of entity e_1 belonging to S, $|S|$ is the total number of seed entities, is calculated as follows:

$$conf(e_1) = \frac{\sum_{e_2 \in S} sim_{sib}(e_1, e_2)}{|S|} \tag{7}$$

Reciprocal Rank. The Reciprocal Rank (RR) determines the reciprocal of the rank at which the initial pertinent document appears [7]. RR is 1 if a pertinent document is found at the first position, $\frac{1}{2}$ if it is found at the second position and so on. Here, a document represents an entity. Therefore, we can calculate the RR of an entity e according to its ranking position, denoted as $RR(e) = \frac{1}{r_e}$, where r_e is the ranking position of the entity e.

WidthExpan Overall Process. Given a seed set S and a list of extracted entities V, we follow [27], since the feature space is huge (i.e. many skip-pattern features are noisy) and V is noisy (i.e. many entities in V are irrelevant to S).

To obtain candidate entities using *skip-pattern* features (see Fig. 3), we apply three steps: (1) To score each skip-pattern feature, we accumulate its strength with entities in S by calculating $score(sk) = \sum_{e \in S} f_{e,sk}$, and select *top_k_sg* skip-pattern features with highest scores. (2) We use sampling without replacement method to generate T subsets of skip-pattern features F_t, where $t = 1, \ldots, T$ and each F_t has a fixed size of *sample-size* features. For each F_t, we select candidate entities from V_{sk} if they have associations with skip-pattern features in F_t. We then calculate similarity scores between the selected candidate entities and the seed entities in S (see Eq. (3)), arrange them based on their scores in descending order, and compute their reciprocal ranks (RRs). (3) From each list L_t, we select *top_k_entity* candidate entities, aggregate their RRs, arrange them in descending order in the final ranked list, and select the *top_k_each_feature* candidate entities.

Similarly, to obtain candidate entities using *entity type* features, we apply three steps: (1) To score each type feature, we accumulate its strength with entities in S by calculating $score(tp) = \sum_{e \in S} f_{e,tp}$, and select *top_k_type* type features with highest scores. (2) We select candidate entities from V_{tp} if they have associations with these *top_k_type* type features. (3) We calculate similarity scores between the selected candidate entities and the seed entities in S (see Eq. (4)), arrange them based on their scores in descending order, compute their RRs, and select the *top_k_each_feature* candidate entities.

To obtain the candidate entities using *term embedding* features, we apply two steps: (1) We combine the previously selected candidate entities of *skip-pattern* and *entity type* features. (2) We calculate similarity scores between these combined candidate entities and the seed entities in S (see Eq. (5)), arrange them based on their scores in descending order, calculate their RRs, and select the *top_k_each_feature* candidate entities.

Finally, we aggregate the reciprocal ranks of the selected candidate entities using these three types of features, arrange them in descending order, and select the *top_k_expand* candidate entities to expand S. For each concept, we set a maximum of *top_k_per_concept* terms. The confidence score of each candidate entity belong to S is calculated using Eq. (7).

Conflict Resolution and Global Optimization. At the end of each iteration, since the supervision signal from each seed entity S is very weak (i.e. only a few annotated terms are provided), we need to ensure that candidate terms introduced in early iterations are high-quality and will not mislead the expansion process later on. When a term appears in multiple concepts during the expansion process, we encounter a "conflict" and aim to resolve it by finding the best concept for that term. Given a set of conflicting terms C, we apply two rules:

1. If a term $c \in C$ is in a seed entity of any concept, we retain c in that concept and remove it from the others, then skip the next rule assuming the correctness of the initialized seed entities.
2. For each term $c \in C$, we compare its confidence score across all concepts, retain it in the concept where it has the highest score, and delete it from other concepts.

Finally, we employ a global optimization on every concept to filter noisy terms with sibling similarity scores below a predefined *threshold*. Let us note that the variables T, *sample-size*, *top_k_sg*, *top_k_entity*, *top_k_each_feature*, *top_k_type*, *top_k_expand*, *top_k_per_concept*, and *threshold* are hyperparameters, that will be set in the experiments.

4.3   Location Recognition and Disambiguation

To identify geographical location entities in narrative texts, we utilize Named Entity Recognition (NER). NER is a popular data preprocessing task that seeks to locate and classify named entities mentioned in unstructured text into predefined categories such as person names, organizations, locations, time expressions, etc. In our study, we utilize several state-of-the-art (SOTA) NLP frameworks, including spaCy [14], FLAIR [1], and Stanza [22].

Geographical location disambiguation is crucial for visualizing migration routes. To pinpoint exact locations on a map, we need to link those recognized by NER to their accurate entries in a KB, a task known as Entity Linking (EL). EL is a common NLP task in practical applications, aiming to match textual entity mentions to KB entries like Wikipedia or Wikidata, serving as canonical entries. In our study, to link location entities to a KB, we propose using a recent and advanced tool called Bi-encoder Entity Linking Architecture, known as BELA [21]. Provided by Meta Open Source, BELA is the first transformer-based, end-to-end, one-pass, and multilingual EL model that efficiently identifies and links entities in texts, covering approximately 16 million entities and 97 languages. It utilizes a bi-encoder architecture that requires a single forward pass through a transformer for end-to-end linking of a passage, regardless of the number of entity mentions present. BELA has been trained on a Wikipedia dataset consisting of approximately 661 million samples, considering all the Wikipedia articles across 97 languages. For details regarding the training of BELA, we refer to Plekhanov et al. [21]. We choose BELA over other multilingual EL systems for several reasons. (1) It is computationally less expensive than other systems, such as [8], making it more practical for real-world applications. (2) For Entity Disambiguation (ED) tasks, it does not require a predefined candidate set for each mention, which is suitable for our case. (3) It disambiguates multiple entities in one pass, which is faster for disambiguation speed, while other systems [4, 8] require a mention encoding pass for each candidate.

BELA can be used for both End-to-End Entity Linking (EL) and Entity Disambiguation (ED) tasks. In our study, we utilize it for ED tasks, focusing on linking the location entities found in narrative texts to the knowledge base (KB) of Wikidata [31].

5   Experiments

We conduct the experiments for *MultiWidthExpan*, location detection and location disambiguation using the datasets presented in Table 1.

For *MultiWidthExpan* and location detection, the experiments are conducted on a computer equipped with Intel(R) Core(TM) i9-10900 CPU @ 2.80 GHz with 62Gib of memory. For location disambiguation using BELA, the experiments are conducted on a GPU machine equipped with Intel XEON Gold 6226R (16 cores @2.9 GHz) and 4 NVIDIA Quadro RTX8000 (48GB graphics processors and 512 Gib of memory). The source codes and instructions for reproducibility are available here.

5.1   Experiments for MultiWidthExpan

We evaluate the quality of the expanded sets using *MultiWidthExpan* by comparing them to those annotated by experts. Given our small corpora, *MultiWidthExpan* is allowed to run until there are no additional quality terms for each concept. Table 2 reports the quantitative results using information retrieval metrics [5]. Hyperparameters in the first column are kept at their default values as in [27], except for top_k_type and $top\_k\_per\_concept$, which are adjusted to adapt to our corpora. As we set $top\_k\_per\_concept = 50$, the metrics in the last column are considered as P@50, R@50, and F1@50. However, after each iteration, since we set a predefined *threshold* ($t \in [0.7, 0.8]$) in the fifth column to filter out noisy terms, many terms fell below this threshold (i.e. no concept exceeds 50 terms in the sixth column, and will be truncated if it does). For the seed S, we discussed with HSS experts and conducted preliminary experiments to select the best entities (around 10% of the overall annotated entities) for each concept.

Despite having a small corpus and weak supervision of initialized terms, experiments show that *MultiWidthExpan* achieves desirable results by expanding many relevant terms from a list containing many noisy terms (see Table 1, only approximately 6% of terms are relevant for both types). Nevertheless, *MultiWidthExpan* expands some noisy terms, especially for *Accommodation*, which has the lowest precision and the highest recall for both types. This implies that while it expands many relevant terms, it also includes many noisy terms. Certain noisy terms share the same skip-pattern features with relevant terms in our corpora. For example, in English narratives, phrases like "I spent one month in one room" and "There is one kitchen" demonstrate that while "room" is a relevant term, "kitchen" is a noisy term. Similarly, in French narratives, phrases like "Je vis dans un foyer..." and "Je suis resté comme ça dans un jardin" show that while "foyer" is a relevant term, "jardin" is a noisy term. As shown in the fifth column, most of the red terms expanded in each concept have very close semantics with other terms inside their own concept but were not considered relevant based on the context of the narratives, as annotated manually by experts. For French narratives, *MultiWidthExpan* achieves higher F1-scores for all concepts compared to English narratives. One reason might be the number of narratives, since we have more narratives in French than in English, thus yielding more high-quality skip-pattern features. Since we rely on the CamemBERT MLM to generate the types of entities for French narratives, this suggests that this model can generate many pertinent types when provided with specific prompts, thus playing an important role in the expansion process.

However, as mentioned in [26], it is challenging to establish a perfect scoring method to obtain the ideal sets of entities, given the diversity and noisiness of unstructured text such as migration narrative texts in our study.

Table 2. Quantitative Results of MultiWidthExpan using Precision (P), Recall (R), and F1-score (F1). Annotated Set: ● missing term in Expanded Set. Expanded Set: ●, ● correct or incorrect expanded term respectively. ● initialized term (not include to calculate P, R, F1).

Type: hyperparameters	Concept	Annotated Set provided by Experts	S	t	Expanded Set generated by MultiWidthExpan	Metrics
English:	Accom.	homes, home, house, houses, building, room, rooms, hotel, tent, tents, bed, apartment, shelter, floor, garage, hostel	home shelter	0.74	home, shelter, shops, parking, kitchen, houses, hotel, door, dormitories, bed, bathroom, floor, house, cabin, building, homes, doors, hostel, toilets, room, tent, tents, garage, shop, rooms, apartment, restaurant, accommodation	P: 53.84% R: 100% F1: 70%
$T=10,$						
sample-size=20,	Means of Transport	autobus, boat, car, cars, foot, taxi, taxis, cab, bus, buses, minibus, van, vans, minivan, minivans, truck, trucks, tractor, train, trains, tram, ship, ferry, plane, airplane, flight, road, walk	boat train plane	0.72	boat, train, plane, airplane, trains, minivan, ship, flight, passengers, tractor, cab, taxi, vans, trucks, petrol, luggage, taxis, ride, car, cars, helicopters, buses, bus, ferry, tram, minivans, minibus, truck, passenger	P: 76.92% R: 80% F1: 78.43%
top_k_sg=200,						
top_k_entity=90,						
top_k_each_feature=50,	Env.	jungle, jungles, forest, forests, trees, seaside, mountain, mountains, desert, hill, river, sea, valley, rocks, beach, coast, island, islands	jungle island	0.70	jungle, island, jungles, coast, region, mountain, hill, desert, sea, forests, mountains, southwest, valley, beach, area, forest, land, river, south, islands, seaside	P: 73.68% R: 87.50% F1: 80%
top_k_type=70,	Family or Friends	family, father, mother, brother, brothers, grandchildren, parents, dad, mum, mom, son, sons, sister, sisters, relatives, relative, cousin, cousins, uncle, wife, husband, kids, child, daughter, daughters, children, grandfather, grandmother, sister-in-law, friends, friend	mom relative daughter	0.75	daughter, mom, relative, child, grandfather, sons, daughters, brothers, relatives, friend, cousin, grandmother, uncle, cousins, sister, marriage, friends, nephew, son, boyfriend, dad, sisters, father, grandchildren, housewife, family, brother, elder, wife, mother, children, parents, husband	P: 83.34% R: 89.28% F1: 86.20%
top_k_expand=10,						
tsp_k_per_concept=50						
French:	Accom.	maison, appartement, chambre, chambres, maisonnette, hôtel, tentes, foyer, ferme, immeuble, domicile, tente, bâtiment, bâtisse, auberge, cabane, église, maisons, asile, salle	apparte-ment tente	0.72	appartement, tente, cabane, foyer, jardin, église, bâtisse, école, étage, bâtiment, asile, rue, village, immeuble, ferme, hôtel, maisonnette, maisons, ville, chambres, auberge, maison, chambre, domicile, salle	P: 73.91% R: 94.44% F1: 82.92%
$T=10,$						
sample-size=20,	Means of Transport	bateau, camion, camions, pickup, marche, routes, pied, transport_commun, autobus, train, avion, convoi, véhicule, véhicules, taxi, taxis, métro, tram, bus, minibus, 4×4, autocar, voiture, voitures, vol, remorque, fourgonnette, route, autoroute, rail	avion taxi métro	0.76	avion, taxi, métro, fourgons, remorque, camions, rail, bateau, vélo, aéroport, camion, convoi, routes, tram, minibus, voiture, train, hélicoptère, bus, autobus, taxis, route, 4×4, véhicule, fourgonnette, autocar, voitures, chauffeur, hélicoptère, véhicules, autoroute	P: 78.57% R: 81.48% F1: 80%
top_k_sg=200,						
top_k_entity=90,						
top_k_each_feature=50,	Env.	mer, forêt, forêts, montagne, désert, brousse, montagnes, collines, rivière, île, jungle, lac, broussaille, océan	forêt mer	0.80	forêt, mer, désert, rivière, forêts, île, océan, brousse, montagne, broussaille, terre, lac, montagnes, jungle, côte	P: 84.61% R: 91.66% F1: 88%
top_k_type=60,	Family or Friends	oncle, oncles, père, frère, grand-frère, ami, amis, grand-père, parent, parents, mère, famille, tante, sœur, sœurs, maman, frères, papa, cousin, cousins, tonton, fils, mari, frangin, cadet, amie, compatriote, compatriotes, compagnon, copine, copain, compagnons, fille, camarade, tuteur	parents frères cousin	0.75	parents, frères, cousin, famille, amie, ami, amis, copine, copain, homme, fils, compatriote, parent, frangin, oncle, oncles, maman, compatriotes, mère, femme, sœur, camarade, grand-frère, compagnon, jeune, cousins, tante, sœurs, frère, papa, mari, grand-père, tonton, pote, père, fille, cadet	P: 88.23% R: 93.75% F1: 90.91%
top_k_expand=10,						
top_k_per_concept=50						

5.2   Experiments for Location Recognition

We evaluate spaCy, FLAIR, and Stanza by comparing their outputs to those annotated by experts. Table 3 reports the evaluations of these pretrained NER models on our corpora in terms of Precision, Recall, and F1-score.

According to the experiments, the pretrained models perform better on the English corpus than on the French corpus by approximately 10% in terms of F1-score. FLAIR achieves the highest F1-score for the English corpus, while spaCy achieves the highest F1-score for the French corpus. Interestingly, Stanza, which performs slightly lower on the English corpus, shows marginally better performance on the French corpus compared to FLAIR.

We observe that these pretrained NER models failed to recognize certain specific cities and small towns in various countries across different narratives in some parts of the texts, especially for French narratives, including *Bogovađa, Alipašino polje, Bazargan, Krnjača, Doğubayazıt, Tavo, Al-Shaykh Maskin, Gbèdjromèdé, Preševo, Kastanas, Orestiada, Polykastro, Horgoš, Sutukoba, Mansa Konko, Pakali Ba, Atatürk, Al-Salameh, Rakovica, Farmakonisi, Leros, Mytilini, Esendere, Sombor, El Jadida, Mohammédia, Alexandroúpoli, Loyané, Marvintsi, Evzonoi, Dojran, Ödemiş, Salmas, Zeytinburnu, Meissen,* and more.

Additionally, they also incorrectly predicted or classified some nationalities (e.g. *Nigérian(s), Syrien(s), Sénégalais, Malien(s), Marocain(e), Africain, Ivoirien(s), Algérien(ne), Guinéen(s),* etc.), names of people (e.g. *Zireg, Lucie, Sami,* etc.), languages (e.g. *Pendjabi, Pashtu, Baloutchi,* etc.), and other entities (e.g. *Western Union, Schengen, Daesh,* etc.) as locations.

Table 3. Comparison of Pre-trained NER models for Location Recognition.

Model	NER-English			NER-French		
	Precision	Recall	F1-score	Precision	Recall	F1-score
Spacy	0.9865	0.9619	0.9736	0.8651	0.9053	**0.8822**
FLAIR	0.9761	0.9756	**0.9755**	0.8615	0.9029	0.8785
Stanza	0.9842	0.9304	0.9561	0.8429	0.9335	0.8813

Table 4. Evaluation of Location Disambiguation using BELA.

Type	Ambiguous entities (countries or cities)	Accuracy
English	*Macedonia, Sombor, Banja, Dimitrovgrad, Skala, Rakovica, Kabal, Balochistan, Esendere, Skenderija*	0.9897
French	*Congo, Souba, Pogo, Siby, Farato, Tinzaouten Koloni, Konna, San, Bondo, Kalehe, Ondo*	0.9780

5.3   Experiments for Location Disambiguation

We evaluate BELA by comparing its output disambiguated locations to those disambiguated by experts. The results are shown in Table 4. The columns from left to right show the type of narratives, the ambiguous entities, and the accuracy.

Experiments show that BELA achieves high accuracy for both types, with performance on the English corpus slightly better than on the French corpus. However, there are some major ambiguous entities listed in the second column. For instance, in English narratives, BELA failed to recognize "Macedonia" as "North Macedonia" instead of the region in Greece. Another entity, "Sombor", a city in Serbia, was predicted as "Sumar", a city in Kermanshah Province, Iran. Similarly, in French narratives, BELA failed to distinguish "Congo" as "Democratic Republic of the Congo" instead of "Republic of the Congo". Another entity, "Souba", a village in the Ségou Region of Mali, was predicted as "Soba", a municipality in Spain. For other entities in the table, they show similar issues.

6   Map Visualization and Discussion with Experts

Figure 1(f) illustrates the process of visualizing the migration routes on a map. First, we employ a pretrained NER model to identify the locations mentioned in a narrative to obtain the tagged locations. Next, a pretrained disambiguation model based on the Wikidata KB is used to disambiguate those tagged locations to obtain their accurate Wikidata IDs. We then submit SPARQL queries to the Wikidata SPARQL endpoint using those Wikidata IDs to retrieve their Geonames IDs. Subsequently, we submit additional SPARQL queries to the Geonames Database [11] using those Geonames IDs to retrieve specific information about those locations, including longitudes and latitudes. Having obtained the longitudes and latitudes of such locations, we can visualize the migration routes on a map using OpenStreetMap [19]. The step-by-step details of this visualization process can be found here.

Our proposed framework has been presented, thoroughly analyzed and discussed with HSS researchers, experts, and the members of our project. It aids in accelerating the analysis of migration routes by automatically extracting relevant information and mapping out the migrants' journeys. Understanding the intricate nature and dynamics of migratory journeys requires examining numerous factors experienced and articulated by migrants during their movement. The initial phase of our framework allows us to derive a comprehensive set of terms from expert-defined concepts, capturing key terms conveyed in the narratives. This approach enables direct interrogation of the narratives by collecting terms associated with each concept as used by the migrants themselves. This understanding highlights various aspects such as the pivotal role of migrant families or friends, the nature of accommodations, modes of transportation, and the diverse environments traversed. Figure 4 and Fig. 5 depict the examples of narrative texts with the highlighted key terms associated with five different concepts: *Location*, *Accommodation*, *Family or Friend*, *Environment*, and *Means of Transport*, in English and French, respectively.

In summary, the knowledge extracted is highly valuable for Humanities and Social Sciences researchers, providing essential assistance in analyzing migratory journeys. Visualizing the itineraries traversed by migrants on a map offers a powerful tool for enhancing observation and comprehension of migration routes. Figure 6 demonstrates five primary *Trans-Saharan* routes traversing four African countries (Morocco, Mauritania, Algeria, and Mali), originating from Senegal, Guinea, Ivory Coast, Burkina Faso, and Nigeria.

LOC
Accommodation
Family Members
Environment
Means of transport

Asadabad is near the Kunar province . I heard that from other friends and from some people going on that way . I knew exactly that way will be easy to go to Europe : From Jalalabad , then Kabul , then Kandahar , then Quetta , then Quetta to the jungle , and from jungle to Iran until Istanbul . I know exactly that I needed to go to that place first , then that place , and then that place . I ask someone where I can sleep , and where I cannot sleep . The night is coming , I think about finding somewhere to sleep . Sometimes in the jungle , give money to someone to have a bed . The taxi driver knew about it . I gave money to him and he told me . In some jungles , my friends passed this way . Those guys tell their stories . Some of them were shot . I am scared of Asadabad . Here it 's too hard , but my life is more dangerous there . I did n't see any hot time because everyday everybody is like Serbian , no fight , nothing just safe and everyone is good , that 's a very safe place . Many Afghans are in Aksaray . No one speaks English , this is a big problem , but Rehan is a good learner . In Turkey , the taxi driver told us how to go . Many guys are waiting . He said he will find something that will help us to cross . In Greece , it 's very dangerous because there is the sea . You can be only 20 people , but they put 60 people on one boat . So , there is a big danger . That way is near but too dangerous . That way is far but less dangerous . There was a guy that the taxi driver knows , and he showed me way . But the person told us : you go on that way and on that way . When we reached there , there were taxis to go to Sofia . That taxi driver took us to a place where we can sleep . But the biggest problem is we do n't know the Bulgarian language . They took our money ; they asked us for hundred dollars to go to Serbia . The taxi took us to the jungle , and again , the same guy we met , he shows us the way : you should go on this way . We did n't know anything about Bulgaria and we cannot go out of the house . We were afraid of the police and the fingerprints . That 's why many of us are going through Bulgaria . It was n't very expensive . Then we move to the jungle , we stayed all day in the jungle . There are houses , so if someone sees you , they will call the police . So better if you stay in the jungle . Then you cross the border . You need to reach the main road to Dimitrovgrad . The guy explained us before . After that , we travelled there by bus , thanks to NGOs . From Istanbul , there are only two ways to go to Europe . One is the sea through Greece , and one is Bulgaria . But people told us to be aware , to be not arrested by police that will take fingerprints and then will deport us from Europe to Bulgaria . We know that if you cross Bulgaria to enter Serbia , then , no problem . When we reached Dimitrovgrad , UNHCR and Red Cross gave us food , explained where we are , and gave us clothes , blankets , and everything , they arrange a ticket for us to go to Belgrade . Now , we are waiting for friends who are still in Bulgaria . We only know about Greece , that we needed to cross the sea . We knew from Greece that we need to go to Serbia and then Hungary . But , when we were in Istanbul , they said you could not go to Hungary , it 's a danger for life . So , we decide to go on that way . It 's a little bit expensive but it 's the safest way . Greece is less expensive but too dangerous . Afghanistan , fear for life ; Turkey is the best place I 've always been ; Bulgaria is the most frightening place that no one can forget , there were too many problems , Bulgarian police and Bulgarian people all treated us very bad ; and Serbia is better than Turkey because of the people , the friends we got here , all the people we met here .

Fig. 4. Example of a narrative text in English.

LOC
Hebergement
Membres de famille
Environnement
Moyens de transport

Bobo Dioulasso, juillet 2009, 06 septembre 2009, j'ai pris cette route parce que j'ai volé l'argent de mon frère pour fuir. C'est quand je suis arrivé à Koutiala au Mali on m'a parlé de cette route. C'est pour cette raison que j'ai tenté de venir ici. C'est des amis que j'ai rencontrés au Mali qui m'ont informé de cette route. Je suis passé par Koutiala, Bamako, Gao, Bordj Badji Mokhtar, Riganne et Bordj Badji Mokhtar où je suis resté. Je n'avais aucune connaissance sur les routes ni la difficulté. J'ai voyagé pour rentrer à Koutiala parce que j'ai peur que mon grand-frère me frappe. Je voulais me retourner à Bobo mais j'avais déjà dépensé beaucoup donc j'ai finalement opté pour le voyage sur l'Europe. Je suis resté avec une famille malienne sous prétexte que je suis orphelin. Après que les amis m'ont parlé de la route j'ai pris un minibus pour aller à Bamako. Après, je suis parti à Gao. J'ai payé 75.000 FCFA (environ 110 euros) pour passer en Algérie. J'ai emprunté le pickup avec une dizaine de migrants. On était très serré dans le pickup. J'étais fatigué et tout le monde criait et demandait au chauffeur d'arrêter le pickup. C'est un très difficile voyage. On a pris deux jours pour arriver à Bordj Badji Mokhtar. Le pickup nous a laissés à environ deux kilomètres du poste frontière. On a marché pour aller au poste. Les policiers ont pris tous les passeports pour le contrôle. J'étais de ceux qui n'ont pas pu traverser la frontière avec la faute de passeport. Alors le lendemain j'ai payé de l'argent à un démarcheur et j'ai finalement traversé la frontière. J'avais besoin de passeport pour continuer le parcours alors j'en ai payé un. J'ai pris le transport commun pour aller à Riganne. Je suis resté là-bas avec des maliens. Je me suis enfin mis à travailler parce que je commençais déjà à en manquer. Un jour, des maliens voulaient continuer le chemin et j'ai fait le chemin avec eux. On a emprunté un autobus. Comme on était au nombre de six subsahariens la police nous a contrôlé beaucoup de fois. Depuis que je suis arrivé ici je suis maintenant très décidé à continuer mon chemin jusqu'en Europe parce qu'il n'y a rien en Afrique. Je suis dans le loyer malien (appartement de trois pièces). Je travaille dans la construction et je vis de cet argent. Les gens sont très sympas et je n'ai pas de dérangements. Je n'ai pas grand contact avec les algériens. Je n'ai pas de contact avec mes parents. Ici la police rôde dans les environs mais ne font pas de rafles. C'est au Tchad (lieu où les migrants s'arrêtent pour chercher du travail que la police vient prendre les gens. Je ne sais vraiment pas ce qu'il faut penser de l'avenir.

Fig. 5. Example of a narrative text in French.

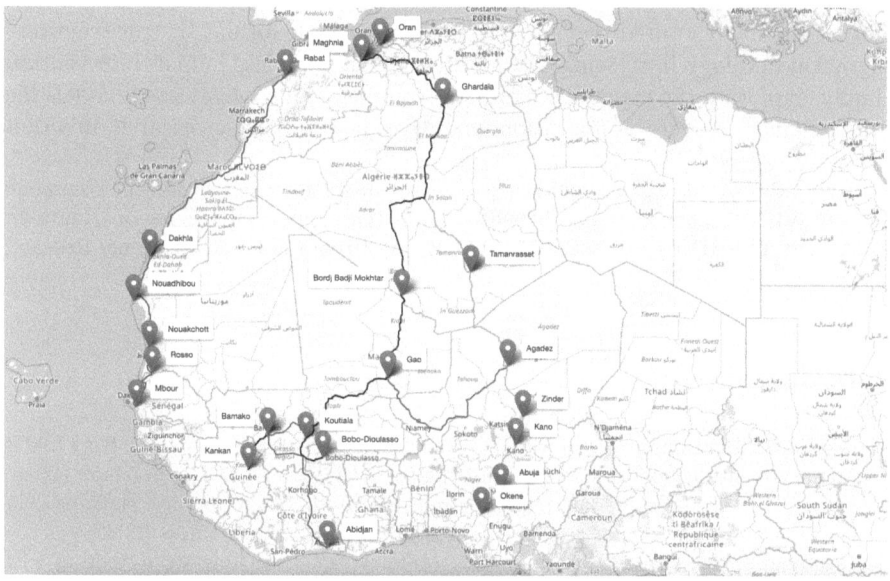

Fig. 6. Itineraries of migration routes from the Trans-Saharan region.

7   Conclusion and Future Works

In this paper, we have presented a text mining approach to leverage the collection of migration narratives in English and French. We first collaborated with HSS experts to annotate the essential concepts, their related terms, and the locations mentioned in the narratives. We then adapted a set expansion algorithm to extract related terms embedded in these narratives in a weakly supervised manner using a small set of annotated terms. We utilized existing NER models to identify locations crossed by migrants, followed by a pretrained disambiguation model to precisely locate them on a map. Experiments were conducted by comparing the output generated by the proposed algorithm and models to those annotated by experts. Finally, we design a tool to visualize the itineraries of migration routes on a map. Insightful discussions with HSS experts concluded that our framework aids their analyses by automatically extracting relevant terms and drawing the itineraries of migrants, providing a deep understanding of migration phenomena.

In the future, we plan to collect more interview texts while considering additional sensitive concepts, such as control and human trafficking. Addressing these non-neutral or politically charged concepts may require a larger dataset of migrant narratives to train and generate specific embeddings, thereby minimizing noisy terms during the expansion process. Additionally, we aim to enhance the performance of NER models, particularly for French, by fine-tuning pretrained models on French narratives and reassessing their effectiveness. Our next goal is to use the extracted terms from each concept to explore their relationships and convert the unstructured text into a machine-readable format by constructing a migration ontology in a (semi-)automatic manner with less human intervention. Finally, exploring the capabilities of more complex and sophisticated models like large language models on migration narratives is a promising research direction.

Acknowledgements. Many thanks to the reviewers for their insightful comments and suggestions. This work has benefited from the support of the region Hauts-de-France and ANR HYCI Project (ANR-22-CE55-0010) of the French National Research Agency.

References

1. Akbik, A., Bergmann, T., Blythe, D., Rasul, K., Schweter, S., Vollgraf, R.: FLAIR: an easy-to-use framework for state-of-the-art NLP. In: NAACL, pp. 54–59 (2019)
2. Bacon, L.: La fabrique du parcours migratoire sur la route des Balkans. Co-construction des récits et écritures (carto)graphiques. Ph.D. thesis (2022)
3. Bojanowski, P., Grave, E., Joulin, A., Mikolov, T.: Enriching word vectors with subword information. Trans. ACL **5** (2017)
4. Botha, J.A., Shan, Z., Gillick, D.: Entity linking in 100 languages. In: EMNLP, pp. 7833–7845 (2020)
5. Carterette, B., Voorhees, E.: Overview of information retrieval evaluation, pp. 69–85 (2011)
6. Chen, Z., Cafarella, M., Jagadish, H.V.: Long-tail vocabulary dictionary extraction from the web. In: WSDM, pp. 625–634 (2016)
7. Craswell, N.: Mean Reciprocal Rank. Springer, Boston (2009)
8. De Cao, N., et al.: Multilingual autoregressive entity linking. Trans. ACL **10** (2022)
9. Frantzi, K., Ananiadou, S., Mima, H.: Automatic recognition of multi-word terms: the c-value/ nc-value method. Int. J. Dig. Libr. **3**, 115–130 (2000)
10. Gantz, J., Reinsel, D.: Extracting value from chaos. IDC iview (2011)
11. GeoNames: Geonames. http://geonames.org/. Accessed 17 June 2009
12. Grave, E., Bojanowski, P., Gupta, P., Joulin, A., Mikolov, T.: Learning word vectors for 157 languages. In: LREC (2018)
13. He, Y., Xin, D.: SEISA: set expansion by iterative similarity aggregation. In: The Web Conference (2011)
14. Honnibal, M., Montani, I., Van Landeghem, S., Boyd, A.: spaCy: industrial-strength natural language processing in python (2020)
15. Hussain, M.N., Bandeli, K.K., Al-khateeb, S., Agarwal, N.: Analyzing shift in narratives regarding migrants in Europe via blogosphere (2018)
16. Ioffe, S.: Improved consistent sampling, weighted minhash and L1 sketching. In: ICDM, pp. 246–255 (2010)
17. Macanovic, A.: Text mining for social science – the state and the future of computational text analysis in sociology. Soc. Sci. Res. (2022)
18. Martin, L., et al.: CamemBERT: a tasty French language model. In: ACL (2020)
19. Nelson, A., de Sherbinin, A., Pozzi, F.: Towards development of a high quality public domain global roads database. Data Sci. J. (2006)
20. Petroni, F., et al.: Language models as knowledge bases? In: EMNLP-IJCNLP (2019)
21. Plekhanov, M., et al.: Multilingual end to end entity linking (2023)

22. Qi, P., Zhang, Y., Zhang, Y., Bolton, J., Manning, C.D.: Stanza: a python natural language processing toolkit for many human languages. In: ACL: System Demonstrations (2020)

23. Robin, N.: Migrations, observatoire et droit. complexité du système migratoire ouest-africain. migrants et normes juridiques. In: HdR. Univ. de Poitiers (2014)

24. Rong, X., Chen, Z., Mei, Q., Adar, E.: EgoSet: exploiting word ego-networks and user-generated ontology for multifaceted set expansion. In: WSDM (2016)

25. Salton, G., Buckley, C.: Term-weighting approaches in automatic text retrieval. Inf. Process. Manag. **24**(5), 513–523 (1988)

26. Shen, J., Wu, Z., Lei, D., Shang, J., Ren, X., Han, J.: SetExpan: corpus-based set expansion via context feature selection and rank ensemble (2019)

27. Shen, J., et al.: HiExpan: task-guided taxonomy construction by hierarchical tree expansion (2019)

28. Shi, S., Zhang, H., Yuan, X., Wen, J.R.: Corpus-based semantic class mining: distributional vs pattern-based approaches. In: COLING (2010)

29. Taylor, W.L.: "Cloze Procedure": a new tool for measuring readability. J. Q. **30**(4), 415–433 (1953)

30. Tong, S., Dean, J.: System and methods for automatically creating lists. US Patent 7,350,187 (2008)

31. Vrandečić, D., Krötzsch, M.: Wikidata: a free collaborative knowledgebase. Commun. ACM **57**(10), 78–85 (2014)

32. Wang, C., Chakrabarti, K., He, Y., Ganjam, K., Chen, Z., Bernstein, P.A.: Concept expansion using web tables. In: WWW (2015)

33. Wang, R.C., Cohen, W.W.: Language-independent set expansion of named entities using the web. In: ICDM, pp. 342–350 (2007)

34. Wu, W., Li, H., Wang, H., Zhu, K.Q.: Probase: a probabilistic taxonomy for text understanding. In: SIGMOD, pp. 481–492 (2012)

35. Öztürk, N., Ayvaz, S.: Sentiment analysis on twitter: a text mining approach to the Syrian refugee crisis. Telemat. Inf. (2018)

A Benchmark to Evaluate LLMs' Proficiency on Italian Student Competencies

Fabio Mercorio[1,2], Mario Mezzanzanica[1,2], Daniele Potertì[3], Antonio Serino[3], and Andrea Seveso[1,2(✉)]

[1] Department of Statistics and Quantitative Methods, University of Milano-Bicocca, Milan, Italy
{fabio.mercorio,mario.mezzanzanica}@unimib.it
[2] CRISP Research Centre, University of Milano-Bicocca, Milan, Italy
andrea.seveso@unimib.it
[3] Department of Economics, Management and Statistics, University of Milano-Bicocca, Milan, Italy

Abstract. Recent advancements in Large Language Models (LLMs) have significantly enhanced their ability to generate and manipulate human language, highlighting their potential across various applications. Evaluating LLMs in languages other than English is crucial for ensuring their linguistic versatility, cultural relevance, and applicability in diverse global contexts, thus broadening their usability and effectiveness. We tackle this challenge by introducing a structured benchmark using the INVALSI tests, a set of well-established assessments designed to measure educational competencies across Italy. Our study makes three primary contributions: First, we adapt the INVALSI tests as a benchmark for automated LLM evaluation, rigorously adapting the test format to suit automated processing while retaining the essence of the original tests. Second, we provide a detailed assessment of current LLMs, offering a crucial reference point for the academic community. Finally, we visually compare the performance of these models against human results. Additionally, our benchmark is publicly available and provided with a comprehensive evaluation suite (https://github.com/Crisp-Unimib/INVALSI-Eval-Suite), ensuring that the benchmark remains a current and valuable resource relevant for advancing industrial-strength NLP applications.

Keywords: Large Language Models · Benchmark · Evaluation

1 Introduction

In recent years, Large Language Models (LLMs) have emerged as a pivotal advancement in the field of Natural Language Processing (NLP) and Artificial Intelligence (AI) [9]. Model evaluation is paramount but difficult since there are various important qualities to consider: models should be precise, resilient, fair, and efficient, among others [26]. Developing language models that function effectively across diverse global languages and evaluating them remains a significant and ongoing challenge [41]. The currently available models often perform highly in English but are lacking in under-represented languages [38]. This is due to factors such as the scarce and lower quality available data [21], smaller contributing communities, and Anglo-centric cultural bias in development [42]. In the current landscape, there is a pressing need for a reliable tool to evaluate models' proficiency in the Italian language, particularly to assess their ability to align with the cultural and linguistic nuances critical for effective deployment in industrial contexts.

The INVALSI (National Institute for the Evaluation of the Education and Training System) test has been crucial in Italy's educational assessment since the 2005-2006 academic year. It evaluates students' competencies in subjects like the Italian language and mathematics at various educational stages. The primary goal is to assess linguistic proficiency, focusing on reading comprehension, grammatical knowledge, and lexical competence [45].

INVALSI tests use real-world language tasks to measure understanding of texts, appropriate vocabulary use, and application of grammatical rules [13,17,43]. The design ensures progressive complexity suitable for each educational level, providing fair and challenging assessments. These tests offer transparent benchmarks for student performance, guiding instructional strategies [31].

Since the test covers a wide range of linguistic and comprehension skills [14], using it to evaluate LLMs can provide a detailed view of a model's proficiency in handling real-world, nuanced language tasks designed for human learners. The test's structured and standardised nature makes it an excellent benchmark for comparing different LLMs with questions culturally and contextually relevant to Italian speakers. However, our findings are applicable across all languages since they assess various general capabilities, such as word formation and text comprehension abilities. Additionally, since it is designed for multiple educational stages, it offers a range of complexity and challenges. This aspect can gauge an LLM's capability at various difficulty levels, reflecting its potential scalability and adaptability across simpler to more complex linguistic tasks.

Given these robust evaluation criteria, this paper aims to establish a benchmark for assessing the performance of large language models by leveraging the INVALSI framework.

1.1 Contributions

The contributions of this work are fourfold:

1. We structure the INVALSI test, a notable national test for Italian students, as a publicly available evaluation benchmark for LLMs[1], making it a valuable resource for those aiming to integrate Italian language services powered by LLMs into their business operations;
2. We perform an in-depth analysis of existing models, using our benchmark, establishing a reference for the research community;
3. We visually display results across several important metrics and compare models' performances to human standards, pinpointing the strengths and weaknesses;

---

[1] We use a subset of tests, handpicked from different years and educational levels, ensuring that we exclude those with questions that are difficult to rephrase or that require analysing images.

4. We make the dataset available along with an evaluation suite, ensuring the replicability of our results and allowing anyone to test their model on the benchmark[2].

The remainder of the paper is structured as follows: Sect. 2 presents related work in the state of the art; Sect. 3 details our data curation process for creating the benchmark; Section sec:results displays the results of multiple models tested against this benchmark. Section 5 discusses these results and identifies limitations; Sect. 6 concludes the paper and outlines proposals for future work.

2   Related Work

A Large Language Model is a deep learning model trained on vast amounts of text data to develop a sophisticated understanding of language structures and semantics. Leveraging the transformer architecture [46], LLMs employ self-attention mechanisms to process sequential data efficiently, exemplified by models such as GPT [35].

Multilingual Models. LLMs have shown multilingual capabilities based on their training on multilingual data [24,44] and vocabulary [10,25,32]. GPT-3 and its successors have shown different capabilities in several languages [3] since their training corpora are, in part, composed of non-English texts. Most recently, smaller size models [20,44], due to the inclusion of multilingual data in the training process, have shown emerging capabilities in German, French, Spanish and Italian but not performing as well in the most prominent training language. Given the peculiarity of the Italian language and the lack of consistency of multilingual models in the Italian language, [15] pioneered the first Italian-adapted GPT-2-based model. The development of low-resource adaptation techniques [16,18] enabled the adaptation of larger models to Italian. Recently [39] instruction-tuned LLaMa with the Alpaca dataset translated into Italian, while [4] implemented Parameter Efficient Fine Tuning (PEFT) [28] using synthetically generated, machine-translated data. Additionally, [5] applied PEFT to LLaMa2 across multiple scales (7B, 13B, 70B). Most recently, [33] adapted an 8B LLaMa3 model to Italian via PEFT.

Available Benchmarks. Available benchmarks aim to evaluate commonsense reasoning [11,47], multi-step mathematical reasoning [12], Question-Answering [27] and reading comprehension capabilities [36]. The Italian NLP community lacks the depth of original language evaluation benchmarks compared to the English community. Some natively English benchmarks, such as [11,47], are commonly used to evaluate LLMs in Italian after being automatically translated. Benchmarks natively Italian are less common. [6] propose a Unified Benchmark for Italian Natural Language Understanding that covers textual entailment, Event detection and classification, factuality classification, sentiment polarity classification, irony detection and hate speech detection. [22] proposes a collaborative benchmark on 13 tasks. Both benchmarks focus on classification-based tasks and do not explore LLM properties, such as common-sense reasoning. Another Italian benchmark is represented by [23], which concentrates solely on Italian

---

[2] https://github.com/Crisp-Unimib/INVALSI-Eval-Suite.

news text summarisation abilities. Additionally, [29] introduced a specialised benchmark for evaluating LLMs on Italian driving license knowledge, demonstrating domain-specific evaluation approaches. More recently, [40] proposed a culture-aware benchmark specifically designed to assess LLMs' understanding of Italian cultural contexts and nuances. In a previous paper [34], the authors structured the INVALSI data to create a benchmark; however, unlike our work, they did not include any open-ended questions. These benchmarks lack a wide range of possible scenarios to evaluate LLMs, thus not allowing a comprehensive evaluation [26].

3   INVALSI Benchmark Curation

We have collected from public sources 58 unique tests, divided into 141 unique units, with 2114 questions and 2808 unique items. Some questions are subdivided into multiple items, each requiring a specific answer.

Data for this study was sourced from the Gestinv[3] database [7]. This database, widely used in Italian educational research and teacher development programs, includes questions from national assessments since 2008, as well as related test materials, statistical reports, and educational tools to enhance the understanding of student learning outcomes across Italy.

The questions' formatting is sometimes not adequately structured for LLM evaluation; for instance, it is occasionally impossible to automatically transcribe the questions into structured fields, necessitating further inspection of images and PDFs. For this reason, we also collected corresponding PDF files and images. Manual inspection was required to ensure accuracy. In cases where questions involved graphical elements, we modified them into a multiple-choice format that was more suitable for analysis. For example, if the task required a student to find and underscore a word, we reformulated the question to allow selection from multiple choices. Similarly, if the task involved drawing a line between two groups of concepts—a common task for younger students—we rephrased it to include choosing the correct association from given options. Generally, we aimed to adapt the questions to a format that allows the model to select the correct answer from a pool of choices if it aligns with the original question type. Figure 1 shows a few illustrative question examples.

3.1   Dataset Characteristics

We have selected 11 tests comprising 31 unique units, 405 questions, and 618 items from the above data. A test consists of two or more different units; each question can have more than one item to answer. The sample of tests was chosen through manual inspection, aiming to include a variety of grades and years, and avoiding those with questions that require image inspection or contain questions that would be difficult to reformulate for language model comprehension.

Table 2 shows the macro area distribution in our benchmark.

"Locate and identify information within the text" is used for all questions aiming to evaluate the capability of identifying various types of information within the provided

---

[3] https://www.gestinv.it/Index.aspx.

Illustrative Examples

Multiple Choice (MC) Question

Question:
In the sentence: "Livia was running in the park when a strong storm broke out," what are the events indicated by the two verbs?

Options:

- A. They are contemporary and have the same duration
- B. They are contemporary and indicate habitual actions
- C. The first event occurs during the second event
- D. The second event occurs during the first event (✓)

Multiple Complex Choice (MCC) Question

Question:
Read this sentence: "The night bird made such an acute sound that frightened the inhabitants of the forest very much."

Indicate whether *The* is a noun or not.
Options:

- A. It's a noun
- B. It's not a noun (✓)

Unique Response (RU) Question

Question:
Where would you put the letter h? Indicate whether or not it is necessary instead of **.

**avevo perso l'autobus così arrivai tardi a scuola.

Options:

- A. Necessary
- B. Not necessary (✓)

Fig. 1. Illustrative examples of the INVALSI benchmark for each question format. (✓) indicates the correct answer. **Note:** the original questions are in Italian, and the translation in English is purely for illustrative purposes.

context. *"Reconstruct the meaning of the text, locally or globally"* assesses how well one can infer and reconstruct the text's context and the encyclopedic knowledge it conveys. Lastly, *"Reflect on the content or form of the text, locally or globally, and evaluate them"* questions aim to evaluate the ability to interpret texts and their shape, expressing an evaluation. The remaining macro areas are designed and structured to evaluate grammatical knowledge. *"Word formation"* aims to assess knowledge about base words and their derivatives, and *"Lexicon and semantics"* aims to assess knowledge about the

Table 1. Distribution of tests, questions, and items by educational grade and question format.

Test Distribution by Grade			
School Grade	# Tests	# Questions	# Items
2nd (Primary School)	2	34	72
5th (Primary School)	2	73	115
6th (Middle School)	2	87	118
8th (Middle School)	2	86	88
10th (High School)	2	75	134
13th (High School)	1	50	91
Question Distribution by Format			
Format	# Questions		# Items
MC	337 (83.2%)		340
MCC	35 (8.6%)		228
RU	33 (8.1%)		50

Table 2. Distribution of questions by section and macro area.

Section	Macro Area	# Questions
Text comprehension	Reconstruct the meaning of the text, locally or globally	177 (43.7%)
	Locate and identify information within the text	108 (26.7%)
	Reflect on the content or form of the text, locally or globally, and evaluate them	33 (8.1%)
Reflection on the language	Lexicon and semantics	29 (7.2%)
	Morphology	24 (5.9%)
	Syntax	18 (4.4%)
	Word formation	7 (1.7%)
	Textuality and pragmatics	5 (1.2%)
	Spelling	4 (1.0%)

semantic relationship between words. The questions belonging to *"Morphology"* category aim to check the competencies with several lexical categories (noun, adjective, etc.) and sub-categories (possessive adjective, proper name, etc.). In contrast, using accents and apostrophes, upper and lowercase letters, etc., is evaluated by the questions categorised as *Spelling*. All the questions within *Syntax* aim to assess the correctness of syntactic rules of Italian written language, and *"Textuality and pragmatics"* aims to evaluate signs of text organisation and cohesion phenomena.

The questions come in three distinct formats, which are:

- *Multiple Choice (MC)*: composed of a question with several answer options, among which only one is correct. It is the most common question format in the selected tests, comprising 337 questions (83.2% of the total) and 340 items. Some questions require the selection of two distinct options, both of which must be correct. The answer choices are typically four, labelled A, B, C, and D.
- *Multiple Complex Choice (MCC)*: composed of input questions and multiple items to answer. It is the second most common type of question, with 38 (9.4%) instances

and 228 items. For each item, one answer from among the two or more available options must be selected, and only one is correct. The question is deemed correct only if all the items are rightly answered.

- *Unique Response (RU)*: involves open-ended questions in which there are no options or suggestions and where only one answer is considered correct (with sometimes a limited number of possible variants). We found 33 (8.1%) RU questions and 50 items in the selected tests.

3.2 Evaluation

The diversity in question formats ensures a comprehensive evaluation of the models' capabilities. 82.5% of the questions follow a standard multiple-choice format with closed options, 9.4% of the questions are multiple binary choices, requiring the model to affirm or deny statements, and 1% of the questions require specific handling, such as adding punctuation to one particular sentence. As seen in Table 1, 91.9% of the questions in the benchmark dataset created are MC and MCC. Consequently, evaluation involves verifying whether the generated answer includes the target answer, which is accomplished through the use of regular expressions. In the case of questions with multiple items, such as MCC, the question is only considered correct if all the items are answered correctly. Our approach is consistent with standard LLM evaluation frameworks, such as OpenAI's simple-evals[4]. We generate responses for open-source models and API-based LLMs and then compare these to the labelled correct answers. We use a temperature of 0 to ensure deterministic output in this setting. Each evaluation has been run exactly once. The benchmark tests models in a zero-shot scenario, requiring them to understand and correctly answer based on their general knowledge or the provided narrative.

Specific strategies for RU questions were developed to cater to their unique requirements. These questions require more than simply selecting an available option; therefore, the prompts were tailored with additional or specific instructions to ensure accurate responses. Each function for generating prompts checks for the presence of context and choices, incorporating them into the prompt if available. This provides the LLM with all pertinent information to answer the question accurately.

Specific evaluation methods include *word matching*, extracting words or phrases and comparing them directly to the answers, making it especially effective for questions that require specific terms or phrases. Another strategy is *pattern matching*: employing regular expressions to detect patterns in the model's output, aiding in evaluating syntactic or grammatical responses. Lastly, we use *BERTScore* [48] to assess the semantic content of answers with a threshold of 0.7 for correctness. This method ensures that responses capture the intended meaning, not just the exact wording, which is vital for complex language tasks where paraphrasing or diverse expressions may still be correct. This threshold has been empirically validated across all model answers. BERTScore utilises BERT's contextual embeddings to accurately evaluate the semantic similarity between responses and reference texts.

---

[4] https://github.com/openai/simple-evals.

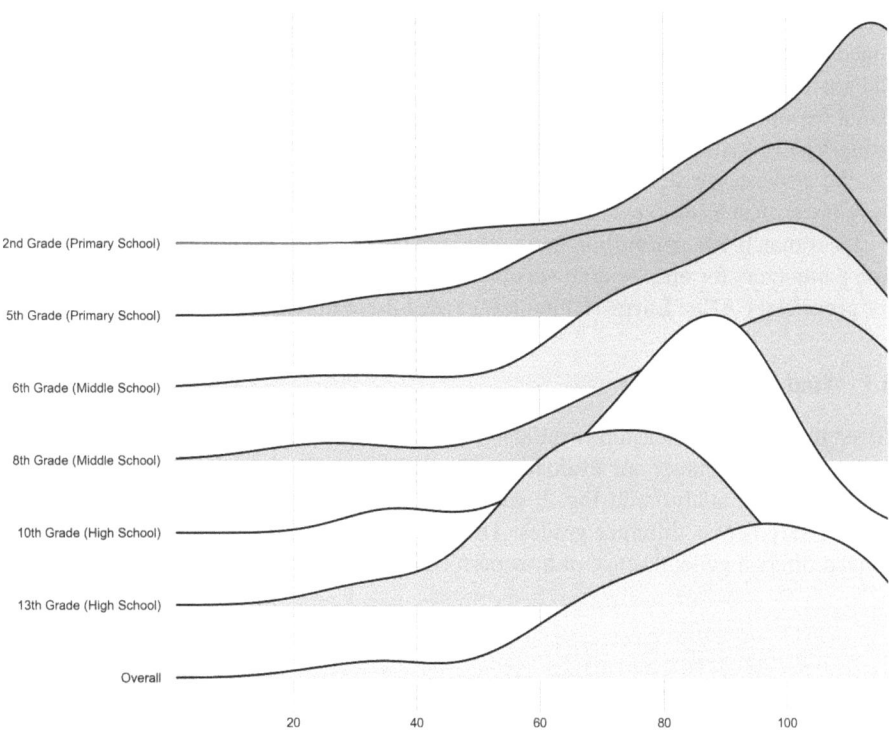

Fig. 2. Visualising the accuracy of various models across different school grades. Each layer represents a different grade level, from 2nd grade in primary school to 13th grade in high school, showing the distribution of performance accuracy for each grade.

4   Results

Model Selection Criteria. We evaluate a variety of notable foundational and fine-tuned models, chosen based on the following characteristics: (i) *Parameter threshold.* Models with at least three billion parameters are included to ensure substantial complexity and language comprehension capacity. (ii) *Temporal range.* Focuses on models published from 2023 onwards to capture recent advancements and influential models. (iii) *Institutional source.* Considers models from prominent organisations like OpenAI and Meta. (iv) *Popular Italian models.* Includes models specifically trained or fine-tuned in Italian.

For closed-source models, we include OpenAI's GPT-4o and GPT-4o-mini [1], both recognised for their advanced language capabilities. Additionally, we consider Anthropic's Claude series, which includes Haiku and Sonnet, each excelling in text generation tasks. Also part of our evaluation is Google's Gemini Pro 1.5 and 2.0 flash [37], as well as Gemma 3 27B. Our selection of open-source models includes Mistral 7B [19] and Mixtral [20]. Furthermore, we examine Meta's LLaMA 3 series models in three different sizes [2] (405B, 70B, 8B). For models specifically tuned to the Italian language, we include Minerva 7B [30], a foundational model trained from scratch in Italian, as well as Almawave's Velvet 14B[5]. We also consider LLaMAntino 3 [33], a model fine-tuned from LLaMa 3, popular models Llama-3.1-8b-Ita[6] and maestrale-chat-v0.4[7]. We did not inspect older versions of Italian models due to their lower performance. We evaluated the open-source models in bf16 format on an NVIDIA H100 80GB PCIe GPU, using VLLM with its default OpenAI-compatible server.

We also categorise the models into three categories by their size. **Small (S)** models have fewer than 8 billion parameters, or for the closed models accessible via API; they cost less than 0.50$ per million input tokens. **Medium (M)** models can go up to 70 billion parameters for open-source versions and cost less than 5$ per million input tokens for proprietary APIs. **Large (L)** models exceed these limits.

4.1 Model Performance

Given the various dimensions available, we present an overall accuracy distribution for each model to conduct our evaluation. The school grade is the most critical variable influencing our analysis; in Fig. 2, we provide a plot illustrating how accuracy distributions vary across different grades. This visual does not detail specific numbers but instead offers a general sense of how performance shifts with grade level, with a more

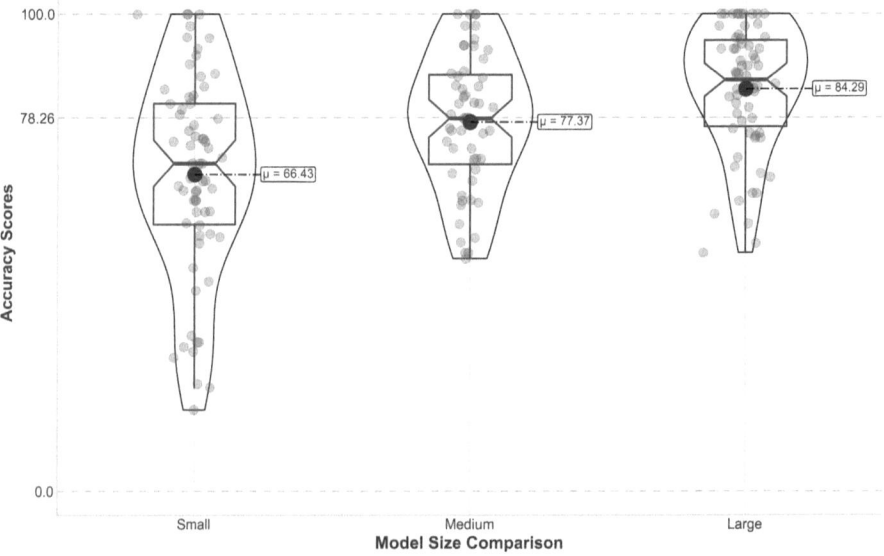

Fig. 3. Distribution of accuracy scores of language models categorised by size: small, medium, and large. Each plot represents the distribution of accuracy scores within each category, with individual data points highlighted, each representing a test taken by a model, and the mean accuracy marked by a horizontal line.

---

[5] Almawave/Velvet-14B.

[6] DeepMount00/Llama-3.1-8b-Ita.

[7] mii-llm/maestrale-chat-v0.4-beta.

detailed analysis to follow. Another intriguing dimension to consider is the impact of model size on performance. In Fig. 3, we present the distribution of scores segmented by the model size.

Detailed Analysis of Question Format and Macro Areas. We then delve into a detailed analysis of how question format influences performance. In Tables 3 and 4, we present the accuracy scores for each model, stratified by both school grade and question format. Due to the stratification and the limited number of questions in some categories, extreme values such as 100 or 0 are more attainable in the sections with few items. The number of questions for each category is indicated in the table headers. The model average is in the last column of Table 4. Similarly, Table 5 shows the performance comparison of AI models across linguistic macro areas.

Table 3. Performance (accuracy %) comparison of AI models across school grades and question formats for grades 2 to 6.

School Grade	2nd Grade (Primary School)	5th Grade (Primary School)			6th Grade (Middle School)		
Question Format (#)	MC (32)	MCC (2)	MC (61)	MCC (6)	RU (6)	MC (72)	MCC (6)	RU (9)
claude-3.7-sonnet	96.3	100.0	100.0	89.8	66.7	64.3	95.2	50.0
claude-3.5-haiku	88.9	100.0	75.0	85.7	58.3	57.1	76.2	0.0
gpt-4o	92.6	100.0	75.0	95.9	75.0	71.4	81.0	37.5
gpt-4o-mini	81.5	0.0	100.0	81.6	58.3	57.1	66.7	0.0
gemini-pro-1.5	92.6	100.0	100.0	81.6	58.3	64.3	83.3	25.0
gemini-2.0-flash	92.6	0.0	100.0	83.7	66.7	71.4	83.3	12.5
gemma-3-27b-it	88.9	100.0	75.0	83.7	33.3	57.1	69.0	12.5
Mistral-Large	88.9	0.0	100.0	85.7	66.7	64.3	81.0	12.5
mistral-nemo	77.8	0.0	75.0	73.5	41.7	71.4	73.8	0.0
llama-3.1-405b	93.8	100.0	100.0	93.9	66.7	71.4	83.3	37.5
llama-3.3-70b	88.9	100.0	75.0	85.7	58.3	78.6	81.0	0.0
llama-3.1-8b	64.2	0.0	50.0	67.3	25.0	64.3	61.9	0.0
■ Velvet-14B	60.5	0.0	50.0	71.4	25.0	35.7	57.1	12.5
■ Llama-3.1-8b-ITA	66.7	0.0	75.0	77.5	33.3	57.1	64.3	0.0
■ LLaMAntino-3-8B	63.0	0.0	50.0	67.3	25.0	42.9	52.4	0.0
■ maestrale-chat-v0.4	67.9	100.0	50.0	71.4	33.3	50.0	61.9	0.0
■ Minerva-7B	23.5	0.0	0.0	40.8	16.7	7.1	33.3	0.0
Models Avg	78.1	47.1	73.5	78.6	47.5	58.0	70.9	11.8

4.2 Comparison with Human Respondents

In evaluating the performance of language models, a critical comparison arises between the responses generated by these models and those of human respondents. We aim to provide insights into the capabilities of language models relative to average human performance.

Not every test we had included the percentage of human accuracies. Specifically, data was available from one test for grade 2; for grades 5 and 6, there were accuracies

Table 4. Performance (accuracy %) comparison of AI models (cont.), for grades 8 to 13 and overall average.

School Grade	8th Grade (Middle School)			10th Grade (High School)			13th Grade (High School)		All Grades
Question Format (#)	MC (81)	MCC (1)	RU (4)	MC (49)	MCC (12)	RU (14)	MC (42)	MCC (8)	Overall
claude-3.7-sonnet	96.3	100.0	100.0	89.8	66.7	64.3	95.2	50.0	92.3
claude-3.5-haiku	88.9	100.0	75.0	85.7	58.3	57.1	76.2	0.0	81.2
gpt-4o	92.6	100.0	75.0	95.9	75.0	71.4	81.0	37.5	90.1
gpt-4o-mini	81.5	0.0	100.0	81.6	58.3	57.1	66.7	0.0	78.3
gemini-pro-1.5	92.6	100.0	100.0	81.6	58.3	64.3	83.3	25.0	85.9
gemini-2.0-flash	92.6	0.0	100.0	83.7	66.7	71.4	83.3	12.5	87.7
gemma-3-27b-it	88.9	100.0	75.0	83.7	33.3	57.1	69.0	12.5	78.3
Mistral-Large	88.9	0.0	100.0	85.7	66.7	64.3	81.0	12.5	85.2
mistral-nemo	77.8	0.0	75.0	73.5	41.7	71.4	73.8	0.0	73.6
llama-3.1-405b	93.8	100.0	100.0	93.9	66.7	64.3	83.3	37.5	90.4
llama-3.3-70b	88.9	100.0	75.0	85.7	58.3	78.6	81.0	0.0	83.7
llama-3.1-8b	64.2	0.0	50.0	67.3	25.0	64.3	61.9	0.0	61.5
■ Velvet-14B	60.5	0.0	50.0	71.4	25.0	35.7	57.1	12.5	57.5
■ Llama-3.1-8b-ITA	66.7	0.0	75.0	77.5	33.3	64.3	64.3	0.0	66.2
■ LLaMAntino-3-8B	63.0	0.0	50.0	67.3	25.0	42.9	52.4	0.0	58.3
■ maestrale-chat-v0.4	67.9	100.0	50.0	71.4	33.3	50.0	61.9	0.0	64.7
■ Minerva-7B	23.5	0.0	0.0	40.8	16.7	7.1	33.3	0.0	28.6
Models Avg	78.1	47.1	73.5	78.6	47.5	58.0	70.9	11.8	64.9

Table 5. Performance (accuracy %) comparison of AI models across macro areas. Categories are abbreviated as: *LI*: Locate and identify information within the text. *RM*: Reconstruct the meaning of the text, locally or globally. *RC*: Reflect on the content or form of the text, locally or globally, and evaluate them. *WF*: Word formation. *LS*: Lexicon and semantics. *MO*: Morphology. *SP*: Spelling. *SY*: Syntax. *TP*: Textuality and pragmatics.

Section	Text Comprehension			Reflection on the Language						Both
Macro Area (#)	LI (108)	RM (177)	RC (33)	WF (7)	LS (29)	MO (24)	SP (4)	SY (19)	TP (5)	Overall
claude-3.7-sonnet	94.4	92.7	81.8	100.0	96.6	87.5	50.0	100.0	100.0	92.3
claude-3.5-haiku	82.4	85.9	81.8	57.1	69.0	83.3	0.0	66.7	100.0	81.2
gpt-4o	89.8	93.8	84.8	100.0	82.8	91.7	0.0	88.9	100.0	90.1
gpt-4o-mini	78.7	84.2	84.8	71.4	62.1	66.7	0.0	61.1	100.0	78.3
gemini-2.0-flash	89.8	89.8	78.8	100.0	79.3	87.5	0.0	94.4	100.0	87.7
gemini-pro-1.5	91.7	88.1	81.8	71.4	82.8	66.7	25.0	83.3	100.0	85.9
gemma-3-27b-it	82.4	81.4	72.7	42.9	62.1	79.2	0.0	83.3	100.0	78.3
Mistral-Large	88.0	87.0	81.8	85.7	79.3	79.2	25.0	88.9	80.0	85.2
mistral-nemo	79.6	81.9	78.8	57.1	48.3	41.7	0.0	44.4	100.0	73.6
llama-3.1-405b	89.8	93.2	87.9	85.7	86.2	83.3	50.0	94.4	100.0	90.4
llama-3.3-70b	88.0	89.3	84.8	71.4	72.4	70.8	0.0	66.7	60.0	83.7
llama-3.1-8b	63.9	72.3	66.7	14.3	41.4	25.0	0.0	38.9	80.0	61.5
■ Velvet-14B	63.9	63.8	66.7	0.0	34.5	33.3	0.0	38.9	80.0	57.5
■ Llama-3.1-8b-ITA	71.3	73.4	75.8	28.6	55.2	33.3	0.0	38.9	60.0	66.2
■ LLaMAntino-3-8B	61.1	66.7	69.7	0.0	41.4	29.2	0.0	44.4	40.0	58.3
■ maestrale-chat-v0.4	66.7	71.2	66.7	57.1	44.8	54.2	0.0	38.9	100.0	64.7
■ Minerva-7B	33.3	33.3	21.2	0.0	13.8	12.5	0.0	33.3	20.0	28.6
Models Avg	77.3	79.3	74.5	55.5	61.9	60.3	8.8	65.0	83.5	64.9

from two tests each; and for grades 8 and 10, accuracies were available from one test each. Unfortunately, no data on human accuracies was available for grade 13.

In Fig. 4, we compare human and model performances. The red lines represent the median of human answers, set at 59.8, to delineate which classes of models perform above this benchmark. This division creates four quadrants: both perform well, neither perform well, humans perform better, and models perform better.

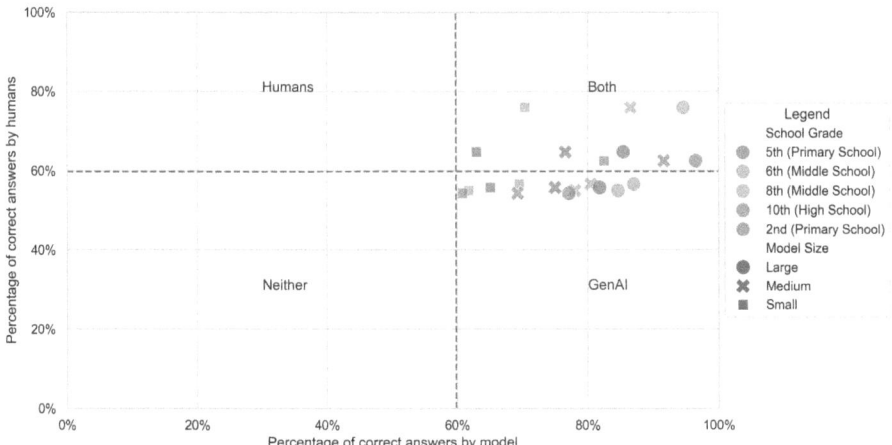

Fig. 4. Scatter plot visualising the accuracy of both human respondents and language models on various tests across different grade levels. The red lines represent the median accuracy of human answers at 59.8%. The graph is divided into four quadrants to categorise the performance: top-right quadrant ("Both"), where both humans and models perform well; top-left quadrant ("Humans"), where humans outperform models; bottom-right quadrant ("GenAI") where models outperform humans; and bottom-left quadrant ("Neither") where neither models nor humans perform well. Each symbol represents the average performance for each model size on a test, and colour coding corresponds to the educational grade level, providing an overview of where AI competes or lags behind human performance. Multiple data points with the same colour and symbol are shown wherever multiple tests for the same school grade exist. (Color figure online)

5 Discussion

Model Performance Across Stratifications. In analysing the performance results of these models, it is evident that models with a higher number of parameters generally demonstrate superior performance compared to those with fewer parameters, as illustrated in Fig. 3. The figure reveals that smaller models exhibit greater variance and dispersion in their accuracy scores than medium and large models. They achieve an average accuracy score of 66.43%. Medium-sized models have a slightly lower average accuracy, compared with the average total accuracy (78.26%), achieving an average score of 77.37%. While the larger sized models score well above average, achieving an accuracy of 84.29%.

Examination of Tables 3 and 4 reveals significant variability in model performance across various school grades.

Models tend to perform better in lower grades, while showing lower accuracy in higher ones. In particular, grade 6 and grade 13 are the grades in which the models have the most difficulty in answering the present questions correctly.

A comparative analysis of LLMs across various macro areas is shown in Table 5. A notable strength of these models is their ability to reconstruct the meaning of text, locally and globally (RM), with an overall accuracy of 79.3%. Conversely, none of the models consistently performed well in the spelling (SP) category, with an overall accuracy of 8.8%. A surprising result is the 83.5% accuracy achieved by the models in question in the Textuality and Pragmatics (TP) category. An example of this category is shown in Fig. 5.

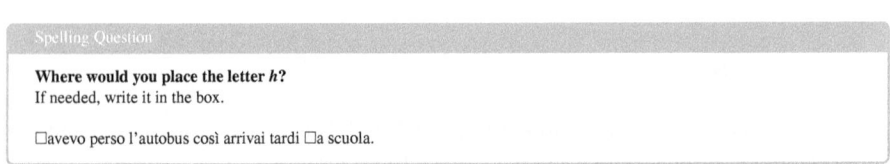

Textuality and Pragmatics Question

In the following sentence, insert the missing punctuation marks. Rewrite the sentence with the missing marks.

Mother called Little Red Riding Hood and told her please go to grandma; bring her these things the butter the eggs and the sugar

Fig. 5. Example of a Textuality and Pragmatics question.

Overall, LLMs exhibit superior performance on average in Text Comprehension tasks compared to Reflection on the Language tasks. This aligns with previous findings in the field of Language Understanding, where these language models can excel at understanding context and drawing inferences based on large contexts because of their generative pre-training and discriminative fine-tuning [35]. Conversely, syntax and morphology tasks require precise, rule-based understanding and application. Although models can produce grammatically correct text, they often encounter difficulties with tasks that demand explicit knowledge of linguistic rules and higher levels of reasoning. None of the models tested could correctly answer all or even the majority of the SP category questions. These questions presented a classical Italian writing task (Fig. 6):

Spelling Question

Where would you place the letter *h*?
If needed, write it in the box.

☐avevo perso l'autobus così arrivai tardi ☐a scuola.

Fig. 6. Example of a Spelling question.

The letter "h" should be placed correctly to answer this question and form the appropriate Italian words. The letter "h" is essential in Italian for distinguishing between certain homophones. The correct placement would differentiate "ho" (I have) and "ha" (he/she has), but in this context, the correct form is "a scuola" (at school), meaning no "h" is needed. Therefore, the sentence reads: "avevo perso l'autobus così arrivai tardi a scuola" (I missed the bus so I arrived late at school). We observed that some of the larger closed models correctly answered one or two of the four spelling questions.

Impact of Model Size on Performance. Large closed-source models achieve superior accuracy on benchmarks, successfully addressing approximately 80-85% of the tasks. The Claude class model exhibits the highest accuracy with *Claude Sonnet 3.7* at 92.3%, while OpenAI's *GPT 4o* model shows an accuracy of 90.1%. In the domain of open weights models, *llama-3.1-405b* achieves an accuracy of 90.4%, while *Mistral-Large* produce a 85.2% accuracy score. Among the Italian pre-trained models, *Minerva-7B* shows an accuracy rate of 28.6% and *Velvet-14B* shows an accuracy of 57.5%.

Whereas among the improved Italian models, *Llama-3.1-8b-ITA*, which is an improved variant of LaMA-3-8b, demonstrates improved performance, achieving a 66.2% success rate, an increase of 4.7% points over the base model.

Overall, the inference for this benchmark with closed-weight models incurred a cost slightly below $50. The dataset comprises approximately 620,000 input million tokens, yielding an average output of 17,000 tokens per model. As of the inference date, the costliest model was ChatGPT 4-o, priced at $5 per million input tokens and $15 per million output tokens.

Comparison of Models with Human Respondents. When evaluating language models, comparing their responses to human respondents is crucial. However, human accuracy data was not uniformly available: it was present for one test in grade 2, two tests each in grades 5 and 6, and one test each in grades 8 and 10, with no data for grade 13. In Fig. 4, we visualise those comparisons. The red lines, representing the median human score 59.8%, identify which models perform above or below this level. This creates four quadrants: both perform well, neither perform well, humans perform better, and models perform better. It is interesting to notice that, while we assume that LLMs' performance would vary linearly with task difficulty, human cognitive development does not follow a linear path in individuals but occurs in stages marked by times of discontinuity [8], especially during adolescence.

5.1   Limitations

Data Availability. The dataset obtained from Gestinv includes all the INVALSI tests on the Italian language; however, a few questions (3 or 4) were missing from certain tests. Moreover, in some tests, particularly those labelled as simulations, a few questions were missing multiple-choice options, rendering the questions unclear. Some metadata was wrongly labelled. These minor issues were identified and rectified through manual intervention.

Potential Shortcomings in Complex Answer Evaluation. A subset of questions (seven in total) posed a significant challenge in the evaluation due to the requirement for subjective judgment to determine the correctness of the answers. These questions necessitate that the generated answers be semantically relevant to the target answers provided as references. The complexity arises because semantic relevance is not always easily quantifiable, leading to potential inconsistencies in assessment. To address this, we employed BERTscore [48] to establish an empirical threshold where answers with a BERT score greater than 0.70 were considered correct, while those below this threshold were deemed incorrect. While this method provided a systematic evaluation approach, it has limitations. In practice, this method has been manually validated to work well in all present cases, and future cases will be carefully monitored.

6   Conclusion and Future Work

This research paper introduces a new benchmark for evaluating large language models by structuring the Italian INVALSI tests. Key contributions include establishing a structured benchmark for the Italian language, extensively assessing current LLMs, and comparing model performances across various dimensions. Due to the increased complexity of language and cognitive tasks at higher levels, models perform better on tasks for lower school grades than on higher ones. Models excel in text comprehension but find reflecting on the Italian language harder. Larger models outperform smaller ones, even those pre-trained and fine-tuned for the Italian language, indicating that extensive training data and complex architectures help handle language task nuances better. We also release the *data* and *evaluation suite* to allow anyone to test their model on our benchmark at https://github.com/Crisp-Unimib/INVALSI-Eval-Suite.

Looking ahead, the research aims to expand the benchmark's scope and utility by *(i) incorporating mathematics and multimodal capabilities* to test the models' abilities to handle linguistic, quantitative, and visual information. *(ii) Increasing the test size* to enhance the robustness of evaluations, reduce variance, and provide a more comprehensive assessment of LLMs' linguistic capabilities.

A   Ethical Considerations

The dataset is composed entirely of publicly available test questions and does not include any confidential information, personal data, or non-public communications. All data and materials used in the collection process are free from personally identifiable information or sensitive content. An ethical review process was unnecessary since the dataset is derived solely from public tests and does not involve human subjects or private data. However, potential misuse risks exist, such as using benchmark results to support or oppose the development of native LLMs specifically tailored to the Italian language. Careful consideration is advised to prevent misinterpretations or unintended consequences when applying the evaluation outcomes.

B   Resource Availability Statement

Our benchmark is accessible at https://doi.org/10.5281/zenodo.15553471 under the MIT license, with no IP-based or other restrictions. Additionally, the code used for the evaluation is available on GitHub[8].

---

[8] https://github.com/Crisp-Unimib/INVALSI-Eval-Suite.

References

1. Achiam, J., et al.: Gpt-4 technical report. arXiv preprint arXiv:2303.08774 (2023)
2. AI@Meta: Llama 3 model card (2024). https://github.com/meta-llama/llama3/blob/main/MODEL_CARD.md
3. Armengol-Estapé, J., Bonet, O.D.G., Melero, M.: On the multilingual capabilities of very large-scale english language models. arXiv preprint arXiv:2108.13349 (2021)
4. Bacciu, A., Trappolini, G., Santilli, A., Rodolà, E., Silvestri, F.: Fauno: the Italian large language model that will leave you senza parole! arXiv preprint arXiv:2306.14457 (2023)
5. Basile, P., Musacchio, E., Polignano, M., Siciliani, L., Fiameni, G., Semeraro, G.: Llamantino: Llama 2 models for effective text generation in Italian language. arXiv preprint arXiv:2312.09993 (2023)
6. Basile, V., Bioglio, L., Bosca, A., Bosco, C., Patti, V.: Uinauil: a unified benchmark for italian natural language understanding. In: Proceedings of the 61st Annual Meeting of the Association for Computational Linguistics, vol. 3: System Demonstrations, pp. 348–356 (2023)
7. Bolondi, G., Gambini, A., Ferretti, F.: Il database gestinv delle prove standardizzate invalsi: Uno strumento per la ricerca: Alcuni esempi di utilizzo nell'ambito della matematica. In: I dati INVALSI: Uno strumento per la ricerca, pp. 43–48. Franco Angeli (2017)
8. Carey, S., Markman, E.M.: Cognitive development. In: Cognitive Science, pp. 201–254. Elsevier (1999)
9. Chang, Y., et al.: A survey on evaluation of large language models (2023). http://arxiv.org/abs/2307.03109
10. Chung, H.W., Garrette, D., Tan, K.C., Riesa, J.: Improving multilingual models with language-clustered vocabularies. arXiv preprint arXiv:2010.12777 (2020)
11. Clark, P., et al.: Think you have solved question answering? Try arc, the ai2 reasoning challenge. arXiv preprint arXiv:1803.05457 (2018)
12. Cobbe, K., et al.: Training verifiers to solve math word problems (2021). https://arxiv.org/abs/2110.14168
13. Corsini, C.: La validità di contenuto delle prove invalsi di comprensione della lettura. Ital. J. Educ. Res. **10**, 46–61 (2013)
14. Corsini, C., Losito, B.: Le rilevazioni invalsi: a che cosa servono? Cadmo: giornale italiano di pedagogia sperimentale: 2, 2013, pp. 55–76 (2013)
15. De Mattei, L., Cafagna, M., Dell'Orletta, F., Nissim, M., Guerini, M.: Geppetto carves italian into a language model. arXiv preprint arXiv:2004.14253 (2020)
16. Dettmers, T., Pagnoni, A., Holtzman, A., Zettlemoyer, L.: Qlora: efficient finetuning of quantized llms. Adv. Neural Inf. Process. Syst. **36** (2024)
17. Guzzo, G.: La competenza grammaticale nelle prove invalsi (2023)
18. Hu, E.J., et al.: Lora: low-rank adaptation of large language models. arXiv preprint arXiv:2106.09685 (2021)
19. Jiang, A.Q., et al.: Mistral 7b. arXiv preprint arXiv:2310.06825 (2023)
20. Jiang, A.Q., et al.: Mixtral of experts. arXiv preprint arXiv:2401.04088 (2024)
21. Kreutzer, J., et al.: Quality at a glance: an audit of web-crawled multilingual datasets. Trans. Assoc. Comput. Linguist. **10**, 50–72 (2022)
22. Lai, M., Menini, S., Polignano, M., Russo, V., Sprugnoli, R., Venturi, G., et al.: Evalita 2023: overview of the 8th evaluation campaign of natural language processing and speech tools for italian. In: Proceedings of the Eighth Evaluation Campaign of Natural Language Processing and Speech Tools for Italian. Final Workshop (EVALITA 2023). CEUR. org, Parma (2023)
23. Landro, N., Gallo, I., La Grassa, R., Federici, E.: Two new datasets for italian-language abstractive text summarization. Information **13**(5), 228 (2022)

24. Li, J., Zhou, H., Huang, S., Cheng, S., Chen, J.: Eliciting the translation ability of large language models via multilingual finetuning with translation instructions. Trans. Assoc. Comput. Linguist. **12**, 576–592 (2024)
25. Liang, D., et al.: Xlm-v: overcoming the vocabulary bottleneck in multilingual masked language models. arXiv preprint arXiv:2301.10472 (2023)
26. Liang, P., et al.: Holistic evaluation of language models. arXiv preprint arXiv:2211.09110 (2022)
27. Lin, S., Hilton, J., Evans, O.: Truthfulqa: measuring how models mimic human falsehoods. arXiv preprint arXiv:2109.07958 (2021)
28. Mangrulkar, S., Gugger, S., Debut, L., Belkada, Y., Paul, S., Bossan, B.: Peft: state-of-the-art parameter-efficient fine-tuning methods (2022). https://github.com/huggingface/peft
29. Mercorio, F., Potertì, D., Serino, A., Seveso, A., et al.: Beep-best driver's license performer: a calamita challenge. In: CEUR Workshop Proceedings, vol. 3878 (2024)
30. Orlando, R., et al.: Minerva llms: the first family of large language models trained from scratch on Italian data. In: Proceedings of the Tenth Italian Conference on Computational Linguistics (CLiC-it 2024) (2024)
31. Pastore, S., Freddano, M., et al.: "questione di feedback": dati invalsi e pratiche di valutazione in classe. In: I dati INVALSI: uno strumento per la ricerca, pp. 89–100. FrancoAngeli (2017)
32. Pires, T., Schlinger, E., Garrette, D.: How multilingual is multilingual bert? arXiv preprint arXiv:1906.01502 (2019)
33. Polignano, M., Basile, P., Semeraro, G.: Advanced natural-based interaction for the Italian language: Llamantino-3-anita (2024)
34. Puccetti, G., Cassese, M., Esuli, A.: The invalsi benchmarks: measuring the linguistic and mathematical understanding of large language models in Italian. In: Rambow, O., Wanner, L., Apidianaki, M., Al-Khalifa, H., Eugenio, B.D., Schockaert, S. (eds.) Proceedings of the 31st International Conference on Computational Linguistics, pp. 6782–6797. Association for Computational Linguistics, Abu Dhabi (2025). https://aclanthology.org/2025.coling-main. 453/
35. Radford, A., Narasimhan, K., Salimans, T., Sutskever, I.: Improving language understanding by generative pre-training (2018)
36. Rajpurkar, P., Zhang, J., Lopyrev, K., Liang, P.: Squad: 100,000+ questions for machine comprehension of text. arXiv preprint arXiv:1606.05250 (2016)
37. Reid, M., et al.: Gemini 1.5: unlocking multimodal understanding across millions of tokens of context. arXiv preprint arXiv:2403.05530 (2024)
38. Ruder, S., et al.: Xtreme-r: towards more challenging and nuanced multilingual evaluation. In: Proceedings of the 2021 Conference on Empirical Methods in Natural Language Processing. Association for Computational Linguistics (2021)
39. Santilli, A., Rodolà, E.: Camoscio: an Italian instruction-tuned llama. arXiv preprint arXiv:2307.16456 (2023)
40. Seveso, A., Potertì, D., Federici, E., Mezzanzanica, M., Mercorio, F., et al.: Italic: an Italian culture-aware natural language benchmark. In: Proceedings of the 2025 Conference of the Nations of the Americas Chapter of the Association for Computational Linguistics: Human Language Technologies, 29 April–4 May 2025, vol. 1: Long Papers), pp. 1469–1478 (2025)
41. Srivastava, A., et al.: Beyond the imitation game: quantifying and extrapolating the capabilities of language models. arXiv preprint arXiv:2206.04615 (2022)
42. Talat, Z., et al.: You reap what you sow: on the challenges of bias evaluation under multilingual settings. In: Proceedings of BigScience Episode# 5–Workshop on Challenges & Perspectives in Creating Large Language Models, pp. 26–41 (2022)
43. Tóth, Z.: Riflettere sulle parole: la formazione delle parole nelle prove invalsi. Lingue antiche e moderne **12**, 277–298 (2023)

44. Touvron, H., et al.: Llama 2: open foundation and fine-tuned chat models. arXiv preprint arXiv:2307.09288 (2023)

45. Trinchero, R.: Il servizio nazionale di valutazione e le prove invalsi. stato dell'arte e proposte per una valutazione come agente di cambiamento. Form@ re-Open Journal per la formazione in rete **14**(4), 34–49 (2014)

46. Vaswani, A., et al.: Attention is all you need. Adv. Neural Inf. Process. Syst. **30** (2017)

47. Zellers, R., Holtzman, A., Bisk, Y., Farhadi, A., Choi, Y.: Hellaswag: can a machine really finish your sentence? arXiv preprint arXiv:1905.07830 (2019)

48. Zhang, T., Kishore, V., Wu, F., Weinberger, K.Q., Artzi, Y.: Bertscore: evaluating text generation with bert. arXiv preprint arXiv:1904.09675 (2019)

Longitudinal Surveys Are Texts: LLM-Enhanced Analysis of School Attendance in New Zealand

Tingrui Qiao[1]([✉]), Caroline Walker[1], Chris Cunningham[2], Adam Jang-Jones[3], Susan Morton[4], Kane Meissel[1], and Yun Sing Koh[1]

[1] University of Auckland, Auckland, New Zealand
{ricky.qiao,caroline.walker,k.meissel,y.koh}@auckland.ac.nz
[2] Massey University, Auckland, New Zealand
C.W.Cunningham@massey.ac.nz
[3] New Zealand Ministry of Education, Wellington, New Zealand
Adam.JangJones@education.govt.nz
[4] University of Technology Sydney, Ultimo, Australia
Susan.Morton@uts.edu.au

Abstract. School attendance is an important factor in educational success and plays a key role in shaping students' academic and social development. Longitudinal surveys provide valuable insights into factors affecting attendance patterns, yet analysing such data presents unique challenges. First, the variation in survey questions across data collection waves complicates the application of standard temporal modelling techniques that assume consistent features over time. Second, conventional methods often one-hot encode survey responses, stripping away contextual meaning within questions and responses. Lastly, open-ended responses are typically omitted, leading to a loss of valuable qualitative insights. To address these challenges, we propose Survey-as-Text Modelling (STM), which represents multi-wave survey questionnaires as coherent textual sequences. By maintaining the textual format, STM allows similar questions across different years to be compared directly rather than existing as independent features. STM also retains the meaning within question-response pairs, preventing loss of information from one-hot encoding and enabling the incorporation of open-ended responses. We apply STM to survey data from *Growing Up in New Zealand* and link it to official attendance records from the *New Zealand Ministry of Education*. We leverage large language models (LLMs) to predict future school attendance from text-based surveys, outperforming existing temporal methods. Beyond predictive accuracy, we propose gradient-guided counterfactual analysis to identify key survey questions influencing the model's decision-making. Our findings highlight the potential of LLMs for survey analysis and provide data-driven insights that can inform policy and intervention strategies.

Keywords: Longitudinal Survey · Large Language Models · School Attendance

B. Pfahringer et al. (Eds.): ECML PKDD 2025, LNAI 16020, pp. 310–327, 2026.
https://doi.org/10.1007/978-3-662-72243-5_18

1 Introduction

School attendance is an important determinant of academic achievement, social development, and long-term well-being [20]. Attendance is shaped by a wide range of factors, including mental health [10], parental support [31], socioeconomic status [21], school experiences [22], and external disruptions such as the COVID-19 pandemic [29]. Data from *Growing Up in New Zealand* (GUiNZ) [34], the country's largest ongoing longitudinal study on child well-being, which tracks over 6,000 children from before they were born, provides an opportunity to examine these influences. GUiNZ collects data through repeated data collection waves, where participants provide survey responses at different ages, capturing evolving socioecological factors over time. By linking this data with official attendance records from the *New Zealand Ministry of Education*, we are able to analyse how multiple factors interact over time to shape attendance patterns.

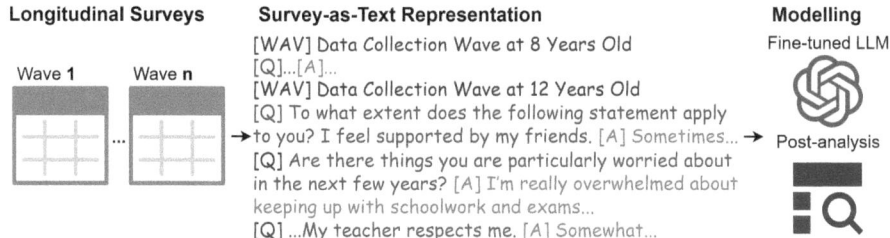

Fig. 1. In Survey-as-Text Modelling, survey data from multiple data collection waves is retained as natural text representation where special delimiters are used to separate survey waves, questions, and responses. The text representation is processed by a fine-tuned large language model for attendance prediction.

Analysing longitudinal survey data presents challenges to existing temporal modelling methods. First, the variation in survey questions across waves disrupts the assumption of the same features being collected over time at regular intervals. This poses difficulties for existing methods such as Recurrent Neural Networks (RNNs) [42] and Transformers [53,56], which often assume structured input sequences with consistent features across observations or time steps. However, in longitudinal surveys, questions evolve due to shifting research priorities and external factors; for instance, earlier waves from GUiNZ include questions on experience starting school, while later waves focus on the impact of COVID-19 on schooling. Additionally, data collection occurs at irregular intervals, with some variables collected at certain waves but omitted in others; for example, the New Zealand index of socioeconomic deprivation [2] is recorded at ages six, eight, and twelve, while questions about material hardship are asked at ages six and twelve but not at age eight, further complicating feature alignment. Second, conventional methods often one-hot encode survey responses, leading to a loss of contextual meaning within questions and responses. For example, responses to "children feel they belong to school when they start school" and "children feel they are connected to school during lockdown" may be treated as entirely separate variables, losing their relationship in meaning, or collapsed into a single category, ignoring the differences in context. One-hot encoding forces models to rely on statistical associations rather than textual meaning, limiting their ability to capture nuanced relationships in survey data. Lastly, conventional approaches struggle to incorporate open-ended responses, which often contain valuable qualitative insights. Since these responses cannot be easily one-hot encoded, they are frequently excluded from analysis. For example, responses to "What is the most worrying thing during the COVID-19 lockdown?" can reveal key concerns affecting school attendance, but existing methods lack a structured way to integrate this information. These limitations highlight the need for a more flexible approach that can preserve contextual meaning, handle irregular survey structures, and incorporate qualitative responses into predictive modelling.

To address these limitations, we propose Survey-as-Text Modelling (STM), which represents longitudinal survey data in its natural textual format rather than converting it into structured tabular variables. By leveraging large language models (LLMs), which have been pretrained on vast amounts of text data, STM can model survey data while preserving its original structure and meaning. STM mitigates the challenge of irregular survey structures caused by evolving questions across waves. Instead of treating missing or modified variables as a structural problem requiring imputation or manual feature alignment, STM processes survey responses as continuous textual sequences, allowing similar questions asked at different waves to be compared within context rather than treated as separate features. This enables the model to generalise across changes in wording or focus of questions, ensuring better alignment of information across survey waves. The time information of each wave can also be described within the text representation, indicating the time duration between each wave. Furthermore, STM retains the contextual meaning of survey questions and responses and leverages LLMs' ability to understand texts to maintain the conceptual connection between similar but distinct questions (e.g., school engagement at different time points) and to recognise differences in phrasing and context. This allows the model to capture deeper relationships between responses rather than treating them as isolated categorical variables. Additionally, STM directly incorporates open-ended responses by integrating them naturally within the textual representation, allowing LLMs to extract meaningful insights alongside structured survey responses. This provides a richer understanding of subjective factors influencing attendance, such as personal experiences, concerns, and motivations, that would otherwise be omitted from quantitative models.

Beyond predictive modelling, interpretability is essential for deriving insights from survey data. Therefore, we propose gradient-guided counterfactual analysis to identify the most influential survey items in attendance predictions. By aggregating gradients at the question level, we highlight which questions and responses contribute most to the model's decision. However, gradient-based attribution alone provides only ranked importance of survey items and does not determine which specific responses can consistently influence model decisions. To address this, we assess model sensitivity by iteratively swapping responses with values sampled from participants in the opposite attendance category, following the ranked importance of survey items based on question-level gradients. We identify the minimal number of swaps required to flip a participant's classification and analyse which questions appear most frequently in these minimal swaps, highlighting the key factors influencing attendance predictions. Our main contributions are as follows:

1. We propose **Survey-as-Text Modelling (STM)**, which preserves the textual format of surveys and leverages LLMs to predict future school attendance. The text representation allows STM to address challenges in feature alignment, evolving contexts, and open-ended responses.
2. To improve interpretability, we introduce **gradient-guided counterfactual analysis** to identify influential survey items and evaluate how response variations impact model decision-making.
3. By linking *Growing Up in New Zealand* survey data with official attendance records from the *Ministry of Education*, our approach provides insights into potential factors influencing school attendance, supporting policymakers in data-driven decision-making and targeted interventions.

2   Related Work

Longitudinal Analysis. Longitudinal studies provide valuable insights by tracking individuals or groups over time, enabling researchers to identify temporal patterns, developmental changes, and underlying trends [49]. Conventional statistical methods, such as latent growth models and autoregressive approaches, rely on strong assumptions, including lack of multicollinearity, specific data distributions, and homoscedasticity [9]. These methods struggle with high-dimensional data, limiting flexibility in complex real-world applications [41]. Machine learning and deep learning offer a more adaptable alternative by capturing non-linear and higher-order relationships. Jin et al. [18] used Long Short-Term Memory to predict malnutrition from longitudinal patient records. Adler et al. [1] applied gradient boosting to track mental health symptoms using longitudinal mobile sensing data. Nitski et al. [36] explored Transformers, Temporal Convolutional Networks, and Recurrent Neural Networks for long-term mortality prediction in liver transplant recipients. These methods rely on fixed feature sets across time, making them less suited to longitudinal surveys where questions evolve, responses carry contextual meaning, and open-ended data remains underutilised. Our approach treats survey responses as natural text, enabling LLMs to address these challenges within a unified framework.

LLMs for Time Series. LLMs have been increasingly explored for time series modelling, demonstrating their ability to capture complex temporal dependencies. Existing approaches aim to enhance LLMs' ability to process numerical time series directly or align time series data with LLMs' natural language capabilities. Xue et al. [51] encode numerical inputs and outputs within prompts to adapt LLMs for time series tasks, while Zhou et al. fine-tune LLM input and output layers for time series modelling. Cao et al. [5] decompose trend, seasonal, and residual components within prompts to improve distribution adaptation. Other methods attempt to bridge time series with language processing: Jin et al. [19] align time series patches with text modality and supplement inputs with textual dataset descriptions, Sun et al. [44] map time series embeddings to LLM token spaces, and Pan et al. [37] employ semantic-informed prompt learning for cross-modal alignment. While these methods adapt LLMs for structured time series data, they primarily treat time series as numerical sequences and lack direct contextual information. In contrast, our approach models longitudinal surveys as text, leveraging LLMs' language understanding to handle evolving questions, irregular structures, and open-ended responses, making it fundamentally different from numerical time series modelling.

LLMs Interpretability. Interpreting the predictions of LLMs has been a growing area of research, with various methods developed to explain model decisions. Local surrogate models [12] and local interpretable models [11] approximate LLM predictions using simpler models, but they rely on sampling-based approximations and do not directly reveal which variables drive predictions in structured survey responses. Concept bottleneck models [45] enforce interpretability by mapping predictions to predefined concepts; however, in our setting, survey questions already serve as well-defined interpretable variables, making additional concepts unnecessary. Self-explanation techniques [16,39] generate textual justifications for LLM outputs but can suffer from hallucination and may not consistently align with the true decision-making process. Attribution-based methods such as Shapley values [33] estimate the contribution of individual input components, while gradient-based attribution [43] analyses the sensitivity of predictions to input perturbations. However, these techniques operate at the token level, making it difficult to aggregate influence at the question-response level, which is essential for understanding survey-based predictions. Our approach, gradient-guided counterfactual analysis, first aggregates gradients at the question level to identify influential survey items, then iteratively swaps responses and observes prediction changes to reveal their impact on model decisions.

3   Survey-as-Text Modelling

We introduce Survey-as-Text Modelling (STM), a framework that leverages LLMs to process survey responses in their natural textual form. Section 3.1 details STM's text-based modelling and fine-tuning for classification, while Sect. 3.2 introduces gradient-guided counterfactual analysis to identify influential survey items and assess response swaps' impact on predictions.

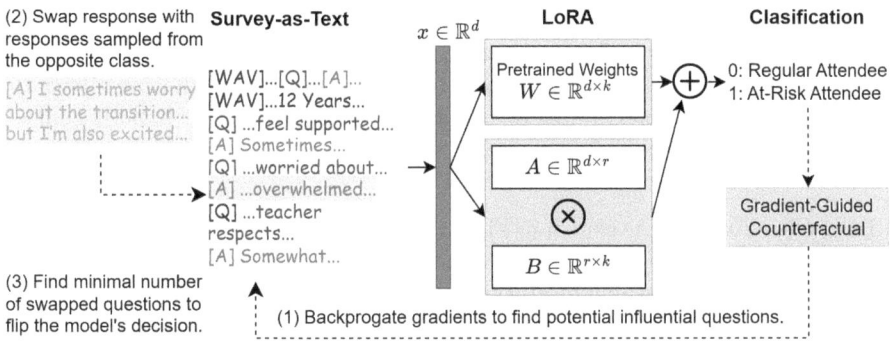

Fig. 2. Survey-as-Text Modelling processes longitudinal surveys as text. A Low-Rank Adaptation (LoRA) fine-tuned LLM is used for classification, where pretrained weights $W \in \mathbb{R}^{d \times k}$ remain frozen, and low-rank adaptation matrices $A \in \mathbb{R}^{d \times r}$ and $B \in \mathbb{R}^{r \times k}$ are learned during finetuning. Here, d represents the input embedding dimension, k is the output dimension of the layer, and r is the rank of LoRA. Gradient-based attribution identifies potential influential questions, and counterfactual swaps reveal key variables that impact classification.

3.1 Modelling Survey with LLMs

Problem Definition. Given a longitudinal survey collected over T waves, each wave is represented as $X^t = \{(q_i^t, x_i^t)\}_{i=1}^{D^t}$, where each (q_i^t, x_i^t) denotes a survey question q_i^t and its corresponding response x_i^t. The number of questions D^t varies across waves, meaning that certain questions may be missing in some waves. The objective is to train a classification model $\mathcal{C}$ with parameters $\Theta_\mathcal{C}$ to predict a categorical target variable $\hat{Y}$ using responses from past survey waves as input: $\hat{Y} = \mathcal{C}(\{X^1, X^2, \ldots, X^{T-1}\}; \Theta_\mathcal{C})$. The classification output $\hat{Y}$ is a discrete label corresponding to predefined categories. Unlike time-series classification, where the input consists of structured numerical sequences $X \in \mathbb{R}^{D \times T}$ with a fixed set of D features across all time steps, our formulation allows the number of features to vary per wave, meaning $D^t \neq D^{t'}$ for some $t \neq t'$, reflecting the evolving nature of survey design.

Text Representation. We represent each wave X^t as a structured text sequence. As shown in Fig. 1, each wave begins with a textual description that explicitly marks the data collection period, such as *"Data Collection Wave at 6 Years Old (2015)"*, providing temporal context and allowing the model to distinguish between different survey waves. Each question-response pair (q_i^t, x_i^t) is structured in its natural form and concatenated sequentially within each wave. We introduce a set of special delimiter tokens: [WAV] is inserted before each wave description to explicitly mark temporal boundaries, [Q] is placed before each question q_i^t, and [A] precedes its corresponding response x_i^t. This structured encoding ensures that the model preserves semantic relationships between questions and responses while maintaining the sequential flow of information across survey waves. Missing responses are explicitly represented using the placeholder text *"missing"*, allowing the model to recognize patterns of missingness without relying on statistical imputation. This structured text representation allows the model to leverage its pretraining on natural language, effectively handling survey evolution across waves while preserving semantic and temporal coherence.

LLMs Finetuning. As shown in Fig. 2, to model longitudinal survey data in its natural textual format, we fine-tune a pretrained LLM using Low-Rank Adaptation (LoRA) [15], a parameter-efficient tuning method that introduces trainable low-rank update matrices while freezing the original model weights. This approach allows adaptation to survey-based classification tasks with reduced computational overhead. During fine-tuning, we appended a classification head to the LLM to predict attendance categories based on past survey responses. The model is optimised using cross-entropy loss.

3.2   Gradient-Guided Counterfactual Analysis

Gradient-Based Attribution. To identify the most influential survey questions and responses in determining the model's decision, we compute the gradient of the model's output probability with respect to the input tokens. Given a trained classifier $\mathcal{C}$ with parameters Θ_C, the predicted probability is denoted as $P(\hat{Y} \mid X; \Theta_C)$. During inference, we first perform a forward pass through the model, encoding the survey input $X = \{(q_i^t, x_i^t)\}_{i=1}^{D^t}, t \in 1, \ldots, T$, which consists of concatenated question-response pairs formatted in text. The final classification probability $P(\hat{Y} \mid X; \Theta_C)$ is obtained from the softmax layer over the logits. To determine the impact of each response x_i^t on the prediction, we compute the gradient of $P(\hat{Y} \mid X; \Theta_C)$ with respect to the input embeddings $\nabla_{E(x_i^t)} P(\hat{Y} \mid X; \Theta_C)$, where $E(x_i^t)$ is the embedding representation of the response x_i^t after tokenization. Since the gradient is computed at the token level, we must aggregate it to obtain an importance score for each question-response pair. We achieve this by leveraging our special delimiter tokens, which explicitly separate each survey item in the text format. Let x_i^t denote the response to the i-th question q_i^t in wave t, and let its corresponding tokenized representation be $\{v_k^i\}_{k=1}^{T_i}$, where v_k^i is the k-th token of x_i^t, and T_i is the total number of tokens in the response after tokenization. To determine the contribution of each question-response pair to the classification decision, we compute a question-level importance score $S(x_i^t)$ by aggregating the gradient magnitudes of all tokens within x_i^t:

$$S(x_i^t) = \frac{1}{T_i} \sum_{k=1}^{T_i} \left\| \nabla_{E(v_k^i)} P(\hat{Y} \mid X; \Theta_C) \right\|_1.$$

Here, $\nabla_{E(v_k^i)} P(\hat{Y} \mid X; \Theta_C)$ represents the gradient of the predicted class probability with respect to the embedding of a token v_k^i, and $\| \cdot \|_1$ denotes the $L1$ norm, capturing the absolute contribution of each token. Normalising by T_i

ensures that responses of different token lengths do not disproportionately influence ranking, allowing fair comparison across survey items. To obtain an overall ranking of influential survey items, we further aggregate $S(x_i^t)$ across all participants, computing the mean importance of each question-response pair across the dataset. This allows us to determine which survey items contribute most to attendance classification, guiding interpretability and further analysis.

Minimal Response Swaps. While gradient-based attribution identifies which survey responses influence predictions, it does not directly determine their effect on classification outcomes. To address this, we conduct counterfactual evaluation through minimal response swaps, measuring how sensitive predictions are to changes in survey responses. For each participant classified as an at-risk attendee, we iteratively replace responses with alternative responses observed in participants classified as regular attendees. The swaps are performed in order of importance, starting with the question-response pair with the highest gradient-based attribution score. Given a participant's survey representation X, we define a modified version X' in which responses are systematically substituted. At each step, the most influential response x_i^t is replaced with an alternative response $\tilde{x}_i^t$ drawn from a pool of responses observed in the regular attendee group. The classification model $\mathcal{C}(X'; \Theta_C)$ is re-evaluated after each swap, and the process continues until the prediction flips to a regular attendee: $\mathcal{C}(X; \Theta_C) \neq \mathcal{C}(X'; \Theta_C)$. The same process is repeated for participants classified as regular attendees. The number of swapped questions required to induce this change, denoted as the minimal swap count, provides a measure of how easily a classification outcome can be altered for each participant. This counterfactual evaluation complements gradient-based attribution by refining the identification of survey responses with the greatest impact on classification outcomes. By analysing the distribution of minimal swap counts across the dataset, we gain further insight into the relative importance of different survey items in shaping attendance classification.

Aggregating Insights Across Participants. To derive population-level insights, we measure the importance of each question by counting how often it appears in the minimal swap sets across all participants. A question appearing frequently across many minimal swap sets suggests it plays a key role in distinguishing attendance categories, whereas less frequent occurrences indicate factors that are influential only for specific subgroups. This approach provides a measure of which survey items most consistently impact classification outcomes.

4   Experiments

We evaluate Survey-as-Text Modelling (STM) for school attendance classification using longitudinal survey data from Growing Up in New Zealand (GUiNZ), linked with official attendance records. We detail experimental settings in Sect. 4.1. To benchmark STM, we compare it against machine learning, recurrent, convolutional, transformer-based, and LLM-based models in Sect. 4.2. Beyond predictive performance, we introduce gradient-guided counterfactual analysis to interpret STM's decision-making by identifying influential survey items that can flip the model's prediction. Additionally, we analyse the effectiveness of parameter-efficient fine-tuning techniques, compare various missing data imputation strategies, and evaluate the fairness of classification results among ethnicities in Sect. 4.3.

4.1   Experimental Settings

Dataset. We use longitudinal survey data from GUiNZ [34], linked with official school attendance records from the Ministry of Education (MoE). Our study focuses on three survey waves collected at ages six, eight, and twelve, capturing key socioecological factors influencing school attendance. Attendance rates are derived from MoE's administrative records, calculated as the percentage of total recorded minutes present rather than the Ministry's half-day classification system. This granular, minute-based approach results in a slightly lower attendance percentage than MoE's official business rules. We categorise students into two groups: regular attendees, with attendance above 90%, and at-risk attendees, which includes all students below this threshold. The at-risk attendee category encompasses students with varying levels of absenteeism, including irregular, moderate, and chronic absenteeism. After filtering for students who participated in all three waves and removing those with missing attendance records, our final dataset consists of 3,844 participants, comprising 3,077 regular attendees and 767 at-risk attendees. We include variables related to mental health, socioeconomic status, parental support, school experiences, and COVID-19 disruptions, including open-ended questions such as asking what the biggest worry is for the future. The selected variables have an average of 3% missing rate.

Baseline Methods. We evaluate our approach against five categories of baseline models: machine learning models, Recurrent Neural Networks (RNNs), convolutional models, transformer-based models, and LLM-based approaches. For Machine learning models, we include XGBoost [6], and Random Forest (RF) [4]. We exclude logistic regression due to its reliance on manual feature engineering and the high dimensionality introduced by interaction terms. Similarly, traditional longitudinal methods, such as mixed-effects models and latent growth models, are not included because they are primarily designed for modelling individual trajectories or estimating population-level trends rather than performing multivariate temporal classification. RNN-based models, including RNN [32], Long Short-Term Memory (LSTM) [13], and Gated Recurrent Unit (GRU) [8], capture sequential dependencies in structured time series data. Convolutional models, such as Temporal Convolutional Networks (TCN) [48], use hierarchical convolutions to model temporal patterns. Transformer-based models, including Transformer [47], Autoformer [50], Crossformer [55], FEDformer [57], Informer [56], iTransformer [26], Nonformer [27], and PatchTST [35], leverage self-attention mechanisms to enhance long-range dependency modeling. Finally,

LLM-based models, such as TEST [44], S^2IP-LLM [37], FPT [58], and Time-LLM [19], adapt pre-trained language models for time series tasks through reprogramming, embedding alignment, or prompt-based learning.

Evaluation. We evaluate model performance using standard classification metrics, including accuracy, precision, recall, F1 score, Area Under the Receiver Operating Characteristic Curve (AUROC), and Area Under the Precision-Recall Curve (AUPRC). We apply stratified splitting with 60% for training, 20% for validation, and 20% for testing across attendance categories.

Data Preprocessing. For STM, we describe each wave in text and use special delimiters to separate questions and responses, maintaining the natural structure of survey data. In contrast, for other methods, we transform the data into a tabular format by merging similar questions across waves into the same variable and interpolating variables that were not collected in certain waves from past waves to ensure alignment across time points. For handling missing data, STM preserves missing responses as explicit text "missing" to allow the model to learn patterns around missingness, while for tabular models, we apply KNN imputation [25] to estimate missing values based on similar participants.

Experimental Setup. Given the sensitive nature of the survey data, we employ a locally hosted model to ensure data privacy and compliance with ethical guidelines. We fine-tune LLaMA-3.1-8B using LoRA with a classification head for school attendance prediction. The same backbone model is used for all LLM-based time series methods to ensure a fair comparison. The model is trained for 10 epochs with a batch size of 16 and a learning rate of 1×10^{-4}. We optimise the model using the AdamW optimiser with weight decay regularisation to prevent overfitting. For evaluation, we perform 30 independent runs with different random seeds (1–30) and report the mean and standard deviation of classification metrics. Statistical significance is assessed using the Wilcoxon signed-rank test, and the best-performing results with statistical significance are highlighted in bold. All experiments are conducted on NVIDIA A100 GPUs.

4.2 Main Results

Attendance Level Classification. Table 1 presents the performance comparison of STM against baseline methods. STM outperforms all baselines across all evaluation metrics. These results demonstrate the effectiveness of STM in capturing complex relationships in longitudinal survey data. Unlike baseline models that rely on fixed tabular structures or numerical encodings, STM attempts to preserve the contextual meaning of survey responses and adapts to evolving question formats. This flexibility allows STM to outperform existing temporal modelling methods, which are not designed to process survey data in their natural textual form.

Table 1. Performance comparison of baseline methods for attendance prediction.

Model	Accuracy	Precision	Recall	F1 Score	AUROC	AUPRC
RF [4]	73.5 ± .3	69.0 ± .2	70.4 ± .4	69.7 ± .4	69.8 ± .3	68.6 ± .4
XGBoost [6]	75.2 ± .2	71.1 ± .1	71.4 ± .4	71.2 ± .4	72.5 ± .2	70.4 ± .3
RNN [32]	78.0 ± .4	75.2 ± .3	73.6 ± .2	74.4 ± .3	75.2 ± .4	72.6 ± .3
LSTM [13]	80.3 ± .4	76.9 ± .4	76.5 ± .2	76.7 ± .3	77.3 ± .4	75.1 ± .3
GRU [8]	79.6 ± .3	75.7 ± .2	76.0 ± .5	75.8 ± .4	75.9 ± .4	74.9 ± .5
TCN [48]	81.2 ± .4	78.1 ± .4	78.0 ± .2	78.0 ± .2	78.0 ± .2	76.2 ± .1
Transformer [47]	80.1 ± .3	76.4 ± .5	76.2 ± .2	76.3 ± .3	77.4 ± .3	76.0 ± .2
Informer [56]	83.5 ± .2	81.0 ± .5	79.6 ± .4	79.6 ± .1	79.7 ± .1	79.3 ± .2
Autoformer [50]	84.0 ± .1	80.9 ± .2	79.8 ± .1	79.8 ± .2	81.3 ± .4	79.3 ± .3
FEDformer [57]	82.9 ± .4	79.7 ± .1	79.6 ± .5	79.6 ± .1	80.2 ± .2	77.6 ± .5
Nonformer [27]	83.8 ± .3	80.4 ± .3	79.3 ± .3	79.8 ± .2	80.1 ± .2	78.8 ± .4
PatchTST [35]	85.2 ± .2	81.0 ± .2	80.8 ± .2	80.9 ± .2	82.2 ± .2	79.3 ± .1
Crossformer [55]	84.5 ± .3	81.2 ± .4	81.1 ± .1	81.1 ± .3	81.6 ± .2	80.7 ± .2
iTransformer [26]	83.3 ± .3	78.9 ± .5	79.5 ± .3	79.2 ± .5	80.6 ± .2	78.2 ± .3
FPT [58]	85.8 ± .1	81.8 ± .4	81.2 ± .1	81.5 ± .4	83.2 ± .4	80.5 ± .5
TEST [44]	86.4 ± .1	83.3 ± .3	82.4 ± .4	82.8 ± .2	82.4 ± .3	81.0 ± .4
Time-LLM [19]	87.2 ± .4	82.7 ± .1	82.7 ± .3	82.7 ± .4	85.0 ± .4	81.5 ± .3
S^2IP-LLM [37]	86.1 ± .2	84.3 ± .3	82.7 ± .3	83.5 ± .2	84.7 ± .4	82.4 ± .2
STM (Ours)	**92.0 ± .1**	**89.2 ± .2**	**90.9 ± .4**	**90.0 ± .4**	**89.7 ± .2**	**88.3 ± .1**

Influential Survey Questions. To examine the model's decision-making process, we analyse the most influential survey questions identified through gradient-guided counterfactual analysis. Across all participants, the number of minimal swaps required to flip an at-risk attendee to a regular attendee is, on average, four swaps, with a maximum of eight. Conversely, flipping a regular attendee to an at-risk attendee requires a mean of three swaps and a maximum of six. Figure 3 presents the frequency of survey items appearing in minimal swaps when flipping classifications in either direction. The model is most sensitive to mental health, followed by bullying experiences, family support, and teacher fairness, all from Age 12. The deprivation index also plays a significant role, along with residential mobility from Wave Eight, suggesting that past relocations still contribute to classification shifts. Open-ended concerns about the future and sleep quality only appear in the maximal swaps for at-risk attendees transitioning to regular attendees, indicating they contribute to fine-grained adjustments rather than early decision shifts.

4.3   Further Analysis

Parameter-Efficient Finetuning Methods. Table 2 presents the performance of different fine-tuning approaches for LLMs in longitudinal survey clas-

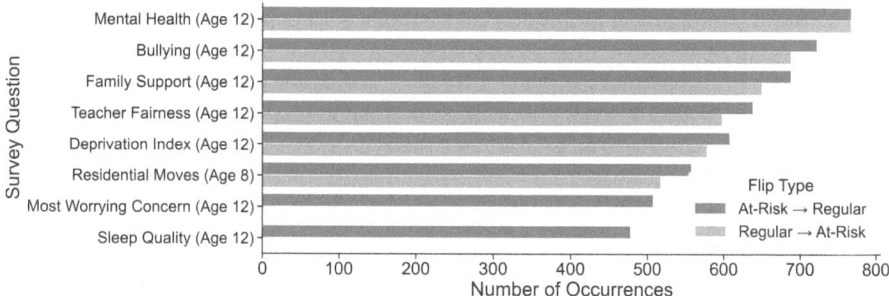

Fig. 3. Survey items most frequently appear in minimal swaps when flipping classification labels. Minimal swaps refer to the smallest number of response changes needed to flip a model's prediction between at-risk and regular attendees.

Table 2. Performance comparison of different finetuning methods for LLMs.

Method	Accuracy	Precision	Recall	F1 Score	AUROC	AUPRC
Zero-shot	75.2 ± .5	70.1 ± .6	65.4 ± .7	67.7 ± .4	72.8 ± .5	64.9 ± .6
Few-shot	78.5 ± .4	73.3 ± .5	69.7 ± .6	71.5 ± .5	76.2 ± .4	68.1 ± .5
Full Fine-Tuning	91.5 ± .1	88.7 ± .2	90.2 ± .3	89.4 ± .3	89.2 ± .2	87.8 ± .1
Adapters [14]	91.1 ± .2	88.3 ± .3	89.8 ± .4	89.0 ± .3	88.9 ± .3	87.3 ± .3
Prefix [24]	90.8 ± .2	88.0 ± .3	89.4 ± .4	88.7 ± .2	88.5 ± .3	87.0 ± .3
Prompt [23]	90.5 ± .3	87.6 ± .4	89.0 ± .5	88.3 ± .2	88.2 ± .4	86.7 ± .4
LoRA [15]	**92.0 ± .1**	**89.2 ± .2**	**90.9 ± .4**	**90.0 ± .1**	**89.7 ± .2**	**88.3 ± .1**

sification. Zero-shot learning achieves the lowest performance, indicating that using a pretrained LLM without task-specific finetuning is insufficient. Few-shot tuning provides a moderate improvement but remains limited in effectively capturing survey patterns. Full fine-tuning demonstrates strong performance but requires significantly more computational resources. Among parameter-efficient methods, LoRA achieves the highest accuracy at 92.0% and the strongest recall at 90.9%, outperforming adapters, prefix-tuning, and prompt-tuning, which exhibit slightly lower but comparable performance. While full fine-tuning performs well, LoRA matches or surpasses it across all metrics with substantially reduced computational overhead. These results highlight the effectiveness of LoRA in adapting LLMs for longitudinal survey classification while maintaining efficiency.

Missing Data. Table 3 compares different missing data handling methods in longitudinal survey classification with STM. Traditional imputation techniques, such as mean and median imputation, yield the lowest performance, indicating their limited effectiveness in reconstructing missing information. More advanced methods, including KNN [25], XGBoost-based imputation [28], Monte Carlo

Table 3. Comparison of imputation methods with explicit "missing" text.

Method	Accuracy	Precision	Recall	F1 Score	AUROC	AUPRC
Mean	89.0 ± .5	86.5 ± .4	87.2 ± .5	86.8 ± .4	87.0 ± .5	85.5 ± .5
Median	89.2 ± .4	86.8 ± .4	87.4 ± .4	87.1 ± .3	87.3 ± .4	85.8 ± .5
KNN [25]	91.7 ± .2	88.5 ± .3	90.1 ± .4	89.3 ± .3	89.0 ± .3	87.5 ± .3
XGBoost [28]	91.8 ± .2	88.8 ± .3	90.3 ± .3	89.5 ± .2	89.3 ± .3	87.9 ± .3
MIWAE [30]	91.7 ± .2	88.6 ± .3	90.2 ± .3	89.4 ± .2	89.2 ± .3	87.7 ± .3
GAIN [52]	91.6 ± .3	88.4 ± .3	90.1 ± .3	89.2 ± .3	89.1 ± .3	87.6 ± .3
Text (Ours)	92.0 ± .1	**89.2 ± .2**	**90.9 ± .4**	**90.0 ± .1**	89.7 ± .2	88.3 ± .1

Importance-Weighted Autoencoder (MIWAE) [30], and Generative Adversarial Imputation Nets (GAIN) [52], leverage statistical and machine learning-based imputation strategies to infer missing responses, improving overall classification performance. However, our approach, which retains missing responses as explicit tokens rather than imputing values, achieves similar performance, demonstrating that LLMs can implicitly model missingness without requiring explicit data reconstruction. These results suggest that imputing missing responses may not be necessary when using LLMs, as they can naturally infer meaningful patterns from the surrounding context.

Fairness Evaluation. While ethnicity is not included as a predictor in our model, we assess fairness by evaluating Equal Opportunity, which compares true positive rates across ethnic groups, and Equalised Odds, which ensures both false positive and false negative rates remain consistent [54]. We examine classification performance across five major groups specific to the New Zealand setting: European, Māori, Pacific, Asian, Middle Eastern, Latin American, and African ethnicities (MELAA) and Others. For the children belonging to more than one ethnic group, we record their ethnicity in the priority order of Māori, Pacific, Asian, MELAA and others, and Europeans. These groups reflect the diverse composition of the GUiNZ cohort, which aligns with birth demographics in Auckland at the time of recruitment [34]. Statistical analysis using the Kruskal-Wallis test finds no significant differences in true positive rates or false positive rates across ethnicities, indicating that classification outcomes are consistent across demographic groups.

5   Conclusion

We proposed Survey-as-Text Modelling (STM) to address challenges in analysing longitudinal survey data, including irregular feature alignment, evolving context, and the integration of open-ended responses. By representing survey data as text and leveraging LLMs, STM preserves contextual meaning and enables more flexible predictive modelling compared to conventional tabular approaches.

Our results demonstrate that STM significantly outperforms traditional machine learning models, transformer-based methods, and LLM-based time-series models across all evaluation metrics. Additionally, we introduced gradient-guided counterfactual analysis to enhance interpretability by identifying the most influential survey items affecting attendance classification. This analysis revealed that recent social, emotional, and economic factors play a crucial role in distinguishing attendance patterns. These findings contribute to the methodological advancement of longitudinal survey analysis and provide data-driven insights for policymakers seeking to improve school attendance.

Acknowledgment. We thank the *Growing Up in New Zealand* team and the *New Zealand Ministry of Education* for providing access to data, and acknowledge the support and contributions of the *Our Voices* team and study investigators. This research was funded by the *Our Voices* programme (Endeavour grant UOAX1912), supported by the Ministry of Business, Innovation and Employment (2019–2025). The study was conducted in accordance with the Declaration of Helsinki, and all procedures involving human subjects were approved by the Ministry of Health's Northern B Health and Disability Ethics Committee. Consent was obtained from all participants and their parents or guardians. Tingrui Qiao is supported by the University of Auckland Doctoral Scholarship and CSGST travel award from the School of Computer Science, University of Auckland.

A   List of Variables

1. **New Zealand Deprivation Index (NZDep)**: an area-based measure of socioeconomic deprivation in New Zealand based on nine Census variables.
2. **Crowding groups**: how many people live in the house.
3. **Easy access to school**: whether this is a deciding factor for choosing a school.
4. **Resource provided by the school**: whether the ability of the school to provide good resources is a deciding factor for choosing a school.
5. **Children's physical needs**: degree of satisfaction from mother.
6. **Children's learning needs**: degree of satisfaction from mother.
7. **Children's social and emotional needs**: degree of satisfaction from mother.
8. **Children's culture needs**: degree of satisfaction from mother.
9. **Difficulty starting school**: level of difficulty and how long the difficulty lasts.
10. **Parental support**: whether the mother is confident she knows how to help her children do well at school.
11. **Belong to school (mother)**: mother feels comfortable and welcomed when visiting the school.
12. **Belong to school (children)**: children feel they belong to their school.
13. **Number of moves after the last wave**.
14. **Form of transport and duration of transport**.
15. **Put up with feeling cold**.

16. **Gone without fresh fruit or vegetables.**
17. **Centre for Epidemiologic Studies Short Depression Scale (CES-D-R 10):** a concise self-report tool to assess depressive symptoms, comprising 10 items rated on a 4-point Likert scale, with higher total scores indicating greater depressive symptomatology.
18. **Work status of the mother.**
19. **Household income groups.**
20. **Housing tenure.**
21. **Rurality.**
22. **Time and energy for parenting.**
23. **Home atmosphere.**
24. **Children have enough friends and are treated well by them.**
25. **Children are bullied at school.**
26. **Culture acceptance at school.**
27. **Gender acceptance at school.**
28. **Sleeping quality.**
29. **Children feel supported by their family.**
30. **Children feel supported by their friends.**
31. **Miss school due to COVID-19.**
32. **Financial stress due to COVID-19.**
33. **People getting along at home during COVID-19.**
34. **Worries and fears of social mixing during COVID-19.**
35. **Teachers respect and are fair to children.**
36. **School work stress.**
37. **Things the children look forward to for the next few years.**
38. **Things the children worry about for the next few years.**

Table 4. Performance comparison of different LLM backbones for school attendance classification.

Backbone	Accuracy	Precision	Recall	F1 Score	EiCAT
BERT [7]	83.2 ± .3	80.5 ± .4	81.0 ± .5	80.7 ± .4	5.9 ± .3
GPT-2 [40]	85.0 ± .3	82.7 ± .3	83.1 ± .4	82.9 ± .3	1.6 ± .4
Mistral-7B [17]	92.0 ± .2	89.3 ± .3	91.0 ± .3	90.1 ± .3	11.5 ± .3
Qwen1.5-7B [3]	92.1 ± .1	89.2 ± .3	90.9 ± .4	90.0 ± .3	10.9 ± .3
LLaMA-3.1-8B [46]	92.0 ± .1	89.2 ± .2	90.9 ± .4	90.0 ± .1	11.2 ± .1

B   LLM Backbones

To assess the impact of different language model architectures on school attendance classification, we evaluate STM using a range of local, smaller-scale LLM backbones. This experiment ensures that our approach remains effective across different models while addressing data privacy constraints by using locally hosted models. Table 4 presents the results, showing that STM achieves consistent performance across various backbones, with all models in the LLM category performing within a close range. Smaller models such as BERT [7] and GPT-2 [40] exhibit lower performance. Apart from performance metrics, we also measured the bias within the LLMs in the New Zealand context through the EiCAT score [38]. We found that LLMs tend to have lower biases than smaller models such as BERT and GPT-2, as shown by the larger EiCAT scores.

References

1. Adler, D.A., Wang, F., Mohr, D.C., Choudhury, T.: Machine learning for passive mental health symptom prediction: generalization across different longitudinal mobile sensing studies. PLoS ONE **17**(4), e0266516 (2022)
2. Atkinson, J., Salmond, C., Crampton, P.: Nzdep2013 index of deprivation. Wellington: Department of Public Health, University of Otago **5541**, 1–64 (2014)
3. Bai, J., et al.: Qwen technical report. arXiv preprint arXiv:2309.16609 (2023)
4. Breiman, L.: Random forests. Mach. Learn. **45**, 5–32 (2001)
5. Cao, D., et al.: Tempo: prompt-based generative pre-trained transformer for time series forecasting. arXiv preprint arXiv:2310.04948 (2023)
6. Chen, T., Guestrin, C.: Xgboost: a scalable tree boosting system. In: SIGKDD, pp. 785–794 (2016)
7. Devlin, J., Chang, M.W., Lee, K., Toutanova, K.: BERT: pre-training of deep bidirectional transformers for language understanding. In: Burstein, J., Doran, C., Solorio, T. (eds.) Proceedings of the 2019 Conference of the North American Chapter of the Association for Computational Linguistics: Human Language Technologies, vol. 1 (Long and Short Papers), pp. 4171–4186. Association for Computational Linguistics, Minneapolis (2019). https://doi.org/10.18653/v1/N19-1423
8. Dey, R., Salem, F.M.: Gate-variants of gated recurrent unit (gru) neural networks. In: MWSCAS, pp. 1597–1600. IEEE (2017)
9. Erceg-Hurn, D.M., Mirosevich, V.M.: Modern robust statistical methods: an easy way to maximize the accuracy and power of your research. Am. Psychol. **63**(7), 591 (2008)
10. Finning, K., et al.: The association between anxiety and poor attendance at school– a systematic review. Child Adolesc. Mental Health **24**(3), 205–216 (2019)
11. Harder, F., Bauer, M., Park, M.: Interpretable and differentially private predictions. In: Proceedings of AAAI, vol. 34, pp. 4083–4090 (2020)
12. Heyen, H., Widdicombe, A., Siegel, N.Y., Perez-Ortiz, M., Treleaven, P.: The effect of model size on llm post-hoc explainability via lime. arXiv preprint arXiv:2405.05348 (2024)
13. Hochreiter, S., Schmidhuber, J.: Long short-term memory. Neural Comput. **9**(8), 1735–1780 (1997)
14. Houlsby, N., et al.: Parameter-efficient transfer learning for nlp. In: ICML, pp. 2790–2799. PMLR (2019)
15. Hu, E.J., et al.: Lora: low-rank adaptation of large language models. ICLR **1**(2), 3 (2022)

16. Huang, S., Mamidanna, S., Jangam, S., Zhou, Y., Gilpin, L.H.: Can large language models explain themselves? A study of llm-generated self-explanations. arXiv preprint arXiv:2310.11207 (2023)
17. Jiang, A.Q., et al.: Mistral 7b (2023). https://arxiv.org/abs/2310.06825
18. Jin, B.T., Choi, M.H., Moyer, M.F., Kim, D.A.: Predicting malnutrition from longitudinal patient trajectories with deep learning. PLoS ONE **17**(7), e0271487 (2022)
19. Jin, M., et al.: Time-llm: time series forecasting by reprogramming large language models. arXiv preprint arXiv:2310.01728 (2023)
20. Kearney, C.A., Benoit, L., Gonzálvez, C., Keppens, G.: School attendance and school absenteeism: a primer for the past, present, and theory of change for the future. In: Frontiers in Education, vol. 7, p. 1044608. Frontiers (2022)
21. Klein, M., Sosu, E.M., Dare, S.: Mapping inequalities in school attendance: the relationship between dimensions of socioeconomic status and forms of school absence. Child Youth Serv. Rev. **118**, 105432 (2020)
22. Laith, R., Vaillancourt, T.: The temporal sequence of bullying victimization, academic achievement, and school attendance: A review of the literature. Aggress. Violent. Beh. **64**, 101722 (2022)
23. Lester, B., Al-Rfou, R., Constant, N.: The power of scale for parameter-efficient prompt tuning. arXiv preprint arXiv:2104.08691 (2021)
24. Li, X.L., Liang, P.: Prefix-tuning: optimizing continuous prompts for generation. arXiv preprint arXiv:2101.00190 (2021)
25. Liao, S.G., et al.: Missing value imputation in high-dimensional phenomic data: imputable or not, and how? BMC Bioinformatics **15**, 1–12 (2014)
26. Liu, Y., et al.: itransformer: inverted transformers are effective for time series forecasting. arXiv preprint arXiv:2310.06625 (2023)
27. Liu, Y., Wu, H., Wang, J., Long, M.: Non-stationary transformers: exploring the stationarity in time series forecasting. NeuraIPS **35**, 9881–9893 (2022)
28. Madhu, G., Bharadwaj, B.L., Nagachandrika, G., Vardhan, K.S.: A novel algorithm for missing data imputation on machine learning. In: 2019 International Conference on Smart Systems and Inventive Technology (ICSSIT), pp. 173–177. IEEE (2019)
29. Maltezou, H.C., Ledda, C., Sipsas, N.V.: Absenteeism of healthcare personnel in the covid-19 era: a systematic review of the literature and implications for the post-pandemic seasons. In: Healthcare, vol. 11, p. 2950. MDPI (2023)
30. Mattei, P.A., Frellsen, J.: Miwae: deep generative modelling and imputation of incomplete data sets. In: ICML, pp. 4413–4423. PMLR (2019)
31. McConnell, B.M., Kubina, R.M.: Connecting with families to improve students' school attendance: a review of the literature. Prevent. School Fail. Alternat. Educ. Children Youth **58**(4), 249–256 (2014)
32. Medsker, L.R., Jain, L., et al.: Recurrent neural networks. Des. Appl. **5**(64–67), 2 (2001)
33. Mohammadi, B.: Explaining large language models decisions using shapley values. arXiv preprint arXiv:2404.01332 (2024)
34. Morton, S.M., et al.: Cohort profile: growing up in New Zealand. Int. J. Epidemiol. **42**(1), 65–75 (2013)
35. Nie, Y., Nguyen, N.H., Sinthong, P., Kalagnanam, J.: A time series is worth 64 words: long-term forecasting with transformers. arXiv preprint arXiv:2211.14730 (2022)
36. Nitski, O., et al.: Long-term mortality risk stratification of liver transplant recipients: real-time application of deep learning algorithms on longitudinal data. Lancet Digital Health **3**(5), e295–e305 (2021)

37. Pan, Z., Jiang, Y., Garg, S., Schneider, A., Nevmyvaka, Y., Song, D.: s^2ip-llm: semantic space informed prompt learning with llm for time series forecasting. In: ICML (2024)
38. Pang, B., Qiao, T., Walker, C., Cunningham, C., Koh, Y.S.: Libra: measuring bias of large language model from a local context. In: European Conference on Information Retrieval, pp. 1–16. Springer, Heidelberg (2025). https://doi.org/10.1007/978-3-031-88708-6_1
39. Qiao, T., Walker, C., Cunningham, C., Koh, Y.S.: Thematic-lm: a llm-based multi-agent system for large-scale thematic analysis. In: Proceedings of the ACM on Web Conference 2025, pp. 649–658 (2025)
40. Radford, A., Wu, J., Child, R., Luan, D., Amodei, D., Sutskever, I., et al.: Language models are unsupervised multitask learners. OpenAI Blog **1**(8), 9 (2019)
41. Sheetal, A., Jiang, Z., Di Milia, L.: Using machine learning to analyze longitudinal data: a tutorial guide and best-practice recommendations for social science researchers. Appl. Psychol. (2023)
42. Sherstinsky, A.: Fundamentals of recurrent neural network (rnn) and long short-term memory (lstm) network. Physica D **404**, 132306 (2020)
43. Srinivas, S., Fleuret, F.: Rethinking the role of gradient-based attribution methods for model interpretability. arXiv preprint arXiv:2006.09128 (2020)
44. Sun, C., Li, H., Li, Y., Hong, S.: Test: text prototype aligned embedding to activate llm's ability for time series. arXiv preprint arXiv:2308.08241 (2023)
45. Tan, Z., Chen, T., Zhang, Z., Liu, H.: Sparsity-guided holistic explanation for llms with interpretable inference-time intervention. In: Proceedings of AAAI, vol. 38, pp. 21619–21627 (2024)
46. Touvron, H., et al.: Llama: open and efficient foundation language models. arXiv preprint arXiv:2302.13971 (2023)
47. Vaswani, A., et al.: Attention is all you need. NeuraIPS **30** (2017)
48. Wan, R., Mei, S., Wang, J., Liu, M., Yang, F.: Multivariate temporal convolutional network: a deep neural networks approach for multivariate time series forecasting. Electronics **8**(8), 876 (2019)
49. White, R.T., Arzi, H.J.: Longitudinal studies: designs, validity, practicality, and value. Res. Sci. Educ. **35**, 137–149 (2005)
50. Wu, H., Xu, J., Wang, J., Long, M.: Autoformer: decomposition transformers with auto-correlation for long-term series forecasting. NeuraIPS **34**, 22419–22430 (2021)
51. Xue, H., Salim, F.D.: Promptcast: a new prompt-based learning paradigm for time series forecasting. IEEE TKDE **36**(11), 6851–6864 (2023)
52. Yoon, J., Jordon, J., Schaar, M.: Gain: missing data imputation using generative adversarial nets. In: ICML, pp. 5689–5698. PMLR (2018)
53. Zeng, A., Chen, M., Zhang, L., Xu, Q.: Are transformers effective for time series forecasting? In: Proceedings of AAAI, vol. 37, pp. 11121–11128 (2023)
54. Zhang, J., Bareinboim, E.: Equality of opportunity in classification: a causal approach. NeuraIPS **31** (2018)
55. Zhang, Y., Yan, J.: Crossformer: transformer utilizing cross-dimension dependency for multivariate time series forecasting. In: ICLR (2023)
56. Zhou, H., et al.: Informer: beyond efficient transformer for long sequence time-series forecasting. In: Proceedings of AAAI. vol. 35, pp. 11106–11115 (2021)
57. Zhou, T., Ma, Z., Wen, Q., Wang, X., Sun, L., Jin, R.: Fedformer: frequency enhanced decomposed transformer for long-term series forecasting. In: Proceedings of ICML, pp. 27268–27286. PMLR (2022)
58. Zhou, T., Niu, P., Sun, L., Jin, R., et al.: One fits all: power general time series analysis by pretrained lm. NeuraIPS **36**, 43322–43355 (2023)

Engineering and Technology

Graph Neural Networks for Jamming Source Localization

Dania Herzalla[1]([✉]), Willian T. Lunardi[1], and Martin Andreoni[1,2]

[1] Technology Innovation Institute, Abu Dhabi, United Arab Emirates
{dania.herzalla,willian.lunardi,martin.andreoni}@tii.ae
[2] Computer Science Department, Khalifa University of Science and Technology, Abu Dhabi, United Arab Emirates

Abstract. Graph-based learning provides a powerful framework for modeling complex relational structures; however, its application within the domain of wireless security remains significantly underexplored. In this work, we introduce the first application of graph-based learning for jamming source localization, addressing the imminent threat of jamming attacks in wireless networks. Unlike geometric optimization techniques that struggle under environmental uncertainties and dense interference, we reformulate the localization as an inductive graph regression task. Our approach integrates structured node representations that encode local and global signal aggregation, ensuring spatial coherence and adaptive signal fusion. To enhance robustness, we incorporate an attention-based Graph Neural Network (GNN) that adaptively refines neighborhood influence and introduces a confidence-guided estimation mechanism that dynamically balances learned predictions with domain-informed priors. We evaluate our approach under complex Graph Neural Network (GNN) environments with various sampling densities, network topologies, jammer characteristics, and signal propagation conditions, conducting comprehensive ablation studies on graph construction, feature selection, and pooling strategies. Results demonstrate that our novel graph-based learning framework significantly outperforms established localization baselines, particularly in challenging scenarios with sparse and obfuscated signal information. Our code is available at https://github.com/tiiuae/gnn-jamming-source-localization.

Keywords: Graph-based learning · Graph Neural Networks · Graph regression · Wireless security · Jamming source localization

1 Introduction

Graphs serve as a fundamental framework for representing complex relationships and interactions in real-world systems. Many highly successful machine

---

D. Herzalla and W. T. Lunardi—These authors contributed equally.

Supplementary Information The online version contains supplementary material available at https://doi.org/10.1007/978-3-662-72243-5_19.

learning applications are based on graph-based learning [15]. Although explored in numerous domains, the application of graph-based learning to wireless security remains underexplored. In particular, jamming source localization, a task essential for mitigating the threat of interference to the availability of wireless communication, presents a promising avenue for research. In this study, we investigate the application of a novel graph-based learning framework to perform an inductive graph-level regression task to predict the location of a jammer in complex RF environments.

The ubiquitous and growing dependence on wireless networks for everyday connectivity and mission-critical operations introduces significant security vulnerabilities. As jamming attacks transmit intentional interference across communication channels, they lead to degradation and severing of wireless links [12]. The repercussions of such attacks are severe, leading to disruptions in essential services and operational hazards [18]. Although countermeasures such as frequency hopping have been explored, their effectiveness is limited against advanced jammers such as reactive, follow-on, and barrage that adaptively pursue target frequencies creating dense interference across multiple channels [13]. Unlike avoidance techniques that passively adjust the network to evade interference, jammer localization provides a direct mitigation strategy, wherein network administrators can deploy countermeasures such as physical neutralization or geofencing to restore network reliability regardless of the attack strategy [18].

Classical jammer localization methods rely on geometric and optimization-based techniques to estimate the jammer's position. However, they degrade in real-world RF environments due to noise and multipath effects [11]. Their dependence on idealized propagation models limits adaptability to stochastic RF dynamics. To overcome these limitations, we introduce a novel graph-based formulation of the jamming localization problem, leveraging attention-based GNNs to adaptively extract spatial and signal-related patterns from measurements. Additionally, we propose Confidence-guided Adaptive Global Estimation (CAGE), a confidence-guided estimation mechanism that dynamically balances GNN-based predictions with domain-informed priors, improving robustness in varying deployment conditions. Rather than treating localization as a geometric optimization problem, we redefine it as a graph regression task, where node features encode key RF and spatial characteristics, and the graph structure captures local and global signal dependencies. Our contributions are as follows:

- We present the first application of GNNs to jamming source localization in wireless networks by reformulating the problem as an inductive graph regression task.
- We propose a graph-based learning framework with structured node representations for local and global signal aggregation. We also introduce a confidence-guided estimation mechanism to balance GNN predictions with domain-informed priors.
- We conduct comprehensive ablation studies on graph construction and model design, analyzing the impact of node connectivity, feature selection, pooling strategies, downsampling techniques, and graph augmentations on localization performance and model robustness.

- We benchmark against well-known localization methods in challenging environments, consistently outperforming established baselines, with emphasized improvements in scenarios characterized by sparse and obscured signal information.

The remainder of this paper is organized as follows. Section 2 reviews related work, highlighting existing approaches to jamming source localization and their limitations. Section 3 formally defines the problem, detailing the network configuration, jammer characteristics, and underlying assumptions. Section 4 presents a learning framework that dynamically integrates data-driven representations with inductive priors. Section 5 reports experimental results, demonstrating the effectiveness of our approach under various network conditions. Finally, we conclude by discussing key findings and future research directions.

2 Related Work

2.1 Jamming Source Localization

Jamming source localization has been widely studied using range-free and range-based algorithms. Range-free algorithms perform localization using network topology-related properties, without relying on the physical characteristics of the incoming signals [8]. These methods are useful in infrastructure-limited environments, however, they suffer from degraded accuracy in sparse or unevenly distributed networks [17,18]. In contrast, range-based methods utilize geometric optimization to estimate the distance to the source using the measurement of various physical properties such as Received Signal Strength Indicator (RSSI), Time of Arrival (ToA), and Time of Arrival (ToA) [8]. While these methods generally achieve higher accuracy, obtaining measurements such as ToA and AoA rely on specialized and calibrated hardware and are susceptible to errors where multipath effects introduce significant biases [19].

Many of the existing jammer localization approaches are validated under theoretical propagation models, such as free-space path loss, which fails to capture the complexities of real-world settings. Furthermore, many evaluations fail to include diversity in attack scenarios, sampling strategies, and long-range jamming effects [11]. To address these limitations, we evaluate our method on diverse network configurations, leveraging the Log Distance Path Loss (LDPL) [3] model to account for realistic signal propagation conditions (See Appendix D).

As our method leverages spatial and signal information exclusively, we focus on methods that similarly harness this information for localization. We benchmark our approach against established range-free and range-based localization techniques: Weighted Centroid Localization (WCL) [17], Least Squares (LSQ) [18], Path Loss (PL) [10], Maximum Likelihood Estimation (MLE) [10], and Multilateration (MLAT) [20]. These baselines serve as reference points to assess the robustness and adaptability of our graph-based framework.

2.2   Graph Neural Networks for Localization

GNNs have demonstrated strong capabilities in regression tasks by capturing spatial dependencies within graph-structured data, such as in molecular property prediction and material science [9]. Beyond these domains, GNNs have also been applied to pose regression problems, including camera pose estimation [14] and human pose tracking [21], where they refine node and edge representations to improve motion prediction and spatial consistency. Their effectiveness in localization tasks has also gained attention, particularly in wireless and sensor network applications. GNNs have been applied to RF-based localization, including WiFi fingerprinting-based indoor localization [6], where they leverage RSSI signals to construct graphs and improve positioning accuracy. More recent works extend GNNs for network localization beyond Wi-Fi, addressing challenges such as dynamic network topologies and mobility-induced signal variation [3].

While these advancements highlight the growing potential of GNNs for network localization, their application to jamming source localization remains unexplored. This gap presents an opportunity to adapt GNNs to interference localization, addressing unique challenges under adversarial conditions.

3   Problem Definition

The problem addressed in this study is the localization of a wireless jammer, an adversarial interference source that disrupts communications by emitting intentional interference signals to degrade legitimate wireless communication.

Network Configuration. The network consists of N devices, either static or dynamic, deployed in a D-dimensional space, where $\mathcal{A} \subset \mathbb{R}^D$ defines the geographic area of interest and $N \geq 1$. Each device i records signal measurements over time, forming a set of samples:

$$\mathcal{S}_i = \{s_i^1, s_i^2, \ldots, s_i^T\}, \quad s_i^t = (\mathbf{x}_i^t, \eta_i^t)$$

where s_i^t denotes a measurement taken at position $\mathbf{x}_i^t$ with an associated noise floor value η_i^t in dBm at time t. Note that η_i^t, referred to as the *noise floor*, is commonly treated as jamming signal strength, where here it represents the combined effect of jammer interference and baseline environmental noise floor. Signal attenuation and propagation effects are modeled using the empirical LDPL model to simulate Non-line-of-sight (NLOS) conditions; refer to Appendix D for details.

This formulation accommodates both *static* and *dynamic* sampling scenarios. In the static case, devices remain at fixed locations but are likely distributed over space. In contrast, in the dynamic case, devices move through space, collecting measurements at different positions over time.

Jammer Characteristics. The jammer is located at an unknown position $\mathbf{x}_j \in \mathcal{A}$ and emits interference signals that elevate the noise floor of nearby devices. The interference strength varies spatially due to distance attenuation and propagation effects such as shadowing and multipath fading. The sampled region, denoted as $\mathcal{R} \subseteq \mathcal{A}$, is the subset of $\mathcal{A}$ where devices collect noise floor measurements. Although the jammer's position satisfies $\mathbf{x}_j \in \mathcal{A}$, it does not necessarily hold that $\mathbf{x}_j \in \mathcal{R}$, i.e., $\mathbf{x}_j \in \mathcal{A} \backslash \mathcal{R}$ is possible. We evaluate localization methods in scenarios where the jammer affects areas beyond the sampled region, testing their ability to infer positions outside direct measurement zones.

Objective. Given the set of samples collected by N devices, denoted as $\mathcal{S} = \{\mathcal{S}_1, \mathcal{S}_2, \ldots, \mathcal{S}_N\}$, the goal is to infer $\mathbf{x}_j$ based on the spatial distribution of measured noise floor levels. This problem is inherently challenging due to environmental noise and uncertainty affecting signal propagation, complex spatial correlations between noise floor levels and jammer interference, and the need to generalize beyond observed regions where no direct measurements are available.

4   Graph-Structured Learning for Jammer Localization

Given the set of collected measurements $\mathcal{S} = \{\mathcal{S}_1, \mathcal{S}_2, \ldots, \mathcal{S}_N\}$, we represent the sampled signal space as a graph $G = (V, E)$, where nodes in V correspond to individual measurement instances $s_i^t \in \mathcal{S}_i$, and edges E define spatial relationships between them. Edges are established using K-Nearest Neighbors (KNN), where for each node v_i, an edge set is constructed as $E = \{(v_i, v_j) \mid v_j \in \mathcal{N}_k(v_i)\}$, where $\mathcal{N}_k(v_i)$ denotes the set of k nearest neighbors of v_i in the Euclidean space. To enforce the spatial attenuation principle of jamming signals, each edge (v_i, v_j) is assigned a weight w_{ij} that decays exponentially with the Euclidean distance as:

$$w_{ij} = \frac{e^{-d_{ij}} \left(e - e^{d_{ij}}\right)}{e - 1}, \tag{1}$$

where $d_{ij} = \frac{\|\mathbf{x}_i - \mathbf{x}_j\|}{d_{\max}}$ is the normalized Euclidean distance between nodes v_i and v_j, with $d_{\max} = \max_{(v_i, v_j) \in E} \|\mathbf{x}_i - \mathbf{x}_j\|$.

Since message passing in the graph relies on node and edge attributes, we define a structured representation that incorporates both spatial and signal characteristics. Each node $i \in V$ is assigned a feature vector:

$$X_i = (\tilde{\eta}_i, \mathbf{x}_i^{\mathrm{sph}}, \mathbf{x}_i^{\mathrm{cart}}, \mathcal{F}_i^{\mathrm{local}}). \tag{2}$$

where $\tilde{\eta}_i$ is the normalized noise floor value and $\mathbf{x}_i^{\mathrm{sph}}$ represents the normalized angular representation:

$$\mathbf{x}_i^{\mathrm{sph}} = (r_i, \sin\theta_i, \cos\theta_i, \sin\phi_i, \cos\phi_i), \tag{3}$$

where r_i is the radial distance from the origin, and (θ_i, ϕ_i) are the azimuth and elevation angles of the measured position. We additionally incorporate the normalized cartesian coordinate representation $\mathbf{x}_i^{\text{cart}} = (\tilde{x}_i, \tilde{y}_i, \tilde{z}_i)$ to maintain direct Euclidean relationships between nodes.

To encode spatial correlations and local noise floor variations within the graph, we define $\mathcal{F}_i^{\text{local}}$, which characterizes the local noise floor distribution within each node's neighborhood:

$$\mathcal{F}_i^{\text{local}} = \{\text{median}(\eta_{\mathcal{N}_k(i)}), \max(\eta_{\mathcal{N}_k(i)}), \Delta\eta_i, \mathbf{x}_i^{\text{wcent}}, d_i^{\text{wcent}}\},$$

where $\text{median}(\eta_{\mathcal{N}_k(i)})$ and $\max(\eta_{\mathcal{N}_k(i)})$ provide local statistical summaries of the noise floor levels, $\Delta\eta_i$ represents the deviation of the node's noise level from the mean noise level within its neighborhood, and $\mathbf{x}_i^{\text{wcent}}$ and d_i^{wcent} correspond to the *local weighted centroid* and its distance from the node v_i, respectively:

$$\mathbf{x}_i^{\text{wcent}} = \frac{\sum_{j \in \mathcal{N}_k(i)} \eta_j' \mathbf{x}_j}{\sum_{j \in \mathcal{N}_k(i)} \eta_j'}, \quad d_i^{\text{wcent}} = \|\mathbf{x}_i - \mathbf{x}_i^{\text{wcent}}\|, \quad \Delta\eta_i = \eta_i - \frac{1}{|\mathcal{N}_k(i)|} \sum_{j \in \mathcal{N}_k(i)} \eta_j,$$

where $\eta_j' = 10^{\eta_j/10}$ represents the noise floor level converted to linear scale.

For dynamic scenarios where devices move while collecting measurements, the graph representation is extended to incorporate temporal dependencies. Each node $i \in V$ retains its spatial attributes while additionally capturing motion through two features: the *direction vector* and the *temporal signal variation*. These measurements, computed between consecutive positions, are given, respectively, as:

$$\mathbf{d}_i = \mathbf{x}_i^{t+1} - \mathbf{x}_i^t, \quad \Delta\eta_i^{\text{temp}} = \eta_i^{t+1} - \eta_i^t.$$

The final node feature vector for dynamic scenarios is given by:

$$X_i = (\tilde{\eta}_i, \mathbf{x}_i^{\text{sph}}, \mathbf{x}_i^{\text{cart}}, \mathcal{F}_i^{\text{local}}, \mathbf{d}_i, \Delta\eta_i^{\text{temp}}). \tag{4}$$

4.1 Learning Spatial Relations with Attention-Based Graphs

Graph-based learning enables the model to capture structured dependencies in the jammer interference field, allowing for improved generalization across spatial regions. However, effective learning in this setting requires handling two key challenges: (1) signal measurements are inherently noisy due to environmental conditions, leading to unreliable observations, and (2) the importance of neighboring nodes varies depending on both their spatial proximity and their reliability in capturing interference effects. Traditional GNN architectures, such as Graph Convolutional Networks (GCNs) [5], perform uniform neighborhood aggregation, which limits their ability to weigh the informativeness of spatially adjacent nodes. Our approach follows Graph Attention Network (GAT) [16], incorporating an adaptive weighting mechanism that dynamically refines neighborhood influence, ensuring that message passing prioritizes nodes with reliable signal information while attenuating contributions from potentially misleading observations.

Let $X \in \mathbb{R}^{|V| \times F}$ represent the matrix of raw node features, where each node v_i has an initial feature vector $h_i^{(0)} = X_i \in \mathbb{R}^F$. Before computing attention, node features are first transformed at each layer l using a learnable weight matrix $\mathbf{W}^{(l)}$. The updated node representation at layer $l+1$ is computed through the aggregation function denoted as:

$$h_i^{(l+1)} = \text{ReLU}\left(\sum_{j \in \mathcal{N}_i} \alpha_{ij}^{(l)} \mathbf{W}^{(l)} h_j^{(l)}\right). \tag{5}$$

The attention coefficients $\alpha_{ij}^{(l)}$, weighted by w_{ij}, determine the relative importance of each neighboring node v_j to node v_i and are computed as:

$$\alpha_{ij}^{(l)} = \frac{w_{ij} \exp\left(\text{LeakyReLU}\left(\mathbf{a}^T[\mathbf{W}^{(l)}h_i^{(l)} \| \mathbf{W}^{(l)}h_j^{(l)}]\right)\right)}{\sum_{k \in \mathcal{N}(i)} w_{ik} \exp\left(\text{LeakyReLU}\left(\mathbf{a}^T[\mathbf{W}^{(l)}h_i^{(l)} \| \mathbf{W}^{(l)}h_k^{(l)}]\right)\right)}, \tag{6}$$

where $\mathbf{a} \in \mathbb{R}^{2F'}$ is a learnable attention weight vector, with $2F'$ corresponding to the concatenation of intermediate node embeddings of dimension F'. Here, $(\cdot)^T$ denotes transposition, $\|$ represents vector concatenation, and w_{ij} is given by Eq. (1). In our implementation, we utilize multi-head attention as originally proposed in [16], where multiple independent attention mechanisms operate in parallel. The resulting node embeddings are concatenated across attention heads, except in the final layer, where they are averaged.

4.2 Supernode-Guided Adaptive Estimation

Prior work [17] establishes that WCL, a simple localization method based on weighted averaging of anchor positions, achieves low localization error when node density around jammer's position is high and placement is radially symmetric, with error decreasing as the number of nodes increases. Building on this, we expand the graph definition to incorporate WCL as a domain-informed prior, leveraging it under dense and symmetrical sampling conditions while introducing an adaptive confidence weighting mechanism for effective integration within the learning framework.

Global Context Encoding with Domain-Guided Priors. We extend the graph representation $G = (V, E)$ by introducing a *supernode* v_s, which encodes a structured global prior by representing the weighted centroid of the measurement space based on noise floor levels. The augmented graph is defined as:

$$G' = (V', E'), \quad \text{where} \quad V' = V \cup \{v_s\}, \quad E' = E \cup \{(v_i \to v_s) \mid v_i \in V\}. \tag{7}$$

Each node $v_i \in V$ is connected to the supernode via a directed edge $(v_i \to v_s)$ with weight w_{is} given by Eq. (1). This connectivity structure ensures that the supernode functions as a global aggregator, primarily influencing the computation of a confidence weight α (later defined in Eq. (12)) while remaining decoupled from the GNN regression process, thereby preventing direct bias from the

WCL prior. The spatial position and noise level of the supernode are defined as:

$$\mathbf{x}_{\text{super}} = \frac{\sum_{i \in V} w_i \mathbf{x}_i}{\sum_{i \in V} w_i}, \quad \eta_{\text{super}} = \frac{\sum_{i \in V} w_i \eta_i}{\sum_{i \in V} w_i}, \quad \text{where } w_i = \frac{\eta_i'}{\sum_{j \in V} \eta_j'}. \quad (8)$$

Here, w_i represents the normalized weight assigned to each node v_i. Since the feature vector for each node, as defined in Eq. 2, is a function of position, noise, and neighboring nodes, we also expand the feature representation for v_s.

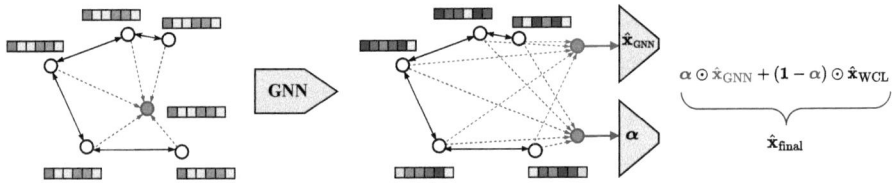

Fig. 1. Overview of the proposed jammer localization framework. A graph is constructed where nodes represent spatial and signal instances, and edges capture spatial relationships. The encoder processes the graph to learn spatial correlations. The final jammer position is estimated through an adaptive combination of the GNN prediction and WCL prior, controlled by a learned confidence weight.

Confidence-Guided Adaptive Position Estimation. The estimated jammer position is computed as a five-tuple normalized angular representation combining the GNN-based prediction with the domain-informed WCL prior. The GNN-based position estimate is obtained by applying a linear transformation to a pooled representation of the node embeddings:

$$\hat{\mathbf{x}}_{\text{GNN}} = \mathbf{W}_{\text{GNN}} h_{\text{graph}} + \mathbf{b}_{\text{GNN}}, \quad (9)$$

where $\hat{\mathbf{x}}_{\text{GNN}} = (\hat{r}, \hat{s}_\theta, \hat{c}_\theta, \hat{s}_\phi, \hat{c}_\phi)$ represents the predicted position, with $\mathbf{W}_{\text{GNN}} \in \mathbb{R}^{5 \times F'}$ and $\mathbf{b}_{\text{GNN}} \in \mathbb{R}^5$ as learnable parameters. The graph representation h_{graph} of G' is computed using an element-wise max pooling operation over all node embeddings, excluding the supernode:

$$h_{\text{graph}} = \max_{v_i \in V} h_i^{(L)}, \quad (10)$$

where $h_i^{(L)}$ is the final embedding of node v_i after L layers of attention-based aggregation given in Eq. (5). To determine the confidence weights $\alpha = (\alpha_1, \alpha_2, \alpha_3, \alpha_4, \alpha_5)$, the supernode representation h_{super} is passed through a linear transformation followed by a sigmoid activation:

$$\alpha = \sigma(\mathbf{W}_\alpha h_{\text{super}} + \mathbf{b}_\alpha), \quad (11)$$

where $\alpha \in \mathbb{R}^5$ is a five-dimensional confidence vector, with each α_d corresponding to one of the five output components in the normalized angular representation.

The parameters $\mathbf{W}_\alpha \in \mathbb{R}^{5 \times F'}$ and $\mathbf{b}_\alpha \in \mathbb{R}^5$ are learnable, and sigmoid $\sigma(\cdot)$ ensures that $0 < \alpha_d < 1$. Finally, the predicted jammer position is computed as:

$$\hat{\mathbf{x}}_{\text{final}} = \boldsymbol{\alpha} \odot \hat{\mathbf{x}}_{\text{GNN}} + (1 - \boldsymbol{\alpha}) \odot \hat{\mathbf{x}}_{\text{WCL}}, \tag{12}$$

where $\odot$ denotes element-wise multiplication, and $\hat{\mathbf{x}}_{\text{WCL}}$ is the five-tuple normalized angular representation of the WCL estimate.

This formulation allows the model to adaptively balance the reliance on the GNN-based prediction and the structured WCL prior, ensuring robustness across varying sampling densities and spatial distributions. The corresponding graph-based formulation and adaptive position estimation process are illustrated in Fig. 1, showing the transformation from raw signal measurements to the final position estimate through graph construction, GNN encoding, and confidence-weighted integration of the WCL prior.

4.3   Training Strategy and Loss Function

To enable adaptive estimation, we define a loss function that minimizes localization error by optimizing the weighted combination of the GNN-based estimate and the WCL prior. Given a batch of training instances $\mathcal{B}$, the loss function for adaptive estimation is formulated as:

$$\mathcal{L}_{\text{Adapt}} = \frac{1}{|\mathcal{B}|} \sum_{m \in \mathcal{B}} \left\| \hat{\mathbf{x}}_j^{(m)} - \left(\boldsymbol{\alpha}^{(m)} \odot \hat{\mathbf{x}}_{\text{GNN}}^{(m)} + (1 - \boldsymbol{\alpha}^{(m)}) \odot \hat{\mathbf{x}}_{\text{WCL}}^{(m)} \right) \right\|^2, \tag{13}$$

where $\hat{\mathbf{x}}_j^{(m)}$ is the ground truth jammer position in the normalized angular representation, $\hat{\mathbf{x}}_{\text{GNN}}^{(m)}$ is the predicted position from the GNN model, and $\hat{\mathbf{x}}_{\text{WCL}}^{(m)}$ is the WCL-based position estimate. The confidence vector $\boldsymbol{\alpha}^{(m)} \in \mathbb{R}^5$ is learned from the supernode representation and dynamically balances the contribution of the two estimations.

Encouraging Independent Learning of the GNN Regressor. While the confidence mechanism allows optimal weighting of WCL and GNN estimates, an inherent risk of optimizing Eq. (13) alone is that the GNN regressor might learn primarily as a residual corrector for WCL rather than as an independent position estimator. To prevent this, we introduce an additional loss term that enforces direct learning of the jammer's position by the GNN. This leads to the joint loss formulation:

$$\mathcal{L}_{\text{CAGE}} = \frac{1}{2} \left(\mathcal{L}_{\text{GNN}} + \mathcal{L}_{\text{Adapt}} \right) + \lambda \sum_{m \in \mathcal{B}} (1 - \boldsymbol{\alpha}^{(m)})^2, \tag{14}$$

where

$$\mathcal{L}_{\text{GNN}} = \frac{1}{|\mathcal{B}|} \sum_{m \in \mathcal{B}} \left\| \hat{\mathbf{x}}_j^{(m)} - \hat{\mathbf{x}}_{\text{GNN}}^{(m)} \right\|^2. \tag{15}$$

Here, $\mathcal{L}_{\text{GNN}}$ ensures that the GNN independently learns to predict the jammer's position without being influenced by WCL, while $\mathcal{L}_{\text{Adapt}}$ (as defined in Eq. (13)) optimizes the weighted combination of GNN and WCL estimates, ensuring that the model learns to assign appropriate confidence to each based on spatial conditions. The final term in Eq. (14) penalizes deviations of $\boldsymbol{\alpha}^{(m)}$ from 1, reducing over-reliance on WCL. For simplicity, we set $\lambda = 0$ in our experiments while retaining this term for flexibility.

Note that in the experimental evaluation, we refer to our proposed method as CAGE. For clarity in comparisons, Multilayer Perceptron (MLP), GCN, Principal Neighbourhood Aggregation (PNA) and GAT operate on graph G and are trained with Eq. (15) with the final estimate given by $\hat{\mathbf{x}}_{\text{GNN}}$, while CAGE is evaluated on the augmented graph G' and the adaptive confidence-weighted estimation, trained with Eq. (14).

5   Experimental Evaluation

We evaluate CAGE across static and dynamic environments under the LDPL model. In the static setting (Sect. 5.1), fixed nodes with varying positions and densities are considered, with the jammer positioned either inside or outside the sampled region $\mathcal{R}$ to study spatial effects. In the dynamic setting (Sect. 5.2), a device moves in 3D space, approaching and encircling the jammer to assess localization accuracy across angles and distances. Ablation studies in Sect. 5.3 and Appendix A evaluate the impact of node features, edge construction, graph augmentations, global pooling, and downsampling techniques. Details on data generation, node spatial arrangements, jammer characteristics, and signal propagation environments varied in our experiments are provided in Appendix D, and an analysis of confidence weighting is presented in Sect. 5.3.

We compare CAGE against classical methods (WCL [18], LSQ [18], PL [10], MLAT [20], MLE [10], MLP) and graph-based learning methods (GCN [5], PNA [1], GAT [16]). As previously described, while MLP, GCN, PNA, and GAT operate on G, CAGE leverages augmented graph G' with the supernode, incorporating graph attention mechanisms alongside confidence-weighted estimation for adaptive localization. Models are trained using AdamW with a one-cycle cosine annealing scheduler. Hyperparameter tuning details, including model architectures and optimizer settings, are provided in Appendix C. Appendix 5.3 describes the downsampling techniques applied in the dynamic experiments. All experiments are conducted over three indcpendent trials with different random seeds to ensure robust evaluation, reporting the mean and standard deviation of Mean Absolute Error (MAE) and Root Mean Squared Error (RMSE) as the primary evaluation metrics.

5.1   Static Evaluation for Jamming Localization

To analyze the impact of node arrangements and coverage on localization accuracy, we evaluate performance in a static setting where devices remain fixed at

Table 1. RMSE in jammer localization for static scenarios, averaged over three trials with different seeds. Results are split by sampling geometry. MAE results are provided in Appendix B Table 8.

	Method	Jammer within ($\mathbf{x}_j \in \mathcal{R}$)					Jammer outside ($\mathbf{x}_j \in \mathcal{A} \backslash \mathcal{R}$)					Mean
		C	T	R	RD	Mean	C	T	R	RD	Mean	
RMSE	WCL	53.6	65.6	39.7	54.1	53.3	201.6	241.1	254.6	234.0	232.8	143.1
	PL	159.5	115.0	121.3	114.6	127.6	357.3	314.4	365.2	336.2	343.3	235.5
	MLE	123.2	112.5	116.5	362.3	178.6	295.8	302.9	318.3	1002.7	479.9	329.3
	MLAT	158.1	125.5	110.4	98.1	123.1	346.8	329.7	353.4	309.3	334.8	229.0
	LSQ	299.0	268.9	146.7	487.5	300.5	495.6	440.5	568.8	713.9	554.7	427.6
	MLP	54.1	46.1	34.7	42.6	44.4	95.7	120.3	120.6	125.0	115.4	79.9
	GCN	51.6	44.2	36.1	49.3	45.3	91.5	115.1	117.7	124.3	112.2	78.8
	PNA	50.8	41.3	30.6	38.8	40.4	91.1	115.0	113.9	119.7	109.9	75.2
	GAT	49.7	41.1	30.1	39.2	40.0	89.6	113.7	114.3	117.6	108.8	74.4
	CAGE	**42.8**	**36.5**	**27.9**	**35.7**	**35.7**	**77.2**	**101.4**	**104.1**	**107.3**	**97.5**	**66.6**

predefined locations. Each instance consists of nodes randomly placed within the geographic area $\mathcal{A} = \{(x, y) \in \mathbb{R}^2 \mid 0 \leq x, y \leq 1500\}$, following circular, triangular, rectangular, or uniformly random layouts. These configurations define the sampling region $\mathcal{R} \subseteq \mathcal{A}$, where noise floor measurements are collected. The jammer's position $\mathbf{x}_j$ is also randomly assigned within $\mathcal{A}$, independently of node placement, resulting in two distinct localization scenarios: when $\mathbf{x}_j \in \mathcal{R}$, proximity to the source yields more precise sampling of interference, whereas when $\mathbf{x}_j \in \mathcal{A} \backslash \mathcal{R}$, localization relies on extrapolation from peripheral observations.

Table 1 presents the jammer localization performance across various methods in the static experiment as measured by RMSE. MAE results are provided in Appendix B Table 8. The classical localization methods exhibit significantly higher errors across all sampling scenarios. Among them, WCL performs best with an overall RMSE of 143.1 m, while LSQ yields the worst performance. The suboptimal performance of path-loss-based approaches (PL, MLE, MLAT, LSQ) is likely attributed to their dependency on estimating the path loss exponent (γ) and jammer transmit power (P_t^{jam}) in order to estimate the jammer position [10]. The GNN-based approaches consistently outperform these classical methods. CAGE delivers the highest overall performance, achieving an RMSE of 66.6 m, followed by GAT with an RMSE of 74.4 m, improving localization accuracy as compared to WCL by 114.9%.

A significant performance gap is observed based on whether the jammer is located inside or outside the sampled region $\mathcal{R}$. Localization outside $\mathcal{R}$ is inherently more challenging due to extrapolation beyond measured signals. Classical methods like WCL perform well within densely and radially symmetric sampled regions [17], resulting in an RMSE of 53.3 m (inside). However, the performance sharply declines when extrapolating, with RMSE increasing to 232.8 m (outside). In contrast, GAT demonstrates better robustness, with RMSE rising moderately from 40.0 m (inside) to 108.8 m (outside). CAGE achieves the lowest errors overall, with RMSE of 35.7 m (inside) and 97.5 m (outside). Notably, the circular topology significantly enhances performance when the jammer is outside $\mathcal{R}$ by maximizing angular diversity and preserving directional information, as supported by the principles guiding the use of circular antenna arrays in direction-finding applications [4]. These findings highlight the critical role of spatial coverage and the superior robustness of GNN-based methods for long-range jammer localization.

5.2 Dynamic Evaluation for Jamming Localization

We evaluate localization performance in a dynamic 3D environment where a mobile device travels through space while tracking a jamming source. The trajectory follows an encirclement pattern, where the device converges toward the jammer while collecting measurements from varying distances and angles. This experiment enables the analysis of localization performance under varying observational constraints, evaluating how well methods estimate the jammer's position with limited initial data and how accuracy evolves as additional spatially diverse measurements are incorporated. During training, we employ random cropping of trajectory segments to expose the model to varied subsequences of the jamming encounter, enhancing robustness to partial observations and improving generalization across different trajectory lengths.

Table 9 presents the jammer localization performance for various methods in the dynamic experiment for MAE. RMSE results are provided in Appendix B Table 2. The results are categorized by distance intervals, where each column represents a different proximity range between the jammer and the nearest sampled measurement. The final column reports the overall mean across trajectories. Notably, WCL achieves an RMSE of 11.6 m in the closest range ($d \in [50,0]$). However, at larger distances ($d > 500$), WCL degrades significantly with an RMSE of 372.4 m. CAGE leverages confidence-weighted estimation to adaptively integrate WCL's structured prior with the GNN-based predictions, resulting in the most consistent and robust performance. With an RMSE of 5.7 m in $d \in [50,0]$, CAGE significantly outperforms both WCL and GAT. Interest-

Table 2. RMSE in jammer localization along dynamic trajectories, reported across distance intervals to the jammer and averaged over three trials. The final column reports the mean RMSE across the full trajectory. MAE results are provided in Appendix B Table 9.

	Method	Distance to the Jammer (m)					Mean
		$d > 500$	$d \in [500, 200]$	$d \in [200, 100]$	$d \in [100, 50]$	$d \subset [50, 0]$	
RMSE	WCL	372.4	253.1	111.8	45.4	11.6	66.6
	PL	379.8	312.6	190.0	104.2	41.4	100.5
	MLE	510.5	463.9	148.4	92.9	6486.9	5493.5
	MLAT	275.2	234.3	183.9	147.0	99.1	124.7
	MLP	$182.1_{\pm9.7}$	$114.8_{\pm7.8}$	$49.1_{\pm3.2}$	$28.3_{\pm1.2}$	$19.0_{\pm1.0}$	$35.0_{\pm0.7}$
	GCN	$161.5_{\pm4.3}$	$91.1_{\pm1.2}$	$34.2_{\pm0.1}$	$19.1_{\pm0.4}$	$10.8_{\pm0.2}$	$25.6_{\pm0.3}$
	PNA	$214.1_{\pm7.3}$	$129.5_{\pm5.2}$	$56.9_{\pm2.4}$	$34.9_{\pm1.7}$	$24.9_{\pm1.1}$	$41.5_{\pm1.2}$
	GAT	$131.0_{\pm13.6}$	$70.0_{\pm0.2}$	$33.2_{\pm1.5}$	$17.8_{\pm0.6}$	$9.6_{\pm0.5}$	$21.3_{\pm0.6}$
	CAGE	$\mathbf{104.0_{\pm5.9}}$	$\mathbf{53.4_{\pm0.2}}$	$\mathbf{23.5_{\pm0.7}}$	$\mathbf{14.0_{\pm0.4}}$	$\mathbf{5.7_{\pm0.2}}$	$\mathbf{15.7_{\pm0.1}}$

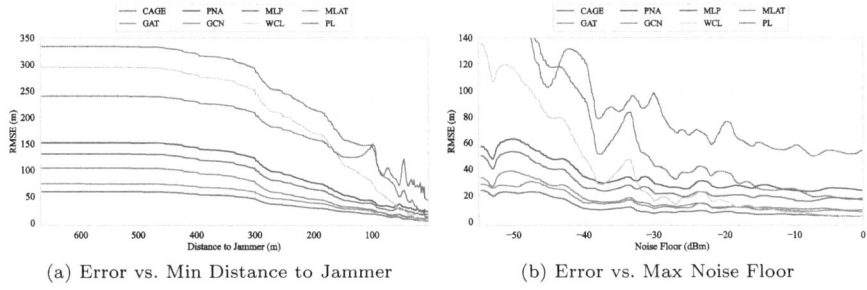

(a) Error vs. Min Distance to Jammer   (b) Error vs. Max Noise Floor

Fig. 2. Localization performance as a function of (a) minimum distance to the jammer and (b) maximum noise floor.

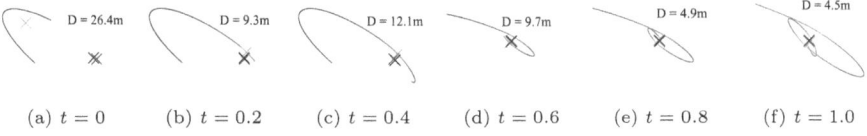

(a) $t = 0$ (b) $t = 0.2$ (c) $t = 0.4$ (d) $t = 0.6$ (e) $t = 0.8$ (f) $t = 1.0$

Fig. 3. Localization accuracy along a single trajectory. The red cross-mark is the jammer position, orange is WCL, and blue is the CAGE prediction. (Color figure online)

ingly, while CAGE integrates WCL as a prior, its benefits extend beyond dense, symmetric scenarios. The performance gap is particularly evident in sparse sampling conditions, where CAGE maintains significantly lower error than WCL and GAT, highlighting its ability to generalize beyond the expected advantages of structured priors.

Figure 2 shows localization performance trends over varying distances to the jammer and noise floor conditions. In Fig. 2(a), WCL performs well at short distances, surpassing GAT only when very close to the jammer (∼20 m). While GAT demonstrates greater robustness along most of the trajectory, its performance is consistently surpassed by CAGE. Figure 3 visually compares localization predictions along a trajectory, demonstrating progressive refinement after initial attack detection.

5.3   Ablation Study

CAGE Components. We perform an ablation study to assess the contribution of individual components in the CAGE architecture, as detailed in Table 3. The columns $\mathcal{L}_{GNN}$ and $\mathcal{L}_{Adapt}$ indicate the use of graph-based and adaptive losses, respectively, as defined in Sect. 4. "SN" and "SN Edges" denote the presence of a supernode and its edge connections. "Con." represents the confidence weight (α) layer (linear or 3-layer MLP with ReLU activations and final sigmoid), while "Con. In" and "Reg. In" indicate the input data for the confidence weight layer and regressor, respectively. "Con. Out" indicates whether a single shared confidence weight is used for all predicted coordinates or separate weights are pro-

Table 3. Ablation study on CAGE components.

Loss		Configurations						$\hat{x}_{final}$	$\hat{x}_{GNN}$
$\mathcal{L}_{GNN}$	$\mathcal{L}_{Adapt}$	SN	SN Edges	Con.	Con. In	Reg. In	Con. Out		
✓	✗	✗	–	–	–	◐	–	–	21.3±0.6
✗	✓	✓	Undirected	Linear	○	◐	Single	22.2±0.2	253.8±40.1
✗	✓	✓	Undirected	Linear	●	●	Single	21.3±0.7	247.4±30.8
✗	✓	✓	No edges	Linear	●	●	Single	20.6±0.1	155.8±32.2
✗	✓	✓	No edges	Linear	○	◐	Single	19.7±0.3	119.1±9.2
✗	✓	✓	Directed	Linear	○	◐	Single	19.4±0.3	102.9±6.9
✗	✓	✓	Directed	MLP	○	◐	Single	18.2±1.1	117.1±4.7
✗	✓	✓	Directed	MLP	○	◐	Multiple	17.7±0.4	153.0±17.1
✓	✓	✓	Directed	MLP	○	◐	Single	16.6±0.8	16.8±0.8
✓	✓	✓	Directed	MLP	○	◐	Multiple	15.7±0.1	16.2±0.0

duced for each. Finally, $\hat{x}_{final}$ and $\hat{x}_{GNN}$ represent the estimated position using the marked loss functions in the table and the GNN-only prediction, respectively. The symbols ●, ◐, and ○ denote pooled graph representations with the supernode, without the supernode, and exclusively using the supernode.

Results show that replacing bidirectional edges with directed edges improves accuracy, using an MLP instead of a linear layer reduces RMSE, and multiple confidence outputs outperform a single output. Training with $\mathcal{L}_{CAGE}$ enables the GNN regressor to function properly, achieving an RMSE of 16.2 compared to 153.0 m without it, with adaptive estimation reaching 15.7.

Confidence Weighting in CAGE. We analyze how the $\mathcal{L}_{CAGE}$ loss shapes confidence weight assignment in CAGE by comparing two training setups: one using only $\mathcal{L}_{Adapt}$ and another incorporating the full $\mathcal{L}_{CAGE}$ loss. Confidence weights are plotted against the jammer's distance to assess how the choice of loss function influences the model's reliance on the WCL prior versus GNN-based predictions. This experiment uses the dynamic trajectory data described in Sect. 5.2, where measurements are collected while encircling the jammer from varying distances and angles. This setup yields conditions where the GNN can best leverage wide spatial context at long ranges, while WCL becomes increasingly reliable at close distances due to the dense, radially symmetric sampling created by the encircling motion.

When trained solely with $\mathcal{L}_{Adapt}$ (Fig. 4a), the model assigns relatively low confidence weights across all distances. This suggests a persistent reliance on WCL, even in regions where GNN-based predictions should dominate. Since $\mathcal{L}_{Adapt}$ optimizes the blended prediction without enforcing a direct learning signal for the GNN, the model tends to treat it as a correction mechanism rather than as an independent estimator. In contrast, training with $\mathcal{L}_{CAGE}$ (Fig. 4b) yields high initial confidence in the GNN prediction ($\alpha \approx 1$), especially at large distances. As the distance to the jammer decreases, confidence in WCL increases, indicating that the model learns when the WCL prior becomes more reliable, particularly in the densely sampled, radially symmetric regions near the jammer.

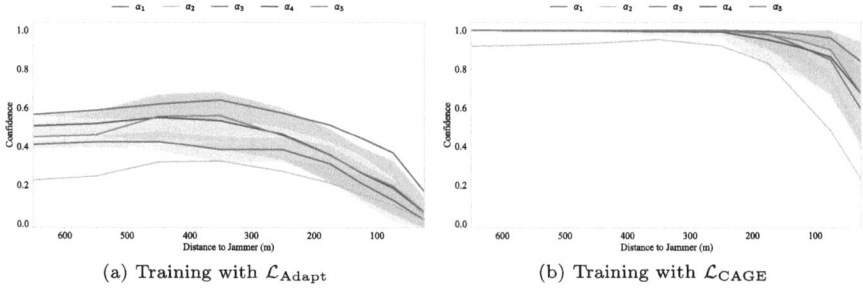

(a) Training with $\mathcal{L}_{\text{Adapt}}$ (b) Training with $\mathcal{L}_{\text{CAGE}}$

Fig. 4. Effect of training loss on confidence weighting in CAGE. (a) Training with $\mathcal{L}_{\text{Adapt}}$ causes over-reliance on WCL due to low GNN confidence. (b) Training with $\mathcal{L}_{\text{CAGE}}$ increases initial GNN confidence, sharpening near the jammer.

Table 4. Ablations on augmentations, global pooling, and neighborhood size.

(a) Varying number of k nearest neighbors.

k	3	5	7	11
RMSE	**54.7**±0.1	57.3±0.0	60.2±0.2	64.9±0.2

(b) Global pooling strategies.

Pooling	Sum	Mean	Max	Att
RMSE	72.2±0.3	84.1±0.2	**52.9**±0.1	61.7±0.3

(c) Graph- and Feature-level augmentations.

Aug	None	Rotation	Crop	Drop Node	Feat. Noise
RMSE	54.7±0.1	58.9±0.1	54.5±0.1	**52.9**±0.1	54.6±0.1

(d) Performance of combined augmentation strategies.

Aug	Crop+DN	DN+Feat Noise	Crop+Feat Noise
RMSE	55.5±0.1	**53.0**±0.1	55.3±0.2

This improvement stems from the explicit GNN supervision provided by $\mathcal{L}_{\text{GNN}}$, resulting in a more structured confidence-weighting mechanism and improved localization robustness.

Figure 4b also reveals that among all confidence weights, α_2, which corresponds to $\sin(\theta)$ in the final estimation, remains slightly lower than the others, even at large distances. This suggests that while the model generally prioritizes GNN-based predictions, it continues to rely on the WCL azimuth as a stable directional reference. Although we used $\lambda = 0$ in this work, tuning λ in Eq. (14) may further improve performance by better balancing the model's reliance on different components.

Graph Construction, Pooling, and Augmentations. We investigate how different graph construction strategies, pooling methods, and augmentation techniques influence model performance, as summarized in Table 4. A lower neighborhood size ($k = 3$) yields the best RMSE, with larger k leading to over-smoothing [7]. Among global pooling strategies, max pooling performs best. For augmentations, DropNode [2] at a 0.2 drop rate offers the greatest improvement, and the combination of DropNode and feature noise achieves the best perfor-

Table 5. Ablation study of downsampling techniques on high-resolution dynamic path data under LDPL model. The retained number of nodes is denoted by $|V|$.

$|V|$	Window averaging				Spatial binning with noise filtering			
	$t_{0.0-0.2}$	$t_{0.4-0.6}$	$t_{0.8-1.0}$	Mean	$t_{0.0-0.2}$	$t_{0.4-0.6}$	$t_{0.8-1.0}$	Mean
200	74.5	22.1	13.2	38.7	78.4	21.6	10.5	40.5
600	63.2	21.8	14.7	34.3	63.5	16.3	9.8	31.7
800	57.1	23.9	15.7	32.2	59.3	15.3	10.4	29.7
1000	54.6	23.4	16.5	**31.4**	54.5	13.7	9.8	**27.4**

mance overall. See Appendix A for further results on feature engineering and augmentations.

Downsampling Strategies for High-Resolution Signal Graphs. High-frequency sampling in Software Defined Radio (SDR) systems produces dense graphs with thousands of nodes (approx. 6000 per instance in our dynamic dataset; see Appendix D, Table 11). To reduce computational cost while preserving key signal characteristics, we apply downsampling prior to graph construction. We compare two methods: (1) *window averaging*, which operates on the raw sequence of samples by dividing it into $|V|$ segments based on sample count and averaging the position and noise values within each; and (2) *spatial binning with noise filtering*, which groups samples into fixed $1\,\mathrm{m}^3$ spatial bins based on their positions, averages the position and noise values within each bin, and retains only the $|V|$ bins with the highest average noise, as high-noise regions are more informative [10].

Table 5 presents results from the downsampling ablation experiment. Each segment $t_{\ell,u}$ denotes a subinterval of the normalized trajectory, with ℓ and u indicating the lower and upper bounds of the time fraction. The results indicate that spatial binning with noise filtering consistently outperforms window averaging, particularly in later segments. Following these results, we adopt the spatial boning with noise filtering with $|V| = 1000$ for all our experiments.

6   Conclusion

This work presents CAGE, the first graph-based framework for jamming source localization that reformulates the problem as an inductive graph regression task. Our approach integrates attention-based GNNs with a confidence-weighted fusion mechanism that adaptively balances learned predictions with structured spatial priors. Experiments across diverse static and dynamic scenarios demonstrate that CAGE consistently outperforms both classical and learning-based baselines. Through detailed ablations, we show that our design choices significantly enhance model robustness and performance. Future work includes incorporating temporal GNNs, analyzing the impact of the confidence weighting parameter λ, and evaluating cross-domain generalization beyond simulated environments.

References

1. Corso, G., Cavalleri, L., Beaini, D., Liò, P., Veličković, P.: Principal neighbourhood aggregation for graph nets. In: Advances in Neural Information Processing Systems (2020)
2. Do, T.H., Nguyen, D.M., Bekoulis, G., Munteanu, A., Deligiannis, N.: Graph convolutional neural networks with node transition probability-based message passing and dropnode regularization. Expert Syst. Appl. **174**, 114711 (2021)
3. Etiabi, Y., et al.: Metagraphloc: a graph-based meta-learning scheme for indoor localization via sensor fusion. arXiv preprint arXiv:2411.17781 (2024)
4. Häfner, S., Käske, M., Thomä, R.: On calibration and direction finding with uniform circular arrays. Int. J. Antennas Propag. **2019**(1), 1523469 (2019)
5. Kipf, T.N., Welling, M.: Semi-supervised classification with graph convolutional networks. In: International Conference on Learning Representations (2017)
6. Lezama, F., Larroca, F., Capdehourat, G.: On the application of graph neural networks for indoor positioning systems. In: Machine Learning for Indoor Localization and Navigation, pp. 239–256. Springer (2023)
7. Li, Q., Han, Z., Wu, X.M.: Deeper insights into graph convolutional networks for semi-supervised learning. In: Proceedings of the AAAI Conference on Artificial Intelligence, vol. 32 (2018)
8. Liu, H., X, W., Chen, Y., Liu, Z.: Localizing jammers in wireless networks. In: 2009 IEEE International Conference on Pervasive Computing and Communications, pp. 1–6 (2009)
9. Merchant, A., Batzner, S., Schoenholz, S.S., Aykol, M., Cheon, G., Cubuk, E.D.: Scaling deep learning for materials discovery. Nature **624**(7990), 80–85 (2023)
10. Nardin, A., Imbiriba, T., Closas, P.: Jamming source localization using augmented physics-based model. In: ICASSP 2023 - 2023 IEEE International Conference on Acoustics, Speech and Signal Processing (ICASSP), pp. 1–5 (2023)
11. Niu, Z., Li, H., Zhou, X., Huang, J.: Overview of jammer localization in wireless sensor networks. In: 2020 IEEE 9th Joint International Information Technology and Artificial Intelligence Conference (ITAIC), vol. 9, pp. 9–13 (2020)
12. Pelechrinis, K., Koutsopoulos, I., Broustis, I., Krishnamurthy, S.V.: Lightweight jammer localization in wireless networks: system design and implementation. In: GLOBECOM 2009 - 2009 IEEE Global Telecommunications Conference, pp. 1–6 (2009)
13. Pirayesh, H., Zeng, H.: Jamming attacks and anti-jamming strategies in wireless networks: a comprehensive survey. IEEE Commun. Surv. Tutorials **24**(2), 767–809 (2022)
14. Turkoglu, M.O., Brachmann, E., Schindler, K., Brostow, G.J., Monszpart, A.: Visual camera re-localization using graph neural networks and relative pose supervision. In: 2021 International Conference on 3D Vision (3DV), pp. 145–155 (2021)
15. Veličković, P.: Everything is connected: graph neural networks. Curr. Opin. Struct. Biol. **79**, 102538 (2023)
16. Veličković, P., Cucurull, G., Casanova, A., Romero, A., Liò, P., Bengio, Y.: Graph attention networks. In: International Conference on Learning Representations (2018)
17. Wang, J., Urriza, P., Han, Y., Cabric, D.: Weighted centroid localization algorithm: theoretical analysis and distributed implementation. IEEE Trans. Wireless Commun. **10**(10), 3403–3413 (2011)

18. Wei, X., Wang, Q., Wang, T., Fan, J.: Jammer localization in multi-hop wireless network: a comprehensive survey. IEEE Commun. Surv. Tutorials **19**(2), 765–799 (2017)
19. Yan, W., Wang, J., Yin, F., Tian, Y., Zoubir, A.M.: Attentional graph neural networks for robust massive network localization. arXiv preprint arXiv:2311.16856 (2023)
20. Yang, J., Lee, H., Moessner, K.: Multilateration localization based on singular value decomposition for 3d indoor positioning. In: 2016 International Conference on Indoor Positioning and Indoor Navigation (IPIN), pp. 1–8 (2016)
21. Yang, Y., Ren, Z., Li, H., Zhou, C., Wang, X., Hua, G.: Learning dynamics via graph neural networks for human pose estimation and tracking. In: Proceedings of the IEEE/CVF Conference on Computer Vision and Pattern Recognition, pp. 8074–8084 (2021)
22. Zhang, M., Li, P.: Nested graph neural networks. Adv. Neural. Inf. Process. Syst. **34**, 15734–15747 (2021)

Preserving the World Heritage: Post-earthquake Monitoring Based on Structural Break Testing with Deep Temporal Convolutional Features

Francesco Dente[1,2(✉)], Andy Combey[1], Alix Lhéritier[3], Rodrigo Acuna-Agost[3], and E. Diego Mercerat[1]

[1] Université Cote d'Azur, CEREMA, IRD, CNRS, Observatoire de la Cote d'Azur, Géoazur, Valbonne, France
diego.mercerat@cerema.fr, francesco.dente@eurecom.fr,
andy.combey@geoazur.unice.fr
[2] EURECOM, Biot, France
[3] Amadeus, Sophia Antipolis, France
{alix.lheritier,rodrigo.acunaagost}@amadeus.com

Abstract. Built heritage faces nowadays increasing vulnerability due to the combined impact of climatic, seismic, and anthropogenic forcings. In this context, vibration-based monitoring has become a key non-invasive method for assessing the integrity of historical buildings. However, little attention has been given to the development of automatic tools, which are crucial for rapid and effective decision-making. This study examines San Cristobal Church, a 17th-century building located in the UNESCO World Heritage site of Cusco, Peru. The church has been continuously monitored during 17 months using a seismic sensor located on one of its walls. First, we develop machine learning models to predict the church's natural frequencies based only on weather data. Then, we analyze deviations from the expected frequency variations to detect anomalies that may indicate structural changes in the building, especially following strong transient events such as earthquake-induced motions. We evaluate multiple machine learning approaches, including Ridge Regression, Feed-forward Neural Networks, and Temporal Convolutional Networks, with the latter outperforming other models in capturing nonlinear temporal dependencies. To estimate the post-seismic recovery time of the natural frequencies following a Mw 4.2 earthquake occurred in August 13th, 2024, we employ the Bai-Perron test for structural break detection on the learned deep temporal convolutional features. As this recovery time is influenced by the damage state, changes in its duration can reflect alterations in masonry mechanical properties. By accurately assessing the post-seismic recovery time, our methodology offers a promising approach for developing early warning systems to identify damage in historical buildings.

© The Author(s), under exclusive license to Springer Nature Switzerland AG 2026
B. Pfahringer et al. (Eds.): ECML PKDD 2025, LNAI 16020, pp. 349–365, 2026.
https://doi.org/10.1007/978-3-662-72243-5_20

Keywords: Structural Health Monitoring · Historical Masonry · Vibration Analysis · Temporal Convolutional Networks · Structural Break Analysis · Bai-Perron Test

1   Introduction

In the 21st century, preserving and protecting the cultural heritage is among the principal missions of UNESCO organization. This heritage faces increasing vulnerability due to the combined impact of climatic, seismic, and anthropogenic forcings. In the field of Structural Health Monitoring (SHM), the characterization of the dynamic response of structures—to both continuous environmental and transient seismic loadings—is widely recognized as an effective tool for identifying the modal properties of existing structures [12,15,17].

In particular, the use of ambient vibration instead of external artificial excitation is highly valuable, as it is quick and easy to implement for structural health assessment and is often integrated into continuous monitoring systems [28]. This approach enables a data-driven evaluation of structural conditions, which is particularly beneficial for heritage structures where invasive testing methods should be avoided. As highlighted by numerous studies, variations in the natural frequencies of buildings have been observed both during and after earthquakes [7,27], even in the absence of structural damage [9]. If no permanent structural damage occurs, the frequency shifts gradually diminish over time, normally returning to pre-seismic values. The duration of this recovery period depends on the mechanical properties of the materials and the damage state of the structure [1,16,19]. However, the effects of environmental factors can mask and complicate an accurate estimation of this recovery period. A proper understanding of the environmental response is essential to develop a reliable model that distinguishes between transient environmental effects and actual structural changes.

Unlike reinforced concrete structures, historical masonry buildings exhibit complex responses that are less studied; the lack of experimental data, and consequently robust models, limits preservation strategies for these heritage structures. No research has focused on the nonlinear elastic response (recovery period) of historical buildings, mainly due to the complexity of their behavior. This highlights the need to better understand the factors influencing their response using machine learning algorithms. While some studies are emerging in Western Europe, particularly in Italy [2,13,21,25], the field remains largely unexplored elsewhere. Studying and better characterizing the seismic response of historical buildings is promising for improving the assessment of their structural health and damage state.

This research focuses on Peru, which has a unique heritage of traditional masonry structures made of stone and earthen materials, distinct from the typical materials used in European historical masonry. The goal is to develop innovative, efficient and lightweight computational tools for a more accurate evaluation of their structural health. This study focuses on the San Cristobal Church,

Fig. 1. a) San Cristobal church from Cusco city centre, view from the South. The small green triangle indicates the position of the Raspberry Shake sensor. Modified from Martin St-Amant - Wikipedia - CC-BY-SA-3.0. b) Interior of the church with the Raspberry Shake sensor: small white box on the window sill. (Color figure online)

a 17th-century colonial building in the UNESCO World Heritage site of Cusco, Peru (Fig. 1). The church has been continuously monitored for 17 months using a tri-axial Raspberry Shake (3C) velocimeter to record its response to ambient and transient vibrations. In addition, environmental data, including temperature, humidity, wind speed, atmospheric pressure, and rainfall, have been collected from a weather station in Cusco located 3.2 km from the site. The unique value of our dataset is that it includes the recording of a $M_w 4.2$ earthquake that occurred on August 13, 2024, which temporarily altered the church's dynamic properties. A key contribution of this study is to focus on a historical masonry structure built using stone and earthen materials (known as "adobe") Such materials are underrepresented in the literature and, to the best of our knowledge, no prior machine learning study has attempted to model their environmental response. Although previous work [29,30] examined the response of earthen masonry to weather conditions, they do not develop predictive models.

Our approach is to develop machine learning models capable of predicting the church's natural frequencies under normal environmental conditions, establishing a baseline response of the undamaged structure. By doing so, we aim to predict the natural frequency variations induced by weather parameters, allowing us to identify non-predicted deviations as a proxy for detecting structural anomalies.

The key focus of this work is to estimate the post-seismic recovery period of the structure's dynamic properties. This estimation is crucial: when an earthquake affects a structure, its natural frequency should not return to its previous value if significant damage has occurred. However, with only a single sensor, localized damage elsewhere may not always be detectable from the data. As a result, the natural frequency could appear to recover even if there is some damage in parts of the church that are not monitored. Laboratory experiments and data from reinforced concrete buildings suggest that the recovery period is directly related to the degree of heterogeneity of the materials and therefore with their mechanical properties [16, 26]. Consequently, a change in recovery period may indicate evolving masonry properties, even in the absence of visible damage. This leads us to our primary research hypothesis: machine learning can assess, model, and predict these recovery periods, potentially identifying structural changes before they result in visible, significant damage.

In summary, the contributions of this paper are twofold: i) we develop and compare different machine learning models to predict the natural frequency of the San Cristobal Church using exclusively environmental parameters before the earthquake, assumed as the undamaged state; ii) we use a methodology based on structural break testing with Deep Temporal Convolutional Features to refine the estimate of post-seismic recovery time.

2   Methodology

Our methodology has three main components: (i) data preprocessing and feature engineering, (ii) predictive modeling of the natural frequency under normal conditions using machine learning, and (iii) post-seismic recovery period estimation based on structural break testing with deep temporal convolutional features.

2.1   Data Collection and Preprocessing

The dataset consists of two primary data sources: i) Seismic data recorded by a triaxial seismometer installed in the south wall of the church's nave, at a height of around 6 m, with a sampling rate of 100 Hz. The natural frequencies are extracted from this data using the Random Decrement Technique [10, 11]; ii) Environmental data obtained from a Davis Vantage Pro 2 weather station located approximately 3.2 km from the church, providing 10 min resolution measurements of temperature, humidity, wind speed, atmospheric pressure, and rainfall. To align the environmental data with the seismic data, all time series are downsampled to an hourly resolution. Weather parameters are averaged, except for rainfall, which is summed. Additionally, missing values are estimated using linear interpolation, as the gaps are short, with a maximum of one week of missing data. In July 2023, we carried out the Operational Modal Analysis [8] of the church from which several structural modes were identified. In the present paper, we focus specifically on the wandering of the natural frequency corresponding to the first torsional mode of the bell tower (around 6.7 Hz), as it is the most excited mode at the sensor location and provides a clean time series with minimal uncertainty. The complete time series is shown in Fig. 2.

2.2   Predictive Modeling

To predict the natural frequency from environmental data, we evaluate multiple machine learning models:

- **Baseline Linear Model**: Ridge Regression [18] is used as a baseline to benchmark more complex models. Linear models are commonly applied in SHM, as noted in [23, 24].
- **Feedforward Neural Network**: a feedforward neural network (FNN) is implemented to model nonlinear dependencies between environmental parameters and the natural frequency. The model is trained using the Adam optimizer with mean squared error as the loss function, and early stopping is applied to prevent overfitting.
- **Temporal Convolutional Networks**: To better capture temporal dependencies, we consider Temporal Convolutional Networks (TCN) [20]. A TCN is a generic 1D-convolutional architecture for sequence prediction with additional key characteristics: (i) It employs causal convolutions, ensuring that the output at time t depends only on the current and past inputs. (ii) A simple causal convolution can only look back at a history (receptive field) that grows linearly with the network depth. To efficiently capture long-range dependencies, dilated convolutions are used, expanding the receptive field exponentially with respect to the number of hidden layers. The transformation of an input sequence $\mathbf{x}_0^t$ through a hidden dilated causal convolutional layer is defined as

$$h^{(l)}(s) = \sum_{i=0}^{k-1} f^{(l)}(i) x_{s-di} \, , \; \forall s \in \{0, \dots, n-k\} \, , \tag{1}$$

where $h^{(l)}(s)$ is the output of the convolutional layer at position s in layer l, $f^{(l)}(i)$ is the learnable convolutional filter at layer l with i indexing the filter coefficients, k is the filter size and d is the dilation factor, which controls the spacing between kernel elements. (iii) Residual connections facilitate stable training, allowing the TCN to model long-term dependencies by stacking multiple layers. Finally, differently from a standard sequence prediction TCN, we focus only on the final time step: $\hat{y}_t = f(x_0, x_1, ..., x_t)$ where $\mathbf{x}_0^t \equiv x_0, x_1, \dots, x_t$ is the input sequence, and $\hat{y}_t$ is the predicted output corresponding to time t. The model is trained using the Adam optimizer with mean squared error as the loss function, and early stopping is applied to prevent overfitting. The final prediction is obtained through a linear layer, which maps the extracted deep convolutional features to the output.

2.3   Structural Break Testing

As the building's natural frequency responds to weather variations, we cannot assess its recovery by considering the variation of the frequency alone. Instead, our approach is to identify changes in the frequency response to the weather variables. In Economics and Statistics, Structural Break Analysis aims at identifying changes over time in the parameters of regression models, called *structural breaks*. The Bai-Perron (BP) sequential test [4, Sec. 5.2.2][5, Sec. 5.3] identifies an unknown number of structural breaks in linear regression models and assesses their statistical significance, by estimating them one at a time as in [3]. After

$l \geq 0$ breaks $\hat{T}_1, \ldots, \hat{T}_l$ have been found (when $l = 0$, the sequence is empty), the test considers an additional break at each possible location within each subsample defined by the l breaks (or within the whole sample, if $l = 0$). Let $\hat{T}_0 = 0$ and $\hat{T}_{l+1} = T$, with T being the sample size, and $S_T(\hat{T}_1, \ldots, \hat{T}_m)$ denote the sum of squared residuals obtained by fitting a linear model on each of the subsamples defined the break points $\hat{T}_1, \ldots, \hat{T}_m$. Then, the following statistic is considered to test the null hypothesis of l breaks $\hat{T}_1, \ldots, \hat{T}_l$ against the alternative of $l + 1$ breaks:

$$F_T(l + 1 \mid l) = \left\{ S_T\left(\hat{T}_1, \ldots, \hat{T}_l\right) \right. \tag{2}$$
$$\left. - \min_{1 \leq i \leq l+1} \inf_{\tau \in \Lambda_{i,\eta}} S_T\left(\hat{T}_1, \ldots, \hat{T}_{i-1}, \tau, \hat{T}_i, \ldots, \hat{T}_l\right) \right\} / \hat{\sigma}^2$$

where

$$\Lambda_{i,\eta} = \left\{ \tau; \hat{T}_{i-1} + \left(\hat{T}_i - \hat{T}_{i-1}\right) \eta \leq \tau \leq \hat{T}_i - \left(\hat{T}_i - \hat{T}_{i-1}\right) \eta \right\}$$

with η being a parameter defining the minimal length between two adjacent breaks and $\hat{\sigma}^2$ a consistent estimate of the variance of the disturbance σ^2 under the null hypothesis. Critical values for this statistic are provided in [4, Table II]. When $F_T(l + 1 \mid l)$ is above the critical value, the null is rejected and the value of τ minimizing the second term of the right-hand side Eq. 2 is retained as the $l + 1$-th break and appended to the previous list of breaks. The test starts with $l = 0$ breaks and keeps increasing l by 1 as long as the null hypothesis is rejected and a maximum number of breaks is not reached. The linear assumption allows the optimization problem to be efficiently solved, resulting in $O(T)$ complexity for the entire procedure.

To extend the structural break analysis to a non-linear framework, our approach consists in processing the raw weather features using the learned TCN and taking the output of the last hidden layer as input features for the structural break analysis—thus replacing the last linear layer of the TCN by the linear models fitted by the BP test. As shown in Sect. 3.5, we use this test to estimate the length of the recovery process and finally assess if it recovered at all by concatenating the time series before the earthquake with that after the hypothesized recovery and testing for breaks—no rejection supporting the full recovery hypothesis, up to a type II error.

3   Application Case: San Cristobal Church

We now present the results obtained with our methodology on the frequency response of the San Cristobal Church to the weather conditions.

The code and the dataset necessary to reproduce the results can be found at: https://github.com/francdente/SHM-post_earthquake_monitoring and https://zenodo.org/records/15641078.

3.1 Experimental Setup

Temporal Constraints and Limited Data Availability. A key challenge is maintaining temporal relationships in the data, ensuring that validation and test sets occur strictly after the training set to prevent the model from predicting the past using future data. This issue is particularly critical for highly seasonal datasets such as ours, which has distinct wet and dry seasons. If the training set consists of dry season data while the validation set is from the rainy season, the model may struggle to generalize, making validation results less meaningful. Even with time series cross-validation [6], which preserves temporal order, validation and test splits may still fail to represent the full distribution, particularly in cases of strong seasonality. The dataset consists of approximately one year and four months of data, whereas at least two years would be ideal to better capture seasonal variations in the validation and test sets. This limitation is complicated by the occurrence of an earthquake on August 13, 2024, which disrupts normal structural behavior, leaving only about a year of usable pre-earthquake data. To mitigate this constraint, only 10% of the pre-earthquake data is allocated for validation when training neural networks. This allows the network to be trained on nearly a full year of pre-earthquake data, reducing the risk of overfitting while still maintaining a sufficient validation set to evaluate performance.

Challenges with Neural Networks and Cross-Validation. Time series cross-validation poses challenges for neural networks, primarily due to training size bias, where increasing training data in each split artificially improves performance, making comparisons difficult. Additionally, small training splits in early folds can be problematic as neural networks require large datasets in relation to the number of parameters they have to perform well. Smaller training splits in early cross-validation iterations result in underperforming models, and these results are not representative of the network's true potential.

Dataset Partitioning. Following the previous considerations, the dataset was partitioned according to the earthquake of August 13. The pre-earthquake period is used for training, including validation data, while the post-earthquake period is designated as the test set. The post-earthquake test set may not fully represent the generalization error of the model due to the sudden frequency disturbance caused by the earthquake and the gradual recovery of elastic properties. The recovery duration depends on material properties and structural damage [16, 19]. Since no visible damage is observed and the frequency value return to pre-earthquake levels, there is no evidence of significant structural damage. Thus, the period during which the frequency had not yet stabilized is classified as abnormal behavior. To determine a first naive estimate of the recovery duration, we applied a conservative moving average with a 12-day window to identify when frequency values returned to pre-earthquake levels ($f = 6.76$ Hz). This resulted in around 2.5 months of estimated recovery period. The natural frequency values calculated after this period are assumed to reflect normal behavior and are used to estimate the generalization error of the predictive model. This setup is visually

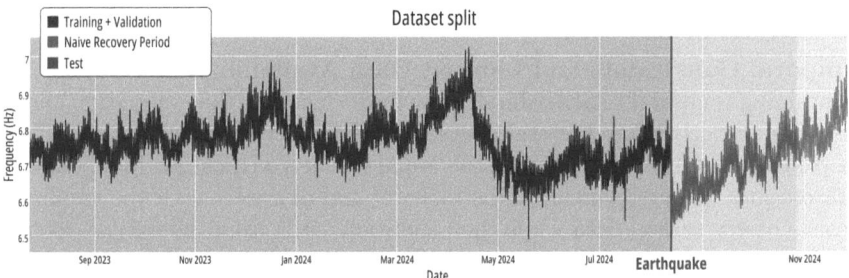

Fig. 2. Visual representation of dataset splits.

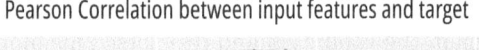

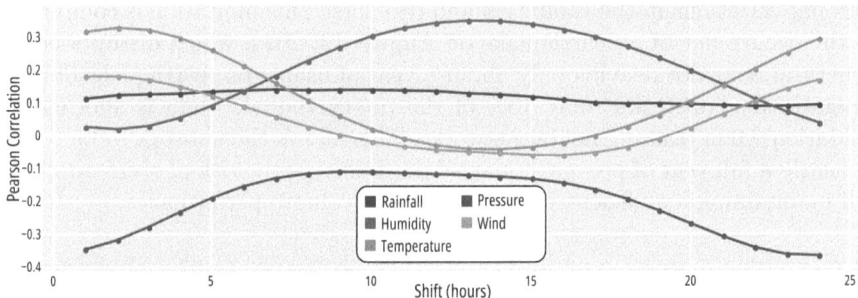

Fig. 3. Pearson correlation between weather parameters and natural frequency at different shifts. The x-axis represents the time shift (up to 24 h in the past), while the y-axis shows the correlation coefficient for each weather variable.

shown in Fig. 2. It allows both the evaluation of the model generalization under normal conditions and the investigation of the lingering effects of the earthquake on the structure. By applying our methodology, we aim to refine the estimate of the recovery period, moving beyond the naive assumptions made during the preliminary analysis.

Evaluation Metric: Root Mean Squared Error (RMSE). We use the Root Mean Squared Error (RMSE) as the primary evaluation metric, as it is widely adopted in regression tasks and retains the same unit as the target variable (Hz), providing an intuitive measure of error magnitude.

3.2   Feature Engineering

Feature engineering is essential for enhancing the performance of linear models. This section focuses on modeling the impact of past weather conditions and examining the correlation between weather variables and natural frequencies over various time shifts. To effectively capture these relationships, we use both shifted weather values and rolling window averages as newly crafted features.

Rolling Windows Features. Using only current weather values (t) ignores past influences, while adding multiple lagged values increases model complexity and risks overfitting. To address this, rolling window averages are used to capture past trends and cumulative effects. Window sizes are treated as hyper-parameter.

Correlation Analysis. To better understand the relationships between input weather features and natural frequency, we compute the correlation coefficients for various weather parameters with different time shifts. Figure 3 shows the correlations across these shifts. Shifting weather data significantly improves correlation for humidity and temperature, with temperature changes linked to thermal expansion and humidity showing a 13-hour lag due to its anti-correlation with temperature. A longer analysis indicates that rainfall has the highest correlation with natural frequency after 4.4 days (106 h), likely due to moisture absorption in adobe walls[1] and soil saturation effects on the foundation. Based on these findings, the original values of temperature, humidity, and rainfall at time t are replaced with their respective lagged counterparts: temperature ($t - 2$ h), humidity ($t - 13$ h), and rainfall ($t - 106$ h).

3.3   Ridge Regression

Training Strategy and Feature Engineering. We optimize key hyperparameters using time series cross-validation [6] with 3 splits, as implemented in `TimeSeriesSplit` from `scikit-learn`. For the regularization weight, values of 0.1, 1, 10, 100, and 1000 are tested. Rolling window sizes are also explored, with different ranges for each variable. For pressure and temperature, window sizes from 0 to 300 past hours are evaluated in increments of 50, as the correlation analysis highlights the importance of recent values. For humidity and rainfall, window sizes from 0 to 600 past hours are tested in increments of 50, as past values in the correlation analysis appear to have a significant influence.

Results and Observations. We evaluate the Ridge Regression model against a dummy model that predicts the mean of the training set. Cross-validation optimization selects the best hyperparameters: a regularization weight of 0.1, a rolling window of 450 h for rainfall, and 150 h for temperature, with no rolling window for pressure, humidity, or wind speed. Ridge Regression outperforms the dummy model but still struggles to capture natural frequency peaks accurately. Table 1 summarizes the RMSE values for both models. Poorly modeled peaks in natural frequency often coincide with periods of heavy rainfall in Cusco. Comparing models with and without a past window for rainfall (Fig. 4) reveals that aggregating past rainfall data significantly improves peak prediction. Simply including rainfall as a feature without applying a past window does not enhance performance, highlighting the importance of capturing cumulative effects (see

---

[1] Adobe walls, composed of earth, clay, and straw, offer good insulation but are highly susceptible to moisture from prolonged rainfall.

Table 1. Comparison of RMSE values for Ridge Regression with (w) and without (w/o) past rainfall window and Dummy Model.

Model	Train RMSE	Validation RMSE	Test RMSE
Dummy Model	0.0659	0.0788	0.0917
Ridge Regression (w/o)	0.0545	0.0599	0.0459
Ridge Regression (w)	**0.0469**	**0.0521**	**0.0414**

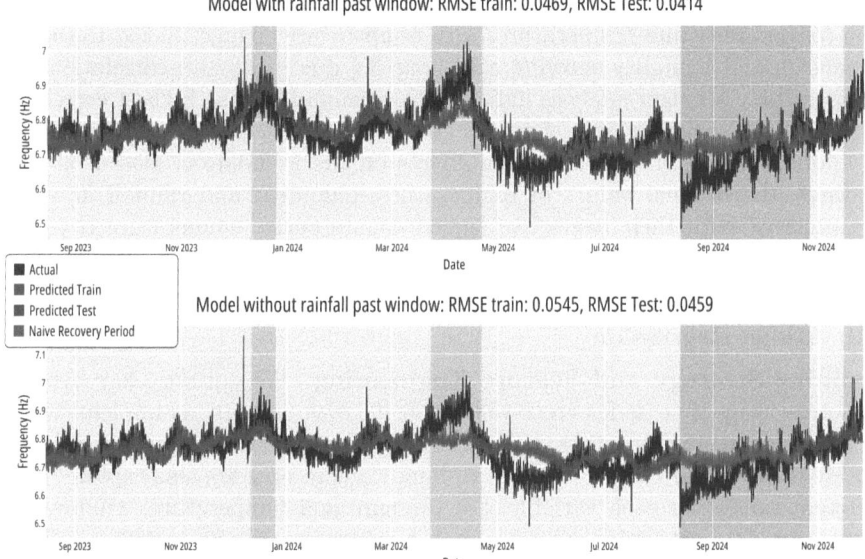

Fig. 4. (Top) Ridge Regression results **with** the rainfall past window as a feature, peaks are better modeled. (Bottom) Ridge Regression results **without** the rainfall past window as a feature, the model struggles to capture peaks and completely fails in capturing the peak in the test set. Poorly modeled peaks are highlighted in red. (Color figure online)

Fig. 5). This is evident in the test set, where early rainfall in 2024 caused a peak that the model without past aggregation failed to capture. These findings suggest that prolonged rainfall impacts the structure, likely through moisture absorption in adobe walls or changes in the foundation.

3.4 Temporal Convolutional Networks

Training Strategy and Feature Engineering. Our implementation of the TCN is based on the PyTorch-TCN library.[2] As in Sect. 3.1, we adopt a fixed train-validation-test partitioning strategy. The training set consists of 90% of the

---

[2] available at https://github.com/paul-krug/pytorch-tcn.

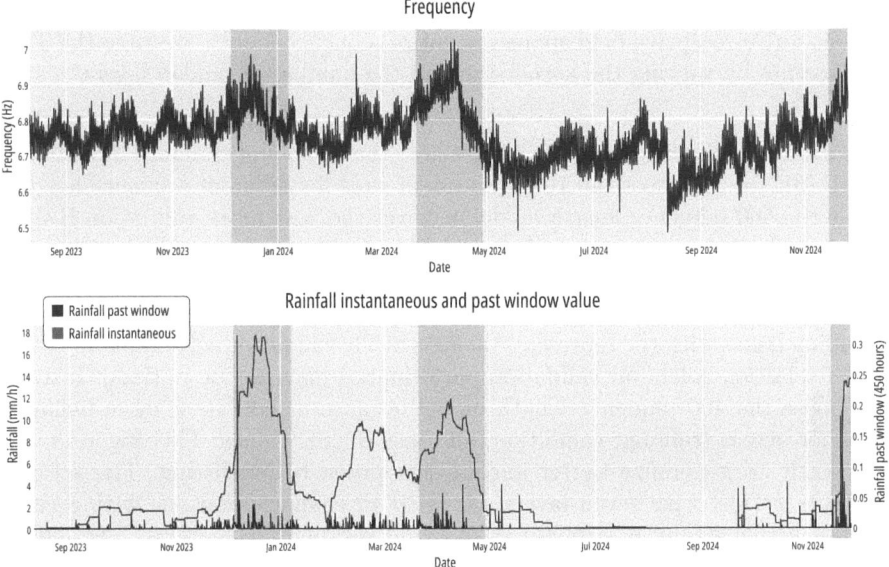

Fig. 5. (Top) Natural frequency time series with the three poorly modeled peaks highlighted. They correspond to periods where the model struggles to accurately predict the natural frequency. (Bottom) Instantaneous rainfall values (measured in millimeters over a one-hour period) and the past rainfall rolling window (450-hour window). The past window feature aligns well with these peaks, suggesting its effectiveness in capturing the cumulative effects of rainfall.

Table 2. Comparison of RMSE values (mean ± standard error of the mean) for TCNNs trained with different sequence lengths across 10 independent runs.

Sequence Length	Train RMSE	Validation RMSE	Test RMSE
400	0.0229 ± 0.0003	0.0306 ± 0.0001	$\mathbf{0.0349 \pm 0.0001}$
500	$\mathbf{0.0229 \pm 0.0002}$	$\mathbf{0.0298 \pm 0.0000}$	0.0375 ± 0.0001
600	0.0244 ± 0.0004	0.0320 ± 0.0001	0.0364 ± 0.0003

pre-earthquake data, while the validation set, comprising 10%, is used to monitor overfitting and select the best model based on validation loss. The test set includes post-earthquake data after a naive recovery period and is used solely to evaluate the model's generalization performance. Since TCNs process sequential data, raw instantaneous input features are used without rolling window transformations, and the sequence length determines how far back the model can analyze past data. To deal with the randomness of the training process, instead of relying on a single training run, 10 independent TCN models are trained for 25 epochs at each sequence length, and the mean and standard deviation of their RMSEs are reported. Based on findings from previous models, where rolling rainfall windows (450 h for Ridge Regression) improved performance, we evaluate sequence lengths ranging from 400 to 600 time steps. To ensure that the network's receptive field spans the entire sequence length, we tune the TCN architecture by varying the kernel size and the number of hidden layers.

Results and Observations. Table 2 shows the mean and standard deviation of the RMSE values across the 10 independent runs for different sequence lengths. While the 500 sequence length model achieves the best mean validation RMSE, we select the 400 sequence length model. The decision to select the latter model is based on the real-world nature of this case study. Unlike a specific benchmark dataset, real-world data often presents challenges, as discussed in Sect. 3.1, including issues with the representativeness of the validation set, therefore basing model selection solely on validation performance may not be optimal. Instead, we choose the 400 sequence length model because it exhibits a more balanced behavior across training, validation, and test RMSE values. This suggests that it is likely to generalize better and be less prone to overfitting. The selected model is a TCN with seven layers (six with 16 channels and one with 8 channels), a kernel size of 6, dropout of 0.3, and residual connections. The output from the final TCN layer is processed through two fully connected layers (8 → 4 → 1) to generate the final prediction. We also show results of a Feedforward Neural Network (FFNN) with three fully connected layers (128, 64, and 1 neurons, respectively), batch normalization, LeakyReLU activation, and dropout, in which we performed feature engineering by adding a rolling window mean of past values for the rainfall feature. This choice was motivated by our observations from Ridge Regression, where incorporating such transformations improved the ability to model peak values. The results in Fig. 6 show that while the FFNN performs better than Ridge Regression in capturing peak values, it still struggles to accurately model the peak occurring between March and May. As a result, in certain intervals, the residuals during the normal period are almost as high as those observed during the anomalous period. In contrast, the TCN model provides a more stable and well-behaved solution. As seen in Fig. 6, the residuals are better distributed, and the RMSE values further confirm its better performance. The other key advantage of TCNs is their ability to learn temporal dependencies directly from raw data, eliminating the need for manually engineered features like rolling window averages. Table 3 summarizes the comparison across different architectures, where the TCN achieves the best performance.

3.5   Structural Break Testing

Our primary goal is to automatically identify the end of the post-earthquake recovery period and refine the naive estimate of 2.5 months. To achieve this, we implement the BP sequential test presented in Sect. 2.3, by using the `dosequa` function provided in the R package `mbreaks` [22]. We perform the test using a 1% significance level, which means that only breakpoints with strong statistical evidence for a structural change are retained. The package requires a minimum segment length for reliable breakpoint detection. We set this value to 5% of the

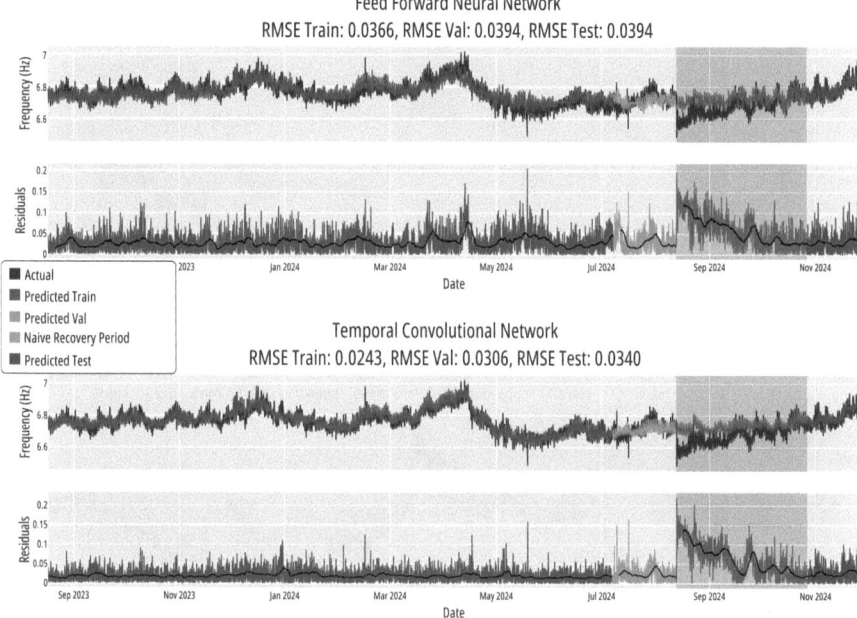

Fig. 6. (Top) Feedforward Neural Network results with rolling window feature engineering (window size 600). While peak modeling improves compared to Ridge Regression, the residuals remain problematic, suggesting further limitations. (Bottom) Temporal Convolutional Neural Network results of the best model across the 10 training runs with sequence length 400.

Table 3. Comparison of RMSE values for the best-performing models across different architectures. For TCN, RMSE values of the best training run are reported. TCN achieves the best performance.

Model	Train RMSE	Test RMSE	Overall RMSE
Ridge Regression	0.0469	0.0414	0.0465
Feedforward Neural Network	0.0366	0.0394	0.0371
Temporal Convolutional Network	**0.0243**	**0.0340**	**0.0308**

total dataset length, which is the smallest allowed by the package. We set a maximum of 10 breaks, which is the largest value allowed by the package.

Results and Observations. Figure 7a shows the result of our approach that combines the BP test with Deep Temporal Convolutional features, on the whole time series. The $F_T(l + 1 \mid l)$ statistic (denoted supF) representing the gain in SSR obtained by splitting at a given break (see Sect. 2.3) is shown on the top. The test correctly identifies a structural break corresponding to the earthquake (Date 4) and two breaks after suggesting two important steps of the recovery

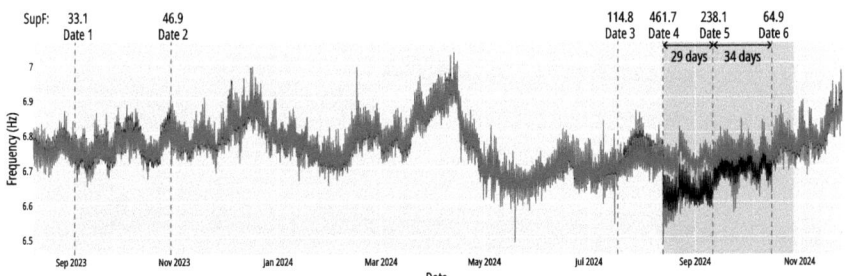

(a) Result of the BP test using Deep Temporal Convolutional Features as input.

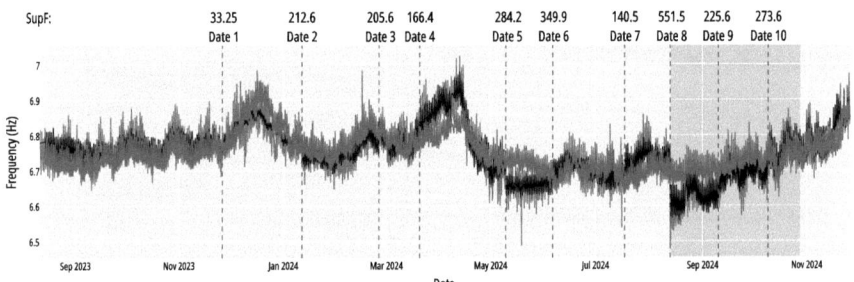

(b) Result of the BP test using Ridge Regression features as input (see Section 3.3).

Fig. 7. Structural Breaks: The black curve represents the predictions with one linear model per segment, the red one corresponds to predictions using a single linear model, and the blue one represents the actual values. In a), Date 4 corresponds to the earthquake, while Date 6 indicates the end of the recovery period. The grayed segment corresponds to the naive estimate. (Color figure online)

process. Before the earthquake, three breaks are detected, however, the breaks at Date 1 and Date 2 have a much lower supF statistic compared to the others. The detection of Date 3 can be attributed to the fact that it marks the beginning of the validation set, where the model exhibits a higher RMSE compared to the training set. Finally, as explained in Sect. 2.3, we concatenate the portion of the time series between Date 3 and 4 of Fig. 7a (i.e., just before the earthquake)[3] with the portion after Date 6 (i.e., after the supposed recovery) and run the test on it, resulting in a non rejection of the null hypothesis (i.e., the recovery). The linear approach (see Fig. 7b), while correctly identifying the recovery period, detects the maximum allowed 10 breaks, many of which may not reflect actual structural changes. In contrast, our method avoids spurious breakpoints, providing a more reliable interpretation and reducing the risk of false positives, especially in less evident cases. These results demonstrate that our approach provides a more

---

[3] We do not use previous segments since they belong to the training set and would induce a break due to the difference between training and test set as for Date 3.

precise estimate of the recovery period, improving upon both the initial naive estimate and the results obtained with the linear approach.

4 Conclusions

This study combined machine learning and statistical methods to analyze the relationship between environmental factors and the natural frequency of a historical adobe church. By developing predictive models based on environmental parameters, we established a baseline response that enabled the detection of anomalies potentially linked to changes in the building's structure.

Our findings demonstrate that incorporating past weather data, particularly a rolling window for rainfall, significantly improves predictions. Ridge Regression served as a useful baseline, but it struggled to capture complex nonlinear dependencies. In contrast, Temporal Convolutional Networks effectively modeled temporal dependencies, outperforming other approaches in predictive accuracy, as they could naturally take into account the time-delayed dynamic response of the church to changes in weather parameters. The achievement of a reliable baseline response model using exclusively weather data demonstrates that a large portion of the observed frequency variations can be explained by environmental conditions. Furthermore, our novel approach combining deep temporal convolutional features with the Bai-Perron test allowed us to refine the estimation of the post-seismic recovery period and to conclude that San Cristobal Church has completely recovered its dynamic behavior on October 15th, 63 days after the Mw 4.2 earthquake of August 13th, 2024.

By accurately assessing the post-seismic recovery time, our methodology provides a promising approach for developing early warning systems to detect damage in historical buildings. This capability is particularly valuable for heritage conservation, where non-invasive monitoring solutions are essential for preserving structural integrity. Heritage management is generally reactive, with interventions occurring only after damage has already taken place [14]. This approach is costly and, in some cases, too late to preserve the building's authenticity. The ability to detect subtle changes, prior to damage, in the mechanical properties of masonry could improve risk assessment strategies and support more effective maintenance interventions.

References

1. Astorga, A., Guéguen, P.: Structural health building response induced by earthquakes: material softening and recovery. Eng. Rep. **2**(9), e12228 (2020)
2. Azzara, R.M., De Roeck, G., Girardi, M., Padovani, C., Pellegrini, D., Reynders, E.: The influence of environmental parameters on the dynamic behaviour of the san frediano bell tower in lucca. Eng. Struct. **156**, 175–187 (2018)
3. Bai, J.: Estimating multiple breaks one at a time. Economet. Theor. **13**(3), 315–352 (1997)
4. Bai, J., Perron, P.: Estimating and testing linear models with multiple structural changes. In: Econometrica, pp. 47–78 (1998)

5. Bai, J., Perron, P.: Computation and analysis of multiple structural change models. J. Appl. Economet. **18**(1), 1–22 (2003)
6. Bergmeir, C., Benítez, J.M.: On the use of cross-validation for time series predictor evaluation. Inf. Sci. **191**, 192–213 (2012)
7. Bodin, P., Vidale, J., Walsh, T., Çakir, R., Çelebi, M.: Transient and long-term changes in seismic response of the natural resources building, Olympia, Washington, due to earthquake shaking. J. Earthquake Eng. **16**(5), 607–622 (2012)
8. Brincker, R., Zhang, L., Andersen, P.: Modal identification of output-only systems using frequency domaindecomposition. Smart Mater. Struct. **10**(3), 441 (2001)
9. Çelebi, M.: On the variation of fundamental frequency (period) of an undamaged building—a continuing discussion. In: International Conference on Experimental Vibration Analysis for Civil Engineering Structures, Porto (2007)
10. Cole, H.A., Jr.: On-line failure detection and damping measurement of aerospace structures by random decrement signatures. Technical report, NASA (1973)
11. Combey, A., Mercerat, D.E., Gueguen, P., Langlais, M., Audin, L.: Postseismic survey of a historic masonry tower and monitoring of its dynamic behavior in the aftermath of le teil earthquake (ardèche, france). Bull. Seismol. Soc. Am. **112**(2), 1101–1119 (2022)
12. Ewins, D.J.: Exciting vibrations: the role of testing in an era of supercomputers and uncertainties. Meccanica **51**(12), 3241–3258 (2016). https://doi.org/10.1007/s11012-016-0576-y
13. Falchi, F., Girardi, M., Gurioli, G., Messina, N., Padovani, C., Pellegrini, D.: Deep learning and structural health monitoring: temporal fusion transformers for anomaly detection in masonry towers. Mech. Syst. Signal Process. **215**, 111382 (2024)
14. Feilden, B.M.: Between Two Earthquakes: Cultural Property in Seismic Zones. Getty Publications (1987)
15. Gattulli, V., Lepidi, M., Potenza, F.: Dynamic testing and health monitoring of historic and modern civil structures in Italy. Struct. Monit. Maint. **3**(1), 71–90 (2016)
16. Guéguen, P., Brossault, M.A., Roux, P., Singaucho, J.C.: Slow dynamics process observed in civil engineering structures to detect structural heterogeneities. Eng. Struct. **202**, 109833 (2020)
17. Gueguen, P., et al.: Testing buildings using ambient vibrations for earthquake engineering: a European review. In: Proceedings of the 2nd European Conference on Earthquake Engineering and Seismology (2ECEES), Istanbul (2014)
18. Hoerl, A.E., Kennard, R.W.: Ridge regression: biased estimation for nonorthogonal problems. Technometrics **12**(1), 55–67 (1970)
19. Johnson, P., Sutin, A.: Slow dynamics and anomalous nonlinear fast dynamics in diverse solids. J. Acoust. Soc. Am. **117**(1), 124–130 (2005)
20. Lea, C., Flynn, M.D., Vidal, R., Reiter, A., Hager, G.D.: Temporal convolutional networks for action segmentation and detection. In: Proceedings of the IEEE Conference on Computer Vision and Pattern Recognition, pp. 156–165 (2017)
21. Lorenzoni, F., Caldon, M., da Porto, F., Modena, C., Aoki, T.: Post-earthquake controls and damage detection through structural health monitoring: applications in l'aquila. J. Civ. Struct. Heal. Monit. **8**, 217–236 (2018)
22. Nguyen, L., Yamamoto, Y., Perron, P.: mbreaks: Estimation and inference for structural breaks in linear regression models [computer software manual]. R package version **1**(0) (2023)
23. Peeters, B., Roeck, G.: One-year monitoring of the z24-bridge: environmental effects versus damage events. Earthq. Eng. Struct. Dyn. **30**(2), 149–171 (2001)

24. Peeters, B., Maeck, J., De Roeck, G.: Vibration-based damage detection in civil engineering: excitation sources and temperature effects. Smart Mater. Struct. **10**(3), 518 (2001)
25. Pellegrini, D., Padovani, C., Messina, N., Girardi, M., Carrara, F., Falchi, F.: Deep learning for structural health monitoring: an application to heritage structures. Mater. Res. Proc. **26** (2022)
26. Van Den Abeele, K.A., Carmeliet, J., Johnson, P., Zinszner, B.: Influence of water saturation on the nonlinear elastic mesoscopic response in earth materials and the implications to the mechanism of nonlinearity. J. Geophys. Res. Solid Earth **107**(B6), ECV-4 (2002)
27. Vidal, F., Navarro, M., Aranda, C., Enomoto, T.: Changes in dynamic characteristics of lorca rc buildings from pre-and post-earthquake ambient vibration data. Bull. Earthq. Eng. **12**, 2095–2110 (2014)
28. Williams, E.F., Heaton, T.H., Zhan, Z., Lambert, V.R.: Variability in the natural frequencies of a nine-story concrete building from seconds to decades. Seismic Rec. **2**(4), 237–247 (2022)
29. Zonno, G., Aguilar, R., Boroschek, R., Lourenço, P.B.: Analysis of the long and short-term effects of temperature and humidity on the structural properties of adobe buildings using continuous monitoring. Eng. Struct. **196**, 109299 (2019)
30. Zonno, G., Aguilar, R., Boroschek, R., Lourenço, P.B.: Experimental analysis of the thermohygrometric effects on the dynamic behavior of adobe systems. Constr. Build. Mater. **208**, 158–174 (2019)

Fostering Responsibility in Email Marketing: A Contextual Restless Bandit Framework

Ibtihal El Mimouni[1,2(✉)] and Konstantin Avrachenkov[1]

[1] INRIA Sophia Antipolis, Biot, France
{ibtihal.el-mimouni,k.avrachenkov}@inria.fr
[2] Smartprofile, Valbonne, France

Abstract. Email marketing is increasingly criticized due to ethical concerns, as bulk email campaigns often result in spam, reduced engagement, and negative user experiences. In addition, there is increasing awareness of the environmental impact, as these large-scale campaigns contribute to carbon emissions. To address these issues, we introduce QWIC-Fair (Q-learning Whittle Index with Context and Fairness), an algorithm that operates within a Contextual Restless Multi-Armed Bandit framework. QWIC-Fair leverages implicit feedback to learn the dynamics of user interactions and thus target users with relevant content. In this model, each user represents an arm of the bandit, evolving as a Markov Decision Process that captures state transitions reflecting their interactions with email contents, while accounting for contextual information. The algorithm also incorporates a fairness constraint to ensure balanced selection and to avoid repetitive targeting of the same users. The experiments conducted, using synthetic and real-world data, show that QWIC-Fair outperforms existing email marketing approaches.

Keywords: Reinforcement learning · Restless bandits · Whittle index · Q-learning · Fairness · Recommender systems · Responsible email marketing

1 Introduction

In today's digital landscape, email marketing has become an essential tool for businesses to reach out to potential customers [12]. However, the volume of emails sent daily raises ethical and environmental issues, particularly with traditional marketing strategies that often deliver generic content to large market segments. This results in high spam rates [23], a negative user experience [22], and a tarnished domain reputation [44]. Moreover, these practices also contribute to digital carbon emissions: a typical email has a carbon footprint that ranges between 0.3g and

---

Supplementary Information The online version contains supplementary material available at https://doi.org/10.1007/978-3-662-72243-5_21.

26g of CO_2, while an email with an attachment can reach up to 50g of CO_2 [5,36]. Individual emails may have a relatively small carbon footprint, but the cumulative effect of poorly targeted campaigns can be significant: in 2023, an estimated 347 billion emails were sent and received around the world [37].

These challenges are compounded by the fact that user engagement is not static: preferences and responsiveness shift over time due to factors such as seasonal trends or changes in personal preferences. As a result, traditional static or myopic approaches, which optimize only for immediate user response, often fail to capture these evolving patterns. This can lead to over-targeting of active users while neglecting others, resulting in disengagement and unfairness. Moreover, bulk campaigns frequently deliver irrelevant content, which not only contributes to user fatigue but also increases the carbon footprint by generating unnecessary emails. To address these issues, personalization is key. It allows for tailored offers that align with users' interests, enhancing engagement [28,41] and reducing the likelihood of emails being marked as spam. By targeting effectively, marketers can achieve better results with fewer emails, thereby minimizing the digital carbon footprint associated with mass campaigns.

Building on this principle of personalization, we propose to frame the problem as a sequential decision-making task using the Contextual Restless Multi-Armed Bandit framework. We model each user as an evolving arm, represented by a context-augmented Markov decision process that captures user's state transitions based on their email interactions. Within this framework, we introduce Q-learning Whittle Index with Context and Fairness (QWIC-FAIR). The algorithm operates in an episodic manner. Each episode consists of L time steps, during which actions are taken using an epsilon-greedy strategy. This involves either randomly exploring users or exploiting by selecting users based on the highest Whittle indices, which are a measure of the value of activating a particular user. QWIC-FAIR functions on two distinct timescales: on a fast timescale, it updates the Q-values by adjusting estimates of the expected cumulative reward for each state-action-context triplet. On a slow timescale, it updates the Whittle indices. At the end of each episode, the learning agent evaluates a fairness constraint to ensure balanced targeting among users. Specifically, it identifies under-selected users and prioritizes their selection in the following iterations. We showcase the effectiveness of QWIC-FAIR by comparing it to baselines often used in email marketing, using two simulators: one built from real-world data and another from synthetic data.

Our contributions can be summarized as follows: (1) We introduce a Contextual Restless Multi-Armed Bandit framework designed for email Recommender Systems (RS), where we consider each user as an arm of the bandit. (2) We design a practically relevant algorithm called QWIC-FAIR, which leverages context-aware Whittle index-based Q-learning, and incorporates a fairness constraint, thereby ensuring equitable selection of the users. (3) Our approach promotes ethical email marketing practices by guiding user selection to prevent spamming and to reduce the carbon footprint associated with bulk email campaigns. (4) Experiments, using both real and synthetic data, demonstrate the effectiveness of QWIC-FAIR.

The paper is structured as follows: Sect. 2 reviews the related literature. Section 3 presents restless bandits and introduces the Whittle index policy. Section 4 formalizes the contextual restless bandit problem and explains the email recommender application. Section 5 details the proposed algorithm. Section 6 outlines the experiments conducted and discusses the results.

2   Related Work

2.1   Bandits in Recommenders

Recommender Systems (RS) [40] have proven to be an effective tool [24] in guiding users through large pools of content, products, and services by suggesting the most pertinent items. RS are now broadly implemented across multiple industries [16,30,43], using various methods such as collaborative and content-based filtering [13,34]. Despite their popularity, these methods have some limitations, notably when favoring some popular items and limiting the exploration of potentially relevant ones. To address the exploration-exploitation dilemma, Multi-Armed Bandits (MAB) [10,25,50] have been explored in recommenders. These algorithms balance discovering new options, and exploiting previous knowledge about items that have been previously recommended. A more advanced type of bandits that incorporate contextual information (such as user demographics, time, or device) are the Contextual Multi-Armed Bandits (CMAB). LinUCB, proposed by Li et al. [27], is one the most popular CMAB algorithms. The authors solve the problem of personalized news recommendations at Yahoo!. However, even CMAB models may fall short in environments where user behavior keeps changing over time. To address this, Restless Multi-Armed Bandits (RMAB) emerged, allowing arms to evolve over time, even when not selected by the agent. Most bandit algorithms for recommenders consider each arm as the item to recommend [27,31]. In our work, we model each user as an arm.

2.2   Restless Bandits

Restless bandits have become very popular over the years, finding applications in different domains such as healthcare [6], web crawling [2], and communication networks [1]. For our RS use case, our study leverages seminal research on RMAB: Whittle [51] introduced the Whittle index policy, which allows for the activation of M arms on average by calculating an index for each arm and selecting top M arms with the highest indices. Building on Whittle's work, there has been a surge of interest in developing algorithms to calculate the Whittle index. For instance, Avrachenkov and Borkar [3] focused on the time-average criterion and developed a tabular algorithm that converges to the Whittle index. Various other approaches have been proposed to tackle the RMAB problem, including index policies [15,32,49] and Reinforcement Learning (RL) techniques [47,52]. Another line of research that is related to ours is the growing literature on fairness in RMAB. Some authors focused on quota-based fairness [19,35], while others studied satisfying the fairness among the allocated resources [7]. Other works explored soft fairness where fairness constraints are considered on average [26,46].

2.3   Contextual Restless Bandits

A particularly promising direction is the combination of contextual and restless bandits, coined as Contextual Restless Multi-Armed Bandits (CRMAB). While the incorporation of context has been explored in contextual MAB [9,27], research on CRMAB remains limited. To the best of our knowledge, the only works that address CRMAB are by Chen and Hou [11], who proposed a model-based online learning algorithm that combines index policies with a dual decomposition framework, allowing for simultaneous learning of the arm models and decision-making. They applied their algorithm to smart grid optimization. On the other hand, Liang et al. [29], developed a Bayesian CRMAB approach tailored to public health interventions. They used Thompson sampling and relied on informative priors to model arm behavior. In contrast, our method is model-free, using Q-learning to learn arm dynamics from observed interactions. Moreover, in addition to reward maximization, our approach ensures balanced exposure across arms by incorporating a fairness constraint.

3   Preliminaries

3.1   Restless Bandits

The RMAB problem is a generalization of the MAB framework. Unlike the classical bandit problems, restless bandits model a more realistic scenario where arms evolve over time regardless of whether they are selected. As a result, computing optimal policies becomes PSPACE-hard [33], and the exploration-exploitation trade-off is further complicated by the need to balance learning both active and passive arms.

Let us consider a RMAB with N arms, each evolving according to a Markov Decision Process (MDP). At each time step t, the agent selects a subset of M arms to activate, where $M < N$. The state of arm i at time t is denoted by $s_i(t) \in \mathcal{S}$, where $\mathcal{S}$ is the finite state space of the arm.

The state of each arm is controlled by the action chosen. Specifically, let $a_i(t)$ be the action taken on arm i at time t, where $a_i(t) = 1$ if arm i is activated, and $a_i(t) = 0$ if left passive. The state transition probabilities are defined as:

$$P(s_i(t+1) = s'|s_i(t) = s, a_i(t) = a) = P_{s,s'}^{i,a}, \tag{1}$$

where $P_{s,s'}^{i,a}$ is the probability of transitioning from current state s to next state s' for arm i under action a.

Each arm generates a reward depending on its state and the action taken. Let $r_i(s_i(t), a_i(t))$ denote the reward obtained from arm i at time t, at state $s_i(t)$, when action $a_i(t)$ is taken. The goal is to determine a policy π, that specifies which arms to activate at each time step, to maximize the expected cumulative reward. Under the total discounted criterion ($\gamma \in (0, 1)$ being the discount factor) and infinite horizon, the objective is to solve the following:

$$\max_{\pi} \mathbb{E} \left[\sum_{t=0}^{\infty} \sum_{i=1}^{N} \gamma^t \, r_i(s_i(t), a_i(t)) \right], \tag{2}$$

subject to the constraint that no more than M arms can be active simultaneously:

$$\sum_{i=1}^{N} a_i(t) \leq M, \quad \forall t \geq 0. \tag{3}$$

RMAB problems are computationally expensive [33]. Consequently, researchers have proposed approximation techniques to make these problems more tractable. One particularly significant advancement in this area is the Whittle index heuristic [51].

3.2   Whittle Index

Whittle's index policy utilizes the concept of Lagrangian relaxation to address the complexities of the RMAB problem. Whittle proposed to relax the constraint (3) to apply on average, rather than strictly, by incorporating a Lagrange multiplier, denoted $\tilde{\lambda}$. The objective function becomes the following:

$$\max_{\pi} \mathbb{E} \left[\sum_{t=0}^{\infty} \sum_{i=1}^{N} \gamma^t \left(r_i(s_i(t), a_i(t)) + \tilde{\lambda}(1 - a_i(t)) \right) \right]. \tag{4}$$

This relaxation allows the RMAB problem to be decoupled into N independent subproblems, each solved by the associated Bellman equation for the state value function:

$$V_i(s) = \max_{a \in \{0,1\}} \left[a \left(r_i(s, 1) + \gamma \sum_j p_i(j|s, 1) V_i(j) \right) \right.$$
$$\left. + (1 - a) \left(r_i(s, 0) + \tilde{\lambda} + \gamma \sum_j p_i(j|s, 0) V_i(j) \right) \right]. \tag{5}$$

We rewrite Eq. (5) as a function of the state-action pair, which determines the Q-values that reflect the expected future rewards of taking an action in a given state:

$$Q_i(s, a) = \begin{cases} r_i(s, 1) + \gamma \sum_j p_i(j|s, 1) V_i(j), & \text{if } a = 1, \\ r_i(s, 0) + \tilde{\lambda} + \gamma \sum_j p_i(j|s, 0) V_i(j), & \text{if } a = 0. \end{cases} \tag{6}$$

Whittle interpreted the Lagrange multiplier $\tilde{\lambda}$ as a subsidy for passivity. Accordingly, the Whittle index λ is defined as the smallest subsidy that makes the agent indifferent between choosing an arm i ($a_i = 1$) or not choosing it ($a_i = 0$). The RMAB problem is (Whittle) indexable if the set of states for which it is optimal to activate the arm increases monotonically with λ. For a given state k, $\lambda(k)$ is determined such that the expected reward from activating and not activating the arm are equal:

$$Q(k, 1) = Q(k, 0). \tag{7}$$

The objective is to learn the Whittle indices λ by solving (7).

4   Problem Formulation

4.1   An Email Recommender System

In RS, ethically collected user feedback [18], that respects user privacy and consent, is crucial for enhancing personalization and improving the performance of these systems. It is categorized into: *Explicit feedback* [4], which involves direct inputs from users such as ratings, reviews, likes, or explicitly stated preferences. This type of feedback offers precise insights into user preferences because it reflects their evaluations. However, explicit feedback is not always available as it relies on users actively providing it. On the other hand, *Implicit feedback* [20] is gathered passively through users' interactions with the system. It includes data such as browsing history, purchase frequency, shares, time spent on certain items, etc. This form of feedback tends to be more abundant providing a rich source of data for inferring user preferences.

An email RS benefits from a substantial amount of implicit feedback including actions like opening emails, clicking on call-to-action buttons, unsubscribing, etc.

In our work, we model an email RS as a sequential decision-making problem, specifically as a contextual restless bandit. Our goal is to maximize user engagement while minimizing unnecessary emails. This not only enhances user satisfaction and reduces the risk of email fatigue but also helps address the environmental challenges discussed in Sect. 1.

4.2   A Contextual Restless Bandit

Let $\mathcal{U} = \{u_1, u_2, \ldots, u_N\}$ be the finite collection of N heterogeneous users, where each user u_i is an arm of the CRMAB. Each user behaves according to a Contextual Markov Decision Process (CMDP) [17]. CMDP extends traditional MDP by incorporating contextual information that influences both the dynamics of the environment and the rewards associated with different actions.

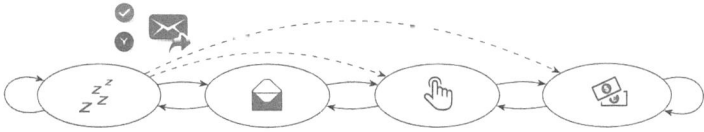

Fig. 1. Users are modeled as Markov decision processes, with state transitions reflecting engagement levels (idle, open, click, purchase).

We define a CMDP by the tuple $(\mathcal{S}, \mathcal{A}, \mathcal{C}, P, r)$, where the state space $\mathcal{S} = \{s_1, s_2, \ldots, s_{|\mathcal{S}|}\}$ represents the users' implicit feedback. We consider fully observable states corresponding to four levels of engagement, as shown in Fig. 1. *Open* is when the user opens an email, *click* is when the user clicks on a link within the email, *purchase* refers to buying a product, *idle* indicates no interaction.

The context space $\mathcal{C} = \{c_1, c_2, \ldots, c_{|\mathcal{C}|}\}$ captures side information that could include the special features of the campaign (e.g. seasonal promotions), user's features (e.g. age, location, segment). Contexts enrich the data from which the system learns.

The actions correspond to the type of emails to send to users, each with a different content, such as offering promotions, showcasing product features, and inviting feedback, etc. This multi-action setup adds another layer of complexity, which we will address in an extended version of the current work. To simplify, for now, we only consider the two-action CRMAB framework. Thus, the action space is $\mathcal{A} = \{0, 1\}$, where $a = 1$ is the active action of sending a promotional email, and $a = 0$ is the passive action of not sending it.

The probability that user u transitions from state s to state s', given action a, and context c is: $P_{s,s'}^{u,a,c}$ following the notation in Eq. (1).

The reward is a function of the current state, context, action, and next state, denoted as $r : \mathcal{S} \times \mathcal{C} \times \mathcal{A} \times \mathcal{S} \mapsto \mathbb{R}$. It is designed by assigning a reward value for an email open, a higher reward for a click, and a highest reward for a purchase, while taking into account the contexts and the action taken. For instance, suppose we have two users: u_1, a young professional living in an urban area, and u_2, a retired individual living in a suburban area. Without adding context, the system might treat both users the same way and send them identical offers, potentially leading to lower engagement. Incorporating context into the reward function allows the recommender to learn the types of actions (promotional offers) that yield the best outcomes (user engagement) in different contexts.

The goal is to maximize the discounted cumulative reward over infinite time horizon, subject to the constraint (3) that, at time step t, no more than M out of N users can be chosen:

$$\max_{\pi} \mathbb{E}\left[\sum_{t=0}^{\infty} \sum_{i=1}^{N} \gamma^t \, r_{u_i}(s_{u_i}(t), c_{u_i}, a_{u_i}(t), s_{u_i}(t+1))\right]. \tag{8}$$

For ease of notation, we will refer to the reward as r.

5   Algorithm: QWIC-FAIR

QWIC-FAIR leverages Q-learning, a model-free RL technique [48], alongside the Whittle index policy [51]. It uses a two-timescale stochastic approximation scheme [8] where both control and parametric optimization occur simultaneously. The algorithm incorporates contextual information to guide informed decision-making based on user interaction dynamics. It also constrains selection with fairness criteria to ensure balanced targeting, and to prevent repeatedly activating the same users.

Algorithm 1. Q-learning Whittle Index with Context & Fairness (QWIC-FAIR)

1: **Initialize** Q_table and λ_table, fairness threshold η, episodes $E_{episodes}$, time steps L, exploration parameter ϵ, discount factor γ, set of under-selected arms $\tilde{\mathcal{U}} = \emptyset$, $selection\_count$ to track arms' selections, $average\_reward$ to track arms' average reward across episodes, engagement threshold τ, interval to check inactive arms H
2: **for** $e = 1$ to $E_{episodes}$ **do**
3:     **for** $t = 1$ to L **do**
4:         /* Exploration-Exploitation */
5:         **if** Uni[0,1] $< \epsilon$ **then**
6:             Randomly select M arms from the set $\tilde{\mathcal{U}}$
7:             Fill remaining slots (if any) by selecting arms from the complement of $\tilde{\mathcal{U}}$
8:         **else**
9:             Select top M arms from the set $\tilde{\mathcal{U}}$ with the highest Whittle indices
10:            Fill remaining slots (if any) by selecting arms from the complement of $\tilde{\mathcal{U}}$
11:        **end if**
12:        /* Update selection counters and $\tilde{\mathcal{U}}$ */
13:        **for** each $selected\_arm$ **do**
14:            $selection\_count\,[selected\_arm] \leftarrow selection\_count\,[selected\_arm]+1$
15:            Remove $selected\_arm$ from the set $\tilde{\mathcal{U}}$ (if $selected\_arm \in \tilde{\mathcal{U}}$)
16:        **end for**
17:        Take actions $a(t)$, observe next states $s(t+1)$, contexts c, and rewards $r(t)$
18:        /* On a faster timescale, update the Q-values */
19:        **for** k in S **do**

$$Q(s(t), a(t), k, c) \leftarrow Q(s(t), a(t), k, c) + \alpha(t)\Big[(1 - a(t))(r(t) + \lambda(k, c))$$
$$+ \, a(t)r(t) + \gamma \max_{a' \in \{0,1\}} Q(s(t+1), a', k, c) - Q(s(t), a(t), k, c)\Big]$$

20:        **end for**
21:        /* On a slower timescale, update the Whittle indices */
22:        **for** k in $\mathcal{S}$ **do**
23:            **for** c in $\mathcal{C}$ **do**
24:                $\lambda(k, c) \leftarrow \lambda(k, c) + \beta(t)\Big(Q(k, 1, k, c) - Q(k, 0, k, c)\Big)$
25:            **end for**
26:        **end for**
27:    **end for**
28:    /* Fairness constraint */
29:    $\tilde{\mathcal{U}} = \{arm \mid selection\_count[arm] < \eta\,L\}$
30:    $selection\_count \leftarrow \{arm : 0\}$ for all arms
31:    /* Put non-engaging arms to sleep */
32:    **if** $e \equiv 0 \mod H$ **then**
33:        $\mathcal{Z} = \{arm \mid average\_reward[arm] < \tau\}$
34:        $\tilde{\mathcal{U}} = \{arm \mid selection\_count\,[arm] < \eta\,L \text{ and } arm \notin \mathcal{Z}\}$
35:    **end if**
36: **end for**

QWIC-FAIR operates in an episodic manner, where each episode is of length L. The entire time horizon is denoted by T. Let $E_{episodes}$ be the total number of episodes until time T, hence we have: $T = L\,E_{episodes}$. The episodic structure allows to periodically check the fairness constraint defined as follows:

Definition 1 (Fairness constraint). *Let $\mathcal{U} = \{u_1, u_2, \ldots, u_N\}$ be the set of N arms, and let L be the length of an episode. The fairness constraint is satisfied if, in each episode, we have:*

$$selection\_count[u_i] \geq \eta L, \quad \forall u_i \in \mathcal{U}, \tag{9}$$

where selection_count$[u_i]$ is the number of times arm u_i is selected during an episode e, and $\eta \in [0,1]$ is a fairness threshold. The fairness constraint ensures that, at the end of each episode, each arm $u_i \in \mathcal{U}$ was selected at least ηL times. If selection_count$[u_i] < \eta L$, the arm u_i is added to the set of under-selected arms $\tilde{\mathcal{U}}$[1], and is prioritized in the subsequent episode.

In our QWIC-FAIR algorithm, each arm u_i corresponds to an individual user. When clear from the context, we use the terms *arms* and *users* interchangeably. Thus, in an episode e, the set of under-selected arms $\tilde{\mathcal{U}}$ contains users who were targeted less frequently than others during that episode.

Each episode consists of L time steps. At each time step t, the algorithm employs an epsilon-greedy strategy to balance exploration and exploitation (see lines 4 → 11 of Algorithm 1):

- With probability ϵ, it explores the state-action-context space by randomly selecting arms from the set of under-selected users $\tilde{\mathcal{U}}$. If $|\tilde{\mathcal{U}}| < M$, the algorithm fills the remaining slots by selecting additional arms from the set: $\mathcal{U} \setminus \tilde{\mathcal{U}} = \{u_i \in \mathcal{U} \mid u_i \notin \tilde{\mathcal{U}}\}$.
- With probability $1 - \epsilon$, the algorithm exploits its current knowledge by selecting M users with the highest Whittle indices. Again, the algorithm first considers under-selected users by selecting the top M from $\tilde{\mathcal{U}}$ to ensure that fairness constraints are met. If $|\tilde{\mathcal{U}}| < M$, the remaining slots are filled by selecting arms with the highest Whittle indices from the complement of $\tilde{\mathcal{U}}$. This way the Whittle index policy respects the constraint (3).

For every selected user, the algorithm increments their selection counter, which tracks how often they are targeted during the episode. If the selected user $\in \tilde{\mathcal{U}}$, they are removed from this set for the remainder of the episode. This ensures that they are no longer prioritized as under-selected users for the rest of the current episode (see lines 12 → 16 of Algorithm 1).

Once the users are selected, the algorithm executes the actions $a(t)$, and observes the resulting next states $s(t + 1)$, contexts c, and rewards $r(t)$. Next, it updates the Q-values and Whittle indices, following a two-timescale stochastic approximation approach with asynchronous iterates (see lines 17 → 26 of

---

[1] The maximum size of $\tilde{U}$ is $N - M$. This occurs when the algorithm repeatedly selects the same subset of M users. To ensure that all users in $\tilde{U}$ are covered throughout the episode, the minimum number of time steps required is: $L \geq \lceil \frac{N-M}{M} \rceil$.

Algorithm 1). Specifically, on a fast timescale, it updates the Q-values:

$$Q(s(t), a(t), k, c) \leftarrow Q(s(t), a(t), k, c) + \alpha(t) \Big[(1 - a(t))(r(t) + \lambda(k, c))$$
$$+ a(t)r(t) + \gamma \max_{a' \in \{0,1\}} Q(s(t+1), a', k, c) - Q(s(t), a(t), k, c) \Big], \tag{10}$$

and, on a slow timescale, it updates the Whittle indices:

$$\lambda(k, c) \leftarrow \lambda(k, c) + \beta(t)(Q(k, 1, k, c) - Q(k, 0, k, c)). \tag{11}$$

In the above, $\alpha(t)$ and $\beta(t)$ are the learning rates for the Q-values and the Whittle indices, respectively, with $\beta(t) = o(\alpha(t))$, as the Whittle index estimates need to be updated less frequently. We fix:

$$\alpha(t) = \frac{C}{\left\lceil \frac{t}{5000} \right\rceil}, \quad \beta(t) = \frac{C'}{1 + \left\lceil \frac{t \log t}{5000} \right\rceil} \mathbf{I}\{t \mod N \equiv 0\}, \tag{12}$$

This ensures that:

- $\sum_{t=0}^{\infty} \alpha(t) = \infty$ and $\sum_{t=0}^{\infty} \alpha(t)^2 < \infty$: $\alpha(t)$ must decrease sufficiently slowly to ensure that the algorithm can explore the environment over time, while also decreasing quickly enough to guarantee convergence to the optimal Q-values.
- $\sum_{t=0}^{\infty} \beta(t) = \infty$ and $\sum_{t=0}^{\infty} \beta(t)^2 < \infty$: $\beta(t)$ must decrease gradually enough to allow continuous learning of Whittle index estimates, but also quickly enough to ensure the estimates eventually converge to their true values.

The theoretical guarantees from [3] include convergence of the Q-values and of the Whittle index estimates for each state. For our tabular setting, for time-independent context, the learning process inherits these convergence guarantees. Concerning time-dependant context, one may choose α and β to be small constant values with the condition that $\beta << \alpha$.

At the end of each episode, the algorithm checks the fairness criterion by reviewing the selection count for each user. Users who were under-selected are added to the set $\tilde{U}$. The elements of this set are prioritized in the subsequent episode, ensuring a more balanced targeting approach over time. The algorithm resets the selection counter for all users, to prepare for the next episode (see lines 28 $\rightarrow$ 30 of Algorithm 1). While fairness is important to ensure equitable selection among users, strictly adhering to the fairness constraint can sometimes lead to suboptimal outcomes. For instance, some users might consistently remain in the *idle* state, showing little to no engagement. Continuing to target these users can reduce system performance. To address this, after every H episodes, the algorithm identifies a set $\mathcal{Z}$ of users who exhibit low engagement by calculating the average reward of each user across previous episodes. If a user's average reward falls below a threshold τ, they are classified as non-engaging and added to $\mathcal{Z}$. We say that these users are *put to sleep*.

The threshold τ can either be set as a constant, or it can be a dynamic threshold that changes throughout episodes. For example, if we set τ to the

20th percentile of user rewards, it would be the value below which 20% of the rewards fall. Meaning that, in an episode e, if the 20th percentile of user rewards is 0.5, then τ would be 0.5. Users with rewards below this 0.5 threshold would be considered non-engaged and added to $\mathcal{Z}$. By periodically putting inactive users to sleep, the algorithm shifts its focus to users that are more likely to engage: users in $\mathcal{Z}$ are excluded from $\tilde{\mathcal{U}}$, so even though they would be flagged as under-selected, they are deprioritized in the following episode due to their low engagement (see lines $31 \rightarrow 35$ of Algorithm 1).

The episodic setting aligns well with the email RS, where campaigns are typically sent at regular intervals. An episode could represent a week or a month, with each time step corresponding to an email campaign or a decision to interact with a user.

6   Experiments and Results

6.1   Baselines

In our experiments, we compare QWIC-FAIR against the following baselines:

Table 1. Baseline policies used for comparison with QWIC-FAIR (Code available at: https://github.com/cloud-commits/QWIC-Fair.).

Policy	Definition
RANDOM	Selects users randomly without considering engagement information, which is fair in expectation.
MYOPIC	Selects users who are most likely to result in conversions, based on immediate rewards.
FAIR-MYOPIC	Selects users based on immediate rewards, while incorporating the fairness constraint.
ROUND-ROBIN	Selects users in a cyclic order. This is by nature a fair policy because it guarantees equal distribution of email sends across all users.

We choose to compare with these baselines because they are currently used by Smartprofile [42], our partner company specializing in B2B digital marketing, and are often adopted by marketers in emailing. The objective is to demonstrate the practical improvements of our proposed method over existing emailing industry standards.

6.2   Real Dataset

We use a real-world dataset provided by Smartprofile. The dataset is a sample from one of their clients' data, which was gathered with user consent and adheres to GDPR [14] regulations. The sample includes 10,000 distinct users, which is

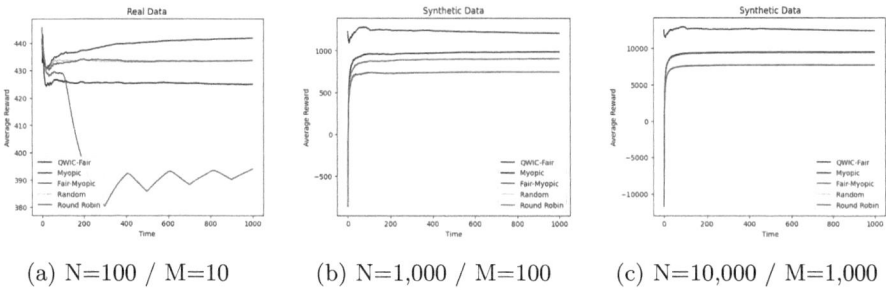

(a) N=100 / M=10   (b) N=1,000 / M=100   (c) N=10,000 / M=1,000

Fig. 2. Average rewards of different policies over a time horizon of $T = 1,000$. (a) shows results with real data; (b) and (c) show results with synthetic data. N is the total number of arms, and M^3 (In a typical setup of Smartprofile, M represents 10% of N available users. We also use this ratio in our experiments.) is the number of selected arms. The fairness threshold is $\eta = 10\%$, the exploration parameter is $\epsilon = 0.3$, and the discount factor is $\gamma = 0.9$.

representative of small to medium-sized email marketing businesses. However, the proposed algorithm can scale to larger datasets involving millions of users. In fact, once Whittle indices are inferred from the modest-sized dataset, they can be immediately transferred to a dataset of million users: the application of Whittle indices is just a sorting procedure with complexity of $O(n \log n)$.

Analyzing user logs revealed that more than 60% of users exhibit low engagement. This indicates that most users are likely to remain in an *idle* state, with low probabilities of transitioning to more active states such as *clicking*, or *purchasing*. This results in data sparsity, which makes it challenging to have accurate model predictions about user behavior. To overcome this limitation, we developed a simulator that draws on the transitions observed in the real dataset. Despite initially having data from over 10,000 users, we could only reliably construct irreducible MDPs for 100 users due to sparse interactions and limited contextual features in the initial dataset. We used location as the primary time-independent contextual feature in this model.

We also explored a publicly available dataset, "messages-demo", provided by the REES46 Customer Data Platform project [38]. This dataset, accessible on Kaggle [39], contains messaging campaigns from a medium-sized retail company, delivered through various channels, including email, web and mobile push notifications, and SMS. Each message in the dataset is associated with detailed statistics, such as delivery, open, click, purchase events, and negative feedback (unsubscribes, spam complaints, and bounces). While we initially considered this dataset for our experiments, we encountered challenges when focusing solely on email interactions. In fact, after filtering the data to include only email-related events, we found that the number of interactions per user was insufficient to construct representative transition matrices. This sparsity posed a challenge for our modeling framework, which requires adequate user interaction data to train effectively.

The REES46 data structure and content are very similar to the data provided by Smartprofile, which we used in our experiments. We encourage readers to explore this publicly available dataset as it is a useful resource for experimenting with similar algorithms and studying user interactions across multiple communication channels.

6.3   Synthetic Dataset

The purpose of the synthetic simulation is to enhance the modeling of user behavior by generating a richer dataset. To achieve this, we collaborated with our partner company Smartprofile, leveraging their expertise to accurately reflect email industry standards in the simulator's design. To provide a comprehensive representation of varied user behaviors, we categorized users into four distinct engagement levels: low, medium, high, and very high; and designed corresponding transition matrices for each class. We incorporated time-independent contextual features such as user location, age, and marital status, derived from distributions provided by INSEE [21]. Since the model is based on CMDP, having well-calibrated transition matrices is essential. We tested various setups. Plots (b) and (c) of Fig. 2 illustrate the scenario where low user engagement is prominent, just like in the real dataset.

6.4   Results and Discussion

Performance plots in Fig. 2 show that QWIC-FAIR exceeds the policies, presented in Table 1, in terms of average rewards, for both synthetic and real-world data. In plot (a) of Fig. 2, which uses real data, QWIC-FAIR shows significant improvement over the other policies, particularly in the initial time steps, where it quickly converges to a higher average reward. Plots (b) and (c) of Fig. 2, using synthetic data, also show that QWIC-FAIR leads to higher rewards. The gap between QWIC-FAIR and the other policies widens as the data size increases.

If fairness is omitted, standard Whittle-index-based Q-learning (QWIC) focuses solely on maximizing cumulative reward and does not inherently prevent repeated selection of high-reward arms. This can lead to fairness issues such as over-targeting some users while neglecting others, especially in domains where equitable exposure and long-term user engagement are important. While tuning parameters like ϵ in the ϵ-greedy strategy may help broaden exploration, this does not guarantee balanced exposure across users. QWIC-FAIR addresses this by enforcing an episodic fairness constraint that ensures under-selected users are prioritized in subsequent episodes. This introduces a natural trade-off between fairness and immediate reward: in some real-world scenarios, user engagement follows a heavy-tailed Pareto distribution, where a small fraction of users drive most conversions. Allocating recommendations to less engaged users can reduce short-term reward, especially in early episodes when the system is still exploring. The relevance of this trade-off depends on application goals. In email marketing, fairness is operationally preferred as over-targeting users risks unsubscribes and spam complaints, affecting both campaign effectiveness and sender reputation. Thus, fairness is not only an ethical consideration, but also a strategic requirement.

Smartprofile also provided data on carbon emissions from one of their email campaigns, estimating that a bulk campaign sent to around 197,000 users resulted in 789.16 kg of CO_2 emissions, whereas targeting only 17,885 users produced an estimated 71.54 kg of CO_2. This suggests that for a setting where $M \simeq 0.1 N$, carbon emissions are reduced by approximately 90%. These estimates highlight that shifting to a more targeted approach can significantly reduce the environmental impact of email campaigns.

In this paper, we focused on a binary-action setting within the CRMAB framework, where the two actions are either to send a recommendation (active) or not send it (passive). However, the CRMAB framework can naturally extend to a multi-action setting, where different actions correspond to recommending various items. For instance, this is particularly relevant in sequential recommender systems [45]. Such systems are widely used in e-commerce and entertainment platforms, to suggest complementary or related products to users based on their interactions: when a user shows interest in a product by clicking on it (state S_1), the system may recommend the item (e.g., a smartphone). If the user purchases the item, they transition to a new state (S_2). This process repeats as the system dynamically recommends additional items, such as a smartwatch or headphones, based on the user's evolving engagement.

Beyond email marketing, this framework can be adapted for advertisements across other channels such as web push notifications, mobile app notifications, or even chatbot interactions. For example, in a mobile shopping app, the system could recommend various items via in-app notifications depending on the user's browsing behavior, purchase history, or demographic profile.

A key advantage of the CRMAB framework is its ability to model user behavior as a dynamic, evolving process. By capturing state transitions, it allows for personalized recommendations that adapt to changes in user preferences over time. This is particularly valuable in dynamic environments where user interests may shift rapidly, such as during seasonal sales or promotional campaigns.

7   Conclusion and Future Work

To our knowledge, we are the first to propose utilizing Whittle index-based Q-learning for CRMAB, and we are the first to propose an application of restless bandits for responsible email marketing. Our algorithm, QWIC-FAIR, models implicit user feedback as state transitions in a context-augmented MDP to learn user interaction dynamics while ensuring equitable user selection through a fairness constraint. Experiments on both synthetic and real-world data showed that QWIC-FAIR outperforms common email marketing approaches.

Our solution leverages context information by incorporating it into the Q-learning process, allowing the algorithm to adjust its actions based on both user states and contextual factors. While we used a tabular Q-learning method for initial validation, this approach effectively demonstrates the integration of context in decision-making. For larger context spaces, our future work will explore advanced methods such as function approximation to handle increased complexity. Additionally, we aim to incorporate multiple actions and conduct A/B testing to evaluate the algorithm's impact on customer behavior.

Acknowledgments. This research was conducted in collaboration between INRIA and NSP/Smartprofile (www.smartp.com), with support from the ANRT (Association Nationale de la Recherche et de la Technologie). Special thanks to our colleague Hervé Baïle from NSP/Smartprofile for his help throughout this project.

References

1. Akbarzadeh, N., Mahajan, A.: Restless bandits with controlled restarts: indexability and computation of whittle index. In: 58th IEEE Conference on Decision and Control, CDC 2019, Nice, France, December 11-13, 2019, pp. 7294–7300. IEEE (2019). https://doi.org/10.1109/CDC40024.2019.9029182

2. Avrachenkov, K.E., Borkar, V.S.: Whittle index policy for crawling ephemeral content. IEEE Trans. Control. Netw. Syst. **5**(1), 446–455 (2018). https://doi.org/10.1109/TCNS.2016.2619066

3. Avrachenkov, K.E., Borkar, V.S.: Whittle index based q-learning for restless bandits with average reward. Autom. **139**, 110186 (2022). https://doi.org/10.1016/j.automatica.2022.110186

4. Bennett, J., Lanning, S.: The netflix prize. In: Proceedings of KDD Cup and Workshop, vol. 2007, p. 35. New York (2007). https://api.semanticscholar.org/CorpusID:1978078

5. Berners-Lee, M.: How bad are bananas?: The carbon footprint of everything. Profile Books (2020)

6. Biswas, A., Aggarwal, G., Varakantham, P., Tambe, M.: Learn to intervene: an adaptive learning policy for restless bandits in application to preventive healthcare. In: Zhou, Z. (ed.) Proceedings of the Thirtieth International Joint Conference on Artificial Intelligence, IJCAI 2021, Virtual Event / Montreal, Canada, 19-27 August 2021, pp. 4039–4046. ijcai.org (2021). https://doi.org/10.24963/ijcai.2021/556

7. Biswas, A., Killian, J.A., Diaz, P.R., Ghosh, S., Tambe, M.: Fairness for workers who pull the arms: an index based policy for allocation of restless bandit tasks pp. 1321–1328 (2023). https://dl.acm.org/doi/10.5555/3545946.3598779

8. Borkar, V.S.: Stochastic approximation with two time scales. Syst. Control Lett. **29**(5), 291–294 (1997). https://www.sciencedirect.com/science/article/pii/S0167691197900153

9. Bouneffouf, D., Rish, I., Aggarwal, C.: Survey on applications of multi-armed and contextual bandits. In: 2020 IEEE Congress on Evolutionary Computation (CEC), pp. 1–8. IEEE (2020)

10. Chapelle, O., Li, L.: An empirical evaluation of thompson sampling. In: Shawe-Taylor, J., Zemel, R.S., Bartlett, P.L., Pereira, F.C.N., Weinberger, K.Q. (eds.) Advances in Neural Information Processing Systems 24: 25th Annual Conference on Neural Information Processing Systems 2011. Proceedings of a meeting held 12-14 December 2011, Granada, Spain, pp. 2249–2257 (2011). https://doi.org/10.5555/2986459.2986710

11. Chen, X., Hou, I.: Contextual restless multi-armed bandits with application to demand response decision-making. CoRR **abs/2403.15640** (2024). https://doi.org/10.48550/arXiv.2403.15640

12. Chittenden, L., Rettie, R.: An evaluation of e-mail marketing and factors affecting response. J. Target. Meas. Anal. Mark. **11**, 203–217 (2003). https://doi.org/10.1057/palgrave.jt.5740078

13. Ekstrand, M.D., Riedl, J., Konstan, J.A.: Collaborative filtering recommender systems. Found. Trends Hum. Comput. Interact. **4**(2), 175–243 (2011). https://doi.org/10.1561/1100000009

14. GDPR: General data protection regulation (2025). https://gdpr-info.eu/. Accessed 16 Jan 2025

15. Glazebrook, K.D., Mitchell, H., Ansell, P.: Index policies for the maintenance of a collection of machines by a set of repairmen. Eur. J. Oper. Res. **165**(1), 267–284 (2005)

16. Gomez-Uribe, C.A., Hunt, N.: The netflix recommender system: algorithms, business value, and innovation. ACM Trans. Manag. Inf. Syst. **6**(4), 13:1–13:19 (2016). https://doi.org/10.1145/2843948

17. Hallak, A., Castro, D.D., Mannor, S.: Contextual markov decision processes. CoRR **abs/1502.02259** (2015). http://arxiv.org/abs/1502.02259

18. Hemker, S., Herrando, C., Constantinides, E.: The transformation of data marketing: how an ethical lens on consumer data collection shapes the future of marketing. Sustainability **13**(20), 11208 (2021)

19. Herlihy, C., Prins, A., Srinivasan, A., Dickerson, J.P.: Planning to fairly allocate: probabilistic fairness in the restless bandit setting. In: Proceedings of the 29th ACM SIGKDD Conference on Knowledge Discovery and Data Mining, pp. 732–740 (2023). https://doi.org/10.1145/3580305.3599467

20. Hu, Y., Koren, Y., Volinsky, C.: Collaborative filtering for implicit feedback datasets. In: Proceedings of the 8th IEEE International Conference on Data Mining (ICDM 2008), December 15-19, 2008, Pisa, Italy, pp. 263–272. IEEE Computer Society (2008). https://doi.org/10.1109/ICDM.2008.22

21. INSEE: National institute of statistics and economic studies (2025). https://www.insee.fr/en/accueil. Accessed 16 Jan 2025

22. Jenkins, S.: The Truth About Email Marketing. FT Press (2008)

23. (source: Kaspersky), S.: Global spam volume as percentage of total e-mail traffic from 2011 to 2023 (2025). https://www.statista.com/statistics/420400/spam-email-traffic-share-annual/. Accessed 16 Jan 2025

24. Ko, H., Lee, S., Park, Y., Choi, A.: A survey of recommendation systems: recommendation models, techniques, and application fields. Electronics **11**(1), 141 (2022)

25. Lattimore, T., Szepesvári, C.: Bandit Algorithms. Cambridge University Press, Cambridge (2020)

26. Li, D., Varakantham, P.: Avoiding starvation of arms in restless multi-armed bandits, pp. 1303–1311 (2023). https://doi.org/10.5555/3545946.3598777

27. Li, L., Chu, W., Langford, J., Schapire, R.E.: A contextual-bandit approach to personalized news article recommendation. In: Rappa, M., Jones, P., Freire, J., Chakrabarti, S. (eds.) Proceedings of the 19th International Conference on World Wide Web, WWW 2010, Raleigh, North Carolina, USA, April 26-30, 2010, pp. 661–670. ACM (2010). https://doi.org/10.1145/1772690.1772758

28. Lian, Z., Nath, R.: A conceptual model for effective email marketing. In: 17th International Conference on Computer and Information Technology, ICCIT 2014, pp. 250–256. IEEE (2014). https://doi.org/10.1109/ICCITechn.2014.7073103

29. Liang, B., Xu, L., Taneja, A., Tambe, M., Janson, L.: A Bayesian approach to online learning for contextual restless bandits with applications to public health. CoRR **abs/2402.04933** (2024). https://doi.org/10.48550/arXiv.2402.04933

30. Liu, J., Dolan, P., Pedersen, E.R.: Personalized news recommendation based on click behavior. In: Rich, C., Yang, Q., Cavazza, M., Zhou, M.X. (eds.) Proceedings of the 15th International Conference on Intelligent User Interfaces, IUI 2010, Hong Kong, China, February 7-10, 2010, pp. 31–40. ACM (2010). https://doi.org/10.1145/1719970.1719976

31. Meshram, R., Manjunath, D., Gopalan, A.: A restless bandit with no observable states for recommendation systems and communication link scheduling. In: 54th IEEE Conference on Decision and Control, CDC 2015, Osaka, Japan, December 15-18, 2015, pp. 7820–7825. IEEE (2015). https://doi.org/10.1109/CDC.2015.7403456

32. Niño-Mora, J.: Restless bandits, partial conservation laws and indexability. Adv. Appl. Probab. **33**(1), 76–98 (2001). http://www.jstor.org/stable/1428442

33. Papadimitriou, C.H., Tsitsiklis, J.N.: The complexity of optimal queueing network control. In: Proceedings of the Ninth Annual Structure in Complexity Theory Conference, Amsterdam, The Netherlands, June 28 - July 1, 1994, pp. 318–322. IEEE Computer Society (1994). https://doi.org/10.1109/SCT.1994.315792

34. Pazzani, M.J., Billsus, D.: Content-based recommendation systems. In: The Adaptive Web: Methods and Strategies of Web Personalization, pp. 325–341. Springer, Cham (2007)

35. Prins, A., Mate, A., Killian, J.A., Abebe, R., Tambe, M.: Incorporating healthcare motivated constraints in restless bandit based resource allocation. NeurIPS 2020 Workshops: challenges of Real World Reinforcement Learning, Machine Learning in Public Health (Best Lightning Paper), Machine Learning for Health (Best on Theme), Machine Learning for the Developing World (2020)

36. Project, T.C.L.: The carbon cost of an email (2022). https://carbonliteracy.com/the-carbon-cost-of-an-email/. Accessed 16 Jan 2025

37. (source: Radicati), S.: Number of sent and received e-mails per day worldwide from 2017 to 2026 (2022). https://www.statista.com/statistics/456500/daily-number-of-e-mails-worldwide/. Accessed 16 Jan 2025

38. REES46: Rees46 CDP for ecommerce (2025). https://rees46.com/en/cdp. Accessed 22 Jan 2025

39. REES46-Datasets: Direct messaging campaigns dataset overview (2025). https://www.kaggle.com/code/mkechinov/direct-messaging-campaigns-dataset-overview/input?select=messages-demo.csv. Accessed 22 Jan 2025

40. Resnick, P., Varian, H.R.: Recommender systems. Commun. ACM **40**(3), 56–58 (1997)

41. Singh, G., Singh, H., Shriwastav, S.: Improving email marketing campaign success rate using personalization. Adv. Anal. Appl. 77–83 (2019)

42. Smartprofile: Smartprofile (2025). https://smartp.com/. Accessed 10 June 2025

43. Smith, B., Linden, G.: Two decades of recommender systems at amazon.com. IEEE Internet Comput. **21**(3), 12–18 (2017). https://doi.org/10.1109/MIC.2017.72

44. Taylor, B.: Sender reputation in a large webmail service. In: CEAS 2006 - The Third Conference on Email and Anti-Spam, July 27-28, 2006, Mountain View, California, USA (2006). http://www.ceas.cc/2006/listabs.html#19.pdf

45. Wang, S., Hu, L., Wang, Y., Cao, L., Sheng, Q.Z., Orgun, M.A.: Sequential recommender systems: challenges, progress and prospects. In: Kraus, S. (ed.) Proceedings of the Twenty-Eighth International Joint Conference on Artificial Intelligence, IJCAI 2019, Macao, China, August 10-16, 2019, pp. 6332–6338. ijcai.org (2019). https://doi.org/10.24963/ijcai.2019/883

46. Wang, S., Xiong, G., Li, J.: Online restless multi-armed bandits with long-term fairness constraints. In: Proceedings of the AAAI Conference on Artificial Intelligence, vol. 38, pp. 15616–15624 (2024). https://doi.org/10.1609/aaai.v38i14.29489

47. Wang, S., Huang, L., Lui, J.C.S.: Restless-ucb, an efficient and low-complexity algorithm for online restless bandits (2020). https://proceedings.neurips.cc/paper/2020/hash/89ae0fe22c47d374bc9350ef99e01685-Abstract.html

48. Watkins, C.J.C.H., Dayan, P.: Technical note q-learning. Mach. Learn. **8**, 279–292 (1992). https://doi.org/10.1007/BF00992698

49. Weber, R.R., Weiss, G.: On an index policy for restless bandits. J. Appl. Probab. **27**(3), 637–648 (1990). http://www.jstor.org/stable/3214547

50. White, J.: Bandit Algorithms for Website Optimization. O'Reilly (2013)

51. Whittle, P.: Restless bandits: Activity allocation in a changing world. J. Appl. Probab. **25**(A), 287–298 (1988)

52. Xiong, G., Wang, S., Yan, G., Li, J.: Reinforcement learning for dynamic dimensioning of cloud caches: a restless bandit approach. IEEE/ACM Trans. Netw. (2023)

Contextual Hypernetwork for Adaptive Prediction of Laser-Induced Colors on Quasi-random Plasmonic Metasurfaces

Thibault Girardin[1,3]($\boxtimes$), Nathalie Destouches[1,2], and Amaury Habrard[1,2,3]

[1] Université Jean Monnet Saint-Etienne, CNRS, Institut d'Optique Graduate School, Laboratoire Hubert Curien UMR 5516, 42023 Saint-Etienne, France
{thibault.girardin,nathalie.destouches,amaury.habrard}@univ-st-etienne.fr
[2] Institut Universitaire de France (IUF), 42023 Paris, France
[3] Centre Inria de Lyon, Villeurbanne, France

Abstract. Laser processing is a rapid, versatile, and low-cost technology to print images on large surfaces. When applied to very thin films embedded with disordered metallic nanoparticles, known as quasi-random plasmonic metasurfaces, it generates colors that vary with the observation mode, making it valuable for visual security applications. Predicting these colors in different modes from the knowledge of laser processing parameters and the initial state of the metasurface can accelerate the industrialization process. However, there is no general physical model able to make this prediction accurately in various modes. In order to address this issue, this paper proposes a data-driven approach for learning deep models on experimental data able to predict the colors observed in different environments for a large range of laser processing parameters. We leverage a framework that learns jointly a shared latent space for multiple environments together with a contextual representation specific to each. This contextual representation is generated by an hypernetwork conditioned on an interpretable context vector. This context vector can be learned from few data allowing fast adaptation to new environments. This approach demonstrates that a single model can learn to predict a large range of colors across different environments. Its effectiveness is demonstrated through its ability to rapidly adapt to new scenarios with minimal data and to serve as an improved weight initializer for fine-tuning when larger datasets are available. Source code and datasets are available on Gitlab (https://gitlab.univ-st-etienne.fr/gt101872/ECML25-Hypernetwork-ColorPrediction-metasurface.

Keywords: Deep Learning · Hypernetwork · Domain Adaptation · Nanoplasmonic · Color Science

Supplementary Information The online version contains supplementary material available at https://doi.org/10.1007/978-3-662-72243-5_22.

1   Introduction

Metasurfaces are ultrathin optical surfaces made of periodic metallic or dielectric nanostructures that strongly interact with light, and have found applications such as nano-antennas, sensors or optical filters [3,4,25]. Introducing different types of disorder into optical metasurfaces can enhance their performance or create unique optical properties [14]. The use of lasers to control the opto-geometrical properties of random optical metasurfaces provides the flexibility to shape their optical properties at the micrometer scale over large areas in a rapid process [27]. Laser processing is mainly used on plasmonic metasurfaces since metallic nanostructures can be reshaped and reorganized through photo-induced physical and chemical mechanisms [17,19]. Laser-induced self-organization mechanisms can also introduce order in initially random distribution of metallic nanostructures as demonstrated with continuous-wave [6,15], and femtosecond lasers [16]. The resulting quasi-random plasmonic metasurfaces feature dichroic colors that have been recently used to create multiplexed images observable under white light [7]. Image multiplexing is based on the ability to create sets of metasurfaces that show the same colors in some observation modes and different colors in others, and to organize these metasurfaces appropriately on the surface to display different images in the different observation modes. This laser-induced printing technology has great promise in visual security applications for the protection of secure documents from counterfeiting [5].

The industrial application of this technology requires the ability to reproduce on different substrates the laser-induced colors observed in different modes with an accuracy that is below the smallest color difference perceived by the human eye. Since the laser-induced colors depend on the initial state of the random plasmonic metasurface, and since this state may vary slightly over time due to uncontrolled variations in the fabrication process, it is useful to predict accurately the colors that can be produced on a given sample from a limited number of measurements. Unfortunately, due to the complex physical and chemical processes that occur in the metasurface during laser processing, physical models do not precisely predict the morphological transformations of the metasurface and thus the colors it may ultimately display in different observation modes.

One solution is to consider data driven models. Deep learning-based methods have been successfully used in nanophotonics to infer possible designs from given optical responses [11,12,18,21,22,30] or to predict optical properties [1,8,10,26]. In the context of color prediction, one solution has been developed in [20] with a deep learning model for predicting color spectra from laser parameters. However, this model is not able to generalize to new environment such as novel initial state of the substrate, requiring to learn a specific model for each setting.

In order to overcome this drawback, we propose in this paper a new framework for efficient prediction of laser-induced colors on plasmonic metasurfaces. Our contribution is three-fold. We first propose to learn a deep learning model that predicts the colors directly in the CIE LAB color space from laser parameters. This model is used to provide a shared latent space among training environments. Second, we use a contextual hypernetwork to adapt the shared represen-

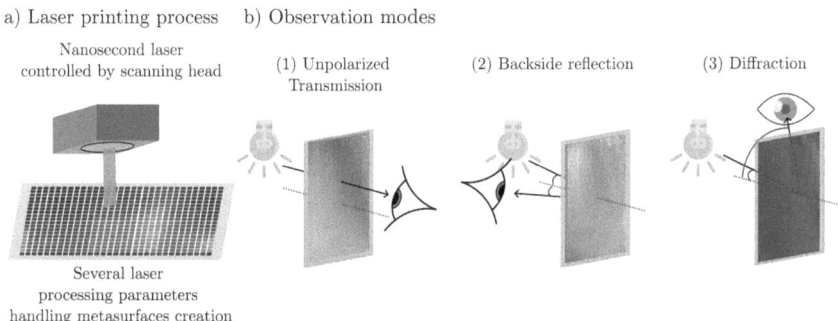

Fig. 1. Color production rationale. (a) Colors are produced by scanning a laser over the thin film. (b) Processed surface are observed in different modes such as transmission (1), specular reflection (2) or diffraction (3) displaying different ranges of colors. (Color figure online)

tation to new environments. Inspired by previous works on adaptive dynamics [13], this hypernetwork is parametrized by a context vector modeling the peculiarities of a particular environment and that can be learned efficiently from few data. Finally, we provide an experimental study on real data showing the interest of the proposed setup for multi-environment color prediction.

The paper is organized as follows. The problem definition and the related work are introduced in Sect. 2. We present in Sect. 3 our hypernetwork-based deep learning architecture. Section 4 is dedicated to our experimental study. We conclude in Sect. 5.

2 Problem Definition and Related Work

2.1 Color Production Rationale

Quasi-random plasmonic metasurfaces of square shape and micrometer area are created by laser processing of a thin layer of TiO_2 containing silver nanoparticles [5]. Each square is laser printed with a specific set of laser paremeters and the color of the squares is measured in different observation modes (see Fig. 1). Production rationale is detailed in Appendix Sect. 2.

2.2 Color Prediction Problem

The color prediction problem consists in learning a model capable of mapping the produced color of a quasi random metasurface from d laser processing parameters. Colors are computed, with respect to the D65 illuminant, from the measured and normalized spectra in several observation modes which are expressed in CIE LAB space, a 3-dimensional perceptually uniform color space (See Appendix Sect. 1 for further details on color theory and color spaces). The learning problem can then be formalized as follows. Let $\mathcal{X} \subset \mathbb{R}^d, \mathcal{Y} \subseteq \mathbb{R}^3$ be respectively the

Reference	LAB(50, -1, 52)	LAB(50, -1, 52)	LAB(50, -1, 52)	LAB(50, -1, 52)
Sample	LAB(50, 1.5, 52)	LAB(50, -3, 52)	LAB(45.8, -1.64, 52.3)	LAB(50, 15, 52)
ΔE94	0.28	1.12	4.22	8.93

Fig. 2. Evolution of measured color shifts with $\Delta E94$ for similar but different pair of colors modeled by their LAB coordinates, illustrating the necessity to be close to 1 to minimize perceived color differences (best viewed in color). (Color figure online)

space of laser processing parameters and the color coefficients in the CIE LAB space. We denote by $\mathcal{D}_e$ a dataset of colors from $\mathcal{X} \times \mathcal{Y}$ that can be obtained from a particular observation environment e. We denote by $\mathcal{E}$, the set of all possible environments, each environment corresponding to a particular experimental configuration where the colors are measured.

The objective is to learn a neural network model $f_\theta : \mathcal{X} \to \mathcal{Y}$, parameterized by a weight vector θ. Given a dataset of N elements $\mathcal{D}_e = \{(x_{e,i}, y_{e,i})\}_{i=1}^{N}$, the loss function is defined with respect to the $\Delta E94$ measure, a weighted RMSE loss allowing to measure human perceived color differences.

$$\mathcal{L}(\theta, \mathcal{D}_e) = \sum_{i=1}^{N} \Delta E_{94}\left(y_{e,i}, f_\theta(x_{e,i})\right). \tag{1}$$

Illustrated in Fig. 2, the goal is to learn a model able to make target color prediction with a small $\Delta E94$. A value below or at least close to 1 corresponds to situations where the colors are indistinguishable by a human eye.

2.3 Related Work

Deep Learning is widely used to solve design and properties prediction problem in nanophotonics applications, mainly from simulated datasets. As highlighted in [2] in the context of plasmonic color prediction, learning from experimental data is difficult. Data acquisition is by nature costly and subject to experimental noise which may lead to small datasets of low quality. In this context, transfer learning has already been used for simulated optical properties [24] or inverse design prediction [32]. However, there is no widely known work in this community considering a learning process based entirely on experimental data and transfer learning. By the lack of simulation model for our random plasmonic metasurfaces, we aim at solving a fully experimental data-driven transfer problem.

In domain adaptation, feature-based methods such as DANN [28] or DA-DETR [31], aims at learning robust intermediate representations across different domains or tasks to improve transfer accuracy. While popular, these approaches are not directly adapted to our setting since we have a small number of input features that remain the same across the different environments. Instance-based adaptation methods such as WANN [23] learns a reweighting model to correct the co-variate shift between domains or samples but this assumption is not directly adapted to our setting. Multi-task learning has the objective to deal with multiple tasks but adaptation to new tasks exists essentially for classification [29]. Meta-learning approaches such as [9], which aims to adapt to a new domain with few (gradient) adaptation steps, are very appealing in the context of low data regimes. Recently, CoDA [13] proposed a generalization of these approaches with the use of an hypernetwork allowing efficient adaptation with few samples to new domains in the context of dynamical models. In this paper, our objective is to adapt this strategy to our real problem of color prediction across different environments.

3   Hypernetwork for Contextual Adaptation

This section introduces the adaptation rule used to train our hypernetwork and how parameters are updated in the training and adaptation phase.

3.1   Architecture and Adaptation Principles

Our model follows a similar strategy as CoDA [13]. The principle is to allow the color prediction model f_θ to adapt to colors induced in different environments. The idea is to condition the model on observed samples from environment $\mathcal{D}_e$. This conditioning is done by using a network A_ϑ parametrized by a set ϑ containing weights variation for f_{θ^e} to adapt to an environment e with respect to:

$$\theta^e = A_\vartheta(\mathcal{D}_e) = \theta^s + \delta\theta^e, \ \vartheta = \{\theta^s, \{\delta\theta^e\}_{e\in\mathcal{E}}\}, \tag{2}$$

where $\theta^s \in \mathbb{R}^{d_\theta}$ is a vector of shared parameters and $\delta\theta^e \in \mathbb{R}^{d_\theta}$ corresponds to a vector of parameters specific to an environment $\mathcal{D}_e$. The set ϑ represents the parameters to be learned by the network. The environment-specific parameters will be obtained by a contextual hypernetwork introduced in the next subsection.

3.2   Contextual Hypernetwork

The Hypernetwork principle is illustrated in Fig. 3. The idea is to estimate $\delta\theta^e$ from the linear decoding of a context vector specific to an environment $\mathcal{D}_e$ and denoted $\kappa_e \in \mathbb{R}^{d_\kappa}$. Let $W \in \mathbb{R}^{d_\theta \times d_\kappa}$ the matrix parameter of the linear decoder, the adaptation problem can be rewritten as:

$$A_\vartheta(\mathcal{D}_e) = \theta^s + W\kappa_e, \vartheta = \{W, \theta^s, \{\kappa_e\}_{e\in\mathcal{E}}\}. \tag{3}$$

We consider $d_\kappa \ll d_\theta$. This allows us to learn a low-dimensional subspace of specific parameters which is better suited to limit overfitting, in particular in low data regimes. From an adaptation point of view, considering that the shared parameters θ^s and W have been learned, adapting to a new environment e implies to learn only κ_e which represents very few parameters to infer to adapt the color prediction model to this environment.

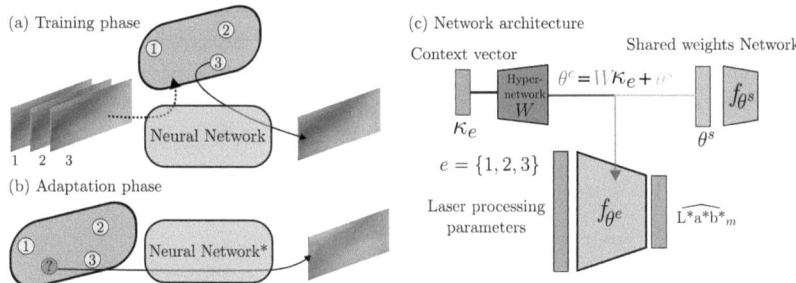

Fig. 3. Principle of the approach. During the training phase (a) the model learns parameters from all the training environments. In the adaptation phase, the model can explore the induced latent space freely to find the best context vector coordinates to adapt to a new task. Adapting to a given task is always obtained by combining the shared parameters between all the environments with the addition of a specific variation conditioned by the context vector κ_e (c).

3.3   Learning and Adaptation Loops

In this part, we introduce two important aspects of the method: the training phase and the adaptation one.

From given training samples of a set of training environments $\mathcal{E}_{tr} \subseteq \mathcal{E}$, the training phase aims at learning the shared initial weights, the shared decoder and the context vectors according to the following optimization problem in Eq. 4:

$$\min_{\theta^s, W, \{\kappa_e\}_{e\in\mathcal{E}_{tr}}} \sum_{e\in\mathcal{E}_{tr}} \left(\mathcal{L}(\theta^s + W\kappa_e, \mathcal{D}_e) + \lambda_\kappa ||\kappa_e||_2^2 + \lambda_W \sum_{i=1}^{d_\theta} ||W_{i,:}||^2\right) \quad (4)$$

with an L_2 regularization on the context vectors and a mixed $L_{2,1}$ regularization on the W matrix to induce sparsity, λ_κ and λ_W serve as hyperparameters.

Once the model is trained, θ^s and W are fixed, so that only the context vectors κ_e of a set of new environments $\mathcal{E}_{adapt} \subseteq \mathcal{E}$ need to be learned during the adaptation phase with Eq. 5:

$$\min_{\{\kappa_e\}_{e\in\mathcal{E}_{adapt}}} \sum_{e\in\mathcal{E}_{adapt}} \mathcal{L}(\theta^s + W\kappa_e, \mathcal{D}_e). \quad (5)$$

where $\mathcal{L}$ refers to the $\Delta E94$ introduced in Eq. 1 The pseudo code Algorithm 1 shows how the model is trained. Note that in practice we initialize the shared weights θ^s by optimizing the loss $\sum_{e\in\mathcal{E}_{tr}} \mathcal{L}(\theta^s, \mathcal{D}_e)$ leading to the initialization θ^{init} which can be seen as a pre-trained network without contextual information.

4   Experiments

This section is devoted to our experimental study. We first introduce the used datasets, how they are pre-processed and prepared for the different learning

---

Algorithm 1. Model training and adaption pseudo-codes

Training:

1: **Input:** $\mathcal{E}_{tr} \subset \mathcal{E}, \{\mathcal{D}_{e_{tr}}\}_{e_{tr} \in \mathcal{E}_{tr}}$

2: $\vartheta = \{W, \theta^s, \{\kappa_{e_{tr}}\}_{e_{tr} \in \mathcal{E}_{tr}}\}$ where $W \in \mathbb{R}^{d_\theta \times d_\kappa}, \theta^s \in \mathbb{R}^{d_\theta}$

3: Randomly initialize W, and set $\forall e_{tr} \in \mathcal{E}_{tr}, \kappa_{e_{tr}} = \mathbf{0} \in \mathbb{R}^{d_\kappa}, \theta^s = \theta^{\text{init}} \in \mathbb{R}^{d_\theta}$

4: **while** stopping criterion is not reached **do**

5: $\quad \vartheta \leftarrow \vartheta - \eta \nabla_\vartheta \left(\sum_{e_{tr} \in \mathcal{E}_{tr}} \left(\mathcal{L}(\theta^s + W\kappa_{e_{tr}}, \mathcal{D}_{e_{tr}}) + \lambda_\kappa ||\kappa_{e_{tr}}||_2^2 + \lambda_W \sum_{i=1}^{d_\theta} ||W_{i,:}||^2 \right) \right)$

6: **end while**

Adaptation on a new environment:

1: **Input:** $e_{\text{adapt}} \in \mathcal{E}_{\text{adapt}} \subset \mathcal{E}; \mathcal{D}_{e_{\text{adapt}}}$

2: Trained $W \in \mathbb{R}^{d_\theta \times d_\kappa}, \theta^s \in \mathbb{R}^{d_\theta}$ and $\kappa_{e_{\text{adapt}}} = \mathbf{0} \in \mathbb{R}^{d_\kappa}$

3: **while** stopping criterion is not reached **do**

4: $\quad \kappa_{e_{\text{adapt}}} \leftarrow \kappa_{e_{\text{adapt}}} - \eta \nabla_{\kappa_{e_{\text{adapt}}}} \left(\mathcal{L}(\theta^s + W\kappa_{e_{\text{adapt}}}, \mathcal{D}_{e_{\text{adapt}}}) \right)$

5: **end while**

---

experiments. Then, we present our learning setup before presenting the results, which are then analyzed both quantitatively and qualitatively. Finally, we propose an ablation study and a context size study to substantiate our parameters selection. Note that the code and the dataset are available as supplementary material and on Gitlab.

4.1   Dataset

We use the dataset presented in [20] that contains a set of real colors measurements obtained from the principle introduced in Sect. 2.1. Among the existing observation modes, we consider **two modes** presented in Fig. 1: the unpolarized transmission (Tunpol) and the Backside Reflection (BR). The data are obtained by varying 5 laser parameters: the laser power, the laser repetition rate (frep), the laser scan speed, the interline distance between laser lines and the laser polarization[1] state. Both datasets contain 9600 samples with the exact same laser parameters linked to their respective color L*a*b* coefficients. Additional information are given in Appendix Sect. 2.

We define different sub-environments of observation according to the laser polarization state parameter which corresponds to 4 possible laser polarization angles: 0, 30, 60 and 90°. Then, the laser prediction consists in predicting the colors in the CIE LAB space according to the other 4 laser parameters across the different laser polarization environments. For each of the two datasets, we define 4 specific environment subsets: $\mathcal{D}_{\{\text{Tunpol,BR}\}\{0,30,60,90\}}$, each of them containing 2400 samples. As illustrated in Fig. 4, the color shifts between different subsets is different enough to require an adaptation, we can note that the BR mode is more challenging than the Tunpol one.

To minimize the influence of the experimental noise during the learning process, a two-step pre-processing method is applied on the L*a*b*/scan-speed

---

[1] Note that the laser polarization used to process the metasurface should not be confused with unpolarized transmission which refers to the non polarization of the illuminant used to acquire the dataset.

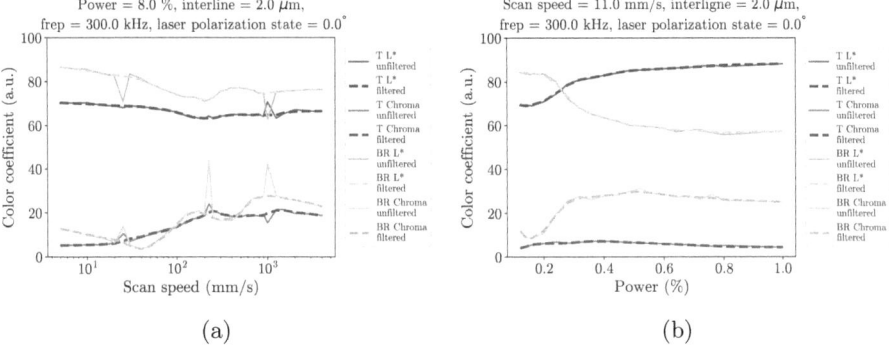

Path	$\Delta E94$ T	$\Delta E94$ BR
(1)	1.28±0.72	3.13±1.93
(2)	1.21±0.76	2.14±1.32
(3)	1.01±0.78	1.99±1.20
(4)	2.08±1.36	3.90±2.24
(5)	1.94±1.13	4.27±2.75
(6)	1.60±1.14	2.26±1.22

Fig. 4. Mean color shifts and their respective standard deviation between each sub-dataset in each observation mode with respect to the laser parameters. A path (i) indicates the average $\Delta E94$ between the colors obtained with respect to the two laser polarization angles linked by the path, for each of the two observation modes. For example (2) compares the colors between the 30° and 60° polarization angles for the same laser parameters.

(a)   (b)

Fig. 5. Evolution of color coefficients over Scan speed (a) and Power (b). Chroma is defined as $C = \sqrt{a^{*2} + b^{*2}}$.

correlation curves. A Hampel filter (Algorithm 2) removes outliers and a polynomial filter (Algorithm 3) enforces smoothness to color coefficients according to their laser processing parameters. Illustrated in Fig. 5, outliers within correlation curves are removed while preserving the natural evolution of the colors. Laser processing parameters are minmax-normalized (with scan-speed log-normalized) and the color coefficients are normalized according to the defined bounds of each channel with $L^* \in [0, 100]$ and $a^*, b^* \in [-128, 128]$ allowing adaption on partially known environments. Model learning is done by a train/validation/test split following a 80/10/10 ratio for each specific environment dataset. Splitting is done at the laser parameters level ensuring that the same parameters appear in the same split for each environment. Each experiment is repeated 4 times.

4.2   Experimental Setup

We present in this section the different learning setups considered in our study.

Adaptation Setup. Given one observation mode, we consider the 4 settings where three of the four datasets are given as training environments and the last one is considered for the adaptation phase corresponding to the target environment.

Base-Architecture. The architecture of our color prediction model corresponds to a 8 layer feed forward neural networks with 128 neurons on each layer activated by ReLU. Only the last hidden layer weights are linearly activated. The size of the context vector is fixed to 3.

Pre-training. We first begin to pre-train the shared parameters θ^s on a sample where we associate to each laser parameters the mean of the colors of the 3 datasets used in training[2]. Training is achieved over 800 epochs and a batch size of 64, using an Adam optimizer with a step scheduler after 300 epochs and a learning rate of 0.0015.

Hypernetwork Training and Adaptation (Hnet). For the training phase, θ^s is initialized with pre-trained weights mentioned above. The hypernetwork parameters and context vectors are then adjusted with the mean response of the three datasets and then frozen[3]. The training uses the same learning parameters as pre-training with $\lambda_\kappa = 1e{-}3$ and $\lambda_W = 1e{-}6$ for the regularization hyperparameters.

Adaptation is performed with a small data regime on the adaptation dataset with increasing data size drawn from its associated training sample: [5, 10, 20, 40, 80, 160, 320], these include laser parameters already seen in training phase by construction. Here, in addition to the test error that measures the generalization over unseen laser parameters during training, we also measure the error on half of the training sample of the adaptation environment that is not used during adaptation to measure the generalization to laser parameters unseen during adaptation but considered during training. Adaption is made on 100 epochs using Adam with no scheduling and a learning rate of 0.003.

0-Shot and Fine-Tuning (0-shot, FT). 0-shot consists in evaluating each pre-trained model without updating any weights. We also perform a fine-tuning on all the models parameters for 500 epochs using Adam with a learning rate of 0.0001 and step scheduling after 300 epochs. We use the same increasing data as for the adaptation phase of the hypernetwork.

Hypernetwork Adaptation and Fine-Tuning (HnetFT). Models obtained after the adaptation phase of the hypernetwork are also fine-tuned following the aforementioned protocol using exactly the same datafold as in adaption. Epochs are reduced to 400 with scheduling starting at 200 to align with fine-tuning tasks.

---

[2] On Tunpol dataset, using only ΔE94 could occasionaly make the model diverging. As a workaround model's parameters are updated with MSE during the first epoch and the rest of the training is done with ΔE94.

[3] We have noticed nevertheless that it is more efficient to freeze the shared weights after the pre-training than learning them together with the other two sets of parameters.

Training from Target with Low Data (Target). A model is trained using only the data available in the adaptation phase with 40 and 320 samples, following the pre-training learning setup.

Instance Based WANN (WANN). An adaptation is performed using the WANN model [23] and is tested using 40 and 320 samples from the target environment of the adaptation phase. The weighted network used is a 3 layer network with 64 neurons each using ReLU activation. Learning parameters are the same as in fine-tuning.

Metrics. To monitor the performance of the model in each adaptation scenario three metrics are considered: the accuracy defined as the percentage of color predictions that have a $\Delta E94$ below to 1.5 with respect to the ground truth, the average $\Delta E94$ mean values over the test sample and the associated $\Delta E94$ standard deviation. Results are averaged on the 4 repetitions.

4.3   Unpolarized Transmission

Results comparing FT models and Hnet models in Tunpol are displayed in Figs. 6 and 7. In the very low data regimes, the Hnet based models are able to provide the best or a competitive performance. Fine-tuning the different models improves the results when the number of target data increases. The HnetFT model provides always for the best result for all data sizes. It must be noticed that using the Hnet model only reaches a plateau justifying the need for a subsequent model fine-tuning, but we can notice that the Hnet models provide a relevant initialization for fine-tuning. Generalization to unseen laser parameters during training is rather good for all models. Table 1 provides numerical values on two problems for

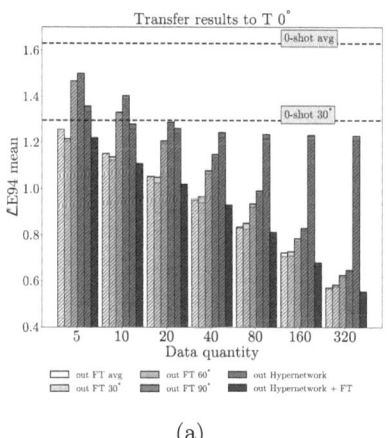
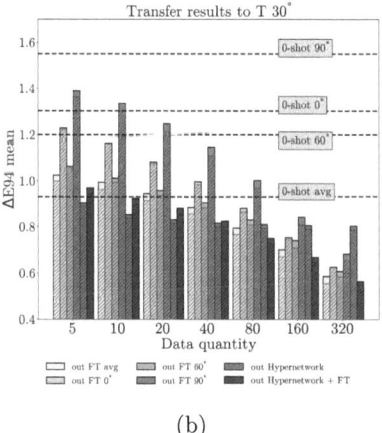

(a)   (b)

Fig. 6. Transfer results in Tunpol for $0°$ and $30°$ laser polarization states. Smooth bars correspond to results on test samples, hatched ones to unseen laser parameters during adaptation phase.

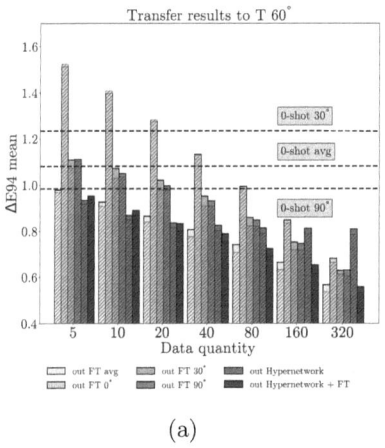

(a)

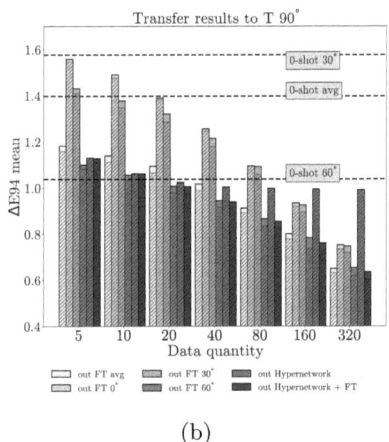

(b)

Fig. 7. Transfer results in Tunpol for 60° and 90° laser polarization states. Smooth bars with thick edge-lines correspond to results on test samples, hatched with thin lines ones to unseen laser parameters during adaptation phase.

Table 1. Test results of different models in Tunpol for adaptation to 0° and 60° degrees environments. Evaluation is done between Hnet and the finetuned pretrained models. WANN uses the weights resulting to the best 0-shot adaptation.

Exp Name	To 0°			To 60°		
	$\Delta E94$ mean	$\Delta E94$ std	Accuracy (%)	$\Delta E94$ mean	$\Delta E94$ std	Accuracy (%)
0-shot	1.30 ± 0.03	0.74 ± 0.04	69.90 ± 1.42	0.98 ± 0.04	0.79 ± 0.013	84.69 ± 1.33
Target-320	0.86 ± 0.07	0.83 ± 0.19	56.98 ± 3.23	0.92 ± 0.07	0.85 ± 0.12	71.09 ± 3.78
FT-320	0.57 ± 0.03	0.52 ± 0.12	95.28 ± 1.86	0.57 ± 0.05	0.47 ± 0.08	95.21 ± 2.12
Hnet-320	1.23 ± 0.04	0.75 ± 0.08	73.61 ± 2.27	0.80 ± 0.02	0.57 ± 0.03	89.34 ± 0.55
HnetFT-320	$\mathbf{0.55 \pm 0.05}$	$\mathbf{0.45 \pm 0.03}$	$\mathbf{96.04 \pm 0.90}$	$\mathbf{0.56 \pm 0.03}$	$\mathbf{0.45 \pm 0.07}$	$\mathbf{95.76 \pm 1.33}$
WANN-320	1.26 ± 0.03	0.71 ± 0.05	71.66 ± 2.52	1.05 ± 0.03	0.85 ± 0.10	82.93 ± 1.33
Target-40	1.98 ± 0.10	1.57 ± 0.19	49.01 ± 6.05	2.08 ± 0.27	1.64 ± 0.32	46.46 ± 5.97
FT-40	0.95 ± 0.06	0.78 ± 0.12	85.00 ± 2.69	0.81 ± 0.05	0.47 ± 0.08	89.69 ± 2.42
Hnet-40	1.24 ± 0.04	0.76 ± 0.09	73.39 ± 2.27	0.82 ± 0.02	0.58 ± 0.03	89.30 ± 0.96
HnetFT-40	$\mathbf{0.93 \pm 0.09}$	$\mathbf{0.73 \pm 0.06}$	$\mathbf{85.44 \pm 2.51}$	$\mathbf{0.79 \pm 0.05}$	$\mathbf{0.58 \pm 0.07}$	$\mathbf{90.48 \pm 2.32}$
WANN-40	1.27 ± 0.03	0.71 ± 0.05	71.67 ± 2.57	1.05 ± 0.03	0.85 ± 0.10	82.93 ± 1.50

fixed target learning data sizes. The HnetFT models lead to the best accuracy with a variance reduction trend in terms of $\Delta E94$. The evolution of the mean ΔE_{94} in validation and test shown in Fig. 8 highlights a reduction of overfitting for Hnet and HnetFT compared to FT making them more invariant to the used data-folds. Finally, the performance decrease between the best model with 320 data folds and the fully train one (Full results in Appendix Sect. 3) is of 73% for 0° and 60% for 60°.

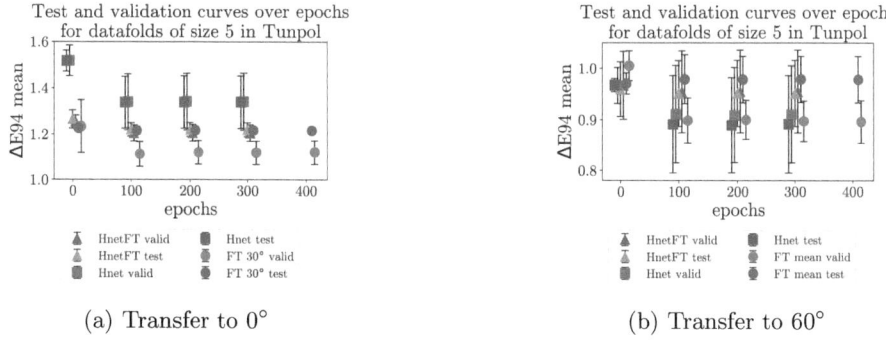

(a) Transfer to 0°   (b) Transfer to 60°

Fig. 8. Evolution of $\Delta E94$ in test and validation in Tunpol every 100 epochs. Hnet epochs are extended up to 300. More results in Appendix Sect. 3.

4.4 Backside Reflection

Results comparing FT models and Hnet models in BR are displayed in Figs. 9 and 10. The same observations made for Tunpol can be made for BR, *i.e.* HnetFT always provides the best adaption model. Numerical results in Table 2 confirm that HnetFT leads to best accuracy with better variance. Test and validation curves in Fig. 11 show the same benefits as depicted in Tunpol. The performance decrease between the best model with 320 data folds and the fully train one is similar to Tunpol with 73% for 0° and 54% for 60° (Full results in Appendix Sect. 3). The results are nevertheless less good than the ones obtained in transmission confirming the difficulty of the task.

Table 2. Test results for different model in BR for adaptation to 0° and 60° polarization states. Evaluation is done between Hnet and the finetuned pretrained models. WANN uses the weights resulting to the best 0-shot adaptation.

Exp Name	To 0°			To 60°		
	$\Delta E94$ mean	$\Delta E94$ std	Accuracy (%)	$\Delta E94$ mean	$\Delta E94$ std	Accuracy (%)
0-shot	3.00 ± 0.19	1.81 ± 0.11	22.29 ± 2.42	2.00 ± 0.09	1.18 ± 0.04	38.12 ± 5.72
Target-320	1.68 ± 0.18	1.30 ± 0.12	56.98 ± 3.23	1.60 ± 0.18	1.30 ± 0.12	60.21 ± 2.47
FT-320	1.22 ± 0.04	0.87 ± 0.07	72.19 ± 1.66	1.15 ± 0.04	0.84 ± 0.08	75.87 ± 2.93
Hnet-320	3.00 ± 0.18	1.79 ± 0.10	21.88 ± 2.70	1.78 ± 0.02	1.06 ± 0.05	47.01 ± 1.47
HnetFT-320	$\mathbf{1.21 \pm 0.06}$	$\mathbf{0.86 \pm 0.06}$	$\mathbf{74.44 \pm 3.53}$	$\mathbf{1.13 \pm 0.04}$	$\mathbf{0.84 \pm 0.10}$	$\mathbf{76.32 \pm 2.78}$
WANN-320	3.09 ± 0.13	1.86 ± 0.13	19.60 ± 2.58	2.02 ± 0.03	1.32 ± 0.08	38.75 ± 1.78
Target-40	6.23 ± 1.03	4.13 ± 0.92	8.19 ± 2.45	5.88 ± 0.65	3.73 ± 0.44	5.65 ± 2.71
FT-40	2.14 ± 0.13	1.38 ± 0.14	39.08 ± 3.98	1.78 ± 0.09	1.08 ± 0.09	48.08 ± 4.53
Hnet-40	3.05 ± 0.17	1.79 ± 0.12	20.79 ± 3.11	1.82 ± 0.06	1.07 ± 0.05	45.35 ± 3.02
HnetFT-40	$\mathbf{2.08 \pm 0.14}$	$\mathbf{1.35 \pm 0.15}$	$\mathbf{40.76 \pm 4.41}$	$\mathbf{1.65 \pm 0.09}$	$\mathbf{1.01 \pm 0.09}$	$\mathbf{52.71 \pm 4.40}$
WANN-40	3.10 ± 0.13	1.87 ± 0.13	18.75 ± 2.95	2.03 ± 0.03	1.32 ± 0.09	37.92 ± 2.54

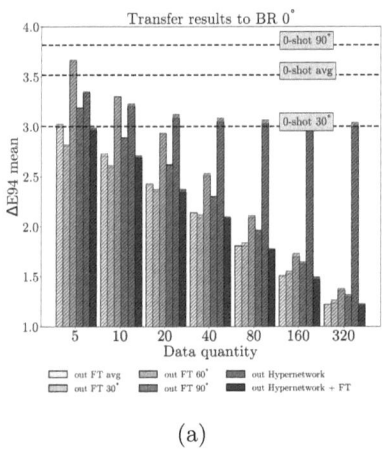
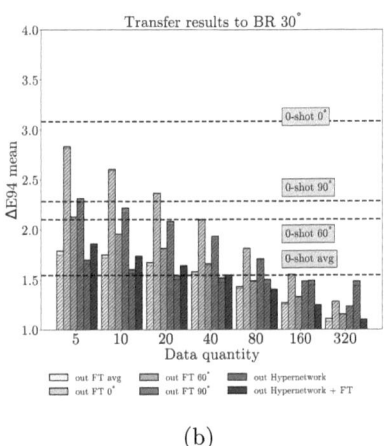

(a)   (b)

Fig. 9. Transfer results in BR for 0° and 30° laser polarization angles. Smooth bars with thick edge-lines correspond to results on test samples, hatched with thin lines ones to unseen laser parameters during adaptation phase.

4.5   Qualitative Analysis on the Learned Environments

In this section, we provide a qualitative analysis of the context vectors learned with Hnet models by displaying their projection in 2D in Figs. 12 and 13. The heatmap indicates the adaptation error in terms of $\Delta E94$ in the considered space. For each adaptation task, even in the smallest data regime, the learned context vector is close to the one corresponding to the best $\Delta E94$ (green diamond). As the data quantity increases, context vectors get closer to the optimal one while becoming less and less scattered across the latent space. Two behaviors can be identified: one where the optimum is between two training environments as in Figs. 12b or 13b , and one where the optimum is close to one training environment such as in Figs. 12a or in 13a . These behaviors are directly related to the proximity of the training environments to the target ones. For example in Tunpol from Fig. 6, when transferring to 0° the best model performs closely to the fine-tuned 30° model and this is what is found in Fig. 12a , while the reverse is not true for adaptation to 30° (See Appendix Sect. 4.). This shows that learned context vectors can be interpreted to give some insights on the closeness of different environments. Predicted colors are also closer to the expected color variations using Hnet as seen in Fig. 14a and b for low data regime adaptation. With only five datapoints, Hnet has already reproduced some of the mapping compared to the Finetuned model. In BR, 0-shot delivers better performance which is consistent with previous numerical results. This highlights the capability of the model to quickly match new color trends.

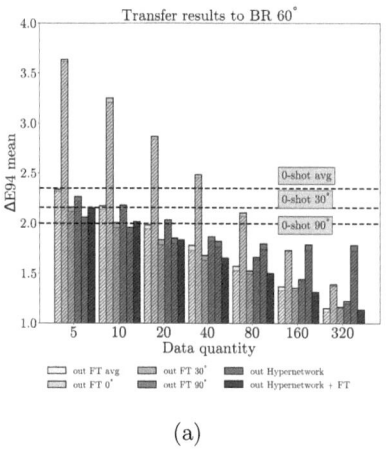
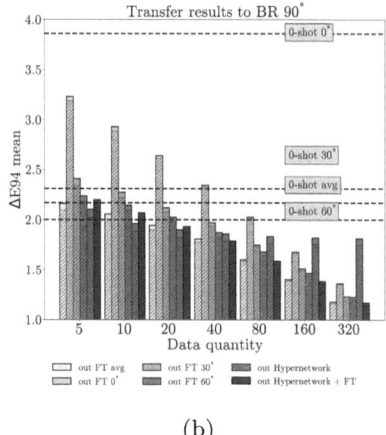

(a)   (b)

Fig. 10. Transfer results in BR for 60° and 90° laser polarization angles. Smooth bars with thick edge-lines correspond to results on test samples, hatched with thin lines ones to unseen laser parameters during adaptation phase.

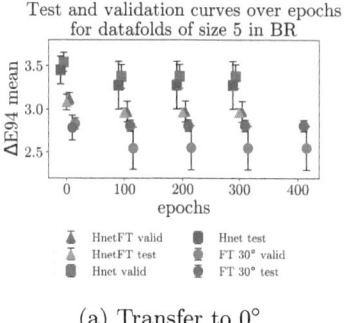
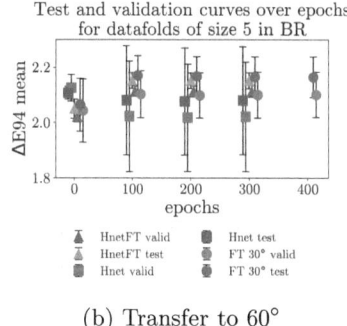

(a) Transfer to 0°   (b) Transfer to 60°

Fig. 11. Evolution of $\Delta E94$ in test and validation in BR every 100 epochs. Hnet epochs are extended up to 300. More results in Appendix Sect. 3.

4.6   Ablation Studies

The study is performed to highlight the impact of the introduced regularization and pre-training on the adaptation quality. The adaption task used is toward 60° in Tunpol and BR. Evaluation is done on Hnet with datafolds of size 320. Results are reported in Table 3. If it is clear to see the benefits of pretraining and freezing on the adaptation results, it is hardly the case for the different regularizations. However, adding a regularization during the training helps to reduce the variance of each metrics, so that adaptation becomes more invariant to the datasets used to generate the latent space. It is chosen to apply a regularization on both decoder and context vector but a more in-depth hyperparameters tuning could enhance adaptation quality.

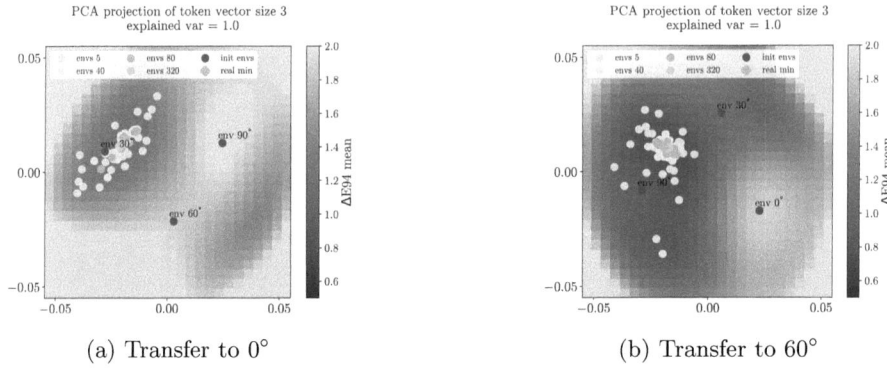

(a) Transfer to 0°   (b) Transfer to 60°

Fig. 12. Shared latent space visualization in Tunpol using PCA projection. More results in Appendix Sect. 4.

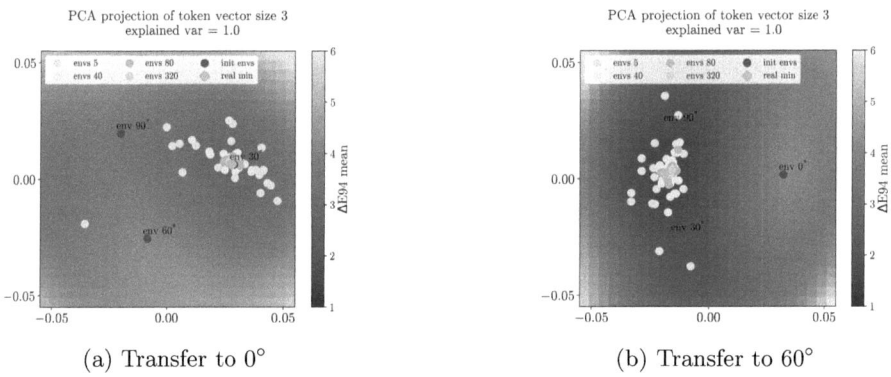

(a) Transfer to 0°   (b) Transfer to 60°

Fig. 13. Shared latent space visualization in BR using PCA projection. More results in Appendix Sect. 4.

4.7 Context Vectors Size Study

We use the same learning condition as for the ablation study on frozen pretrained weights. Context size varies from 1 to 4 and results are showed in Table 4. As performance increases an optimum is found at size 3 with less variance on the metrics compared to size 2 and 4.

Algorithm 2. Hampel filter algorithm
X, k refer respectively to a 1D or 2D signal and the sliding window size.

1: **Input:** $X = \{x_i\}_{i \in \{0,...,N\}, N \in \mathbb{N}}$, $k \in \mathbb{N}^*$
2: **for** $x_i \in X$ **do**   ▷ Boundary conditions are taken into account for $i > N + k$ and $i < k + 1$
3:      $m \leftarrow \text{median}(x_{i-k}, ..., x_i, ..., x_{i+k})$
4:      $\sigma \leftarrow \kappa \text{median}(|x_{i-k} - m|, ..., |x_i - m|, ..., |x_{i+k} - m|)$ ▷ here $\frac{\sigma}{\kappa}$ refers to the median absolute deviation and $\kappa \approx 1.4826$
5:      **if** $|x_i - m| > n\sigma$ **then** $x_i \leftarrow m$ **endif**
6: **end for**

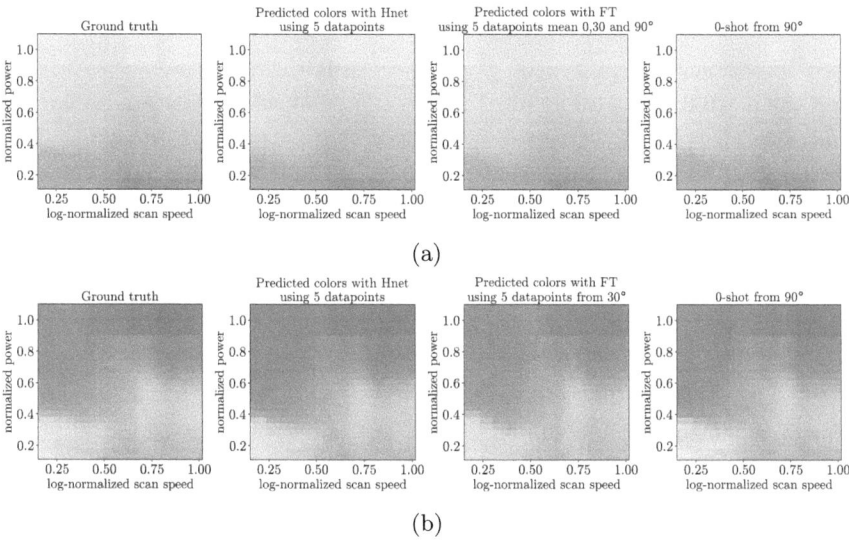

Fig. 14. Tunpol (a) and BR (b) colors comparison between real data and predicted ones given at 60° for repetition rate of 300 kHz and interline distance of 2 μm. More results in Appendix Sect. 4.

Table 3. Test results for ablation study.

Exp Name	Tunpol			BR		
	ΔE94 mean	ΔE94 std	Accuracy (%)	ΔE94 mean	ΔE94 std	Accuracy (%)
no-pretraining						
no reg	7.88 ± 0.23	5.18 ± 0.37	3.44 ± 2.32	8.04 ± 3.40	4.20 ± 1.31	4.20 ± 3.66
Only λ_W	10.24 ± 7.69	3.30 ± 2.18	10.31 ± 12.42	8.55 ± 1.52	3.98 ± 1.52	5.07 ± 7.11
Only λ_κ	11.58 ± 6.69	10.66 ± 1.66	1.94 ± 1.54	$11.74 + 8\ 02$	$3.19 \perp 1.67$	7.78 ± 12.33
λ_W and λ_κ	$9\ 53 \pm 7.62$	2.93 ± 2.16	19.62 ± 31.75	11.00 ± 1.03	4.98 ± 0.33	0.83 ± 0.59
pre-training						
no reg	1.16 ± 0.20	0.77 ± 0.17	75.73 ± 9.70	1.84 ± 0.06	1.02 ± 0.08	43.06 ± 4.18
Only λ_W	3.17 ± 2.91	2.26 ± 2.20	47.64 ± 30.29	1.84 ± 0.03	1.01 ± 0.06	43.06 ± 2.49
Only λ_κ	1.55 ± 0.66	1.03 ± 0.35	64.69 ± 20.59	1.91 ± 0.05	1.07 ± 0.10	41.08 ± 1.66
λ_W and λ_κ	1.70 ± 0.24	1.00 ± 0.07	50.00 ± 11.86	1.82 ± 0.04	1.02 ± 0.06	44.51 ± 1.34
frozen-pretraining						
no reg	0.81 ± 0.01	0.57 ± 0.17	90.21 ± 0.52	1.74 ± 0.02	1.04 ± 0.05	49.41 ± 3.47
Only λ_W	0.80 ± 0.02	0.57 ± 0.03	90.07 ± 0.99	1.77 ± 0.04	1.04 ± 0.08	46.42 ± 2.49
Only λ_κ	0.79 ± 0.01	0.55 ± 0.02	91.18 ± 0.77	1.75 ± 0.01	1.03 ± 0.06	48.12 ± 2.33
λ_W and λ_κ	0.80 ± 0.02	0.57 ± 0.03	89.34 ± 0.55	1.78 ± 0.02	1.06 ± 0.05	47.01 ± 1.47

Table 4. Test results for context Vector Size study.

Exp Name	Tunpol			BR		
	ΔE94 mean	ΔE94 std	Accuracy (%)	ΔE94 mean	ΔE94 std	Accuracy (%)
context size: 1	0.99 ± 0.04	0.61 ± 0.05	83.82 ± 2.80	1.78 ± 0.04	1.02 ± 0.04	45.17 ± 3.26
context size: 2	0.80 ± 0.02	0.56 ± 0.02	90.42 ± 0.62	1.77 ± 0.03	1.07 ± 0.06	47.71 ± 2.68
context size: 3	0.80 ± 0.02	0.57 ± 0.03	89.34 ± 0.55	1.78 ± 0.02	1.06 ± 0.05	47.01 ± 1.47
context size: 4	0.80 ± 0.02	0.57 ± 0.03	90.17 ± 1.48	1.75 ± 0.03	1.05 ± 0.07	47.64 ± 3.06

Algorithm 3. Savitsky-Golay filter algorithm X, k, P refer respectively to a 1D or 2D signal, the sliding window size and the maximum polynomial order.

1: **Input:** $X = \{x_i\}_{i \in \{0,\dots,N\}, N \in \mathbb{N}}$, $(k, P) \in \mathbb{N}^{*2}$
2: $\hat{y} \leftarrow [\,]$
3: **for** $x_i \in X$ **do**
4:     $y \leftarrow \sum_{p=0}^{P} \alpha_p x^p$
5:     Minimize $\sum_{i=-k}^{k} \left(y_{k+i} - \sum_{p=1}^{P} \alpha_p x_{k+1}^p \right)^2$
6:     $\hat{y}_k \leftarrow \sum_{p=0}^{P} \alpha_p x_k^p$
7: **end for**

5   Conclusion

This work introduces adaptative color prediction models for nanophotonics applications based on a contextual hypernetwork. In a real-world experimental case scenario, the proposed model demonstrates its ability to adapt quickly and automatically to unseen environments in low data regimes while preventing strong overfitting. Our study indicates that the model needs to be refined by a fine-tuning procedure but its quality is good enough to ensure a good adaptation. The visualization of the context vectors can be interpreted to identify similar environments which could help the practitioner to identify close tasks. In low data-regime, the model matches more closely to ground truth's color variations than the other methods. Overall, this work provides a general framework for color adaptation that can offer many application perspectives for learning adaptive models. Future work aims at integrating a priori physical knowledge to help the model to adapt faster to a wider range of environments.

Impact Statement. Our work focuses on a machine learning model for the prediction of laser-induced colors in nanophotonics. This work is essentially an applicative work for an engineering task. There are many potential consequences of using our work on other domains or tasks, none which we feel must be specifically highlighted here.

Acknowledgments. This work has been funded by a public grant from the French National Research Agency under the "France 2030" investment plan, which has the reference EUR MANUTECH SLEIGHT - ANR-17-EURE-0026.

Disclosure of Interests. The authors have no competing interests to declare that are relevant to the content of this article.

References

1. An, S., et al.: Deep neural network enabled active metasurface embedded design. Nanophotonics **11**(17), 4149–4158 (2022)
2. Baxter, J., Calà Lesina, A., Guay, J.M., Weck, A., Berini, P., Ramunno, L.: Plasmonic colours predicted by deep learning. Sci. Rep. **9**(1), 8074 (2019)
3. Bibbò, L., Khan, K., Liu, Q., Lin, M., Wang, Q., Ouyang, Z.: Tunable narrowband antireflection optical filter with a metasurface. Photon. Res. **5**(5), 500–506 (2017)
4. Casaletti, M., Valerio, G., Quevedo-Teruel, O., Burghignoli, P.: An overview of metasurfaces for thin antenna applications. C R Phys. **21**(7–8), 659–676 (2020)
5. Dalloz, N., et al.: Anti-counterfeiting white light printed image multiplexing by fast nanosecond laser processing. Adv. Mater. **34**(2), 2104054 (2022)
6. Destouches, N., et al.: Self-organized growth of metallic nanoparticles in a thin film under homogeneous and continuous-wave light excitation. J. Mater. Chem. C **2**, 6256–6263 (2014)
7. Destouches, N., et al.: Laser-empowered random metasurfaces for white light printed image multiplexing. Adv. Funct. Mater. **31**(18), 2010430 (2021)
8. Dinsdale, N.J., et al.: Deep learning enabled design of complex transmission matrices for universal optical components. ACS Photonics **8**(1), 283–295 (2021)
9. Finn, C., Abbeel, P., Levine, S.: Model-agnostic meta-learning for fast adaptation of deep networks. In: Precup, O., Teh, Y.W. (eds.) International Conference on Machine Learning, vol. 70, pp. 1126–1135. PMLR, 06–11 August 2017
10. Jia, Y., Qian, C., Fan, Z., Cai, T., Li, E.P., Chen, H.: A knowledge-inherited learning for intelligent metasurface design and assembly. Light Sci. Appl. **12**(1), 82 (2023)
11. Jiang, J., Chen, M., Fan, J.A.: Deep neural networks for the evaluation and design of photonic devices. Nat. Rev. Mater. **6**(8), 679–700 (2021)
12. Khoram, E., Wu, Z., Qu, Y., Zhou, M., Yu, Z.: Graph neural networks for metasurface modeling. ACS Photonics **10**(4), 892–899 (2023)
13. Kirchmeyer, M., Yin, Y., Dona, J., Baskiotis, N., Rakotomamonjy, A., Gallinari, P.: Generalizing to new physical systems via context-informed dynamics model. In: International Conference on Machine Learning, pp. 11283–11301. PMLR (2022)
14. Lalanne, P., Chen, M., Rockstuhl, C., Sprafke, A., Dmitriev, A., Vynck, K.: Disordered optical metasurfaces: basics, properties, and applications. Adv. Opt. Photon. **17**(1), 45–113 (2025)
15. Le, V.D., et al.: Understanding and exploiting the optical properties of laser-induced quasi-random plasmonic metasurfaces. ACS Appl. Opt. Mater. **2**(3), 373–385 (2024)
16. Liu, Z., et al.: Three-dimensional self-organization in nanocomposite layered systems by ultrafast laser pulses. ACS Nano **11**(5), 5031–5040 (2017). pMID: 28471649
17. Liu, Z., Vitrant, G., Lefkir, Y., Bakhti, S., Destouches, N.: Laser induced mechanisms controlling the size distribution of metallic nanoparticles. Phys. Chem. Chem. Phys. **18**, 24600–24609 (2016)
18. Liu, Z., Zhu, D., Rodrigues, S.P., Lee, K.T., Cai, W.: Generative model for the inverse design of metasurfaces. Nano Lett. **18**(10), 6570–6576 (2018)

19. Ma, H., et al.: Laser-generated Ag nanoparticles in mesoporous TiO2 films: formation processes and modeling-based size prediction. J. Phys. Chem. C **123**(42), 25898–25907 (2019)

20. Ma, H., et al.: Predicting laser-induced colors of random plasmonic metasurfaces and optimizing image multiplexing using deep learning. ACS Nano **16**(6), 9410–9419 (2022)

21. Ma, W., Liu, Z., Kudyshev, Z.A., Boltasseva, A., Cai, W., Liu, Y.: Deep learning for the design of photonic structures. Nat. Photonics **15**(2), 77–90 (2021)

22. Majorel, C., Girard, C., Arbouet, A., Muskens, O.L., Wiecha, P.R.: Deep learning enabled strategies for modeling of complex aperiodic plasmonic metasurfaces of arbitrary size. ACS Photonics **9**(2), 575–585 (2022)

23. de Mathelin, A., Richard, G., Mougeot, M., Vayatis, N.: Adversarial weighting for domain adaptation in regression. CoRR abs/2006.08251 (2020)

24. Peng, R., Ren, S., Malof, J., Padilla, W.J.: Transfer learning for metamaterial design and simulation. Nanophotonics **13**(13), 2323–2334 (2024)

25. Qin, J., et al.: Metasurface micro/nano-optical sensors: principles and applications. ACS Nano **16**(8), 11598–11618 (2022). pMID: 35960685

26. Sadeghli Dizaji, P., Habibiyan, H.: Machine learning with knowledge constraints for design optimization of microring resonators as a quantum light source. Sci. Rep. **15**(1), 372 (2025)

27. Sharma, N., Destouches, N., Florian, C., Serna, R., Siegel, J.: Tailoring metal-dielectric nanocomposite materials with ultrashort laser pulses for dichroic color control. Nanoscale **11**(40), 18779–18789 (2019)

28. Sicilia, A., Zhao, X., Hwang, S.J.: Domain adversarial neural networks for domain generalization: when it works and how to improve. Mach. Learn. **112**(7) (2023)

29. Wang, H., Zhao, H., Li, B.: Bridging multi-task learning and meta-learning: towards efficient training and effective adaptation. In: ICML (2021)

30. Xu, P., Lou, J., Li, C., Jing, X.: Inverse design of a metasurface based on a deep tandem neural network. J. Opt. Soc. Am. B, JOSAB **41**(2), A1–A5 (2024)

31. Zhang, J., Huang, J., Luo, Z., Zhang, G., Lu, S.: DA-DETR: domain adaptive detection transformer by hybrid attention. In: CVPR (2023)

32. Zhu, R., et al.: Phase-to-pattern inverse design paradigm for fast realization of functional metasurfaces via transfer learning. Nat. Commun. **12**(1), 2974 (2021)

Legend-Informed Symbol Recognition in Engineering Diagrams with Self-supervised Learning

Antonia Hain[1]([✉]), Simon Gölzhäuser[1], Nicolas Réhault[1], Thomas Brox[2], and Matthias Demant[1]

[1] Fraunhofer Institute for Solar Energy Systems ISE, Freiburg im Breisgau, Germany
{antonia.hain,simon.goelzhaeuser,nicolas.rehault,
matthias.demant}@ise.fraunhofer.de
[2] University of Freiburg, Freiburg im Breisgau, Germany

Abstract. Engineering diagrams are vital documents in many industries. Historically stored as image data, conversion of such diagrams into modern formats is required for further use and adaptation. Therefore, research towards automated digitization has gained traction. To recognize symbols in the diagrams, recent studies rely on supervised learning, but large labeled datasets are difficult to acquire in industry settings. In this paper, we present a self-supervised approach towards automated recognition of engineering diagram symbols. We validate the method on diagrams from the building sector, where they are used for technical plant planning, installation, and monitoring. The method makes use of diagram legends, which show prototypical examples of the symbols occurring in the diagram. As the legend entries are unique, they can be used to learn embeddings through contrastive learning for a self-supervised classification of diagram symbols. The method circumvents most of the labeling efforts: all symbols are extracted from the set of diagrams with a symbol region detector trained on a synthetic dataset. Then, we train a symbol encoder by contrasting the symbols found inside the legends with each other. The encoder is subsequently used in a matching procedure that classifies unknown diagram symbols by comparing them to the legend examples. Furthermore, it can recognize when symbols do not appear in the legend at all. Generalizing beyond variations in diagram drawing style, this matching procedure achieves over 80% accuracy. The results demonstrate the potential of legends for engineering diagram digitization without the need to invest in labeled datasets.

Keywords: Engineering Diagram · Building Services · Heating, Ventilation and Air Conditioning · Contrastive Learning

1 Introduction

The operation of buildings, specifically heating and cooling systems, contributes significantly to carbon emissions, causing an estimated 26% of global emissions

ⓒ The Author(s) 2026
B. Pfahringer et al. (Eds.): ECML PKDD 2025, LNAI 16020, pp. 403–421, 2026.
https://doi.org/10.1007/978-3-662-72243-5_23

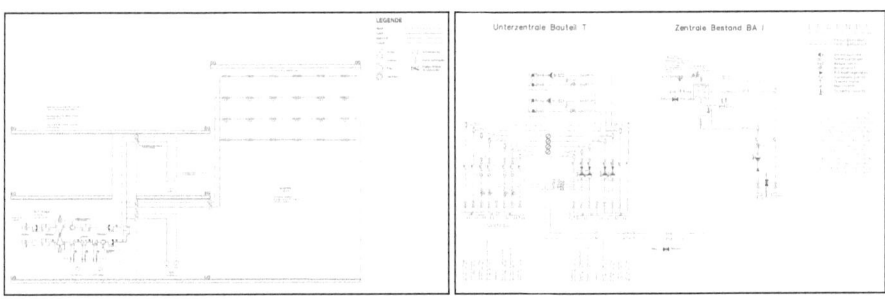

Fig. 1. Exemplary engineering diagrams with different style, coloring and symbols.

related to energy [11]. Therefore, steps towards renovation or operational optimization of heating, ventilation, and air conditioning (HVAC) systems must be taken promptly. However, much effort goes into planning such steps: Before deriving retrofit or optimization measures, existing systems are thoroughly analyzed by reviewing building data and transferring the often decades-old data into a modern CAD format. This entails high workloads for engineers and technicians.

An integral part of building data are engineering diagrams, which illustrate a system's components, using symbols, and its topology. Similar diagrams are used in other industry sectors such as process engineering or electrical engineering. The diagrams may also contain text, tables, or a legend explaining the symbols. Despite existing norms, their style and qualities vary strongly depending on age and source, as shown in Fig. 1. Diagrams may be hand-drawn, scanned or photographed from a print, or provided as a PDF file. In most cases, they therefore do not contain any semantic machine-readable information.

Though considerable advances have been made towards automated recognition and digitization of engineering diagrams, creating a solution that is robust to variation in depiction styles is difficult, especially in regard to diagram symbols. A lack of public and labeled datasets in the domain makes the training of machine learning models for this purpose additionally challenging.

We propose a novel pipeline for the recognition of symbols in engineering diagrams that aims to address these challenges. Instead of attempting to learn all-encompassing representations for a large number of symbols in a supervised manner, we leverage the diagram legends to train a symbol encoder. Our method allows for the recognition of symbols with just one reference example and without the need to predefine classes of symbols to recognize. Furthermore, the method is indifferent to variation in symbol depictions across diagrams, as long as each symbol looks distinguishable from other symbols within the same image.

The approach is a three-step procedure that works without annotations, except for the legend location: First, we generate synthetic data with the aim of representing the gist of what the diagrams look like. Then, we train a generalized symbol detector on the synthetic data, which extracts symbols from the diagrams and corresponding legends. We employ a self-supervised contrastive learning framework to subsequently train an encoder which learns symbol representations based on the legends. The representations produced by the encoder are used to classify symbols in the diagrams by determining the nearest-neighbor legend symbol embedding for each diagram symbol embedding. To identify symbols that are not represented in the legend, we define an embedding distance threshold which adapts to each individual diagram.

Summarized, our contributions are:

– A pipeline for legend-based symbol recognition without symbol annotations
– A diagram symbol detection method, trained entirely on synthetic data
– An encoder model computing symbol embeddings, trained with legend symbols and contrastive learning
– A matching procedure selecting corresponding legend symbols for symbols in the diagrams, and rejecting symbols not present in the legend

2 Related Work

2.1 Engineering Diagram Digitization

Digitization of engineering and architectural diagrams, such as, for example, P&ID, chemical process flow and circuit diagrams, or floor plans, has been an active research area since at least the 1990s [19]. In recent years, diagram digitization research has increasingly shifted from hand-crafted features towards neural networks and deep learning. Extensive literature reviews have been comprised by Moreno-García et al. [19] and Jamieson et al. [12].

Alongside a variety of other relevant data, like text and lines, one essential structure to identify in diagrams are symbols, which require a recognition approach specialized to the data at hand. Recently, mostly supervised learning has been applied to locate and recognize diagram symbols, often with popular object detectors [14,31,34], and occasionally with segmentation networks [24] or a two-step pipeline, where a localization module is followed by classification [21,35]. Various studies have demonstrated high precision and recall; however, for a practical application setting, we identify some drawbacks of this approach. The training needs extensive amounts of data, which has to be labeled by experts. In fact, even finding enough and varied data can be a challenge, where possible solutions include mining images from other scientific publications [32], gathering data via web search [31] or simulation with synthetic data [21]. Aside from this roadblock, strong class imbalance has been identified as another issue in training symbol identification models [5].

Few contributions have attempted to classify symbols without a large training dataset. Paliwal et al. [22] represent symbols as graphs and create embeddings of both the graph and the visual representation. Their method recognizes 25 classes of symbols based on just one example each and still performs comparably to other work. One inherent limitation that remains for this method as described, and in general for supervised learning methods, is that all relevant symbols must be predefined. For each class, sufficiently varied samples must be found which cover the expected distribution, as diagrams in the field show many different variations of the same component types.

While, nowadays, the classification aspect of the symbols is almost always addressed with supervised deep learning, the detection of symbol locations is still sometimes tackled with traditional computer vision techniques [22,35]. This methodology has the advantage of not requiring large amounts of training data, and in that sense, being unsupervised. However, human-engineered feature extractors have the downside of being vulnerable to data variations that were not explicitly addressed in the design of the method.

Few works explore using the diagram legend for symbol identification. In the domain of map digitization, Samet et al. [28] have studied legends for the identification of symbols with traditional template matching. In the engineering drawing domain, Joy and Mounsef [13] used legend symbols to create training data for an object detector. Sarkar et al. [29] used the legend to classify symbols, testing both SIFT [18] descriptors and a convolutional neural network trained with labeled symbols, in which SIFT achieved better results. Symbol localization was performed with a Faster R-CNN [26] that learned from annotated data. In this work, we also utilize a Faster R-CNN for detection, but trained with synthetic data, bypassing the need for symbol annotation. Similarly, we classify the symbols using the legend, but use a self-supervised learning approach to train a symbol encoder.

Newly, foundation models such as large language models (LLMs) have been on the rise, showing an impressive body of knowledge that can be readily applied to many domains. While we are not aware of any publications using LLMs to digitize complex engineering diagrams, the application of such models may seem intuitive. For this scenario, we however see some challenges: First, many diagram images have thousands of pixels on both axes, but cannot be downsized without rendering small symbols unrecognizable. Therefore, an LLM would have to process a diagram in many small excerpts, which is costly due to the models' complexity. Further, an LLM would need to return accurate symbol locations to allow for subsequent reconstruction of the full diagram, which current models are not specifically trained for. In a pre-test run by us with GPT 4-o [20], we also found that the model's knowledge without finetuning is not sufficient to recognize symbols beyond common types. The model also tends to overlook symbols and to produce false results rather than admitting uncertainty. For these reasons, while engineering diagram recognition with LLMs does not seem out of reach with proper model finetuning and appropriate prompts to address these hindrances, we explore a more lightweight approach in this work.

2.2   Non-supervised Representation Learning

Unsupervised, semi-supervised and self-supervised learning advance steadily, in part motivated by the effort and cost of data labeling. While semi-supervised learning still makes use of a small set of labeled data, unsupervised and self-supervised methods aim at utilizing data without any labels. A popular technique is *representation learning*. The goal of representation learning is to distill data

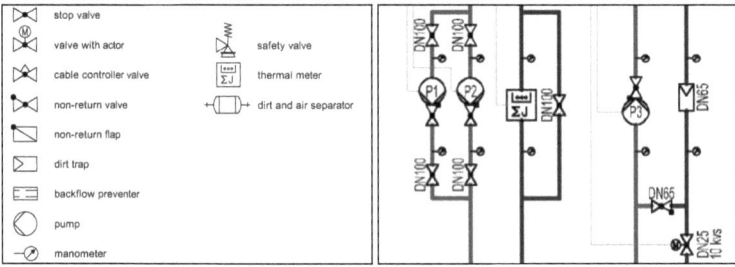

Fig. 2. Legend depicting different kinds of symbols (left) and an excerpt of the diagram in which the legend is placed (right).

into a less complex set of features preserving the key identifiers of each data point, allowing for comparison of data points with simple computations.

Generative models are one popular branch of representation learning which synthesize data similar to a given distribution [23]. To do so, the models implicitly learn to embed the key features of the data, allowing for the use of the embeddings in tasks such as classification. Well-known models include Generative Adversarial Networks (GANs) [6] and autoencoders.

Another field in representation learning is contrastive learning, where the model is instructed on which points in the data are similar and which are different. The data points are passed through a twin network [16] of identical architecture and weights. Similar data points then ought to produce similar embeddings, and dissimilar points different embeddings. This is enforced by, for example, using a contrastive loss [7] or triplet loss [30], which we also use in our approach. Without labels, samples "similar" to a reference data point can be created with augmentation. In recent years, the contrastive learning framework has been adapted for more complex and data-intensive scenarios, e.g. through facilitating the use of many dissimilar pairings with momentum contrast [9] and memory banks [33] or by embedding the input images in a patch-wise manner [2,8]. For industrial anomaly detection, it has also been shown that patch embeddings can be taken from intermediate layers of pre-trained networks, presenting an alternative to training a specialized network on labeled domain data [27].

3 Legend-Informed Symbol Recognition

3.1 Properties of Engineering Diagrams and Legends

Legends are present in many engineering diagrams and provide useful information regarding the component symbols in the diagram. As seen in the examples in Fig. 1, legends are table-like structures that are usually provided on the side of the diagrams. For simplicity, we will call symbols found inside the bounds of the legend *legend symbols*, and the symbols outside the legend *diagram symbols*.

Figure 2 shows an exemplary legend and an excerpt of the corresponding diagram, taken from the same image file. Within one diagram, legend symbols often share similarities in drawing style and coloring. One legend may contain multiple visually similar symbols showing variations of the same component.

From the excerpt, it is evident that matching the diagram symbols to the legend symbols is not trivial: Although the legend contains all symbols in the excerpt and is intuitively usable to human readers, the diagram symbols are not drawn in the exact same way as they appear in the legend. Aside from rotation and scaling differences, outlines may be thicker, thinner, or blurry, and the appearance is additionally changed by the lines connecting the symbols. This challenges more traditional computer vision methods like template matching. As the symbols contain a lot of whitespace and only a few lines, we are also wary of using autoencoders or patch embeddings - even minor image transformations, such as translation or scaling, could be punished strongly in a classical autoencoder setting, and small patches of the images may not always be meaningful.

However, we observe the following properties of legends that make contrastive learning an interesting option for this data:

(1) Each symbol is unique within the legend
(2) Diagram symbols (mostly) appear in the legend

Property (1) can be exploited to mine positive and negative pairings out of the given data, and property (2) can subsequently be used to find labels for the diagram symbols. It is important to note that while, in our observation, property (1) is nearly always true, there are exceptions to (2). Real-life data is imperfect; many legends are indeed incomplete and additional objects appear in the diagrams. However, we find that most legends do represent the majority of diagram symbols, such that applying the method will nevertheless considerably decrease the effort needed for digitizing the documents.

3.2   Method Overview

The proposed legend-informed symbol recognition pipeline is summarized in Fig. 3 and consists of three main parts: First, synthetic data emulating the symbols and diagrams is created using simple drawing functions and randomization. Then, symbols in the diagrams are detected using a generalized symbol region detector, i.e. an object detection neural network that is indifferent to the specific classes of the symbols. After symbol detection, an embedding encoder is trained on the legend symbols with contrastive learning. Finally, we compute embeddings for all symbols with this encoder, which enables for comparison of diagram symbols and the legend counterparts.

Crucially, the method can be trained with minimal annotation effort: The symbol detector is trained entirely on synthetic data, whose creation requires only superficial knowledge of the diagrams' appearance. The embedding encoder also needs knowledge of only two things: (1) the locations of all symbols in the diagram - which can be determined using the detector - and (2) the location of the legend itself, to group the symbols into diagram and legend symbols.

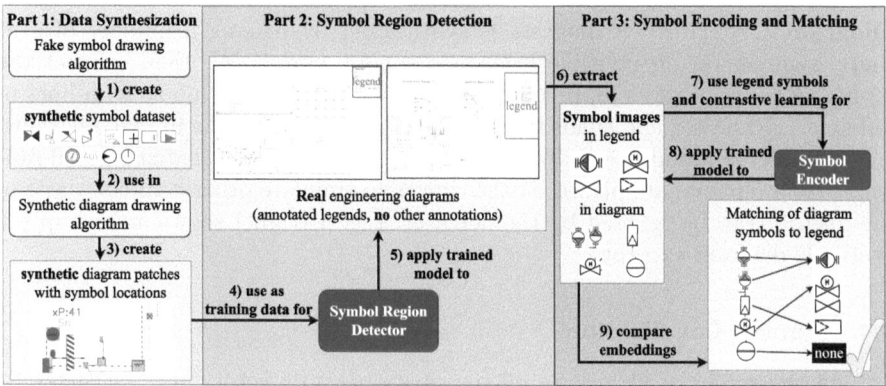

Fig. 3. Overview of the pipeline. Data is shown in orange, basic algorithms in gray and the neural networks in pink boxes. The method's steps are written along the arrows. (Color figure online)

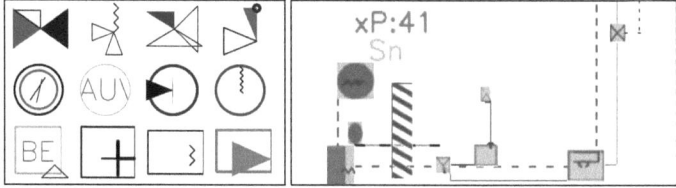

Fig. 4. Synthetic data symbols (left) and an exemplary synthetic diagram excerpt with symbols highlighted in yellow (right). (Color figure online)

Therefore, the only annotations we use are those of the legend locations. Even this can likely be determined automatically, e.g. with a table detection method. Given the low effort needed to point out the legend and the immediate tradeoff in method stability, we however assume here that the legend location is known.

3.3 Synthetic Data Creation

Symbol Creation: For the symbol detector training, we first create a set of symbol-like illustrations using randomized drawing algorithms. The synthetic data is designed to simulate various component types without representing specific symbols. Rather than focusing on the details, the detector is encouraged to recognize what symbols generally look like and in which contexts they appear. Examples can be viewed in Fig. 4 (left). Each image follows one of three basic shape types which imitate the symbol shapes typically seen in the diagrams. This main shape is drawn first and is either a combination of triangles (top row), a circle (middle row) or a rectangle (bottom row). Straight and zig-zag lines or other basic geometric shapes are randomly added to the symbols. Circle and rectangle components may also include letters. Parameters like line strength, gray value, font scale and size are all randomized within pre-set bounds.

Diagram Creation: A diagram is synthesized by placing a number of synthetic symbols on an invisible grid on a square canvas. We then connect the bounding boxes of random, but most often spatially close, symbols with lines of different thicknesses and shades, some of which are dashed like in real diagrams. Additionally, randomly generated rectangles, some with cross-hatching, and random text fragments are placed on the canvas to simulate other common parts of the diagrams to be ignored by the detector. Fig. 4 (right) shows an exemplary synthetic diagram excerpt.

3.4   Symbol Localization

To find the symbols, we use an off-the-shelf object detector, such as Faster R-CNN [26] or a detector from the YOLO series [25]. The network only knows one foreground class and is trained exclusively on the synthetic diagrams. During inference on real data, we first detect text elements in the diagram with the CRAFT text detector [1] and remove them. Due to the large size of the diagrams, the networks cannot process them as one. Instead, we employ a sliding window approach, in which square excerpts are taken from the diagram and evaluated by the detectors one by one. Since the diagrams often contain a lot of whitespace, the approach skips excerpts which contain only one unique gray value, and as such appear empty, to avoid unnecessary forward passes and speed up processing.

3.5   Diagram-to-Legend Symbol Matching

To learn an embedding function which can be used to match diagram symbols to the legend symbols, we employ a contrastive learning framework using the legend, and a lightweight convolutional encoder, described in the following subsections.

Contrastive Learning on Legend Symbols: Property (1) as given in Sect. 3.1 is the backbone for the training of our method. Knowing that legend symbols are unique allows for the design of a self-supervised method which learns to find similarities between different augmentations of the same legend symbol, and differences between one legend symbol and others. Specifically, we use a triplet loss [30], in which each triplet is drawn from the legends in the dataset. The loss function is

$$L(a, p, n) = \max(0, d(a, p) - d(a, n) + m) \qquad (1)$$

where a denotes the embedding of an anchor symbol, p and n respectively denote embeddings of "positive"/"negative" symbols that match/do not match the anchor, $d(x, y)$ refers to the Euclidean distance between two embeddings x and y, and m is a predefined margin that is sought to be enforced between the distances of positive pairs and negative pairs.

To form a triplet, a random legend symbol is retrieved from the dataset to serve as the anchor, then augmented and embedded using the encoder. The same symbol with different augmentations is used for the positive, matching, symbol. For the negative example, another symbol from the same legend is taken and augmented. As we are dealing with data points that would be considered highly similar in a broader image classification task, the encoder must learn to distinguish small details. Therefore, instead of retrieving the negative symbol randomly, we first embed all other symbols within the anchor's legend, and then pick a random symbol within the three closest matches. This is to ensure that the algorithm drives apart the most similar symbols, without getting stuck contrasting against the same neighbor over and over.

Augmentations are crucial for successful contrastive training [3]. Our approach particularly relies on extensive augmentation, since the anchor and the positive sample are based on the same symbol. To reflect all the potential differences in depiction between legend and diagram symbols described in Sect. 3.1, a variety of augmentations are randomly applied, such as rotation, erosion and dilation, padding and cropping, addition of lines, color shade changes, and noise.

Encoder Network: The encoder is a lightweight neural network with three convolutional layers (using a 7×7 kernel in the first layer and 3×3 kernels after), with ReLU activation functions and 2D Max Pooling placed in between. The block of convolutional layers is followed by a linear layer, which is then normalized to a unit vector, becoming the symbol's embedding. The normalization step ensures that the maximal distance between two embeddings is known and a reasonable margin for the triplet loss function can be chosen.

Matching Procedure: Diagram symbols are matched to the legend symbols with the smallest Euclidean distance in the embedding space. To recognize false-positive symbol detections and symbols not represented in the legend, we add a threshold to our embedding matching method. If no legend symbol embedding is within this distance, the diagram symbol is rejected. Depending on diagram style and quality, the legend symbols may be more or less similar to the diagram symbols. To account for this, the threshold t adapts to each diagram, s.t.

$$t = m + \min_{q \in Q; l \in L} (d(q, l)) \tag{2}$$

where m is the margin used in the triplet loss training, $d(q, l)$ is the Euclidean distance between symbol embeddings q and l, Q is the set of diagram (query) symbols embeddings, and L is the set of legend symbol embeddings within the diagram. In other words, the threshold is the sum of the desired minimal embedding distance between different symbols, and the smallest distance between any diagram and legend symbol embeddings in the respective diagram.

4   Experiments

4.1   Experimental Setup

Data: Our dataset consists of 141 diagrams, acquired from industrial partners[1]. The diagrams were converted from PDF format to grayscale images with 300 dpi to preserve detail. This results in image sizes of around 2300–7900 pixels on the smaller axis and 3300–27,500 pixels on the larger axis, with a median of around 30 MP in total. The diagrams contain five to 800 symbols, with a median of 105.

A test set of 21 diagrams was created to reflect diagrams that are likely encountered in daily use. Due to the sliding window processing, this amounted to over 8000 input patches for the symbol detection, excluding the ignored white-space excerpts.

We selected the test diagrams manually to ensure that various drawing styles, symbols, qualities and complexities were covered. Some diagrams have the same source and were thus drawn with similar templates. The full dataset contains around 20 different drawing styles, but is imbalanced regarding their prevalence. For example, one template was highly common with 57% of diagrams drawn in this style, while other styles only occurred once or twice. Random test data selection would therefore likely favor styles that happened to be common in our data, while not every dataset may contain such imbalances. Note that two diagrams being drawn with the same template does not necessarily entail that the set of symbols used in both diagrams or their legends is the same.

We evaluate multiple scenarios designed to reflect different use cases: (1) As the symbol matching is self-supervised, we test its effectiveness on the data it was bootstrapped on, by testing on seven diagrams whose legends were also used in training. This models a case in which the method is trained to digitize one set of diagrams without considering future use on unseen data. (2) Another third of the test diagrams was excluded from training, but follows similar templates as training diagrams. This models a case where the symbol recognition method is already trained and a user wants to apply it on new incoming data made with the same software or templates as training diagrams. (3) The final third of the test set were neither used in training, nor drawn with a known template, therefore representing a case where a user wants to use the pre-trained method on entirely new incoming diagrams, e.g., from a different building project, made by a collaborator who uses a different template, or which are hand-drawn.

In the human annotations created with the VGG Image Annotator [4] for evaluation purposes, the test diagram legends contain three to 35 symbols, the diagrams themselves between 34 and 484 symbols. Note that in the full pipeline, with bounding boxes generated by the detector, these values may differ due to detection errors.

Detector: As the symbol region detector, we use a Faster R-CNN with Mobile-NetV3-Large [10] backbone, pre-trained on the COCO dataset [17]. 10,000 fake

---

[1] Due to industrial restrictions, the dataset and code for this project can not be published at this time.

symbols were created for each of the three types - triangles, circle and rectangle - as basis for the synthetic diagrams. The synthetic diagrams are created on-the-fly during training. We use around 34,000 synthetic samples with a batch size of 16, therefore training for around 2125 steps. We train with Adam Optimizer [15] and evaluate precision and recall.

Encoder and Matching: The encoder transforms 64×64 grayscale images into a 15-dimensional embedding vector. We parameterize the triplet loss with margin $m = 0.5$ and train with Adam Optimizer and a batch size of 64. Training stops when the symbol-to-legend assignments in the test set have changed less than 3% per epoch, averaged over the last 50 epochs. For evaluation, we build a confusion matrix of all symbol-to-legend assignments. Symbols not appearing in the legend, which are therefore not to be matched, are classified as a special symbol type which we call *rejects*, and considered separately in the statistics. The results are quantified in classification accuracy, precision and recall, both over the entire test dataset and averaged over the individual diagrams. To separate the performance of the symbol matching procedure from that of the detector, our evaluation considers two cases: One, where near-perfect detections are assumed, using manually annotated bounding boxes, and one for the entire pipeline, using detections made by the object detector.

The results are compared to those of a SIFT matching procedure implemented as proposed in [29]. This baseline approach matches symbols by computing a similarity score between 0 and 1 for each potential diagram-legend match. We enable for rejections by setting a threshold for this similarity. Here, we assume a hypothetical optimal thresholding method, and use the threshold yielding the best accuracy for each individual diagram, which we determine experimentally. For an additional baseline comparison that is not influenced by the rejections, we ignore all reject symbols, remove the rejection mechanisms and report the symbol matching accuracy in the absence of a negative class.

4.2   Experimental Results

Detector: Qualitative and quantitative detection results can be viewed in Fig. 5. The detector achieves up to around 72% precision and recall when the necessary IoU to match a detected box to the ground truth is 0.5. The precision-recall curves show that the metrics are strongly affected by changes in this threshold. False positive detections typically occur at text fragments that were not found by the text detector, and line crossings. Symbols that are not detected are most often very large or small, or drawn in a style that differs from the average symbol, for example more intricate drawings with little whitespace.

Encoder and Matching: Table 1 shows quantitative results of our symbol encoding and the matching algorithm, and of the baseline SIFT approach, on the full test set. With accurate symbol detections, sourced from human annotations, our procedure for matching/rejection achieves an overall accuracy of 83.7%, with

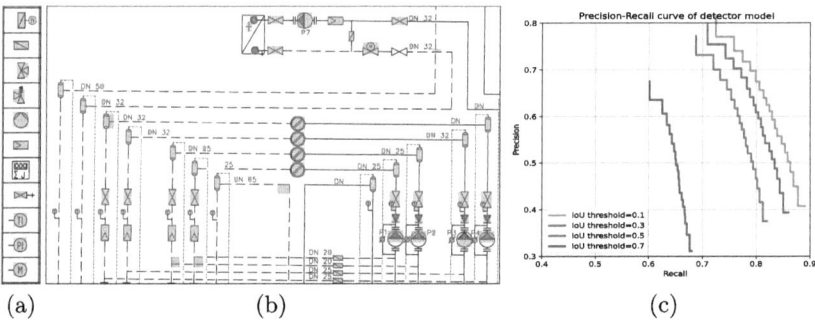

(a)   (b)   (c)

Fig. 5. Symbol region detection results, highlighted in yellow, on (a) a legend and (b) a diagram excerpt (a text detector is used to remove text beforehand, but the original image is displayed here for readability), and (c) the precision-recall curves on the test set. Each curve shows the precision and recall values modulated by the confidence threshold that is used to filter detections. The diagram shows curves for multiple Intersection over Union (IoU) thresholds, influencing which boxes are considered a match to a ground truth box. (Color figure online)

precision and recall of 94.6% and 82.7% for the symbols which are represented in the legend. The precision and recall of rejects are 59.3% and 87.4%. Notably, precision is therefore much higher for symbols listed in the legends compared to the reject symbols. Averaged over the diagrams instead of over all symbols, the numbers are similar, but the sample standard deviations indicate strong differences across the diagrams: On some diagrams, near-perfect accuracy is reached, and around 70% on others. Our method thereby considerably outperforms the SIFT approach with this data, achieving over 20pp higher accuracy.

Using the symbol detections of our object detector, the overall accuracy is slightly lower at 80.9%. In this scenario, the precision discrepancy between the true positive symbols and rejects was much smaller. Upon visual inspection, this is because false positive symbol detections - which are not present in the human annotations - are rejected very reliably, raising the average performance on the reject group of symbols. However, both precision and recall for the symbols listed in the legend are about 10% lower than in the reference case, and detections with inaccurate bounding boxes can cause errors. Our proposed method again achieves higher scores than the SIFT method, with over 18pp higher accuracy. A visual result of the entire inference pipeline with both symbol detection and matching is displayed in Fig. 6.

If the need for rejections is removed, our method correctly matches 93.3% (annotation bounding boxes) and 86.0% (detector bounding boxes) of the symbols, more than SIFT with 66.4% and 56.3%, respectively.

Table 2 shows exemplary success and failure cases. Evidently, the symbols are rarely confused with each other and most errors stem from the rejection mechanism. For example, symbols are falsely rejected if their diagram representation diverges strongly from the legend representation, e.g. due to lower quality

Table 1. Quantitative symbol matching results with our method and a baseline SIFT approach. Column 1 states whether the symbol bounding boxes used for training and evaluation were sourced from human annotations or from the object detector. Column 2 states whether the metrics were averaged over all symbol types in the test set, or averaged over the diagrams, and whether rejects were left out from the statistic. *Acc.* = accuracy, P_S/R_S = precision/recall of symbols matching one of the legend symbols, P_R/R_R = precision/recall of rejects.

BBoxes	Statistic	Acc.	P_S	R_S	P_R	R_R
		Proposed Method				
Annotation	overall	**83.7%**	**94.6%**	**82.7%**	**59.3%**	**87.4%**
Annotation	diagram aver-age (±stddev)	**83.4%** (±10.5pp)	**95.2%** (±6.2pp)	**81.9%** (±11.5pp)	57.0% (±29.1pp)	**83.7%** (±21.4pp)
Detector	overall	**80.9%**	**85.1%**	**71.4%**	**77.5%**	**91.8%**
Detector	diagram aver-age (±stddev)	**81.0%** (±8.2pp)	**84.4%** (±11.2pp)	**71.4%** (±12.4pp)	**77.3%** (±12.9pp)	**90.2%** (±12.5pp)
Annotation	overall, no rejects	**93.3%**	-	-	-	-
Detector	overall, no rejects	**86.0%**	-	-	-	-
		SIFT-based Method [29] (Baseline)				
Annotation	overall	62.0%	63.8%	62.7%	55.7%	59.4%
Annotation	diagram aver-age (±stddev)	63.2% (±15.6pp)	67.6% (±16.4pp)	59.8% (±22.3pp)	58.5% (±24.3pp)	52.4% (±32.4pp)
Detector	overall	61.7%	50.3%	44.0%	71.8%	82.2%
Detector	diagram aver-age (±stddev)	62.3% (±16.0pp)	52.7% (±18.5pp)	42.8% (±25.2pp)	71.0% (±16.8pp)	82.6% (±11.6pp)
Annotation	overall, no rejects	66.4%	-	-	-	-
Detector	overall, no rejects	56.3%	-	-	-	-

or alterations in drawing style. Outside of the legend, most symbol types are represented with coherent drawing styles, such that in this case, a number of instances of the same symbol type may be misclassified. Therefore, errors are not evenly distributed across symbols, but focus on specific types. Conversely, reject symbols are most likely falsely matched if a similar symbol is listed in the legend. However, the perceived general intra-diagram symbol similarity did not inherently cause issues: For example, one diagram contained exclusively rectangular symbols with little variation, which were matched with 97% accuracy. Regarding the three potential use cases reflected in the test data as described in Sect. 4.1, we do not observe a clear trend outside the inter-diagram standard deviation: On diagrams also seen in training (case 1), the method achieved an average accuracy of 82.1%/83.8% using the annotated/detector bounding boxes, respectively. On diagrams with similar templates to those seen in training (case

Table 2. Exemplary symbol matching success and failure cases. Each column, top to bottom, shows a query (diagram) symbol, the legend match chosen by our method, and the correct match in the legend. "-" indicate rejections, where no legend symbol was found within threshold distance/the symbol type was not listed in the legend.

	success cases	failure cases
query symbol	⊤ⅼ ◢ ⃠ ⋈ ◺ ◉ ✳ ◯	◺ ⚡ ⊓ ◔ ◪ ⓘ ◡ ✕
matched symbol	⊤ⅼ ◤ ⊘ ⋈ ◿ ◉ ⋈ ◯	- - ⊓ - ◪ Ⓜ - ⋈
correct symbol	⊤ⅼ ◤ ⊘ ⋈ ◿ ◉ ⋈ ◯ ◺◺	- ◔ ◪ ⓣ ◐ ⋈

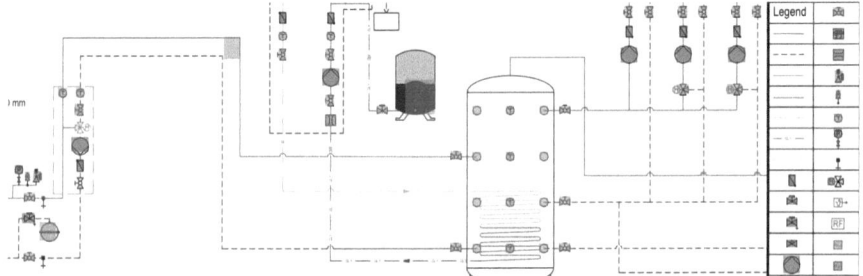

Fig. 6. Result of entire detection and matching pipeline on a diagram excerpt and the corresponding legend. Diagram symbols are marked in the color of the matched legend symbols. Gray boxes indicate detections which were not matched to any legend symbol. (Color figure online)

2), accuracy was 87.5%/79.2%. On test diagrams with a style fully unknown to the model (case 3), accuracy was 80.5%/78.7%.

5   Discussion

Our symbol detector demonstrates promising results on complex data, despite having been trained only on synthetic data that was created based on superficial observation of the diagrams' properties. However, the bounding box locations appear to be inaccurate, as seen by the influence of the IoU threshold on the precision-recall curve. Detecting and removing text elements was essential, as the symbol detector did not reliably ignore leftover text, despite seeing text in the training data. Failure to detect very large or small symbols may be explained by limitations of the object detector or the sliding window detection method. However, the detector also struggled with symbols of uncommon style, indicating that it may rely on the look of the symbols rather than their context, such as lines. On the other hand, legend symbols, which appear without this context, were therefore detected as reliably as the diagram symbols. This is important because missing a legend symbol could lead to many diagram symbols not being matched. To this end, high detection recall is also preferred over precision, since false positives can still be removed in the matching process. In general, our symbol detection strategy serves as a proof of concept for a scenario where labeled data cannot be obtained at all. Notable improvements are likely possible if, for example, datasets similar to the application area are available, the data is less diverse, or labeling a small amount of data is feasible. Finetuning of the text detection component to technical documentation texts and diagram data could also be explored to improve text removal results and, consequently, those of the following pipeline steps.

The symbol-to-legend matching trained with contrastive learning correctly assigns a majority of symbols with little confusion between symbols on both the diagrams used in training and diagrams that were not available at training time, where we observed no clear trend comparing various test scenarios. On our data, the method outperforms a SIFT approach as used in previous literature addressing the challenge of recognizing diagram symbols with a legend in a non-supervised manner. In many difficult cases, such as low-quality symbols, hand-drawn symbols or accidentally cropped symbols due to bounding box detection errors, the correct match is still found with sufficient confidence. If those difficulties are even more pronounced, errors are however more likely to occur. One thing to keep in mind is that this promising performance is likely dependent on the number and diversity of diagrams available for the initial training.

We find that the main challenge is identifying rejects, i.e. symbols not listed in the legend, without causing too many false rejections in the process. As seen in the results of an experiment case where the rejects are removed, over 90% accuracy may be possible when the rejection mechanism becomes unnecessary. While in our scenario, our thresholding method has shown good success, the results varied strongly depending on the diagram and factors such as the ratio between the amount of symbols represented in the legend and those which were not. Overall, the method tended to reject more symbols than necessary.

We also find that the matching and rejection procedure should be able to adapt to each diagram and that a universal threshold is likely unsuited: Dependent on factors such as the difference between the legend depictions and those used in the actual diagrams, the actual embedding distances varied and did not always adhere to the triplet loss margin.

An inherent challenge is posed by compound symbols. In our data, this kind of symbol is not consistently depicted in the legends: Sometimes, a compound symbol is given its own legend explanation; an example can be seen in Fig. 2, where the symbol *valve with actor* is a compound of the *stop valve* and a motor symbol. In other cases, often even within the same legend, compound symbols are explained only through their separate building blocks. As a result, the same building block may appear in a legend multiple times, softening the uniqueness property of the legend symbols. However, we find that our data did not contain enough such cases to strongly disturb the training. For these reasons, we decide against attempting to merge compound symbols automatically, which the detector usually identifies as separate entities. Having the user indicate which symbols should be merged after the recognition process would be a practical solution to this challenge and can likely be done with reasonable effort.

Overall, the results show that the method can be highly beneficial for users in the field despite the mentioned shortcomings. Manual labeling of the diagram symbols is tedious, error-prone, and takes twenty to thirty minutes per diagram in our data, while our method processed the test diagrams in an average of less than fifteen seconds on a machine equipped with a NVIDIA Quadro RTX 8000 (48 GB) GPU. If the legend is highly incomplete or there is none at all, the encoder embeddings could instead be used to cluster symbols and, thereby, recognize which symbols show the same component. In a practical setting, a user could be presented with each recognized symbol along with the corresponding original excerpts of the diagram image, which can facilitate cross-checking of the results and correction of errors. The user could also manually add missing symbols to the legend, which are likely common symbols known to experts in the field, and may have therefore been omitted. Because the encoder is very lightweight, the matching could be recalculated with an adapted legend almost instantly. Another possible avenue for expansion and improvement of the method may be to subsequently integrate an adequate human-in-the-loop approach which finetunes the recognition based on such user feedback.

6   Conclusion and Outlook

We presented a pipeline for automated symbol recognition in engineering diagrams, based on diagram symbol legends. Our method needs minimal labeling and delivered promising results on real diagrams from the building sector, where data is often proprietary and labeling is costly. We found that most symbols can be localized with a model trained only on synthetic data, and that the uniqueness of symbols in a legend can be utilized for a contrastive learning approach for symbol embeddings. This subsequently enabled us to identify symbols by matching them to the legend. The approach successfully recognized symbols on test diagrams even of unseen drawing style, and is not limited to a predefined set of symbol classes. For a practical setting, this means that the method could be applied to new diagrams outside of the distribution available for training. Therefore, we demonstrated the potential to achieve a notable decrease in the effort needed for diagram digitization. Future research could explore alternative symbol region detection strategies or symbol matching algorithms, with a focus on reliable separation between the symbols represented in the legend from those which are not. In practice, the method will be validated by HVAC engineers in a web-based application that we developed, providing functionalities to digitize, modify, and complete diagrams.

Although we designed our method for the building sector, similar problems could conceivably be addressed in other fields with a similar approach. We therefore believe that the methodology can be valuable in any field facing high workload with digitization of schematics and diagrams, if the data contains legends.

Acknowledgments. This study is funded by a PhD scholarship granted to the first author by the German Federal Environmental Foundation (DBU), and by the German Federal Ministry for Economic Affairs and Climate Action through the project DiMASH (FKZ 03EN1067 A). We thank Serdar Yilmaz of Scherr+Klimke AG as well as Simon Glatz and Niklas Broghammer of Maurer Energie- und Ingenieurleistungen GmbH & Co. KG for provisioning the engineering diagrams used in this study.

Disclosure of Interests. The authors have no competing interests to declare that are relevant to the content of this article.

References

1. Baek, Y., Lee, B., Han, D., Yun, S., Lee, H.: Character region awareness for text detection. In: CVPR, pp. 9365–9374 (2019)
2. Caron, M., et al.: Emerging properties in self-supervised vision transformers. In: ICCV (2021)
3. Chen, T., Kornblith, S., Norouzi, M., Hinton, G.: A simple framework for contrastive learning of visual representations. In: III, H.D., Singh, A. (eds.) ICML. Proceedings of Machine Learning Research, vol. 119, pp. 1597–1607 (2020)
4. Dutta, A., Zisserman, A.: The VIA annotation software for images, audio and video. In: ACM Multimedia, pp. 2276–2279 (2019)
5. Elyan, E., Jamieson, L., Ali-Gombe, A.: Deep learning for symbols detection and classification in engineering drawings. Neural Netw. **129**, 91–102 (2020)
6. Goodfellow, I., et al.: Generative adversarial nets. In: Ghahramani, Z., Welling, M., Cortes, C., Lawrence, N., Weinberger, K. (eds.) NIPS, vol. 27, pp. 2672–2680 (2014)
7. Hadsell, R., Chopra, S., LeCun, Y.: Dimensionality reduction by learning an invariant mapping. In: CVPR, vol. 2, pp. 1735–1742 (2006)
8. Hamilton, M., Zhang, Z., Hariharan, B., Snavely, N., Freeman, W.T.: Unsupervised semantic segmentation by distilling feature correspondences. In: ICLR (2022)
9. He, K., Fan, H., Wu, Y., Xie, S., Girshick, R.: Momentum contrast for unsupervised visual representation learning. In: CVPR, pp. 9729–9738 (2020)
10. Howard, A., et al.: Searching for mobilenetv3. In: ICCV, pp. 1314–1324 (2019)
11. IEA: Energy systems buildings database (2024). https://www.iea.org/energy-system/buildings. Accessed 11 Mar 2025
12. Jamieson, L., Moreno-García, C., Elyan, E.: A review of deep learning methods for digitisation of complex documents and engineering diagrams. Artif. Intell. Rev. **57**, 136 (2024)
13. Joy, J., Mounsef, J.: Automation of material takeoff using computer vision. In: IAICT, pp. 196–200 (2021)
14. Kim, H., et al.: Deep-learning-based recognition of symbols and texts at an industrially applicable level from images of high-density piping and instrumentation diagrams. Expert Syst. Appl. **183**, 115337 (2021)
15. Kingma, D.P., Ba, J.: Adam: a method for stochastic optimization. In: Bengio, Y., LeCun, Y. (eds.) ICLR (2015)
16. Koch, G., Zemel, R., Salakhutdinov, R.: Siamese neural networks for one-shot image recognition. In: ICML (2015)
17. Lin, T.Y., et al.: Microsoft coco: common objects in context. In: Fleet, D., Pajdla, T., Schiele, B., Tuytelaars, T. (eds.) ECCV, pp. 740–755 (2014)

18. Lowe, D.: Object recognition from local scale-invariant features. In: ICCV, vol. 2, pp. 1150–1157 (1999)
19. Moreno-García, C.F., Elyan, E., Jayne, C.: New trends on digitisation of complex engineering drawings. Neural Comput. Appl. **31**(6), 1695–1712 (2019)
20. OpenAI: Hello gpt-4o (2024). https://openai.com/index/hello-gpt-4o/. Accessed 11 Mar 2025
21. Paliwal, S., Jain, A., Sharma, M., Vig, L.: Digitize-pid: automatic digitization of piping and instrumentation diagrams. In: Gupta, M., Ramakrishnan, G. (eds.) PAKDD, pp. 168–180 (2021)
22. Paliwal, S., Sharma, M., Vig, L.: Ossr-pid: one-shot symbol recognition in p&id sheets using path sampling and GCN. In: IJCNN, pp. 1–8 (2021)
23. Payandeh, A., Baghaei, K.T., Fayyazsanavi, P., Ramezani, S.B., Chen, Z., Rahimi, S.: Deep representation learning: fundamentals, technologies, applications, and open challenges. IEEE Access **11**, 137621–137659 (2023)
24. Rahul, R., Paliwal, S., Sharma, M., Vig, L.: Automatic information extraction from piping and instrumentation diagrams. In: Marsico, M.D., di Baja, G.S., Fred, A.L.N. (eds.) ICPRAM, pp. 163–172 (2019)
25. Redmon, J., Divvala, S., Girshick, R., Farhadi, A.: You only look once: unified, real-time object detection. In: CVPR, pp. 779–788 (2016)
26. Ren, S., He, K., Girshick, R., Sun, J.: Faster R-CNN: towards real-time object detection with region proposal networks. In: Cortes, C., Lawrence, N., Lee, D., Sugiyama, M., Garnett, R. (eds.) NIPS, vol. 28, pp. 91–99 (2015)
27. Roth, K., Pemula, L., Zepeda, J., Schölkopf, B., Brox, T., Gehler, P.: Towards total recall in industrial anomaly detection. In: CVPR, pp. 14318–14328 (2022)
28. Samet, H., Soffer, A.: Magellan: map acquisition of geographic labels by legend analysis. Int. J. Doc. Anal. Recogn. **1**, 89–101 (1998)
29. Sarkar, S., Pandey, P.K., Kar, S.: Automatic detection and classification of symbols in engineering drawings. arXiv preprint arXiv:2204.13277 (2022)
30. Schroff, F., Kalenichenko, D., Philbin, J.: Facenet: a unified embedding for face recognition and clustering. In: CVPR, pp. 815–823 (2015)
31. Stinner, F., Wiecek, M., Baranski, M., Kümpel, A., Müller, D.: Automatic digital twin data model generation of building energy systems from piping and instrumentation diagrams. In: ECOS, pp. 2854–1865 (2021)
32. Theisen, M.F., Flores, K.N., Schulze Balhorn, L., Schweidtmann, A.M.: Digitization of chemical process flow diagrams using deep convolutional neural networks. Digital Chem. Eng. **6**, 100072 (2023)
33. Wu, Z., Xiong, Y., Yu, S.X., Lin, D.: Unsupervised feature learning via non-parametric instance discrimination. In: CVPR, pp. 3733–3742 (2018)
34. Xiao, X., Li, Z., Zhao, S., Yang, L., Zhao, F., Ge, C.: Improved p&id symbol detection algorithm based on yolov5 network. In: SMC, pp. 120–126 (2023)
35. Yu, E.S., Cha, J.M., Lee, T., Kim, J., Mun, D.: Features recognition from piping and instrumentation diagrams in image format using a deep learning network. Energies **12**(23), 4425 (2019)

Denoising Diffusion Implicit Models for Laser-Plasma Accelerator Simulation Trained With Physical Constraint Loss

Matěj Jech[1,2(✉)], Gabriele Maria Grittani[2], Carlo Maria Lazzarini[2], and Alexander Kovalenko[1]

[1] Czech Technical University in Prague, Thákurova 9,Prague, Czechia
{jechmate,alexander.kovalenko}@fit.cvut.cz
[2] The Extreme Light Infrastructure ERIC,Za Radnicí 835,Dolní Břežany, Czechia
{matej.jech,gabrielemaria.grittani,carlomaria.lazzarini}@eli-beams.eu

Abstract. The paper addresses simulating laser wakefield electron acceleration experiments by using a novel training methodology for probabilistic diffusion models with adherence to the foundational physical principles. The methodology allows overcoming the inability of the common generative machine learning models to capture external data manifold constraints due to the nature of training. Laser wakefield electron acceleration is a highly complex non-linear phenomenon with a developed approximation theory, which, however, falls short in many extreme cases. Applying a model trained with physical constraint loss to simulate these experiments demonstrates strong performance and produces results that are positively evaluated by experts in the field. Moreover, due to the embedded physical information, it can extrapolate outside the range of training input data, based on the known physics of the process. This approach shows immense potential for using generative models in the modeling of complex scientific experiments, which helps in efficient experiment planning and optimization. We evaluate the generative models using Wasserstein distance calculated between distributions of charge of electrons at corresponding energies. This metric provides a robust quantification of the similarity between the predicted and reference electron energy spectra.

Keywords: Diffusion models · Laser wakefield electron acceleration · Physics-informed machine learning · Generative modeling

1 Introduction

Despite the overall success of probabilistic diffusion models in image generation [1], their application remains largely confined to entertainment and design, possessing significant underrepresentation in the broader practical domain. The limitations that hinder the application of probabilistic diffusion models in other domains arise from learning solely from visual and textual representations that

B. Pfahringer et al. (Eds.): ECML PKDD 2025, LNAI 16020, pp. 422–437, 2026.
https://doi.org/10.1007/978-3-662-72243-5_24

often do not reflect in learning of an actual world model. One of such limitations is the use of physical constraints in generated data [2]. Physics-informed neural networks [3–5] (PINNs) are a powerful tool for efficient learning the distribution of data adherent to the foundational physical principles. PINNs help in reducing the required amount of data by embedding physics as part of the loss function. This helps achieve more scientifically reasonable results given fewer experimental observations, as we do not rely solely on passive information present in the dataset. By incorporating physical constraints and specific we can enhance the model's ability to generate data that adheres to real-world physical phenomena.

One promising application of such physics-constrained diffusion models is in the optimization of particle accelerators. These powerful scientific instruments enable us to study the fundamental properties of matter and the universe [6]. One of the most significant discoveries made using particle accelerators is the Higgs boson, a fundamental particle that gives other particles mass. The Large Hadron Collider at CERN [7], the world's largest and most powerful particle accelerator, discovered the Higgs boson in 2012 [8], confirming a key prediction of the Standard Model of particle physics [9]. However, the development of laser-plasma accelerators has enabled significant miniaturization of particle accelerators, making them indispensable in various scientific fields. These devices are workhorses in myriad fields of science, blasting out fundamental particles and generating intense beams of X-rays for studies of biomolecules and materials. Using laser wakefield acceleration (LWFA) [10,11], kilometers-long devices [12] can be scaled down into a centimeters scale and, for example, the Large Hadron Collider, the biggest and most powerful of them all, potentially could fit in a classroom.

However, despite the main advantage - the compact size - laser wakefield electron accelerators are characterized by a plethora of non-linearly dependent parameters along with a high sensitivity to their changes [13]. Furthermore, these experiments are influenced by stochastic-like influences from temperature, lighting conditions, material deterioration or even other unknown sources. This makes the development and optimization of them a difficult task [14]. Therefore at the moment obtaining high-quality laser-plasma accelerated electron beams poses a significant challenge, given its crucial role in numerous applications of healthcare, notably in medical imaging [15,16], radiation medicine [17,18] and cancer treatment [19]. Additionally, they are invaluable in future research domains that would require accelerated particles, offering more compact and efficient alternatives to traditional accelerators. This process requires the careful manipulation of various interconnected physical phenomena, including plasma wave generation, electron injection, betatron radiation, and beam phase space evolution. The simulation of these processes demands sophisticated numerical methods and high-performance computational resources to solve the governing equations, namely Maxwell's and relativistic fluid equations. Conducting experiments to optimize these beams is complex and costly due to the nonlinear, transient nature of laser-plasma interactions and the plethora of instabilities that arise. Furthermore, the experimental parameter space is extremely high-dimensional, encompassing numerous variables from both the laser system (such as pulse energy, duration, and focusing conditions) and electron acceleration (including plasma density, interaction length, and injection conditions). This multitude of inter-connected parameters creates a prohibitively large search space for optimizing experimental outcomes.

To address these challenges, the adoption of artificial intelligence and generative deep learning models, such as Denoising Diffusion Probabilistic Models (DDPM) or those based on Nonequilibrium Thermodynamics, can prove beneficial. Diffusion models, which employ physics-inspired diffusion processes to iteratively refine a random initial state into a sample from the target distribution, have gained significant recognition for their capability to model complex, inherently probabilistic, high-dimensional distributions. In their comprehensive review, Däpp et al. [20] provided a detailed analysis of machine learning applications in laser-plasma science, demonstrating how various data-driven techniques have transformed experimental design, theoretical modeling, and diagnostic analysis

These models can be used to conditionally generate novel electron beam spectra based on the input parameters, effectively augmenting the search space without necessitating additional expensive and time-consuming experiments. This approach allows for more efficient exploration of the parameter space and increases the probability of identifying optimal conditions.

By integrating reinforcement learning agents [21] or other optimization algorithms [22] with the diffusion model, the search process can be guided more efficiently, learning the complex dependencies within the data. Feedback from the experiments, based on the parameters suggested by the model, can be utilized to further refine the model, thereby enhancing its predictive power and the quality of the generated samples. Consequently, this approach establishes a virtuous cycle of learning and optimization, demonstrating the potential of combining physics and AI to tackle this complex challenge. Bayesian optimization has already proven to be a viable tool for LWFA experimental parameter tuning achieving an increase in both stability and electron energy [13,14].

Therefore the present article is focused on developing a probabilistic diffusion model that takes into account physical theory related to particle acceleration induced by laser. Given the complexity of the data from the experiments and, often, the high cost of scientific trials, generative models based on physics-informed probabilistic diffusion models for spectral generation can be extremely beneficial for experimental design as they can support and accelerate scientific discovery by augmenting a search space for the conducted experiments.

2   Laser-Plasma Accelerator Setup

The key apparatus in these experiments was the laser system, operating at a frequency of 1 kHz and delivering high pulse energy at approximately 26 mJ. This multi-cycle, 15 fs pulse laser, based on optical parametric chirped pulse amplification (OPCPA) technology, was pivotal in enabling laser wakefield acceleration

(LWFA). Unlike earlier systems requiring single-cycle pulses, the design proved capable of achieving electron beam energies up to 50 MeV at a high repetition rate, showcasing a 25% energy spread and 2 mrad beam divergence. [23]

The laser was directed toward a gas target, composed either of pure nitrogen or a nitrogen-helium mixture of gases. Upon laser interaction, the gas undergoes ionization, forming plasma. As the laser traverses the plasma, it generates a wakefield in its trail. Electrons within the plasma are then drawn into this wakefield and accelerated to high energies, essentially "surfing" [24] in a trajectory parallel to the laser's path. The accelerated electron beam is directed toward a spectrometer equipped with a LANEX Fast Back scintillator screen. The interaction of electrons with the screen results in luminescence at the points of impact, enabling their detection and capture via a camera [25].

Another aspect of this setup is the incorporation of a 5mm aluminum slit and a magnetic dipole positioned before the screen. The magnet's role is to deflect the electron beam, causing a displacement relative to the beam's original path. By analyzing this displacement and applying a deflection curve specific to the experimental setup geometry, it is possible to measure the energy levels of the electrons striking the screen. The slit is used to center the spectrometer on the average electron beam pointing. A detailed illustration of the experimental setup is depicted in Fig. 1, providing a comprehensive visual overview of the entire process and apparatus.

During the experiments, the electron beams were generated with energies reaching up to 50 MeV, additionally characterized by a low energy spread. It was observed that small changes in the laser and plasma parameters significantly affected the energy distribution of accelerated electrons. [23]

3   Data Processing Pipeline

The dataset obtained from the scientific group exhibited a high level of noise, resulting in grainy images. To mitigate this, the data was preprocessed using a median filter with a kernel size of 5. A larger kernel did not appear to improve noise removal significantly. Additionally, the images were taken by the camera with a damaged sensor making parts of the images contain irrelevant outlying values. These parts were manually set to 0 as is usually the background value. Fortunately, these errors never appear near the electron beams and therefore such treatment is sufficient.

The Lanex screen, which is hit by accelerated electrons, has black dots arranged in a cross shape to facilitate distance calculations. These dots obscured the image and needed to be removed. This process was automated using a dot-detection algorithm. The image is first converted to binary using adaptive thresholding. The main parameters are *blockSize*, which controls the size of the neighborhood used to calculate the segmentation threshold, and C, a constant subtracted from the mean of the neighborhood to obtain the final threshold value. After experimentation, these parameters were set to 51 and 4 respectively. The dots were then detected using the circle Hough transform

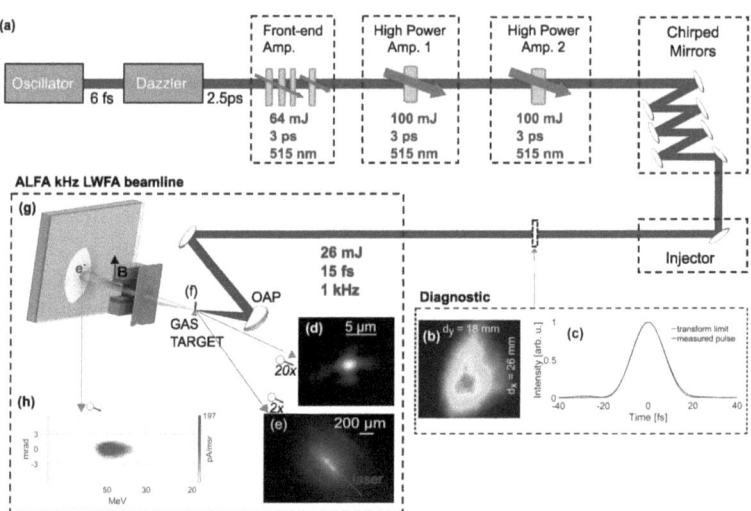

Fig. 1. From [23]: Experimental setup of the laser-plasma accelerator. (a) The laser system. (b, c, e) Various laser-related diagnostics. (d) View of the focal spot of the laser. (f) The gas-jet target of the laser. (g) Electron spectrometer. (h) Electron-beam trace projected on the Lanex screen.

[26]. The OpenCV [27] implementation was used with the following parameters: $minDist=20$, $param1=50$, $param2=7$, $minRadius=0$, $maxRadius=10$. This resulted in more detected dark dots in the image than actually present, which is preferable to the alternative. The black dots were then removed by interpolating along the x axis, meaning that the "removal" of non-existent dots had minimal effect on the resulting image given the gradient-like nature of the images.

In addition to the data with the magnet in the aperture, which is used to measure the energy of the electrons, there are corresponding datasets without the magnet used to acquire the position of the electron beam. This position is then used as a reference point when calculating the energy of the accelerated particles. The position of the electron beam was estimated by summing all images of a given experiment and then searching for the position of the maximum in the summed image. This point of highest intensity is taken as the center of the electron beam.

The original images contained large areas either outside of the Lanex itself or far from the electron beam pointing pixel, that did not contain any valuable information. The images were cropped to a height of 256 pixels and width of 512 pixels, with the electron pointing pixel fixed at coordinates [128, 62] (vertical and horizontal position). This position was selected because the vertical axis is similarly important, and on the horizontal axis, the deflection by the magnet occurs towards positive values of x. However, the image size was still excessive to be used as an input for training a DDIM with many convolutional layers and would require more VRAM than was available for this project. Cropping the images to a smaller size of 64 by 128 pixels resulted a significant information loss as many training data contained only lower energy electrons which would be deflected outside of the new horizontal image range. To overcome this issue, the images were resized using bilinear interpolation to a final size of 64 by 128 pixels before being used for training. At the end of the sampling process used for image generation, the images were resized back to the original size. Due to the gradient-like nature of most of the images, this process of repeating interpolation does not result in much loss in the fine detail of the images. The preprocessing pipeline demonstrated on one data sample can be seen in Fig. 2. The preprocessed dataset can be downloaded from this link.

The dataset consists of folders of images of electron spectra from 22 experiments with varying values of the following parameters:

- **E** - energy of the laser (12–26 mJ)
- **P** - pressure of the gas jet (10–38 Bar)
- **gas** - type of gas (Nitrogen or Helium/Nitrogen mixture)
- **ms** - acquisition time of the camera/opening time of the gas valve (10–40 ms)
- **gain** - gain setting on the camera

In the process of training the model, only a subset of the parameters, specifically **E**, **P**, and **ms**, were incorporated into the conditional vector. The rationale behind this selection was based on the relevance and variability of these parameters in the context of the experiments.

The parameter **gas**, which denotes the type of gas used in the experiments, was deliberately excluded from the conditional vector. This decision was driven by the fact that only two experiments were conducted using a gas mixture, while the rest employed Nitrogen. Consequently, the **gas** parameter exhibited very little variation across the dataset, rendering it less informative for the purpose of training the model.

Furthermore, both **gain** and **ms** are parameters that influence the brightness of the captured images. However, the **gain** parameter was not included in the conditional vector. The influence of the **gain** setting on the image brightness is deterministic, meaning it follows a predictable and consistent pattern. Therefore, its effect can be accounted for by subtracting it from the images during the preprocessing stage. This allows the model to focus on learning from the more variable and informative aspects of the data, potentially improving its performance and generalization ability.

The data was collected using a Basler aca2040-25gm camera. According to the official documentation [28], the formula for calculating gain is:

$$\text{Gain} = 20 * \log_{10}(\text{GainRaw}/32) \tag{1}$$

Here, *GainRaw* is the value set within the Basler Pylon Viewer through which camera settings were adjusted during the experiment. After recalculating the value of *Gain* from decibels (dB) to linear units, the gain value is used to adjust the brightness of the image. However, it was experimentally found that subtracting the gain value from the dataset causes the network to perform poorly during training. It is assumed to be caused by weak signal from dataset features. Therefore, the gain value was left as is. This may result in some inaccuracies when accessing the intensity of the generated samples which corresponds to the total charge of the accelerated electrons. However, this inaccuracy was deemed unsubstantial and a better alternative to poor training performance.

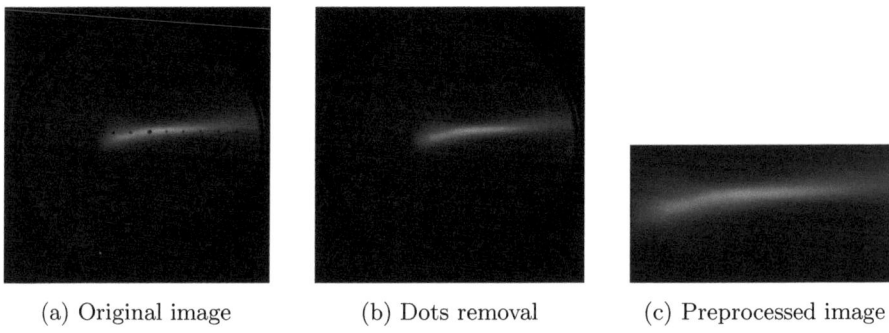

(a) Original image   (b) Dots removal   (c) Preprocessed image

Fig. 2. Data preprocessing pipeline.

4   Methodology

The full implementation can be found in the github repository including training, validation, sampling and all hyperparameters.

4.1   Denoising Diffusion Implicit Model

The proposed diffusion process adheres to the following distribution as introduced by Song et al. [29]:

$$q(\mathbf{X}_{t-1}|\mathbf{X}_t, \mathbf{X}_0) = \mathcal{N}(\sqrt{\alpha_{t-1}}\mathbf{X}_0 + \sqrt{1 - \alpha_{t-1} - \sigma_t^2}\frac{\mathbf{X}_t - \sqrt{\alpha_t}\mathbf{X}_0}{\sqrt{1 - \alpha_t}}, \sigma_t^2 I) \quad (2)$$

For the α_t noising parameters the cosine schedule was chosen based on its superior performance over a linear schedule [30].

The objective function for this model is most commonly defined as the MSE between the removed noise, $\tilde{\epsilon}_t$ and the actual noise ϵ_t, that was added during step t in the forward diffusion process. This is calculated over a batch of size B, as shown in the following equation:

$$MSE = \frac{1}{B}\sum_{j=1}^{B}(\epsilon_{t_j} - \tilde{\epsilon}_{t_j})^2 \quad (3)$$

The input image is processed through a U-Net architecture [31], which is composed of three downsampling and upsampling blocks. The initial processing stage involves a double-convolution block, which applies a 2D convolutional layer, group normalization, and a GELU activation function twice in succession. Following this, the first downsampling block is applied, which consists of a 2D maxpooling layer and two subsequent double-convolution blocks.

In addition to images, the network processes the settings vector and the noising step number. The settings vector, denoted as y, is processed through a block of layers, which includes batch normalization, a linear layer, and a SiLU activation. The noising step number, denoted as t, is encoded using positional encoding to provide the model with more nuanced information about the noise step beyond a single integer value. The tensors y and t are combined and serve as inputs to the network's Down and Up blocks, where they undergo further processing through a SiLU activation [32] and a linear layer before being added to the tensors derived from the image data. This approach equips the model with both conditional information and the remaining number of noise steps to be eliminated.

At the network's core, there are three double-convolution blocks, succeeded by the upsampling phase. The Up block mirrors the structure of the Down block, except for an upsampling layer replacing the maxpooling layer to enlarge the tensor dimensions. Layers are concatenated with a skip connection, utilizing the output from the corresponding Down block.

Each Down and Up block is followed by a SelfAttention [33] block. Initially, the input is reshaped to conform to the data ordering expected by the MultiheadAttention layer and is then normalized using layer normalization. The output is subsequently combined with the original input, followed by a sequence of layer normalization, linear transformation, GELU activation [34], and another linear transformation. Prior to reshaping the output to maintain consistency with the network's data ordering, the output of the MultiheadAttention layer is added once more. Overall the architecture of the model was hand-tailored, however we leveraged transfer learning [35] and used a subset of pre-trained convolutional filters from previous implementation of a DDPM model [36]. A simplified scheme of the architecture can be seen in Fig. 3.

The enhanced DDIM sampling sequence, as described in [29], was implemented utilizing the source code for the diffusion autoencoder [37]. This implementation leverages the underlying DDPM noising schedule to derive a new schedule with a reduced number of steps. Furthermore, it offers the flexibility to distribute the new steps non-uniformly, enabling a more precise focus on specific segments of the denoising process. A sample $\mathbf{X}_{t-1}$ can be generated from a sample $\mathbf{X}_t$ using the following equation [29]:

$$\mathbf{X}_{t-1} = \sqrt{\alpha_{t-1}} \underbrace{\left(\frac{\mathbf{X}_t - \sqrt{1-\alpha_t}\epsilon_\theta^{(t)}(\mathbf{X}_t)}{\sqrt{\alpha_t}} \right)}_{\text{predicted } \mathbf{X}_0} + \underbrace{\sqrt{1 - \alpha_{t-1} - \sigma_t^2} \cdot \epsilon_\theta^{(t)}(\mathbf{X}_t)}_{\text{direction pointing to } \mathbf{X}_t} + \underbrace{\sigma_t \epsilon_t}_{\text{random noise}}$$

(4)

Upon completion of the sampling process, the output image is reshaped to the desired dimensions. In the final implementation, this step is crucial for generating

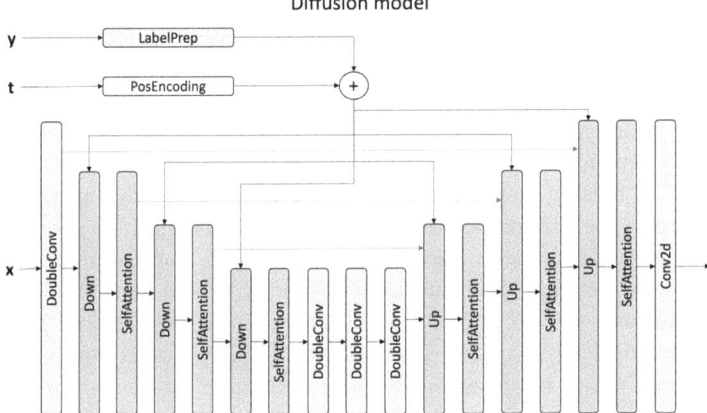

Fig. 3. A schematic of the model architecture. Black arrows show the flow of data, red arrows signify skip connections. (Color figure online)

the image in its original size, as the training dataset was previously rescaled to minimize computational demands.

4.2   Physical Constraint Loss

The physical constrained loss is defined in two parts corresponding to different aspects of the experiments. First, the ability of the model to precisely model the energy and charge of electrons is tested. This loss function is further referred to as L_{phys1}. Second, the model is penalized for generating electrons left of the electron-pointing beam. Such particles would have beyond infinite energy as their distance to the beam-pointing pixel relative to the magnet is negative. The loss corresponding to this constraint is termed L_{phys2}.

Both L_{phys1} and L_{phys2} use a partially noised image. L_{phys1} compares an image partially altered by the noise distribution learned by the model and an image noised by the forward diffusion process. L_{phys2} uses an image partially denoised by the model. Both L_{phys1} and L_{phys2} are controlled during training by a scheduled weight parameter. This weight is parameterized by the current denoising step number t. During the first steps where t is high, the constraint losses are virtually unused since the image is too noisy to discern any real features. For the schedule of the weight, a cosine schedule was chosen as it mirrors the approach used in the forward diffusion process. The formula for the scheduling is defined as:

$$\text{weight}_{\text{phys}}(t) = 0.5 \times \left(1 + \cos\left(\frac{t}{1000} \times \pi\right)\right) \tag{5}$$

Electron Beam Spectra Simulation. From each image of the accelerated electrons the total charge of electrons at a certain energy level can be calculated.

This is based on the distance of the deflected electrons from the original position of the electron beam. A training image, along with its calculated electron beam spectrum, is visualized in Fig. 4.

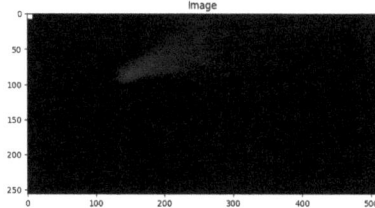 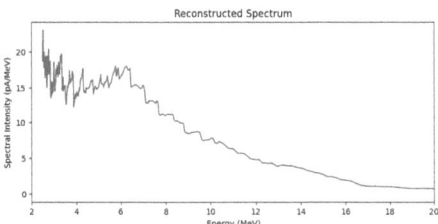

Fig. 4. An image from the training dataset with the 1D spectrum calculation. The image is rendered in monochrome, with a colormap applied to enhance visual clarity and facilitate easier interpretation.

This calculation is used for the first part of the physics constraint loss by calculating it from an image noised by the forward diffusion process and an image noised by the distribution learned by the model. This encourages the model to learn the distribution of noise more precisely by ensuring the noising process has little or no effect on the calculation of the spectra. The spectrum in MeV is calculated by using the deflection curve of the magnet inserted into the aperture. In the original script, this is done by interpolating between measured points of the curve of the magnet. For ease of loss computation we use a double exponential decay function:

$$f(d) = a_1 e^{-\lambda_1 d} + a_2 e^{-\lambda_2 d} \tag{6}$$

fitted as:

$$\hat{f}(d) \approx 77.86 e^{-0.47d} + 19.91 e^{-0.04d} \tag{7}$$

The spectrum is then calculated by taking the horizontal sum of the image denoted as x_{sum} into:

$$S(j) = \left\{ \frac{x_{\text{sum}}[j]}{\hat{f}(j-1) - \hat{f}(j)} \mid j \in \mathbb{Z}, 62 \leq i < \text{len}(\mathbf{X}) \right\} \tag{8}$$

where 62 is the position of the electron pointing pixel (point of infinity) and $\text{len}(\mathbf{X})$ is the horizontal size of the image. The spectrum is then calibrated by $C = 3.706$ which is a conversion value from pixel intensity to nA/MeV, the acquisition time t_{acq} and gain g by

$$S_{\text{MeV}}(x) = \frac{S(x) \cdot C}{t_{\text{acq}} \cdot g} \tag{9}$$

for a final loss of:

$$L_{\text{phys1}} = \text{MSE}\left(S_{\text{MeV}}(\mathbf{X}_t), S_{\text{MeV}}(\hat{\mathbf{X}}_t)\right) \tag{10}$$

where $\hat{\mathbf{X}}_t$ is the image noised by the reverse process learned by the model.

Electron Beam Pointing Pixel. The second part of the loss uses the fact that no electrons should appear left of the electron-pointing pixel as they would have an impossible higher than infinite energy. It uses a transition smoothed by a sigmoid function applied over the image. First, for defining the sigmoid transition at the correct area we need to define a calculation of horizontal distance as:

$$d_{X_i} = \{(i - 62) \cdot 0.137 \mid i \in \mathbb{Z}, -62 \leq i < \text{len}(\mathbf{X}) - 62\} \tag{11}$$

where 62 is the position of the electron beam, 0.137 is the ratio of pixels to millimeters specific to the experimental camera setup, i is the horizontal index of the pixel and $\text{len}(\mathbf{X})$ is the horizontal size of the image. This is then used in the final loss function as:

$$L_{phys2} = \frac{1}{n} \sum_{i=1}^{n} \left(\mathbf{X}\left(1 - \frac{1}{e^{-2 \cdot d\mathbf{x}_i}}\right)\right) \tag{12}$$

This approach to penalization, which is informed by the physical properties of the system under study, contributes to the robustness and accuracy of the model's performance. This enhances the model's ability to generate meaningful and reliable outputs. This condition could have been also fulfilled by a hard constraint where this area would not be generated by the model. However, the training data shows that some electrons do seldom appear in this region due to specific interactions with the magnetic field and therefore their distribution is also worthwhile to simulate.

5   Evaluation Metrics

We implemented a targeted cross-validation approach to evaluate our models, wherein each model underwent five training iterations. For each iteration, one experiment was withheld as a validation set. The five experiments were selected to maximize diversity in both experimental parameters and electron spectra distributions, ensuring robust evaluation across varied conditions.

Following the standard procedure for evaluating generative models we first used the Fréchet Inception Distance (FID) [38] metrics. Nevertheless, we argue that since the feature embeddings captured by the Inception model are designed for natural images they are consequently not suitable for evaluation of the nuanced physical properties present in electron spectra data.

Therefore, to address this limitation, we propose a more dataset specific evaluation approach based on the Wasserstein distance [39], which enables direct comparison of charge distributions across energy bins. For each validation experiment and its generated counterpart, we compute the one-dimensional spectra of charge versus electron energy according to Eqs. 8 and 9. Our methodology then calculates the Wasserstein distance between real and generated charge distributions for each energy bin, as formulated in Eq. 13:

$$W_w(\text{val}, \text{gen}) = \frac{1}{N} \sum_{i=1}^{N} w_i \cdot W_1(P_{\text{val}_i}, P_{\text{gen}_i}) \tag{13}$$

where W_w represents the weighted Wasserstein metric, N is the total number of energy bins, w_i is the weight assigned to the i-th energy bin, and $W_1(P_{\text{val}_i}, P_{\text{gen}_i})$ is the Wasserstein distance between the probability distributions of charge in the i-th energy bin for validation and generated samples, respectively.

This formulation offers significant flexibility for physics-specific evaluation. By adjusting the weight vector $\{w_i\}_{i=1}^{N}$, researchers can emphasize particular regions of interest in the energy spectrum. For instance, setting $w_i = 0$ for low-energy bins and $w_i = 1$ for high-energy bins enables focused evaluation of peak acceleration performance, which is often critical in electron acceleration experiments. The validation metric for each experiment is computed as the weighted mean across all bins, providing a comprehensive yet customizable assessment of model performance.

6   Results

The evaluation process was performed for a vanilla DDIM training approach and for the PCDDIM (physically constrained DDIM) introduced in this paper. The only difference between these two models and their training and sampling regime is the presence of the physical constraint loss in the PCDDIM. All of the training and validation models can be accessed from this link. The results can be seen in Table 1 over various classifier-free guidance [40] values. The results are averaged across various step counts ranging from 10 to 30 totaling 10 different runs per model and CFG value. The Wasserstein distance metric as described in Sect. 5 was used for energy bins corresponding to 30 McV or higher, disregarding the lower energy electrons and focusing more on peak energy. Across both models and metrics we can see a decrease in sampling quality as CFG increases. This is attributed to the recent findings in [41].

Furthermore, the increased accuracy of the PCDDIM can be seen in its ability to produce samples outside of the training data parameters range. From Fig. 5 it is apparent that the PCDDIM suggests electrons are being accelerated at laser energies of 40 mJ and above which is well aligned with other LWFA experimental data even though such experiments were not included in the training dataset. The proposed method can be further tested and validated outside the scope of available experimental data by using Particle-in-Cell (PIC) simulation data and comparing them to the generated results. [42]

Table 1. Comparison of Wasserstein distance and FID metrics for DDIM and PCDDIM models across different CFG values.

Metric	Model	CFG Values							
		1	2	3	4	5	6	7	8
Wasserstein	DDIM	**5.43**	9.56	13.95	16.34	19.33	21.46	22.13	23.47
	PCDDIM	17.98	16.94	17.17	19.38	21.01	24.4	23.62	27.73
FID	DDIM	107.11	111.56	111.74	114.20	115.75	116.03	118.41	121.11
	PCDDIM	**97.12**	101.32	103.49	104.99	106.62	107.57	108.70	109.29

(a) DDIM   (b) PCDDIM

Fig. 5. Comparison of average results between DDIM and PCDDIM when sampling at higher laser energies.

7   Conclusion

This paper presents a novel methodology that integrates physical principles into generative denoising diffusion models applied for the optimization of laser-plasma accelerators. The approach demonstrates notable improvements in modeling complex, high-dimensional distributions associated with laser wakefield electron acceleration experiments. By embedding physical constraints into the model's training process, PCDDIM not only improves the FID metric but also offers robust extrapolation capabilities beyond the range of training data. Additionally, due to the ability of the PCDDIM to operate outside of the training inputs, the outputs from the model were recognized by the experts in the field as more credible overall.

The above-described approach can be used for the conditional generation of multidimensional spectral data under physics constraints in various fields. This approach is believed to accelerate scientific discoveries by augmenting the search space of the experiments. Combination of PCDDIM with agent-based or other type of optimization can be a step forward in the efficient experimental design. The PCDDIM can be adapted to be used in other applications modeling highly non-linear interactions and parameter dependencies. The physical constraints need to be tailored specifically for each application and used within the proposed training scheme.

A specific metric tailored for electron spectra simulation was developed by comparing the distributions of charge over energy levels between generated and real samples. This offers a flexible approach to evaluation as one can assign significance to parts of the spectra. This can be used in optimization tasks by utilizing sampling settings which more closely model desirable parts of the spectrum.

Acknowledgments. This work was supported by the Student Summer Research Program 2023 of FIT CTU in Prague. This work was supported by the National Science Foundation and Czech Science Foundation under NSF-GACR collaborative Grant No. 2206059 from the NSF and Czech Science Foundation Grant No. 22-42963L.

Disclosure of Interests. The authors have no competing interests to declare that are relevant to the content of this article.

References

1. Croitoru, F.A., Hondru, V., Ionescu, R.T., Shah, M.: Diffusion models in vision: a survey. IEEE Trans. Patt. Analy. Mach. Intell. (2023)
2. Gori, M., Betti, A., Melacci, s.: A constraint-based approach. Elsevier, Machine Learning (2023)
3. Karniadakis, G.E., Kevrekidis, I.G., Lu, L., Perdikaris, P., Wang, S., Yang, L.: Physics-informed machine learning. Nat. Rev. Phys. **3**(6), 422–440 (2021)
4. Li, Z., Shu, D., Barati Farimani, A.: A physics-informed diffusion model for high-fidelity flow field reconstruction. **478**, 111972 (2022). ISSN 0021-9991. https://doi.org/10.1016/j.jcp.2023.111972
5. Bastek, J. H., Sun, W., Kochmann, D.M.: Physics-informed diffusion models (2024)
6. Sessler, A.: Engines of discovery: a century of particle accelerators. World Sci. (2014)
7. Myers, S.: The large hadron collider 2008–2013. Int. J. Mod. Phys. A **28**(25), 1330035 (2013)
8. Aaboud, M., et al.: Evidence for the associated production of the HIGGS boson and a top quark pair with the atlas detector. Phys. Rev. D **97**(7), 072003 (2018)
9. Gaillard, M.K., Grannis, P. D., Sciulli, F.J.: The standard model of particle physics. Rev. Modern Phys. **71**(2), S96 (1999)
10. Tajima, T., Dawson, J.M.: Laser electron accelerator. Phys. Rev. Lett. **43**(4), 267–270 (1979). ISSN 0031-9007. https://doi.org/10.1103/physrevlett.43.267
11. Sprangle, P., Esarey, E., Ting, A., Joyce, G.: Laser wakefield acceleration and relativistic optical guiding. Appl. Phys. Lett. **53**(22), 2146–2148 (1988)
12. Gibney, E.: How the revamped large hadron collider will hunt for new physics. Nature **605**(7911), 604–607 (2022). ISSN 1476-4687. https://doi.org/10.1038/d41586-022-01388-6
13. Jalas, S., et al.: Bayesian optimization of a laser-plasma accelerator. **126**(10), 104801. ISSN 1079-7114. https://doi.org/10.1103/physrevlett.126.104801
14. Shalloo, R.J., et al.: Automation and control of laser wakefield accelerators using bayesian optimization **11**(1). ISSN 2041-1723. https://doi.org/10.1038/s41467-020-20245-6
15. Brümmer, T., Debus, A., Pausch, R., Osterhoff, J., Grüner, F.: Design study for a compact laser-driven source for medical x-ray fluorescence imaging. Phys. Rev. Accelerators Beams, **23**(3), 031601 (2020). ISSN 2469-9888. https://doi.org/10.1103/physrevaccelbeams.23.031601

16. Cole, J.M., et al.: Laser-wakefield accelerators as hard x-ray sources for 3d medical imaging of human bone. Sci. Reports **5**(1) (2015). ISSN 2045-2322. https://doi.org/10.1038/srep13244

17. Chiu, C., et al.: Laser electron accelerators for radiation medicine: a feasibility study. Med. Phys. **31**(7), 2042–2052 (2004). ISSN 2473-4209. https://doi.org/10.1118/1.1739301

18. Giulietti, A.: Laser-driven particle acceleration towards radiobiology and medicine. BMPBE, Springer, Cham (2016). https://doi.org/10.1007/978-3-319-31563-8

19. Nicks, B.S., Tajima, T., Roa, D., Nečas, A., Mourou, G.: Laser-wakefield application to oncology. Int. J. Modern Phys. A **34**(34), 1943016 (2019). ISSN 1793-656X. https://doi.org/10.1142/s0217751x19430164

20. Döpp, A., Eberle, C., Howard, S., Irshad, F., Lin, J., Streeter, M.: Data-driven science and machine learning methods in laser-plasma physics. https://doi.org/10.48550/ARXIV.2212.00026

21. Mehta, V., Paria, B., Schneider, J., Ermon, S., Neiswanger, W.: An experimental design perspective on model-based reinforcement learning. arXiv preprint arXiv:2112.05244 (2021)

22. Greenhill, S., Rana, S., Gupta, S., Vellanki, P., Venkatesh, S.: Bayesian optimization for adaptive experimental design: a review. IEEE Access **8**, 13937–13948 (2020)

23. Lazzarini, C.M., et al.: Ultrarelativistic electron beams accelerated by terawatt scalable khz laser. Phys. Plasmas **31**(3) (2024). ISSN 1089-7674. https://doi.org/10.1063/5.0189051

24. Tajima, T., Yan, X.Q., Ebisuzaki, T.: Wakefield acceleration. Rev. Modern Plasma Phys. **4**(1), 1–72 (2020). https://doi.org/10.1007/s41614-020-0043-z

25. Zymak, I., et al.: Characterization of KHZ repetition rate laser-driven electron beams by an inhomogeneous field dipole magnet spectrometer. Photonics **11**(12), 1208 (2024). ISSN 2304-6732. https://doi.org/10.3390/photonics11121208

26. V C Hough, P.: Method and means for recognizing complex patterns (1962). URL https://patents.google.com/patent/US3069654A/en

27. Bradski, G.: The OpenCV Library. Dr. Dobb's Journal of Software Tools (2000)

28. Basler, A.G.: Gain - basler product documentation. https://docs.baslerweb.com/gain (2023). Accessed (2024)

29. Song, J., Meng, C., Ermon, S.: Denoising diffusion implicit models. https://doi.org/10.48550/ARXIV.2010.02502

30. Dhariwal, P., Nichol, A.: Improved denoising diffusion probabilistic models. https://doi.org/10.48550/ARXIV.2102.09672

31. Ronneberger, O., Fischer, P., Brox, T.: U-net: convolutional networks for biomedical image segmentation. https://doi.org/10.48550/ARXIV.1505.04597

32. Nwankpa, C., Ijomah, W., Gachagan, A., Marshall, S.: Activation functions: Comparison of trends in practice and research for deep learning. arXiv preprint arXiv:1811.03378 (2018)

33. Vaswani, A., et al.: Attention is all you need (2017). https://doi.org/10.48550/ARXIV.1706.03762

34. Hendrycks, D., Gimpel, K.: Gaussian error linear units (gelus). arXiv preprint arXiv:1606.08415 (2016)

35. Shin, H.-C., et al.: Deep convolutional neural networks for computer-aided detection: CNN architectures, dataset characteristics and transfer learning. IEEE Trans. Med. Imaging **35**(5), 1285–1298 (2016)

36. Karras, T., Aittala, M., Aila, T., Laine, S.: Elucidating the design space of diffusion-based generative models. https://doi.org/10.48550/ARXIV.2206.00364

37. Preechakul, K., Chatthee, N., Wizadwongsa, S., Suwajanakorn, S.: Diffusion autoencoders: toward a meaningful and decodable representation. https://doi.org/10.48550/ARXIV.2111.15640

38. Heusel, M., Ramsauer, H., Unterthiner, T., Nessler, B., Hochreiter, S.: Gans trained by a two time-scale update rule converge to a local nash equilibrium. Adv. Neural Inf. Process. Syst. 30 (NIPS 2017) (2017). https://doi.org/10.48550/ARXIV.1706.08500

39. Kantorovich, L.V.: Mathematical methods of organizing and planning production. Manage. Sci. **6**(4), 366–422 (1960). ISSN 1526-5501. https://doi.org/10.1287/mnsc.6.4.366

40. Ho, J., Salimans, T.: Classifier-free diffusion guidance. https://doi.org/10.48550/ARXIV.2207.12598

41. Kynkäänniemi, T., Aittala, M., Karras, T., Laine, S., Aila, T., Lehtinen, J.: Applying guidance in a limited interval improves sample and distribution quality in diffusion models. InProc, NeurIPS (2024)

42. Valenta, P., Esirkepov, T.Z., Ludwig, J.D., Wilks, S.C., Bulanov, S.V.: Bayesian optimization of electron energy from laser wakefield accelerator (2025). https://doi.org/10.1103/knh7-hbr3

RAID: Root Cause Anomaly Identification and Diagnosis

Joël Roman Ky[1,2（✉）], Bertrand Mathieu[3], Abdelkader Lahmadi[1], Minqi Wang[3], Nicolas Marrot[3], and Raouf Boutaba[4]

[1] Université de Lorraine, CNRS, Inria, LORIA, 54000 Nancy, France
abdelkader.lahmadi@loria.fr
[2] University of Luxembourg, Esch-sur-Alzette, Luxembourg
joel.ky@uni.lu
[3] Orange Innovation, Lannion, France
{bertrand2.mathieu,minqi.wang,nicolas.marrot}@orange.com
[4] David R. Cheriton School of Computer Science, University of Waterloo, Waterloo, Canada
rboutaba@uwaterloo.ca

Abstract. Wi-Fi networks are widely used for modern connectivity but remain vulnerable to impairments such as bandwidth fluctuations, interference, packet loss and latency spikes. These challenges make it difficult to support latency-sensitive applications like Cloud Virtual Reality (Cloud VR), which offloads intensive computation to remote servers to reduce local hardware requirements but demands high throughput and ultra-low latency. Consequently, Wi-Fi network degradations can severely impact the Quality of Experience (QoE) of such applications. Traditional Root Cause Diagnosis (RCD) approaches rely on expert-defined rules or supervised ML (Machine Learning) models that require extensive labeled datasets. This dependence on manual labeling makes them costly, time-consuming, and impractical for real-world Wi-Fi diagnostics.

To overcome these limitations, we introduce RAID (Root cause Anomaly Identification and Diagnosis), a two-stage ML framework that diagnoses Wi-Fi performance issues using time series KPIs collected directly from the Wi-Fi access point, with Cloud VR serving as a use case. RAID combines contrastive learning-based anomaly detection with a lightweight classifier to categorize network impairments. We evaluate RAID, with a real-world Cloud VR use case, in a testbed using NVIDIA CloudXR and a Meta Quest 2, collecting Wi-Fi performance metrics on the access point, under controlled conditions. Results demonstrate that RAID outperforms existing RCD methods, achieving high accuracy even with minimal labeled data. Compared to conventional supervised and self-supervised time series models, RAID offers a scalable, real-time solution with a good trade-off between training efficiency and inference speed, making it well-suited for practical deployment in dynamic Wi-Fi network environments.

© The Author(s), under exclusive license to Springer Nature Switzerland AG 2026
B. Pfahringer et al. (Eds.): ECML PKDD 2025, LNAI 16020, pp. 438–455, 2026.
https://doi.org/10.1007/978-3-662-72243-5_25

Keywords: Wi-Fi Networks · Root Cause Diagnosis · Cloud VR · Anomaly Detection · Contrastive Learning · Time Series Classification

1   Introduction

Wi-Fi has become the dominant access technology for modern networks, offering flexibility and convenience. However, unlike wired connections, Wi-Fi is inherently unreliable due to environmental factors, interference from coexisting devices, bandwidth fluctuations, latency spikes, and packet loss. These impairments make it challenging to support the new generation of latency-sensitive applications, which demand both high throughput and ultra-low latency to maintain seamless performance. These emerging applications such as cloud gaming, telemedicine, cloud robotics, and Cloud Virtual Reality (Cloud VR) particularly suffer from these Wi-Fi limitations. Cloud VR, for instance, offloads intensive computation to remote servers, allowing for lightweight and cost-effective VR headsets. However, delivering high-resolution (4K–8K) immersive experiences requires substantial bandwidth (≥ 80 Mbps) and ultra-low latency (≤ 20 ms), making reliable performance over Wi-Fi networks a critical challenge. Network degradations in this context lead to lag, visual artifacts, and even cybersickness, ultimately disrupting immersive VR interactions.

Root Cause Diagnosis (RCD) plays a crucial role in identifying, predicting, and mitigating Wi-Fi-related network issues. Traditional RCD approaches rely on expert-defined heuristics to analyze Key Performance Indicators (KPIs). While useful in simple scenarios, these methods are manual, time-consuming, and struggle to scale in modern dynamic wireless environments. Recent advancements in Machine Learning (ML) and Time Series Classification (TSC) have enabled automated analysis of KPIs data, capturing temporal dependencies for improved anomaly detection. However, supervised TSC methods require large labeled datasets, which are costly and time-intensive to annotate, limiting their real-world applicability. As a result, there is a growing need for data-driven RCD approaches that reduce dependency on labeled data while maintaining high accuracy.

To address these challenges, we propose Root cause Anomaly Identification and Diagnosis (RAID), a two-stage ML framework for diagnosing Wi-Fi performance degradation, with Cloud VR used as a representative use case. In Stage one, a contrastive learning-based anomaly detection model differentiates normal from anomalous KPI patterns without requiring labeled samples. In Stage two, once anomalies are detected, a lightweight supervised classifier categorizes them into specific Wi-Fi impairments. We evaluate RAID using time series KPIs collected from a real-world Cloud VR testbed that emulates realistic network degradations under controlled conditions, using off-the-shelf devices and equipment, with user traffic generated by the Cloud VR game Beat Saber. This setup ensures that all collected data are real and representative of operational deployments. Although our experiments focus on Cloud VR, the RAID framework itself is domain-agnostic and can be readily applied to other root cause diagnosis scenarios by adapting the input KPIs. Our results demonstrate that RAID outperforms existing methods, even with limited labeled data, offering a scalable, efficient, and real-time root-cause diagnosis solution for Wi-Fi networks supporting latency-sensitive applications. Specifically, the key contributions of this paper are as follows:

- We set up a controlled Wi-Fi testbed that faithfully replicates an operational network setup using the same commercial hardware. This environment can replicate real-world network impairments, enabling reproducible and realistic evaluation of Cloud VR performance under degraded conditions.
- We introduce a novel two-stage framework that combines contrastive learning-based anomaly detection with supervised classification to effectively detect and diagnose Wi-Fi impairments.
- We perform extensive empirical evaluations using time series KPI datasets collected from our testbed, comparing our proposed solution with state-of-the-art time series classification models.
- Our solution demonstrates strong performance even in low-label scenarios, highlighting its ability to generalize with minimal supervision. Additionally, it offers a balanced trade-off between moderate training time and low inference latency, making it well-suited for real-time deployment in practical Wi-Fi diagnostic applications.

2   Related Work

ML-Based Network Root Cause Diagnosis: Root Cause Diagnosis aims to identify the sources of network anomalies such as degraded performance or failures. The rise of ML has led to supervised and unsupervised approaches for network diagnosis. Supervised methods [10,11,21] have been used to troubleshoot Wi-Fi impairments [21] and classify home network issues using transformers [11]. Unsupervised approaches such as the two-stage VAE-MLP framework by Fida et al. [13] detect bottlenecks in cloudified 5G networks. Our work extends these efforts by incorporating contrastive learning for anomaly detection, reducing reliance on labeled data while enhancing root cause classification for low-latency Wi-Fi environments.

Time Series Classification: Time Series Classification (TSC) plays a key role in network diagnostics. Traditional approaches include distance-based [2], interval-based [9], shapelet-based [4], and ensemble-based [3] methods. More recently, deep learning architectures [30,31] have improved classification performance but require extensive labeled data. Self-Supervised Learning (SSL) has emerged as a scalable alternative, with frameworks like T-Loss [14], TNC [22], TS-TCC [12], TF-C [29] or TS2Vec [28] to further improve feature extraction by learning meaningful representations from unlabeled data. Our method leverages a two-stage TSC approach, where anomaly detection precedes classification, ensuring more accurate impairment diagnosis.

Anomaly Detection Techniques: Anomaly Detection (AD) methods span statistical models and deep learning approaches. Statistical methods include parametric (ARIMA [26], Gaussian-based [18]) and non-parametric (KDE [5]). Distance-based [6] and spectral-based [19] methods analyze distributional patterns, while isolation-based models [17] identify anomalies based on recursive partitioning. Deep learning-based AD captures complex temporal dependencies using autoencoders (AEs, VAEs) [25], gaussian models [32], RNN-based methods [20], and transformer-based solutions [23]. Contrastive learning further enhances AD, with models like COCA [24], ContrastAD [16], and CARLA [8] improving representation learning, while DCdetector [27] refines spatial-temporal feature extraction. Our approach integrates contrastive learning in a two-stage RCD framework, effectively detecting and classifying impairments for real-time Cloud VR over Wi-Fi.

3   Proposed Method

We propose RAID, a two-stage root cause diagnosis framework for Cloud VR over Wi-Fi, formulated as a time series classification problem. Given a dataset $\mathcal{D}_{train} = \{(w_1, y_1), \ldots, (w_T, y_T)\}$ of multivariate time series KPIs, RAID consists of **1) an Anomaly Detection stage:** that identifies deviations from normal network behavior using contrastive learning and **2) a Root Cause Classification stage** that classifies detected anomalies into specific impairment types (Fig. 1).

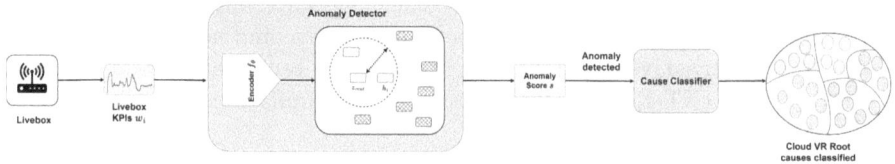

Fig. 1. RAID framework

3.1   Anomaly Detection Stage

The first stage identifies whether a time series is anomalous using a self-supervised anomaly detection approach based on contrastive learning. This approach eliminates the need for labeled data by leveraging only normal data collected during Cloud VR sessions without Wi-Fi impairments. Our anomaly detection module builds upon CATS (Contrastive learning for Anomaly detection in Time Series), a framework introduced in our previous work [15] that has demonstrated superior performance in time series anomaly detection. CATS enhances anomaly detection through synthetic anomaly generation and contrastive loss formulations, leveraging temporal dependencies to improve representation learning. Specifically, the anomaly detection model is trained using a combined global and temporal contrastive loss $\mathcal{L} = \frac{1}{2}(\mathcal{L}_{TCL} + \mathcal{L}_{GCL})$, ensuring robust detection of anomalous patterns.

We briefly summarize the components of the anomaly detector below, and refer the reader to [15] for a detailed analysis of its design choices and experimental validation.

– **Data augmentation:** From an input window w_i, it generates a set of time series views through positive data augmentations such as jittering and scaling $\{w_i^+, w_{i+N}^+\}$, and introduces synthetic anomalies via masking or trend perturbations w_i^-.

– **Encoder:** Maps the augmented time series into a low-dimensional latent space $h_i = f_\theta(w_i)$. The encoder architecture is model-agnostic, supporting convolutional, recurrent, or transformer-based models.

– **Projection head:** A non-linear MLP that refines the latent representations for contrastive learning $z_i = g_\theta(h_i)$.

– **Temporal contrastive loss:** Utilizes a differentiable variant of DTW (Soft-DTW) to learn temporal similarities in representations using a triplet of views.

$$\mathcal{L}_{TCL} = \frac{1}{N} \sum_{i=1}^{N} \max\left(D^\gamma(h_i^+ - h_{i+N}^+) - D^\gamma(h_i^+ - h_i^-) + m, 0\right) \quad (1)$$

where $D^\gamma(.)$ is the Soft-DTW divergence measure, and m is the margin parameter (the minimum distance between positive and negative samples).

– **Global contrastive loss:** Uses a Normalized Temperature-Scaled Cross-Entropy Loss (NT-Xent) to learn global feature similarities with an extended set of negative pairs.

$$\mathcal{L}_{GCL} = \frac{1}{2N} \sum_{i \in \mathcal{B}^+} \log \frac{\exp(sim(z_i, z_{i+N})/\tau)}{\sum_{j \in \mathcal{B}, j \neq i} \exp(sim(z_i, z_j)/\tau)} \quad (2)$$

where $\mathcal{B}$ is the set of all views, N is the batch size, τ is the temperature hyperparameter, and $sim(.)$ is the cosine similarity.

– **Anomaly scoring:** After training, anomalies are detected by calculating the distance between the latent representation of an unseen time series and the centroid of normal representations. If the score exceeds a predefined threshold, the instance is classified as anomalous.

$$s(\tilde{w}_t) = \mathcal{D}(f_\theta(\tilde{w}_t), z_{cent}) = \mathcal{D}(\tilde{z}_t, \frac{1}{N_{train}} \sum_{i=1}^{N_{train}} z_i) \quad (3)$$

where $\mathcal{D}$ is the Euclidean distance.

3.2 Root Cause Classification

Once an anomaly is detected, the next step is to determine its underlying root cause. This stage is framed as a supervised classification problem, where the objective is to map each detected anomaly to a predefined class of root causes $\{cause_1, cause_2, \ldots, cause_{K-1}\}$. To ensure efficiency and simplicity, we use a shallow classifier such as logistic Regression or SVM despite the various techniques for supervised TSC that were proposed in the literature. This approach, as shown in the following sections, achieves high accuracy with minimal computational overhead, making it suitable for real-time deployment.

4 Testbed

In this section, we introduce our testbed, designed for controlled experiments to assess Cloud VR performance over Wi-Fi while systematically injecting real-world network impairments.

4.1 Wi-Fi Testbed for Controlled Experiments

To systematically evaluate Wi-Fi's impact on Cloud VR performance, we developed a controlled Wi-Fi testbed (Fig. 2), designed to replicate real-world network impairments while maintaining precise experimental control. The testbed consists of two primary layers:

– **Infrastructure layer:** The infrastructure layer provides the core hardware setup for Cloud VR streaming and controlled Wi-Fi experimentation thanks to four Faraday cages used to isolate equipment from external electromagnetic interference. It comprises a Cloud VR system based on a CloudXR streaming setup, where a high-performance server (equipped with Intel Xeon W2235 CPU @ 3.8 GHz, 32 GB RAM, and NVIDIA RTX 3090 Ti) renders OpenVR applications using GPU acceleration and streams VR content wirelessly to a Meta Quest 2 headset (in cage 1). It also includes a Wi-Fi network environment that consists of two Wi-Fi APs: AP1 (in cage 2) that serves as the primary network for Cloud VR streaming and is used for both normal and coverage experiments and AP2 (in cage 4) that introduces network interference thanks to a traffic generator generating competing UDP to a station (in cage 3). The Faraday cages are interconnected using coaxial cables to transmit Wi-Fi signals, and Radio Frequency (RF) attenuators are employed to simulate variations in signal strength during experiments.
– **Control and Automation layer:** This layer ensures reproducibility and facilitates real-time monitoring, automation, and data collection. It includes a VR PC controller connected to the VR headset via USB, responsible for managing headset settings and collecting performance metrics, such as KPIs from OVR Metrics tools[1] or quality-of-service (QoS) statistics from CloudXR. The

---

[1] https://developers.meta.com/horizon/downloads/package/ovr-metrics-tool/.

controller also automates game sessions using the Meta Quest Autodriver[2]. Additionally, this layer features an attenuator controller that configures and manages RF attenuators via APIs, enabling automated signal attenuation adjustments through FastAPI. Furthermore, the Livebox controller manages the Livebox via Telnet to collect Wi-Fi KPIs every 3 s. A local ELK Stack database aggregates data from all controllers for post-experiment analysis.

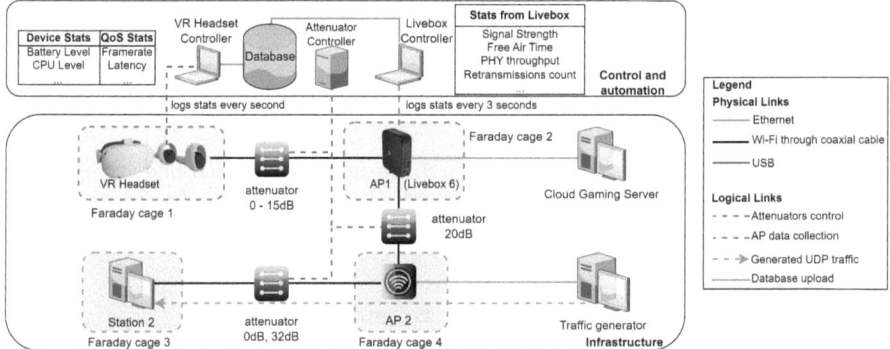

Fig. 2. Wi-Fi testbed for Cloud VR scenarios

4.2   Experimental Scenarios

Cloud VR experiments were conducted using the Beat Saber VR game as a benchmark across 2.4 GHz and 5 GHz Wi-Fi bands. Three experimental scenarios were evaluated:

- **Normal**: VR sessions under optimal conditions (RSSI: −45 dB (2.4 GHz), −65 dB (5 GHz), txops = 100%), with 5x 300 s sessions per band;
- **Coverage**: Signal attenuation simulated via RF attenuators at different RSSI levels (−55 to −65 dB for 2.4 GHz and −80 to −90 dB for 5 GHz). Further degradation was limited by system constraints: VR disconnects below −65 dB for 2.4 GHz, and −65 dB was the highest achievable for 5 GHz.;
- **Interference**: Interference was introduced by the station connected to AP2, occupying 9% to 15% of the transmission opportunities (txops) available on AP1 once the game started.

---

[2] https://developers.meta.com/horizon/documentation/unity/ts-autodriver.

4.3 Data Collection

With this testbed, three types of data can be collected: **i) Application-Level Metrics** that are extracted from the OVR Metrics Tool and CloudXR stack; **ii) Livebox-Level Metrics**: collected from the Wi-Fi AP, including RSSI, noise levels, airtime, MCS index, retry rates, and bitrate statistics; and **iii) Raw Traffic Captures**.

While the network impairments in our testbed are emulated in a controlled setting, the data used in this study is entirely real, collected directly from commercial hardware (Livebox, CloudXR stack, and Meta Quest 2) during representative Cloud VR sessions. The impairment scenarios are carefully designed to reproduce typical real-world conditions such as signal degradation, and interference. This setup enables reproducible experimentation while preserving the complexity and variability inherent to practical Wi-Fi deployments, thanks to the use of physical RF manipulation, real-time VR streaming, and traffic dynamics generated by actual application workloads, including interference created through competing traffic injected via a neighboring access point.

5 Evaluation Setup

5.1 Dataset Description

To evaluate our proposed solution, we utilize the time series datasets collected from the experimental testbed. Although our setup gathers KPIs from both the VR headset and the CloudXR stack, which provide insights into QoS and QoE during VR sessions, this study focuses exclusively on data retrieved from the Livebox. This choice is motivated by the practical accessibility of these metrics for network operators, who own and manage the Livebox. Leveraging these metrics for RCD allows for the development of smarter APs and more intelligent network management solutions, aligning closely with the operational needs of network operators.

The dataset consists of 112 time series features extracted from the Livebox. These features include signal strength indicators (e.g., RSRP, RSSI), transmission performance metrics (e.g., txops), channel utilization measures (e.g., air time), among others, offering a comprehensive view of Wi-Fi performance in various conditions. Monitoring was performed at a frequency of one sample every three seconds. To facilitate analysis, the data is structured into overlapping time series windows, each spanning 10 time steps (30 s per window). In total, the dataset (presented in Table 1) contains 13,657 time series windows, which are partitioned into training and testing subsets using a 70:30 split ratio categorized into three classes, corresponding to distinct experimental scenarios during data collection.

5.2 Competing Solutions

To demonstrate the effectiveness of RAID, we compare it against several baseline including one-stage and two-stage TSC models.

Table 1. Dataset Summary

Class	Train	Test	Features	Time Steps
Normal	4718	1924	112	10
Coverage	2984	1270	112	10
Interference	1822	939	112	10
Total	9524	4133	112	10

One-Stage Models

– **1-NN-DTW:** A nearest-neighbor classifier with Dynamic Time Warping (DTW), a strong baseline for time series classification [2].

We also include SSL time series representation learning methods that undergo pretraining before classification with an SVM classifier with an RBF kernel following the protocol outlined in [14].

– **T-Loss** [14]: A SSL approach that uses triplet loss with time-based negative sampling for generalizable representations.
– **TS-TCC** [12]: A SSL framework that combines weak/strong augmentations with temporal/contextual contrastive learning.
– **TS2Vec** [28]: A framework that learns both instance-wise and temporal-wise representations via a hierarchical contrastive objective.

Two-Stage Models. For the two-stage models, we replace RAID's anomaly detector with alternative unsupervised AD methods which are:

– **iForest** [17]: An isolation-based model that recursively partitions feature space to isolate anomalies.
– **USAD** [1]: Uses dual autoencoders in a min-max game with the first learns to reconstruct data and the second attempts to differentiate between true data and reconstructions.
– **SimCLR** [7]: A contrastive learning framework adapted for time series that learn representations from augmented views of data and can be used for AD.

5.3   Evaluation Metrics

We evaluate the performance of our root-cause diagnosis models using well-known multi-class classification metrics, including weighted Precision (P), weighted Recall (R), weighted F1-score (F1), Accuracy (Acc), and Normalized Accuracy (N-Acc). These metrics are defined as follows:

– **Precision:** The macro-weighted precision is the weighted average of precision values computed for each class, w_i being the proportion of class i:

$$P = \sum_{i=1}^{K} w_i \times P_i, \quad P_i = \frac{TP_i}{TP_i + FP_i} \tag{4}$$

- **Recall:** The macro-weighted recall is the weighted average of recall values computed for each class, w_i being the proportion of class i:

$$R = \sum_{i=1}^{K} w_i \times R_i, \quad R_i = \frac{TP_i}{TP_i + FN_i} \quad (5)$$

- **F1-Score:** The macro-weighted F1-score is the harmonic mean of macro-weighted Precision and Recall. This metric coupled P and R are suitable for imbalanced datasets.

$$F1 = 2 \times \frac{P \times R}{P + R} \quad (6)$$

- **Accuracy:** The fraction of correctly classified samples over the total number of samples. This metric is widely used and easy to interpret.
- **Normalized Accuracy (N-Acc):** This metric adjusts the balanced accuracy ($bac = \frac{1}{K} \sum_{i=1}^{K} w_i \times R_i$) which is the weighted average of the recall of each class with respect to the accuracy of random guessing (bac_{RG}), ensuring that random predictions score 0 while perfect predictions score 1. It is more interpretable and suitable for imbalanced datasets.

$$\text{N-Acc} = \frac{bac - bac_{RG}}{1 - bac_{RG}} \quad (7)$$

5.4 Implementation Details

All datasets are normalized and split into training and testing sets. The architecture and hyperparameters of the anomaly detection stage in RAID are directly inherited from our prior work on CATS [15]. Specifically, we employ a dilated CNN with 10 residual blocks as encoder and a three-layer MLP with ReLU activations as projection head. As the anomaly detection module is reused without modification, we do not repeat the extensive evaluation conducted on CATS, which includes ablation studies on the loss components and augmentation strategies. This paper focuses instead on the integration of the detection module into a complete root cause diagnosis pipeline and its evaluation in a realistic Wi-Fi testbed setting. The model is trained for 100 epochs using the Adam optimizer with a learning rate of 10^{-3} and a batch size of 512. Competing models are trained using their official implementations with consistent optimization settings. The classification stage is performed via an SVM with an RBF kernel, with hyperparameters tuned via grid search.

All experiments were conducted on an Ubuntu 22.04 with an AMD Ryzen 9 5900X CPU and an NVIDIA RTX 3090 Ti GPU (24 GB), using PyTorch 2.2.0 and CUDA 12.1. The code and datasets to reproduce all experiments are publicly available.[3]

---

[3] https://github.com/joelromanky/raid.

Table 2. Performance comparison on the datasets. Mean and standard deviation computed over five runs for Cloud VR datasets. Bold values indicate best results and underlined values the second best.

Models	Metrics	Accuracy	N-Accuracy	Precison	Recall	F1-score
One-stage	1-NN-DTW	$51.54_{(\pm 0.11)}$	$26.36_{(\pm 0.17)}$	$56.74_{(\pm 0.09)}$	$51.54_{(\pm 0.11)}$	$52.96_{(\pm 0.10)}$
	T-Loss	$79.47_{(\pm 4.39)}$	$\mathbf{75.22}_{(\pm \mathbf{5.58})}$	$\mathbf{83.98}_{(\pm \mathbf{4.74})}$	$\underline{79.47}_{(\pm 4.39)}$	$79.60_{(\pm 4.53)}$
	TS2Vec	$70.12_{(\pm 5.28)}$	$55.71_{(\pm 6.53)}$	$75.42_{(\pm 3.22)}$	$70.12_{(\pm 5.28)}$	$70.49_{(\pm 4.88)}$
	TS-TCC	$73.78_{(\pm 6.38)}$	$66.17_{(\pm 8.12)}$	$79.29_{(\pm 6.07)}$	$73.78_{(\pm 6.38)}$	$73.86_{(\pm 6.68)}$
Two-stage	iForest	$72.48_{(\pm 2.69)}$	$62.22_{(\pm 4.69)}$	$72.26_{(\pm 3.14)}$	$72.48_{(\pm 2.69)}$	$72.24_{(\pm 2.99)}$
	USAD	$72.22_{(\pm 0.80)}$	$63.39_{(\pm 1.36)}$	$72.72_{(\pm 0.97)}$	$72.22_{(\pm 0.80)}$	$72.38_{(\pm 0.84)}$
	SimCLR	$57.76_{(\pm 3.25)}$	$37.59_{(\pm 4.84)}$	$61.01_{(\pm 2.60)}$	$57.76_{(\pm 3.25)}$	$58.65_{(\pm 3.06)}$
	RAID	$\mathbf{81.83}_{(\pm \mathbf{2.96})}$	$\underline{74.80}_{(\pm 4.19)}$	$\underline{81.85}_{(\pm 3.02)}$	$\mathbf{81.83}_{(\pm \mathbf{2.96})}$	$\mathbf{81.60}_{(\pm \mathbf{3.05})}$

6   Results

6.1   Performance Evaluation

Table 2 summarizes the evaluation results of our solution compared to competing TSC methods using various performance metrics, including accuracy, normalized accuracy, precision, recall, and F1-score. The results highlight the superiority of our approach over both one-stage and two-stage methods.

Evaluation of One-Stage Models. One-stage models, including 1-NN-DTW, T-Loss, TS2Vec, and TS-TCC, directly perform root cause classification without a preliminary anomaly detection step. Among these models, 1-NN-DTW exhibits the lowest overall performance, with an accuracy of 51.54% and an F1-score of 52.96%. Despite being a strong baseline for TSC, it struggles to handle the complex time series data encountered in CloudVR scenarios.

Contrastive learning-based SSL models outperform 1-NN-DTW. Among them, T-Loss emerges as the most effective technique, achieving the highest normalized accuracy (75.22%) and precision (83.98%) within this category. This demonstrates its capability to learn meaningful representations for RCD tasks. TS-TCC follows with an accuracy of 73.78% and an F1-score of 73.86%, while TS2Vec achieves an accuracy of 70.12% and an F1-score of 70.49%.

Evaluation of Two-Stage Models. Two-stage models incorporate a preliminary anomaly detection step, enabling better focus on relevant patterns before root cause classification. iForest and USAD achieve comparable performance, with accuracy scores of 72.48% and 72.22%, respectively. Both models demonstrate strong F1-scores around 72%, yet they fall short of advanced one-stage approaches like T-Loss. Meanwhile, SimCLR performs suboptimally with an accuracy of 57.76% and an F1-score of 58.65%.

Our custom solution significantly outperforms all competing methods across most metrics. It achieves the highest accuracy (81.83%), recall (81.83%), and F1-score (81.60%), demonstrating robustness and effectiveness for CloudVR RCD. While T-Loss marginally outperforms in normalized accuracy and precision, our custom model achieves the best balance across all metrics, establishing it as the most reliable approach in this evaluation.

The superior performance of our solution can be attributed to the efficiency of its anomaly detection stage. As shown in Fig. 3, our solution outperforms other two-stage techniques in detecting anomalies across various well-known metrics. RAID achieves the best overall anomaly detection performance, which directly contributes to its effectiveness in RCD tasks.

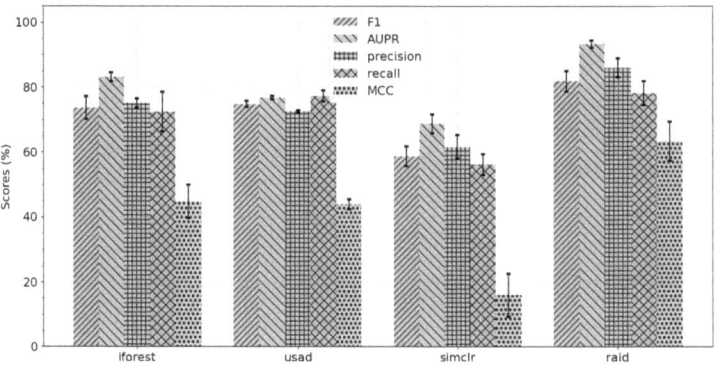

Fig. 3. Results of anomaly detectors of two-stage models.

Per-Class Performance Analysis. Figures 4 and 5 provide a detailed comparison of the per-class performance metrics for T-Loss and our custom solution. Our approach demonstrates a significant advantage in efficiently distinguishing normal scenarios from both coverage and interference scenarios.

For normal scenarios, our solution achieves a notably lower misclassification rate compared to T-Loss, with 1,761 correctly classified normal samples versus 1,350 for T-Loss. This represents a substantial improvement in detecting normal behavior. Additionally, our solution attains perfect classification for interference scenarios, with a recall of 100%, highlighting its robustness in detecting distinct anomaly patterns such as interference.

However, Fig. 5 also reveals the limitations of our solution. It struggles to discriminate coverage scenarios, with a considerable number of coverage windows misclassified as normal. This indicates challenges in capturing the subtle

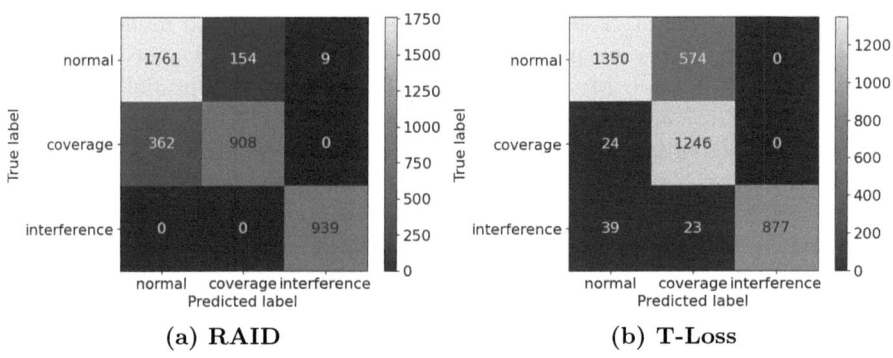

Fig. 4. Confusion matrix

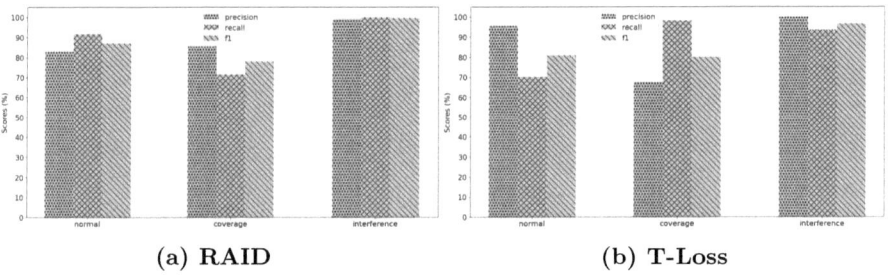

Fig. 5. Per-class precision, recall and F1-score.

variations and transitional patterns between normal and coverage states. In contrast, T-Loss, while less accurate overall, shows a more balanced performance in handling coverage scenarios.

This trade-off underscores the strengths and weaknesses of our model: it is highly effective in detecting clear-cut anomalies but requires further refinement to enhance its sensitivity to nuanced variations between normal and coverage states. Future work could focus on addressing this limitation by incorporating advanced feature extraction techniques or domain-specific data augmentation strategies.

6.2   Efficiency with Few Labels

Figure 6 illustrates the evolution of model performance as the percentage of labeled data increases. The left subplot depicts the accuracy scores across various label ratios, while the right subplot presents the corresponding F1-scores.

At the lowest label ratios (1%-5%), most models exhibit limited performance, reflecting the inherent difficulty of accurate RCD with minimal supervision. However, T-Loss and RAID stand out by achieving relatively higher accuracy and F1 scores, showcasing their ability to generalize effectively even with sparse labeled data. T-Loss benefits significantly from its triplet-based pretraining strategy, which efficiently captures meaningful representations from the unlabeled dataset, thereby enhancing fine-tuning performance. Similarly, the pretraining stage of RAID contributes to its robustness in low-label scenarios by effectively leveraging the anomaly detection process to prioritize relevant patterns.

As the label ratio increases, all models demonstrate steady improvement in performance, highlighting the benefits of additional labeled data. Notably, RAID and T-Loss consistently lead in performance, with our solution exhibiting a steady performance boost. This consistency underscores the robustness of RAID across varying levels of supervision. While T-Loss initially competes closely, its performance shows a slight decline between the 5% and 20% label ratios, coupled with increased variability, indicating potential sensitivity to the quality or distribution of labeled data in these ranges.

The findings from Fig. 6 highlight the efficiency of RAID in leveraging limited labeled data, making it an ideal solution for real-world scenarios where labeling is both expensive and time-consuming. Its performance with sparse labels, along with its stable scalability as more labeled data becomes available, firmly establishes RAID as the most suitable model in this evaluation.

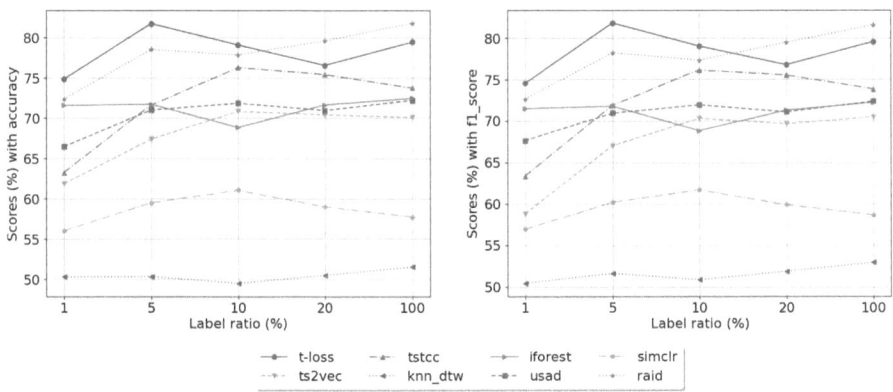

Fig. 6. Performance variation regarding the labels ratio.

6.3   Time Complexity

Figure 7 presents the training time (in seconds) and inference time per time series (in milliseconds) for each of the RCD models. The model with the longest training time is Triplet, which takes approximately 300 s, while the fastest training model is 1-NN-DTW, completing training in 500 ms. In terms of inference time, 1-NN-DTW significantly outpaces other models, with the highest inference time of 1800 ms. In contrast, models such as Triplet or TS-TCC, achieve inference times as low as 0.5 ms.

Our proposed solution, RAID, demonstrates a moderate training time of 200 s and an inference time of 3.5 ms. While this inference time is the second highest among the models compared, it is still well-suited for real-time deployment, especially in our testbed where data is collected at frequent intervals (e.g., every 3 s). This makes RAID an excellent choice for RCD, as it balances moderate training overhead with sufficiently low inference latency, allowing for continuous monitoring and fast anomaly detection. Additionally, being a two-stage model, RAID offers a key advantage: when new causes or anomalies are detected, only the supervised classifier requires retraining. Most of the training time originates from the initial anomaly detection phase, unlike one-stage models that require complete retraining, including the pretraining phase. This makes RAID more efficient for scenarios requiring periodic updates or retraining, reducing overall downtime and resource consumption.

In summary, RAID strikes a practical balance between training efficiency and inference speed, making it highly effective for real-time RCD in dynamic and large-scale network environments.

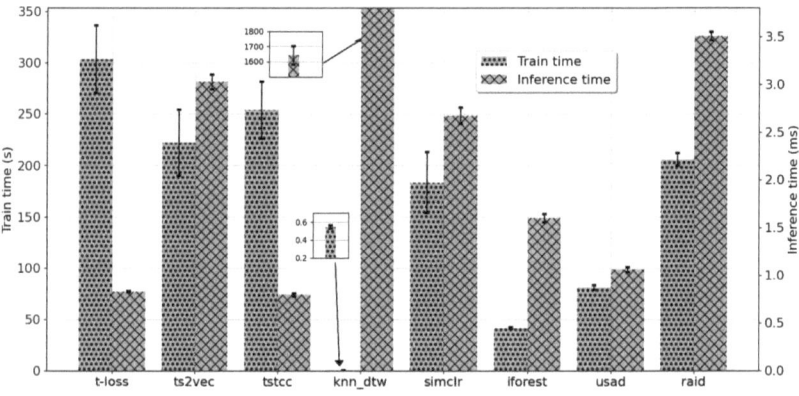

Fig. 7. Time complexity of each model.

7   Conclusion and Future Work

This paper presents a root cause diagnosis approach for identifying network issues in Cloud VR sessions over Wi-Fi networks, utilizing time series KPIs collected from access points. By employing a two-stage ML framework, we demonstrated the effectiveness of our approach compared to traditional time series classification methods. Our proposed architecture, which integrates contrastive learning into the anomaly detection process, has shown significant improvements in both identifying anomalies and diagnosing the root causes of Cloud VR performance issues. This provides a good foundation for future research in real-time diagnostics for cloud-based VR applications. One key strength of our approach is its ability to balance training time and inference speed, making it ideal for real-time diagnostics in dynamic network environments. Moreover, its two-stage design enhances efficiency by restricting retraining to the impairment classifier, thus avoiding full model retraining when new causes are introduced. Although our experimental evaluation focused on Cloud VR over Wi-Fi, the RAID framework is application-agnostic and can be seamlessly adapted to other root cause diagnosis scenarios. By replacing the time series inputs, RAID can be retrained without architectural changes.

Despite the promising results, there are several areas that warrant further exploration and improvement. First, while our model performs well in detecting clear anomaly patterns such as interference, its sensitivity to more nuanced variations—particularly in signal attenuation scenarios—needs to be enhanced. Future work will focus on improving the model's ability to detect subtle transitions between normal and degraded states. Second, scaling the solution to larger and more complex datasets is a priority. Our current framework has been tested in a controlled Cloud VR testbed with only two types of impairments. To improve its robustness, future research should include additional Wi-Fi impairments such as network congestion, hidden terminal issues, and non-Wi-Fi interference. Expanding the test environment to include more diverse real-world conditions, such as home networks where multiple sources of impairments may coexist, will also offer valuable insights. Finally, extending this two-stage model to a multi-modal diagnostic approach could provide a more comprehensive view of the root cause diagnosis process. By incorporating additional data sources, such as application-level performance metrics or raw network PCAP data, the system could offer even more accurate and proactive detection of network impairments. These enhancements will be crucial for addressing the growing demands of next-generation low-latency applications like Cloud VR.

Acknowledgments. This work is partially funded by a ANR - French government grant under the France 2030 program, project SPIREC of PEPR Cloud (ANR-23-PECL-0006) and the French National Research Agency (ANR) MOSAICO project, under grant No ANR-19-CE25-0012.

Disclosure of Interests. The authors have no competing interests to declare that are relevant to the content of this article.

References

1. Audibert, J., Michiardi, P., Guyard, F., Marti, S., Zuluaga, M.A.: Usad: unsupervised anomaly detection on multivariate time series. In: Proceedings of the 26th ACM SIGKDD International Conference on Knowledge Discovery & Data Mining, pp. 3395–3404 (2020)
2. Bagnall, A., Lines, J., Bostrom, A., Large, J., Keogh, E.: The great time series classification bake off: a review and experimental evaluation of recent algorithmic advances. Data Min. Knowl. Disc. **31**, 606–660 (2017)
3. Bagnall, A., Lines, J., Hills, J., Bostrom, A.: Time-series classification with cote: the collective of transformation-based ensembles. IEEE Trans. Knowl. Data Eng. **27**(9), 2522–2535 (2015)

4. Bostrom, A., Bagnall, A.: Binary shapelet transform for multiclass time series classification. In: Madria, S., Hara, T. (eds.) DaWaK 2015. LNCS, vol. 9263, pp. 257–269. Springer, Cham (2015). https://doi.org/10.1007/978-3-319-22729-0_20

5. Cao, V.L., Nicolau, M., McDermott, J.: One-class classification for anomaly detection with kernel density estimation and genetic programming. In: Genetic Programming: 19th European Conference, EuroGP 2016, Porto, Portugal, March 30-April 1, 2016, Proceedings 19, pp. 3–18. Springer, Cham (2016)

6. Chaovalitwongse, W.A., Fan, Y.J., Sachdeo, R.C.: On the time series k-nearest neighbor classification of abnormal brain activity. IEEE Trans. Syst. Man, Cybern.-Part A: Syst. Hum. **37**(6), 1005–1016 (2007)

7. Chen, T., Kornblith, S., Norouzi, M., Hinton, G.: A simple framework for contrastive learning of visual representations. In: International Conference on Machine Learning, pp. 1597–1607. PMLR (2020)

8. Darban, Z.Z., Webb, G.I., Pan, S., Aggarwal, C.C., Salehi, M.: Carla: self-supervised contrastive representation learning for time series anomaly detection. Pattern Recogn. **157**, 110874 (2025)

9. Deng, H., Runger, G., Tuv, E., Vladimir, M.: A time series forest for classification and feature extraction. Inf. Sci. **239**, 142–153 (2013)

10. Dimopoulos, G., Leontiadis, I., Barlet-Ros, P., Papagiannaki, K., Steenkiste, P.: Identifying the root cause of video streaming issues on mobile devices. In: Proceedings of the 11th ACM Conference on Emerging Networking Experiments and Technologies, pp. 1–13 (2015)

11. Dötterl, J., Hemmati Fard, Z.: Classification of home network problems with transformers. In: Proceedings of the 39th ACM/SIGAPP Symposium on Applied Computing, pp. 1081–1087 (2024)

12. Eldele, E., Ragab, M., Chen, Z., Wu, M., Kwoh, C., Li, X., Guan, C.: Time-series representation learning via temporal and contextual contrasting. In: International Joint Conference on Artificial Intelligence (2021)

13. Fida, M.R., Ahmed, A.H., Dreibholz, T., Ocampo, A.F., Elmokashfi, A., Michelinakis, F.I.: Bottleneck identification in cloudified mobile networks based on distributed telemetry. IEEE Trans. Mob. Comput. (2023)

14. Franceschi, J.Y., Dieuleveut, A., Jaggi, M.: Unsupervised scalable representation learning for multivariate time series. In: Advances in Neural Information Processing Systems, vol. 32 (2019)

15. Ky, J.R., Mathieu, B., Lahmadi, A., Boutaba, R.: Cats: contrastive learning for anomaly detection in time series. In: 2024 IEEE International Conference on Big Data (BigData), pp. 1352–1359. IEEE (2024)

16. Li, B., Müller, E.: Contrastive time series anomaly detection by temporal transformations. In: 2023 International Joint Conference on Neural Networks (IJCNN), pp. 1–8. IEEE (2023)

17. Liu, F.T., Ting, K.M., Zhou, Z.H.: Isolation forest. In: 2008 Eighth IEEE International Conference on Data Mining, pp. 413–422. IEEE (2008)

18. Luo, H., Zhong, S.: Gas turbine engine gas path anomaly detection using deep learning with gaussian distribution. In: 2017 Prognostics and System Health Management Conference (PHM-Harbin), pp. 1–6. IEEE (2017)

19. Paffenroth, R., Kay, K., Servi, L.: Robust PCA for anomaly detection in cyber networks. arXiv preprint arXiv:1801.01571 (2018)

20. Su, Y., Zhao, Y., Niu, C., Liu, R., Sun, W., Pei, D.: Robust anomaly detection for multivariate time series through stochastic recurrent neural network. In: Proceedings of the 25th ACM SIGKDD International Conference on Knowledge Discovery & Data Mining, pp. 2828–2837 (2019)

21. Syrigos, I., Sakellariou, N., Keranidis, S., Korakis, T.: On the employment of machine learning techniques for troubleshooting wifi networks. In: 2019 16th IEEE Annual Consumer Communications & Networking Conference (CCNC), pp. 1–6. IEEE (2019)
22. Tonekaboni, S., Eytan, D., Goldenberg, A.: Unsupervised representation learning for time series with temporal neighborhood coding. arXiv preprint arXiv:2106.00750 (2021)
23. Tuli, S., Casale, G., Jennings, N.R.: Tranad: deep transformer networks for anomaly detection in multivariate time series data. arXiv preprint arXiv:2201.07284 (2022)
24. Wang, R., et al.: Deep contrastive one-class time series anomaly detection. In: Proceedings of the 2023 SIAM International Conference on Data Mining (SDM), pp. 694–702. SIAM (2023)
25. Xu, H., et al.: Unsupervised anomaly detection via variational auto-encoder for seasonal kpis in web applications. In: Proceedings of the 2018 World Wide Web Conference, pp. 187–196 (2018)
26. Yaacob, A.H., Tan, I.K., Chien, S.F., Tan, H.K.: Arima based network anomaly detection. In: 2010 Second International Conference on Communication Software and Networks, pp. 205–209. IEEE (2010)
27. Yang, Y., Zhang, C., Zhou, T., Wen, Q., Sun, L.: Dcdetector: dual attention contrastive representation learning for time series anomaly detection. In: Proceedings of the 29th ACM SIGKDD Conference on Knowledge Discovery and Data Mining, pp. 3033–3045 (2023)
28. Yue, Z., et al.: Ts2vec: towards universal representation of time series. In: AAAI Conference on Artificial Intelligence (2021)
29. Zhang, X., Zhao, Z., Tsiligkaridis, T., Zitnik, M.: Self-supervised contrastive pre-training for time series via time-frequency consistency. Adv. Neural. Inf. Process. Syst. **35**, 3988–4003 (2022)
30. Zhao, B., Lu, H., Chen, S., Liu, J., Wu, D.: Convolutional neural networks for time series classification. J. Syst. Eng. Electron. **28**(1), 162–169 (2017)
31. Zheng, Y., Liu, Q., Chen, E., Ge, Y., Zhao, J.L.: Exploiting multi-channels deep convolutional neural networks for multivariate time series classification. Front. Comp. Sci. **10**(1), 96–112 (2016). https://doi.org/10.1007/s11704-015-4478-2
32. Zong, B., et al.: Deep autoencoding gaussian mixture model for unsupervised anomaly detection. In: International Conference on Learning Representations (2018)

A Dynamic Ensemble and Replaying Model for Online Marine Sensor Data Prediction

Xiang Li[1,2(✉)], Xi Fu[1,2], Congqi Lin[3], Xiangkai Wang[1,2], Yuhang Zhang[1,2], Hao Wang[1,2], Zhigang Zhao[1,2(✉)], Meihong Yang[1,2], and Yinglong Wang[1,2]

[1] Key Laboratory of Computing Power Network and Information Security, Ministry of Education, Shandong Computer Science Center (National Supercomputer Center in Jinan), Qilu University of Technology (Shandong Academy of Sciences), Jinan, China
[2] Shandong Provincial Key Laboratory of Computing Power Internet and Service Computing, Shandong Fundamental Research Center for Computer Science, Jinan, China
[3] Johns Hopkins University, Baltimore, USA
{xiangli,zhaozhg}@sdas.org

Abstract. Deep learning excels in time-series data mining, yet offline-trained models often degrade when faced with dynamic marine observation data. To address this, we propose a brain-inspired online learning and replay framework for efficient marine time-series data prediction. The proposed framework tackles concept drift not only by updating the parameters of its internal modules but also by employing an attention mechanism to adaptively assign importance to these modules, and incorporating a neuroscience-inspired memory replay mechanism for reinforcing past knowledge. Unlike traditional deep learning models reliant on extensive historical data, our framework enables cold-start learning and inference, making it ideal for environmental monitoring stations with limited data where offline models struggle to generalize. We further introduce the first marine data prediction benchmark dataset MarineDrift-1.0, covering key marine environmental indicators with natural conecpt drift. Experiments on this dataset demonstrate the model's superior performance over state-of-the-art methods. Notably, the framework is model-independent, allows seamless integration with various models, delivering strong results even with simple architectures.

Keywords: ocean · time series · concept drift · online deep learning · variational auto-encoders

1 Introduction

In recent years, the rapid expansion of Internet of Things (IoT) systems has driven the real-time generation of massive time-series data from sensors and devices, particularly in environmental monitoring such as ocean observation.

© The Author(s), under exclusive license to Springer Nature Switzerland AG 2026
B. Pfahringer et al. (Eds.): ECML PKDD 2025, LNAI 16020, pp. 456–473, 2026.
https://doi.org/10.1007/978-3-662-72243-5_26

Ocean buoys equipped with multi-parameter sensors continuously collect critical marine data including water temperature, salinity, wind speed, and pollution levels. Forecasting such data provides technical support for monitoring dynamic marine ecosystem evolutions, early environmental risk warnings, and scientific decision-making.

Though Deep learning (DL) models have demonstrated effectiveness in time series data forecasting [1,2]. These models require sufficient training data and assume static input-output relationships. In contrast, marine sensor time series data often exhibits fluctuating patterns with evolving underlying distributions (Concept Drift or Distribution Shift) [3–5]. As shown in Fig. 1, a marine sensor time series consists of segments with distinct distributions. The drift disrupts the assumption of stationarity, Thus current Deep Learning approaches face the challenge of **Stability-Plasticity Dilemma** [6]. As data evolves unpredictably, static forecasting models experience a decline in performance.

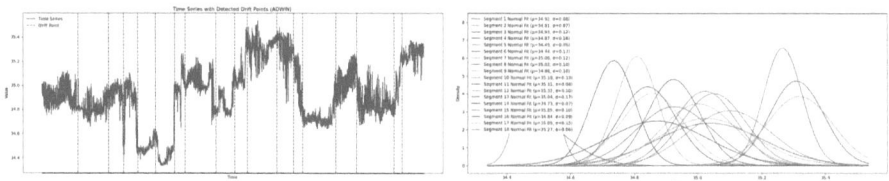

Fig. 1. Conceptual drift occurs in a marine time-series data stream, which can be divided into 18 distinct segments with ADWIN algorithm, each exhibiting a different distribution.

This challenge has sparked extensive research into methods for addressing concept drift in time series analysis [7]. There are two distinct but interconnected approaches: Online Learning (**active mode**) and Incremental Learning (**lazy mode**). Online learning relies on scalable and efficient algorithms to sequentially process training instances from a data stream, one by one, to learn the model [8–10]. On the other hand, incremental learning updates the model when a batch of data instances arrives [11]. In this paper, we focus methods in the context of active mode. There is still room for improvement in active mode methods specific to marine time series data, the motivation of this work is as follows:

- **Motivation 1 (Enhancing Model Adaptability):** Existing online models primarily adjust hidden layer parameters while overlooking structural adaptation. Given numerous marine variables and monitoring scenarios, customized model designs are impractical, necessitating self-evolving architectures that autonomously balance model capacity with environmental demands.
- **Motivation 2 (Catastrophic Forgetting Prevention):** MLP-based models inherently suffer from catastrophic forgetting [12], where new knowledge acquisition overwrites previous patterns [13]. Many existing approaches rely on storing and ensembling historical models to incorporate past knowledge. However [14], storing intermediate models can quickly become unmanageable on resource-constrained marine observation devices.

– **Motivation 3 (Cold Start Learning):** In under-monitored environments, the lack of sufficient historical data hampers the development of deep learning (DL)-based online learning models, as they typically require pre-existing data to warm up the model, followed by online learning and inference on the data stream (e.g., FSNet [15] and OneNet [16]). We prefer a 'Cold Start' learning paradigm that can be applied directly to the stream, quickly adapting to target time series data without initial training.

To address these challenges, we propose a **B**rain-inspired **R**eplay **A**daptive **I**ncremental **N**etwork built on a **V**ariational **A**utoencoder (BRAIN-VAE). The model integrates two neuro-inspired strategies: A modular attention mechanism that emulates functional specialization in brain regions, where distinct neural modules dynamically reconfigure their contributions for specific temporal patterns, akin to how visual and auditory cortices process separate patterns. A generative memory replay system that mitigates catastrophic forgetting by synthesizing pseudo-experiences of historical patterns through latent space generation, mirroring hippocampal-neocortical interactions in memory consolidation. Furthermore, we introduce the **MarineDrift-1.0** dataset—the first open-source dataset specifically designed for ocean data mining with natural concept drift. Experimental results on this dataset show BRAIN-VAE significantly outperforms all baselines in cold-start settings.

2   Backgrounds and Related Works

2.1   Learning on Time Series with Concept Drift

Concept drift is prevalent in sensor time - series data due to unpredictable factors like environmental changes and pollutant accumulation. Some prior studies have tackled this issue from the Domain Adaptation perspective in Transfer Learning, e.g., the ADARNN model [17]. However, these methods are limited to offline training of pre-available time series data. Online Learning methods include the Dynamically Scalable Network (DEN) [18], Deep Evolutionary Denoising Autoencoder (DEVDAN) [19] and Neural Networks with Dynamically Evolved Capacity (NADINE) [12], which evolves the structure dynamically and adjust the representational capacity; the HSN-LSTM [20], the first to embed an Adaptive Hybrid Spike (AHS) module in LSTM for stream-based prediction in concept-drift environments; and the FSNet [15] and OneNet [16] models employ a dynamic adaptive mechanism and enhance the effectiveness of online learning through a complementary learning paradigm, representing the most advanced methods in the current field of time-series online learning.

2.2   Catastropical Forgetting and Brain Memory Replay

Deep neural networks (DNNs) excel in diverse tasks but suffer from catastrophic forgetting during sequential learning, losing previously acquired knowledge [13]. For example, LSTM/RNN models experience exponential decay of long-term memory, degrading performance as critical temporal patterns are rapidly forgotten [21]. Conventional replay-based approaches mitigate forgetting by ensembling past learned models [14], but these methods are computationally inefficient and impractical for real-time IoT systems due to storage constraints. In contrast, the human brain employs scalable Memory Replay during sleep/awake SWR events, where the hippocampus coordinates neocortical reactivation to stabilize memories [22,23]. The Complementary Learning Systems (CLS) Theory posits that this process consolidates experiences via hippocampal-neocortical interactions [24]. **Notably, brain replay abstract representations of learned patterns rather than raw data [25], suggesting no need for full historical data storage.** Inspired by this mechanism, we propose a generative replay neural network for marine time-series forecasting. Our model enables efficient continuous learning in resource-constrained IoT environments.

3   Methodology

3.1   Problem Definition

Online learning algorithms feature instantaneous forecasting and learning. The model iteratively updates parameters using per-data-point loss and gradients. Let $X = x_0, x_1, ..., x_t, ..., x_T$ denote real-time time-series data from a sensor, where T is unbounded. Under the online setting, data arrives sequentially: for forecasting at time t, only historical data $x_0, x_1, ..., x_{t-1}$ are available. The model generates predictions $\hat{x}^t$ using this past window, then updates parameters with the loss computed from the observed x^t. For multi-step forecasting with horizon $h > 1$, the target sequence $\{\hat{x}_t, \hat{x}_{t+1}, ..., \hat{x}_{t+h}\}$ is predicted, and loss is computed once the entire window is observed.

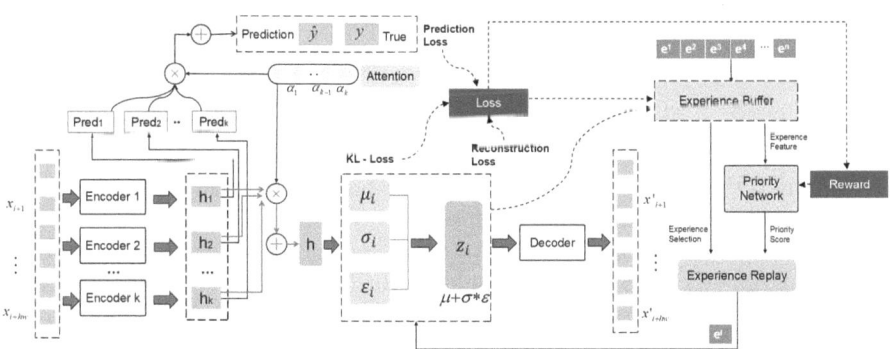

Fig. 2. The proposed online learning framework for dynamic marien time series data forecasting.

3.2   Overall Structure of the BRAIN-VAE

The BRAIN-VAE model integrates several key functions, including VAE-based generative learning mechanism, attention mechanisms, online learning mechanism, and brain-inspired replay mechanism. Accordingly, the BRAIN-VAE model is structured into three pathways, are shown in Fig. 2:

- The **VAE-based encoder-decoder pathway** for capturing latent representations of time series data and generating reconstructions.
- The **Attention-based forecasting fusion pathway**, which dynamically weights the contributions of different layers for real-time prediction.
- The **Brain-inspired memory replay pathway**, which implement a generative replay mechanism to retain previously learned experience and prevent catastrophic forgetting

3.3   VAE Based Encoder-Decoder Pathway

The BRAIN-VAE model is built upon the Variational Autoencoder (VAE) structure, a generative model that is capable of learning distribution parameters (mean and variance) of latent factors and generating data based on learned distributions.

- **Encoder**: Given an input sequence $x = \{x_i, x_{i+1}, \ldots, x_T\}$, the encoder outputs the mean (μ) and variance (σ^2) of the latent variables. These latent variables z are sampled from a Gaussian distribution:

$$
\begin{aligned}
h &= \sum_{k=1}^{K} \alpha_k h_k \\
\mu_z &= f_{linear}^{\mu}(h) \\
\sigma_z &= f_{linear}^{\sigma}(h)
\end{aligned}
\tag{1}
$$

Let h denote the concatenated hidden representations derived from the internal encoders. The attention weight α for the concatenation operation is computed through the proposed attention-based forecasting fusion pathway, which will be elaborated in the subsequent section.

- **Reparameterization Trick**: To enable backpropagation during training, the reparameterization trick is employed. Instead of directly sampling z from $\mathcal{N}(\mu_z, \sigma_z^2)$, a random noise vector ε is sampled from a standard normal distribution, and z is sampled by:

$$
z = \mu_z + \sigma_z \cdot \varepsilon, \quad \varepsilon \sim \mathcal{N}(0, 1)
\tag{2}
$$

This reparameterization allows the latent space to remain differentiable, thus facilitating gradient-based optimization.

- **Decoder**: The decoder reconstructs the input data by generating x' from the sampled latent variables:

$$x' = f_{decoder}(z) \tag{3}$$

The reconstruction loss is minimized to ensure that the latent space captures meaningful information.

3.4 Attention-Based Forecasting Fusion Pathway

Dynamic representational capacity adjustment is vital for time-series forecasting under concept drift [19,26]. Specifically, we aim to develop a model capable of performing efficient inference with a 'cold start' fashion while dynamically adapting its representational capacity to the evolving stream. We realize it through a complementary inference pathway integrating internal encoders' information and dynamically balancing contributions via an attention mechanism.

The BRAIN-VAE model supports integrating multiple time-series encoders as internal modules, thereby enhancing the learning capability of temporal representations. The BRAIN-VAE model synthesizes its forecast by assigning weighted importance to the predictions generated at each module. Modules contributing less relevant information to the current forecast receive lower weights, resulting in a final prediction that aggregates the forecasts from all internal modules as a weighted sum, formulated as:

$$
\begin{aligned}
h_k &= f_{encoder}^k(x) \\
y_{pred}^k &= f_{pred}^k(h_i) \\
y_{pred} &= \sum_{k=1}^{K} \alpha_i y_{pred}^k
\end{aligned}
\tag{4}
$$

$f_{encoder}(*)$ and $f_{pred}(*)$ transforms the original sequence x into intermediate representation and localized forecasts, and h_i represents the hidden representation of the ith module. The weight α_i is recalculated dynamically through the following re-weighting mechanism. To update the model iteratively, we incorporate the re-weighting operation, which is implemented based on an feed forward neural network based Attention Network, formulated as:

$$\alpha_k = f_{attention}(h_k) \tag{5}$$

This dynamic attention mechanism adaptively adjusts module contributions via softmax-normalized weights, quantifying their importance in capturing time-varying patterns. Unlike fixed-weight architectures, this enables rapid cold-start convergence while allowing modules to dynamically specialize based on input characteristics, enhancing adaptability to evolving data distributions and improving prediction accuracy.

3.5   Brain-Inspired Memory Replay Pathway

Drawing on cognitive neuroscience, we incorporate a brain-inspired replay mechanism into the BRAIN-VAE model. Instead of replaying or generating the original raw data, it internally replays high-level hidden representations. This concept stems from the discovery in human brain hippocampal memory reactivation process that reactivating abstract representations tied to past experiences. Important components related to the replay strategy is described as follows:

Experience Replay Buffer. Define the replay buffer $\mathcal{D} = \{e_i\}_{i=1}^T$ where each stored experience e_i contains:

- Experience index $i \in \mathbb{R}$
- Latent mean $\mu_z^{(i)} \in \mathbb{R}^{Z_{\dim}}$
- Latent variance $\sigma_z^{(i)} \in \mathbb{R}^{Z_{\dim}}$
- loss $\mathcal{L}_{BRAIN\_VAE}^{(i)}$

Priority Scoring Function. Define the priority network $\theta_{priority} : \mathbb{R}^{d_\phi} \to \mathbb{R}$ with input feature vector, the feature vector is built based on the stored experience:

$$\phi^{(i)} = \left[\mu_z^{(i)}, \sigma_z^{(i)}, \mu_z^{(t)}, \sigma_z^{(t)}, \mathcal{L}_{BRAIN\_VAE}^{(i)}, \mathcal{L}_{BRAIN\_VAE}^{(t)}, \Delta d^{(i,t)} \right] \tag{6}$$

The temporal difference is calculated by $\Delta d^{(i,t)} = t - i$, it reflects the influence of the past experience in time i to data in current time t. Priority score (expected reward) is calculated on the feature:

$$R_{expected}^{(i)} = \theta_{priority}(\phi^{(i)}) \tag{7}$$

Selection Strategy. The z selection and replay policy is as follows:

$$P_{select}(e_i) = \begin{cases} 1, & \text{if } i = \arg\max_j R_{expected}^{(j)} \\ 0, & \text{otherwise} \end{cases} \tag{8}$$

Inspired by reinforcement learning, we introduce the reward-based optimization strategy that leverages the experience feature $\phi^{(i)}$ to compute a performance-based reward signal. This reward quantifies the prediction performance enhancement achieved through experience replay of the selected experience e_i This strategy ensures that the model consolidates both new and previously learned information to enhance online prediction with a low-cost fashion.

3.6   Loss Functions and Parameter Optimization

For the BRAIN-VAE, the most important learning objective is to minimize the forecast bias, hence we need first define the forecast bias in objective function. The **Forecast Loss** function include the forecast loss of each module and the ensemble forecast loss, as follows:

$$
\begin{aligned}
\mathcal{L}_{P_j} &= \sum_{h=1}^{H} MSE\left(y_{j,h}{}', y_{j,h}\right) \\
\mathcal{L}_P &= \sum_{h=1}^{H} MSE\left(\sum_{k=1}^{K} \alpha_k y'_{k,h}, y_{k,h}\right)
\end{aligned}
\tag{9}
$$

In addition to the loss function of forecast, the training of the BRAIN-VAE model also needs the guidance of two other loss functions. One of them is the Kullback-Leibler divergence loss (KL loss), which serves to measure the difference between the posterior distribution $q(z|x)$ and the standard normal distribution $p(z)$. The **KL-loss** is defined as:

$$
\mathcal{L}_{KL} = -0.5 * \sum_{m=1}^{Z_{\mathrm{dim}}} (1 + \log(\sigma_m^2) - \mu_m^2 - \sigma_m^2)
\tag{10}
$$

The other is **Reconstruction loss**, which can be L1 or L2 Loss, as follows:

$$
\mathcal{L}_{Rec} = MSE(x, x')
\tag{11}
$$

Finally, in order to optimize the BRAIN-VAE model, we need to minimize the above four losses simultaneously, namely:

$$
\mathcal{L}_{BRAIN\_VAE} = \sum_{k=1}^{K} \mathcal{L}_{P_j} + \mathcal{L}_P + \mathcal{L}_{KL} + \mathcal{L}_{Rec}
\tag{12}
$$

For the Priority Network, we introduce the reward-based optimization strategy, the reward signal is based on prediction improvement. The larger the loss decrease after replay, the higher the reward assigned, as follows:

$$
R_{actual}^{(i)} = \underbrace{\mathcal{L}_{BRAIN\_VAE}^{(i)}}_{\text{pre-replay}} - \underbrace{\mathcal{L}_{BRAIN\_VAE}^{(i)}}_{\text{post-replay}}
\tag{13}
$$

The Priority Network loss **Priority Loss** is as follows:

$$
\mathcal{L}_{priority}^{i} = \left(R_{expected}^{(i)} - R_{actual}^{(i)}\right)^2
\tag{14}
$$

The training process is illustrated as follows:

Algorithm 1. Optimization Procedure for BRAIN-VAE Model

1: Initialize main model θ_{main} and priority network $\theta_{\mathrm{priority}}$
2: **for** each time step $t = 1$ to T **do**
3:     Generate prediction $\mathbf{y}_t$ and latent $\mathbf{z}_t$
4:     Compute loss $\mathcal{L}_{BRAIN-VAE}^t$ before replay and store experience e_t in $\mathcal{D}$
5:     **if** $t \bmod K = 0$ **and** $|\mathcal{D}| > 0$ **then**
6:         Build feature vector on $\mathcal{D}$ and compute priority scores (expected reward) for
            the stored experiences $R_{expected}^{(i)} = \theta_{priority}(\phi^{(i)})$
7:         Select experience e_i from $\mathcal{D}$ with top priority score
8:         Replay the selected experience and compute loss of the replayed experience,
            and update the main model θ_{main}.
9:         Recompute the loss $\mathcal{L}_{BRAIN-VAE}^t$ for current time t after replay, get the
            actual reward (prediction improvement) $R_{actual}^{(t)}$
10:         Compute the reward loss of the Priority Network, and update the the model
            $\theta_{\mathrm{priority}}$;
11:     **end if**
12: **end for**

In practice, we can set the replay frequency $K = 1$, and at the end of each round of forecast, the model adjusts itself based on the instantaneous loss before the coming rounds. The error derivatives of BRAIN-VAE model are backpropagated to each of the internal module to adjust the corresponding parameters.

4   Experiments

4.1   Experimental Data, Metrics and Environment

The MarineDrift-1.0 dataset is constructed using in-situ near-real-time marine observation data from buoy networks under the MO category of the Copernicus Marine Service[1] dataset currently contains six critical physical and biogeochemical parameters essential for monitoring marine environmental dynamics: sea temperature (TEMP), salinity (PSAL), dissolved oxygen concentration (DOX1), turbidity (TUR4), chlorophyll-a concentration (CPHL), and horizontal wind speed (WSPD). To ensure data representativeness, we implement a two-stage concept drift detection framework. First, the ADWIN (Adaptive Windowing) algorithm dynamically identifies concept drift phase through adaptive time window adjustments. Second, the Wasserstein distance metric quantifies the magnitude of detected drifts, providing an interpretable measure of distributional divergence between sequential data segments (Table 1).

In this work, for experimental validation, we curated challenging subsets from the MarineDrift-1.0 dataset exhibiting substantial distributional shifts. These subsets provide a rigorous testbed for evaluating model adaptation capabilities under realistic marine environmental non-stationarity conditions. Each time

---

[1] https://data.marine.copernicus.eu/product/INSITU_GLO_PHYBGCWAV_DISC
RETE_MYNRT_013_030/files?subdataset=cmems_obs-ins_glo_phybgcwav_
mynrt_na_irr_202311--ext--history.

Table 1. Statistics Information of Selected Experimental Data from MarinShift-1.0

Dataset	Domain	# Time Series	Min Length	Mean Length	Max Length	Total Observations	Forecast Horizon
CPHL	BGC	5	6376	46391.6	70000	231958	{1,24,48}
DOX1	BGC	5	14524	38249.4	79046	191247	{1,24,48}
PSAL	Physical oceanography	5	11701	17179.8	28987	85899	{1,24,48}
TEMP	Physical oceanography	5	12796	19321.2	34361	96606	{1,24,48}
TUR4	BGC	5	4398	9214.8	15542	46074	{1,24,48}
WSPD	Meteorological	5	8045	34417	75595	172085	{1,24,48}

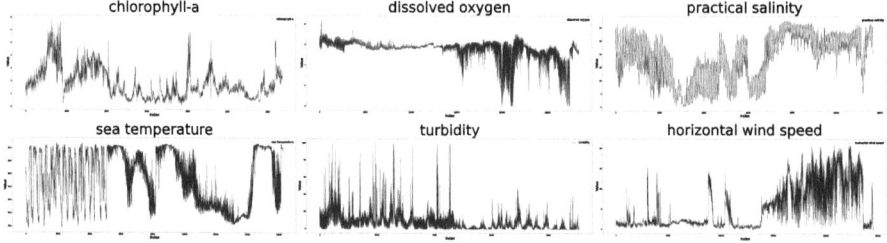

Fig. 3. Representative examples of concept drift in 6 key types of marine observational time series data.

series was split into warm-up (30%) and online-inference (70%) phases. The warm-up data serves to train traditional offline models and several online learning models that need warm-up phase, also used to normalize the online-inference data. The online-inference data is used for performance validation across all methods (Fig. 3).

4.2 Experimental Settings

Settings for BRAIN-VAE: The BRAIN-VAE model employs a three-module architecture, each adopts the encoder structure of TS2Vec, as follows:

Module 1 (Global Feature Extraction Module): This module is dedicated to extracting global contextual information from the entire historical time series window. By encoding the input sequence as a holistic entity, it aims to capture long-term dependencies and macroscopic patterns that span the entire segment, such as trends and seasonality. The module synthesizes and refines feature representations across all time steps to generate a single, fixed-dimensional context vector. This vector is subsequently fed into a linear regressor to produce predictions from a macro-level perspective.

Module 2 (Local Feature Extraction Module): This module focuses on capturing local patterns within the original univariate time series. It employs a TS2Vec framework with an input dimensionality of 1 to process the raw univariate time series, leveraging hierarchical dilated convolution operations to extract multi-scale temporal features. For prediction, this module exclusively extracts and utilizes the output feature vector from the final time step of the sequence. Finally, this feature vector is mapped to the prediction space via a linear regressor.

Module 3 (Temporal Feature Enhancement Module): This module integrates additonal 7-dimensional timestamp features (minute, hour, day of week, day of month, day of year, month, and week of year) and concatenates them with the original time series data to form an 8-dimensional input. Significantly improving the model's ability to capture periodic, seasonal, event-driven patterns, and complex temporal dependencies across scales in ocean.

The dimensionality of latent variable z is set to 8. In terms of the Attention Network and Priority Network, we both set up 2 hidden layers with 50 neurons in each layer.

Settings for Baselines: Considering that BRAIN-VAE is fundamentally a deep learning model, we compared it with several representative deep learning models for time series data prediction. This includes models without online learning capabilities, as well as models designed for online learning. The detailed settings for the baselines are shown in Table 2. **RNN-LSTM** [27]; 2) **Transformer** [28] and its variants 3) **Informer** [29], 4) **FEDFormer** [30], and 5) **Autoformer** [31]; 6) **NBeats** [32], the M-Competition 2020 champion; Pre-trained time series model 7) **PatchTST** [33]; and 8) **AdaRNN** [34], a domain adaptation framework employing Temporal Distribution Matching.

Online Learning Models includes: 1) **HSN-LSTM** [20], which integrates an Adaptive Hybrid Spike module and dual attention mechanisms into LSTM for concept drift-aware stream prediction; 2) **NADINE** [12], a dynamic neural network that evolves its architecture by pruning/growing hidden units/layers based on drift detection; 3) **FSNet** [15], inspired by Complementary Learning Systems theory to combine fast learning with slow adaptation via temporal pattern memory; and 4) **OneNet** [16], which dynamically combines temporal/cross-variable dependency models using reinforcement learning within an online convex programming framework. FSNet and OneNet are state-of-the-art (SOTA) models that serve as strong baselines in online time-series forecasting.

Settings for Ablation Study: To evaluate the brain replay mechanism's impact, we designed three variants: **BRAIN-VAE-RER** (random experience replay), **BRAIN-VAE-WRE** (without experience replay), and **BRAIN-VAE-PER** (priority experience replay via PriorityNetwork that we adopt). Ablation experiments were also conducted to assess encoder architecture sensitivity by substituting the original three Ts2Vcc-based encoders with TCN (**BRAIN-VAE-TCN**). Additionally, we tested the model's performance without attention mechanisms, referred to as **BRAIN-VAE-woAttn**.

4.3   Experimental Results and Discussion

We conducted a comparative evaluation of the BRAIN-VAE model against baseline methods. As shown in Table 3 and Fig. 4, the BRAIN-VAE model not only excels in prediction accuracy but also demonstrates remarkable stability across

Table 2. Parameter Settings for Comparison Methods

Offline Methods	
RNN-LSTM	dimension of LSTM hidden layer: 200 number of LSTM layers: 2 use of bias in LSTM: True
NBeats	stack types: {H-1: generic}, {H-24,H-48: [trend, seasonality]} number of blocks per stack: 3 hidden layer units: 256
{Transformer Informer Autoformer FEDformer}	model dimension: 512 feedforward network dimension: 2048 number of attention heads: 8 number of encoder layers: 3 number of decoder layers: 1 attention factor: 3
PatchTST	model dimension: 128 feedforward network dimension: 256 number of encoder layers: 3 number of attention heads: 8 patch length: 16 stride: 8
AdaRNN	RNN hidden layer dimension: 64 number of RNN layers: 2 number of domains: 2 data model: TDC distribution distance function: adversarial distance
Online Methods	
HSN-LSTM	membrane potential time constant, τu: 64 spike time constant, τa: 32 initial threshold, $c0$: 4e-2 dynamic range control parameter, $d0$: 1.8 time step, dt: 0.01(10 ms)
NADINE	network type: stacked initial hidden layers: 1 stabilization period: 20 anomaly threshold 1: chi2inv(0.99, 168) chi2inv(0.999, 168) forgetting factor: 0.98 drift detection error thresholds: {0.001 (drift), 0.005 (warning)}
FSNet	feed-forward network dimension: 2048 model hidden layer dimension: 512 number of decoder layers: 1 number of encoder layers: 2 number of attention heads: 8 sparse attention factor: 5 test batch size: 1 online learning model: full training method: fsnet
OneNet	model dimension: 32 feed-forward network dimension: 128 number of attention heads: 8 number of encoder layers: 2 number of decoder layers: 1 sparse attention factor: 5 test batch size: 1 online learning model: full

Table 3. Performance of the BRAIN-VAE model and baseline models.

Model	CPHL						DOX1					
	H = 1		H = 24		H = 48		H = 1		H = 24		H = 48	
	RMSE	MAE	RMSE	MAE	RMSE	MAE	RMSE	MAE	RMSE	MAE	RMSE	MAE
BRAIN-VAE	**0.1200**	**0.0348**	**0.2752**	**0.1303**	**0.3561**	**0.1744**	**0.1284**	0.2431	**0.3233**	**0.1835**	**0.4143**	**0.2493**
RNN-LSTM	1.2129	0.7007	1.2791	0.7697	1.2873	0.7759	1.5160	1.0581	1.7229	1.2775	1.8434	1.3923
NBeats	0.3128	0.1357	0.5346	0.2595	0.6535	0.3253	0.3593	0.2442	0.6490	0.3887	0.7792	0.5021
Transformer	0.7835	0.3957	1.0258	0.5666	1.0278	0.5759	0.7265	0.4107	1.0493	0.6573	1.2220	0.8219
Informer	0.8494	0.4298	0.9944	0.5613	1.0740	0.6297	0.8116	0.4744	1.1784	0.7544	1.2083	0.8098
FEDformer	0.2812	0.1259	0.5834	0.3167	0.6682	0.3679	0.3048	0.1818	0.6862	0.4198	0.7637	0.4753
Autoformer	0.3950	0.1915	0.6145	0.3434	0.7136	0.3996	0.4002	0.2570	0.7143	0.4603	0.7865	0.5178
PatchTST	0.2743	0.1150	0.5068	0.2558	0.6132	0.3176	0.2712	0.1387	0.6224	0.3659	0.7106	0.4298
AdaRNN	0.6563	0.4481	0.7884	0.5313	1.0645	0.6720	0.3310	0.2046	0.9604	0.7031	0.9843	0.7004
HSN-LSTM	0.6525	0.3446	0.8595	0.4563	0.9336	0.5106	0.6184	0.3243	0.8875	0.5427	1.0505	0.6711
NADINE	0.4007	0.1741	0.6803	0.3809	0.8394	0.4884	0.4465	0.1847	1.2152	0.6640	1.6422	0.9133
FSNet	0.4020	0.2028	0.3435	0.1777	0.3909	0.2031	0.6235	0.4459	0.5898	0.3069	0.5625	0.3499
OneNet	0.2343	0.0938	0.4560	0.2317	0.4958	0.2581	0.2165	0.1099	0.5497	0.3331	0.5721	0.3712

Model	PSAL						TEMP					
	H = 1		H = 24		H = 48		H = 1		H = 24		H = 48	
	RMSE	MAE	RMSE	MAE	RMSE	MAE	RMSE	MAE	RMSE	MAE	RMSE	MAE
BRAIN-VAE	**0.2953**	**0.1340**	**0.9480**	**0.5856**	**1.2242**	**0.8045**	**0.2198**	**0.0994**	**0.6287**	**0.3842**	**0.8412**	**0.5137**
RNN-LSTM	4.2336	3.4063	4.8702	4.0146	5.5061	4.6823	3.2687	2.4213	4.2192	3.1841	4.4146	3.3858
NBeats	0.8107	0.5186	1.8068	1.1749	2.2441	1.5172	1.0030	0.6786	1.5496	0.9989	2.1463	1.4210
Transformer	0.8027	0.5094	2.4351	1.7783	3.3364	2.4657	1.2431	0.7707	2.7991	1.8921	3.4034	2.4428
Informer	1.3949	0.9856	2.4642	1.7923	3.1687	2.3294	1.7742	1.2145	2.8586	2.0476	3.2066	2.3762
FEDformer	0.6396	0.3796	2.2741	1.6161	2.5236	1.8353	0.8266	0.5282	1.7587	1.2064	2.0894	1.4110
Autoformer	1.2059	0.8755	2.3049	1.6566	2.9015	2.1718	1.1957	0.8272	1.8325	1.3267	2.0443	1.5037
PatchTST	0.6136	0.3350	1.8009	1.1721	2.3252	1.5422	0.7651	0.4506	1.5439	0.9190	1.8213	1.0751
AdaRNN	1.0281	0.8156	4.0677	3.3787	3.9977	3.2982	1.0847	0.8079	2.8720	2.3254	3.3872	2.5916
HSN-LSTM	0.9187	0.5960	2.0921	1.5183	2.6806	2.0383	1.3076	0.8061	2.3727	1.6801	2.8312	2.0698
NADINE	2.0536	0.5998	5.3457	2.9008	6.8524	3.9764	1.2894	0.5368	3.4520	1.6377	5.2622	2.6760
FSNet	1.6107	1.0467	4.5993	2.0053	2.5862	1.4668	1.6133	0.9453	2.2440	1.4468	2.4191	1.6479
OneNet	0.5730	0.3291	1.7088	1.2038	2.0060	1.4595	0.6825	0.4075	1.2452	0.8421	1.6971	1.2028

Model	TUR4						WSPD					
	H = 1		H = 24		H = 48		H = 1		H = 24		H = 48	
	RMSE	MAE	RMSE	MAE	RMSE	MAE	RMSE	MAE	RMSE	MAE	RMSE	MAE
BRAIN-VAE	**1.3968**	**0.5463**	**2.8633**	**1.5436**	**3.0698**	**1.7291**	**0.6496**	**0.3076**	**1.5595**	**0.9558**	1.7178	1.1927
RNN-LSTM	7.0597	5.5112	7.2619	5.6497	7.6757	6.1001	4.5227	3.1496	4.9202	3.4894	5.0434	3.6070
NBeats	3.9913	2.2494	4.8533	2.7216	5.1332	3.0728	1.9122	1.1723	2.9384	2.0149	3.6390	2.5035
Transformer	5.1282	3.7572	5.9702	4.3753	6.6822	4.9547	2.6666	1.6509	3.7313	2.5430	4.3578	2.9860
Informer	5.0593	3.4409	6.4531	4.8229	7.1578	5.5133	2.8657	1.8281	4.1323	2.8662	4.3691	3.0360
FEDformer	4.3692	2.7313	5.1605	3.3677	5.6446	3.7936	1.8921	1.2258	2.7489	1.9040	2.9713	2.0751
Autoformer	4.2407	2.5758	4.9667	3.1035	5.2695	3.3313	2.1136	1.3943	2.6700	1.8512	2.9566	2.0761
PatchTST	3.9400	2.0615	4.5397	2.4823	4.9003	2.7783	1.8384	1.1825	2.5421	1.7481	2.8270	1.9613
AdaRNN	4.7166	3.0292	6.4782	4.8479	6.1856	4.4350	1.8935	1.2347	3.4822	2.3841	3.9063	2.7208
HSN-LSTM	4.4713	2.9312	6.0312	4.3518	6.5432	4.9223	2.2278	1.3779	3.3015	2.2822	3.8957	2.7278
NADINE	4.7241	2.6707	5.6897	3.4842	6.6388	4.4067	2.3424	1.5615	3.5149	2.4989	3.8332	2.7577
FSNet	4.0991	2.1153	4.8031	2.9947	5.4131	3.7947	1.9539	1.2961	1.7099	1.1518	**1.7038**	**1.1465**
OneNet	3.2020	2.1984	3.9796	2.6236	4.4182	3.1360	1.4301	0.8046	2.6530	1.7941	2.9708	1.9418

[a] We conducted 2340 experiments in total, and it is not feasible to present them all specifically. All data presented above are the average results across time-series instances of each marine data type. The detailed tables can be obtained by contacting the author.

different prediction horizons and diverse data types, showcasing a clear advantage over the baseline methods. These results highlight the model's robustness in handling marine time series data, particularly in addressing distributional shifts. Notably, our approach was rigorously validated under cold-start settings without any warm-up data. In contrast, all other methods, including state-of-the-art baselines such as FSNet and OneNet, rely on warm-up data for initialization. Furthermore, our analysis reveals that FSNet exhibits less robustness compared to OneNet and, in some cases, fails to outperform even offline methods.

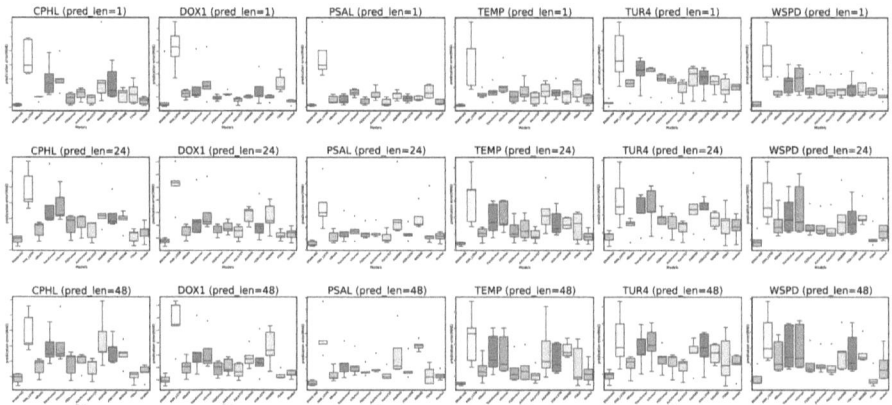

Fig. 4. A box plot comparison of model performance across the experimental datasets, presenting results in a consistent order from left to right: BRAIN-VAE, RNN-LSTM, NBeats, Transformer, Informer, FEDformer, Autoformer, PatchTST, AdaRNN, HSN-LSTM, NADINE, FSNet, and OneNet.

In the ablation study, as illustrated in Fig. 5, the choice of replay mechanism significantly impacts the performance of the BRAIN-VAE model. Specifically, the BRAIN-VAE-PER variant, which employs Prioritized Experience Replay, performs better than other models in the vast majority of cases. Meanwhile, the BRAIN-VAE-RER variant, which employs a random experience selected replay mechanism, performs notably worse than even those models that do not utilize any replay mechanism at all. This comparison strongly demonstrates that the strategy of strategically selecting samples for replay is effective and helps the model to learn better. Additionally, it was observed that removing the attention-based fusion module (BRAIN-VAE-woAttn) results in a noticeable decline in predictive performance, underscoring the critical role of the attention layer in the model's effectiveness. The BRAIN-VAE model is designed to seamlessly integrate any type of time series model as its internal module; even when incorporating relatively simple structures such as TCN (Temporal Convolutional Network), the model achieves competitive performance, showcasing its flexibility and robustness in handling diverse time series data.

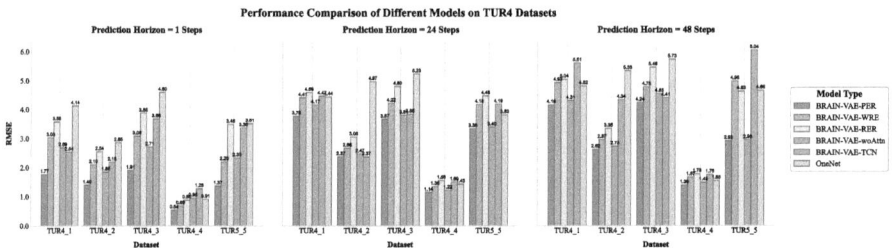

Fig. 5. Performance comparison of BRAIN-VAE variants on 5 time series in TUR4 datasets across prediction horizons (1, 24, 48 steps) using RMSE.

To gain deeper insights into the importance reweighting behavior and the dynamics of the latent variable, we conducted a case study using the PSAL-3 dataset. As shown in Fig. 6, the attention weights across the three modules exhibit dynamic adjustments rather than remaining static throughout the online learning process. Notably, a significant change in weight allocation occurs during periods of data distribution shift. Specifically, Module-1 tends to contribute less in high-frequency data segments, while BRAIN-VAE assigns higher weights to Module-2, which is better suited for capturing and adapting to high-frequency patterns. To further investigate the behavior of the latent variable z, we selected several time points to extract its distribution parameters and plotted the corresponding probability density. The results demonstrate that the distribution of z undergoes continuous changes over time, reflecting its dynamic adaptation to the evolving patterns in the time series.

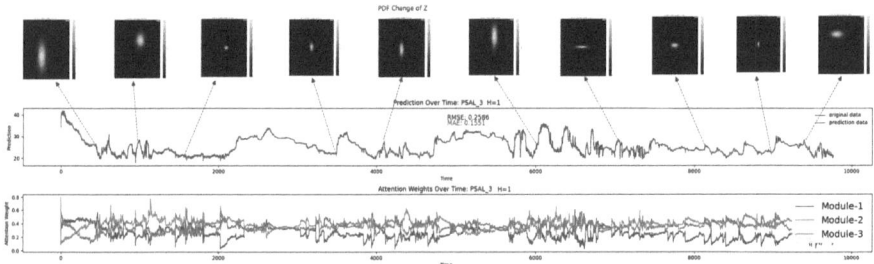

Fig. 6. An illustration of the probability density of z (the lantent representation space is set as 2) change across Prediction Steps for PSAL-3 data.

4.4   Performance and Deployment Considerations

The operational deployment of online learning models in large-scale systems requires careful consideration of computational efficiency and scalability. Our implementation shows that edge devices in the network have limited computational capacity, making them unable to support complex AI algorithms—especially in high-throughput environments. Therefore, our deployment architecture adopts a compute-offloading paradigm: sensor data skips local processing and is directly streamed to a centralized computing facility, the National Supercomputing Center in Jinan. As a core partner in the ocean observation network, the center handles data collection, processing, and analysis. Specifically, we design a supercomputing-parallelized architecture to handle massive concurrent data streams, distributing high-throughput intelligent computations across thousands of cores. Each stream is assigned to an individual core for end-to-end online learning and inference, addressing the inability of edge devices to perform AI model inference services in high-throughput scenarios. This centralized, high-performance framework meets BRAIN-VAE's computational needs and provides a robust, scalable solution for deploying advanced AI in marine monitoring systems.

5   Conclusion

In this work, we propose BRAIN-VAE, an online deep learning model tailored for marine observation data forecasting. BRAIN-VAE integrates a variational autoencoder backbone with an attention mechanism to effectively fuse information from multiple modules, enabling robust generalization capabilities for handling marine data with concept drift. Notably, BRAIN-VAE operates efficiently in cold-start scenarios without the need for pre-training or storing historical models. Instead, it employs a generative replay mechanism that reconstructs hidden representations of past data distributions, akin to a 'hippocampus', to serve as pseudo-replay data. This allows the model to 'review' past experiences most relevant to the current patterns, making it particularly well-suited for long-term, real-time processing of marine observation data streams. Additionally, we introduce MarineDrift-1.0, the first dataset specifically designed to study concept drift in marine observation data. This dataset provides a valuable resource for evaluating forecasting models in marine environments. To promote further research and reproducibility, we make the source code and MarineDrift-1.0 dataset publicly available at: https://github.com/muzixiang/BRAIN-VAE.

Despite the model's strong performance, several promising enhancement directions exist. The current univariate BRAIN-VAE framework, featuring a modular architecture that decouples generative memory replay, multi-module dynamic ensembling, and VAE-based representation learning, can naturally scale to multivariate scenarios. Future work will integrate multivariate encoders and cross-attention layers to model inter-variable dependencies—requiring no infrastructure modifications. Additionally, the model lacks systematic sensitivity analysis of hyperparameters, e.g., the replay frequency and the number of replayed experiences. Furthermore, we will quantify the model's performance in catastrophic forgetting scenarios by introducing a dedicated dataset and evaluating retention of historical knowledge. Finally, we aim to enrich the MarineDrift dataset with complex periodic patterns and multivariate samples.

Acknowledgments. This work was supported by the Major Innovation Project for the Integration of Science, Education, and Industry of Qilu University of Technology (Shandong Academy of Sciences) (2024GH24, 2023JBZ02, 2023HYZX01), the Jinan '20 New Colleges and Universities' Funded Project (202333043), the Key Research and Development Program of Shandong Province (Major Scientific and Technological Innovation Project) (2024CXGC010111), and the Shandong Province Taishan Scholar Climbing Program Project (NO.tspd20240814).

References

1. Torres, J.F., Hadjout, D., Sebaa, A., Martínez-Álvarez, F., Troncoso, A.: Deep learning for time series forecasting: a survey. Big Data **9**(1), 3–21 (2021)
2. Wen, Q., et al.: Transformers in time series: a survey. arXiv preprint arXiv:2202.07125 (2022)
3. Gama, J., Žliobaitė, I., Bifet, A., Pechenizkiy, M., Bouchachia, A.: A survey on concept drift adaptation. ACM Comput. Surv. (CSUR) **46**(4), 1–37 (2014)
4. Agrahari, S., Singh, A.K.: Concept drift detection in data stream mining: a literature review. J. King Saud Univ.-Comput. Inf. Sci. **34**(10), 9523–9540 (2022)
5. Nguyen, N.T., Heldal, R., Pelliccione, P.: Concept-drift-adaptive anomaly detector for marine sensor data streams. Internet Things 101414 (2024)
6. Grossberg, S., Grossberg, S.: How does a brain build a cognitive code? Studies of mind and brain: neural principles of learning, perception, development, cognition, and motor control pp. 1–52 (1982)
7. Yuan, L., et al.: Recent advances in concept drift adaptation methods for deep learning. In: IJCAI, pp. 5654–5661 (2022)
8. Hoi, S.C., Sahoo, D., Lu, J., Zhao, P.: Online learning: a comprehensive survey. Neurocomputing **459**, 249–289 (2021)
9. Sahoo, D., Pham, Q., Lu, J., Hoi, S.C.: Online deep learning: learning deep neural networks on the fly. In: Proceedings of the 27th International Joint Conference on Artificial Intelligence, pp. 2660–2666 (2018)
10. Zhang, S.S., Liu, J.W., Zuo, X., Lu, R.K., Lian, S.M.: Online deep learning based on auto-encoder. Appl. Intell. **51**(8), 5420–5439 (2021)
11. Lu, Y., Cheung, Y.m., Tang, Y.Y.: Dynamic weighted majority for incremental learning of imbalanced data streams with concept drift. In: IJCAI, pp. 2393–2399 (2017)
12. Pratama, M., Za'in, C., Ashfahani, A., Ong, Y.S., Ding, W.: Automatic construction of multi-layer perceptron network from streaming examples. In: Proceedings of the 28th ACM International Conference on Information and Knowledge Management, pp. 1171–1180 (2019)
13. French, R.M.: Catastrophic forgetting in connectionist networks. Trends Cogn. Sci. **3**(4), 128–135 (1999)
14. Wang, H., Li, M., Yue, X.: Inclstm: incremental ensemble lstm model towards time series data. Comput. Electr. Eng. **92**, 107156 (2021)
15. Pham, Q., Liu, C., Sahoo, D., Hoi, S.C.: Learning fast and slow for online time series forecasting. arXiv preprint arXiv:2202.11672 (2022)
16. Wen, Q., et al.: Onenet: enhancing time series forecasting models under concept drift by online ensembling. In: Advances in Neural Information Processing Systems, vol. 36 (2024)

17. Du, Y., et al.: Adarnn. In: Proceedings of the 30th ACM International Conference on Information &; Knowledge Management, October 2021
18. Yoon, J., Yang, E., Lee, J., Hwang, S.J.: Lifelong learning with dynamically expandable networks. arXiv preprint arXiv:1708.01547 (2017)
19. Ashfahani, A., Pratama, M., Lughofer, E., Ong, Y.S.: Devdan: deep evolving denoising autoencoder. Neurocomputing **390**, 297–314 (2020)
20. Zheng, W., Zhao, P., Chen, G., Zhou, H., Tian, Y.: A hybrid spiking neurons embedded lstm network for multivariate time series learning under concept-drift environment. IEEE Trans. Knowl. Data Eng. 1 (2022)
21. Zhao, J., Huang, F., Lv, J., Duan, Y., Qin, Z., Li, G., Tian, G.: Do rnn and lstm have long memory? In: International Conference on Machine Learning, pp. 11365–11375. PMLR (2020)
22. Ji, D., Wilson, M.A.: Coordinated memory replay in the visual cortex and hippocampus during sleep. Nat. Neurosci. **10**(1), 100–107 (2007)
23. Tambini, A., Davachi, L.: Awake reactivation of prior experiences consolidates memories and biases cognition. Trends Cogn. Sci. **23**(10), 876–890 (2019)
24. Kumaran, D., Hassabis, D., McClelland, J.L.: What learning systems do intelligent agents need? complementary learning systems theory updated. Trends Cogn. Sci. **20**(7), 512–534 (2016)
25. Pezzulo, G., Van der Meer, M.A., Lansink, C.S., Pennartz, C.M.: Internally generated sequences in learning and executing goal-directed behavior. Trends Cogn. Sci. **18**(12), 647–657 (2014)
26. Gama, J., Rodrigues, P.P., Spinosa, E., Carvalho, A.: Knowledge discovery from data streams. In: Web Intelligence and Security, pp. 125–138. IOS Press (2010)
27. Hu, Y., Yan, L., Hang, T., Feng, J.: Stream-flow forecasting of small rivers based on lstm. arXiv preprint arXiv:2001.05681 (2020)
28. Li, S., et al.: Enhancing the locality and breaking the memory bottleneck of transformer on time series forecasting. In: Advances in Neural Information Processing Systems, vol. 32 (2019)
29. Zhou, H., et al.: Informer: beyond efficient transformer for long sequence time-series forecasting. In: Proceedings of the AAAI Conference on Artificial Intelligence, vol. 35, pp. 11106–11115 (2021)
30. Zhou, T., Ma, Z., Wen, Q., Wang, X., Sun, L., Jin, R.: Fedformer: frequency enhanced decomposed transformer for long-term series forecasting. In: International Conference on Machine Learning, pp. 27268–27286. PMLR (2022)
31. Wu, H., Xu, J., Wang, J., Long, M.: Autoformer: decomposition transformers with Auto-Correlation for long-term series forecasting. In: Advances in Neural Information Processing Systems (2021)
32. Oreshkin, B.N., Carpov, D., Chapados, N., Bengio, Y.: N-beats: neural basis expansion analysis for interpretable time series forecasting. arXiv preprint arXiv:1905.10437 (2019)
33. Nie, Y., Nguyen, N.H., Sinthong, P., Kalagnanam, J.: A time series is worth 64 words: long-term forecasting with transformers (2022)
34. Du, Y., et al.: Adarnn: adaptive learning and forecasting of time series. In: Proceedings of the 30th ACM International Conference on Information & Knowledge Management, pp. 402–411 (2021)

Supply Framework of Physical Machine Demand in Elastic Computing Service

Zhanyu Liu[1], Xudong Zhang[2], Zhidong Hu[2], Xiejing Li[2], Fei Peng[2], Jian Zhou[2], Siyu Deng[2], and Guanjie Zheng[1(✉)]

[1] Shanghai Jiao Tong University, Shanghai, China
{zhyliu00,gjzheng}@sjtu.edu.cn
[2] Alibaba Cloud Computing, Hangzhou, China
{yulan.zxd,huzhidong.hzd,xiejing.lxj,xinyou.pf,xuming,
desy.dsy}@alibaba-inc.com

Abstract. In the context of Elastic Computing Service (ECS), ensuring an adequate supply of physical machines to meet the varying computing demands is crucial for sustaining high performance and low cost. In industrial practices, different from the typical resource allocation problem that allocates the computing demand into servers, provision of physical servers is a supply chain problem that predicts the future demand for physical machines based on forecasts derived from historical vCPU usage and potential future customer needs, particularly for those customers with high demand. This provision process encompasses three main stages: customer text demand analysis, future demand forecasting, and the allocation of physical servers. However, each stage presents specific challenges. Firstly, large demands from customers are often ambiguously expressed. Secondly, the forecasting process is complicated to model due to the scarce, spiky, and ambiguous nature of the data. Thirdly, the conversion of forecasted vCPU demand into actual physical server quantities is inefficient and ineffective. To address these issues, we propose a novel framework for physical server provisioning. Initially, client requests are aggregated and processed using Large Language Model to extract Potential Future Demand (PFD). Subsequently, future vCPU demand is predicted based on PFD data through a specialized forecasting model tailored with PFD-specific optimizations. Finally, physical machine allocation is executed employing a hierarchical bin-packing algorithm enhanced by heuristic selection and integer programming. Extensive experiments demonstrate the effectiveness and efficiency of the proposed framework with over 60% accuracy improvement and 90% fragment reduction on average compared with the baselines. This framework has been applied to the real industrial scenario of Alibaba Cloud.

Keywords: time series forecasting · elastic computing service · cloud computing

Z. Liu—Work was done during Alibaba Cloud Computing intership.

B. Pfahringer et al. (Eds.): ECML PKDD 2025, LNAI 16020, pp. 474–491, 2026.
https://doi.org/10.1007/978-3-662-72243-5_27

1   Introduction

In Elastic Computing Service (ECS), provisioning physical machines to meet client computing demands is a critical supply-chain challenge [2, 8, 19, 42] distinct from traditional resource allocation. Unlike static server distribution, this requires forecasting future infrastructure needs using historical vCPU usage data and proactive customer demand signals, including support tickets where clients explicitly request supply solutions for anticipated large-scale requirements or report immediate shortages. These client-initiated communications serve as critical inputs for procurement planning, enabling timely equipment orders and deployment scheduling to preempt gaps between supply and demand.

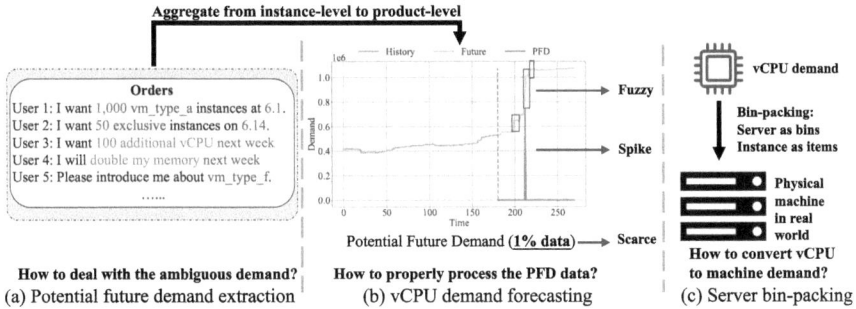

Fig. 1. The challenges in physical machine demand supplement task in elastic computing service.

The process of supplying the physical machine in the cloud service consists of three stages in the industrial practice, as shown in Fig. 1. Firstly, the clients, especially those with big demand, would request resources ahead of time in the Orders. The requests will be aggregated and processed to potential future demand (PFD) focusing on virtual CPU (vCPU) demand. Furthermore, the future vCPU demand will be predicted based on the historical vCPU demand and PFD data. Finally, the physical machine supply allocation is executed which aims to use physical machines with minimum cost to satisfy the predicted vCPU demand. The generated physical machine could offer a reasonable reference for the downstream procurement department.

However, the task of supplementing physical machines in real-world industrial applications is highly complex. As illustrated in Fig. 1, this challenge involves several pivotal factors: (1) managing ambiguous large demand requests from the users, (2) effectively processing PFD data to accurately forecast the future vCPU demand, and (3) optimizing physical machine allocation strategies to reduce overall costs. In particular, during the first stage, client-provided requests are often vague and unstructured, making it challenging to directly extract precise data points, such as dates, exact vCPU requirements, and the quantity of instances needed. Moreover, the second stage involves difficulties in integrating

PFD data with predictions concerning future vCPU demand. This complexity arises due to the characteristics of the PFD data since it is non-zero on only 1% of data samples (indicating scarcity), the non-zero values tend to be large (indicating sparsity), and there is often a discrepancy between real demand and the PFD data (indicating fuzziness). Finally, a gap exists between vCPU demand and actual physical machine provisioning that translating the demand into a concrete number of servers while minimizing costs is a complex task.

In this paper, we develop a deployed comprehensive framework aimed at systematically forecasting and processing future vCPU and physical machine demand while addressing the identified challenges. Our framework initially employs LLM-enhanced techniques to accurately interpret and structure requests provided by clients. Specifically, we utilize the in-context learning ability of LLM to enhance the understanding of client text inputs. Furthermore, we introduce a specialized time series forecasting model tailored for PFD-based vCPU prediction. This model includes multiple modules to manage the challenges of scarcity, sparsity, and fuzziness in vCPU demand prediction respectively. Finally, physical machine demand is determined using a hierarchical bin-packing algorithm to meet the forecasted vCPU requirements. Our contributions ould be summarized as follows:

- To the best of our knowledge, we are the first to systematically address the physical machine demand supplement task in industrial cloud computing supply-chain applications.
- We propose a supply framework of physical machine demand that seamlessly integrates algorithms from LLM, time series forecasting, and bin-packing. This framework effectively addresses challenges related to ambiguous client requests, complex PFD data, and efficient server provisioning.
- We conduct extensive experiments on real-world industrial datasets of Alibaba Cloud. The results validate the effectiveness of our framework and significant performance boost in demand prediction and resource allocation.

2   Related Work

2.1   Demand Forecasting

Demand forecasting is essential not only in cloud computing but also in a variety of other domains [1, 24, 32]. In industrial applications, effective forecasting could enhance resource management and operational efficiency across various scenarios. For instance, [43] employs an LSTM-based method [12] to forecast the number of tourists in different countries. Similarly, [9] utilizes ARIMA and linear models to predict company sales. Moreover, [33] compares statistical and machine learning methods for daily demand forecasting. However, there is a noticeable gap in methods tailored for demand forecasting in cloud computing, where PFD data significantly impacts the demand curve. In the academic realm, time series forecasting has been extensively studied due to its pivotal role in various downstream applications such as traffic management [22, 26, 27] and energy management [13,18], where its implementation is often facilitated through the application of graph modeling [16,17,25]. Numerous methods have been developed to enhance time series forecasting, each focusing on different aspects of data modeling [7,23]. Some approaches leverage transformer-based architectures [34] to capture cross-channel and temporal dependencies. Notable examples include Autoformer [38], Pyraformer [20], Informer [45], FEDFormer [46], and iTransformer [21]. Recently, [40] evaluated the performance of these transformer-based methods and concluded that linear methods could achieve greater effectiveness and efficiency. Consequently, linear-based models and convolution-based models have demonstrated superior performance, such as PatchTST [29], TimesNet [37], Mamba [10], CMamba [41] and TimeMixer [36]. However, these academic methods are typically evaluated on datasets related to energy, weather, and traffic, which exhibit high periodicity, stable trends, and similar data distributions across different nodes. This contrasts sharply with real industrial data related to vCPU and server demand, which are characterized by high volatility and are significantly influenced by PFD data.

2.2   Resource Allocation

Resource allocation is a fundamental component of cloud computing, primarily focused on the efficient distribution of computational resources to satisfy user demands while minimizing operational expenses [19,28]. Traditional mechanisms for resource allocation often rely on heuristic methods such as First-Fit, Best-Fit, and Worst-Fit algorithms [4]. In addition to heuristic methods, some approaches employ price-based greedy algorithms, which are applicable in scenarios like cloud gaming, where resource allocation decisions are influenced by pricing strategies [5]. Other methods involve prediction-based algorithms that dynamically adjust resource allocation based on predicted future demands [39]. Optimization techniques such as integer programming have also been extensively utilized for resource allocation and scheduling to achieve optimal results [11,14,31]. In recent years, deep reinforcement learning (DRL) methods have emerged as promising solutions for the resource allocation problem [3,15,44]. Nevertheless, the integration of accurate demand forecasting with resource allocation remains an underexplored area. While deep learning and optimization methods have made significant strides in addressing resource allocation challenges, their effectiveness can be further enhanced by incorporating precise demand forecasts.

3   Preliminary

Definition 1 (Physical Machine). *A **Physical Machine** is a hardware machine in a data center that provides computational resources, including CPU, memory, storage, and network bandwidth.*

Definition 2 (Virtual CPU). *A **Virtual CPU** (vCPU) represents a portion of physical CPU resources allocated to a virtual machine (VM). Each vCPU is* *scheduled and managed by the hypervisor or virtualization engine. In the industrial application, we focus on demand forecasting for product-level vCPU to guarantee the robustness of the prediction result.*

Definition 3 (Potential Future Demand). *Potential Future Demand (PFD) describes the requirement for computational resources based on the mined order data. PFD is critical for effective demand forecasting, helping to ensure that supply meets demand while minimizing costs and optimizing performance.*

Definition 4 (Instance, Product, Order). *An **Instance** is a single deployment of a virtual machine configured according to specific customer requirements. A **Product** includes a range of cloud service instances with varying computational ability, as well as consistent configurations of other services such as networking and physical machines. An **Order** refers to a formalized communication, typically text-based, between the customer and customer support, aimed at obtaining additional information or making requests regarding specific products. In this paper, we aim to forecast vCPU demand at the product level to ensure the robustness of the results and subsequently divide this forecast to the instance level for optimized downstream physical machine demand allocation.*

Problem 1 (Demand Forecasting). Given T-day historical vCPU demand data $\mathbf{X}^{t-T+1:t}$ and auxiliary information of the PFD data $\mathbf{P}^{t+1:t+T'}$ extracted from the orders, the aim of demand forecasting is to learn a model $f(\cdot)$ to forecast future T' days vCPU demand data $\mathbf{X}^{t+1:t+T'}$. Formally, it could be formulated:

$$[\mathbf{X}^{t-T+1}, \cdots, \mathbf{X}^t, \mathbf{P}^{t+1:t+T'}] \xrightarrow{f(\cdot)} [\mathbf{X}^{t+1}, \cdots, \mathbf{X}^{t+T'}].$$

Problem 2 (Physical Machine Allocation). Basically, this problem is a vector bin-packing problem (VBP). Given the forecasted vCPU demand data $\mathbf{X}^{t+1:t+T'}$ obtained from the demand forecasting model $f(\cdot)$, the objective of physical machine allocation is to optimally assign these CPU demands of product-level of certain day $\mathbf{X}^{T'}$ to the instances of different type $[\mathbf{I}_0, \mathbf{I}_1, \cdots, \mathbf{I}_n]$, where each instance has its size of CPU c_i and memory m_i. The physical machine allocation problem is converted to a bin-packing problem that instances $[\mathbf{I}_0, \mathbf{I}_1, \cdots, \mathbf{I}_n]$ serve as items and physical machines $[\mathbf{S}_0, \mathbf{S}_1, \cdots, \mathbf{S}_m]$ serve as bins. Each physical machine $\mathcal{S}_i$ has its cpu capacity $\bar{c}_i$, memory capacity $\bar{m}_i$, and cost $\bar{o}_i$. The bin-packing problem can be formulated as $\min \sum_{j=1}^m \bar{o}_j y_j$, which is subject to

$$\sum_{i=1}^n c_i a_{ij} \leq \bar{c}_j y_j, \ \sum_{i=1}^n m_i a_{ij} \leq \bar{m}_j y_j, \ \sum_{j=1}^m a_{ij} = 1, \ \forall i \in \{1, \ldots, n\}, \forall j \in \{1, \ldots, m\},$$

where a_{ij} is a binary variable indicating whether instance i is assigned to server j ($a_{ij} = 1$) or not ($a_{ij} = 0$) and y_j is a binary variable indicating whether server j is used ($y_j = 1$) or not ($y_j = 0$).

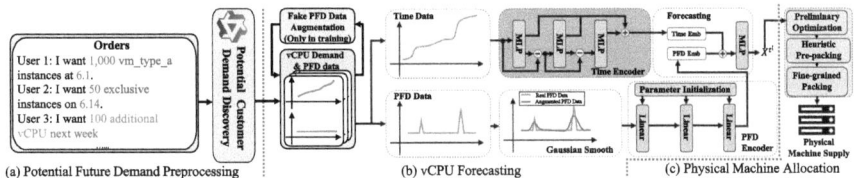

Fig. 2. Illustration of our framework for physical machine supplement.

4   Method

In this section, we detail our comprehensive framework for provisioning physical machines within the elastic computing service, as shown in Fig. 2. Firstly, the Potential Future Demand (PFD) Extraction Module leverages LLM to extract potential vCPU future demand derived from incoming orders of large demand. Subsequently, the vCPU Forecasting Module utilizes separate modeling techniques for historical time series data and PFD data to accurately forecast future vCPU demand. Finally, the Physical Machine Allocation Module employs a multi-stage approach to ensure efficient resource allocation.

4.1   PFD Preprocessing Module

Goal: The primary challenge in extracting future demand lies in the ambiguous nature of the textual input provided by the users with large demand, as depicted in Fig. 2(a). To address this, the Potential Future Demand (PFD) Extraction Module employs the ability of in-context learning (ICL) of LLM to convert unstructured text into structured entity tuples. This structured PFD data can then be seamlessly integrated into the downstream vCPU forecasting module, facilitating accurate and reliable demand prediction.

Input and Output. The PFD Preprocessing Module processes the textual reports derived from orders. Example texts of these inputs are provided in Fig. 2(a). This module translates these ambiguous requests by Qwen2.5-7B[1] LLM into clear and structured data such as (UserID, Quantity, InstanceType, Date) to enhance the accuracy of the forecasting process.

Potential Customer Demand Discovery. To interpret the requests from the users, we propose the ICL-enhanced Potential Customer Demand Discovery module, as shown in Tab 1. The module integrates structured system configurations with contextual learning to extract structured demand tuples (UserID, Quantity, InstanceType, Date) from heterogeneous inputs, including user information and requests. First, it integrates **system configurations**, such as the current date and ECS knowledge base defining VM specifications, to ensure

---

[1] https://github.com/QwenLM/Qwen2.5.

Table 1. ICL-enhanced prompt of Potential Customer Demand Discovery.

Potential Customer Demand Discovery

[System Config]
Current Date: {Weekday}, {YYYY-MM-DD}
ECS Knowledge Base: {vm_type_a: this VM contains 4 vcpu and ...}
[Task] Extract (UserID, Quantity, InstanceType, Date) tuples from:
1. User Context → [Existing Resources/Contracts]
2. Current Request → [Natural Language]
[In-Context Examples]
UserID: User1. Context: {User_Instances: None, ...}
Request: "I want 1,000 vm_type_a instances at 6.1"
Output: (User1, 1000, vm_type_a, 2024.6.1)
      ......
[New Request]
UserID: {UserX}, Context: {User_Summary}, Request: {Natural Language Text}

---

temporal relevance and technical grounding. Then, it formalizes a **structured extraction task** targeting (UserID, Quantity, InstanceType, Date) tuples, explicitly bridging user context (e.g., existing instances) and natural language requests. Subsequently, **in-context examples** demonstrate schema alignment that colloquial expressions like "6.1" are mapped to standardized formats by leveraging the system configuration, while VM type definitions from the knowledge base disambiguate technical terms. Finally, the **new request** combines summarized user profiles with raw textual queries, enabling joint reasoning to infer the coming user request. This hierarchical design supports scalable adaptation to updated VM types or policies through the knowledge base, ensuring industrial-grade robustness in demand extraction.

4.2   vCPU Forecasting Module

Goal: As shown in Fig. 1 (b), the main challenges in forecasting the vCPU demand encompass several critical aspects: (1) the PFD data is **scarce**, with only 1% of the dates containing non-zero PFD data; (2) most of the non-zero PFD data consists of **spikes**, characterized by sudden, large values; (3) the PFD demand data is not consistently aligned with the actual demand, as customers often provide **fuzzy** future demand requests and fail to purchase instances punctually. Consequently, in this subsection, we propose three modules to address these challenges separately.

Input and Output. The vCPU Forecasting Module takes two inputs: the T-day historical vCPU demand data $\mathbf{X}^{t-T+1:t}$ and the future T'-day PFD data $\mathbf{P}^{t+1:t+T'}$. The output generated by this module is the forecasted vCPU demand for the future T' days, denoted as $\mathbf{X}^{t+1:t+T'}$.

Fake PFD Augmentation. To mitigate the **scarcity** of the PFD data in training, we propose the Fake PFD Augmentation Module, as shown in Fig. 3. This module aims to enhance the volume and variability of the training data, improving the robustness of the forecasting models. The intuition behind this module is based on the observation that if the customers request a specific amount of vCPU for a future date, they are likely to purchase a similar amount around that time. Initially, we randomly select a subset of the existing training samples. For each selected sample, we generate a fake PFD dataset, denoted as $\mathbf{P}'$, which includes a small, random number of randomly distributed non-zero entries. These non-zero values are crafted to replicate the characteristics observed in real PFD data, such as spikes and variability in magnitude. Subsequently, we incorporate this synthetic PFD data $\mathbf{P}'$ with the corresponding future vCPU demand data $\mathbf{X}$ of the selected samples by adding the synthetic PFD data with a random scaling factor. This integration process aims to simulate realistic demand patterns, thereby allowing the model to generalize more effectively and adapt to the sparsity and irregularities that are typical of real-world PFD data.

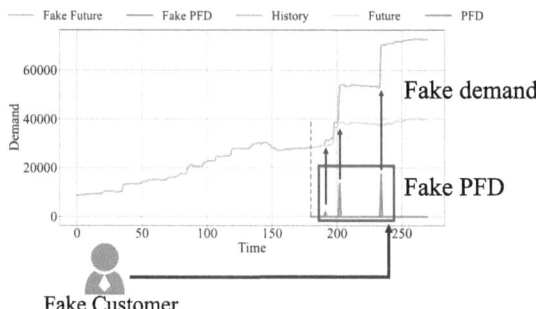

Fig. 3. Illustration of Fake PFD Data Augmentation

Gaussian Smoothing Augmentation. The **spiked** PFD data could harm the performance of the downstream prediction model since the spike values may distort the learning process and lead to overfitting or inaccurate predictions. To alleviate the impact of spiked data in the forecasting process, we introduce the Gaussian Smoothing Augmentation module. This method aims to smooth the spike in the PFD data and keep the information of the vCPU demand, thus helping the models to generate stable output and learn robust knowledge, as shown in Fig. 2(b). Specifically, each spiked value in $\mathbf{P}^k$ is converted into a Gaussian distribution and aggregated to form $\hat{\mathbf{P}}$, as represented in Eq. 1.

$$\hat{\mathbf{P}}^t = \sum_{k=1}^{T'} \mathbf{P}^k \frac{1}{\sigma_1 \sqrt{2\pi}} e^{-\frac{(t-k)^2}{2\sigma_1^2}} \tag{1}$$

Gaussian Center Parameter Initialization. In practice, the PFD data is **fuzzy** and often does not precisely align with the actual demand, as customers may purchase instances approximately around the projected date rather than on the exact date, as depicted in Fig. 1(b). Consequently, the PFD data is highly correlated with the actual demand, exhibiting temporal locality where the PFD at day t ($\hat{\mathbf{P}}^t$) is significantly related to the actual demand on nearby dates. To effectively utilize the PFD data for forecasting demand, we incorporate this temporal locality into the initialization of the model, thereby leveraging prior knowledge to enhance the training process, as shown in Fig. 4. For a linear model W that encodes the PFD data, we can express this relationship:

$$\hat{\mathbf{P}}^t_{out} = \sum_{i=1}^{T'} \hat{\mathbf{P}}^i W_{it}, \tag{2}$$

where $\mathbf{P}^{\hat{i}}_{out}$ is the output data of position t. Given the temporal locality of the PFD data, the parameter matrix should exhibit the following characteristic:

$$W^{tt} \geq W^{it} \quad \forall i \in \{1, 2, \ldots, T'\}. \tag{3}$$

Accordingly, we initialize the parameter matrix using a column-wise Gaussian distribution. By denoting the t-th column of the parameter matrix as w^t, this initialization can be described as:

$$w^t \sim \mathcal{N}(t, \sigma_2). \tag{4}$$

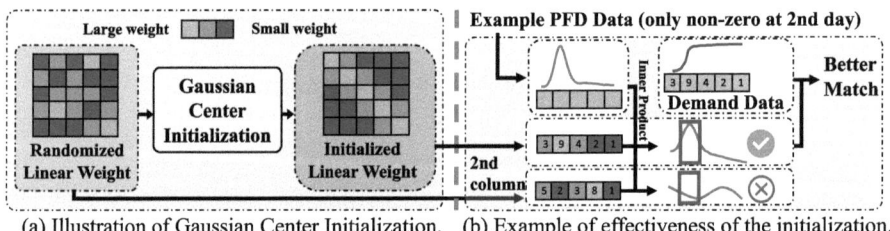

(a) Illustration of Gaussian Center Initialization.   (b) Example of effectiveness of the initialization.

Fig. 4. Gaussian Center Initialization. (a) This panel depicts the initialized linear parameter matrix. (b) This panel provides a practical example on a PFD data with only potential demand on the 2nd day. It shows that the Gaussian Center Initialized parameter of the 2nd column has highest weight on the 2nd slot, thereby enhancing the demand of the 2nd day and generate accurate embedding.

Forecasting. To model the temporal data, we utilize a forecast-backcast model based on N-BEATS [30] to generate time embeddings. In each layer of this model, a Multi-Layer Perceptron (MLP) is used to process the input data H_i (where $H_0 = \mathbf{X}^{t-T+1:t}$), producing two types of embeddings: forecast embedding fo_i and backcast embedding ba_i at the i-th layer.

$$fo_i, ba_i = MLP(H_i) \tag{5}$$

The input to the subsequent layer is then computed as the difference between H_i and ba_i and the final time embedding is obtained by summing the forecast embeddings across all layers:

$$H_{i+1} = H_i - ba_i, \quad H_{time} = \sum_i fo_i. \tag{6}$$

Finally, the time embedding H_{time} is combined with the PFD embedding H_{PFD}, and a final MLP layer is used to forecast the future vCPU demand:

$$\hat{\mathbf{X}}^{t+1:t+T'} = MLP(H_{time} + H_{PFD}). \tag{7}$$

For the training of the forecasting model, we use the Mean Square Error (MSE) as the loss function.

$$\mathcal{L} = \sum_{i=t+1}^{t+T'} (\hat{\mathbf{X}}^i - \mathbf{X}^i)^2 \tag{8}$$

4.3 Physical Server Allocation Module

Goal: In the previous subsection, we get the predicted future vCPU demand. Nevertheless, to supply this demand, the downstream purchasing department needs the actual physical machine demand and there is a gap between the vCPU demand and the physical machine demand. Consequently, the Physical Server Allocation Module is designed to bridge this gap by mapping the predicted vCPU demand to tangible physical server demand.

Input and Output. The input of this module is the predicted future vCPU demand $\mathbf{X}^{t+1:t+T'}$. In practice, we use the vCPU demand of the final day $\mathbf{X}^{t+T'}$ as the target demand and convert it into the instances of different type $[\mathbf{I}_0, \mathbf{I}_1, \cdots, \mathbf{I}_n]$ by the selling ratio of different instances to get a robust estimation. The output of this module is the usage of physical machines, including the machine list $[\mathbf{S}_0, \mathbf{S}_1, \cdots, \mathbf{S}_m]$ and indicator $y_{1:m}$.

Preliminary Optimization. In this subsection, we first utilize the instance demand $[\mathbf{I}_0, \cdots, \mathbf{I}_n]$ and the physical server types $[\mathbf{R}_0, \cdots, \mathbf{R}_k]$ to get a initial physical server lists $[\mathbf{S}_0, \cdots, \mathbf{S}_m]$. The primary constraints ensure that the CPU and memory capacities of the physical servers meet the requirements of the instances. This is formulated as:

$$\sum_{i=1}^{n} c_i \leq \sum_{i=1}^{k} \hat{c}_i N_i \quad \sum_{i=1}^{n} m_i \leq \sum_{i=1}^{k} \hat{m}_i N_i, \tag{9}$$

where $\hat{c}_i$, $\hat{m}_i$, and N_i represent the CPU, memory, and the number of physical server types $\mathbf{R}_i$. Additionally, we incorporate a constraint on the fragment space ratio to ensure that the available fragmented space can ideally accommodate an instance. This is expressed as:

$$\frac{\sum_{i=1}^{k} \hat{m}_i N_i - \sum_{i=1}^{n} m_i}{\sum_{i=1}^{k} \hat{c}_i N_i - \sum_{i=1}^{n} c_i} \geq r, \tag{10}$$

where r is the mem/CPU ratio, which is set to 2. By solving this optimization problem using cvxpy [6], we could get the initial quantities of each physical machine N_i and subsequently convert it to the physical machine list $[\mathbf{S}_0, \cdots, \mathbf{S}_m]$.

Heuristic Pre-packing. To alleviate the redundancy of the intermediate result, we formalize the problem to a two-dimensional bin-packing problem. However, directly optimize the problem with integer programming is highly costly since the quantity of instance is too large. Consequently, we propose to first use a Heuristic Pre-packing based on a bin-centric best-fit algorithm to reduce the scale of the problem. We sort the physical server and pack the server with a larger capacity first. To pack the server, we compute the cosine similarity between its remaining capacity and the demand of each instance in both memory and CPU dimensions and repeatedly. Then, we pack the instance with the highest cosine similarity to the server. By iteratively applying this heuristic packing method, we can significantly reduce the scale of the problem and achieve an effective, scalable solution to the bin-packing problem.

Fine-Grained Packing. Following the Heuristic Pre-packing phase, the set of physical servers $[\mathbf{S}_0, \cdots, \mathbf{S}_m]$ may contain some residual fragmentation and redundancy (about 5% of the total servers on average). Consequently, we process the remaining servers and instances by the integer-programming-based Fine-grained Packing module to enhance the efficiency. Firstly, **Index-Independent Optimization** eliminates instance and server indices, focusing on their quantities. Let n and m be the number of instances and servers, and p and q the number of instance and server types, with $p \ll n$ and $m \ll q$. Directly packing instances into servers has a complexity of $O(n^m)$, which is impractical. The Index-Independent Optimization reduces this to $O(p^q)$, simplifying the problem. Then, the **Instance Type Merging** technique merges instances with similar CPU and memory capacities, thus reducing the number of instance types from p to p', where $p' < p$. This further lowers the time complexity of the packing process from $O(n^m)$ to $O(p'^q)$. Finally, we utilize cvxpy [6] to optimize this problem to get the vector $y_{1:m}$ that indicates whether each physical server is used.

5   Experiment

5.1   Experiment Setting

The framework is evaluated in the real vCPU demand data for 31 different products from Alibaba Cloud, spanning the period from January 2018 to April 2023.

The experiment comprises two parts. All of the experiments were conducted on an NVIDIA A10 GPU.

- In vCPU Forecasting, we follow the setting of previous time series forecasting research on benchmark datasets [35,46] that segment the dataset with continuous sliding windows of 270 days and utilize historical vCPU data of 180 days to forecast the future vCPU data of subsequent 90 days. We search the hyper-parameters σ_1 and σ_2 within the set $\{1, 3, 7\}$, and synthesize fake PFD data using 10% of the training set of the original dataset. Additionally, within the Fake PFD Augmentation module, we randomly allocate up to three days of fake customer demand to each sample. We use Root Mean Squared Error (RMSE), Mean Absolute Error (MAE), and Mean Absolute Percentage Error (MAPE) as the metrics.

$$RMSE = \sqrt{\frac{1}{T'}\sum_{i=1}^{T'}(\mathbf{X}^i - \hat{\mathbf{X}}^i)^2}, MAE = \frac{1}{T'}\sum_{i=1}^{T'}|\mathbf{X}^i - \hat{\mathbf{X}}^i|, MAPE = \frac{1}{T'}\sum_{i=1}^{T'}|\frac{\mathbf{X}^i - \hat{\mathbf{X}}^i}{\mathbf{X}^i}| \tag{11}$$

- In Physical Server Allocation, we utilize the predicted vCPU as the input. In practical industrial scenarios, the demands for different products necessitate allocation to distinct types of physical servers. To assess the efficacy and efficiency of the proposed allocation method, we use the predicted vCPU requirements for the one with largest demand in the 31 products, assigning its demands to three specific types of physical servers accordingly.

Table 2. Overall performance of the vCPU () demand forecasting task on the real data of Alibaba Cloud from January 1, 2018, to April 1, 2023. The mean and standard deviation of the results in five runs are shown. In each column, the best result is highlighted in bold and grey. All numbers are in units of 1k.

	Day 7			Day 30			Day 90		
	RMSE	MAE	MAPE(%)	RMSE	MAE	MAPE(%)	RMSE	MAE	MAPE(%)
Autoformer	147.53±14.98	104.25±19.93	81.82±24.64	171.34±8.52	114.70±14.62	82.36±24.84	245.91±20.69	155.71±17.30	89.29±16.12
Pyraformer	546.63±60.09	154.84±17.64	21.54±7.09	504.12±33.92	159.87±27.98	23.93±8.35	483.47±26.35	179.57±10.78	40.87±2.04
Informer	403.77±38.04	135.09±11.50	36.78±8.65	382.19±24.68	131.01±7.86	39.16±8.30	383.61±23.33	151.86±12.45	48.80±4.39
FEDformer	69.50±12.26	46.83±7.56	31.28±4.15	97.09±7.32	58.53±7.93	34.26+6 96	181.70±19.52	83.41±11.56	32.46±7.70
MICN	57.53±5.18	25.46+? 33	0.22±2.47	88.66±2.84	37.31±2.55	12.56±2.74	166.54±6.32	73.83±3.86	28.74±6.68
iTransformer	47.37±3.18	20.48±1.53	6.95±0.33	89.12±4.17	36.24±1.49	10.46±0.38	169.69±2.30	68.54±1.63	20.46±0.75
PatchTST	62.11±19.65	31.30±10.88	9.87±3.67	95.52±8.65	45.39±2.95	13.75±0.35	209.67±23.55	93.44±13.21	27.37±4.91
Mamba	105.80±4.47	51.60±2.65	16.82±1.10	149.29±7.21	73.79±4.11	25.43±1.35	367.35±132.28	134.68±39.77	46.92±27.06
NLinear	26.71±4.04	15.24±6.28	11.27±9.58	64.32±3.10	29.50±6.56	13.28±10.22	158.84±2.00	70.07±3.31	24.04±7.14
Ours	**21.79±0.53**	**8.09±0.39**	**2.62±0.43**	**58.16±0.93**	**22.35±0.33**	**6.66±0.25**	**148.10±1.48**	**57.30±0.63**	**17.02±0.29**

5.2 vCPU Forecasting Overall Performance

Baseline. We select nine well-acknowledged baselines to evaluate the performance of our proposed module on the vCPU forecasting task. We utilize the hyperparameter of the original papers for the baseline models. Moreover, these baselines are fed with the PFD embedding processed by a three-layer MLP.

- Transformer-based methods: These methods employ the Transformer [34] as the backbone model, incorporating specific optimizations tailored for time series analysis, including adjustments for trend and seasonal patterns. The comparison encompasses models such as **Autoformer** [38], **Pyraformer** [20], **Informer** [45], **FEDformer** [46].
- Linear-based methods: These methods utilize the linear network or convolutional neural network (CNN), including **MICN** [35], **PatchTST** [29], **NLinear** [40], **Mamba** [10]. Note that when the input is single-channel, the **iTransformer** [21] is reduced to the linear model.

Overall Performance. We report the forecasting accuracy of the vCPU demand on days 7, 30, and 90 in Table 2. From the analysis of the table, several key observations emerge: (1) The proposed framework consistently outperforms state-of-the-art (SOTA) baselines across all experimental settings. (2) In comparison to transformer-based methods, our framework shows a remarkable improvement: 67.74% in RMSE, 74.99% in MAE, and 79.72% in MAPE. This suggests that the transformer-based approaches do not align well with the characteristics of vCPU demand data, likely due to their assumption of a pronounced trend and seasonal patterns. The observed superior performance signifies that our straightforward model effectively captures the underlying patterns in vCPU demand data, learning robust knowledge from them. (3) When compared with linear-based methods, our framework exhibits performance enhancements of 38.48% in RMSE, 47.35% in MAE, and 54.35% in MAPE. Notably, linear-based methods outperform transformer-based methods, consistent with the findings of [40], where linear models are noted for their robustness in time series forecasting. Moreover, the substantial performance gains underscore the efficacy of the specialized PFD data modeling approach of our framework.

Table 3. Ablation Study of vCPU demand forecasting. The mean and standard deviation of the results in five runs are shown. In each column, the best result is highlighted in bold and grey. All numbers are in units of 1k.

	Day 7			Day 30			Day 90		
	RMSE	MAE	MAPE(%)	RMSE	MAE	MAPE(%)	RMSE	MAE	MAPE(%)
Base	24.56±1.01	9.83±0.25	3.44±0.14	77.44±4.66	31.01±1.31	7.76±0.50	214.75±11.72	84.72±4.87	21.29±1.39
Base+P	23.54±0.37	8.81±0.18	3.09±0.10	66.36±3.05	25.52±1.61	6.91±0.68	177.24±3.02	66.35±1.56	18.97±1.30
Base+P+F	22.79±0.39	8.51±0.13	2.83±0.05	61.15±3.47	23.64±1.37	6.75±0.48	161.42±8.47	62.04±3.84	18.29±2.45
Base+P+F+A	**21.79±0.53**	**8.09±0.39**	**2.62±0.43**	**58.16±0.93**	**22.35±0.33**	**6.66±0.25**	**148.10±1.48**	**57.30±0.63**	**17.02±0.29**

5.3   vCPU Forecasting Ablation Study

In this section, we will verify the effectiveness of the proposed modules in the vCPU Forecasting framework. We define **Base** as a straightforward MLP model that utilizes raw vCPU time series and PFD data. The enhanced model,

Base+P, incorporates Gaussian Center Parameter Initialization. Further optimizations are defined as **Base+P+F**, which includes Fake PFD Augmentation, and **Base+P+F+A**, which integrates Gaussian Smoothing Augmentation. The result is shown in Table 3. From the table, we can observe that (1) The integration of Gaussian Center Parameter Initialization (in the **Base+P** model) results in a substantial improvement in performance. This enhancement underscores the significance of embedding prior knowledge, which facilitates the model in acquiring more effective and robust representations. (2) The incremental additions of Fake PFD Augmentation and Gaussian Smoothing Augmentation (in the **Base+P+F** and **Base+P+F+A** models, respectively) contribute further to the accuracy and reliability of the model. These results collectively demonstrate that each augmentation not only enhances the predictive capability of the MLP but also reinforces the stability and generalization of the forecasting framework.

Table 4. The baseline comparison of Physical Server Allocation module. The mean and standard deviation are reported. In each column, the best result is highlighted in bold and grey.

Methods	1000 Instances (n = 1000)			5000 Instances (n = 5000)			10000 Instances (n = 10000)		
	Packing Density(%)	Fragment (%)	Solving Time (s)	Packing Density(%)	Fragment (%)	Solving Time (s)	Packing Density(%)	Fragment (%)	Solving Time (s)
First-Fit-B	66.74±7.37	32.73±7.04	1.86±1.90	65.35±5.65	34.54±5.61	6.59±1.79	73.58±4.82	26.36±4.77	**12.49±0.87**
First-Fit-I	96.56±1.45	2.52±1.30	**1.05±0.52**	96.52±1.40	3.39±1.44	**6.24±1.22**	97.84±0.83	2.03±0.74	14.52±4.24
Best-Fit-B	97.31±1.30	1.68±0.98	2.63±1.09	98.06±0.26	1.23±0.60	19.51±2.86	97.42±1.54	2.22±1.98	46.78±9.84
Best-Fit-I	84.89±10.61	4.30±6.67	12.51±12.64	87.36±14.73	2.30±4.22	191.75±37.13	91.66±6.73	5.05±4.46	387.85±33.40
IP	98.71±1.48	0.49±0.57	120.00±0.00	88.96±8.36	5.29±4.22	120.00±0.00	89.09±3.02	5.13±1.54	120.00±0.00
Ours	**99.40±0.74**	**0.05±0.12**	11.31±3.09	**99.63±0.70**	**0.06±0.11**	23.66±3.18	**99.54±0.73**	**0.05±0.08**	43.59±10.37

5.4   Physical Server Allocation Result

In this section, we will verify the efficacy and efficiency of the proposed Physical Server Allocation module in different problem scales by employing several performance metrics:

- Packing Density: Calculated as $\frac{1}{2}\left(\frac{Demand\_CPU}{Supplied\_CPU} + \frac{Demand\_Mem}{Supplied\_Mem}\right)$.
- Fragment: The remaining space ratio that cannot accommodate any instance.
- Solving Time: The average time required to solve each forecasted result.

We compare our module with several baseline methods including both instance-centric and server-centric algorithms. Specifically, we consider the First-Fit algorithm, which assigns the current instance to the first available server (-I) or places the first available instance onto the current server (-S); the Best-Fit algorithm, which allocates the instance to a server (-I) or the server to an instance (-S) based on the highest cosine similarity in resource capacity; and an Integer Programming (IP) approach that directly formulates the instance-server assignment as a linear programming problem, with a 120-second time constraint imposed to mitigate computational complexity while maintaining solution feasibility. The results summarized in Table 4 lead to two key observations: (1) our proposed module outperforms the baseline methods significantly while maintaining an acceptable computational cost, and (2) the Packing Density and Fragment metrics remain robust and stable across various problem scales, thereby substantially reducing costs.

6   Conclusion

In this work, we introduce a novel framework for provisioning physical machines in elastic computing services. The framework incorporates a PFD Preprocessing module to structure PFD data from text inputs, a vCPU Forecasting Module to precisely predict future vCPU requirements by modeling the PFD data, and a Physical Server Allocation Module to efficiently translate these vCPU demands into actual physical server allocations. In the future, we will aim at further optimize the efficiency and efficacy of the framework.

Acknowledgment. This work was sponsored by National Key Research and Development Program of China under Grant No.2022YFB3904204, National Natural Science Foundation of China under Grant No. 62102246, 62272301, and Provincial Key Research and Development Program of Zhejiang under Grant No. 2021C01034. This work was supported by Alibaba Research Intern Program.

References

1. Abolghasemi, M., Beh, E., Tarr, G., Gerlach, R.: Demand forecasting in supply chain: the impact of demand volatility in the presence of promotion. Comput. Ind. Eng. **142**, 106380 (2020)
2. Al-Dhuraibi, Y., Paraiso, F., Djarallah, N., Merle, P.: Elasticity in cloud computing: state of the art and research challenges. IEEE Trans. Serv. Comput. **11**(2), 430–447 (2017)
3. Chen, Z., Hu, J., Min, G., Luo, C., El-Ghazawi, T.: Adaptive and efficient resource allocation in cloud datacenters using actor-critic deep reinforcement learning. IEEE Trans. Parallel Distrib. Syst. **33**(8), 1911–1923 (2021)
4. Coffman, E.G., Csirik, J., Galambos, G., Martello, S., Vigo, D., et al.: Bin packing approximation algorithms: Survey and classification. In: Handbook of combinatorial optimization, pp. 455–531. Springer (2013)
5. Deng, Y., Li, Y., Tang, X., Cai, W.: Server allocation for multiplayer cloud gaming. In: Proceedings of the 24th ACM International Conference on Multimedia, pp. 918–927 (2016)
6. Diamond, S., Boyd, S.: CVXPY: A python-embedded modeling language for convex optimization. J. Mach. Learn. Res. **17**(83), 1–5 (2016)
7. Ding, J., Liu, Z., Zheng, G., Jin, H., Kong, L.: Condtsf: one-line plugin of dataset condensation for time series forecasting. arXiv preprint arXiv:2406.02131 (2024)

8. Dong, H., et al.: Predictive job scheduling under uncertain constraints in cloud computing. In: IJCAI, pp. 3627–3634 (2021)
9. Feizabadi, J.: Machine learning demand forecasting and supply chain performance. Int J Log Res Appl **25**(2), 119–142 (2022)
10. Gu, A., Dao, T.: Mamba: Linear-time sequence modeling with selective state spaces. arXiv preprint arXiv:2312.00752 (2023)
11. Heinz, S., Ku, W.-Y., Beck, J.C.: Recent improvements using constraint integer programming for resource allocation and scheduling. In: Gomes, C., Sellmann, M. (eds.) CPAIOR 2013. LNCS, vol. 7874, pp. 12–27. Springer, Heidelberg (2013). https://doi.org/10.1007/978-3-642-38171-3_2
12. Hochreiter, S., Schmidhuber, J.: Long short-term memory. Neural Comput. **9**(8), 1735–1780 (1997)
13. Hong, T., Pinson, P., Wang, Y., Weron, R., Yang, D., Zareipour, H.: Energy forecasting: a review and outlook. IEEE Open Access J. Power Energy **7**, 376–388 (2020)
14. Ibrahim, H., Aburukba, R.O., El-Fakih, K.: An integer linear programming model and adaptive genetic algorithm approach to minimize energy consumption of cloud computing data centers. Comput. Electr. Eng. **67**, 551–565 (2018)
15. Islam, M.T., Karunasekera, S., Buyya, R.: Performance and cost-efficient spark job scheduling based on deep reinforcement learning in cloud computing environments. IEEE Trans. Parallel Distrib. Syst. **33**(7), 1695–1710 (2021)
16. Kang, Z., Liu, Z., Pan, S., Tian, L.: Fine-grained attributed graph clustering. In: Proceedings of the 2022 SIAM International Conference on Data Mining (SDM), pp. 370–378. SIAM (2022)
17. Kipf, T.N., Welling, M.: Semi-supervised classification with graph convolutional networks. arXiv preprint arXiv:1609.02907 (2016)
18. Le Cam, M., Daoud, A., Zmeureanu, R.: Forecasting electric demand of supply fan using data mining techniques. Energy **101**, 541–557 (2016)
19. Li, F.: Cloud-native database systems at alibaba: opportunities and challenges. Proc. VLDB Endowment **12**(12), 2263–2272 (2019)
20. Liu, S., et al.: Pyraformer: low-complexity pyramidal attention for long-range time series modeling and forecasting. In: International Conference on Learning Representations (2021)
21. Liu, Y., et al.: Itransformer: inverted transformers are effective for time series forecasting. arXiv preprint arXiv:2310.06625 (2023)
22. Liu, Z., Ding, J., Zheng, G.: Frequency enhanced pre-training for cross-city few-shot traffic forecasting. In: Joint European Conference on Machine Learning and Knowledge Discovery in Databases, pp. 35–52. Springer (2024)
23. Liu, Z., Hao, K., Zheng, G., Yu, Y.: Dataset condensation for time series classification via dual domain matching. In: Proceedings of the 30th ACM SIGKDD Conference on Knowledge Discovery and Data Mining, pp. 1980–1991 (2024)
24. Liu, Z., Liang, C., Zheng, G., Wei, H.: Fdti: fine-grained deep traffic inference with roadnet-enriched graph. In: Joint European Conference on Machine Learning and Knowledge Discovery in Databases, pp. 174–191. Springer (2023)
25. Liu, Z., Zeng, C., Zheng, G.: Graph data condensation via self-expressive graph structure reconstruction. In: Proceedings of the 30th ACM SIGKDD Conference on Knowledge Discovery and Data Mining, pp. 1992–2002 (2024)
26. Liu, Z., Zheng, G., Yu, Y.: Cross-city few-shot traffic forecasting via traffic pattern bank. In: Proceedings of the 32nd ACM International Conference on Information and Knowledge Management, pp. 1451–1460 (2023)

27. Liu, Z., Zheng, G., Yu, Y.: Multi-scale traffic pattern bank for cross-city few-shot traffic forecasting. ACM Trans. Knowl. Discov. Data **19**(4), 1–24 (2025)
28. Nahir, A., Orda, A., Raz, D.: Resource allocation and management in cloud computing. In: 2015 IFIP/IEEE International Symposium on Integrated Network Management (IM), pp. 1078–1084. IEEE (2015)
29. Nie, Y., Nguyen, N.H., Sinthong, P., Kalagnanam, J.: A time series is worth 64 words: long-term forecasting with transformers. arXiv preprint arXiv:2211.14730 (2022)
30. Oreshkin, B.N., Carpov, D., Chapados, N., Bengio, Y.: N-beats: neural basis expansion analysis for interpretable time series forecasting. arXiv preprint arXiv:1905.10437 (2019)
31. Rezvani, M., Akbari, M.K., Javadi, B.: Resource allocation in cloud computing environments based on integer linear programming. Comput. J. **58**(2), 300–314 (2015)
32. Seyedan, M., Mafakheri, F.: Predictive big data analytics for supply chain demand forecasting: methods, applications, and research opportunities. J. Big Data **7**(1), 1–22 (2020). https://doi.org/10.1186/s40537-020-00329-2
33. Spiliotis, E., Makridakis, S., Semenoglou, A.A., Assimakopoulos, V.: Comparison of statistical and machine learning methods for daily sku demand forecasting. Oper. Res. Int. J. **22**(3), 3037–3061 (2022)
34. Vaswani, A., et al.: Attention is all you need. Adv. Neural Inf. Process. Syst. **30** (2017)
35. Wang, H., Peng, J., Huang, F., Wang, J., Chen, J., Xiao, Y.: Micn: multi-scale local and global context modeling for long-term series forecasting. In: The Eleventh International Conference on Learning Representations (2023)
36. Wang, S., et al.: Timemixer: Decomposable multiscale mixing for time series forecasting. arXiv preprint arXiv:2405.14616 (2024)
37. Wu, H., Hu, T., Liu, Y., Zhou, H., Wang, J., Long, M.: Timesnet: temporal 2D-variation modeling for general time series analysis. In: The Eleventh International Conference on Learning Representations (2022)
38. Wu, H., Xu, J., Wang, J., Long, M.: Autoformer: decomposition transformers with auto-correlation for long-term series forecasting. Adv. Neural. Inf. Process. Syst. **34**, 22419–22430 (2021)
39. Xiao, Z., Song, W., Chen, Q.: Dynamic resource allocation using virtual machines for cloud computing environment. IEEE Trans. Parallel Distrib. Syst. **24**(6), 1107–1117 (2012)
40. Zeng, A., Chen, M., Zhang, L., Xu, Q.: Are transformers effective for time series forecasting? In: Proceedings of the AAAI conference on artificial intelligence, vol. 37, pp. 11121–11128 (2023)
41. Zeng, C., Liu, Z., Zheng, G., Kong, L.: Cmamba: channel correlation enhanced state space models for multivariate time series forecasting. arXiv preprint arXiv:2406.05316 (2024)
42. Zhang, G., Ravishankar, M.: Exploring vendor capabilities in the cloud environment: a case study of alibaba cloud computing. Inf. Manag. **56**(3), 343–355 (2019)
43. Zhang, Y., Li, G., Muskat, B., Law, R.: Tourism demand forecasting: a decomposed deep learning approach. J. Travel Res. **60**(5), 981–997 (2021)
44. Zhang, Y., Yao, J., Guan, H.: Intelligent cloud resource management with deep reinforcement learning. IEEE Cloud Comput. **4**(6), 60–69 (2017)

45. Zhou, H., et al.: Informer: beyond efficient transformer for long sequence time-series forecasting. In: Proceedings of the AAAI Conference on Artificial Intelligence, vol. 35, pp. 11106–11115 (2021)
46. Zhou, T., Ma, Z., Wen, Q., Wang, X., Sun, L., Jin, R.: Fedformer: frequency enhanced decomposed transformer for long-term series forecasting. In: International Conference on Machine Learning, pp. 27268–27286. PMLR (2022)

Improving Pricing Recommendations Using Nearest Neighbors Retrieval Via Contrastive Learning and Hard Negatives Mining

Eyal Mazuz[1](✉), Gilad Fuchs[2], Alex Nus[2], Lior Rokach[1], and Bracha Shapira[1]

[1] Ben-Gurion University of the Negev, Beersheba, Israel
{mazuze,liorrk,bshapira}@post.bgu.ac.il
[2] eBay, Netanya, Israel
{gfuchs,alnus}@ebay.com

Abstract. Accurately determining selling prices for listings in online marketplaces poses a significant challenge due to the lack of universally recognized identifiers, such as Global Trade Item Numbers (GTIN) or Universal Product Codes (UPC). This lack of uniformity results in inconsistencies across product descriptions, titles, attributes, and features, complicating price prediction efforts. Traditional approaches for price prediction have predominantly relied on manually engineered features or direct price predictions from textual and image data, often failing to capture the nuanced differences between similar products. While transformer architectures have been widely used in e-commerce for item recommendation and retrieval tasks, these applications focus mainly on single-modal retrieval and do not address the complexities of pricing.

In this paper, we introduce a novel approach to price recommendation by leveraging item retrieval methods enhanced with hard negatives during training. Incorporating hard negatives improves the quality of the generated embeddings, enabling more effective differentiation between similar listings with significantly different prices. This methodology focuses on understanding the contextual relationships and characteristics of listings relative to one another, rather than solely focusing on direct price prediction.

By integrating contrastive learning with both price and aspects-based hard negatives, our approach better distinguishes between similar listings, significantly advancing price recommendation methods. Our research addresses this gap, aiming to significantly enhance the accuracy and effectiveness of pricing strategies. Extensive evaluations show that our method substantially improves pricing accuracy and enhances retrieval accuracy compared to existing approaches. We present extensive analysis and demonstrate successful deployment to production environment.

Supplementary Information The online version contains supplementary material available at https://doi.org/10.1007/978-3-662-72243-5_28.

Keywords: Recommender Systems · Information Retrieval ·
Contrastive Learning · Hard-Negatives

1   Introduction

Providing explainable and accurate selling prices for listings, particularly in the online marketplace, is a complex task, largely due to the absence of universally recognized identifiers like Global Trade Item Numbers (GTIN) or Universal Product Codes (UPC). Moreover, there is no standardized process for sellers when posting listings online, leading to inconsistencies in how listings are described. Factors like item titles, attributes, and features can vary greatly between listings, or in some cases, may be completely omitted. These inconsistencies make it particularly challenging to identify similar listings based on a given seed item, complicating price estimation and comparison efforts. In this study, we focus on one of the most popular categories on the eBay marketplace: "Trading Cards." This category is known for its significant price volatility, making it particularly intriguing and valuable for analysis and improvement (Fig. 1 and Table 1).

Previous research in price recommendation has primarily relied on manually extracted features, a process that is both time-consuming and requires domain expertise [23]. Some studies has explored direct recommendation of prices using textual and image features [15], but these approaches often suffer from limited coverage and a lack of explainability.

Transformer architectures have been widely employed in e-commerce for item recommendation systems [18,27,28] and have recently been adapted to item retrieval tasks [8,12,31]. However, most existing approaches focus on aligning

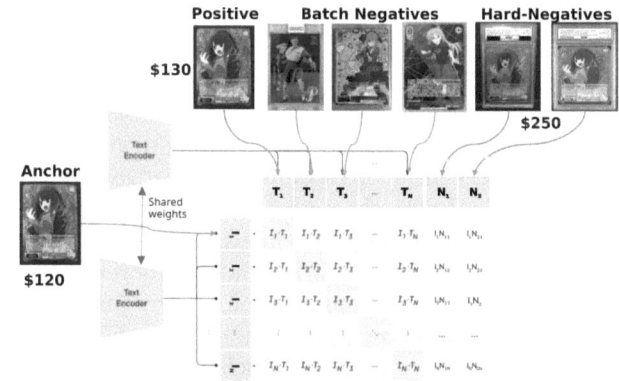

Fig. 1. Overview of the Training Process with Hard Negatives: We train a Siamese Neural Network to boost similarity among co-clicked pairs and reduce similarity between different listings. Using Multiple Negatives Ranking Loss with hard negatives refines the embeddings. The displayed prices show that listings with similar appearances can have drastically different prices.

Table 1. Hard Negative Mining Example: Although the listing titles differ, they represent the same player, team, year, and grading. In contrast, the hard-negative example is nearly identical except that it's a "Blue Refractor" (blue background instead of dark gray), a detail that significantly impacts its value compared to the co-clicked pair.

Type	Co-clicked		Hard-Negative
Image			
Title	2024 Topps Chrome Black - Yoshinobu Yamamoto #18 - GEM MINT 10	Graded 2024 Topps Chrome Black Yoshinobu Yamamoto #18 RC Baseball Card PSA 10	2024 Topps Chrome Black Yoshinobu Yamamoto RC **Blue Refractor** /75 PSA 10 Dodgers
Price	$134.59	$160.00	$299.99

embeddings across different modalities for the same product, rather than learning embeddings for similar products through image-to-text, text-to-image, or query-to-product tasks.

In this paper, we propose an enhanced approach to price recommendation using nearest neighbor retrieval by integrating hard negatives into the training process of existing models. Incorporating hard negatives improves the quality of embeddings generated during training [10], enabling more effective differentiation between similar listings with significantly different prices. This advancement has the potential to substaintially improve accuracy and reliability in online pricing strategies. Our approach addresses the pricing challenge through a streamlined, single-network training process, reducing development complexity and eliminating the need for manual feature extraction.

To the best of our knowledge, the combination of textual inputs with hard negatives that are jointly based on both price and listings' aspects has not been previously explored in the field of recommender systems. Thus, our research introduces a novel approach with the potential to significantly improve the accuracy and effectiveness of price reecommendation methods. By employing this unique strategy, we aim to uncover new insights and develop advanced methodologies in the domain of price recommendation and recommendation systems.

Moreover, we demonstrate how this method has been successfully deployed in a production environment, where it has delivered superior performance and proven effective in real-world applications.

2   Related Work

Assisting sellers in pricing their products is valuable across various marketplace domains, including e-commerce, tourism, and more. Traditional approaches, such as those used in the Kaggle Mercari Price Suggestion Challenge [1], relied heavily on extensive feature engineering and regression models for price prediction. By leveraging the BERT encoder, which effectively captures rich contextual and semantic information directly from textual data, the need for extensive feature engineering is eliminated, allowing listing title embeddings to be used instead.

Recent solution relate to E-commerce pricing include embeddings of different modalities, including textual, visual and structured data. The vector representation is then used as input for a trained model. For example, [15] built a price recommendation approach based on listings images and text descriptions. In [9] CNN and LSTM are combined and receive as input both text and visual features.

Although multi-modal data is a common approach, our experiments show that product titles alone provide the most accurate information for pricing, with images offering no performance improvement and, in some cases, even degrading model performance. This result supports an earlier finding by [21] which combined images and text features, and reached a similar conclusion.

Our work builds upon the study by [11], which identified a trade-off between semantic similarity and price accuracy. This trade-off was partially managed by a multi-task network that trained a BERT-based Siamese dual encoder in parallel with a BERT model incorporating a regression layer (Title2Price). The Title2Price model directly learns the pricing of listings, while the Siamese model does not have access to any price-related information. Our work focuses on improving the Siamese encoder by incorporating pricing information through data processing and hard-negative mining. Our approach significantly enhances the Siamese model's pricing accuracy while maintaining its semantic similarity capabilities. As a result, our approach enables the pricing challenge to be addressed with a single network training, simplifying both the development process and its subsequent use in production settings.

3   Methods

In this section, we present our proposed pipeline for product price guidance, which consists of four key stages: training product embeddings, using these embeddings to index previously purchased products in a KNN index, retrieving the k nearest neighbors of new products, and finally using the retrieved products for price prediction. We begin by outlining our data preparation approach followed by contrastive learning training, and a discussion on the hard-negative mining process. Finally, we describe our retrieval strategy and the implementation of the pricing mechanism.

3.1   Data Preparation

In recent years, contrastive learning has become a common approach for training large, generalized models applicable to many downstream tasks [4,19,24]. This method maps similar examples close together in the embedding space while learning to separate the dissimilar ones. With efficient training, it naturally organizes data into well-separated clusters, enabling simpler and more efficient applications in various downstream tasks.

Recently, similar approaches have been proposed for language models [13, 26]. Building upon previous work [25], our approach involves training Siamese Neural Networks [2, 20] based on the BERT architecture [6].

To construct our training dataset, we first filter search queries to remove those with fewer than six words, ensuring co-clicked listings are similar (e.g., a query like "sports cards" might yield dissimilar listings). A pair is considered positive if the same user clicks both listings under the same query. These positive pairs are then aggregated and further filtered based on aspects, price ratio (i.e., ensuring the price difference stays within a threshold), entity extraction, and other criteria to minimize false positives.

Since attributes are user-defined and often incomplete, many listings lack full attribute details. However, sellers usually include key information (such as player name, team, year, rarity, and grading) in the title. Therefore, we focus on generating rich embedding representations solely for the listings' titles.

3.2   Model Architecture

Given mini-batch of n positive pairs:

$$B = \{(a_i, b_i)\}_{i=1}^{n} \tag{1}$$

Let a and b be a pair of positive listings. We feed each into a BERT model and extract the final hidden layer:

$$E_{a_i} = BERT(a_i), \quad \text{with} \quad E_{a_i} = \langle e_1, e_2, \ldots, e_n \rangle.$$

Let e_i (and similarly b_i) denote the embedding for the i-th token; we then pool these to form a single title embedding.

$$u_i = Pooler(E_{a_i}); \quad v_i = Pooler(E_{b_i}) \tag{2}$$

Since our dataset contains only positive pairs, we generate pseudo-negatives by considering mismatched pairs within each batch as negatives. This enables the use of the Multiple Negative Ranking Loss [3, 16] during training. Specifically, we compute cosine similarity between all pairs (a_i, b_j) for $i, j = 1, \ldots, n$:

$$s_{i,j} = \frac{\langle u_i, v_j \rangle}{\|u_i\|_2 \|v_j\|_2}$$

This yields an $n \times n$ similarity matrix. The loss function is defined as:

$$\mathcal{L}_{Siamese} = -\sum_{i=1}^{n} \log \frac{\exp(s_{i,i})}{\sum_{j=1}^{n} \exp(s_{i,j})}$$

3.3   Hard-Negatives Mining

Contrastive learning depends on in-batch negatives, which can be limiting when the negatives are too dissimilar. For example, if our goal is to learn detailed animal embeddings, a batch with two dog images and several car images won't challenge the model. With only obvious negatives like cars, the model may fail to capture the subtle differences between similar animal images.

To address this issue, we avoid using only in-batch negatives and enrich the data with "hard negatives" [14].

With this modification, our training batches are now structured as follows:

$$B = \{(a_i, b_i, h_{i_1}, \ldots, h_{i_m})\}_{i=1}^n \tag{3}$$

Now when constructing our similarity matrix we end up with a matrix that its shape is $n * (n + m)$ where m is the number of hard-negatives added to each example in our training data.

$$\begin{pmatrix} a_1 \\ a_2 \end{pmatrix} \begin{matrix} (b_1 \ b_2 \ b_3 \ h_1 \ h_2) \\ \begin{pmatrix} s_{11} \ s_{12} \ s_{13} \ s_{1h_1} \ s_{1h_2} \\ s_{21} \ s_{22} \ s_{23} \ s_{2h_1} \ s_{2h_2} \end{pmatrix} \end{matrix}$$

Given that our input data consists of listings' titles, relying on hard negatives based solely on this data is not optimal. Traditional hard-negative mining processes usually focus on finding examples that are "close enough" in similarity to the positive pairs [14, 29]. However, similar titles do not always correspond to significant price differences. For example, a "Red iPhone" and a "Green iPhone" may differ in color but typically share the same price. If we base our hard-negative mining on the titles alone, we risk introducing many false positives into our model. This approach is inefficient in our e-commerce pricing context.

Instead, we opt for a different mining approach that is more suitable for price recommendation. During the dataset generation, in addition to the positive pairs we mine "negative pairs" by applying two relaxation rules to our preprocessing pipeline. First, we remove some of the aspect constraints; instead of requiring that pairs match in all aspects such as team, player, year, grader, graded status, variety, etc., we allow mismatches in some attributes.

We remove predicates that could yield similar listings with significant price differences; for example, the grade of a card—a measure of its condition by a professional grading service. Two cards may be identical except that one is graded PSA 10 (mint condition) and the other PSA 6 (fair condition), leading to price differences of hundreds or thousands of dollars.

Secondly, we invert the price ratio requirement. Instead of requiring the price ratio between two cards to be below a threshold for positive pairs, we set a threshold that requires it to be above a specified value. These augmentations help capture listings that are nearly identical except for a minor detail making one card worth \$200 and another \$1,000.

After generating the negative pairs dataset, we have two datasets—one for positive and one for negative pairs. Given their largely overlapping preprocessing,

---

Algorithm 1: Hard-negatives mining

Data: P- positive-pairs dataset, N- negative-pairs dataset, K- hard negative
       size

Result: D- Final dataset with k hard negatives per example

1 $J \leftarrow pd.DataFrame()$;

2 **for** (a, b) *in* $[(a_i, a_i), (a_i, b_i), (b_i, a_i), (b_i, b_i)]$ **do**

3      $J_i \leftarrow pd.merge([P, N], how = inner, left\_on = a, right\_on = b)$;

4      $J \leftarrow pd.concat([J, J_i], axis = 0)$;

5 **end**

6 $J \leftarrow J.groupBy(by = [query, a, b])$;

7 $J[b] \leftarrow J.apply(list, J[b])$;

8 $J \leftarrow J[J[b].len >= K]$ **# Drop rows with $\leq$ k negatives**

9 $J[b] \leftarrow random.sample(J[b], K)$ **# pick k random negatives**

10 $Negatives \leftarrow pd.DataFrame(J[b], columns = [Neg_1, \ldots, Neg_k])$;

11 $D \leftarrow pd.concat([P, Negatives], axis = 1)$;

12 **return** D

---

some listings appear in both. As described in Algorithm 1, we first perform an inner join between the datasets to create (anchor, positive, negative) triples, then group all negatives for each positive pair.

Because our training requires a fixed number of hard negatives, we filter out rows with fewer than K negatives, randomly select K negatives per positive pair, and combine them into a single dataset.

3.4   Retrieval and Pricing

To identify similar listings for pricing, we use a k-nearest neighbors (KNN) approach, searching for listings with cosine similarity that meets a predefined threshold. This threshold was determined by a grid search process - multiple candidate thresholds were evaluated using a train-validation-test split. The grid search involved testing various thresholds on the training set, tuning the threshold based on performance on the validation set, and finally choosing the optimal threshold based on its ability to generalize to the test set.

For efficient nearest neighbor search and retrieval, we utilized the Faiss library [17], a high-performance tool specifically designed for fast similarity search in large datasets. Faiss allows efficient indexing and retrieval of embeddings. The Faiss implementation we used is an optimized algorithms for both exact and approximate nearest neighbor search, depending on the data characteristics and performance requirements. This enable to quickly and accurately fetch nearest neighbors that are most similar to a given listing, making the pricing recommendation process both fast and scalable.

For the final predicted price, several pricing strategies were evaluated, with the best strategy selected through a grid search (similar to the approach used above for determining the optimal similarity threshold). Specifically, we explored various price percentiles, the exponential moving average, and a modified version of k-nearest neighbors (KEN), which allows soft thresholding and a larger recall set per query [11].

4   Experiments and Results

In this section, we present our evaluation. We begin by presenting our datasets, followed by definition of our evaluation metrics. Finally we present our results, discuss their implication and perform an ablation study to further investigate our approach.

Table 2. Aspect Mismatch retrieval results. X-HN signifies the number of hard-negatives used during training. ↓ indicates lower is better.

AMP@5	CLIP-Image	CLIP-Text	Resnet	Title2Price	ViT	ViLT	eBERT 1-HN
Graded ↓	11.2	14.7	12.1	9.4	**3.9**	6.7	7.2
Sport ↓	3.3	3.3	3.15	12.2	5.5	3.2	**3.1**
Season ↓	31.8	29.4	24.6	35.1	31.2	**21.0**	26.4
Manufacturer ↓	15.5	11.2	12.1	19.2	15.2	**10.6**	12.9
Set ↓	46.8	44.5	**33.2**	45.5	43.0	37.3	36.2
Player Athlete ↓	10.3	6.3	9.6	25.5	20.1	**5.9**	10.6
Team ↓	21.0	16.9	**15.8**	30.2	30	17.5	17.7
Grade ↓	59.0	45.0	27.7	20.6	39.7	12.6	**11.2**
Variation ↓	76.7	50.8	52.1	60.7	55.3	70.1	**49.7**
Professional Grader ↓	22.9	7.3	**4.1**	15.0	8.2	8.7	9.5
Autographed ↓	6.9	6.5	6.2	7.3	**4.8**	5.2	5.3

Table 3. Retrieval-based pricing accuracy results. X-HN signifies the number of hard-negatives used during training. ↑ indicates higher is bette.

Price Accuracy	CLIP-Image	CLIP-Text	Resnet	Title2Price	ViT	ViLT	eBERT 1-HN
P(20) ↑	32.8%	38.4%	47.1%	49.1%	39.2%	42.4%	**53.1%**
MAE ↓	853.8	672.5	468.7	**264.0**	685.9	652.3	325.8
Recall ↑	69.7%	67.6%	71.2%	**71.7%**	68.5%	68.1%	70.5%

4.1   Data

In our experiments we use two types of datasets:

1. Co-clicked dataset: listings pairs that were clicked in the same eBay search session. It consists of 240,000 co-clicked listing pairs.

2. Vault dataset: Simulates eBay's vault listings, which are high-value items stored and secured by eBay. It includes a sample of 20k listings with known sold prices for validation and hyper-parameter tuning, as well as a 10k listing sample for testing over a two-week period.

Both datasets consist of structured key-value pairs representing listing attributes (e.g., "Player Name": "LeBron James"). We use the co-clicked dataset to train our models using the "Multiple Negative Ranking Loss". The Vault dataset was segmented into validation, and test sets using a time-ordered split and is used to evaluate our models on their retrieval and pricing performance. The overlap between the co-clicked data and the Vault test set is negligible ($< 0.001\%$) The Vault dataset, which simulates eBay's high-value, secured listings, is crucial for evaluating our models' retrieval and pricing performance. By using a dataset of real-world, high-value items, we can ensure that our models are robust and accurate in a production setting where precise pricing and efficient retrieval of these expensive cards are paramount. This is especially important for Vault listings, as these items are often rare and unique, making accurate pricing a challenging task. In addition, our actual production use-case required the development of a model capable of accurately pricing these high-value items, which is a complex problem due to the rarity and variability of such products.

4.2   Metrics

Our primary metric for price guidance is P(20), Additionally we also calculate P(20)-Smooth, "Attribute Mismatch Percentage" (AMP), Mean Absolute Error (MAE), and Recall. The seed items used for evaluation are taken from the Vault dataset, as outlined in Sect. 4.1.

1. **P(k)**- This calculates the percentage of successfully retrieved cards that their listing price is at most a certain percentage away from the seed item. Since card prices have small variations in them (not all sellers sell at the exact same price), this metric captures the ability of the model to retrieve similar priced cards.

   for each query listing $a \in A$, and a set of seed listings S and their prices, P(k) is then defined as:

   $$P(k) = \frac{\mathbb{1}\{|\frac{P_a - P_s}{P_a}| \leq \frac{k}{100} + \delta\}}{|A|} \qquad (4)$$

   where P_a and P_s are the prices of a and s respectively, and δ is a smoothing factor when dealing with low-priced listings.

2. **MAE**- The average absolute difference between the seed item's price and the prices of the retrieved listings

   $$\frac{\sum_{i=1}^{n} |y_i - x_i|}{n}$$

3. **AMP@K**- measures the percentage of successfully retrieved cards whose listing attributes match the seed item attributes.
   Since retrieval is based on the listing title embedding, this metrics captures the model's ability to retrieve correct cards.
   For each attribute a, and a set of seed listings S that contain a value for this attribute, we take the k nearest neighbors $NN_k(s)$ for each listing $s \in S$. AMP is then defined as:

$$AMP@K(S,a) = 100 * \frac{\sum_{s \in S} \sum_{r \in NN_k(s)} \mathbb{1}\{a(s) \neq a(r), a(r) \neq \emptyset\}}{\sum_{s \in S} \sum_{r \in NN_k(s)} \mathbb{1}\{a(r) \neq \emptyset\}}$$

4. **Recall**- The percentage of listings that a successful retrieval could be performed.

Table 4. Effect of Modalities in Multi-Modal Models: The model correctly identifies similarity between a seed listing and its co-clicked pair. However, when the title is kept but the image is replaced with a random one, similarity remains high, while using the correct image with an incorrect title causes a sharp drop. This indicates that the model primarily relies on text over visual cues.

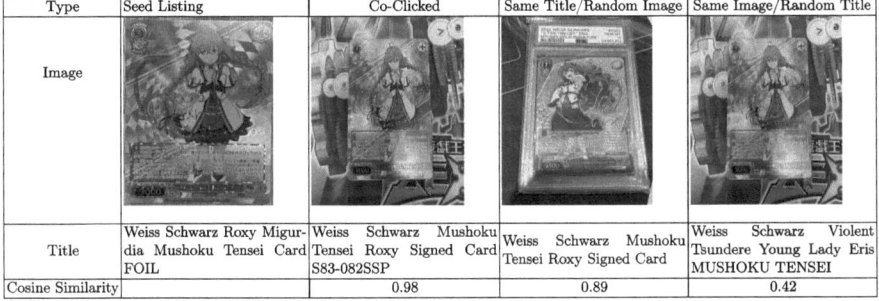

Type	Seed Listing	Co-Clicked	Same Title/Random Image	Same Image/Random Title
Image				
Title	Weiss Schwarz Roxy Migurdia Mushoku Tensei Card FOIL	Weiss Schwarz Mushoku Tensei Roxy Signed Card S83-082SSP	Weiss Schwarz Mushoku Tensei Roxy Signed Card	Weiss Schwarz Violent Tsundere Young Lady Eris MUSHOKU TENSEI
Cosine Similarity		0.98	0.89	0.42

4.3   Training

Our main approach and model is eBERT [5], a domain-adapted version of BERT that achieves better performance in e-commerce settings. Encoder-based models have shown great success in dominating embedding tasks [22], as they offer great balance between efficiency and performance. The decision to use a BERT-based architecture is also motivated by the high traffic volume on our marketplace, necessitating a system that can efficiently handle large-scale data in real time.

We compared our eBERT with hard negatives to different approaches and architectures across various modalities (image/text) and tasks (contrastive learning, regression, multi-class classification). All models, except ResNet and Title2Price, were trained using the same contrastive learning approach (see Sect. 3), hyperparameters, and datasets. Title2Price was adapted from [11], and ResNet was trained using multi-class classification [30]. Each model was trained on 8 GPUs for 120 epochs using the Adam optimizer with a weight decay of 0.01, a linear scheduler with warm-up, and an initial learning rate of $2 \cdot 10^{-5}$.

4.4 Results

As can be seen in Table 2 and Table 3, Title2Price achieved the lowest MAE due to its regression-based training that directly predict the prices from titles. However, Title2Price achieved poor performance on aspect matching compared to eBERT. CLIP-text also achieves subpar results because it isn't trained on titles and can't capture the hidden relationships that exist between the tokens in titles. Notably, Our eBERT approach with hard-negatives outperformed all other models on the P(20) metric at the same recall range, suggesting that supplementing the training process with price-based hard negatives allows the model to identify price-sensitive words in titles and leads to more accurate price predictions.

When comparing the performance of image-based models (such as CLIP-Image, ResNet, and ViT) to text-based models (like BERT and Title2Price), we observe a decline in performance for the image-based models as seen previously [7]. This degradation is likely due to the weaker signal from images, which obstructs the training process compared to using the listings' titles. When a new listing is created on eBay, sellers typically include comprehensive information to stand out and help buyers make informed decisions. This information often encompasses details such as player, team, year, rarity, grade, and more. Essentially, a listing title is a collection various aspects and attributes, and the inclusion or exclusion of specific terms can be easily distinguished, aiding in understanding their impact on pricing—for example, "graded" versus "ungraded" or "PSA 10" versus "PSA 4". Conversely, extracting this information from images is more challenging. Image models lack the domain knowledge necessary to grasp certain subtleties solely from visual data, such as the year a card was printed and its effect on price, or the relationship between the player and the team. These limitations make retrieval-based pricing a more difficult task for image-based models compared to their text-based models. In Appendix A, we explore a setting that image-based models are on par with text-based models.

In our experiments, the multi-modal vision-text model ViLT outperforms purely image-based models. This is primarily because ViLT ignores the image when embedding the listing and relies mainly on the signal that the titles provide. Table 4 shows a representative example: when ViLT is fed the images and titles of co-clicked listings, it recognizes them as similar (cosine similarity = 0.98). In contrast, replacing the title in one listing with a random title causes the cosine similarity to drop significantly (0.42), whereas replacing an image with a random image only modestly reduces the similarity (0.89). These results, consistently observed across multiple examples, indicate that ViLT's superior performance over image-based models like CLIP or ViT is largely driven by its reliance on textual information.

4.5 Hard-Negatives Ablation

We conducted an ablation study to evaluate the contribution of the hard-negatives to our model's performance. As shown in the results presented in

Table 5, we observed that incorporating a single hard-negative into our training scheme enhances pricing performance.

When increasing the number of hard-negatives during training we experience a decrease in our metrics performance. This effect is similar to those reported in [10] (We refer the readers to appendix B in [10]) due to decreased batch size needed to train with more hard-negatives. Furthermore, we also observe that aspects not used in creating the negative set (See Subsect. 3.3), such as, "Parallel Variety", "Professional Grader", and "Autographed", have better aspect matching. This aligns with the idea that hard-negative training allows for better separation between related examples that result in notable price difference.

Since k hard-negatives adds a $k \times n \times d_k$ additional operations between embedding vectors of size $u \in d_k$, and due to the fact that most system have limited amount of memory, the only option is to reduce the batch size, which negates the benefits of having very large batch sizes when applying contrastive learning methods. This trade-off might explain the decrease in performance when increasing the number of hard-negatives from one to four.

Table 5. Effect of hard-negatives on price guidance in text models. X-HN signifies the number of hard-negatives used during training. ↑ indicates higher is better, while a ↓ indicates lower is better.

AMP@5	eBERT	eBERT 1-HN	eBERT 4-HN
Graded ↓	**5.4**	7.2	7.8
Sport ↓	3.1	3.1	**3.0**
Set ↓	37.5	**36.2**	36.6
Player Athlete ↓	**9.6**	10.6	10.0
Professional Grader ↓	**10.2**	11.2	11.3
Variation ↓	53.5	49.7	**47.9**
Autographed ↓	5.7	5.3	**5.2**
Price Accuracy	eBERT	eBERT 1-HN	eBERT 4-HN
P(20) ↑	51.7%	**53.1%**	52.6%
MAE ↓	404.8	**325.8**	358
Recall ↑	**71.7%**	70.5%	71.4%

4.6 Production Deployment

One of the services eBay provides to its users is the 'eBay Price Guide', specifically developed for collectible and sports trading cards enthusiast. We applied the hard-negative mining approach to develop production-ready models for both sports and collectible cards. During inference, the listing title is sent to a service node, which generates an embedding and performs an index lookup to retrieve a shortlist of similar listings. These candidates are then used to calculate the recommended price based on a defined similarity threshold. As shown in Table 6, a comparison of our models with the existing production models (which rely on keyword search) demonstrates improvement in both price accuracy and recall. Based on these results, our models were deployed to production in 2024, replacing the previous models. Given this improvement, the models are expected to be also deployed in 2025 to assist sellers during the listing process.

Table 6. Comparing our nard-negative based approach to eBay Price Guide production models.

Sport Cards	P(20)	Recall
Production	55%	54.2%
Our Model	**64%**	**62%**
Collectible Cards	P(20)	Recall
Production	62.7%	48%
Our Model	**63.8%**	**73%**

5   Discussion and Conclusion

In this paper, we propose a retrieval-based pricing method for trading cards that enhances training using hard-negative mining. Unlike prior approaches that rely solely on input data (e.g., comparing similar texts or applying image augmentations), our method leverages the idea that small item variations can lead to significant price differences. We generate hard negatives based on price and aspect differences, resulting in pairs nearly identical to the original co-clicked pair except for one trait that causes large price variations. While we currently use domain knowledge to identify these aspects, this process can be automated by analyzing their values and correlations with prices.

Allowing for better pricing of trading cards, improve the experience of both shoppers and sellers, as accurate prices would allow seller to know what prices to set in order to guarantee selling their trading card, and for shoppers knowing the current price trends for their desired purchases will help making better purchases.

We evaluated our approach against text-based (CLIP-text), regression (Title2Price), and image-based models (CLIP-image, ViT, Resnet) using a common test set and multiple pricing and aspect metrics. Image-based models underperformed compared to title-based ones, emphasizing that explicit details in listing titles offer a stronger signal for pricing than images, which often provide less clear information. This underscores the challenge of relying on images for price prediction in e-commerce.

Furthermore, we determined that adding additional hard-negatives to our training, without changing the batch size improve pricing accuracy, and partial aspect accuracy compared to training without them.

Future work can explore different strategies or settings in which models can benefit from incorporating images into their training process.

Disclosure of Interests. The authors have no competing interests to declare that are relevant to the content of this article.

A   Collection Set Performance

Table 7. Performance of ViT model compared to BERT in a low-priced and short title setting. a smoothing factor of $2 was added due to low prices in collection cards.

AMP@5	eBERT	ViT
Graded ↓	7.06	**4.0**
Sport ↓	12.25	**9.4**
Set ↓	**33.6**	40.1
Player Athlete ↓	**11.8**	41.1
Professional Grader ↓	**17.0**	21.7
Variation ↓	**53.3**	71.4
Autographed ↓	10.1	**5.5**
Price Accurracy	eBERT	ViT
$P(20)$ $\delta = 2$ ↑	60.8%	**63.8%**
MAE ↓	20.9	**18.3**
Recall ↑	57.5%	**57.9%**

As observed, text-based models achieve top results in retrieval-based price guidance due to the strong signal provided by detailed titles. In contrast, image-based models have underperformed, even though images can offer useful, complementary information. We aim to investigate when image-based models—specifically ViT—can match text-based models like BERT.

For this experiment, we use the same training settings but switch our evaluation dataset to a "Collection set." Unlike the vault dataset, which features high-priced listings with detailed titles, the Collection set has no lower price bound and includes cards priced as low as $1. We select a seed test set containing titles with five words or fewer, then evaluate BERT and ViT, both trained with the same contrastive learning loss, on this new dataset.

As shown in Table 7, ViT achieves results comparable to BERT when only short titles are used. Sellers usually employ descriptive titles to attract buyers, providing a strong signal for text-based models like eBERT. However, with short titles, eBERT has fewer tokens and less information to extract, while the image signal remains constant. Although listings with short titles represent only about 0.65% of the Collection set, these results suggest that image-based models can be particularly valuable in domains where text is less informative.

References

1. Ali, A.A.S., Seker, H., Farnie, S., Elliott, J.: Extensive data exploration for automatic price suggestion using item description: Case study for the kaggle mercari challenge. In: Proceedings of the 2nd International Conference on Advances in Artificial Intelligence, ICAAI 2018, Barcelona, Spain, October 06–08, 2018. pp. 41–45. ACM (2018). https://doi.org/10.1145/3292448.3292458
2. Bromley, J., Guyon, I., LeCun, Y., Säckinger, E., Shah, R.: Signature verification using a "siamese" time delay neural network. In: Advances in Neural Information Processing Systems, vol. 6 (1993)
3. Cao, Z., Qin, T., Liu, T.Y., Tsai, M.F., Li, H.: Learning to rank: from pairwise approach to listwise approach. In: Proceedings of the 24th International Conference on Machine Learning, pp. 129–136 (2007)
4. Chen, T., Kornblith, S., Norouzi, M., Hinton, G.: A simple framework for contrastive learning of visual representations. In: Proceedings of the 37th International Conference on Machine Learning, ICML 2020, JMLR.org, Vienna (2020)
5. Dahlmann, L., Lancewicki, T.: Deploying a BERT-based query-title relevance classifier in a production system: a view from the trenches. arXiv preprint arXiv:2108.10197 (2021)
6. Devlin, J., Chang, M.W., Lee, K., Toutanova, K.: BERT: pre-training of deep bidirectional transformers for language understanding. arXiv preprint arXiv:1810.04805 (2018)
7. Di, W., Sundaresan, N., Piramuthu, R., Bhardwaj, A.: Is a picture really worth a thousand words? -on the role of images in e-commerce. In: Proceedings of the 7th ACM International Conference on Web Search and Data Mining, pp. 633–642 (2014)
8. Dong, X., et al.: M5product: a multi-modal pretraining benchmark for e-commercial product downstream tasks. arXiv preprint arXiv:2109.04275 **4** (2021)
9. Fathalla, A., Salah, A., Li, K., Li, K., Francesco, P.: Deep end-to-end learning for price prediction of second-hand items. Knowl. Inf. Syst. **62**(12), 4541–4568 (2020). https://doi.org/10.1007/s10115-020-01495-8
10. Feng, F., Yang, Y., Cer, D., Arivazhagan, N., Wang, W.: Language-agnostic BERT sentence embedding. arXiv preprint arXiv:2007.01852 (2020)
11. Fuchs, G., et al.: Pricing the nearly known-when semantic similarity is just not enough. In: eCom@ SIGIR (2023)
12. Gao, D., et al.: Fashionbert: text and image matching with adaptive loss for cross-modal retrieval. In: Proceedings of the 43rd International ACM SIGIR Conference on Research and Development in Information Retrieval, pp. 2251–2260 (2020)
13. Gao, T., Yao, X., Chen, D.: Simcse: simple contrastive learning of sentence embeddings. arXiv preprint arXiv:2104.08821 (2021)
14. Guo, M., et al.: Effective parallel corpus mining using bilingual sentence embeddings. arXiv preprint arXiv:1807.11906 (2018)
15. Han, L., Yin, Z., Xia, Z., Tang, M., Jin, R.: Price suggestion for online second-hand items with texts and images (2020)
16. Henderson, M., et al.: Efficient natural language response suggestion for smart reply. arXiv preprint arXiv:1705.00652 (2017)
17. Johnson, J., Douze, M., Jégou, H.: Billion-scale similarity search with GPUS. arXiv preprint arXiv:1702.08734 (2017)
18. Kang, W.C., McAuley, J.: Self-attentive sequential recommendation. In: 2018 IEEE International Conference on Data Mining (ICDM), pp. 197–206. IEEE (2018)

19. Khosla, P., et al.: Supervised contrastive learning. In: Advances in Neural Information Processing Systems, vol. 33, pp. 18661–18673 (2020)
20. Koch, G., Zemel, R., Salakhutdinov, R., et al.: Siamese neural networks for one-shot image recognition. In: ICML Deep Learning Workshop, vol. 2, pp. 1–30. Lille (2015)
21. Li, B., Liu, T.: An analysis of multi-modal deep learning for art price appraisal. In: 2021 IEEE Intl Conference on Parallel & Distributed Processing with Applications, Big Data & Cloud Computing, Sustainable Computing & Communications, Social Computing & Networking (ISPA/BDCloud/SocialCom/SustainCom), pp. 1509–1513 (2021)
22. Muennighoff, N., Tazi, N., Magne, L., Reimers, N.: MTEB: massive text embedding benchmark. arXiv preprint arXiv:2210.07316 (2022). https://doi.org/10.48550/ARXIV.2210.07316
23. Pal, N., Arora, P., Sundararaman, D., Kohli, P., Palakurthy, S.S.: How much is my car worth? a methodology for predicting used cars prices using random forest (2017)
24. Radford, A., et al.: Learning transferable visual models from natural language supervision. arXiv preprint arXiv:2103.00020 (2021)
25. Reimers, N.: Sentence-BERT: sentence embeddings using siamese BERT-networks. arXiv preprint arXiv:1908.10084 (2019)
26. Shen, D., Zheng, M., Shen, Y., Qu, Y., Chen, W.: A simple but tough-to-beat data augmentation approach for natural language understanding and generation. arXiv preprint arXiv:2009.13818 (2020)
27. Si, Z., et al.: When search meets recommendation: Learning disentangled search representation for recommendation. In: Proceedings of the 46th International ACM SIGIR Conference on Research and Development in Information Retrieval, SIGIR 2023, pp. 1313–1323. Association for Computing Machinery, New York (2023). https://doi.org/10.1145/3539618.3591786
28. Sun, F., et al.: Bert4rec: sequential recommendation with bidirectional encoder representations from transformer. In: Proceedings of the 28th ACM International Conference on Information and Knowledge Management, pp. 1441–1450 (2019)
29. Tan, W., Heffernan, K., Schwenk, H., Koehn, P.: Multilingual representation distillation with contrastive learning. arXiv preprint arXiv:2210.05033 (2022)
30. Yang, F., et al.: Visual search at ebay. In: Proceedings of the 23rd ACM SIGKDD International Conference on Knowledge Discovery and Data Mining, pp. 2101–2110 (2017)
31. Yao, S., Tan, J., Chen, X., Zhang, J., Zeng, X., Yang, K.: Reprbert: distilling BERT to an efficient representation-based relevance model for e-commerce. In: Proceedings of the 28th ACM SIGKDD Conference on Knowledge Discovery and Data Mining, pp. 4363–4371 (2022)

Graph Neural Networks for Automatic Addition of Optimizing Components in Printed Circuit Board Schematics

Pascal Plettenberg[1]([⊠]), André Alcalde[2], Bernhard Sick[1], and Josephine M. Thomas[1]

[1] Intelligent Embedded Systems, University of Kassel, 34121 Kassel, Germany
{plettenberg,bsick,josephine.thomas}@uni-kassel.de
[2] CELUS GmbH, 80339 Münche, Germany
andre.alcalde@celus.io

Abstract. The design and optimization of Printed Circuit Board (PCB) schematics is crucial for the development of high-quality electronic devices. Thereby, an important task is to optimize drafts by adding components that improve the robustness and reliability of the circuit, e.g., pull-up resistors or decoupling capacitors. Since there is a shortage of skilled engineers and manual optimizations are very time-consuming, these best practices are often neglected. However, this typically leads to higher costs for troubleshooting in later development stages as well as shortened product life cycles, resulting in an increased amount of electronic waste that is difficult to recycle. Here, we present an approach for automating the addition of new components into PCB schematics by representing them as bipartite graphs and utilizing a node pair prediction model based on Graph Neural Networks (GNNs). We apply our approach to three highly relevant PCB design optimization tasks and compare the performance of several popular GNN architectures on real-world datasets labeled by human experts. We show that GNNs can solve these problems with high accuracy and demonstrate that our approach offers the potential to automate PCB design optimizations in a time- and cost-efficient manner.

Keywords: Graph Neural Networks · Printed Circuit Boards · Electronic Design Automation

1 Introduction

The development of high-quality electronic devices relies heavily on the design of Printed Circuit Board (PCB) schematics, which define all required components and their connections to each other. Usually, new PCB schematics undergo several design iterations, and first functional drafts are optimized based on experience according to some "best practices". Thereby, one important task for engineers is to add components like pull-up resistors or decoupling capacitors to the

Supplementary Information The online version contains supplementary material available at https://doi.org/10.1007/978-3-662-72243-5_29.

circuit, which reduce the failure risk and increase the robustness against external disturbances.

In most cases, these types of PCB design optimizations are implemented manually, which is time-consuming and error-prone. Since the additional components are not needed for immediate functionality, they are often neglected. High time pressure on engineers in the development process, and the shortage of skilled engineers in the market contribute to that as well. Consequently, non-optimal PCB schematics result in more frequent prototype iterations and higher troubleshooting costs in later development stages. Furthermore, they reduce the overall lifetime of the final product, resulting in an increased amount of electronic waste that is difficult to recycle.

Electronic Design Automation (EDA) tools are essential for streamlining the process of designing, testing, and verifying electronic designs. These tools have become even more sophisticated since Machine Learning (ML) methods have been integrated into EDA due to the increasing amount of available data [9]. While ML-based EDA tools have been mainly developed for integrated circuits (ICs), the automation of PCB schematics, which include both analog and digital components, is more difficult due to larger design spaces, and existing tools are often limited to rule-based design verifications.

Electronic circuits can be naturally represented as graphs and Graph Neural Networks (GNNs) have emerged as a powerful tool that extends the scope of Deep Learning from Euclidean to graph-structured data. Therefore, GNNs offer great potential for learning meaningful representations of PCB schematics that can be used to automate optimization tasks. However, one big problem is the translation of the huge variety of available information on the PCB components (e.g., types and names) into standardized, numerical node features, especially when dealing with real-world datasets. Furthermore, most GNN models from the literature are either used for prediction tasks on the level of single nodes [6] or edges [30], whereas adding a new component with exactly two terminals requires the classification of node pairs.

Present Work. In this work, we propose a GNN-based approach for automating the placement of optimizing components in PCB schematics. Thereby, we represent PCB schematics as bipartite graphs (see Sect. 3) and predict the positions of new components with a node-pair-level classification model (see Sect. 4). In Sect. 5, we evaluate our approach on large real-world datasets labeled by human experts, thereby focusing on three specific PCB design optimization tasks, each involving the addition of a different optimizing component: (i) **Pull-up** and **pull-down resistors** for ensuring a defined voltage level on floating nets. (ii) **RC filters** on reset pins for preventing unintentional resets from voltage glitches. (iii) **Decoupling capacitors** for reducing high-frequency noise in supply and ground nets. We train our model to perform these tasks using different GNN architectures from the literature and compare their performances.

Main Contributions.

- We propose a bipartite graph representation for PCB schematics involving a method for constructing node and edge attributes from non-standardized component names in real-world data using a pre-trained language model.
- We propose a GNN-based node-pair-level prediction model for the placement of additional optimizing components in PCB schematics.
- We perform extensive experiments on real-world datasets, demonstrating that GNNs can predict the positions of new components with high accuracy.

The code for our model and example graph samples from our dataset are available at https://github.com/pasplett/pcb-node-pair-gnn.

2   Related Work

Machine Learning for Electronic Design Automation. In the last years, many studies have investigated the usage of ML methods for EDA [9]. These studies mainly focused on digital circuit design, including several stages of the design flow such as logic synthesis [7,29], placement [15], and routing [1,27]. In analog design, however, ML-based automation is more difficult due to larger design spaces and varying specifications [14]. Some notable approaches are reinforcement learning for circuit topology optimization [21] as well as ML-assisted analog circuit sizing [3]. However, these approaches do not exploit the graph structure of electronic circuits.

Graph Learning for Electronic Design Automation. Since electronic circuits can be naturally represented as graphs, GNNs have recently become more and more popular in the field of EDA [20]. Again, while the majority of studies focus on the digital EDA flow [4,16,23], there are also some GNN-based approaches for analog EDA, such as ParaGraph [18] for the prediction of net parasitic capacitances, GANA [12] for automated netlist annotation and Circuit Designer [25] for transistor sizing. Most recently, CktGNN [5] was introduced as a nested GNN framework with a pre-designed subgraph basis and has been successfully applied for analog circuit topology design and device sizing. While all of these approaches utilize the graph structure of electronic circuits, they are tailored to different use cases and are not applicable to the specific PCB optimizations that we focus on in our work.

Graph Neural Networks for Circuit Design Completion. Closest to our work is the study by Said et al. [19], which explores the usage of graph neural networks for the design completion of partially designed analog circuits. Thereby, the missing component is first identified using a graph classification, and the placement of the new component within the circuit is then treated as a link prediction problem. However, predicting the connectivity of a new component using link prediction frameworks like GAE [10] or SEAL [30] is difficult because

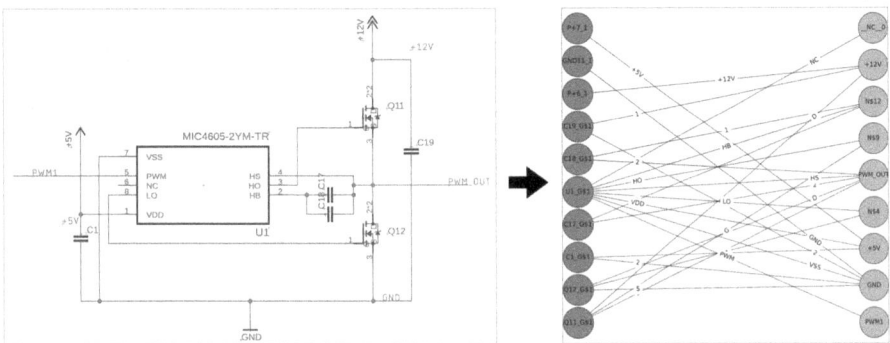

Fig. 1. An exemplary PCB circuit diagram and the corresponding bipartite graph representation. Symbols (e.g., resistors or capacitors) are represented by red nodes, nets (e.g., supply or ground nets) are represented by green nodes, and pins (e.g., component terminals) are represented by edges.(Color figure online)

it involves the prediction of links to isolated nodes and the individual links have to be predicted independently. Here, we focus on adding new components for specific PCB schematic optimization tasks with practical relevance. Thereby, the number of connections for a new component is known in advance, so we can treat the problem as a node-pair-level prediction task rather than a combination of graph classification and link prediction.

3 Graph Representation of PCB Schematics

We represent PCB schematics as bipartite graphs with two distinct sets of nodes: Nets and symbols. Thereby, net nodes (e.g., ground or supply nets) are always connected to symbol nodes (e.g., components like resistors, capacitors, or ICs) and vice versa, but no connections are allowed between nodes within the same set. The edges of the graph represent the pins, i.e., the terminals or connection points of the symbol nodes. Since a symbol may be connected to the same net node via multiple pins, the resulting graphs can be multi-relational, i.e., allow for multiple parallel edges. An example of the proposed graph representation of PCB schematics is given in Fig. 1.

Node Attributes. The node input features contain two types of information: The type and the name of the node. The node type is a binary variable, which takes the value 0 for a net node and the value 1 for a symbol node. The node names are stored as strings within the raw schematics file, e.g. "GND" or "C1_G$1". We use a pre-trained language model to convert the node names into numerical embeddings. For this purpose, we utilize the model all-MiniLM-L6-v2 from the SentenceTransformers Python package [17], which transforms any input string into a numerical vector containing 384 values. The model is a distilled version of a large Transformer model, which was trained on a diverse

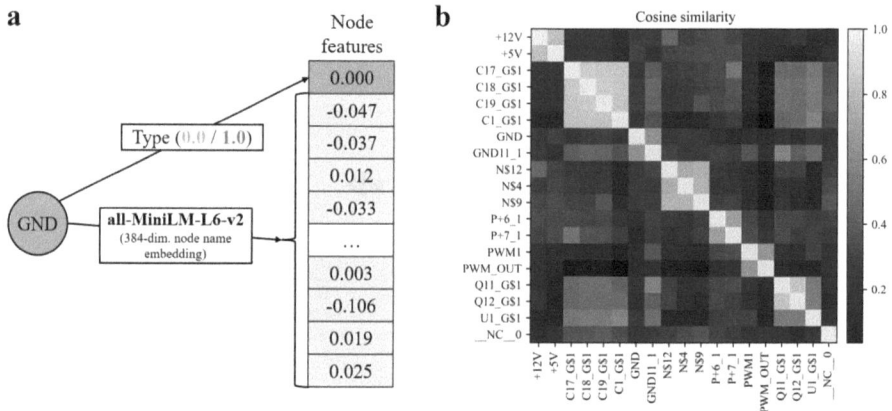

Fig. 2. a Composition of the input node features from node type and node name embedding. **b** Cosine similarity between sentence transformer embeddings of all symbol and net node names in an example PCB circuit diagram. Thereby, embeddings of similar node names exhibit higher cosine similarities.

language dataset containing over 1 billion training pairs [26]. Note that such a lightweight language model is sufficient for our purposes since the node names in our dataset are rather short. However, other general-purpose language models could be used as well. We leave the analysis of the influence of different language models on the prediction accuracy for future work.

The resulting node name embedding is concatenated to the single node type value resulting in the final 385-dimensional node input feature vector (see Fig. 1a).

Edge Attributes. Similar to the node names, we also use the pre-trained sentence transformer model to convert the pin names into 384-dimensional edge attributes. Furthermore, since standard GNN architectures cannot properly handle multi-relational graphs, we combine parallel edges into a single edge by summing up the individual pin name embeddings and concatenating an additional edge feature representing the number of parallel pins represented by the final edge.

Applicability to Real-World Data. Our approach for representing PCB schematics as graphs is very flexible and requires a minimum amount of pre-processing, because the type of a PCB component, e.g., a resistor, capacitor, or IC, is implicitly encoded in the node features via the name embeddings. Therefore, identifying component types manually is not necessary, making the approach especially suitable for real-world datasets with non-standardized component names. Figure 1b shows the cosine similarity between the name embeddings of all nodes in the example PCB circuit diagram from Fig. 1. Note that small name variations (e.g., "C1", C17", "C18") result in similar sentence transformer embeddings, whereas nodes with very different names (e.g., "+5V" and "C17_G$1") exhibit a much lower cosine similarity. This analysis indicates that the selected language model is sufficient for generating well-separated latent representations of the node names.

4 Node Pair Prediction for PCB Component Addition

Our aim is to optimize the robustness and reliability of PCB designs by adding new relevant components and predicting their position within the circuit. In most cases, these new components are either resistors or capacitors, which is why we assume that the new circuit component is a two-terminal component, i.e., it is connected to exactly two net nodes. The task is to predict the pair of net nodes between which the new component has to be inserted.

Node Pre-filtering. A straightforward approach would be to calculate node representations using GNNs and then predict a probability score for each possible pair of net nodes. However, in large circuits with hundreds of nodes, this approach may become computationally expensive because the number of possible node pairs increases quadratically. Furthermore, the approach could lead to training instabilities since the dataset can be extremely imbalanced: Only a few node pairs have a positive training label.

Therefore, we develop a strategy for reducing the number of node pairs that need to be checked during the prediction. First, we can restrict the search to net nodes because the inserted component is a symbol that cannot be directly connected to other symbol nodes. Second, we can sort out net nodes that are very unlikely to be connection points for the new circuit component. For example, the resistor of an RC filter is never connected to a ground net. This pre-filtering can be done with an MLP that predicts for each net node, whether it serves as a connection point for a new component. The resulting probability scores assigned by the pre-filter can be used to identify a set of unlikely candidates and exclude them from the actual pairwise node prediction.

Model Architecture. Our overall model is depicted in Fig. 3. The input to the model is the graph representation of a PCB schematic, as described in the previous section. It contains the input node features, a combination of the node type and name, as well as edge attributes containing the pin name embeddings. An arbitrary GNN can be used to process the graph and calculate hidden node representations. The final node representations are passed to the pre-filtering MLP, which assigns a probability score to each net node representation. All net nodes with a probability score higher than a predefined threshold θ are passed to the node pair prediction module. This module is another MLP that performs a final prediction on the concatenation of two node representations. Thereby, this prediction is only performed for all possible pairs of nodes that were not

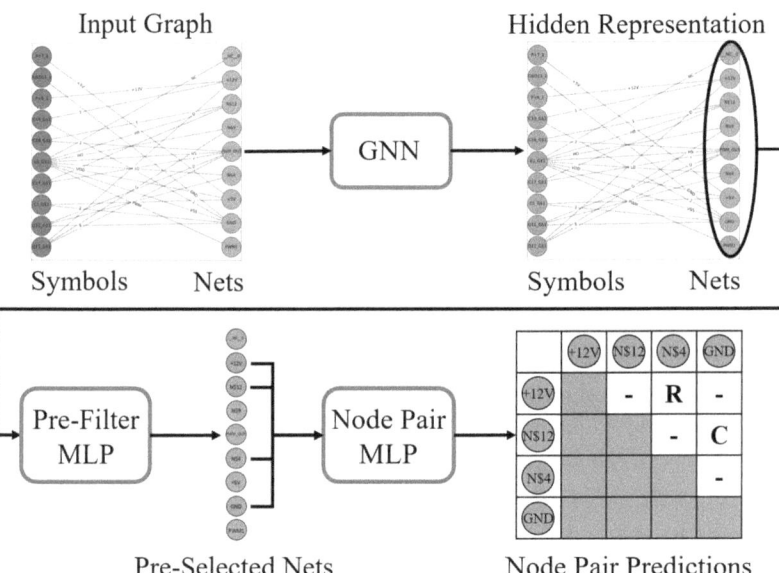

Fig. 3. Model architecture for the GNN-based node-pair-level prediction for PCB component addition. The GNN output representations of the net nodes are passed to the pre-filter MLP, which identifies individual net nodes with a high probability of serving as a connection point to the new component. The filtered node representations are concatenated pairwise and passed to a second MLP, which performs a task-specific prediction on each of these node pairs. In this example, the node pair MLP performs a multiclass classification to predict the new component's position and type (R or C).

sorted out by the pre-filtering MLP. Note that the threshold θ can be treated as an additional hyperparameter.

Task-Specific Model Output. The final output of the node pair prediction depends on the specific learning task. It could be a binary classification if the type of the new component is known, and a multiclass classification if there are multiple possible classes of components. Finally, it could also be a regression if the task is to predict the number of parallel components to insert between a specific pair of nodes.

5   Experiments

We validate our approach by performing experiments on three specific use cases, each corresponding to the addition of a different component for the optimization of the PCB design. These design optimizations increase the robustness of the PCB and are usually performed manually by human engineers in a time-consuming and error-prone process.

Table 1. Dataset statistics. Percentages are calculated with respect to the average number of nodes per graph.

Dataset	Pull-Ups/-Downs	RC-Filters	Decoupling Caps.
No. of Graph Samples	2396	849	944
Avg. No. of Nodes	122.6	123.5	100.1
Min. No. of Nodes	7	7	6
Max. No. of Nodes	702	637	500
Avg. No. of Edges	174.4	175.7	139.0
Avg. No. of Added Nodes	2.8 (2.3%)	2.1 (1.7%)	1.4 (1.4%)

First, we perform a binary classification to predict the positions of additional pull-up- and pull-down resistors. Second, we train a model on inserting RC filters on digital reset pins, which corresponds to a multiclass classification since the model has to distinguish also between resistor and capacitor. Finally, we investigate the addition of decoupling capacitors, which we treat both as a simplified binary classification task ("Add at least one capacitor or not") and as a regression task ("How many parallel capacitors should be placed at this position?").

5.1 Datasets, Models, and Experimental Setting

Datasets. We generated three large datasets of labeled PCB schematics, one for each optimization task. The schematics were optimized and labeled manually by human experts in electrical engineering. Thereby, each pair of net nodes in each circuit of the dataset received a label $\hat{y}_{pair}$ according to the specific task (binary, multiclass, or regression). Additionally, we generated binary labels $\hat{y}_{node}$ for each net node indicating whether it serves as a connection point for at least one new component or not. These single-node labels are used to train the pre-filter MLP. Statistics of the three resulting datasets can be found in Table. 1. All three datasets contain a large number of unique graphs of varying sizes ranging from 6 nodes up to huge graphs with more than 700 nodes. On average, between one and three new nodes are added per graph. This means that only a small fraction of all possible net node pairs receive a positive label, resulting in a strong class imbalance.

GNN Models. In all experiments, we apply our node pair prediction model with different GNN backbones. Thereby, we consider the baseline models GCN [11] and GIN [28] as well as GINe [8], a modification of GIN that includes edge attributes. Furthermore, we experiment with several widely used attention-based GNN models: GAT [24], GATv2 [2], and GraphTransformer (GT) [22]. All three models are taking edge attributes into account. As an additional baseline, we also compare to an "MLP-only" version of our model, where the pre-filter MLP and the node pair MLP are applied directly to the input node features without any message-passing layers in between. In this way, we can specifically investigate the influence of the graph structure on the model performance.

Experimental Setting. We split each dataset into train, validation, and test sets with ratios $80/10/10\%$ and perform a 9-fold cross-validation. Additionally, we perform a small grid search for hyperparameter optimization (see Table. 2 for details). For each training run, we use the AdamW optimizer [13], a batch size of 128, and perform early stopping with a patience of 20 epochs using the task-specific evaluation metric. The loss function is composed of a binary cross-entropy loss term BCE responsible for the training of the pre-filter MLP, and a task-specific node pair term L_{task} for the training of the node pair MLP:

$$L = BCE(y_{\text{node}}, \hat{y}_{\text{node}}) + L_{\text{Task}}(y_{\text{pair}}, \hat{y}_{\text{pair}}). \tag{1}$$

Note that both loss terms also contribute to training the GNN layers.

Table 2. Overview of the hyperparameters used in the experiments.

Hyperparameter	Values
Hid. Dimension	16, 32, 64
Num. of GNN Layers	1, 2, 3
Attention Heads	1, 4
Learning Rate	0.001, 0.0005, 0.0001
Threshold θ	0.0, 0.1, ..., 0.7

5.2 Optimization Task 1: Adding Pull-Up and Pull-Down Resistors

Technical Background. Pull-up and pull-down resistors are two-terminal components placed between one specific net on the design and, in the case of pull-ups, a supply net, and in the case of pull-downs, a ground net. When placed, these components help to ensure that the voltage on the selected design net is brought to a defined known value in case the design net is left floating. There are many possible reasons for the usage of pull-ups and pull-downs, including functionality, reliability, and best practices. In a functional safety example, if a MOSFET transistor is not being actively driven, a pull-down resistor can ensure that the transistor is definitely turned off.

Task-Specific Model. We approach this optimization task as a binary classification on the node pair level, where a positive label corresponds to the placement of a pull-up or pull-down resistor. We do not differentiate explicitly between pull-up and pull-down resistors, since the component is the same in both cases and the function of the resistor follows straight from its position within the circuit. Thus, the node pair MLP has a single output node and for the loss term L_{Task}, we use another binary cross-entropy loss function:

$$L_{\text{Task}}(y_{\text{pair}}, \hat{y}_{\text{pair}}) = BCE(y_{\text{pair}}, \hat{y}_{\text{pair}}). \tag{2}$$

Due to the extreme class imbalance in the dataset, we use the Area Under the Precision-Recall Curve (AUPRC) as our evaluation metric, which is a robust metric for scenarios with an underrepresented positive class that focuses on the trade-off between precision and recall. We calculate the AUPRC over the predictions for all possible pairs of net nodes in each graph. Thereby, all predictions for node pairs that are not evaluated by the node pair MLP (because at least one of the two nodes was sorted out by the pre-filter MLP) are set to negative labels (no component insertion at this position). Therefore, the AUPRC metric reflects both errors resulting from node pair misclassifications as well as errors resulting from incorrect filtering by the pre-filter MLP.

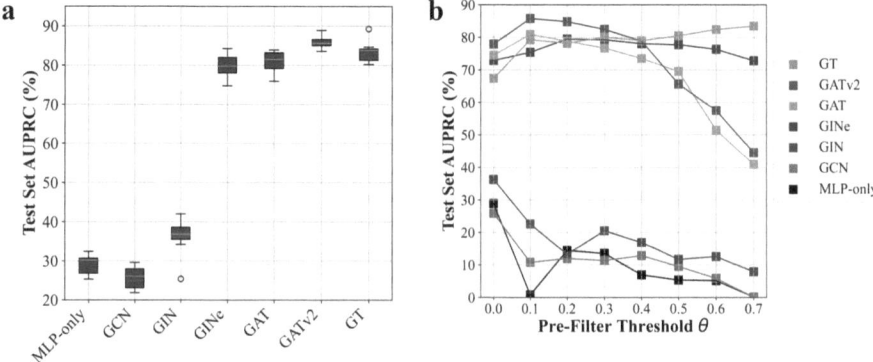

Fig. 4. a Area under the precision-recall curve (AUPRC) on the test set for the best hyperparameter configuration of all model variants for the pull-ups/-downs insertion task. **b** Sensitivity of the pull-ups/-downs insertion performance on the pre-filter threshold θ for all model variants.

Results. Figure 4a shows the AUPRC on the test set for all considered models. Thereby, we only consider the best hyperparameter configurations, which are reported in the Appendix (see Material). First, it is noticeable that the model variants MLP-only, GCN and GIN show a much lower performance compared to all other models. These three models do not consider edge features, which appear to be very important for this specific task. A possible reason for this is that the names of the target connection points are sometimes chosen generically (e.g., "N$2"), whereas the names of the connected pins, i.e., the edge attributes, may reveal more information on their function. The more advanced GNN variants

GINe, GAT, GATv2, and GT all consider edge attributes and exhibit a much higher AUPRC of more than 80 %. Among these models, GATv2 performs best with an AUPRC of 85.8 %.

The influence of the pre-filter threshold θ on the task performance is investigated in Fig. 4b. For the models with an edge-feature dependency, the performance drops when no pre-filter is used ($\theta = 0$). This underlines the importance of the pre-filter beyond computational efficiency: It also stabilizes the training process and increases the performance. The best performances are mostly achieved with a small threshold between 0.1 and 0.3, whereas the AUPRC decreases steadily for higher θ.

These results indicate that it is better to not sort out too many nodes in the pre-filter step, since the node pair MLP is capable of correcting false positive predictions by the pre-filter. However, if the pre-filter MLP has too many false negatives (high θ), the associated node pairs are not evaluated by the node pair MLP anymore and are instead automatically set to a negative label. Only the GT model appears to be an exception here: The test set performance increases for higher θ due to very accurate pre-filtering.

The models without edge-feature dependency (MLP-only, GCN, and GIN) often do not converge and show very low performance. In this case, the AUPRC decreases even more when a pre-filter is used, because these models do not learn sufficiently meaningful node representations. Thus, the pre-filter MLP predicts too many false negatives that the node pair MLP cannot correct anymore.

5.3   Optimization Task 2: Adding RC Filters on Digital Reset Pins

Technical Background. Circuit schematics containing digital logic, especially programmable devices such as microprocessors and microcontrollers, require the special handling of the reset signal pin to prevent unintentional reset events, leading to functional issues in the final product. Commonly, reset pins are built to be "active-low", meaning they should be tied to the supply voltage to stay inactive. However, due to noise created by power supplies and the processor, voltage glitches can be present in the supply line, creating these unintentional reset events. Therefore, it is advisable to always have a simple RC filter between the supply net and the reset pin, in order to smooth out the voltage level noise and prevent issues. An RC filter is composed of a resistor connected between the supply net and the reset net, and a capacitor connected between the reset net and the ground net.

Task-Specific Model. We treat the placement of the RC filters as a multiclass classification task, where the node pair MLP has three output nodes, each corresponding to one of the three possible class labels: Resistor, capacitor, or none. For the loss term L_{task}, we use a cross-entropy loss function:

$$L_{\text{Task}}(y_{\text{pair}}, \hat{y}_{\text{pair}}) = CEL(y_{\text{pair}}, \hat{y}_{\text{pair}}). \tag{3}$$

As an evaluation metric, we utilize the AUPRC with macro-averaging, i.e., the unweighted mean of the separate metrics for all three classes.

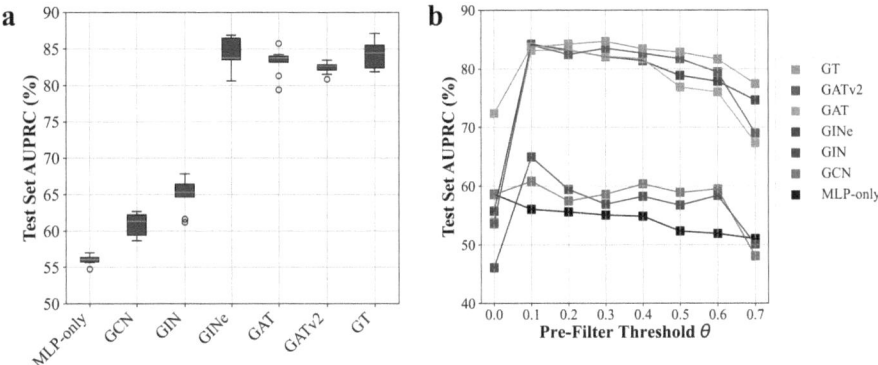

Fig. 5. a Area under the precision-recall curve (AUPRC) with macro-averaging on the test set for the best hyperparameter configuration of all model variants for the RC filter insertion task. **b** Sensitivity of the RC filter insertion performance on the pre-filter threshold θ for all model variants.

Results. Figure 5a shows the AUPRC on the test set for all considered models. First, it is noticeable that the model variants MLP-only, GCN and GIN again show a much lower performance compared to all other models, emphasizing the importance of the edge attributes for the identification of reset pins. Overall, the MLP-only variant shows the lowest performance of all models, which underlines the importance of the graph structure for this learning task. The attention-based GNN variants GAT, GATv2, and GT, as well as the GINe model, exhibit a very similar performance of nearly 85 % AUPRC.

The influence of the pre-filter threshold θ on the task performance is investigated in Fig. 5b. For all models, except the MLP-only variant, the performance drops significantly when no pre-filter is used ($\theta = 0$). Furthermore, the models with edge-feature dependency exhibit a slow performance decrease for increasing θ.

5.4   Optimization Task 3: Adding Decoupling Capacitors to Supply

Technical Background. Most electronic circuits have at least one supply net, used to provide power to integrated circuits, and one ground net, which is the current return net back to the supply. Both supply and ground nets are shared among many components in an electronic design, and therefore it is important to make sure the operation of one integrated circuit does not interfere with the operation of another one. To prevent these undesired interactions through the supply net, decoupling capacitors are placed. They are connected as close as possible between supply and ground nets, which can "short-circuit" high-frequency noise created by digital integrated circuits and make sure both supply and ground nets remain clean. This helps to contain this noise and avoid interferences, as well as to reduce the levels of electromagnetic emission from the final device.

Task-Specific Model. We approach this optimization task from two perspectives simultaneously. First, we consider it as a binary classification task with the goal of predicting whether at least one decoupling capacitor has to be inserted between a pair of net nodes or not. For different reasons, however, engineers are often placing multiple decoupling capacitors in parallel, e.g., to ensure stability over a wider range of frequencies. Therefore, we also perform a regression and predict the exact number of parallel capacitors that engineers would insert at a certain position in the circuit.

We utilize two separate node pair MLPs for this task, one for the binary classification with outputs z_{pair} and one for the regression with outputs y_{pair}. For the binary classification, we use the binary cross-entropy loss function and for the regression, we utilize the mean-squared error. We further assign a weight α to the regression loss term to control its influence on the training process:

$$L_{Task}(z_{pair}, y_{pair}, \hat{y}_{pair}) = BCE(z_{pair}, \hat{z}_{pair}) + \alpha \cdot MSE(y_{pair}, \hat{y}_{pair}). \quad (4)$$

Thereby, the labels $\hat{z}_{pair}$ are computed as

$$\hat{z}_{pair} = \begin{cases} 1, & \hat{y}_{pair} \geq 1 \\ 0, & \text{otherwise.} \end{cases} \quad (5)$$

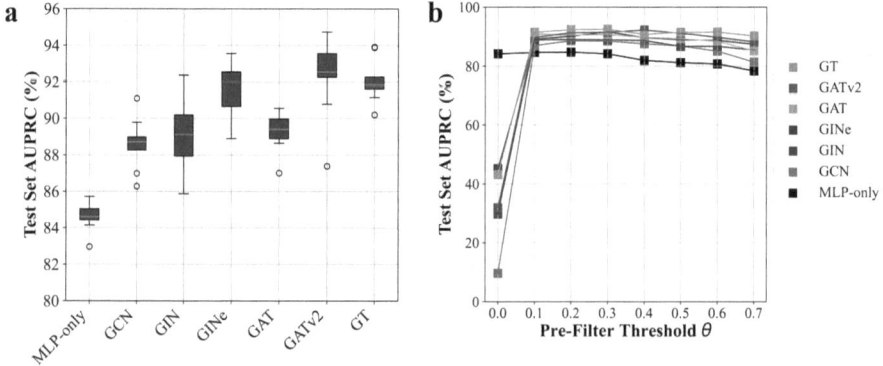

Fig. 6. a Area under the precision-recall curve (AUPRC) on the test set for the best hyperparameter configuration of all model variants for the decoupling capacitor insertion task (treated as a binary classification). **b** Sensitivity of the decoupling capacitor insertion performance on the pre-filter threshold θ for all model variants.

Binary Classification Results. For the evaluation of the binary classification, we utilize the AUPRC metric again. Figure 6a shows the AUPRC on the test set for all considered models. Again, the MLP-only variant shows the lowest performance among all models, although it performs much better than on the other tasks. This indicates that the graph structure and local node neighborhood are less relevant for the decoupling capacitor insertion task. Furthermore, GNNs that include edge attributes (GINe, GAT, GATv2, and GT) only show a slightly better performance compared to GCN and GIN. Therefore, we conclude that the node features, i.e., node types and names, are the most important features for the prediction of decoupling capacitor additions. A possible reason for this is that supply and ground nets, which are the relevant connection points for decoupling capacitors, mostly have well-defined names, making them easily identifiable by their node features alone.

Figure 6b shows the sensitivity of the test set AUPRC on the pre-filter threshold θ. Here, the performance drops drastically when no pre-filter is used ($\theta = 0$) and decreases slightly for increasing θ. Only the MLP-only variant shows an acceptable performance without any pre-filter.

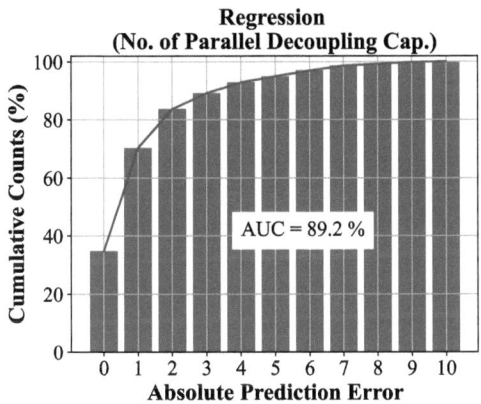

Fig. 7. Cumulative counts of absolute errors of the GATv2 model variant for the prediction of the number of parallel decoupling capacitors to insert at a given position in the circuit. In approx. 70% of the cases, the prediction deviates from the ground truth by at most 1.

Regression Results. For the evaluation of the regression, we first round the outputs of the regression MLP to integers. Next, we calculate the absolute prediction error for all non-zero labels. Figure 7 shows the cumulative counts of absolute prediction errors for the GATv2 model variant with $\alpha = 0.1$. In approximately 70 % of the cases, the predicted number of parallel decoupling capacitors at a given position deviates from the ground truth by at most 1. The overall area under the curve is 89.2 %, indicating that the model can give a good estimation of the number of parallel decoupling capacitors, despite lacking some information that engineers would take into account when solving this problem, e.g., component values or market availability of certain capacitors.

6   Conclusion

In this paper, we presented a Graph Neural Network (GNN)-based approach for automating the addition of new components in Printed Circuit Board (PCB) schematics to optimize their robustness and reliability. Thereby, we represented PCB schematics as bipartite graphs and trained a node-pair-level classification on three real-world PCB datasets manually labeled by human experts, each focusing on the addition of different optimizing components with high practical relevance: Pull-up/-down resistors, RC filters, and decoupling capacitors.

Our results show that GNNs, especially architectures that consider edge attributes, can learn meaningful representations of PCB schematics and provide a significant performance gain on all optimization tasks compared to the usage of pure multi-layer perceptrons. Furthermore, we found that pre-filtering promising connection points for the new components using a separate multi-layer perceptron stabilizes the training process and increases the overall model performance. In summary, the accuracy of our approach is high enough to increase the automation level of the PCB design optimization process and support engineers in developing more durable electronic devices more efficiently, leading to considerable time and cost savings.

In the future, we want to further enhance the model performance by investigating the usage of other graph types for the representation of PCB schematics (e.g., hypergraphs) as well as more specialized GNN architectures such as heterogeneous GNNs. Furthermore, we want to consider additional information from the PCB schematics that has not been exploited so far, e.g., component values like resistances or capacities. Finally, we plan to extend the scope of our graph-based approach to other PCB design optimization tasks involving not only the addition of new components but also the merging, splitting, or removal of existing ones.

Acknowledgments. This study was funded by the German Federal Ministry of Research, Technology, and Space (funding code 16ME0877). We also thank Clara Holzhüter for her helpful feedback.

Disclosure of Interests. The authors have no competing interests to declare that are relevant to the content of this article.

References

1. Barboza, E.C., Shukla, N., Chen, Y., Hu, J.: Machine learning-based pre-routing timing prediction with reduced pessimism. In: Proceedings of the 56th Annual Design Automation Conference 2019, pp. 1–6 (2019)
2. Brody, S., Alon, U., Yahav, E.: How attentive are graph attention networks? In: International Conference on Learning Representations (2022)
3. Budak, A.F., Gandara, M., Shi, W., Pan, D.Z., Sun, N., Liu, B.: An efficient analog circuit sizing method based on machine learning assisted global optimization. IEEE Trans. Comput. Aided Des. Integr. Circuits Syst. 41(5), 1209–1221 (2021)

4. Cheng, R., Yan, J.: On joint learning for solving placement and routing in chip design. Adv. Neural. Inf. Process. Syst. **34**, 16508–16519 (2021)
5. Dong, Z., Cao, W., Zhang, M., Tao, D., Chen, Y., Zhang, X.: Cktgnn: circuit graph neural network for electronic design automation. In: International Conference on Learning Representations (2023)
6. Hamilton, W., Ying, Z., Leskovec, J.: Inductive representation learning on large graphs. Adv. Neural Inf. Process. Syst. **30** (2017)
7. Hosny, A., Hashemi, S., Shalan, M., Reda, S.: Drills: deep reinforcement learning for logic synthesis. In: 2020 25th Asia and South Pacific Design Automation Conference (ASP-DAC), pp. 581–586. IEEE (2020)
8. Hu, W., et al.: Strategies for pre-training graph neural networks. In: International Conference on Learning Representations (2020)
9. Huang, G., et al.: Machine learning for electronic design automation: a survey. ACM Trans. Design Autom. Electr. Syst. (TODAES) **26**(5), 1–46 (2021)
10. Kipf, T.N., Welling, M.: Variational graph auto-encoders. arXiv preprint arXiv:1611.07308 (2016)
11. Kipf, T.N., Welling, M.: Semi-supervised classification with graph convolutional networks. In: International Conference on Learning Representations (2017)
12. Kunal, K., et al.: Gana: graph convolutional network based automated netlist annotation for analog circuits. In: 2020 Design, Automation and Test in Europe Conference and Exhibition (DATE), pp. 55–60. IEEE (2020)
13. Loshchilov, I., Hutter, F.: Decoupled weight decay regularization. In: International Conference on Learning Representations (2019)
14. Mina, R., Jabbour, C., Sakr, G.E.: A review of machine learning techniques in analog integrated circuit design automation. Electronics **11**(3), 435 (2022)
15. Mirhoseini, A., et al.: Chip placement with deep reinforcement learning. arXiv preprint arXiv:2004.10746 (2020)
16. Mirhoseini, A., et al.: A graph placement methodology for fast chip design. Nature **594**(7862), 207–212 (2021)
17. Reimers, N., Gurevych, I.: Sentence-bert: Sentence embeddings using siamese bert-networks. arXiv preprint arXiv:1908.10084 (2019)
18. Ren, H., Kokai, G.F., Turner, W.J., Ku, T.S.: Paragraph: layout parasitics and device parameter prediction using graph neural networks. In: 2020 57th ACM/IEEE Design Automation Conference (DAC), pp. 1–6. IEEE (2020)
19. Said, A., Shabbir, M., Broll, B., Abbas, W., Völgyesi, P., Koutsoukos, X.: Circuit design completion using graph neural networks. Neural Comput. Appl. **35**(16), 12145–12157 (2023)
20. Sánchez, D., Servadei, L., Kiprit, G.N., Wille, R., Ecker, W.: A comprehensive survey on electronic design automation and graph neural networks: theory and applications. ACM Trans. Design Autom. Electr. Syst. **28**(2), 1–27 (2023)
21. Settaluri, K., Haj-Ali, A., Huang, Q., Hakhamaneshi, K., Nikolic, B.: Autockt: deep reinforcement learning of analog circuit designs. In: 2020 Design, Automation and Test in Europe Conference and Exhibition (DATE), pp. 490–495. IEEE (2020)
22. Shi, Y., Huang, Z., Feng, S., Zhong, H., Wang, W., Sun, Y.: Masked label prediction: unified message passing model for semi-supervised classification. In: Proceedings of the Thirtieth International Joint Conference on Artificial Intelligence (2021)
23. Shrestha, P., Savidis, I.: Eda-ml: Graph representation learning framework for digital ic design automation. In: 2024 25th International Symposium on Quality Electronic Design (ISQED), pp. 1–7. IEEE (2024)

24. Veličković, P., Cucurull, G., Casanova, A., Romero, A., Lio, P., Bengio, Y.: Graph attention networks. In: International Conference on Learning Representations (2018)
25. Wang, H., et al.: GCN-RL circuit designer: Transferable transistor sizing with graph neural networks and reinforcement learning. In: 2020 57th ACM/IEEE Design Automation Conference (DAC), pp. 1–6. IEEE (2020)
26. Wang, W., Wei, F., Dong, L., Bao, H., Yang, N., Zhou, M.: Minilm: deep self-attention distillation for task-agnostic compression of pre-trained transformers. Adv. Neural. Inf. Process. Syst. **33**, 5776–5788 (2020)
27. Xie, Z., et al.: Routenet: routability prediction for mixed-size designs using convolutional neural network. In: 2018 IEEE/ACM International Conference on Computer-Aided Design (ICCAD), pp. 1–8. IEEE (2018)
28. Xu, K., Hu, W., Leskovec, J., Jegelka, S.: How powerful are graph neural networks? In: International Conference on Learning Representations (2019)
29. Yu, C., Xiao, H., De Micheli, G.: Developing synthesis flows without human knowledge. In: Proceedings of the 55th Annual Design Automation Conference, pp. 1–6 (2018)
30. Zhang, M., Chen, Y.: Link prediction based on graph neural networks. Adv. Neural Inf. Process. Syst. **31** (2018)

Explaining Bayesian Optimization by Shapley Values Facilitates Human-AI Collaboration for Exosuit Personalization

Julian Rodemann[1,2(✉)], Federico Croppi[2], Philipp Arens[3], Yusuf Sale[4,5], Julia Herbinger[6], Bernd Bischl[2,5], Eyke Hüllermeier[4,5,7], Thomas Augustin[2], Conor J. Walsh[3,8], and Giuseppe Casalicchio[2,5]

[1] CISPA Helmholtz Center for Information Security, Saarbrücken, Germany
julian.rodemann@cispa.de
[2] Department of Statistics, Ludwig-Maximilians-Universität (LMU), Munich, Germany
[3] John A. Paulson Harvard School of Engineering and Applied Sciences, Harvard University, Cambridge, MA, USA
[4] Institute of Informatics, Ludwig-Maximilians-Universität (LMU), Munich, Germany
[5] Munich Center for Machine Learning (MCML), Munich, Germany
[6] Leibniz Institute for Prevention Research and Epidemiology, Bremen, Germany
[7] German Research Centre for Artificial Intelligence (DFKI), Kaiserslautern, Germany
[8] Wyss Institute for Biologically Inspired Engineering, Harvard University, Cambridge, MA, USA

Abstract. Bayesian optimization (BO) has become indispensable for black box optimization. However, BO is often considered a black box itself, lacking transparency in the rationale behind proposed parameters. This is particularly relevant in human-in-the-loop applications like personalization of wearable robotic devices. We address BO's opacity by proposing ShapleyBO, a framework for interpreting BO proposals by game-theoretic Shapley values. Our approach quantifies the contribution of each parameter to BO's acquisition function (AF). By leveraging the linearity of Shapley values, ShapleyBO can identify the influence of each parameter on BO's exploration and exploitation behaviors. Our method gives rise to a ShapleyBO-assisted human-machine interface (HMI), allowing users to interfere with BO in case proposals do not align with human reasoning. We demonstrate these HMI's benefits for the use case of personalizing wearable robotic devices (assistive back exosuits) by human-in-the-loop BO. Results suggest that human-BO teams with access to ShapleyBO outperform teams without access to ShapleyBO. (**Open Science:** ShapleyBO as well as code and data to reproduce findings available at https://github.com/rodemann/ShapleyBO. This work builds upon the master's thesis of the second author supervised by the

---

Supplementary Information The online version contains supplementary material available at https://doi.org/10.1007/978-3-662-72243-5_30.

last author [18], and substantially extends and formalizes the results presented therein.).

Keywords: Bayesian Optimization · Explainable AI · Interpretable Machine Learning · Shapley Values · Robotics · Human-AI Collaboration

1 Introduction

In artificial intelligence (AI) and machine learning (ML), the black-box nature of increasingly complex models poses serious challenges to end-users and researchers alike. The terms explainable AI (XAI) and interpretable machine learning (IML) – often used interchangeably – describe efforts to help illuminate decision-making processes of ML algorithms, see [6,10] for an overview of this emerging field. While the interpretability of ML models has been extensively studied, less attention has been given to the explanation and interpretation of optimization methods, which, given their frequent use in decision making problems, may benefit particularly from increased transparency.

This paper expands the focus of interpretability to Bayesian optimization (BO) with Gaussian Processes (GPs), an optimization method, frequently used in black-box applications such as hyperparameter optimization of ML models, the sequential design of expensive computer simulations or, real-word experiments, for which gradients are difficult to compute. However, BO algorithms are often perceived as black boxes themselves. Understanding and interpreting such optimizers can increase trust in domains such as human-AI interaction, mitigating the risk for algorithmic aversion [13,19]. In addition, we will show that IML techniques can help accelerate the optimization in collaborative setups between humans and AI. Here, a human can intervene by rejecting or rectifying the proposals made by BO [48]. A better understanding of the algorithm fosters more efficient human-machine interaction, which is key in such applications, as we demonstrate in this work.

We present a method to interpret the BO's proposed parameter configurations through Shapley values, a concept from cooperative game theory that has gained much popularity in IML. Our framework `ShapleyBO` informs users about how much each parameter contributed to the configurations proposed by a BO algorithm. The key idea is to quantify each parameters' contribution to the Acquisition Function (AF) – rather than to the model's predictions, as is customary in IML [28]. Loosely speaking, the AF describes how "attractive" BO considers a given parameter configuration. A Shapley value can thus inform the user how much a single parameter contributes to this attractiveness. Since Shapley values are linear in the contributions they explain, see Axiom 3 in Sect. 2, they can be used to inform us about how much each parameter contributed to each component of any additive AF, such as the popular confidence bound, which is a weighted sum of the predicted mean and standard error. AFs play a critical role in BO as they define a decision metric based on which the optimization proceeds to the following iteration. In forming this decision metric, AFs balance exploration of regions with high uncertainty and exploitation of regions with high expected reward. Efficiently managing this exploration-exploitation trade-off is a central objective behind BO.

Bayesian Optimization has become particularly appealing for applications in which objective function samples are costly to obtain. A prominent example is Human-in-the-Loop (HIL) optimization to customize assistance settings for wearable robotic or prosthetic devices [5,20,54]. The goal of such HIL experiments is to find a set of control parameters that maximize the efficacy of the provided assistance. This efficacy is often evaluated through physiological performance metrics such as (reductions in) metabolic demand or muscles dynamics and more recently expanded to subjective metrics such as user preference. Common to all, it is typically unclear to the user (or researcher), why a certain new parameter combination was chosen by the BO algorithm.

To address this, we propose a Human-Machine Interface (HMI) that allows users to better understand BO's proposals and utilize this understanding in deciding whether to intervene and rectify proposals if they seem undesirable for some reason, e.g., because they do not align with human preferences. Experiments on data from a real-world use case, personalizing assistance parameters for a wearable back exosuit [5,42], suggest that such an understanding can indeed help to intervene more efficiently than without the availability of Shapley values.

We summarize our contributions as follows.

(1) We explain why parameters are proposed in BO by quantifying each parameters' contribution to a proposal through Shapley values.
(2) We further distinguish between parameters that drive exploitation (mean optimization) and exploration (uncertainty reduction) in BO, utilizing the linearity of Shapley values.
(3) Exploratory uncertainty reduction is in turn disentangled into aleatoric uncertainty on the one hand and different epistemic sources of uncertainty on the other hand, which fosters theoretical understanding of BO.
(4) We test ShapleyBO on both noisy and noise-free optimization problems and illustrate its practical benefits, see Sect. 5.
(5) To compute the Shapley values, we adopt a traditional MC sampling strategy, supplemented by a novel algorithm, designed to accurately determine an adequate sample size for Shapley value estimation in BO contexts. This increases the computational efficiency of ShapleyBO, see supplementary material.
(6) We apply our ShapleyBO-based HMI to exosuit customization through human-in-the-loop BO and demonstrate that our method can speed up the procedure through more efficient HMI in a simulation study, see Sect. 6.

2   Background

Bayesian Optimization: BO is a popular derivative-free optimizer for functions that are expensive to evaluate and lack an analytical description. Its origin dates back to [30]. Modern use cases of BO cover engineering, drug discovery and finance as well as hyperparameter optimization and neural architecture search in ML, see e.g. [22,34,43]. BO approximates the target function through a surrogate model (SM). In the case of real-valued parameters, the SM typically is a GP. BO then combines the GP's mean and standard error predictions to construct an AF, which is then optimized to propose new points. Algorithm 1 summarizes BO applied to the problem of minimizing (w.l.o.g.) an unknown ("black-box") objective function[1] $\Psi : \Theta \rightarrow \mathbb{R}, \theta \mapsto \Psi(\theta)$, where Θ is a p-dimensional decision (parameter) space. In the human-in-the-loop setup, a user can intervene by either rejecting a proposal (line 4 in Algorithm 1) or an update (line 6 in Algorithm 1) or by proposing another configuration (line 6 in Algorithm 2), see Sect. 6 for details.

Algorithm 1. Bayesian Optimization

1: create an initial design $D = \{(\theta^{(i)}, \Psi^{(i)})\}_{i=1,\dots,n_{init}}$
2: **while** termination criterion is not fulfilled **do**
3:     **train** SM on data D
4:     **propose** θ^{new} that optimizes $AF(SM(\theta))$
5:     **evaluate** Ψ on θ^{new}
6:     **update** $D \leftarrow D \cup (\theta^{new}, \Psi(\theta^{new}))$
7: **end while**
8: **return** $\arg\min_{\theta \in D} \Psi(\theta)$

Shapley Values: Shapley values are a concept from cooperative game theory, originally introduced by [41], that can be used to measure the contribution of each feature to an ML model prediction [45]. The key idea is to consider each feature as a player in a game where the prediction is the game's payoff, and to distribute this payoff fairly among the players according to their marginal contributions. Shapley values have several desirable properties that make them appealing for interpreting optimization problems. In general, given a set of players $P = \{1, \dots, p\}$ and a value or payout function $v : 2^P \rightarrow \mathbb{R}$ that assigns a value $v(S)$ to every subset (called a *coalition* in game theory) $S \subseteq P$ (such that $v(\emptyset) = 0$), the Shapley value $\phi_j(v)$ of player j is defined as the weighted average of their marginal contributions across all possible coalitions [32]:

$$\phi_j(v) = \sum_{S \subseteq P \setminus \{j\}} \frac{|S|! \, (p-1-|S|)!}{p!} [v(S \cup j) - v(S)] \tag{1}$$

The Shapley value can be justified axiomatically through the properties of dummy player, efficiency, linearity, and symmetry.

- *Dummy Player:* If $v(S \cup \{j\}) = v(S)$ for player j and $\forall S \subseteq P \setminus \{j\}$, then $\phi_j(v) = 0$

---

[1] Also referred to as *target* function.

- *Efficiency:* $\sum_{j=1}^{p} \phi_j(v) = v(P) - v(\emptyset)$
- *Linearity:* Given two games (P, v_1) and (P, v_2) and any $a, b \in \mathbb{R}$, the following holds: $\phi_j(av_1 + bv_2) = a\phi_j(v_1) + b\phi_j(v_2)$
- *Symmetry:* If $v(S \cup \{j\}) = v(S \cup \{l\})$ for players j, l and every $S \subseteq P\backslash\{j,l\}$, then $\phi_j(v) = \phi_l(v)$

The payout function does not require any specific properties and the Shapley value can hence be used in many different applications [23, p.3]. We will particularly rely on the linearity of Shapley values when applying them to AFs in BO, see Sect. 4.

Compared to other IML methods, such as the permutation feature importance [12,21] or the partial dependence plot [24], Shapley values have the main advantage of fairly distributing feature interactions among all involved features to quantify feature contributions. While the features become the players, the payout function is typically set to the expected output of the predictive model conditioned on the values of the features in a coalition, see [28,45] or [1, Equation 2]. Formally, let $\hat{f} : \Theta \to \mathbb{R}$ be a prediction model on feature space Θ and $\tilde{\theta} \in \Theta$ the instance to explain. Then the worth of a coalition of features $S \subseteq \Theta$ is given by $v(S) = \mathbb{E}[\hat{f}(\theta)|\theta_S = \tilde{\theta}_S]$, where $\theta_S, \tilde{\theta}_S \in S$ are the feature vectors $\theta, \tilde{\theta}$ projected onto S.

3   Related Work

As mentioned in Sect. 2, there are only quite mild regularity conditions for a function to be explainable by Shapley values. Consequently, there exists a broad body of research on deploying Shapley values beyond classical prediction functions. Examples comprise the explanation of predictive uncertainty [50] or anomaly detection [46]. There is some work on Shapley-based explanations of optimization algorithms such as evolutionary algorithms [49] or differentiable architecture search (DARTS) in deep learning [52]. There are even efforts to utilize Shapley values to improve optimizers similar to our Shapley-assisted human-BO team. For instance, [51] solves fuzzy optimization problems by integrating Shapley values with evolutionary algortihns and [9] use Shapley values to speed up multi-objective particle swarm optimization grey wolf optimization (PSOGWO).

Generally, there has been a lot of interest in how to incorporate human knowledge in optimization loops recently [2,4,7,8,48,53] and what role IML can play in this regard [31]. This growing interest is not only sparked by fine-tuning large language models through reinforcement learning from human feedback [35], but also by chemical applications [17]. The method we apply to exosuit personalization partly builds on [18], who proposed to interpret BO by Shapley values first. Very recently, Adachi et al. [3] introduced Collaborative and Explainable Bayesian Optimization (CoExBo), building on GP-SHAP (Shapley Values explaining Gaussian Processes) [15], for lithium-ion battery design, a framework that integrates human knowledge into BO via preference learning and explains its proposals by Shapley values. Contrary to our approach, CoExBo first aligns human knowledge with BO by preference learning. In a second step, it then proposes several points and allows the user to select among them based on additionally provided Shapley values, while our Shapley-assisted human-BO team directly uses Shapley values to align a single BO proposal with human proposals.

[14] recently proposed TNTRules, a post-hoc rule-based explanation method of BO. TNTRules finds (through clustering algorithms) subspaces of the parameter space that should be tuned by the user. Similar to our work, it emphasizes the benefits of XAI methods in human-collaborative BO. Contrary to our work, it is a post-hoc method (`ShapleyBO` works online) and focuses on explaining the whole parameter space rather than single BO proposals.

4   Explaining Bayesian Optimization via Shapley Values

In this section, we introduce `ShapleyBO` (see footnote 1) that allows to interpret BO proposals by Shapley values. Transitioning from ML models to AFs, the utilization of the Shapley value becomes remarkably straightforward, as an AF essentially represents a transformed version of a surrogate model's prediction function. Consequently, the Shapley value can be employed with any AF to evaluate the contribution of selected parameter values. Among an array of AF options, the confidence bound appears particularly suited for our approach, due to its intuitive functional form and additive nature. The **confidence bound (CB)** of a parameter vector $\boldsymbol{\theta} \in \boldsymbol{\Theta}$ is defined as

$$cb(\boldsymbol{\theta}) - \hat{\mu}(\boldsymbol{\theta}) - \lambda\hat{\sigma}(\boldsymbol{\theta}), \tag{2}$$

where $\hat{\mu}$ and $\hat{\sigma}$ are mean and standard error estimates by the SM (here: GP), respectively; $\lambda > 0$ is a hyperparameter controlling the exploration-exploitation trade-off. The rationale behind the confidence bound is fairly intuitive: a point is deemed desirable if either (i) the mean prediction $\hat{\mu}$ is low (indicating an anticipation of a low target value, thus *exploiting* existing knowledge) or (ii) the uncertainty prediction $\hat{\sigma}$ is high (indicating limited information about the target function in that area, thus *exploring* this region of the parameter space). Proposing new samples boils down to optimizing this confidence bound. To this end, let minimizing (w.l.o.g.) the confidence bound be a cooperative game along the lines of Sect. 2. It shall be defined as (P, cb), or as two separate games $(P, \hat{\mu})$ and $(P, \hat{\sigma})$, with P being the grand coalition of parameters and $\hat{\mu}$ and $\hat{\sigma}$ the payout functions, respectively. According to the linearity axiom, the cb contribution of any parameter j of the parameter vector $\tilde{\boldsymbol{\theta}}$ to be explained can then be decomposed into the mean contribution $\phi_j(\hat{\mu})$ and the uncertainty contribution $\phi_j(\hat{\sigma})$:

$$\phi_j(cb) = \phi_j(\hat{\mu} - \lambda\hat{\sigma}) = \phi_j(\hat{\mu}) - \lambda\phi_j(\hat{\sigma}) \tag{3}$$

Thus, we can not only evaluate the overall contribution of each parameter θ_j, but also examine how both contributions $\phi(\hat{\mu})$ and $\phi(\hat{\sigma})$ impact and drive the selection of proposed parameter values, shedding some light on the exploration-exploitation trade-off. On the background of recent work on uncertainty quantification [26,27,33], we further aim at disentangling the uncertainty contribution $\phi_j(\hat{\sigma})$ of a parameter θ_j into its epistemic (reducible) and aleatoric (irreducible) part. Aleatoric uncertainty is typically caused by noise. This is particularly relevant in BO if the noise is heteroscedastic, i.e., dependent on $\boldsymbol{\theta}$, since decision makers are often risk-averse. In other words, when deciding among two parameter configurations with equal mean target, most humans tend to opt for the one with lower variation. This motivates a risk-averse optimization problem: $\min_{\boldsymbol{\theta} \in \Theta} f(\boldsymbol{\theta}) - \alpha \cdot \epsilon(\boldsymbol{\theta})$ with $\epsilon(\boldsymbol{\theta})$ some noise that is non-constant in $\boldsymbol{\theta}$ and α the degree of risk-aversion. [29] propose risk-averse heteroscedastic Bayesian optimization (RAHBO) which entails minimizing (w.l.o.g.) the **risk-averse confidence bound (racb):**

$$racb(\boldsymbol{\theta}) = \widehat{\mu}(\boldsymbol{\theta}) - \tau \cdot \widehat{\sigma}(\boldsymbol{\theta}) + \alpha \cdot \widehat{\epsilon}(\boldsymbol{\theta}), \qquad (4)$$

where $\widehat{\epsilon}(\boldsymbol{\theta})$ is an on-the-fly estimate of the noise. Due to $racb$'s additive structure, ShapleyBO can identify each parameter's contribution to epistemic uncertainty

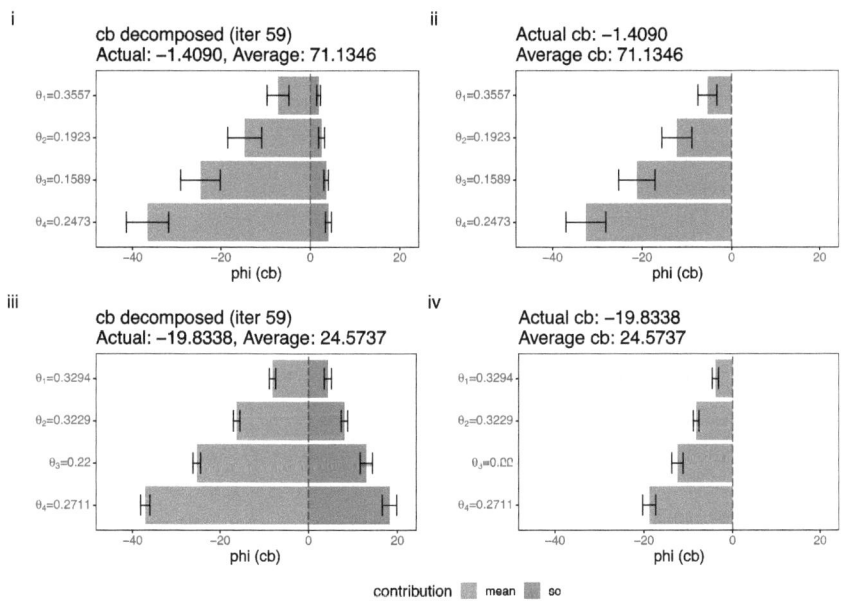

Fig. 1. ShapleyBO results in iteration 59 of BO on $f(\boldsymbol{\theta})$. Plots i and ii for $\lambda = 1$ and plots iii and iv for $\lambda = 10$. Contributions (phi) are averaged over 30 restarts for each λ. On the right, the overall contribution of the parameters is displayed (cb contributions), and on the left the decomposition into $\hat{\mu}$ (red, "mean") and $\hat{\sigma}$ (blue, "se") contributions. Recall that cb is minimized. Vertical axis includes the average distance of the proposed configuration from their optimum for a better interpretation. Error bars show one standard deviation. Actual: cb of actually proposed point. Average: Mean cb over all parameters. (Color figure online)

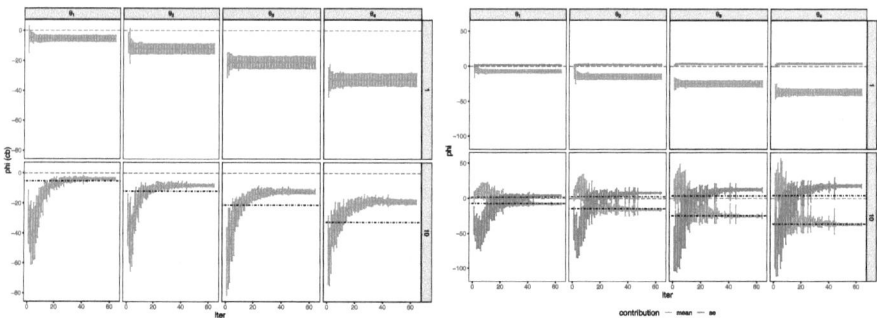

Fig. 2. Contributions curves for hyper ellipsoid optimization. Plot on top displays cb contributions for parameters (vertical) and λ (horizontal); beneath its decomposition into $\hat{\mu}$ (red, "mean") and $\hat{\sigma}$ (blue, "se") contributions, averaged over 30 restarts, error bars show one standard deviation. The black dot-dashed line in the $\lambda = 10$ plots displays the average contribution of the parameters in the $\lambda = 1$ run. (Color figure online)

reduction through $-\tau \cdot \hat{\sigma}(\boldsymbol{\theta})$ and to aleatoric uncertainty *avoidance* through $\alpha \cdot \hat{\epsilon}(\boldsymbol{\theta})$. By filtering out these exploratory contributions, the remainder of a parameter's overall Shapley value can be identified as the parameter's contribution to mean optimization through $\hat{\mu}(\boldsymbol{\theta})$ (exploitation).

5   Experimental Validation

A deployment on synthetic functions allows us to validate our method, because we can formulate concrete expectations for the contributions based on the known functional form of the synthetic target function. We select a hyper-ellipsoid function, where the parameters' partial derivatives grow in j. Thus, we expect the Shapley values of parameters in BO to be higher the higher their j.

Hyper-Ellipsoid Function: Firstly, we select a hyper-ellipsoid function (Eq. 5), where the partial derivatives of the parameters grow with j. Thus, we expect ShapleyBO to identify parameters with higher j as more influential in BO. We illustrate ShapleyBO by optimizing

$$f : [-5.12, 5.12]^4 \rightarrow \mathbb{R}_0^+ ; \boldsymbol{\theta} \mapsto f(\boldsymbol{\theta}) = \sum_{j=1}^{4} j \cdot \theta_j^2 \tag{5}$$

where f is separable and strictly convex with a unique minimizer $\boldsymbol{\theta}^* = (0, 0, 0, 0)^T$ with $f(\boldsymbol{\theta}^*) = 0$. To control for the stochastic behavior of BO, 30 repetitions of the optimization process with a bugdet of 60 function evaluations are run. Results in each iteration are then averaged over all repetitions.

As expected in light of the partial derivatives of $f(\boldsymbol{\theta})$, the contribution of θ_j grows with j, see Figs. 1 and 2. In contrast, uncertainty exhibits a diminutive and adverse effect. The uncertainty measurement $\hat{\sigma}$ for the recommended

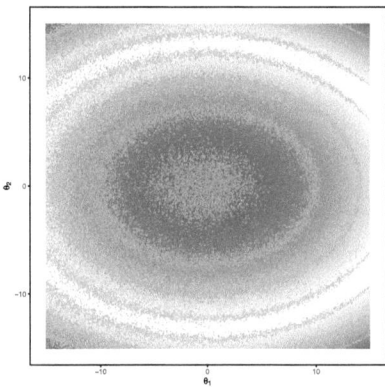 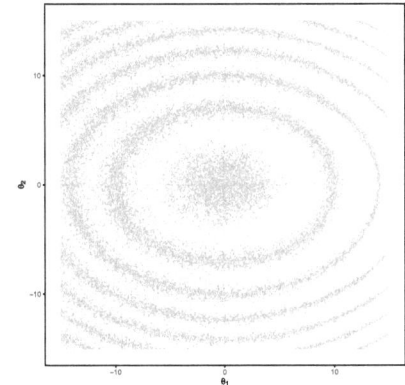

Fig. 3. Contour plots of noisy ellipsoid function $g(\boldsymbol{\theta}) + \boldsymbol{\epsilon}(\boldsymbol{\theta})$, see Eqs. 6 and 7. Red: low values of $g(\boldsymbol{\theta}) + \boldsymbol{\epsilon}(\boldsymbol{\theta})$; blue: high values of $g(\boldsymbol{\theta}) + \boldsymbol{\epsilon}(\boldsymbol{\theta})$. It becomes evident that the noise $\boldsymbol{\epsilon}(\boldsymbol{\theta})$ varies more w.r.t. θ_1, while $g(\boldsymbol{\theta})$ is stronger affected by θ_2. (Color figure online)

Table 1. Results of `ShapleyBO` for exemplary iterations 1 and 2 of BO with risk-averse confidence bound (Eq. 4) on heteroscedastic target function $g(\boldsymbol{\theta})$ (Eq. 7).

iteration	j	$\phi_j(\hat{\mu})$	$\phi_j(\hat{\sigma})$	$\phi_j(\hat{\epsilon})$	$\phi_j(racb)$
1	θ_1	−100.2	2.4	−13.9	−111.8
1	θ_2	−163.1	2.2	1.5	−159.4
2	θ_1	−87.8	2.4	−37.7	−123.1
2	θ_2	−165.6	1.6	3.3	−160.3

Table 2. Results of `ShapleyBO` averaged over all 60 iterations and all 30 BO restarts with risk-averse confidence bound (Eq. 4) on heteroscedastic target function $g(\boldsymbol{\theta})$ (Eq. 7).

j	$\overline{\phi_j}(\hat{\mu})$	$\overline{\phi_j}(\hat{\sigma})$	$\overline{\phi_j}(\hat{\epsilon})$
1	−48.48	4.20	−87.27
2	−157.73	6.88	0.24

setup falls below the average, thus yielding a positive payout (negative contributions). Opting for a setup with an uncertainty estimate beneath the average is deemed a strategic compromise towards enhancing mean values at the expense of exploration. `ShapleyBO` facilitates a nuanced allocation of this trade-off across parameters, see both Figs. 1 and 2. We also study how the contributions change in the course of the optimization. Respective contribution paths are shown in Fig. 2. Throughout the optimization process, the emphasis shifts from reducing uncertainty to prioritizing mean reduction, leading BO to favor configurations that perform well over those with high uncertainty. This transition is marked by a crossing in the contribution curves, see Fig. 2, indicating a preference for mean reduction over uncertainty reduction.

Heteroscedastic Target Function: Secondly, we illustrate `ShapleyBO` on a two-dimensional ellipsoid function with noise depending on $\boldsymbol{\theta}$, see Sect. 4 for details. That is, we minimize $g(\boldsymbol{\theta}) + \boldsymbol{\epsilon}(\boldsymbol{\theta})$, where

$$g\colon [-15, 15]^2 \to \mathbb{R}_0^+$$

$$\boldsymbol{\theta} \mapsto g(\boldsymbol{\theta}) = \sum_{i=1}^{2} i \cdot \theta_i^2 \tag{6}$$

and

$$\epsilon(\boldsymbol{\theta}) = 30 \cdot |\theta_1 - 15| + 0.3 \cdot |\theta_2 - 15|. \tag{7}$$

The noise grows strongly in θ_1, but only moderately in θ_2. Figure 3 shows contours of $g(\boldsymbol{\theta}) + \epsilon(\boldsymbol{\theta})$. It becomes evident that the function varies stronger w.r.t. θ_2 than w.r.t. θ_1, while the noise is strongly affected by θ_1 and almost constant in θ_2. Hence, we expect the respective Shapley values for aleatoric (see Eq. 4) uncertainty contributions to be high for θ_1 and low for θ_2, and vice versa for exploitation (mean optimization).

We run BO on $g(\boldsymbol{\theta}) + \epsilon(\boldsymbol{\theta})$ with risk-averse confidence bound ($racb$), see Eq. 4; we again average over 30 restarts of BO with 60 iterations each. ShapleyBO delivers contributions for each θ_j to each of $racb$'s components in each of BO's iterations. Table 1 has the results for exemplary iterations 1 and 2. Table 2 shows the contributions averaged over all $i \in \{1, \ldots, 60\}$ iterations and all $r \in \{1, \ldots, 30\}$ restarts. For instance, the averaged mean contributions of parameter j are

$$\overline{\phi}_j(\hat{\mu}) = \frac{1}{30} \sum_{r=1}^{30} \frac{1}{60} \sum_{i=1}^{60} \phi_{j,r,i}(\hat{\mu}). \tag{8}$$

It becomes evident that θ_2 is more important for the mean minimization than θ_1, while the latter contributes more to aleatoric uncertainty (noise) avoidance.

Summing up, the applications on both homo- and heteroscedastic target functions demonstrated that ShapleyBO manages to disentangle contributions of different parameters to different objectives of BO, thus providing valuable insights both into BO's inner working (see Figs. 1, 2 and Table 1) and about the target function itself (see Table 2).

6   Shapley-Assisted Human Machine Interface

The ability to interpret BO can be particularly useful for Human-In-the-Loop (HIL) applications, where users observe each step in the sequential optimization procedure. In this case, ShapleyBO can inform users online; that is, while the optimization is still running, about why certain actions were chosen over others, instead of providing such explanations after the experiment has concluded. More specifically, we consider a human-AI collaborative framework [4,11,14,25,48], in which users can actively participate in the optimization by rejecting BO proposals and instead take actions on their own.

As demonstrated in Sect. 5, Shapley values can provide structural insights on the relative importance of parameters for the optimization by filtering out uncertainty contributions, see $\overline{\phi}_j(\hat{\mu})$ in Table 2 for instance. Our general hypothesis is that basing the decision to intervene on this information will speed up the optimization. The underlying idea is that users can reject proposals in case the respective Shapley values do not align with the user's knowledge about the optimization problem.

To test this hypothesis, we benchmark a `ShapleyBO`-assisted human-AI team against teams without access to Shapley values. To better illustrate this, we consider the real-world use case of personalizing control parameters of a wearable, assistive back exosuit by BO.

6.1   Personalizing Soft Exosuits

Wearable robotic devices, such as exoskeletons and exosuits, have emerged as promising tools in mitigating risk of injury and aiding rehabilitation [42,47]. With an increase in use cases and accessibility to a broader community, it has become apparent that the benefits of such devices can vary substantially between individuals. Besides design choices, which have to be made early on and are therefore often guided by (average) user anthropometrics, important factors influencing device efficacy are the magnitude and timing of assistance.

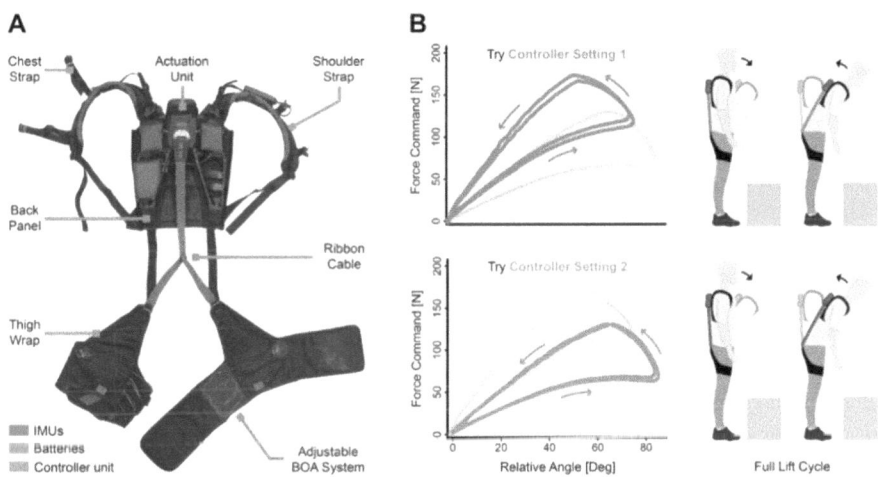

Fig. 4. A: Assistive soft back exosuit. **B**: Force profile example for preference learning. Subjects are asked to compare controllers setting 1 (pink) to 2 (blue). Each option varies in the amount of lowering gain (θ_{low}) and lifting gain (θ_{lif}), see [5]. (Color figure online)

To understand which settings work best for an individual, many studies follow HIL frameworks. These approaches comprise a feedback loop in which the impact of a controller modification on the objective function of interest is measured in real-time, and used to determine a set of control parameters that are likely to improve upon the current optimum in the subsequent iteration. Given that under such conditions there is typically no known analytical relationship between control inputs and objective function outputs, sample efficient, query based methods like BO have had considerable success for such applications [20,54].

Algorithm 2. Human-AI Collaborative BO

1: create an initial design $D = \{(\boldsymbol{\theta}^{(i)}, \Psi^{(i)})\}_{i=1,\ldots,n_{init}}$
2: **while** termination criterion is not fulfilled **do**
3:     **train** SM on data D
4:     **propose** $\boldsymbol{\theta}^{new}$ that optimizes $AF(SM(\boldsymbol{\theta}))$
5:     **If** intervention criterion is fulfilled
6:     $\boldsymbol{\theta}^{new} \leftarrow \boldsymbol{\theta}^{human}$
7:     **End If**
8:     **evaluate** Ψ on $\boldsymbol{\theta}^{new}$
9:     **update** $D \leftarrow D \cup (\boldsymbol{\theta}^{new}, \Psi(\boldsymbol{\theta}^{new}))$
10: **end while**
11: **return** $\arg\min_{\boldsymbol{\theta} \in D} \Psi(\boldsymbol{\theta})$

6.2   Experimental Setup

Here, we explore the potential of `ShapleyBO` for the use-case of preference-based assistance optimization for a soft back exosuit, see Fig. 4. To this end we consider a dataset in which 15 healthy individuals performed a simple, stoop lifting task with a light (2 kg) external load [5]. Details on the dataset can be found in the supplementary material. Preference was queried in a forced-choice paradigm. That is, within each iteration, participants were consecutively exposed to two control parameter settings and asked to indicate which of the two options they preferred for completing the given task. Each of the settings comprised two parameters, referred to as lowering gain θ_{low} and lifting gain θ_{lif}, which govern the amount of lowering and lifting assistance provided by the device, respectively, see also Fig. 4.

This preference feedback was used to compute a posterior utility distribution over the considered parameter domains, relying on a probit likelihood model and a GP prior over the latent user utility as described in [16]. The experiment comprised three separate optimization blocks, in each of which the optimization was running for 12 iterations. To test `ShapleyBO` on this dataset, we averaged the three utility functions for each participant and interpolated by another GP to simulate the user's ground truth utility function. The detailed specifications for both the original BO and the auxiliary BO modeling the human can be found in the supplementary material and in our codebase.

The remaining setup in our experimental study closely follows the one in [48]. That is, the human can intervene in BO by rectifying proposals made by the algorithm, see pseudo code in Algorithm 2. We will compare our `ShapleyBO`-assisted human-BO team against the team in [48, Algorithm 1] and three other baselines (human alone, BO alone, human-BO team with different intervention criterion). We model human decisions by another BO, following [11,48]. This means that $\boldsymbol{\theta}^{human} = (\theta_{lif}^{human}, \theta_{low}^{human})^T$ is found by optimizing an AF modeling human preferences. We use a BO with the same SM and AF as for the outer loop, but with different exploration-exploitation preference and different initial design, representing differing risk-aversion and knowledge of the human, respectively.

Table 3. Intervention Criteria (ICs) for `ShapleyBO`-assisted A4 and baselines A0-A3.

Agent	A0	A1	A2	A3	A4
	BO	Human	Param-Team	Venkatesh et al. [48]	Shap-Team
IC	never	always	$\theta_{lif}^{new}, \theta_{low}^{new}$	k-th iteration	$\phi_{lif}^{new}(\hat{\mu}), \phi_{low}^{new}(\hat{\mu})$

All agents (A0, A1, A2, A3, A4) are equal to each other, the only difference being that the `ShapleyBO`-assisted agent intervenes based on Shapley values (A4), while the other agents intervene in each k-th iteration (A3) [48], based on the proposed parameters (A2), always (A1) or completely abstain from intervening (A0), see overview in Table 3. A4 has access to `ShapleyBO` and bases their decision to intervene (line 5 in Algorithm 2) on the alignment of the Shapley values of a BO proposal $\boldsymbol{\theta}^{new} = (\theta_{lif}^{new}, \theta_{low}^{new})$ with the agent's knowledge. More precisely, A4 accepts a BO proposal θ (does not intervene) if

$$\frac{1}{\beta} < \frac{\phi_{lif}^{new}(\hat{\mu})}{\phi_{low}^{new}(\hat{\mu})} \Big/ \frac{1}{T} \sum_{t=1}^{T} \frac{\phi_{lif}^{human}(\hat{\mu})_t}{\phi_{low}^{human}(\hat{\mu})_t} < \beta, \tag{9}$$

where $t \in \{1, \ldots, T\}$ are iterations of the BO modeling the agent and $\phi(\hat{\mu})$ the Shapley mean contributions of $(\theta_{lif}, \theta_{low})$, i.e., the exosuit's lifting and lowering gain, respectively. We discuss different Shapley-based intervention criteria in the supplement. For A2's intervention criterion we consider the alignment of $(\theta_{lif}^{new}, \theta_{low}^{new})$ with the agents knowledge based on the parameter values itself. That is, A3 accepts a BO proposal (does not intervene) if

$$\frac{1}{\beta} < \frac{\theta_{lif}^{new}}{\theta_{low}^{new}} \Big/ \frac{1}{T} \sum_{t=1}^{T} \frac{\theta_{lif,t}^{human}}{\theta_{low,t}^{human}} < \beta. \tag{10}$$

6.3   Results

We simulate 40 personalization rounds with 10 iterations and initial design of size 3 each for all five agents. We compare them with respect to *optimization paths*, which show best incumbent target values (utility) in a given iteration. The BO uses GP as AM and cb with $\lambda = 20$ as AF; the BO modelling human proposals uses GP and cb with $\lambda = 200$ and prior knowledge of 90 data points. For further details on the experiments, please refer to the supplementary material.

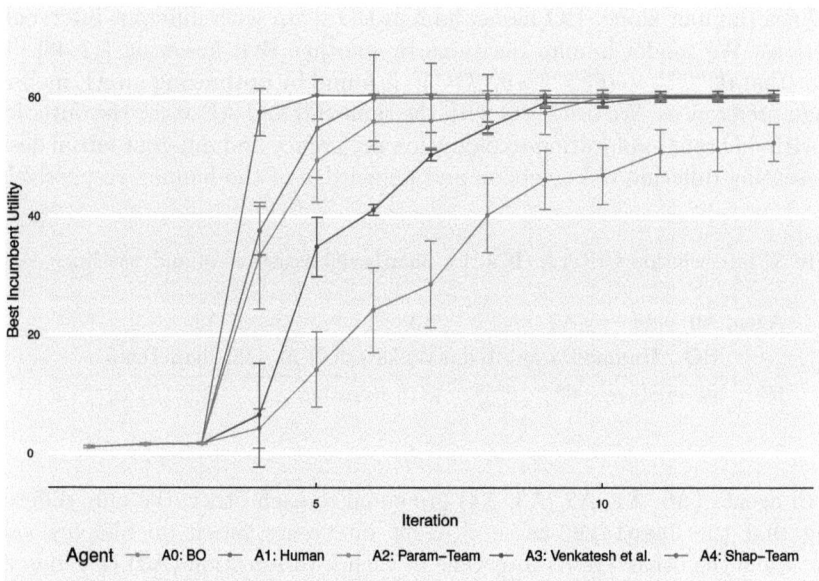

Fig. 5. Results of Agents A0-A4 (see Table 3) in human-AI collaborative BO for simulated exosuit personalization (individual 1) with 10 iterations and 3 initial samples each. Error bars indicate 95% confidence intervals; $k = 2$ for A3, $\beta = 2$ for A2 and A4. Results for remaining individuals can be found in the supplementary material.

Figure 5 exemplarily summarizes results for individual 1; results for remaining 14 individuals as well as experimental details can be found in the supplement. For all 15 subjects, `ShapleyBO`-assisted A4 (Shap-team) on average outperforms human and BO baseline as well as [48] and a team that bases their decision to intervene on the proposed parameters. This latter comparison particularly confirms that Shapley values are a meaningful measure for human-BO alignment that cannot be replaced by another notion of alignment without loss of efficiency. For 10 (among whom is subject 1, see Fig. 5) out of 15 subjects the observed outperformance of the `ShapleyBO`-assisted A4 over competitors is significant at 95% confidence level.

7   Discussion

By quantifying the contribution of each parameter to the proposals, `ShapleyBO` aids in the communication of the rationale behind specific optimization decisions. This interpretability is not only crucial for trust in HIL applications, it also enhances their efficiency in a human-AI collaborative setup. The use case of customizing exosuits illustrates the practical benefits of this approach, suggesting that ShapleyBO is a valuable practical tool for personalizing soft back exosuits.

More generally and beyond exosuits, we conclude that `ShapleyBO` fosters more efficient human-AI collaboration by serving as an explanation interface between the optimization algorithm and humans.

Our paper opens up a multitude of directions for future work. The simulation results in Sect. 6 based on real-world data motivate the actual deployment of Shapley-assisted human-in-the-loop optimization of exosuits in a user study. To this end, the intervention logic used in the simulation study could benefit from an intuitive or visual explanation interface.

On the methodological end, extensions of `ShapleyBO` to multi-criteria BO appear straightforward, as long as additive AFs are used. Moreover, the stability of the Shapley attributions under different BO settings (e.g., kernel or mean choice in Gaussian process, noise, random seeds) might be investigated. A sensitivity analysis along the lines of [36–40] could yield fruitful insights into the robustness of `ShapleyBO`. Moreover, a direct integration of preferences similar to CoExBo [3] might increase the efficiency of human-machine interaction further in a collaborative BO setup.

What is more, a thorough mathematical study of the sublinear regret bounds of BO with confidence bound [44] under Shapley-assisted human interventions might foster theoretical understanding of why Shapley-assisted teams outperform competitors. The theoretical results on general human-AI collaborative BO [48], technically relying on Sobolev spaces, can serve as a starting point for an extended study that explicitly accounts for the `ShapleyBO`-assisted human-machine interface.

Acknowledgments. We thank all three anonymous reviewers for valuable feedback on our work. TA and JR gratefully acknowledge support by the Federal Statistical Office of Germany within the co-operation project "Machine Learning in Official Statistics". JR further acknowledges support by the Bavarian Academy of Sciences (BAS) through the Bavarian Institute for Digital Transformation (bidt) and by the LMU mentoring program of the Faculty of Mathematics, Informatics, and Statistics. YS is supported by the DAAD program Konrad Zuse Schools of Excellence in Artificial Intelligence, sponsored by the Federal Ministry of Education and Research. EH has received funding from the European Union's Horizon Europe research and innovation programme under the Marie Sklodowska-Curie grant agreement No 101073307.

Disclosure of Interests. CJW is an inventor of at least one patent application describing the exosuit components described in the paper that have been filed with the U.S. Patent Office by Harvard University. Harvard University has entered into a licensing agreement with Verve Inc., in which CJW has an equity interest and a board position. The other authors declare that they have no competing interests.

Ehtical Statement. The data used to estimate the utility functions was collected as part of another study [5] for which ethical approval was obtained from the applicable institutional ethical review board.

References

1. Aas, K., Jullum, M., Løland, A.: Explaining individual predictions when features are dependent: more accurate approximations to Shapley values. Artif. Intell. **298**, 103502 (2021)
2. Adachi, M., Chau, S.L., Xu, W., Singh, A., Osborne, M.A., Muandet, K.: Bayesian optimization for building social-influence-free consensus. arXiv preprint arXiv:2502.07166, Accessed 29 May 2025 (2025)
3. Adachi, M., Planden, B., Howey, D.A., Maundet, K., Osborne, M.A., Chau, S.L.: Looping in the human: Collaborative and explainable Bayesian optimization. In: 27th International Conference on Artificial Intelligence and Statistics (AISTATS), vol. 238. PMLR (2024)
4. Akata, Z.E.A.: A research agenda for hybrid intelligence: augmenting human intellect with collaborative, adaptive, responsible, and explainable artificial intelligence. Computer **53**(8), 18–28 (2020)
5. Arens, P., Quirk, D.A., Pan, W., Yacoby, Y., Doshi-Velez, F., Walsh, C.J.: Preference-based assistance optimization for lifting and lowering with a soft back exosuit. Sci. Adv. **11**(15) (2025)
6. Arrieta, A.B., et al.: Explainable artificial intelligence (xai): concepts, taxonomies, opportunities and challenges toward responsible ai. Inf. Fusion **58**, 82–115 (2020)
7. Arun Kumar, A.V., Shilton, A., Gupta, S., Rana, S., Greenhill, S., Venkatesh, S.: Enhanced Bayesian optimization via preferential modeling of abstract properties. arXiv preprint arXiv:2402.17343, Accessed May 28 2025 (2024)
8. Arun Kumar, A.V., et al.: Accelerated experimental design using a human-ai teaming framework. Knowl.-Based Syst. **315**, 113138 (2025)
9. Bakshi, S., Sharma, S., Khanna, R.: Shapley-value-based hybrid metaheuristic multi-objective optimization for energy efficiency in an energy-harvesting cognitive radio network. Mathematics **11**(7), 1656 (2023)
10. Bennetot, A., et al.: A practical tutorial on explainable ai techniques. ACM Comput. Surv. **57**(2), 1–44 (2024)
11. Borji, A., Itti, L.: Bayesian optimization explains human active search. In: Advances in Neural Information Processing Systems, vol. 26 (2013)
12. Breiman, L.: Random forests. Mach. Learn. **45**(1), 5–32 (2001)
13. Burton, J.W., Stein, M.K., Jensen, T.B.: Beyond algorithm aversion in human-machine decision-making. In: Judgment in Predictive Analytics, pp. 3–26. Springer (2023)
14. Chakraborty, T., Seifert, C., Wirth, C.: Explainable Bayesian optimization. arXiv preprint arXiv:2401.13334, Accessed May 29 2025 (2024)
15. Chau, S. L., Muandet, K., Sejdinovic, D.: Explaining the uncertain: stochastic Shapley values for Gaussian process models. In: Advances in Neural Information Processing Systems, vol. 36, pp. 50769–50795 (2023)
16. Chu, W., Ghahramani, Z.: Preference learning with Gaussian processes. In: Proceedings of the 22nd International Conference on Machine Learning, pp. 137–144 (2005)
17. Cisse, A., Evangelopoulos, X., Carruthers, S., Gusev, V.V., Cooper, A.I.: Hypbo: expert-guided chemist-in-the-loop Bayesian search for new materials. arXiv preprint arXiv:2308.11787, Accessed 10 Jun 2025 (2023)
18. Croppi, F.: Explaining sequential model-based optimization (2021), master thesis, LMU Munich

19. Dietvorst, B.J., Simmons, J.P., Massey, C.: Algorithm aversion: people erroneously avoid algorithms after seeing them err. J. Exp. Psychol. Gen. **144**(1), 114 (2015)
20. Ding, Y., Kim, M., Kuindersma, S., Walsh, C.J.: Human-in-the-loop optimization of hip assistance with a soft exosuit during walking. Sci. Robot. **3**(15), eaar5438 (2018)
21. Fisher, A., Rudin, C., Dominici, F.: All models are wrong, but many are useful: learning a variable's importance by studying an entire class of prediction models simultaneously. J. Mach. Learn. Res. **20**(177), 1–81 (2019)
22. Frazier, P., Wang, J.: Bayesian optimization for materials design. In: Information Science for Materials Discovery and Design, pp. 45–75. Springer (2016)
23. Fréchette, A., Kotthoff, L., Michalak, T., Rahwan, T., Hoos, H., Leyton-Brown, K.: Using the Shapley value to analyze algorithm portfolios. In: Proceedings of the AAAI Conference on Artificial Intelligence, vol. 30 (2016)
24. Friedman, J.H.: Greedy function approximation: a gradient boosting machine. Ann. Stat. **29**(5), 1189–1232 (2001)
25. Gupta, S., et al.: Bo-muse: a human expert and ai teaming framework for accelerated experimental design. arXiv preprint arXiv:2303.01684, Accessed 10 Jun 2025 (2023)
26. Hüllermeier, E., Waegeman, W.: Aleatoric and epistemic uncertainty in machine learning: an introduction to concepts and methods. Mach. Learn. **110**(3), 457–506 (2021)
27. Jansen, C., Schollmeyer, G., Blocher, H., Rodemann, J., Augustin, T.: Robust statistical comparison of random variables with locally varying scale of measurement. In: Uncertainty in Artificial Intelligence (UAI). Proceedings of Machine Learning Research (PMLR), pp. 941–952 (2023)
28. Lundberg, S.M., Lee, S.I.: A unified approach to interpreting model predictions. In: Advances in Neural Information Processing Systems (NeurIPS), Curran Associates, Inc. (2017)
29. Makarova, A., Usmanova, I., Bogunovic, I., Krause, A.: Risk-averse heteroscedastic Bayesian optimization. In: Advances in Neural Information Processing Systems, vol. 34, 17235–17245 (2021)
30. Močkus, J.: On Bayesian methods for seeking the extremum. In: Optimization Techniques IFIP Technical Conference, pp. 400–404. Springer (1975)
31. Paleja, R., Ghuy, M., Ranawaka Arachchige, N., Jensen, R., Gombolay, M.: The utility of explainable ai in ad hoc human-machine teaming. In: Advances in Neural Information Processing Systems, vol. 34, pp. 610–623. Curran Associates, Inc. (2021)
32. Peters, H.: Game Theory: A Multi-Leveled Approach. Springer (2015)
33. Psaros, A.F., Meng, X., Zou, Z., Guo, L., Karniadakis, G.E.: Uncertainty quantification in scientific machine learning: methods, metrics, and comparisons. J. Comput. Phys. **477**, 111902 (2023)
34. Pyzer-Knapp, E.O.: Bayesian optimization for accelerated drug discovery. IBM J. Res. Dev. **62**(6) (2018)
35. Rafailov, R., Sharma, A., Mitchell, E., Manning, C.D., Ermon, S., Finn, C.: Direct preference optimization: your language model is secretly a reward model. In: Advances in Neural Information Processing Systems, vol. 36 (2024)
36. Rodemann, J.: Robust generalizations of stochastic derivative-free optimization. master's thesis, LMU Munich (2021)
37. Rodemann, J., Augustin, T.: Accounting for imprecision of model specification in Bayesian optimization. Poster presented at International Symposium on Imprecise Probabilities (ISIPTA) (2021)

38. Rodemann, J., Augustin, T.: Accounting for Gaussian process imprecision in Bayesian optimization. In: International Symposium on Integrated Uncertainty in Knowledge Modelling and Decision Making, pp. 92–104. Springer (2022)

39. Rodemann, J., Augustin, T.: Imprecise Bayesian optimization. Knowl.-Based Syst. **300**, 112186 (2024)

40. Rodemann, J., Fischer, S., Schneider, L., Nalenz, M., Augustin, T.: Not all data are created equal: Lessons from sampling theory for adaptive machine learning. In: International Conference on Statistics and Data Science (ICSDS) (2022)

41. Shapley, L.S.: A value for n-person games. Contrib. Theor. Games **2**(28), 307–317 (1953)

42. Siviy, C., et al.: Opportunities and challenges in the development of exoskeletons for locomotor assistance. Nat. Biomed. Eng. **7**(4), 456–472 (2023)

43. Snoek, J., Larochelle, H., Adams, R.P.: Practical Bayesian optimization of machine learning algorithms. In: Advances in Neural Information Processing Systems, vol. 25, pp. 2951–2959 (2012)

44. Srinivas, N., Krause, A., Kakade, S.M., Seeger, M.W.: Information-theoretic regret bounds for Gaussian process optimization in the bandit setting. IEEE Trans. Inf. Theory **58**(5), 3250–3265 (2012)

45. Štrumbelj, E., Kononenko, I.: Explaining prediction models and individual predictions with feature contributions. Knowl. Inf. Syst. **41**(3), 647–665 (2014)

46. Tallón-Ballesteros, A., Chen, C.: Explainable ai: using Shapley value to explain complex anomaly detection ml-based systems. Mach. Learn. Artif. Intell. **332**, 152 (2020)

47. Toxiri, S., et al.: Back-support exoskeletons for occupational use: an overview of technological advances and trends. IISE Trans. Occupat. Ergon. Hum. Fact. **7**(3–4), 237–249 (2019)

48. Venkatesh, A.K., Rana, S., Shilton, A., Venkatesh, S.: Human-ai collaborative Bayesian optimisation. In: Koyejo, S., Mohamed, S., Agarwal, A., Belgrave, D., Cho, K., Oh, A. (eds.) Advances in Neural Information Processing Systems, vol. 35, pp. 16233–16245 (2022)

49. Wang, Y.C., Chen, T.: Adapted techniques of explainable artificial intelligence for explaining genetic algorithms on the example of job scheduling. Expert Syst. Appl. **237**, 121369 (2024)

50. Watson, D.S., O'Hara, J., Tax, N., Mudd, R., Guy, I.: Explaining predictive uncertainty with information theoretic shapley values. arXiv preprint arXiv:2306.05724, Accessed May 3 2025 (2023)

51. Wu, H.C.: Solving fuzzy optimization problems using Shapley values and evolutionary algorithms. Mathematics **11**(24), 4871 (2023)

52. Xiao, H., Wang, Z., Zhu, Z., Zhou, J., Lu, J.: Shapley-nas: discovering operation contribution for neural architecture search. In: Proceedings of the IEEE/CVF Conference on Computer Vision and Pattern Recognition (CVPR), pp. 11892–11901 (2022)

53. Xu, W., Adachi, M., Jones, C.N., Osborne, M.A.: Principled Bayesian optimization in collaboration with human experts. In: Globerson, A., et al. (eds.): Advances in Neural Information Processing Systems (NeuIPS), vol. 37, pp. 104091–104137. Curran Associates, Inc. (2024)

54. Zhang, J., et al.: Human-in-the-loop optimization of exoskeleton assistance during walking. Science **356**(6344), 1280–1284 (2017)

Enforcing Vector Space Stability in Embeddings with Evolving Vocabularies: A Web-App Behavior Perspective

Asier Rodríguez-González[✉], Ignacio Sisamón Serrano,
Ignacio Esplugues Conca, Daniel Sánchez Santolaya, and Joel Medina Sánchez

BBVA - Behavioral Representation, BBVA AI Factory, Madrid, Spain
{asier.rodriguez.gonzalez,ignacio.sisamon,ignacio.espligues.contractor,
daniel.sanchez.santolaya,joel.medina.sanchez}@bbva.com

Abstract. Embeddings generated from navigation data unlock valuable insights and provide strong baselines for a wide range of applications. However, the dynamic and evolving nature of financial applications presents significant challenges for the stability and adaptability of embedding models, particularly when these embeddings are used as inputs to downstream analytical models. In this paper, an alternative approach for a real-world constraints environment is proposed to address constantly changing vocabularies and dependencies across downstream systems. In order to ensure seamless integration of new elements into an established vector space, and using data from BBVA's application as a case study, a methodology is developed by combining Word2Vec-based embeddings with a two-step pipeline: Embedding Matcher and Space Mirroring. The former is an alignment mechanism that assigns new pages to existing embeddings using Levenshtein distance and cosine similarity. The latter is a technique for embedding projection into the original vector space in which multiple transformation techniques, including SVD, dense layers, ResNet, and GRU-based models, have been compared. The results obtained highlight the effectiveness of preserving semantic integrity and reducing the impact of updates on downstream models while minimizing computational overhead. The proposed approach is applicable to any context that involves dynamic vocabulary data.

Keywords: vector space · stability · embeddings · vocabularies · behavior · navigation · word2vec · client · clustering · aggregation · projection · nlp

1 Introduction

Since the introduction of the embedding concept [14], its use has become widespread due to its simplicity of application and its potential to be adapted for subsequent tasks [24]. However, the representation of non-textual entities has

B. Pfahringer et al. (Eds.): ECML PKDD 2025, LNAI 16020, pp. 543–558, 2026.
https://doi.org/10.1007/978-3-662-72243-5_31

proven to be a key part of the business of many large companies. For example, in music recommendation, Spotify employs embeddings for the representation of its customers [12]. Uber[1] also uses embeddings to represent both its customers and establishments, and then offers appropriate recommendations. Netflix[2] represents its titles as embeddings based on different features of the movie so that other models can then feed on this useful information. These examples showcase the utility of embeddings to link products, regardless of typology and customers [3].

Embeddings have also found application in banking and finance: stock representation [10], transactions [20], using news for recommendation systems; [23] even to represent customers [4,8], where these representations are presented as an opportunity to better understand the context around the customer [27]. Within a financial institution, a large amount of data is generated with a structure that is difficult to represent using traditional machine learning methodologies, such as transactions or user navigation in the application. Specifically in a bank like BBVA, with an App that is a fundamental pillar for the customer, navigation is of great importance[3].

Among the navigation we find key data [29], such as the pages the customers visit, the way they navigate and the time spent on each page, among others. When represented as an embedding, this data allows to carry out quantitative analysis such as identifying browsing patterns or performing clustering to identify similar customers[4] [7,19]. In other words, in addition to providing direct value, embeddings can be considered as baselines and new input features for many other tasks, such as product recommendation systems, pricing or personalization of the users' own browsing experience. By using embeddings, we could reduce feature generation and data mining tasks, which can be very costly with complex and large volumes of data.

However, using embeddings as input to downstream models generates a direct dependency. Although continuously retraining the embedding models can ensure that the representation is updated, this process can alter the structure of the vector space and affect the performance of downstream models and applications that rely on those embeddings. This presents a unique challenge due to the highly dynamic characteristics of the web navigation data, where new pages could constantly emerge, user-interaction patterns evolve thus embeddings should be adjusted accordingly.

2   Problem Definition

Typically, embeddings are learned for a specific purpose, such as the representation of banking products [5]. This approach ensures alignment between the embedding and its purpose, simplifying updates, as embedding retraining occurs

---

[1] Uber - Two tower embeddings.

[2] Netflix - Supporting content decision makers.

[3] BBVA - Spanish banking app with the best reviews on Google.

[4] Instacart - Embeddings to improve search relevance.

without extra dependencies. However, such embeddings are not easily generalizable to other tasks.

In contrast, foundational models often learn embeddings for generic purposes, such as understanding semantic language relationships. These embeddings can be convenient baselines for various use cases, allowing to take advantage of potential features without worrying about the high computational demand required for their development. The embeddings can also be adapted for specific tasks [11,30], leveraging prior learning. Yet, they depend on some sort of foundational model's invariability, because updates in the embedding can degrade the results of specific tasks, which may lead to a need to retrain or readjust the specific use case's models.

This paper presents an approach to foundational models using BBVA navigation data, addressing challenges related to dynamic navigation patterns and the introduction of new app sections. Navigation data in this context includes user sessions, which can be defined as a sequence of visited pages in the App hierarchically organized (i.e., `operative:functionality:detail`). For example, a session that includes a query to the home page, where a money transfer is made, could be coded as follows:

```
global position
operations:index
payments:index
payments:operations payment:index
payments:operations payment:index:savedcontacts
payments:operations payment:conditions
payments:operations payment:confirmation
payments:index
global position:logout
```

Despite a well-defined taxonomy, campaigns, which follow market trends, and custom offers frequently expand the number of pages, introducing challenges in embedding stability, as adding these pages to the vocabulary would require constant retraining of the model. Figure 1 illustrates monthly trends in new pages and campaign-related additions. While new campaign pages constitute a minor percentage of total new pages (∼5%), significant changes in operations or page structures can alter user behavior, impacting the page embeddings. Detecting such changes requires studying embedding drift, which causes updates to the foundational model that involve cascading modifications to downstream models.

3   Dependencies and Restrictions

BBVA's app produces more than 5 million daily navigation sessions, with more than 20 thousand different pages. Preprocessing in state of the art natural language processing models implies many different steps, such as data cleaning, tokenization and padding. Given the large volume of data, these analytical solutions to generate embeddings from scratch are generally very computationally demanding and difficult to be applied when memory and execution times are limited and security and regulatory filters exist. Alternatively, using data subsets

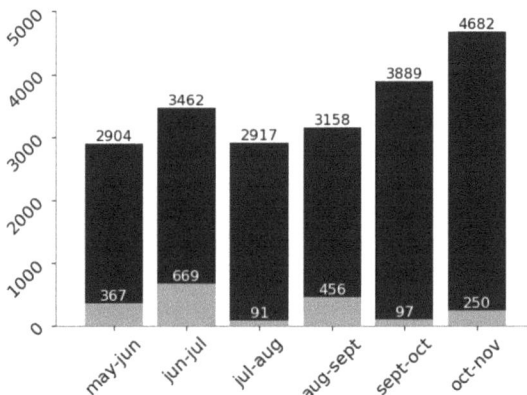

Fig. 1. [Dark Blue] Number of pages appearing for the first time compared to the previous month. [Cyan] Number of pages that are new campaigns each month. (Color figure online)

is an option, but they are hard to make representative and would underutilize BBVA's vast data resources.

For this reason, we chose PySpark's Word2Vec as the framework to develop the embedding models presented in the following sections, encoding each page as a vocabulary token. Spark is a technology that allows us to perform distributed cluster computing to speed up the process and handle the entire data volume without having to use subsets. One significant drawback of PySpark's Word2Vec is its inability to resume training from a previous state, which hinders its flexibility in scenarios requiring incremental learning or continuous model updates.

There is an additional alternative of extending the embeddings matrix within the model and freezing the weights corresponding to the pages previously trained, resuming the training from there and preserving the original structure of the vector space [25]. However, within the bank platform, we face the limitations discussed previously, which prevent us from implementing this solution directly. On the other hand, from the embeddings we could try to self-implement the Word2Vec model (keeping the parameters, the hyperparameters and the architecture fixed) and take control of the whole training. Nevertheless, it is a tedious and computationally very expensive process, so it is not feasible in the current situation (but it is not ruled out in the future in higher-resource scenarios).

All these limitations and restrictions make it necessary to create a method that can keep page embedding stable over a period of time, ensuring that information from new pages entering the app can be incorporated in a useful and secure way for embedding-dependent systems.

4   Methodology

The first step of our methodology consists of generating an embedding through the model e for each of the unique pages visited by users at the moment, $P_1 =$

$\{p_{1,1}, \ldots p_{1,b}\}; P_1 \xrightarrow{e} V_1 \subseteq \mathbb{R}^n$, being V_1 the initial vector space. This process, as mentioned in Sect. 3, uses a Word2Vec model implemented in PySpark to handle the large volume of data processed. To build this vector space, we take as a reference the pages that appear at least ten times in the sessions recorded during a one-year interval, avoiding the use of excessively residual pages to the algorithm and with the aim of capturing representative interaction patterns while minimizing possible seasonal effects within the same year.

A second model, g, is then trained using the same parameters as the initial model but incorporating all newly added pages from the elapsed time since the initial training. This model will generate a new vector space, V_2, where the entire set of pages is denoted as $P_2 = \{p_{2,1}, \ldots p_{2,k}\}; P_2 \xrightarrow{g} V_2 \subseteq \mathbb{R}^n$. For example, if we have detected that the number of pages increases substantially every 3 months, we will train again a model of page embeddings with a time window of one year shifted by 3 months from the time of the initial model training. This model (g) captures all new pages $q \in P_2 \setminus P_1; P_2 \setminus P_1 \neq \varnothing$ that have appeared in this time window, as well as many pages that do not change over time, $r \in P_1 \cap P_2; P_1 \cap P_2 \neq \varnothing$ (Fig. 2).

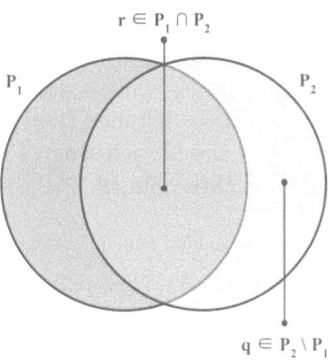

Fig. 2. Set representation of pages in P_1 and P_2.

The next steps aim to integrate the new pages within the previously defined vector space through a function $f : V_2 \to V_1$. This will allow us to update the model with new information and enrich the number of embeddings for all dependent models, avoiding the cascade update of all processes that use embeddings as input, by keeping the original vector space. To achieve this, the process is divided into two complementary stages. Each of them implements its own function:

1. **Embedding Matcher** (f_{EM}): Each new page is compared to existing ones using the Levenshtein distance to identify similarities in page names. Subsequently, the cosine similarity between the corresponding vectors is calculated, allowing us to match pages based on semantic similarity.
2. **Space Mirroring** (f_{SM}): To incorporate the new pages into the original vector space, a projection of their vectors into the existing space is performed.

This process ensures the semantic coherence of the space by allowing the new embeddings to align with the already established representations.

Once completed, the new page embeddings are projected and adjusted to the original vector space. The projection of new embeddings into the original vector space is performed periodically, dynamically incorporating new interactions, and preserving the overall semantic structure of the vector space over time.

4.1   Embedding Matcher

The first step in the flow to keep the vector space as stable as possible is the Embedding Matcher, a component developed within Mercury [6], an inner-course library used in the development of BBVA's analytical processes. As mentioned above, there are pages or campaigns that change monthly, such as the offer of a loan that each month you are granted a different amount, with this amount, or the month of the offer, included in the name of the page for design convenience (i.e., `campaignclick:00000001-this-month-will-be-1600-euros`). This is the reason why all monthly campaigns of this nature could be represented with the same embedding, as they are similar entities, representing the same concept. This process allows for this association of new campaigns and pages that do not yet have a representation but can be matched to an existing embedding in the existing vector space. This is done in a two-step process.

First, the normalized Levenshtein distance (lev) of a new page (q_m) is calculated with the names of pages already existing (P_1), saving the set of pages whose distance is lower than one threshold (θ_1).

$$N_{q_m} = \{n_i \in P_1 : lev(q_m, n_i) < \theta_1\}$$
$$N_{q_1} \cap N_{q_2} \cap \ldots \cap N_{q_m} \neq \varnothing \tag{1}$$

Next, we calculate the cosine similarity (Sc) between the embeddings of all pages in N_{q_m}.

$$S_{q_m} = \{Sc(v_i, v_j) : (v_i, v_j) \in e(N_{q_m}) \times e(N_{q_m}), i < j\} \tag{2}$$

If the average cosine similarity exceeds another threshold ($\overline{S_{q_m}} > \theta_2$), we assign the mean embedding of all pages in N_{q_m} to the new page q_m.

$$f_{EM}(q_m) = \frac{\displaystyle\sum_{v \in e(N_{q_m})} v}{|N_{q_m}|} \tag{3}$$

To select the threshold values, θ_1 is adjusted by taking the maximum threshold ($\theta_1 = 0$) and increasing it until some false positive samples are seen. Then, choosing θ_2 becomes more straightforward, as most of the pages with high Levenshtein distance have a close cosine similarity. This statement can be seen in Fig. 3, where as the value of lev (X-axis) increases, the value of Sc (Y-axis) decreases, concentrating the pages that we will take as a reference for our inference in the upper left corner.

Based on this analysis, the thresholds selected for our use case are $\theta_1 = 0.1$ and $\theta_2 = 0.75$.

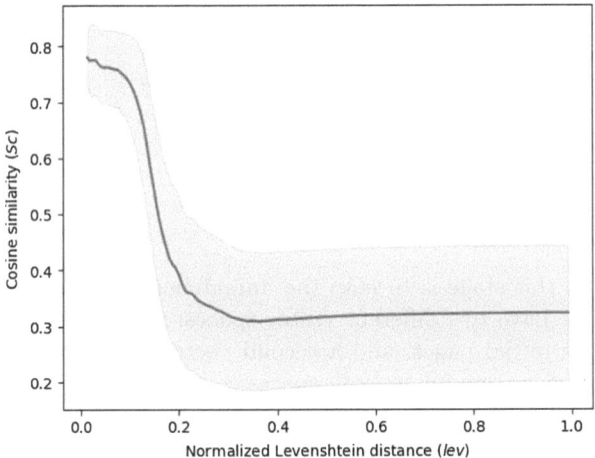

Fig. 3. The X-axis shows the normalization of the discretized Levenshtein distance. The Y-axis shows the average cosine similarity for each discretized value of the Levenshtein distance. The interval around the line refers to the standard deviation for each X-axis value.

Despite the strong correlation between lev and Sc, both thresholds are necessary because there are outliers with low values for both lev and Sc. Thus, by using θ_2, we discard these pages and provide a more precious inference through the Embedding Matcher. Considering that BBVA's app includes multiple frequently asked questions, many of them exhibit high syntactic similarity—mainly due to standardized string formats such as 'faq:1', 'faq:2', 'faq:3', etc. However, this similarity does not necessarily reflect semantic relatedness. Therefore, the use of θ_2 becomes essential to capture deeper content distinctions.

As an example of how the pipeline works (shown in Table 1), consider a new page introduced in November 2023: `campaignclick-loan-month-nov-2023`. First, the Levenshtein distance of the page name is performed with all the names already existing in the vector space of the model. Then, the pages falling behind the threshold $\theta_1 = 0.1$ are chosen.

Next, the cosine similarity between the embedding of `campaignclick-loan-month-nov-2023` and the other pages is calculated. Then, if the average of all the cosine similarities is above the second threshold $\theta_2 = 0.75$, the page is fully matched assigning the embedding of the highest cosine similarity or the mean embedding of all the previous pages.

After completing this process, some pages will be successfully matched with previously existing pages, while others will remain unmatched moving on to the next step: Space Mirroring.

Table 1. Levenshtein and cosine similarity examples for `campaignclick-loan-month-nov-2023`.

Page name	Levenshtein	Cosine similarity
`campaignclick-loan-month-jul-2023`	**0.0909**	**0.92356**
`campaignclick-loan-month-sep-2023`	**0.0909**	**0.91534**
`campaignclick-loan-month-oct-2023`	**0.0607**	**0.89583**
`campaignclick-mortgagge-month-oct-2023`	0.1831	0.69375

4.2   Space Mirroring

The objective of this stage is to map the unmatched new pages to the original vector space. We have two different vector spaces: the original vector space V_1 composed of the initial pages, and a second vector space V_2 composed of the combination of pages present in both spaces, r, and new pages, q. Since vector spaces are learned using different models, r is represented by different vectors.

With the previously defined functions e and g as $P_1 = \{p_{1,1}, \ldots p_{1,b}\}; P_1 \xrightarrow{e} V_1 \subseteq \mathbb{R}^n$ and $P_2 = \{p_{2,1}, \ldots p_{2,k}\}; P_2 \xrightarrow{g} V_2 \subseteq \mathbb{R}^n$, our goal is to learn a function f_{SM} that maps q into the original vector space V_1. We will take advantage of r in order to minimize a specific loss L trying to learn the following function:

$$f_{SM} = \arg\min_{l} L[e(r), l(g(r))] \tag{4}$$

Combining the Embedding Matcher and the Space Mirroring, the final function would be:

$$f : q \to \begin{cases} f_{EM}(q) & \text{for } \overline{S_{q_m}} > \theta_2 \\ f_{SM}(g(q)) & \text{o.w.} \end{cases} \tag{5}$$

4.3   Linear Approach

We initially explored the possibility of using a Singular Value Decomposition (SVD) approach [18] to map the embeddings from the vector space V_2 to the original vector space V_1. The objective was to identify a linear transformation that projects the embeddings from the updated space to the original space. However, for interspace reconstruction and transformation, this approach only captures linear relationships between the dimensions of the matrices.

As expected, this approach proved to be somewhat ineffective due to the non-linear nature of the relationships between the embeddings of the two spaces. The projected SVD transformation did not achieve the expected results and, therefore, led us to opt for more sophisticated approaches.

4.4 Non-Linear Approach

To explore non-linear solutions, we tested various architectures and loss functions on a neural network, with the aim of finding the best mapping from one space to another.

In the case of the loss function, the choices were between Mean Square Error (MSE) [16] and cosine distance. The former because our goal was to have $f(P_2)$ vectors close to V_1; the latter because it may be desirable to maintain the orientation or angle between the output and target vectors.

At the architectural level, and with the assumption that there were no linear relationships between the two spaces, the following configurations are tested and their results are shown in Sect. 5: architectures (**ResNet** [13], **Self-attention** [28] and **GRU** [9]), regularization (**Dropout** [15]), activation (**ReLU** [1]) and optimizer (**Adam** [21]).

4.5 Validation

Measuring the effectiveness of the Embedding Matcher, and thus the value of each threshold, is critical. During calibration, multiple values of each threshold were evaluated through an empirical analysis based on representative examples from different pages and domains. This process allows identifying a balance point where the system minimizes false positives (mismatches) and false negatives (unmatched words), optimizing the performance of the matcher in real scenarios. Although it is possible to automate this selection using optimization algorithms or supervised techniques, the manual approach provides the flexibility to adapt to specific contexts, taking advantage of expert knowledge during development and evaluation iterations.

The Space Mirroring evaluation is carried out in two different ways. First, using only the pages that are common in the initial and updated vector space, a K-Means [2] is trained with the embeddings of the original vector space. Then, an inference is performed with the embeddings of the pages mapped through the mirror function. If the pages with the transformed embedding fall in the same cluster as the original embedding, the transformation is assumed to be accurate since they are very close, and the decision boundaries of the K-Means are maintained in this transformed space (Fig. 4). It effectively measures the consistency of cluster mappings between the two spaces, providing insight into how well the transformations preserve the clustering structure across different vector representations. To make the process more reliable, an iterative process is performed in which the number of clusters (K) increases. The higher the value of K, the more challenging the validation.

Unfortunately, this method is not perfect, as pages that are quite close to a K-Means cluster boundary could have the embedding transformed very close to the original and belong to different clusters, generating a false negative in the metrics. This is why we use a second type of manual validation to complement this first method. It consists of searching by cosine similarity close pages to one taken as a reference in the original vector space and in the transformed

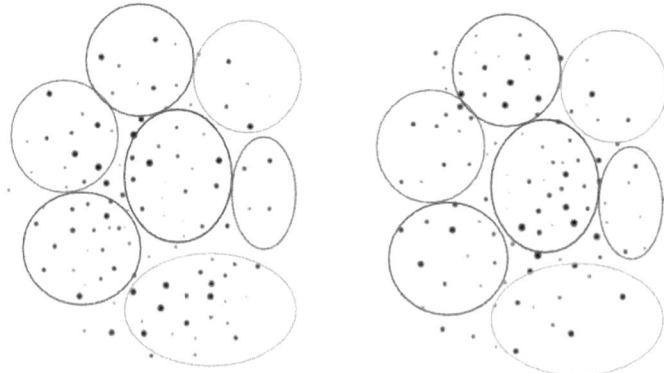

Fig. 4. [Left] K-Means on the original vector space. [Right] K-Means inference on the transformed updated vector space.

vector space. Thus, pages that were previously close should remain close and not have moved away, or at least the uppermost of close pages should be the same, maintaining the isometry. That is, bounding the subset of common pages (r): the vectors in V_1 and the representations of their vectors of V_2 in V_1 ($f(g(r))$) should be close. The results of these validations are presented in Sect. 5.

5   Results

In this section, the theoretical information previously presented will be validated through the results obtained in the experiments carried out. To do so, we can start by comparing different methodologies applicable to the transformation function from one dimensional space to another.

As shown in Table 2, the existence of non-linear relationships between the two vector spaces makes the SVD results one of the worst. Although it does seem to keep the points close since for K = 2 the results are quite good, when we take higher K, the results deteriorate. This is why the best architecture consists of a GRU maintaining the previously learned residuals (GRU + Residuals) which manages to maintain a high accuracy for numerous clusters, and even keeps getting good results with higher K values (for K − 30 it remains at 0.8449).

On the other hand, in manual validation, if we look at an example[5] that is in both vector spaces (Table 3), we find that the distance between pages remains fairly constant, although a new page sneaks into the top of the close ones.

It is important to remember that the mirror function, despite being trained with the common pages in the original and the updated vector spaces, will only be

---

[5] Both examples maintain the structure discussed in the introduction, in which `operative:functionality:detail` is established as the basis for the pages of the app. Thus, the closest pages within an operative will be functionalities of it, with different details.

Table 2. Results of different architectures based on the training of a large set of common pages between the vector spaces V and W.

Architecture	Min. MSE	K-Means Metric			
		K = 2	K = 5	K = 10	K = 15
SVD	0.24971	0.93187	0.86273	0.78838	0.76032
Dense Layer	0.06450	0.94735	0.89819	0.85135	0.83822
ResNet	0.06000	0.94249	0.89320	0.85146	0.84115
Self-attention	0.16750	0.78529	0.39715	0.14127	0.14070
GRU + Residuals	0.05060	0.94631	0.91128	0.87517	0.87517

Table 3. Most similar pages to `expenses:index` in the original and new vector space embedding.

Reference page	Vector space	Most similar pages	Cosine similarity
`expenses:index`	Original	`expenses:index:subcategory`	0.99516
		`expenses:index:category2`	0.93397
		`expenses:index:daily`	0.87933
	New	`expenses:index:subcategory`	0.99566
		`expenses:index:category2`	0.94884
		`expenses:index:modalfeedback`	0.92237
		`expenses:index:daily`	0.90876

applied to those new pages that appear in the vocabulary, so the representation of the previous pages would maintain the original embedding.

The example presented in Table 3 compares the page `expenses:index` with the most similar pages in both the original (V_1) and transformed (V_2) vector space embeddings. Here, `expenses:index` already exists in the original vector space, and we observe how its nearest neighbors are mapped in both spaces.

Table 4. Most similar pages to `financial health rules:index` in the original and new vector space embedding.

Reference page	Vector space	Most similar pages	Cosine similarity
`financial health rules:index`	Original	`financial health rules:index: modalmodalSuccess`	0.91669
		`financial health rules:index:modalList`	0.91379
		`financial health rules:index:modelCreate`	0.89919
	New	`financial health rules:index:modalSuccess`	0.92165
		`financial health rules:index:modalCreate`	0.83532
		`financial health rules:index:modalList`	0.80786

In contrast, Table 4 focus on the page `financial health rules:index`, which is a new page being projected into the original vector space. These tables compare `financial health rules:index`'s most similar pages in both the original and transformed vector spaces. Despite the change in the vector space projection, we find that the closest pages to both `expenses:index` and `financial health rules:index` remain the same, demonstrating that the relative proximity of the nearest neighbors is preserved, even though their spatial positions within the vector spaces have changed.

5.1   Downstream Validation

In order to select candidate models and to ensure that the output embeddings can be used in other downstream tasks, it is necessary to continuously evaluate the procedures performed. For this purpose, an embeddings benchmark module has been developed in the aforementioned BBVA inner-source library, Mercury [6]. This benchmark, based on the MTEB [22], seeks to test them in different specific tasks, assuming that a better result in all tasks globally implies a better quality of the basic embedding. Although the embeddings trained in this document are page embeddings, as discussed above, most of the tasks for which these will be used are directly related to clients, so the benchmark will look at that level of granularity. To achieve the client embeddings, different aggregation methods have been applied to the page embeddings: **Mean Pooling**, **Time Weighted Mean Pooling** and **VLAD** [17].

For the evaluation, a representative sample of customers is used. An embedding of the client data is generated for each customer and a classifier or regressor is trained (depending on the benchmark problem) receiving the embedding as the only input. Through this approach, the variation in the results will correspond uniquely to the embedding model and the chosen aggregation method.

The estimator must be able to successfully predict different variables, such as customer movements, engagement levels, or financial behavior, from this embedding. If the estimator performs well, we can be confident that the embedding encodes the information accurately. The studied evaluators assess diverse aspects of customer data, so if a pooling method consistently outperforms others across different evaluators, it will be selected as the preferred aggregation approach. Some of the used evaluators are:

- **Employed**: the objective is to discern between the employed and those who are not actively working.
- **Engagement**: multi-class problem where a label is identified to represent the transactionality and connection a customer has with BBVA Bank.
- **Expertise**: multi-class problem in which the taxonomy of labels refers to the level of usage that a customer has when navigating the app.

According to Table 5, the random baseline exhibits the lowest performance across all metrics, as expected, with an AUC of 0.5004 for Employed and F1 scores of 0.2223 and 0.1475 for Engagement and Expertise, respectively. Mean Pooling and Time Weighted techniques, both with a dimension of 40, significantly improve the results, achieving AUC values of 0.7395 and 0.7334 for

Table 5. Benchmark evaluators applied to different types of aggregation to generate client embedding. All for a 365-day window.

Aggregation Type	Dimension	Employed AUC	Engagement F1	Expertise F1
Random	40	0.50038	0.22230	0.14750
Mean Pooling	40	0.73951	0.65945	0.41465
Time Weighted	40	0.73340	0.65198	0.39851
VLAD (K = 3)	120	0.77404	0.66929	0.47368
VLAD (K = 5)	200	0.78943	0.69396	0.48591
VLAD (K = 10)	400	0.79829	0.71038	0.52093

Employed, and higher F1 scores for Engagement (0.6594 and 0.6520) and Expertise (0.4147 and 0.3985). Among the VLAD approaches, performance improves as the number of clusters (K) and dimension increase. VLAD (K = 10) achieves the highest results, with an AUC of 0.7983 for Employed, and F1 scores of 0.7104 and 0.5209 for Engagement and Expertise, respectively, demonstrating the effectiveness of larger, more expressive embeddings.

The previously presented results include pages that have been projected back into the original space using the analytical methodology proposed in this work. We observed no variation in the metrics across the different evaluators, indicating that no degradation occurs when employing the pipeline in downstream tasks.

6   Future Work

The restrictions that revolve around the platform, the implementation time, and costs affect this work significantly. Once its effectiveness has been demonstrated and the informative capacity of embeddings as input for other processes has also been proved, the model could be improved. Currently, using a Word2Vec allows us to generate a functional, fast and simple solution. In order to improve it, different alternatives have been identified. Each page is treated independently of the others, but we know that there are operational relationships between them. For example, the hierarchy of pages, where the operation is listed first, followed by details of the operation, can provide a lot of information as they have a significant relationship. Alternatively to Word2Vec, to account for sequence order, any auto-regressive model could be explored.

An interesting technique to take advantage of the capabilities of existing LLMs is the one mentioned by Tan [26]. At its core, navigation could be seen as a graph of interconnected pages. Applying the above methodology, we could use connectors to convert the graph into a set of texts and then represent each of the sessions through an LLM. The complexity of the taxonomy of the pages themselves may require a fine-tuning of the model.

Another potential direction for future work could explore implementing continuous drift detection mechanisms within the BBVA's application to track changes in data distribution over time. This would enable a more targeted response to pipeline obsolescence, reducing reliance on costly full embedding retraining.

7   Conclusions

On several occasions, real problems bring with them restrictions that make it impossible to apply state-of-the-art solutions, so it is necessary to be able to find alternatives. This project presents an architecture that allows updating the embeddings of a constantly changing vocabulary, without altering the original vector space, as it is used as a foundational model that generates many dependencies with subsequent analytical processes.

In the performed tests, it was shown that the proposed method works effectively when dealing with dynamic vocabularies. Firstly, the use of the Embedding Matcher provides a key value by allowing the rapid identification and clustering of similar words based on a threshold that can be parameterized according to the use case. Subsequently, the implementation of Space Mirroring ensures that new words are not only integrated into the existing vector space, but also that they do so while respecting its coherence and minimizing the impact on subsequent analytical dependencies. Finally, automated validation using techniques such as K-Means allow to consistently measure the quality of the fit of the new vectors, ensuring a smooth transition without compromising the stability of the model. Consequently, this approach has been adopted within BBVA's production-ready environment to ensure scalable and reliable embedding updates.

This approach is not only useful in natural language processing contexts with highly dynamic vocabularies, such as the one discussed in this paper, but could also be extended to other domains. For example, applications in recommendation systems that need to constantly adapt to new products or categories, or in the generation of custom embeddings for specific technical domains, such as constantly evolving medical or legal terms. This presents a versatile framework that balances adaptability and stability, offering practical solutions to the challenges of changing vocabularies.

Acknowledgements. The authors extend their sincere gratitude to BBVA for providing the foundation and resources necessary for this research. We thank all our colleagues, with special attention to Mauricio Ciprián and Leonardo Baldassini for the supervision and council, and Álvaro Ibraín for the initial brainstorming from which we ended up with the final proposals.

References

1. Agarap, A.F.: Deep learning using rectified linear units (relu). ArXiv **abs/1803.08375** (2018), https://api.semanticscholar.org/CorpusID:4090379
2. Ahmed, M., Seraj, R., Islam, S.M.S.: The k-means algorithm: a comprehensive survey and performance evaluation. Electronics **9**(8) (2020). https://doi.org/10.3390/electronics9081295, https://www.mdpi.com/2079-9292/9/8/1295

3. Ai, Q., Zhang, Y., Bi, K., Chen, X., Croft, W.B.: Learning a hierarchical embedding model for personalized product search. In: Proceedings of the 40th International ACM SIGIR Conference on Research and Development in Information Retrieval, SIGIR 2017, pp. 645-654. ACM, New York, NY, USA (2017)

4. Baldassini, L., Serrano, J.A.R.: client2vec: towards systematic baselines for banking applications. ArXiv **abs/1802.04198** (2018), https://api.semanticscholar.org/CorpusID:3609178

5. Boulenger, A., Liu, D., Farajalla, G.P.: Sequential banking products recommendation and user profiling in one go. In: Proceedings of the Third ACM International Conference on AI in Finance, ICAIF 2022, pp. 317-324. ACM, New York, NY, USA (2022). https://doi.org/10.1145/3533271.3561697

6. Chaquet, J., Ibrain, A., Santolaya Sánchez, D., Galletero, M., Basaldua, S., Delgado, A.: Mercury: reusable and efficient mlworkflows in finance. In: ACM ICAIF 2024: From Prototype to Production: Deploying Real-World AI/ML Models in the Financial Industry, November 2024, https://openreview.net/forum?id=NBeBMJIWFY

7. Chen, Y., et al.: Clustered embedding learning for recommender systems. In: Proceedings of the ACM Web Conference 2023, WWW 2023, pp. 1074–1084. ACM, New York, NY, USA (2023)

8. Chitsazan, N., Sharpe, S., Katariya, D., Cheng, Q., Rajasethupathy, K.: Dynamic customer embeddings for financial service applications (2021), https://arxiv.org/abs/2106.11880

9. Cho, K., van Merrienboer, B., Çaglar Gülçehre, Bahdanau, D., Bougares, F., Schwenk, H., Bengio, Y.: Learning phrase representations using rnn encoder-decoder for statistical machine translation. In: Conference on Empirical Methods in Natural Language Processing (2014), https://api.semanticscholar.org/CorpusID:5590763

10. Dolphin, R., Smyth, B., Dong, R.: Stock embeddings: Learning distributed representations for financial assets (2022), https://arxiv.org/abs/2202.08968

11. Dušek, R., Galias, C., Wojciechowska, L., Wawer, A.: Improving domain-specific retrieval by nli fine-tuning. Ann. Comput. Sci. Inf. Syst. **Vol. 35**, 949-953 (2023), http://yadda.icm.edu.pl/baztech/element/bwmeta1.element.baztech-1ba6acb7-cd08-4a70-8fde-b28b7cde7a05

12. Hansen, C., et al.: Contextual and sequential user embeddings for large-scale music recommendation. In: Proceedings of the 14th ACM Conference on Recommender Systems, RecSys 2020, pp. 53–62. ACM, New York, NY, USA (2020)

13. He, K., Zhang, X., Ren, S., Sun, J.: Deep residual learning for image recognition. In: 2016 IEEE Conference on Computer Vision and Pattern Recognition (CVPR), pp. 770–778 (2016). https://doi.org/10.1109/CVPR.2016.90

14. Hinton, G.E.: Learning distributed representations of concepts. In: Proceedings of the Annual Meeting of the Cognitive Science Society, vol. 8, no. 1, pp. 1–12 (1986), https://escholarship.org/uc/item/79w838g1

15. Hinton, G.E., Srivastava, N., Krizhevsky, A., Sutskever, I., Salakhutdinov, R.R.: Improving neural networks by preventing co-adaptation of feature detectors. CoRR **abs/1207.0580** (2012), http://arxiv.org/abs/1207.0580, cite arxiv:1207.0580

16. Hodson, T.O., Over, T.M., Foks, S.S.: Mean squared error, deconstructed. J. Adv. Model. Earth Syst. **13**(12), (2021). https://doi.org/10.1029/2021MS002681, https://agupubs.onlinelibrary.wiley.com/doi/abs/10.1029/2021MS002681

17. Ionescu, R.T., Butnaru, A.: Vector of locally-aggregated word embeddings (VLAWE): A novel document-level representation. In: Burstein, J., Doran, C.,

Solorio, T. (eds.) Proceedings of the 2019 Conference of the North American Chapter of the Association for Computational Linguistics: Human Language Technologies, Volume 1 (Long and Short Papers), pp. 363–369. ACL, Minneapolis, Minnesota, June 2019, https://doi.org/10.18653/v1/N19-1033, https://aclanthology.org/N19-1033/

18. Kalman, D.: A singularly valuable decomposition: the svd of a matrix. Coll. Math. J. **27**(1), 2–23 (1996). https://doi.org/10.1080/07468342.1996.11973744

19. Katić, T., Milićević, N.: Comparing sentiment analysis and document representation methods of amazon reviews. In: 2018 IEEE 16th International Symposium on Intelligent Systems and Informatics (SISY), pp. 000283–000286 (2018). https://doi.org/10.1109/SISY.2018.8524814

20. Khazane, A., et al.: Deeptrax: embedding graphs of financial transactions. In: 2019 18th IEEE International Conference On Machine Learning And Applications (ICMLA), pp. 126–133 (2019)

21. Kingma, D.P., Ba, J.: Adam: a method for stochastic optimization. In: International Conference on Learning Representations (ICLR), p. 13. Ithaca, NY: ArXiv (2015), https://arxiv.org/abs/1412.6980

22. Muennighoff, N., Tazi, N., Magne, L., Reimers, N.: MTEB: massive text embedding benchmark. In: Vlachos, A., Augenstein, I. (eds.) Proceedings of the 17th Conference of the European Chapter of the Association for Computational Linguistics, pp. 2014–2037. ACL, Dubrovnik, Croatia, May 2023. https://doi.org/10.18653/v1/2023.eacl-main.148, https://aclanthology.org/2023.eacl-main.148/

23. Ren, J., Long, J., Xu, Z.: Financial news recommendation based on graph embeddings. Decis. Support Syst. **125**, 113115 (2019). https://doi.org/10.1016/j.dss.2019.113115, https://www.sciencedirect.com/science/article/pii/S0167923619301447

24. Su, H., et al.: One embedder, any task: instruction-finetuned text embeddings (2023), https://arxiv.org/abs/2212.09741

25. Tai, W., Kung, H.T., Dong, X., Comiter, M., Kuo, C.F.: exBERT: extending pre-trained models with domain-specific vocabulary under constrained training resources. In: Cohn, T., He, Y., Liu, Y. (eds.) Findings of the Association for Computational Linguistics: EMNLP 2020, pp. 1433–1439. ACL, November 2020, https://doi.org/10.18653/v1/2020.findings-emnlp.129, https://aclanthology.org/2020.findings-emnlp.129/

26. Tan, Y., Zhou, Z., Lv, H., Liu, W., Yang, C.: Walklm: a uniform language model fine-tuning framework for attributed graph embedding. In: Oh, A., Naumann, T., Globerson, A., Saenko, K., Hardt, M., Levine, S. (eds.) Advances in Neural Information Processing Systems, vol. 36, pp. 13308–13325. Curran Associates, Inc. (2023)

27. Tungjitnob, S., Pasupa, K., Suntisrivaraporn, B.: Identifying sme customers from click feedback on mobile banking apps: supervised and semi-supervised approaches. Heliyon **7**, e07761 (2021)

28. Vaswani, A., et al.: Attention is all you need. In: Guyon, I., et al. (eds.) Advances in Neural Information Processing Systems, vol.30. Curran Associates, Inc. (2017)

29. Zhang, J., Bai, B., Lin, Y., Liang, J., Bai, K., Wang, F.: General-purpose user embeddings based on mobile app usage. In: Proceedings of the 26th ACM SIGKDD International Conference on Knowledge Discovery & Data Mining, KDD 2020, pp. 2831–2840. ACM, New York, NY, USA (2020)

30. Zhao, X., et al.: Embedding in recommender systems: a survey (2023), https://arxiv.org/abs/2310.18608

Author Index

B. Pfahringer et al. (Eds.): ECML PKDD 2025, LNAI 16020, pp. 559–561, 2026.
https://doi.org/10.1007/978-3-662-72243-5